EU Intellectual Property Law and Policy

ELGAR EUROPEAN LAW

Series editor: John Usher, *formerly Professor of European Law and Head, School of Law, University of Exeter, UK*

European integration is the driving force behind constant evolution and change in the laws of the member states and the institutions of the European Union. This important series will offer short, state-of-the-art overviews of many specific areas of EU law, from competition law to consumer law and from environmental law to labour law. Whilst most books will take a thematic, vertical approach, others will offer a more horizontal approach and consider the overarching themes of EU law.

Distilled from rigorous substantive analysis, and written by some of the best names in the field, as well as the new generation of scholars, these books are designed both to guide the reader through the changing legislation itself, and to provide a firm theoretical foundation for advanced study. They will be an invaluable source of reference for scholars and postgraduate students in the fields of EU law and European integration, as well as lawyers from the respective individual fields and policymakers within the EU.

Titles in the series include:

EU Consumer Law and Policy
Stephen Weatherill

EU Private International Law
Harmonization of Laws
Peter Stone

EU Public Procurement Law
Christopher H. Bovis

EU Criminal Law and Justice
Maria Fletcher and Robin Lööf with Bill Gilmore

Judicial Review in EU Law
Alexander H. Türk

EU Intellectual Property Law and Policy
Catherine Seville

EU Intellectual Property Law and Policy

Catherine Seville

Vice-Principal and Director of Studies in Law, Newnham College and University Lecturer at the Faculty of Law, University of Cambridge, UK

ELGAR EUROPEAN LAW

Edward Elgar
Cheltenham, UK • Northampton, MA, USA

Published by
Edward Elgar Publishing Limited
The Lypiatts
15 Lansdown Road
Cheltenham
Glos GL50 2JA
UK

Edward Elgar Publishing, Inc.
William Pratt House
9 Dewey Court
Northampton
Massachusetts 01060
USA

A catalogue record for this book
is available from the British Library

Library of Congress Control Number: 2008943825

PEFC
PEFC/16-33-111
CATG-PEFC-052
www.pefc.org

ISBN 978 1 84720 123 2

Typeset by Cambrian Typesetters, Camberley, Surrey
Printed and bound in Great Britain by MPG Books Ltd, Bodmin, Cornwall

The Author and Publisher are grateful to the late John Usher for his support for this book and the Elgar European Law series.

Contents

Preface

My aim in writing this book is to offer a compact and accessible account of EU intellectual property law and policy. It covers the substantive provisions and procedures which apply throughout the EU, making extensive reference to the case law – the sheer volume of which is utterly daunting for students attempting to explore the area on their own. The book is intended to be manageable in terms of length and ease of understanding. Basic material is rehearsed as appropriate, although it is not intended as an introductory book for those entirely unfamiliar with the subjects of intellectual property or EU law. I hope the book will be used as a work of reference, as well as for wider study, so sections stand on their own, with cross-references offered where these will be helpful. Intellectual property is not isolated from other aspects of EU law and policy; it is regarded as a crucial contributor to economic growth and competitiveness, especially in fields of technology. Aspects of the free movement of goods and services, competition law, customs measures, and anti-counterfeiting efforts are all engaged. This work takes a broad view of these interactions, and their impact on law and policy.

It is also essential to set EU intellectual property law in the wider international context necessary for understanding it, and its application to intellectual property law within the EU member states. The exploitation of intellectual property is increasingly global, bringing corresponding pressures for global harmonisation. Often the harmonisation of intellectual property law at the EU level is only partial, so the broader framework is extremely important. This is particularly true of patent law, where the success of the European Patent Convention and other international initiatives has left Community patent law with only a minimal role – thus far. Similarly, the interaction of Community law and national laws may also be very significant. In discussions of this, the book focuses on the harmonised environment. Matters of general application to all member states are discussed, but individual substantive national laws are not. The book is intended to elucidate the framework within which the national intellectual property laws of member states operate. It is thus not tied to any particular national law, although reference is made to national cases where this helps to develop points of interest relevant to the situation within the EU.

Finally, the book also seeks to highlight policy issues and arguments of relevance to the EU, both within the Union, and in its relations with the rest of the world. There is a huge volume of policy material, which may be tricky for the non-specialist to locate and digest; detailed references are given to these sources. There has necessarily been a process of selection, with the focus on offering understanding of the major issues, rather than an exhaustive account of every detail. But the aim has been always to offer guidance and further reading for those wishing to undertake research on particular matters.

Catherine Seville
Newnham College
June 2008

Cases

COURT OF FIRST INSTANCE

COMMISSION DECISIONS

EFTA Court

European Patent Convention decisions

NATIONAL CASES

Canada

Denmark

England and Wales

Estonia

Finland

France

Germany

Legislation

Treaties, conventions and other international instruments

1. Introduction

Intellectual property is increasingly a global commodity. Its intangible nature fits it perfectly for cross-border travel. Technologies of all kinds and in all fields have developed with almost incredible rapidity. As a result, many products of intellectual property may be readily enjoyed by users – both legitimate and illegitimate – all over the world. Intellectual property law has had to respond to these realities. Traditionally, intellectual property rights have been territorial in nature. In an economic world where trade is frequently international, and more and more commonly global, this fact gives rise to difficulties and conflicts between national systems. This engenders efforts towards cooperation and harmonisation at international levels, in an attempt to reduce obstacles to trade, and to increase the general international standard of protection for intellectual property. Such forces are not new; the Paris and Berne Conventions represent significant harmonisation efforts dating from the nineteenth century. However, the current economic significance of intellectual property rights results in evergrowing pressure for harmonisation. These may well be matters of great political importance and delicacy, not simply collections of rules which need tidying up. In some areas – such as patent litigation – there are identifiable, widely acknowledged problems. Although on this particular issue it has thus far proved impossible to resolve differences of opinion among the member states, one hopes that the obvious needs of patent litigants will eventually force a satisfactory outcome. Other initiatives, such as the Draft Criminal Enforcement Directive, raise difficult issues of principle regarding the relationship between the member states and the Community, and provoke discussion as to the appropriate legislative level for such interventions. Looking outwards from the Community, the picture regarding harmonisation initiatives is again mixed. For example, within the TRIPS framework (Agreement on trade-related aspects of intellectual property rights), the EU is contributing constructively to discussions regarding the patenting of biological resources, which is a matter of serious concern to countries who are the source of such resources. Equally, the EU's proposals concerning the harmonisation of geographical indications are being strongly opposed by other countries who regard them as protectionist and unreasonable. In such contexts, harmonisation is more than instrumental, in a narrow sense.

The exploitation and protection of intellectual property is a crucial aspect of the EU's position in the global economy. The Commission has repeatedly emphasised the importance of these rights, which underpin innovation, employment, competition and thus economic growth. Community activity in this field is extensive. There are significant developments in high-level policy matters, and a continuing explosion of case law offering detailed interpretation of the wide range of harmonising measures. Some of these are traditional instruments, harmonising the laws of member states to remove barriers to trade. Many of these concern specific intellectual property rights (or aspects of them), although a few address horizontal aspects of this broad area of law, such as the enforcement of rights. There are also a number of schemes which create unitary systems for the protection of particular intellectual property rights, offering Community-wide protection via a single application. Important though strong intellectual property rights are to the Community, they must nevertheless be compatible with the Community's fundamental principles of free movement and competition. Unless the use of intellectual property rights is checked, their territorial nature will inevitably lead to obstacles to free trade and free competition. The balance is continually contested, both within the single market, and at its borders. The European Court of Justice has had a major impact in this field, creating the doctrine of Community-wide exhaustion of rights. This provides a practical solution to the problem, in which protection of intellectual property rights is ensured, but their use by a right holder to impede free movement or free competition is significantly curtailed. The doctrine has since been adopted in many Community legislative texts. The Commission is also increasingly concerned with wider issues affecting intellectual property, such as counterfeiting. Yet more is promised. Following requests from the European Council, during 2008 the Commission intends to present a comprehensive 'IPR Strategy Communication', addressing the main outstanding non-legislative and horizontal issues in all fields of intellectual property including trade marks, designs, copyright, geographical indications, patents and enforcement.

Although there are many stories of success to be found in the history of these initiatives, it is also necessary to report significant controversies, and numerous fruitless proposals. Harmonisation is not unquestionably 'a good thing', even within the EU, and certainly not for all those affected by intellectual property rights. Interest groups are likely to have strong views as to the appropriate boundaries for the intellectual property rights which most concern them. Those hoping to hold rights will seek strong, wide rights. Those likely to have to pay more as a result of strengthened rights will oppose such expansion. Existing national schemes may work extremely well, in their context, and changes to those systems will be disruptive and expensive. National right holders may be perfectly content to work their rights on a national scale, and may not welcome the prospect of paying for or defending a Community-wide right. Those professionals accustomed to dealing with (say) registration or litigation at a national level will not relish centralisation which diminishes their business. As a result, harmonisation initiatives have been crafted and re-crafted to take account of these factors. It is understandably tempting to harmonise what can be agreed upon for now, leaving more obstinate problems for another day. Although this technique may be fruitful, there is also a risk that, with the central issues already aligned, there is even less incentive to address any intractable controversies which remain. This is evident in a number of areas of intellectual property law, where the substantive rules have been satisfactorily harmonised, leaving procedural matters for the member states. But member states' procedural systems may be very different, leading, perhaps, to inconsistencies in the remedies normally available for breaches of intellectual property rights. Harmonisation of these remedies beyond a certain level of generalisation will almost inevitably generate tensions with member states' general approaches to remedies. It is, unsurprisingly, difficult to reach agreement on modifications to these wider systems, especially if the justification for change arises only in the narrow context of intellectual property rights.

Reviewing the Community law which affects the various specific intellectual property rights, there are areas of strength and areas of weakness. Trade mark law should be counted among the successes of Community harmonisation. It displays both main forms of harmonisation: a Directive harmonising national laws, and a Regulation creating a unitary Community Trade Mark. The substantive laws of member states have been aligned with each other, and are paralleled as closely as possible in the core provisions of Community Trade Mark legislation. The journey has not been easy, however, and followed long negotiations. Even so, much guidance has been required from the European Court of Justice (ECJ) as to the interpretation of the legislative provisions, both major and minor. Community trade mark law starts with a far more open stance towards trade mark registration than many national systems previously had been willing to adopt. Shapes, smells, and even movements now fall within the basic definition of a registrable mark (although their passage to the register is far from guaranteed). National courts took a certain amount of time to adapt to this and other philosophical changes. Lack of clarity in the legislation also caused frustration, at least initially. The volume of case law is immense. However, as the system has matured, understanding has grown, and the central provisions are increasingly well understood. The unitary Community Trade Mark has proved very popular, and co-exists satisfactorily with national systems. It is nevertheless unlikely to displace them in the foreseeable future, given the difficulties inherent in demonstrating Community-wide eligibility for protection. In addition, although much convergence has been achieved, attitudinal differences may still be detected.

Design law within the EU offers a considerable challenge for those with a harmonising brief. The breadth of the design field has led member states to use varieties of copyright, patent, and *sui generis* design protection to cover design products, as well as unfair competition law. Both registered and unregistered rights are common. Even within a single member state it is unlikely that only one form of intellectual property will be engaged. The Commission was faced with a muddle of overlapping schemes of design protection in the member states, and therefore chose to harmonise national laws as best it could, whilst also offering a Community-wide scheme of design protection (both registered and unregistered). For national laws, the Directive harmonises the conditions for obtaining registration, the extent and term of protection, and conditions for refusing or invalidating the right. This still leaves many procedural aspects to the member states, who are, in addition, free to offer additional protection via their own national schemes. The single issue of design protection for spare parts was a stumbling block to agreement for many years, and was shelved in order to allow the rest of the Community initiative to proceed, since this in itself was relatively uncontroversial. The internal market for spare parts is seriously distorted as a result. However, the fundamental issue remains extremely contentious, with national systems divided between liberalisation and protection. This is an example of an area where deferring the problem has not yet resulted in a common perspective. It is, of course, also an area where vested interests (namely, the automotive industry) are extremely powerful. Nevertheless, the Community design regime has so far proved popular, although these are early days. If it is as cheap and convenient as its designers hope, it may perhaps be that it will supplant the confused web of national protection. The transitional period will certainly be a long one.

Arising informally, and covering a diverse range of subject matter, copyright law is also fundamentally difficult to harmonise. The common law and *droit d'auteur* systems approach its protection somewhat differently, and there is significant diversity on particular issues between member states. Digital technology offers the copyright industries both huge opportunities and huge threats. Copying has never been easier. There is, so far, no talk of a unitary Community Copyright. Indeed, it is hard to imagine this ever being conceded by the member states. Instead, there are a number of Directives, the majority of which address particular sectors (rental rights, databases, satellite broadcasting, and so on). Copyright term has been the subject of a horizontal Directive, and the Information Society Directive has also attempted some harmonisation of basic rights and exceptions. Its aspirations, however, were comparatively limited. In this field the Commission's future agenda is directed towards fostering competition and promoting innovation in the exploitation of cross-border rights. Perhaps because they do not pose a direct threat to such activities, substantive issues such as the protection of moral rights, and the authorship and ownership of copyright works, are likely to remain unharmonised. Depending on one's view of convergence, this may be a positive or negative consequence of the complexities inherent in copyright law.

It is in the field of patent law harmonisation that the EU must acknowledge a history of repeated failure. The success of the European Patent Convention makes it clear that it is not patent law itself which presents insuperable problems. But efforts towards a Community patent have time after time become mired in unproductive discussions regarding translations and jurisdictional arrangements. This has been frustrating for patentees, litigants, and the Commission alike. The scale of the problem is the more alarming, given the economic importance of patents, and their significance for growth and innovation in the Community. Thus far, national interests appear to have prevailed over stakeholders' needs for a functioning Community-wide system. Yet one more initiative is currently being tried. There have been some limited sectoral interventions. Regulations have been enacted in the fields of medicinal products and plant protection products. These create a form of *sui generis* protection for innovative products which require extensive and time-consuming testing, to the point where the relatively short duration of general patent protection makes it difficult for a right owner to reap adequate commercial rewards. The Biotechnology Directive was eventually passed, after immense controversy. The proposed Directive on the Patentability of Computer-Implemented Inventions, also contentious, has fared less well.

Intellectual property has offered a broad stage on which a variety of Community harmonisation initiatives have taken a turn. Both political and economic interests have shaped them. At first, the focus was harmonisation in the context of the single market. Increasingly, the Community's regional initiatives are being set in a global context. There are already many examples. The Information Society Directive was required in order that the EC could ratify the WIPO Internet Treaties. The EC is a signatory to the Madrid Agreement, as a result of which Community Trade Mark protection may be extended internationally, and, those applying for a trade mark via an international application may designate the EC as a chosen territory. The EC has recently acceded to the Hague Agreement, which allows protection of a design not only throughout the EU, but also in other member countries of the Hague Agreement, via a single application at WIPO. Community patent law, if it ever develops, will likewise have to take account of the global patent environment. There are risks here. In the field of intellectual property, the pressure to compete with the US and Japan is enormous. If rights are granted according to the wishes of the industries affected, who can mobilise powerful lobbying groups to promote their interests, the path will be towards ever-strengthening protection. Yet if intellectual property rights are to retain their credibility, it is crucial that legislation takes account of the wider public interest, and acknowledges the sometimes negative effects of intellectual property rights. Less developed countries, in particular, are tired of being told that only the industrialised countries' vision of intellectual property is acceptable. The challenge the Community faces is that of listening hard and taking account of such criticisms, given the overwhelming clamour of economic interests. Insensitive or selfish responses to these wider policy considerations are likely to lead to deadlock on global harmonisation, and risk undermining the very rights which it is desired to safeguard.

2. Copyright and related rights

2.1 INTRODUCTION

Copyright is an intangible property right which subsists in various kinds of creative work. It is a comparatively modern concept. Copying on an economic scale was not practical before the invention of printing, demanding huge amounts of time and skill. And at least in some cultures, plagiarism was regarded as immoral. Copyright's origin lies in monopolies of printing which began to develop in the late fifteenth and early sixteenth centuries. Privileges and patents were granted for the exclusive printing of a particular book, or books of a particular kind. Although these privileges might be given to the work's author, very often they would be held by the person who arranged for the printing of the work – a publisher, printer or bookseller. The modern notion of authorial copyright took time to develop. Once books could be produced in quantity, the market for them increased rapidly, and more people could enjoy access to them. Copyright law developed in response to these changes.

A distinction is often made between the common law system of copyright, and the civil law *droit d'auteur* system. The common law system is frequently characterised as primarily concerned with economic rights, and incentives to produce new works. In contrast, the civil law *droit d'auteur* system is portrayed as giving particular priority to the natural rights of authors, and authorial works. It thus takes care to distinguish author's rights from entrepreneurial rights (such as those in sound recordings, broadcasts and cable programmes), these latter being termed *droits voisins* – 'neighbouring rights' or 'related rights'. These images contain elements of truth, though should not be pushed to the point of caricature. The two systems are far from polarised, and have many elements in common. Nevertheless, differences in approach have certainly had an influence on the pattern of harmonisation of copyright law, particularly in the Community context.

The subject matter of copyright has expanded considerably since its earliest concern with printed works. Modern copyright law covers a wide range of cultural products; books, music, plays, art works, dance and mime, films, photographs, computer programs and broadcasts, for example. Copyright protects a number of distinct rights, including the right to copy a work, to distribute it, and to perform it in public. Note, though, that unlike a patent right, it does not prevent use by an independent creator. Furthermore, copyright protects only against the copying of the expression of a copyright work and does not prevent the use of facts or ideas contained within it. Use of the word 'monopoly' to describe copyright is therefore contentious. These factors are used to justify a comparatively extended copyright term, which is a minimum of the author's life plus 50 years under the Berne Convention, and may be longer. Within the EU the basic term is the author's life plus 70 years.

Throughout its history copyright law has been strongly influenced by developments in technology, and this continues. The digital age permits the making of multiple, practically perfect copies, at very low cost. Users of copyright works have been quick to take advantage of the latest digital copying technologies. Copyright holders often argue that stronger copyright protection is necessary. Excessive copyright protection, though, has the potential to harm the public domain and to restrict the creativity which copyright law in theory intends to foster. Legislators face a continuing and difficult challenge in balancing the needs of copyright holders for protection against the needs of the public for access to creative works.

2.2   INTERNATIONAL CONVENTIONS

International aspects of copyright grew in importance during the nineteenth century, as methods of travel and communication increased in safety and efficiency. Business people trying to respond to these increasing markets found themselves at the mercy of copyright 'pirates'. For example, popular British copyright works would be rushed to America, where they were republished in cheap editions and sold in huge quantities to the vast American reading public. The American publisher paid only the publishing costs and did so quite legally. The original publishers would have paid the author for the copyright in the home market, and would have liked to enjoy the fruits of their investment abroad, also.

2.2.1   Early Bilateral Agreements

It became increasingly obvious that a system of international copyright was needed. At first, publishers attempted to create private agreements with publishing houses elsewhere, or to open foreign offices in order to benefit from the various relevant national copyrights. Bilateral treaties offered greater security, however, and a network of such agreements grew in Europe from the late 1820s. By the mid-1870s, many of the most important publishing markets in Europe (France, Belgium, Germany, Holland) were governed, at least to some extent, by a considerable network of bilateral treaties. However, there were still no conventions with much of Europe (notably Holland and Russia), and none with the United States (which took a consistently protectionist line, granting copyrights only to citizens and residents). These were all substantial markets, and in these places 'piratical' editions could be printed, imported, and circulated perfectly legally. Furthermore, in practice these editions circulated widely in convention states and in the British territories overseas, even though here they became piracies.

Although the network of bilateral conventions became quite extensive, the fact that the agreements were far from uniform meant that the resulting protection was neither comprehensive nor systematic. Those intended to benefit found it difficult to ascertain what their rights were, precisely. Without harmonised legal protection, ideally covering a coherent geographic area, individual territories remained vulnerable to smuggled cheap reprints, whatever their particular portfolios of bilateral convention protection. The most satisfactory solution to this problem, logically at least, would have been for all affected countries to adopt uniform, general copyright laws, applicable to foreigners and nationals. The difficulties to be encountered in achieving such a universalist approach are obvious, however, given the diversity of the underlying national systems. In such circumstances, pragmatists are prepared to contemplate the sacrifice of a certain amount of integrity, and to advocate a lesser degree of universality in the interests of reaching agreement. But for those who regard copyright protection as based fundamentally on natural law and principle, the sacrifices inherent in a pragmatic approach bring with them an unacceptable level of compromise, and result in a dilution of the protection which they consider should be absolutely guaranteed.[1]

2.2.2 The Berne Convention

The campaign which resulted in the Berne Convention began in 1858, when a congress of authors and artists met at Brussels. Further congresses were held, notably the 1878 international literary congress, organised by the *Société des gens de lettres* in Paris. A resolution was passed insisting that an author's right was a form of property rather than a legal concession, and that it was a perpetual right. The Paris Congress also established the International Literary Association. This was later expanded to include artists, thus becoming *l'Association littéraire et artistique internationale*, commonly known as *ALAI*. Its main objective was the creation of an international agreement to protect

---

[1]   See Brad Sherman and Lionel Bently, *The Making of Modern Intellectual Property Law* (Cambridge: Cambridge University Press, 1999), 111–18.

literary and artistic copyright.[2] It held annual conferences in various European cities, and its members continued to press for international copyright laws which were universalist in nature. A model law (drafted privately) was discussed at the 1882 Rome Congress. Also at this Congress, a more pragmatic suggestion was put forward: a union of literary property (*une Union de la propriété littéraire*), on the model of the General Postal Union created in 1874.

In September 1883, a conference of interested parties was arranged in Berne. A draft convention of ten articles emerged, founded on a principle of national treatment (familiar from many bilateral conventions).[3] The draft did not cover a number of important matters, including duration of rights. A further conference was held in September 1884, with delegates from ten countries in attendance. The German delegation proposed that a model codification of the law should be the goal, rather than a convention based on the principle of national treatment. This raised a problematic issue: should principle be sacrificed to pragmatism? A further draft was eventually adopted, retaining the principle of national treatment. The French delegates, and some authors' societies, were disappointed by the compromises made in the interests of reaching agreement. However, a *procès-verbal final* positioned international codification as an inevitable future state, if not one presently achievable. Another conference took place in September 1885, again in Berne. The French delegates continued to press for stronger protection for authors. The British delegates lent support to the pragmatists, advocating the principle of national treatment wherever agreement on a uniform rule could not be reached.

A choice had to be made between a uniform convention which would in practice exclude the participation of many countries with weak copyright protection, or a less rigorous convention which would encourage the adherence of a significant number of countries. The Conference finally adopted a pragmatic approach, but the delegations were not unanimous in this. The result was an extremely significant agreement. The 1886 Berne Convention on the Protection of Literary and Artistic Works created a 'Union for the protection of the rights of authors over their literary and artistic works'. The Convention was based on the principle of national treatment. One important exception to this was the term of protection, which was subject to a rule of national reciprocity. Ten states signed the Convention in September 1886, and it came into

---

[2]   *ALAI* is still a significant force in the copyright world. Its objects include 'the defence and propagation of legal principles ensuring international protection of copyright'. See www.alai.org.

[3]   The principle of national treatment requires a country to assimilate foreign nationals to its own nationals, thus giving the foreign national the same level of protection as that accorded to its own nationals under its own law.

force the following year.[4] The signatories were largely European countries, with America a notable non-participant.[5] Given the differences in the legal systems and outlook of the states involved, the level of accord achieved was astonishing. Numa Droz, the Swiss politician who had been President of all the Berne conferences, described the creation of the Union as 'a striking affirmation of the universal conscience in favour of copyright'.[6] Yet self-interest and pragmatism were also involved, with many disagreements of principle remaining unresolved.[7]

The Berne Convention has since been modified a number of times.[8] It now has 163 members.[9] The Convention sets minimum standards for protection which members of the Union must meet. It is still based on the principle of national treatment.[10] The 'enjoyment and exercise' of Berne rights 'shall not be subject to any formality' (such as registration or notice).[11] Berne protection is also independent of the existence of protection in the country of origin of the work. This means that an author's rights and remedies are governed by the laws of the country where protection is claimed.[12] The main exception to this is that if a member state provides for a longer copyright term than the Berne Convention minimum, protection may be denied once protection in the

---

[4] Those signing were Belgium, France, Germany, Great Britain, Haiti, Italy, Liberia, Spain, Switzerland and Tunisia. The French and British governments signed for their colonies and possessions also, whereas the Spanish government reserved its position until the exchange of ratifications one year later. The Convention came into force 5 December 1887, all the signatories except Liberia having ratified it.

[5] America offered no international copyright protection until 1891, and remained outside the Berne Convention until 1988.

[6] *Actes de la Conférence réunie à Berne* (1885), 65.

[7] For the historical background see Catherine Seville, *The Internationalisation of Copyright Law: Books, Buccaneers and the Black Flag in the Nineteenth Century* (Cambridge: Cambridge University Press, 2006), 41–77.

[8] The Berne Convention, concluded in 1886, was revised at Paris in 1896 and at Berlin in 1908, completed at Berne in 1914, revised at Rome in 1928, at Brussels in 1948, at Stockholm in 1967 and at Paris in 1971, and was amended in 1979. It is administered by the World Intellectual Property Organisation (WIPO).

[9] As of April 2008: http://www.wipo.int/export/sites/www/treaties/en/documents/pdf/berne.pdf.

[10] Berne, Art. 5(1). The protection of the Convention applies to authors who are nationals of one of the countries of the Union, for their works, whether published or not; and to authors who are not nationals of one of the countries of the Union, for their works first published in one of those countries: Berne, Art. 3.

[11] Berne, Art. 5(2). This is sometimes called the principle of 'automatic protection'.

[12] Berne, Art. 5(3). This is sometimes called the principle of 'independence of protection'.

country of origin ceases.[13] The expression 'literary and artistic works' includes 'every production in the literary, scientific and artistic domain, whatever may be the mode or form of its expression'.[14] Authors and copyright owners enjoy a number of exclusive rights:

- the right to make reproductions of the work 'in any manner or form';[15]
- the right to perform/recite it in public;[16]
- the right to translate it;[17]
- the right to make adaptations and arrangements of the work;[18]
- the broadcasting right/right of communication to the public.[19]

The Convention acknowledges that there is a need for exceptions to these rights to allow access to copyright works without permissions in a limited number of circumstances (for example, for the purposes of criticism and review, for reporting a current event, for educational purposes, and so on). Exceptions to the reproduction right are subject to the so-called three-step test: they must be confined to 'special cases'; the reproduction must not conflict with a normal exploitation of the work; and must not unreasonably prejudice the legitimate interests of the author.[20] The Convention also provides for

---

[13] Berne, Art. 7(8). There are also exceptions to the principle of national treatment for works of applied art and *droit de suite*: Berne, Art. 2(7), Art. 14*ter* (2).

[14] This includes 'books, pamphlets and other writings; lectures, addresses, sermons and other works of the same nature; dramatic or dramatico-musical works; choreographic works and entertainments in dumb show; musical compositions with or without words; cinematographic works to which are assimilated works expressed by a process analogous to cinematography; works of drawing, painting, architecture, sculpture, engraving and lithography; photographic works to which are assimilated works expressed by a process analogous to photography; works of applied art; illustrations, maps, plans, sketches and three-dimensional works relative to geography, topography, architecture or science'. Berne, Art. 2(1).

[15] Berne, Art. 9. Sound and visual recordings are considered reproductions for the purposes of the Convention.

[16] Berne, Art. 11(1) for the public performance of dramatic, dramatico-musical and musical works, and the right to communicate to the public the performance of such works. Berne, Art. 11*ter* for the public recitation of literary works, and the right to communicate to the public the recitation of such works. In both cases, translations are covered.

[17] Berne, Art. 8 (literary and artistic works); Art. 11(2) (dramatic and musical works).

[18] Berne, Art. 12 (authorising adaptations, arrangements and other alterations of their works); Art. 14 (cinematographic adaptation and reproduction).

[19] Berne, Art. 11*bis*.

[20] Berne, Art. 9(2). See also Art. 10 (use of quotations from a work lawfully made available to the public; illustrations for teaching); Art. 10*bis* (news items; current events).

certain 'moral rights' – the right of attribution and the right of integrity – defined as 'the right to claim authorship of the work and the right to object to any mutilation or deformation or other modification of, or other derogatory action in relation to, the work which would be prejudicial to the author's honor or reputation'. These rights are given to the author alone, and may not be transferred with economic rights.[21] The general rule is that protection must last for the author's life and 50 years thereafter.[22]

2.2.3 The Universal Copyright Convention

The Berne Convention was almost entirely a European instrument (Haiti was briefly a member), and the absence of protection on the American continent was keenly felt. A number of South American states adopted the Montevideo Convention in 1889 (which had many similarities to the Berne Convention, although also some important differences). But this did not become truly pan-American in membership. Two of the five signatory states which ratified the Convention adopted a policy of refusing to accept accessions by non-Latin American states. Although some European states were able to accede to the Montevideo Convention, it did not operate as a truly multilateral international convention. Although a number of other multilateral conventions, involving the states of South and Central America and the USA, were signed in the following decades, no single convention gained universal adherence.[23]

By 1928, Brazil was the only American republic (other than Haiti) which had joined the Berne Convention. Following the Berlin revision of Berne in 1908, however, it seemed not impossible that the Old and New World systems might reach some accommodation. The main sticking point was the insistence on formalities, which were particularly important to the American republics. Although some preparatory steps were taken, World War II interrupted progress. Subsequently it was UNESCO which took the initiative, and the Universal Copyright Convention (UCC) was signed in 1952.[24] This was a completely new treaty, the Berne Convention countries having been unwilling

---

21 Berne, Art. 6*bis*.

22 Berne, Art. 7(1). Exceptions may be made for cinematographic works, anonymous or pseudonymous works (with a minimum 50-year term), and for photographic works and works of applied art in so far as they are protected as artistic works (with a minimum 25-year term).

23 Including the Caracas Convention (1911), and the Pan-American conventions of 1902, 1906, 1910, 1928. For more detail see Sam Ricketson and Jane Ginsburg, *International Copyright and Neighbouring Rights* 2nd ed. (Oxford: Oxford University Press, 2006), 1171–7.

24 Universal Copyright Convention 1952 (revised at Paris on 24 July 1971).

to lower the Berne standard of protection to the point where it would have been attractive to American states, or to allow formalities to be made a condition of protection. The UCC was based (like the Berne Convention) on the principle of national treatment. Those member states which required formalities (such as registration, notice, deposit, local manufacture) were permitted to retain them. However, for non-nationals of that member state, publishing outside that member state's territory, the UCC provides that any formalities shall be regarded as satisfied, if all the copies of the work published with the authority bear the copyright symbol ©, accompanied by the name of the copyright proprietor and the year of first publication placed in such manner and location as to give reasonable notice of claim of copyright.[25] The duration of copyright protection under the UCC was far shorter than that under the Berne Convention, the standard term being the author's life plus 25 years.[26]

Although the UCC guaranteed a lower standard of copyright protection than the Berne Convention, it was useful as a stepping-stone to genuine international copyright relations for many countries – most notably the USA (1954) and the USSR (1973). Nevertheless, its importance has decreased significantly, as more and more states have chosen to join the Berne Union in preference.

2.2.4   The Rome Convention

As has been seen, the Berne Convention covers literary and artistic works, including cinematographic works.[27] It provides no protection for performers, producers of sound recordings, broadcasters or publishers. As copying technology improved and became cheaper, there were growing problems with bootleg recordings and unauthorised films of performances being exploited without the performer's consent. There was opposition to the inclusion of such works within the Berne Convention, particularly from authors' societies, who regarded them as non-creative and derivative.[28] There was also anxiety lest such rights detract from the royalties paid to authors. A separate agreement on these 'neighbouring rights' was therefore negotiated. This was the Rome Convention for the Protection of Performers, Producers of Phonograms and Broadcasting Organisations (1961). It secures protection in performances of performers, in phonograms of producers of phonograms and in broadcasts of

---

[25]   UCC, Art. III.
[26]   UCC, Art. IV.
[27]   Berne, Art. 14.
[28]   Although translations, adaptations and films of works (which the Berne Convention does protect) are likewise 'derivative'.

broadcasting organisations. It currently has 86 signatories.[29] It is administered jointly by WIPO, the ILO, and UNESCO.

Like the Berne Convention, the Rome Convention is founded on the principle of national treatment.[30] Contracting states must grant national treatment to performers if a performance takes place in a member state, if the performance is incorporated in a protected sound recording, or is carried by a protected broadcast.[31] National treatment must be granted to sound recordings produced by a national of a contracting state, first fixed in a contracting state, or first published in a contracting state.[32] National treatment must be granted to broadcasting organisations situated in a contracting state, and to broadcasts transmitted from a contracting state.[33] Each category carries with it certain substantive rights.

Performers may prevent: the broadcasting and the communication to the public of their live performances without their consent; the fixation of their live performances without their consent ('bootlegging'); and the reproduction, without their consent, of such illicit recordings.[34] This is a somewhat limited portfolio of rights, and does not include, for example, the right to control the reproduction, distribution or communication to the public of legitimate recordings of one's performances. Protection must be a minimum of 20 years from the date of fixation of the performance, or 20 years from the date of performance for unfixed performances.[35] However, most national systems significantly exceed the Rome Convention protection periods, at least for performances and phonograms. The most common period is 50 years, the requirement under TRIPS.[36]

Producers of phonograms must be granted the right to authorise or prohibit the direct or indirect reproduction of their phonograms.[37] The contracting state

---

[29] As of June 2008: http://www.wipo.int/export/sites/www/treaties/en/documents/pdf/rome.pdf. The USA is a notable non-signatory, refusing to grant copyright to broadcasting organisations.

[30] Rome, Art. 2.

[31] Rome, Art. 4.

[32] Rome, Art. 5.

[33] Rome, Art. 6.

[34] Rome, Art. 7. 'Performers' are defined as 'actors, singers, musicians, dancers, and other persons who act, sing, deliver, declaim, play in, or otherwise perform literary or artistic works': Rome, Art. 3(a). Contracting states may extend this protection to artists who do not perform literary or artistic works (such as variety and circus artists) by domestic law: Rome, Art. 9.

[35] Rome, Art. 14.

[36] TRIPS, Art. 14.5. The minimum term of protection is 50 years for performers and producers of phonograms, and 20 years for broadcasting organisations.

[37] Rome, Art. 10. 'Phonogram' is defined as 'any exclusively aural fixation of sounds of a performance or of other sounds', and 'producer of phonograms' as 'the

may choose to require the formality of the 'P' symbol (with the date of first publication).[38] If a phonogram published for commercial purposes gives rise to secondary uses (such as broadcasting or communication to the public in any form), a 'single equitable remuneration' must be paid by the user to the performers, or to the producers of phonograms, or to both. The contracting states are free to decide which of these options to pursue, and may exclude the rule altogether, or limit its application.[39] The term of protection must be at least 20 years from the date of fixation.[40]

Broadcasting organisations have exclusive rights to authorise or prohibit the rebroadcasting of their broadcasts, the fixation of their broadcasts, and the reproduction of unauthorised fixations of their broadcasts. They also have the right to control communication to the public of their television broadcasts if such communication is made in places accessible to the public against payment of an entrance fee.[41] Protection must be at least 20 years from the date on which the broadcast took place.[42]

The Rome Convention allows national laws to provide for a number of exceptions to these rights. Specific defences are permitted for private use, use of short excerpts for reporting current events, ephemeral recordings by broadcasting organisations, and use for teaching or scientific research.[43] Where national laws provide exceptions to copyright in literary and artistic works, contracting states may also provide for the same kinds of limitations with regard to Rome Convention rights. However, compulsory licences are permitted only to the extent to which they are compatible with Rome Convention rights.[44]

WIPO's efforts to update the intellectual property rights of broadcasters have been continuing for almost a decade. Radically new types of communications and content distribution over the internet, and growing signal piracy problems, gave the process new urgency. International discussions have taken place to review and upgrade existing international standards, with the aim of ensuring an appropriate balance between stakeholders' various interests, and the interests of the general public. So far the discussions have not been particularly fruitful. There is broad agreement that there should be protection against the growing problem of signal theft. However, there is fierce resistance in

---

person who, or the legal entity which, first fixes the sounds of a performance or other sounds': Rome, Art. 3(b), (c).

[38]   Rome, Art. 11.
[39]   Rome, Art. 12, Art. 16.
[40]   Rome, Art. 14.
[41]   Rome, Art. 13.
[42]   Rome, Art. 14.
[43]   Rome, Art. 15(1).
[44]   Rome, Art. 15(2).

some quarters to the grant of wider exclusive rights (including rights of fixation and reproduction). There are concerns that these might impact adversely technological developments, internet communications, and personal uses (such as home copying).

2.2.5 TRIPS

The WTO's TRIPS Agreement also has had an important impact on copyright law. Before TRIPS, the extent of protection and enforcement of intellectual property rights – not just copyright – varied widely around the world. One of the difficulties with the Berne Convention (for instance) is that it contains no mechanism for ensuring that a signatory meets its obligations, or even of securing a definitive ruling that it is not doing so. Cases of large-scale piracy of books, records and films in non-conforming countries caused tension in trade relations. Intellectual property's increasing economic importance resulted in pressure for internationally agreed trade rules covering intellectual property rights. The TRIPS Agreement attempts to bring intellectual property enforcement under common international rules, and in doing so to establish minimum levels of protection. The basic principles are those of GATT, including national treatment, and most-favoured-nation treatment. The starting point is the obligations of the main international agreements – the Paris Convention, and the Berne Convention. Where these standards of protection are thought to be inadequate, they are supplemented by the TRIPS Agreement. If one state considers that another state is not fulfilling its obligations, it may complain to the WTO, and initiate a 'dispute resolution procedure'. Although the ultimate penalty is trade sanctions, most disputes are resolved at an earlier stage.

TRIPS has a number of specific provisions which affect copyright. The point of departure is the existing level of protection under the Berne Convention. Members are therefore required to comply with the substantive provisions of the Paris Act of 1971 of the Berne Convention (Articles 1 through 21). There is an exception for moral rights (Article 6*bis*).[45] In addition, the TRIPS Agreement clarifies and adds certain specific points – the 'Berne-plus' features. It confirms that copyright protection extends to expressions and not to ideas, procedures, methods of operation or mathematical concepts as such.[46] On the question of copyright term, Article 12 of TRIPS supplements the basic 50-year rule laid down in Article 7 of the Berne Convention. It provides that whenever the term of protection of a work, other than a photographic work or a work of applied art, is calculated on a basis

---

[45] TRIPS, Art. 9.1.
[46] TRIPS, Art. 9.2.

other than the life of a natural person, such term shall be no less than 50 years from the end of the calendar year of authorised publication, or, failing such authorised publication within 50 years from the making of the work, 50 years from the end of the calendar year of making. Importantly, TRIPS requires that *all* limitations or exceptions to exclusive rights comply with the Berne three-step test, and not simply the right of reproduction (the requirement of Berne itself).[47]

Although members are not required to adhere to the Rome Convention, the TRIPS Agreement makes very similar provisions for the protection of performers, producers of phonograms and broadcasting organisations. Performers must be able to prevent the unauthorised fixation of their performance on a phonogram (though audiovisual fixations are not covered), and the reproduction of such fixations. They must also be able to prevent their live performances being broadcast by wireless means or communicated to the public without their authorisation.[48] Producers of phonograms must be granted an exclusive reproduction right, and an exclusive rental right.[49] Broadcasting organisations must have the right to prohibit the unauthorised fixation, the reproduction of fixations, and the rebroadcasting by wireless means of broadcasts, as well as the communication to the public of their television broadcasts. However, it is not necessary to grant such rights to broadcasting organisations, if owners of copyright in the subject matter of broadcasts are provided with the possibility of preventing these acts, subject to the provisions of the Berne Convention.[50] The term of protection for these rights is much greater than that under the Rome Convention, being at least 50 years for performers and producers of phonograms, and 20 years for broadcasting organisations.[51] Conditions, limitations, exceptions and reservations to these rights are allowed only to the extent permitted by the Rome Convention.[52]

A number of issues generated by new technology are addressed by the TRIPS Agreement. Computer programs are to be protected as literary works under the Berne Convention, with the corresponding 50-year minimum term of protection.[53] Databases and other compilations must be protected by copyright 'provided that they by reason of the selection or arrangement of their

---

47   TRIPS, Art. 13.
48   TRIPS, Art. 14.1.
49   TRIPS, Arts. 14.2, 14.4.
50   TRIPS, Art. 14.3.
51   TRIPS, Art. 14.5.
52   TRIPS, Art. 14.6.
53   TRIPS, Art. 10.1. The three-step test requires that exceptions must be confined to 'special cases'; must not conflict with a normal exploitation of the work; and must not unreasonably prejudice the legitimate interests of the author (Berne, Art. 9(2)).

contents constitute intellectual creations'. Databases must be protected regardless of whether they are in machine readable or other form. Protection must not extend to the underlying data, and must be without prejudice to any copyright subsisting in that data.[54] Rental rights must be given to the copyright owners of computer programs, cinematographic works and phonograms.[55]

2.2.6 The WIPO Internet Treaties

The WIPO Copyright Treaty (WCT) and the WIPO Performances and Phonograms Treaty (WPPT), are known together as the WIPO Internet Treaties. These treaties are part of WIPO's so-called 'Digital Agenda', which sets out a series of guidelines and goals for WIPO in seeking to develop practical solutions to the challenges raised by the impact of new technologies on intellectual property rights.[56] But their roots lie also in a history of fruitless efforts to update the Berne Convention, which was last revised in 1971. Negotiations towards this had initially proceeded in parallel with the multinational negotiations that resulted in the TRIPS Agreement (1994). The shape of the intellectual property provisions within TRIPS being clear in late 1991, there seemed little impetus to reach further agreement on a revision of the Berne Convention. WIPO risked losing to the WTO its pre-eminence in the field of authors' rights and neighbouring rights. WIPO seized the initiative, and promoted two new treaties, which sought to go beyond the minimum standards of TRIPS, in particular in areas affected by technological change.[57]

The WIPO Copyright Treaty
The WCT entered into force in 2002, and currently has 65 contracting states.[58]

---

[54]   TRIPS, Art. 10.2. See section 2.36 below: Database Directive.

[55]   TRIPS, Arts. 11, 14.4. With respect to cinematographic works, the exclusive rental right is subject to the so-called impairment test: a member is excepted from the obligation unless rental has led to widespread copying which is materially impairing the exclusive right of reproduction. Rental rights for phonograms are not subject to the impairment test, but are limited by a so-called grandfathering clause, allowing members to maintain in force a system of equitable remuneration of right holders in respect of the rental of phonograms, provided that the commercial rental of phonograms is not giving rise to the material impairment of the exclusive rights of reproduction of right holders.

[56]   http://www.wipo.int/copyright/en/digital_agenda.htm.

[57]   For extensive detail see Jorg Reinbothe and Silke von Lewinski, *The WIPO Treaties 1996* (London: Butterworths, 1992).

[58]   As of 15 April 2008: http://www.wipo.int/export/sites/www/treaties/en/documents/pdf/wct.pdf. Membership of the WCT is open to any member of WIPO, and to certain intergovernmental organisations, including the European Community: WCT, Art. 17.

Its Preamble notes the need for 'adequate solutions to the questions raised by new economic, social, cultural and technological developments', but also recognises the need for a balance between the rights of authors and the wider public interest, particularly 'education, research and access to information'. The WCT restates many of the TRIPS obligations (although now under the umbrella of WIPO), and also goes beyond both TRIPS and the Berne Convention. Contracting parties must comply with Articles 1 to 21 of and the Appendix to the Berne Convention (1971), and (unlike TRIPS) the obligation under Article 6*bis* regarding moral rights is not exempted.[59] The WCT also repeats the TRIPS provision which states that copyright protection extends to expressions and not to ideas, procedures, methods of operation or mathematical concepts as such.[60] Other WCT provisions clarify Berne and TRIPS obligations with respect to computer programs and databases.[61]

The WCT addresses three important authors' rights: the right of distribution, rental right, and the right of communication to the public.[62] The distribution right is somewhat extended beyond the terms of both the Berne Convention and TRIPS.[63] With regard to rental right, the WCT goes further than TRIPS in requiring that it be granted to authors of works embodied in phonograms (not just computer programs and cinematographic works).[64] Perhaps most significant is the grant of an exclusive right of communication to the public. This is the right to authorise any communication to the public, by wire or wireless means, including 'the making available to the public of works in a way that the members of the public may access the work from a

---

[59]   WCT, Art. 1: compare TRIPS, Art. 9(1).

[60]   WCT, Art. 2: compare TRIPS, Art. 9(2).

[61]   WCT, Art. 4: compare Berne, Art. 2; TRIPS, Art. 10(1). WCT, Art. 5, compare Berne, Art. 2, esp. Art. 2(5); TRIPS, Art. 10(2).

[62]   In addition, an Agreed Statement (concerning WCT Art. 1(4)) clarifies the application of the reproduction right in the digital environment and, in particular, the storage of works in digital form in an electronic medium. It states that 'the reproduction right, as set out in Article 9 of the Berne Convention, and the exceptions permitted thereunder, fully apply in the digital environment, in particular to the use of works in digital form. It is understood that the storage of a protected work in digital form in an electronic medium constitutes a reproduction within the meaning of Article 9 of the Berne Convention'.

[63]   WCT, Art. 6 requires that copyright owners are given an exclusive right of 'authorising the making available to the public of the original and copies of their works through sale or other transfer of ownership'. When read with the Agreed Statement concerning Arts. 6 and 7 it is clear that this refers exclusively to 'fixed copies that can be put into circulation as tangible objects'. Compare Arts. 14(1)(i) and 14*bis*(2) of the Berne Convention (which provide a distribution right only in respect of cinematographic works and pre-existing works used for cinematographic adaptation).

[64]   WCT, Art. 7: compare TRIPS, Art. 14. Art. 7(1) is subject to the limitations in Arts. 7(2), 7(3).

place and at a time individually chosen by them'.[65] This covers, for example, on-demand, interactive communication via a web site. Although there were elements of this right in the Berne Convention, the coverage of the newly defined right is more coherent, and includes new methods of distribution through the internet. Another change is that the term of protection of photographs is brought into line with the general minimum term of life plus 50 years.[66] All rights under the WCT are subject to the Berne three-step test, which is a further extension.[67]

In addition to the right of communication to the public, the WCT addresses two other important matters which relate to WIPO's Digital Agenda. Contracting parties must provide adequate legal protection and effective legal remedies against the circumvention of 'effective technological measures' (such as encryption) used by authors in connection with the exercise of their rights.[68] There is also an obligation to provide adequate and effective remedies against those tampering with electronic rights management information. This would include data identifying works or their authors for licensing purposes, or for collecting or distributing royalties.[69]

The WCT's enforcement provisions are much less specific than those in the TRIPS Agreement. Contracting parties must take 'necessary measures' to ensure application of the Treaty, and must ensure that enforcement procedures 'permit effective action' against infringement.[70]

The WIPO Performances and Phonograms Treaty

The WPPT entered into force in 2002, and currently has 64 contracting states.[71] Its Preamble expresses a desire to develop and maintain the protection of the rights of performers and phonogram producers, recognising both 'the questions raised by economic, social, cultural and technological developments', and 'the profound impact of the development and convergence of information and communication technologies on the production and use of performances and phonograms'. As in the WCT, the public interest, 'particularly education, research and access to information', is acknowledged.

---

65   WCT, Art. 8: compare Berne, Arts. 11, 11*bis*, 11*ter*. TRIPS, Art. 9(1) simply includes a reference to these articles, so adds nothing to the Berne requirements.

66   WCT, Art. 9. Berne, Art. 7(4), which stipulates only a 25-year minimum.

67   WCT, Art. 10.

68   WCT, Art. 11.

69   WCT, Art. 12.

70   WCT, Art. 14.

71   As of 28 May 2008: http://www.wipo.int/export/sites/www/treaties/en/documents/pdf/wppt.pdf. Membership of the WPPT is open to any member of WIPO, and to certain intergovernmental organisations, including the European Community: WPPT, Art. 26.

Intended to supplement the Rome Convention, the WPPT does not, however, address the rights of broadcasters. WIPO has been attempting to negotiate new measures to protect broadcasters, but so far without success.[72] As compared to the Rome Convention, several definitions are changed. 'Performers' includes, additionally, 'expressions of folklore'. The definition of 'phonogram' is clarified in order to exclude sounds 'incorporated in a cinematographic or other audiovisual work'. WIPO has attempted to negotiate an agreement on the protection of audiovisual performances, but without success.[73]

For their live ('unfixed') performances, performers must be granted an exclusive right of authorising their broadcasting and communication to the public, and their fixation.[74] These rights are modelled on the 'bootlegging' provision of the Rome Convention, although the WPPT offers a stronger 'exclusive right', rather than 'the possibility of preventing' guaranteed by the Rome Convention.[75] For their performances 'fixed in phonograms', performers have various economic rights: the rights of reproduction, distribution, rental, and making available.[76] Performers are also granted certain moral rights: the right of attribution and the right of integrity. These only apply to 'live aural performances or performances fixed in phonograms'. The effect will be that only recording artists and musicians will enjoy moral rights protection similar to that enjoyed by authors, whereas actors and other performers whose performances are embodied in films or other audiovisual works will not.[77] Producers of phonograms are also granted the same economic rights: the rights of reproduction, distribution, rental, and making available.[78] This represents a considerable strengthening of Rome Convention rights. Performers and producers of phonograms are given the right to share a

---

72   See section 2.24 above: The Rome Convention.
73   WPPT, Art. 2. The United States would like any agreement on the protection of audiovisual performances to contain a rebuttable presumption that performers' economic rights have been transferred to the producer of the film. Others, including the European Union, disagree with this approach. In addition, broadcasters are continuing to press for the widest possible rights, although there is considerable consensus among member states and interest groups that any treaty ought to focus on the issue of signal theft, rather than the creation of new rights for broadcasters – at least if these are unqualified by rights for users and public interest exceptions. The impasse seems unlikely to be resolved in the foreseeable future, and plans for a diplomatic conference have been shelved. See WIPO Press Release (25 June 2007), 'Negotiators Decide to Continue Discussions on Updating Protection of Broadcasting Organisations' PR/2007/498.
74   WPPT, Art. 6.
75   Rome, Art. 7.
76   WPPT, Arts. 7–10.
77   WPPT, Art. 5.
78   WPPT, Arts. 11–14.

single equitable remuneration for secondary uses of phonograms (those published for commercial purposes for broadcasting or for any communication to the public).[79] As under the WCT, contracting parties have an obligation to provide adequate legal protection against the circumvention of technological measures of protection, and the alteration or removal of rights management information.[80]

Exceptions and limitations to rights are permitted only if they satisfy the three-step test.[81] No formalities may be required before the exercise of Treaty rights.[82] The minimum term of protection is 50 years (in line with the TRIPS Agreement, rather than the 20-year term specified in the Rome Convention).[83] The WPPT's enforcement provisions mirror those of the WCT.[84]

2.3   THE INFLUENCE OF THE EUROPEAN UNION

The EU's influence on copyright law has been substantial. Copyright, like other forms of intellectual property, creates problems and raises issues for the Community. Where rights are nationally granted and territorially based, they can function as barriers to the free movement of goods. One obvious solution would be to harmonise the various copyright laws throughout the EU, but this is not so simple as it sounds. Copyright presents particular difficulties. It covers a wide and diverse range of subject matter, so many different interest groups are involved. There is no formal procedure for acquiring copyright (in contrast to patents, trade marks and registered designs, for example), so it is not always easy to see when copyright subsists, and how to impose common rules. There are important dissimilarities in the approach taken by the various member states, some of which stem from different understandings of the role that copyright should play. Systems founded on common law may take a different approach to those founded on *droit d'auteur*. There may be other historical, cultural or political reasons for adopting varying solutions to particular areas of copyright law. The challenge of harmonising copyright is considerable.

---

[79]   WPPT, Art. 15. Contracting parties may regulate the division by national legislation, and are free to limit application of the right, or to state that they will not apply it at all.

[80]   WPPT, Arts. 18, 19.

[81]   WPPT, Art. 16.

[82]   WPPT, Art. 20. The Rome Convention permits certain limited formalities (e.g. Rome, Art. 11).

[83]   WPPT, Art. 17.

[84]   WPPT, Art. 23.

Notwithstanding these difficulties, the task is seen as an important one, for economic reasons. The copyright sector already represents more than 5% of European GDP, and provides employment for more than 3% of the workforce. In 2000, copyright industries contributed more than €1,200 billion to the EU economy, produced 'value added' of €450 billion, and employed 5.2 million people.[85] Within the European Commission, the Internal Market Directorate General has been renamed DG Internal Market and Services, to indicate 'that the department is taking the knowledge economy as its principal focus and aiming to make services, including services supplied across EU borders, the main driver for economic growth and future prosperity'.[86] The copyright and neighbouring rights unit has accordingly been re-baptised, and now deals with 'copyright and the knowledge economy'.

2.3.1 An Early Survey: The Commission's 1988 Green Paper

The Commission first assessed the range of problems facing Community copyright law in its 1988 Green Paper, *Copyright and the Challenge of Technology*.[87] Reading it now, it is striking how extraordinarily rapid the rate of technological change has been in the past two decades, and how much impact this has had in driving changes in the law. Yet the roots of many important contemporary issues are easily traced, even at this early stage. The Commission expressed a number of concerns. In relation to the free movement of goods and services, differences in copyright law obstructed the functioning of the internal market. There was a lack of harmonisation of the content of national rights. An urgent need was perceived for copyright protection in areas of new technology: satellite and cable television, various computer technologies and databases. Improved copying technology was already seen as a two-edged sword: although rapid, high-quality, cheap copying promised enormous benefits to both owners and users of copyright products, it also resulted in unfair competition from pirate products. It was foreseen that digital copying would make national territorial barriers much less meaningful than was the case for physical products. The rhetoric was that access to the global market should be facilitated, thus responding to the challenge, rather than ignoring it. The lack of adequate enforcement of rights, particularly outside the

---

[85]   Single Market News: *Copyright at the Crossroads?* (May 2005): http://ec. europa.eu/ internal_market/smn/smn37/docs/special-feature_en.pdf.

[86]   Tilman Lueder (Acting Head of the Copyright Unit, DG Internal Market and Services) 'Legislative and Policy Developments in the European Union' (April 2005): http://ec.europa.eu/internal_market/copyright/docs/docs/fordham2005_en.pdf.

[87]   *Copyright and Challenge of Technology – Copyright Issues Requiring Immediate Action* ('Green Paper 1988'), COM/88/172.

Community, was highlighted as a serious problem. In terms of copyright's objectives, the Commission expressed a desire that it should stimulate intellectual and artistic creativity, whilst acknowledging the public interest in access to copyright works.

As for solutions, the 1988 Green Paper argued that the focus should be solely on matters which affected the internal market and Community competitiveness, leaving other matters of fundamental convergence to the Berne Convention: 'The Community approach should therefore be marked by a need to address Community problems. Any temptation to engage in law reform for its own sake should be resisted.'[88] The ECJ's approach to exhaustion of rights was seen as effective to remove many of the general barriers to free movement.[89] Areas the Commission highlighted as needing most urgent treatment were: piracy, home copying of sound and audiovisual material, distribution and rental rights in sound and video recordings, protection for computer programs and databases, and limitations on protection for Community right holders in third countries.

Piracy was seen to be a rapidly growing problem, although it was still possible to write that 'piracy in respect of compact discs is so rare as to be unheard of', because of the cost and unavailability of technology.[90] The introduction of DAT tape was feared. It was understood that developing countries would want a balance of protection and access, and were resistant to the inclusion of intellectual property (IP) rights within the General Agreement on Tariffs and Trade (GATT). A survey of member states revealed a divergence of positions on home copying, and conflicting demands from copyright owners and users. On the still-perennial question of levies, the Commission came out against a Community-wide scheme, whilst deliberately expressing no view on individual domestic schemes. A rental right for sound and video recordings, was regarded as a priority, with *Warner Bros.* v. *Christiansen* described as a 'vivid demonstration of the Community dimension' of the problem of lack of harmonisation.[91]

The discussion of computer programs was strongly coloured by anxiety regarding the dominance of the United States in the computer software market. Concerns about conditions of competition, such as interoperability, and the 'bundling' of hardware and software – issues which only grew more controversial – were already prominent. The importance of computer software to the

---

[88] Green Paper 1988, para. 1.4.10.
[89] On Parallel Imports, see section 6.2. Intellectual property in the Community – the free movement of goods (6.2 and 6.3).
[90] Green Paper 1988, para. 2.3.5.
[91] Green Paper 1988, para. 4.9.1. Case 158/86, *Warner Brothers Inc* v. *Christiansen* [1988] ECR 2605 (para. 13).

Community's economy and its industrial and technological future was 'quite apparent'. The Community's software industry had had a 'late start', and needed appropriate legal protection which would 'contribute to an environment favourable to investment and innovation by Community firms, thus permitting the Community industry to catch up with its competitors'. The general preference for a 'copyright solution' to the protection of computer programs (as opposed to a patent or *sui generis* right) was noted. A Directive was regarded as a matter of urgency.[92] Protection for databases was already being considered. The Commission sought to distinguish between databases of copyright works (which it thought should be protected by copyright as compilations), and databases of non-copyright material (where it was looking to protect 'considerable investment', but was wondering whether to do so by copyright or a *sui generis* right).

In terms of external relations, the Commission displayed considerable flexibility. This was perhaps necessarily so, given its reluctance to embark on comprehensive harmonisation of substantive Community copyright law. The Commission expressed willingness to work cooperatively with WIPO, in order to put across the Community point of view. The possibility of Community participation in Diplomatic Conferences, and also perhaps even of EEC membership of WIPO Treaties, had already been raised. The Uruguay round of GATT had been launched in 1986, and would in 1994 spawn the TRIPS Agreement. At this very preliminary stage of negotiations, the Community and Commission welcomed the initiative in so far as it affected intellectual property. In particular, they supported the objectives of better enforcement, the application of GATT principles to the field, the introduction of the dispute settlement procedure, wider adherence to international treaties, and the transposition of basic substantive intellectual property provisions into GATT (at least, where those principles were widely accepted).[93] The Commission was also talking to the OECD Trade Committee, the International Labour Organisation, and the Council of Europe. Finally, it was committed to pursue bilateral agreements where appropriate.

Following further consultations, the Commission issued its Working Programme.[94] The original Green Paper had been criticised for its apparent preoccupation with market issues and entrepreneurial rights, rather than

---

[92] Green Paper 1988, paras. 5.2.1–5.2.13.

[93] Green Paper 1988, para. 7.2.7.

[94] *Follow-up to the Green Paper 1991 – Working Programme of the Commission in the Field of Copyright and Neighbouring Rights* COM(90) 584. For contemporary reactions, see A. Francon, 'Thoughts on the Green Paper' (1989) 139 RIDA 128; M. Moller, 'On the Subject of the Green Paper' (1989) 141 RIDA 22 (1989); Gerhard Shricker, 'Harmonization of Copyright in the EEC' (1989) 20(4) *IIC* 466–84.

authors' rights. The revised proposals redressed this balance somewhat. A host of Directives has followed; covering computer programs, rental and lending rights, neighbouring rights, cable and satellite broadcasting, copyright term, databases, the royalty on resale of an artist's work, and copyright in the 'information society'. Five of the seven copyright Directives are essentially vertical in nature; they protect particular sectors, or focus on particular rights. Only the Term Directive and the Information Society Directive attempt horizontal harmonisation, and it is arguable that the ambitions of even these measures were quite significantly constrained.

Individually negotiated, the various Directives reflect aspects of all the underlying systems they seek to harmonise, sometimes seeming more mishmash than synthesis in terms of their conceptual underpinnings.[95] Perhaps predictably, where there have been differences in approach, the tendency has been to adopt the highest level of protection. The Term Directive offers a good example, whereby the standard term of copyright was raised to the author's life plus 70 years (the then term in Germany), in preference to adopting the life plus 50-year term laid down in the Berne Convention, and in use in many member states at that time. Although such a strategy is in part attributable to political and legislative expediency, a trend to strengthen the position of right holders is also detectable. It should be noted that the degree of harmonisation in these Directives is not always strict. Member states may be allowed significant leeway in certain circumstances, on specific points. There is also a growing tendency to lay down principles of approach rather than comprehensive detail, leaving the member states to adopt rules within this framework which dovetail with their national systems. For example, the Information Society Directive is notable in allowing member states to adopt anywhere between none and 20 optional exceptions to their copyright regimes (although admittedly these must be chosen from an exhaustive list).

2.3.2　The Computer Programs Directive

As has been discussed, the Computer Programs Directive was seen by the Commission as a matter of urgency, and it was the first to be adopted.[96] Its implementation date was 1 January 1993.[97] The Directive's Preamble

---

[95]　See also, Maria Lillà Montagnani and Maurizio Borghi, 'Promises and Pitfalls of the European Copyright Law Harmonization Process' in David Ward (ed.), *The European Union and the Culture Industries: Regulation and the Public Interest* (Aldershot: Ashgate, 2008).

[96]　Directive 91/250 [1991] OJ L 122/42 ('Software Dir.'). A codified version is under discussion: see COM(2008) 23; 2008/0019 (COD) (28 January 2008).

[97]　For further detail see *Report from the Commission to the Council, the*

emphasises that 'computer program technology' is considered 'of fundamental importance for the Community's industrial development'. When the proposal was first mooted, the legislative field was comparatively open, in that only five of the then 12 member states had provisions expressly protecting computer programs. There were also significant differences in the level of protection offered. The Commission was concerned that this would perpetuate or create barriers to intra-Community trade in computer programs, and would deter software companies in the Community. Nevertheless, total harmonisation of the Community framework on the protection of computer programs was not proposed. The preliminary ambition was to remove and prevent differences which adversely affected the functioning of the common market to a substantial degree. The central aims were: to establish that computer programs should be protected under copyright law; to establish who and what should be protected; to define the exclusive rights conferred; and, to determine the term of protection.

The Directive therefore requires member states to protect computer programs, by copyright, as literary works within the meaning of the Berne Convention.[98] The definition of a computer program was also standardised, since there had been considerable differences in the level of originality demanded by member states. Under the terms of the Directive, a computer program must be protected 'if it is original in the sense that it is the author's own intellectual creation'.[99] No other criteria may be applied, although it is made clear that ideas and principles which underlie any element of a computer program, including those which underlie its interfaces, are not protected.[100] The 'author' of a computer program is the person (or persons) who creates it.[101] Note that for computer programs created by employees in the course of their employment, the employer will be granted the copyright, unless the contract provides otherwise. The Directive covers economic rights only (not moral rights).

The owner of copyright in a computer program has a number of exclusive rights, including the right to control the following: its temporary or permanent reproduction (including its loading, displaying, running, transmission or stor-

---

European Parliament and the Economic and Social Committee on the implementation and effects of directive 91/250/EEC on the legal protection of computer programs COM(2000) 199 final.

[98]   Software Dir., Art. 1(1).

[99]   Software Dir., Art. 1(3). At the time this required 12 member states to lower their threshold for granting protection, and the remaining three to raise it.

[100]   Software Dir., Art. 1(2).

[101]   Software Dir., Art. 2(1). This may be a legal person if member states permit this. If collective works are recognised by the legislation of a member state, this legislation will determine who is deemed the program's author.

age); its translation, adaptation and arrangement; and any form of distribution to the public, including rental.[102] Certain acts of secondary infringement are also prohibited.[103] Four exceptions to these exclusive rights are required, and their negotiation was a matter of considerable controversy. Acts 'necessary for the use of the computer program by the lawful acquirer in accordance with its intended purpose' are permitted, as is the making of a back-up copy by a lawful user of the program. A lawful user may also 'observe, study or test the functioning of the program' under certain conditions, to determine its 'ideas and principles'.[104] The most controversial exception allows the decompilation of programs, in certain very limited circumstances, to permit interoperability with other programs. The compromise was intended to limit decompilation to the minimum necessary to achieve interoperability without prejudicing the copyright holder's legitimate interests. Decompilation is permitted where it is 'indispensable' to obtain information needed to achieve interoperability with an independently created program, provided that it is performed by a lawful user of the original program, that the information necessary to achieve interoperability has not previously been made available, and that decompilation is confined to those parts of the original program needed to achieve interoperability. Any information obtained through decompilation must not be used for any other purpose than achieving the interoperability of an independently created computer program; must not be given to others, except when this is necessary for the interoperability of the independently created computer program; and must not be used for the development, production or marketing of a computer program 'substantially similar in its expression', or for any other act which infringes copyright. This exception is subject to the Berne Convention's three-step test.[105]

2.3.3 The Rental Directive

The Rental Directive addresses not only rental and lending rights, but also certain rights related to copyright. At this time, some member states did not provide any neighbouring rights protection at all, and the Commission therefore thought it appropriate to harmonise other basic related rights at the same

---

[102]   Software Dir., Art. 4. Community-wide exhaustion of the distribution right (but with the clear exception of the rental right) is explicitly provided for.

[103]   Software Dir., Art. 7.

[104]   Software Dir., Art. 5.

[105]   Software Dir., Art. 6. Contractual provisions contrary to Art. 6 or to the exceptions provided for in Art. 5(2), (3) are null and void: Art. 9(1). See also Mikko Valimaki and Ville Oksanen, 'DRM Interoperability and Intellectual Property Policy in Europe' [2006] *EIPR* 562–8.

time. The Preamble notes the importance of these rights: to prevent piracy, but also to secure an adequate income for those involved in creative and artistic work, in order to foster the Community's economic and cultural development. The Directive's implementation date was 1 July 1994.[106]

In *Metronome Musik*,[107] the legality of the Directive was challenged by a trader who argued that the rental right encroached upon the fundamental rights of undertakings operating rental businesses (such as his own), including the right freely to pursue a trade. The referring national court was also concerned that the introduction of an exclusive rental right might infringe the principle of exhaustion of rights. Relying on *Warner Brothers* v. *Christiansen*,[108] the ECJ noted that a simple system of royalties on sales made it impossible to guarantee film makers and phonogram producers a remuneration which reflected the number of occasions on which the object was actually hired out, and which secured them a satisfactory share of the rental market. Rental rights were therefore clearly justified on grounds of the protection of industrial and commercial property. Nor did they breach the exhaustion principle, because the purpose and scope of the distribution right is different. Unlike the distribution right, a rental right is not exhausted by sale (or any other act of distribution).[109] The freedom to pursue a trade was not unqualified, and might be restricted if the restrictions corresponded to objectives of general interest and were not disproportionate in achieving those aims. The Court held that the Rental Directive did pursue objectives of general interest, including the economic and cultural development of the Community, and the need to guarantee that authors and performers could 'receive appropriate income and amortise the especially high and risky investments required particularly for the production of phonograms and films'.[110] These objectives could not have been achieved by preserving greater entrepreneurial freedom for those specialising in the commercial rental of films and phonograms, who remained free to negotiate with right holders for authorisation to pursue this business.

Chapter I of the Directive requires that an exclusive right to control rental and lending be given to authors (in respect of their works), performers (in respect of fixations of their performances), phonogram producers (in respect

---

[106]   The original version, Directive 92/100, has now been replaced with a codified version: Directive 2006/115 on rental right and lending right and on certain rights related to copyright in the field of intellectual property (codified version) [2006] OJ L 376/28.

[107]   Case C-200/96, *Metronome Musik GmbH* v. *Music Point Hokamp GmbH* [1998] ECR I-1953.

[108]   Case 158/86, *Warner Brothers Inc.* v. *Christiansen* [1988] ECR 2605.

[109]   Confirmed in Rental Dir., Art. 2(1).

[110]   Case C-200/96, *Metronome Musik GmbH* v. *Music Point Hokamp GmbH* [1998] ECR I-1953 (para. 22).

of their phonograms) and film producers (in respect of their films).[111] However, the exclusive right is qualified in certain respects. The rights may be transferred, assigned or licensed. Under a film production contract, performers are presumed to have transferred their rental rights unless stated otherwise.[112] Member states may provide for a similar presumption with respect to authors.[113] In an attempt to guarantee that creators will enjoy the income from the rental right, the Directive provides for an 'unwaivable right to equitable remuneration' when films or phonograms are rented.[114] Member states' approaches to attribution of authorship in films differed considerably, so the question had to be addressed. Again in an attempt to link rental income to the creator (rather than the entrepreneur), the Directive specifies that the principal director of a cinematographic or audiovisual work must be regarded as one of its authors, although member states may provide for others to be considered as the work's co-authors.[115]

The issue of the unwaivable right to equitable remuneration is contentious. It is argued that without this approach, authors and performers (having little bargaining power) would simply assign their rental rights to the entrepreneur by contract, usually for a minimal flat-rate fee. They would thus not benefit effectively from the new right. If an equitable remuneration is guaranteed, it must be individually negotiated, having regard to the relevant contribution. Payments in such cases should normally be higher. Since the right to equitable remuneration cannot be waived, and may be assigned only for the purposes of administration, this should guarantee a more balanced participation in the economic exploitation of the work. Those arguing against such arrangements

---

[111] Rental Dir., Art. 3(1). Buildings and works of applied art are not covered. 'Rental' means 'making available for use, for a limited period of time and for direct or indirect economic or commercial advantage'. 'Lending' means 'making available for use, for a limited period of time and not for direct or indirect economic or commercial advantage, when it is made through establishments which are accessible to the public': Art. 2(1)(a), (b). This definition covers more than physical copies, and could cover 'pay per view', subscription services, and other online exploitations. The intention was also to *exclude* certain forms of making available (such as making available phonograms or films for the purpose of public performance or broadcasting, making available for the purpose of exhibition, or making available for on-the-spot reference use). Lending does not include making available between establishments which are accessible to the public: Recital 10.

[112] Rental Dir., Art. 3(4). Member states may also provide that the signing of a film production contract has the effect of authorising rental, provided that equitable remuneration is given: Art. 3(6).

[113] Rental Dir., Art. 3(5).

[114] Rental Dir., Art. 5. Member states may provide for the administration of the equitable remuneration right to be handled by collecting societies.

[115] Rental Dir., Art. 2(2).

consider them excessively burdensome and cumbersome for those negotiating and administering them. The concept of equitable remuneration is not defined in the Directive. It was considered by the ECJ in *SENA* v. *NOS*, where the Court declined to dictate specific methods for determining payments, noting that Article 12 of the Rome Convention (which was the inspiration for the Community provision) left it to member states to determine the most relevant criteria within their territory, but stressing that the Community concept of equitable remuneration must be interpreted uniformly in all member states.[116]

One very important exception from Chapter I rights is that member states may derogate from the exclusive lending right, provided that at least authors obtain some remuneration when this occurs. Member states are free to determine this remuneration in the light of their cultural promotion objectives, and may exempt certain categories of establishments from payment.[117] There is a limit to how far this exemption may be carried. For example, the Portuguese law implementing the Directive exempted a vast range of establishments: all state central administrative services, all bodies part of indirect state administration (such as public establishments and public associations), all local administrative services and bodies, all private-law legal persons carrying out functions of a public nature (such as bodies providing administrative services to public and even private schools and universities), and all private non-profit-making institutions. The Commission argued that this amounted to exempting any public lending establishment from the obligation of payment. The ECJ held that the derogation could not be interpreted as allowing for total derogation from the obligation of remuneration. The main objective of the Directive 'is to guarantee that authors and performers receive appropriate income and recoup the especially high and risky investments required particularly for the production of phonograms and films'.[118] Exempting all categories of establishments which engage in public lending from the obligation to pay remuneration would deprive authors of the means to recoup their investments, and would have inevitable repercussions for the creation of new works. This would go directly against the objective of the Directive, and Portugal was held to be in breach of its obligations. Other countries have tried the same approach, and met the same response.[119]

---

[116]   Case C-245/00, *Stichting ter Exploitatie van Naburige Rechten (SENA)* v. *Nederlandse Omroep Stichting (NOS)* [2003] ECR 1251. Here, the Netherlands model was found to be acceptable.

[117]   Rental Dir., Art. 6(1).

[118]   Case C-53/05, *Commission* v. *Portuguese Republic* (6 July 2006) (para. 24).

[119]   Case C-36/05, *Commission* v. *Kingdom of Spain* (26 October 2006); Case C-175/05, *Commission* v. *Ireland* (11 January 2007) [2007] ECDR 8.

The public lending right was a consequence of the growth in public libraries after World War II. Whilst acknowledging the cultural benefits of wide public access to work, authors nevertheless sought remuneration for the increased use of their works, which impacted their sales. Member states responded to this situation in a broad range of ways (and some not at all). Many preferred to provide for lending rights outside the framework of copyright laws. Originally the Commission's Green Paper had not addressed the subject of the public lending right, regarding this as non-commercial. It was later persuaded that it should be included in the Directive, but that member states should be left a very considerable margin of discretion. The issue was hotly debated, and the original Directive provided that, three years after its adoption, the Commission should draw up a report on public lending in the Community.[120] The resulting Report defended the degree of harmonisation provided for by the Directive as an important step forward, if not necessarily the ultimate solution. It considered that the ways in which most member states had transposed the Directive represented an improvement in protection, though acknowledged that it was 'far from obvious' that all member states had complied with their minimum obligations under its terms. The Commission has indicated a willingness to revisit the issue of harmonisation of the public lending right, if necessary. It also has recognised that the media market and the role of libraries are changing profoundly in the digital environment, and that the use of new technologies in public libraries needs to be monitored so that any potential impact on the functioning of the single market, or on rental and lending activities, can be assessed and addressed.

Chapter II of the Directive deals with related rights. Performers have an exclusive right to control the fixation of their unfixed performances,[121] and their broadcasting and communication to the public.[122] They also have a right to a share (with the phonogram producer) of a 'single equitable remuneration' paid for publication or broadcast of a phonogram.[123] They also have a distribution right ('the exclusive right to make available to the public, by sale or otherwise') in respect of their fixed performances.[124] Broadcasting organisations have an exclusive right to control the fixation of

---

[120] *Report from the Commission Committee on the public lending right in the European Union* COM(2002) 502 final.

[121] Rental Dir., Art. 7(1).

[122] Rental Dir., Art. 8(1).

[123] Rental Dir., Art. 8(2). In the absence of agreement between the performers and phonogram producers, member states may determine the conditions under which the remuneration is shared.

[124] Rental Dir., Art. 9(1)(a). The distribution right is exhausted only by first sale in the Community by the right holder or with his consent.

their broadcasts,[125] to control the rebroadcasting of their broadcasts by wireless means, and to control their communication to the public (if entrance is subject to payment of a fee).[126] They also have a distribution right ('the exclusive right to make available to the public, by sale or otherwise') in respect of fixations of their broadcasts.[127] Phonogram producers have a right to a share (with performers) of a 'single equitable remuneration' paid for publication or broadcast of a phonogram.[128] They also have a distribution right ('the exclusive right to make available to the public, by sale or otherwise') in respect of their phonograms.[129] Producers of the first fixations of films have a distribution right ('the exclusive right to make available to the public, by sale or otherwise') in respect of their films.[130] Exceptions to Chapter II rights are permitted for private use, use of short excerpts for reporting current events, ephemeral fixation by a broadcasting organisation by means of its own facilities and for its own broadcasts, and use solely for the purposes of teaching or scientific research. Member states may also provide for the same kinds of exceptions to related rights as they do for copyright in literary and artistic works. All exceptions are subject to the Berne three-step test.[131]

2.3.4   The Satellite and Cable Directive

In 1984 the Commission published a Green Paper on the establishment of a common market in broadcasting.[132] It covered a number of issues, such as the regulation of advertising, but also attempted to address the copyright aspect of trans-frontier broadcasting, with a view to promoting a common market. It proposed a statutory licensing scheme, whereby member states would be obliged to repeal copyright holders' rights to prohibit cable transmission of their works, and replace them with a right to equitable remuneration, exercised

---

[125]   Rental Dir., Art. 7(2). This right applies however the broadcasts are transmitted. A cable distributor does not have this right where it merely retransmits by cable a broadcasting organisation's broadcasts: Art. 7(3).

[126]   Rental Dir., Art. 8(3).

[127]   Rental Dir., Art. 9(1)(d).

[128]   Rental Dir., Art. 8(2). In the absence of agreement between the performers and phonogram producers, member states may determine the conditions under which the remuneration is shared.

[129]   Rental Dir., Art. 9(1)(b).

[130]   Rental Dir., Art. 9(1)(c).

[131]   Rental Dir., Art. 10.

[132]   *Television without Frontiers: Green Paper on the Establishment of the Common Market for Broadcasting, especially by Satellite and Cable* COM(84) 300 final.

only by collecting societies.[133] This remarkable suggestion made no further progress, and the 'Television without Frontiers' Directive (adopted in 1989) did not deal with copyright issues.[134] A subsequent Commission Discussion Paper emphasised that a balancing of rights was needed in order that the European dimension of broadcasting could be fully exploited. It stressed the need for 'adequate' protection of copyright in relation to primary satellite broadcasting, and acknowledged that there should be no compulsory licensing. In relation to cable retransmission, the Commission proposed a system of collective rights management, with a mechanism to ensure that individual right holders could not hold up negotiations 'by excessive demands or conditions which might constitute abuse'.[135]

The Satellite and Cable Directive should be seen against this background.[136] It was intended to break down national barriers and enhance transborder broadcasting and cable retransmission of television programmes within the European Union. It was widely acknowledged that inconsistencies in the approaches of national laws were impeding cross-border satellite broadcasting, undermining legal certainty and discouraging contractual arrangements. The challenge was to achieve improvement in these areas without compromising rights in the underlying copyright works.

Chapter II of the Directive deals with satellite broadcasting. It attempts to prevent the fragmentation of the European market by creating a unitary right of satellite communication which can only be exercised in the country of origin ('uplink') of a satellite transmission.[137] The aim was to impose a common, simple solution. Previous national schemes had made various different choices, perhaps taking into consideration the country where the broadcast originated, the location of the satellite itself, or the countries where the signal could be received ('footprint' countries). Instead, the intention was to allow broadcasters to clear all rights in accordance with the legislation of the signal's country of origin. Certain minimum standards are guaranteed for right holders.

---

[133]   *Television without Frontiers: Green Paper on the Establishment of the Common Market for Broadcasting, especially by Satellite and Cable* COM(84) 300 final, 330–31.

[134]   Directive 89/552/EEC on the coordination of certain provisions laid down by law, regulation or administrative action in Member States concerning the pursuit of television broadcasting activities.

[135]   Broadcasting and Copyright in the Internal Market. Discussion Paper prepared by the Commission of the European Communities on Copyright Questions concerning Cable and Satellite Broadcasts. III/F/5263/80-EN (November 1990), 4–5.

[136]   Directive 93/83 on the coordination of certain rules concerning copyright and rights related to copyright applicable to satellite broadcasting and cable retransmission [1993] OJ L 248/15. Its implementation date was 1 January 1995.

[137]   Satellite Dir., Art. 1(2).

Authors must be given a 'broadcasting right'; an exclusive right for the author to authorise communication to the public by satellite of copyright works.[138] The related rights of performers, phonogram producers and broadcasting organisations are protected in accordance with the Rental Directive (at the minimum).[139] Copyright protection remains unaffected.[140]

Chapter III of the Directive deals with cable retransmission. It sets out a system of compulsory collective management of cable retransmission rights. Member states have an obligation to ensure that when programmes from other member states are retransmitted by cable in their territory the applicable copyright and related rights are observed, and that such retransmission takes place on the basis of contractual agreements between copyright owners, holders of related rights and cable operators.[141] The right to grant or refuse authorisation to a cable operator for a cable retransmission must be exercised through a collecting society.[142] This does not apply to a broadcasting organisation's rights in respect of its own transmission, irrespective of whether the rights concerned are its own or have been transferred to it by other copyright owners and/or holders of related rights.[143] The intention is that collecting societies will negotiate retransmission rights with cable operators and broadcasters.[144]

The Commission was required to report on the application of the Directive and, if necessary, 'make further proposals to adapt it to developments in the audio and audiovisual sector'.[145] The Report frankly acknowledged that the

---

[138]   Satellite Dir., Art. 2.
[139]   Satellite Dir., Art. 4. See also Art. 6.
[140]   Satellite Dir., Art. 2.
[141]   Satellite Dir., Art. 8(1).
[142]   Satellite Dir., Art. 9(1). Right holders may be deemed to have transferred the management of their rights to a collecting society if they have not in fact done so: Art. 9(2). In such a case that society has the power to exercise that right holder's right to grant or refuse authorisation to a cable operator for cable retransmission and, consequently, its mandate is not limited to management of the pecuniary aspects of those rights: Case C-169/05, *Uradex SCRL* v. *Union Professionnelle de la Radio et de la Télédistribution* (RTD) [2006] ECR 4973.
[143]   Satellite Dir., Art. 10. This aim was to offer an alternative to Art. 9, in situations where a broadcasting organisation had acquired all cable retransmission rights and was thus the sole party dealing with the cable operator. However, this is weakened by German legislation, which provides for a right to equitable remuneration for authors, and cable operators can pay this only through a collecting society. Since this does not allow a sole contract to be concluded between the broadcaster and the cable operator, it can make negotiations on cable retransmission more difficult in Germany than in the other member states.
[144]   Negotiations are subject to a right to non-binding mediation (available at the request of either of the parties) and to an obligation on each of the parties not to prevent negotiation improperly: Satellite Dir., Arts. 11, 12.
[145]   Satellite Dir., Art. 14(2).

Directive has not achieved the freedom in trans-border broadcasting which the Commission had hoped.[146] One particular concern is the difficulties which viewers encounter in accessing satellite channels transmitted outside the member state in which they are resident. The Commission regards this as a fetter on the freedom of movement of services, which also affects citizens' ability to exploit the cultural and economic opportunities provided by the internal market. The problem is the proliferation of television channels, many of which are encrypted and accessible by subscription only. Even if potential viewers outside the member state of transmission are willing to pay for access, they are often refused it because the broadcasting organisation does not hold the copyright for the member state where the potential viewers are. This also means that the broadcasting organisation has little incentive to ensure that its programmes are broadcast outside its national market. The problems affect not only pay-TV channels but also uncoded channels, both private broadcasting organisations and public-service broadcasters. Producers tend to sell their programmes to broadcasting organisations on condition that satellite transmissions are encrypted so they cannot be received beyond national borders. Producers can then sell the same programmes to broadcasting organisations in other member states. This practice inevitably fragments the market, and runs counter to the aims of the Directive.

Complete application of the principle of the Directive would involve moving beyond a purely national territorial approach, and would allow the internal market to be a genuine market without internal frontiers for right holders, operators and viewers. The Commission is committed to further research and consultations with the various sectors concerned, to determine how to reconcile the different interests involved with the principle of the free movement of television services. All this has to be done against a background of rapidly changing technology, and rapidly evolving audiovisual services, which will necessarily have an impact on viewers' habits and choices. The Commission remains cautious as to whether the scope of the Directive should be revised in response to these problems and changes. There remains a big question as to whether the Commission's vision is feasible in practice. Although the concept of pan-European television services may be attractive in theory, at the moment it seems unlikely that more than a few specialised broadcasters will want to engage in this expensive practice.[147]

---

[146] *Report from the European Commission on the application of Council Directive 93/83/EEC on the coordination of certain rules concerning copyright and rights related to copyright applicable to satellite broadcasting and cable retransmission* COM(2002) 430 final.

[147] For thoughtful and lively comment on these issues see P.B. Hugenholtz, *Copyright without Frontiers: Is there a Future for the Satellite and Cable Directive?*

2.3.5   The Term Directive

The Term Directive was put in place following *EMI* v. *Patricia*, a case which highlighted the difficulties which an unharmonised regime entailed.[148] EMI had rights to market sound recordings by Cliff Richard in Germany. It objected to sales in Germany of sound recordings lawfully marketed in Denmark, where the sound recording rights had expired. Did the Treaty provisions on the free movement of the goods allow EMI to resist these imports? The exhaustion principle provides that where sound recordings are marketed in the Community by the right owner, or with the right owner's consent, those rights are exhausted by that act of marketing.[149] Here, however, the fact that the sound recordings were lawfully marketed in Denmark was not due to an act of the copyright owner, but to the expiry of the national protection period for sound recording rights. The ECJ observed that 'in the present state of Community law, which is characterized by a lack of harmonization or approximation of legislation governing the protection of literary and artistic property, it is for the national legislatures to determine the conditions and detailed rules for such protection'.[150] The restriction on intra-Community trade was therefore justified, because it was the result of differences between the rules governing the period of protection, and this was inseparably linked to the very existence of the exclusive rights.

Before the Term Directive, most member states had adopted the Berne Convention's minimum requirement for copyright protection, which was 50 years from the author's death. But there were some variations, with Germany providing a 70-year post mortem term, Spain and others 60 years, and so on. For related rights (neighbouring rights) such as performers' rights, rights in phonograms, and rights in broadcasts, there was a much wider degree of variation, since not all member states were party to the Rome Convention. Fifty-year protection was common, although with a range of commencement dates (performance, making, fixation, first communication to the public). But protection in other countries included terms of 20, 25, 30 and 40 years, with

---

Published in Die Zukunft der Fernsehrichtlinie/The Future of the 'Television without Frontiers' Directive, Proceedings of the conference organised by the Institute of European Media Law (EMR) in cooperation with the European Academy of Law, Trier (ERA), Schriftenreihe des Instituts für Europäisches Medienrecht (EMR), Band 29, Baden-Baden: Nomos Verlag 2005. Available at: http://www.ivir.nl/publications/hugenholtz/copyrightwithoutfrontiers.html.

[148]   Case C-341/87, *EMI Electrola GmbH* v. *Patricia Im- und Export* [1989] ECR 79.

[149]   Case C-55/80, *Musik-Vertrieb Membran GmbH* v. *GEMA* [1981] ECR 147.

[150]   Case C-341/87, *EMI Electrola GmbH* v. *Patricia Im- und Export* [1989] ECR 79 (para. 11).

Belgium and the Netherlands offering no specific protection for such rights. The appropriate term for copyright has been a matter of controversy for centuries. The Term Directive adopted a policy of harmonising upwards.[151]

The author of a literary or artistic work within the meaning of the Berne Convention must enjoy copyright for life plus 70 years.[152] Original photographs are included within this.[153] For works of joint authorship, the term runs from the death of the last surviving author.[154] For anonymous or pseudonymous works, the term runs for 70 years from when the work is lawfully made available to the public.[155] Cinematographic and audiovisual works are separately treated. The principal director of such works must be regarded as its author or one of its authors.[156] The term expires 70 years after the death of the last of: the principal director, the author of the screenplay, the author of the dialogue and the composer of music specifically created for the film (whether or not these persons are designated as co-authors).[157]

The term of protection for related rights is essentially 50 years. For performers the term runs from the date of the performance, but if a fixation (recording) of the performance is published within this period the rights run from the date of first lawful publication or communication to the public.[158] The rights of producers of phonograms run from the first fixation, but if the fixation is published, the rights will expire 50 years from the date of first publication. If no lawful publication has been made, and the phonogram has been lawfully communicated to the public within this period, the rights run

---

[151] Directive 93/98 [1993] OJ L 290/9 (in force 1 July 1995). Now replaced by Directive 2006/116 on the term of protection of copyright and certain related rights (codified version) [2006] OJ L 372/12. Recitals 6 and 7 put forward two particular justifications for the upward trend. Firstly, that the 50-year term under the Berne Convention was intended to provide protection for the author and the first two generations of his descendants, but, since the average lifespan in the Community has grown longer, such a term is no longer sufficient to cover two generations. Secondly, that certain member states had granted a term longer than 50 years after the death of the author, to offset the effects of the world wars on the exploitation of authors' works.

[152] Term Dir., Art. 1(1).

[153] A photographic work is to be considered original if it is 'the author's own intellectual creation': Term Dir., Art. 6. Recital 16 explains that this means 'the author's own intellectual creation reflecting his personality'. No other criteria such as merit or purpose may be taken into account. Member states remain free to protect other photographs as they wish.

[154] Term Dir., Art. 1(2).

[155] Term Dir., Art. 1(3).

[156] Term Dir., Art. 2(1).

[157] Term Dir., Art. 2(2).

[158] Term Dir., Art. 3(1).

from the date of the first lawful communication to the public.[159] The rights of producers of the first fixation of a film run from fixation. However, if the film is lawfully published or lawfully communicated to the public during this period, the rights run from the date of first publication or first communication to the public, whichever is the earlier.[160] The rights of broadcasting organisations run from first transmission of a broadcast.[161]

Previously unpublished works published for the first time after copyright protection has expired are covered by a new right (often called the 'publication right'), which is 'equivalent to the economic rights of the author'. It is given to a person who first lawfully publishes or communicates the work to the public, and lasts 25 years from the date of such publication or communication.[162] Member states are also free to protect critical and scientific publications of works which have come into the public domain, for a maximum term of 30 years from first lawful publication.[163] Protection for works from third countries (if the author is not a Community national) is subject to the 'rule of the shorter term'. The terms will expire within the EEA no later than the date of expiry in their country of origin.[164] Note in this context that Community nationals must not be treated differently as a result of any remaining differences in national laws. *Phil Collins* v. *IMTRAT* concerned a concert in California which was recorded without the performer's consent. Copies of the recording were sold in Germany. Collins was not a German national, so could not rely on German law which protected German nationals' performances wherever they had taken place. The United States (the country of performance) was not a signatory to the Rome Convention, so Collins could not invoke this protection either. The German court asked the ECJ whether Collins, as a UK national, was being discriminated against under German law on grounds of nationality – since German nationals were being given more extensive protection than nationals of other member states. The Treaty prohibits 'any discrimination on the grounds of nationality', and this requires 'that persons in a situation governed by Community law be placed on a completely equal footing with nationals of the Member State concerned'.

---

[159]   Term Dir., Art. 3(2). The provision was modified by Art. 11(2) of the Information Society Directive (Directive 2001/29), to address recordings which are communicated to the public before they are published. However, if the rights under the provision as originally set down in the Term Directive had expired, they are not revived by this amendment.

[160]   Term Dir., Art. 3(3). 'Film' is defined as 'a cinematographic or audiovisual work or moving images, whether or not accompanied by sound'.

[161]   Term Dir., Art. 3(4).

[162]   Term Dir., Art. 4.

[163]   Term Dir., Art. 5.

[164]   Term Dir., Art. 7.

Germany was therefore precluded from making the grant of an exclusive right subject to the requirement that the person concerned be a national of that state.[165]

2.3.6 The Database Directive

The Database Directive has been in force since 1 January 1998.[166] The Berne Convention requires its signatories to protect 'collections of literary or artistic works such as encyclopaedias and anthologies which, by reason of the selection and arrangement of their contents, constitute intellectual creations', although such protection must be without prejudice to the copyright in the underlying works.[167] This wording may be interpreted to extend to databases, but in many member states the requirement of originality made it difficult to secure reliable copyright protection for databases. The very issue of whether modern databases form suitable subject matter for copyright protection is somewhat contentious, because in the digital age they may well be the product simply of financial investment (so-called 'sweat-of-the-brow' databases), rather than the original authorial works which form copyright's core subject matter.[168] However, digital technology permits ready access to an immense range and quantity of information, in a form very convenient to the user. Since such databases are readily copied, and, since they may well require significant investment of time and money, there is an argument for some form of intellectual property protection. But there is understandable resistance to bringing such databases within the extensive protection of copyright. The Directive therefore adopts a dual strategy. Firstly, it attempts to harmonise the conditions of copyright protection for databases. Secondly, for those databases which fail to reach the threshold of originality required for copyright, it creates a 15-year

---

[165] Joined Cases C-92/92 and C-326/92, *Phil Collins* v. *Imtrat Handelsgesellschaft* [1993] ECR I-5145. The same applies in cases where the author had already died when the EEC Treaty entered into force in the member state of which he was a national: Case 360/00, *Land Hessen* v. *G Ricordi and Co. Buhnen- und Musikverlag GmbH* [2002] ECR I-5089. Nor may the right of an author to claim copyright protection in a member state be subject to a distinguishing criterion based on the country of origin of the work, even if international conventions provide for protection on the basis of material reciprocity: Case C-28/04, *Tod's SpA* v. *Heyraud SA* [2005] ECR 5781.

[166] Directive 96/9 on the Legal Protection of Databases [1996] OJ L 77/20.

[167] Berne, Art. 2(5).

[168] For different jurisdictions' differing approaches to 'sweat-of-the-brow' copyright see: *Feist Publications Inc.* v. *Rural Telephone Service* (US Supreme Court) 499 US 340 (1991); *CCH Canadian Ltd* v. *The Law Society of Upper Canada* (Supreme Court of Canada) 2004 SCC 13; *Van Dale* v. *Romme* (Dutch Supreme Court), Judgment of 4 January 1991.

sui generis right. This is granted to the maker of a database which shows 'substantial investment' of various forms. The objective was to ensure a clear and appropriate level of protection for database creators and investors in the 'information market' within the EU, encouraging investment in databases whilst safeguarding users' interests.

For the purposes of the Directive, 'database' is defined extremely broadly, as 'a collection of independent works, data or other materials arranged in a systematic or methodical way and individually accessible by electronic or other means'.[169] Paper databases are thus included, as well as electronic ones. The nature of an 'independent' work is not explained in the Directive, but the ECJ has held independent materials to mean 'materials which are separable from one another without their informative, literary, artistic, musical or other value being affected'. The requirement of methodical arrangement 'implies that the collection should be contained in a fixed base, of some sort, and include technical means such as electronic, electromagnetic or electro-optical processes, . . . or other means, such as an index, a table of contents, or a particular plan or method of classification, to allow the retrieval of any independent material contained within it'.[170] Protection does not extend to 'computer programs used in the making or operation of databases accessible by electronic means'.[171] This exclusion suggests that other forms of computer programs may be protected as databases, in appropriate factual circumstances. Another tricky question is how far multimedia works may be protected in their own right as databases.[172]

Copyright protection is extended to 'databases which, by reason of the selection or arrangement of their contents, constitute the author's own intellectual creation shall be protected as such by copyright'.[173] The author of a database has the exclusive right to reproduce it (in whole or in part); to distribute it; to translate, adapt, arrange or alter it; and, to communicate it to the public.[174] A lawful user must have the defence of performing acts which are necessary to access the contents of the databases, and normal use of those

---

[169]   Database Dir., Art. 1(2).
[170]   C-444/02, *Fixtures Marketing Ltd* v. *Organismos Prognostikon Agonon Podosfairou EG* [2004] ECR I-10549 (paras. 29–30).
[171]   Database Dir., Art. 1(3).
[172]   See Tanya Aplin, *Copyright Law in the Digital Society – The Challenges of Multimedia* (Oxford: Hart, 2005).
[173]   Database Dir., Art. 3(1). The author of a database is the natural person who created it, or, where the legislation of a member state permits this, the legal person designated as the right holder by that legislation: Art. 4(1).
[174]   Database Dir., Art. 5. First sale in the Community of a copy of the database by the right holder or with his consent exhausts the right to control resale of that copy within the Community.

contents will not require consent.[175] There is a short list of optional exceptions, which member states may choose to provide for.[176]

The *sui generis* right must be provided where the maker of a database can show 'there has been qualitatively and/or quantitatively a substantial investment in either the obtaining, verification or presentation of the contents' of the database. The right is 'to prevent extraction and/or re-utilization of the whole or of a substantial part, evaluated qualitatively and/or quantitatively, of the contents of that database'.[177] 'Extraction' is defined to mean 'the permanent or temporary transfer of all or a substantial part of the contents of a database to another medium by any means or in any form'. 'Re-utilisation' is defined to mean 'any form of making available to the public all or a substantial part of the contents of a database by the distribution of copies, by renting, by on-line or other forms of transmission'.[178] In addition, 'the repeated and systematic extraction and/or re-utilization of insubstantial parts of the contents of the database implying acts which conflict with a normal exploitation of that database or which unreasonably prejudice the legitimate interests of the maker of the database' will infringe the *sui generis* right. Lawful users may extract and/or reutilise insubstantial parts of the database without infringing, though again the legitimate interests of the maker of the database must not be unreasonably prejudiced.[179] Member states may provide for certain limited exceptions, though these are much narrower than the exceptions for database copyright.[180] The *sui generis* right lasts for 15 years from completion or publication. A substantial change to the contents of a database, if it is considered to be a substantial new investment, qualifies the resulting database for its own term of protection.[181]

---

[175]   Database Dir., Art. 6(1).

[176]   Database Dir., Art. 1(2). These include private copying (though only of a non-electronic database), use of illustrations for teaching or non-commercial scientific research, and use for public security or administrative or judicial procedures. Member states may also provide for 'other exceptions to copyright which are traditionally authorised under national law'. All exceptions are subject to the Berne three-step test.

[177]   Database Dir., Art. 7(1).

[178]   Database Dir., Art. 7(2). As with database copyright, the first sale of a copy of a database within the Community by the right holder or with his consent exhausts the right to control resale of that copy within the Community.

[179]   Database Dir., Art. 8.

[180]   Database Dir., Art. 9. As with database copyright, these include private copying (though only of a non-electronic database), use of illustrations for teaching or non-commercial scientific research, and use for public security or administrative or judicial procedures. However, the 'traditional' copyright exceptions may not be applied. Because the *sui generis* right is not a copyright, there is no requirement that these exceptions should be subject to the Berne three-step test.

[181]   Database Dir., Art. 10.

The Directive has caused considerable controversy. The apparent breadth of its protection, and its potential for indefinite extension, are two recurring criticisms. One major concern initially was that monopolies of information would be created, though the ECJ's narrow interpretation of the scope of the *sui generis* right has substantially reduced this risk.[182] To address this and other concerns, a mechanism for reviewing the application of the right was built into the Directive. The Commission is required to report (every three years), and, in particular, to verify whether the application of the right has led to abuse of a dominant position or any other interference with free competition.[183] Early stakeholder responses to a study undertaken in 2001 included significant criticism. Concerns were expressed that the right was too strong, that the exceptions should be wider, and that some crucial definitions were unclear. A number of users complained about restricted competition in certain areas: such as, the concentration of leading e-journals in a few hands; the creation of *de facto* information monopolies of producers of single source data such as telephone directories, programmes listings or event data. Others argued more positively that database protection fostered competition and economic efficiency, for example, by giving an incentive to license content from more efficient collectors for derivative compilations.[184] The Commission's 2005 report (the first official 'evaluation') concluded that although the *sui generis* right had been introduced to stimulate the production of databases in Europe, it had had no proven impact on it. However, the European publishing industry argued forcefully that *sui generis* protection was crucial to the continued success of their activities, and most respondents to an online survey believed that the new right had brought about legal certainty, reduced the costs associated with the protection of databases, created more business opportunities and facilitated the marketing of databases.[185]

The claim to increased legal certainty is more plausible following several key rulings from the ECJ. There have been four important and controversial

---

[182]   Jerome H. Reichmann and Pamela Samuelson, 'Intellectual Property Rights in Data' (1997) 50 *Vanderbilt Law Review* 51–166; Catherine Colston, '*Sui Generis* Database Right: Ripe for Review' (2001) 3 *Journal of International Law and Technology*; Jacqueline Lipton, 'Databases as Intellectual Property: New Legal Approaches' [2003] *EIPR* 139–45.

[183]   Database Dir., Art. 16(3).

[184]   See the commissioned study, *The Implementation and Application of Directive 96/9/EC on the Legal Protection of Databases* (2001). Available at: http://ec.europa.eu/internal_market/copyright/docs/databases/etd2001b53001e72_en.pdf.

[185]   DG Internal Market and Services working paper, First evaluation of Directive 96/9/EC on the legal protection of databases, para. 1.4., available at: http://ec.europa.eu/internal_market/copyright/docs/databases/evaluation_report_en.pdf.

decisions, offering guidance on central concepts.[186] All involved databases of sporting information. In the *British Horseracing Board (BHB)* case, the claimants maintained a considerable database of information about horses, their owners, trainers and jockeys, and full details of all race meetings. It was claimed that the database cost £4 million per year to maintain. The defendant betting company used some of this information to supply race details to its clients. The ECJ held that this did not amount to infringement. The *sui generis* database right is reserved for databases in which there has been, qualitatively or quantitatively, a substantial investment in the obtaining, verification or presentation of content.[187] However, the concept of 'investment' refers to resources used to seek out existing materials, collect them, verify them and present them in a database.

> The purpose of the protection by the *sui generis* right provided for by the directive is to promote the establishment of storage and processing systems for existing information and not the creation of materials capable of being collected subsequently in a database.[188]

The right thus does not cover resources used for the creation of the materials which make up the contents of the database. In relation to works such as fixture lists, the obtaining and collection of data which makes up the list, and even subsequent verification, do not require any particular effort over and above the creation of the data itself, to which they are inextricably linked. Here, BHB's activities did not require investment which was independent of the resources used by them to create that data in the first instance.[189] This tough approach is an endorsement of aspects of the 'spin-off' doctrine, which is based on the premise that the *sui generis* right is intended to promote investment in European databases, not to protect material which is assembled as a side-effect of other activities. Whatever its basis, the ECJ's distinction between 'creation' of data (unprotected) and 'obtaining and verification of

---

[186]   Case C-338/02, *Fixtures Marketing Ltd* v. *Svenska AB* [2004] ECR I-10497; Case C-444/02, *Fixtures Marketing Ltd* v. *Organismos Prognostikon Agonon Podosfairou EG* [2004] ECR I-10549; Case C-46/02, *Fixtures Marketing Ltd* v. *Oy Veikkaus Ab* ECR I-10365; C-203/02, *British Horseracing Board Ltd* v. *William Hill Organisation Ltd* [2004] ECR 10415. One commentator notes 'the virtual elimination of the *sui generis* right after *William Hill/Fixtures Marketing*': Robert Clark, '*Sui Generis* Database Protection: A New Start for the UK and Ireland?' [2007] *JIPL&P* 97-103, 97.

[187]   Database Dir., Art. 7.

[188]   C-203/02, *British Horseracing Board Ltd* v. *William Hill Organisation Ltd* [2004] ECR 10415, (para. 31).

[189]   C-203/02, *British Horseracing Board Ltd* v. *William Hill Organisation Ltd* [2004] ECR 10415, (paras. 79–80).

contents' (protected) seems likely to be troublesome for the national courts to apply.[190]

The ECJ also offered guidance on infringement, which requires unauthorised extraction or re-utilisation of a 'substantial part' of a database. Both quantitative and qualitative tests must be used. In assessing quality, both the purpose of the third party's use of the data and the intrinsic value of the data are regarded as irrelevant. It thus did not matter that the data extracted and re-utilised by William Hill were vital to the organisation of the horse races, which was BHB's primary responsibility.[191] The ECJ focused instead on the economic justification of the *sui generis* right, which is to afford protection to the maker of the database and guarantee a return on investment in the creation and maintenance of the database. The right to prohibit extraction and/or re-utilisation of all or a substantial part of the contents relates not only to the manufacture of a parasitical competing product but also to any user who, through his acts, causes significant detriment, evaluated qualitatively or quantitatively, to the investment.[192] This finding may prove extremely significant on the facts, because it denies protection to minimal takings which are very valuable to the defendant. Instead, a crucial factor is the scale of the investment (whether human, technical or financial) in that part of the database.[193]

The European Commission is as yet unconvinced that the *sui generis* right is necessary for a thriving database industry, and it put a wide range of policy options on the table in its 2005 evaluation. Responses to stakeholder consultations are currently being considered. Of the 55 responses received, eight

---

[190] See, for example, the UK Court of Appeal's efforts to understand and apply the ECJ's reference in the *BHB* case itself: *British Horseracing Board* v. *William Hill Organisation Ltd* [2005] EWCA Civ. 863. Pill LJ commented (para. 45), 'A distinction is drawn by the ECJ between "obtaining" and "verification" of material, on the one hand, and "creating" it, on the other (paragraphs 31 to 35 of ECJ judgment). I have some difficulty in understanding the use to which the word "create" is put in the judgment and, with respect, whether it is used consistently'. Compare also two recent cases on estate agents' databases (although different rights were relied on in each case); the Dutch decision in *ZAH* (Arnhem City Court, Civil Division in summary proceedings, 16 March 2006), and the Norwegian decision in *Finn No AS* v. *Supersok AS* [2007] ECDR 12.

[191] C-203/02, *British Horseracing Board Ltd* v. *William Hill Organisation Ltd* [2004] ECR 10415, (para. 78).

[192] C-203/02, *British Horseracing Board Ltd* v. *William Hill Organisation Ltd* [2004] ECR 10415, (paras. 45–7).

[193] For more see Tanya Aplin, 'The ECJ Elucidates the Database Right' [2005] *IPQ* 204–21; Mark J. Davison and P. Bernt Hugenholtz, 'Football Fixtures, Horseraces and Spin-offs: The ECJ Domesticates the Database Right' [2005] *EIPR* 113–18; Antoine Masson, 'Creation of Database or Creation of Data: Crucial Choices in the Matter of Database Protection' [2006] EIPR 261–7; Juliet Jenkins, 'Database Rights' Subsistence: Under Starter's Orders' [2006] *JIPL&P* 467–80.

were in favour of repeal of the Directive, three supported withdrawing the *sui generis* right while leaving protection for creative databases unchanged, 26 preferred to see the *sui generis* provisions amended in order to clarify their scope, leaving 26 content to maintain the status quo.[194] There is pressure both for a broader definition of the *sui generis* right (mainly in reaction to the ECJ's narrow interpretation of it) and for more exceptions to it. The Commission must now determine whether further legislative changes are worth pursuing.

2.3.7 The E-Commerce Directive

The E-Commerce Directive was regarded by the Lisbon Summit as a priority both in preparing Europe's transition to a knowledge-based economy, and in boosting competitiveness.[195] The global e-commerce market is growing extremely fast, and the slow response of European industry has concerned the Commission. The Directive aims to ensure that information society services benefit from the internal market principles of free movement, and can be provided throughout the EU if they comply with the law in their home member state. A number of specific harmonised rules have been introduced also, governing the establishment of service providers,[196] transparency requirements for commercial communications,[197] the formation and validity of electronic contracts,[198] the liability of internet intermediaries, codes of conduct, out-of-court dispute settlements, court actions and cooperation between member states. Many of these apply very widely to providers of information society services, and are not specifically related to intellectual property. These will not be discussed in detail in this text.

The Directive's impact on intellectual property is probably strongest in relation to the liability of internet service providers (ISPs). An ISP provides consumers with access to the internet and related services. Formerly the province of phone companies, the technology is now so accessible that ISPs are far more diverse both in their nature and in terms of the services they offer. Some ISPs provide access through local servers or internet cafés, others by running or hosting bulletin boards or web sites, and so on. It has often been

---

[194] Some of the responses supported more than one option. Many are available at: http://ec.europa.eu/internal_market/copyright/prot-databases/prot-databases_en.htm. For possible negative consequences of repeal, particularly in relation to scientific data, see Charlotte Waelde, 'Databases and Lawful Users: the Chink in the Armour' [2006] *IPQ* 256–82.

[195] Directive 2000/31/EC on certain legal aspects of information society services, in particular electronic commerce, in the Internal Market [2000] OJ L 178/1.

[196] E-Commerce Dir., Arts. 4–5.

[197] E-Commerce Dir., Arts. 6–8.

[198] E-Commerce Dir., Arts. 9–11.

suggested that ISPs have more practical power than right holders to address the infringement of intellectual property rights in material found on sites which they control.[199] Predictably, member states were taking different approaches to these questions, and the EU stepped in to ensure a harmonised response. This was not possible through the Information Society Directive exclusively, because liability might have arisen in a number of ways (copyright, defamation, obscenity etc.). Instead, the E-Commerce Directive lays down the necessary framework. The general position is that ISPs are immune from liability. This follows the lead established by the US in the Digital Millennium Copyright Act, and, indeed, the Directive's provisions echo the DMCA's 'safe-harbour' provisions quite closely.[200]

There are three immunities provided for by the E-Commerce Directive:

(a) 'Mere Conduit': Where the service is 'the transmission in a communication network of information provided by a recipient of the service, or the provision of access to a communication network', the ISP will not be liable for the information transmitted, on condition that the provider does not initiate the transmission, does not select the receiver of the transmission, and does not select or modify the information contained in the transmission.[201] In this situation, the ISP is regarded as acting as a mere conduit.

(b) Caching: Where the service consists of 'the transmission in a communication network of information provided by a recipient of the service', the ISP will not be liable 'for the automatic, intermediate and temporary storage of that information, performed for the sole purpose of making more efficient the information's onward transmission to other recipients of the service upon their request'. This immunity is subject to five further conditions that: (1) the provider does not modify the information; (2) the provider complies with conditions on access to the information; (3) the provider complies with rules regarding the updating of the information, specified in a manner widely recognised and used by industry; (4) the provider does not interfere with the lawful use of technology, widely recognised and used by industry, to obtain data on the use of the information; and (5) the provider acts expeditiously to remove or to disable access to the information it has stored upon obtaining actual knowledge of the fact that the information at the initial source of the transmission has been removed from the network, or access to it has been disabled, or that

---

[199] See, for example, Info. Soc. Dir., Recital 59.
[200] Victoria McEvedy, 'The DMCA and the Ecommerce Directive' [2002] *EIPR* 65–73.
[201] E-Commerce Dir., Art. 12(1).

a court or an administrative authority has ordered such removal or disablement.[202]

(c) Hosting: Where the service consists of the storage of information provided by a recipient of the service, the ISP will not be liable for the information stored at the request of that recipient, on condition that: the provider does not have actual knowledge of illegal activity or information and, as regards claims for damages, is not aware of facts or circumstances from which the illegal activity or information is apparent; or the provider, upon obtaining such knowledge or awareness, acts expeditiously to remove or to disable access to the information.[203]

In all these three cases the ISP is exempted from liability for damages and criminal sanctions, but may be subject to injunctive relief, in accordance with member states' legal systems. ISPs providing these services may not be subject to a general obligation to monitor the information which they transmit or store, nor to a general obligation actively to seek facts or circumstances indicating illegal activity. However, member states are free to establish procedures by which ISPs must promptly inform the competent public authorities of alleged illegal activities undertaken or information provided by recipients of their service, or by which ISPs must provide the competent authorities with information identifying the recipients of their storage services.[204] Member states are free to establish procedures governing the removal or disabling of access to information.[205]

2.3.8 The Information Society Directive

On the adoption of the Information Society Directive, Internal Market Commissioner Frits Bolkestein observed:

> Not only is this Directive the most important measure ever to be adopted by Europe in the copyright field but it brings European copyright rules into the digital age. Europe's creators, artists and copyright industries can now look forward with

---

[202]   E-Commerce Dir., Art. 13(1).

[203]   E-Commerce Dir., Art. 14(1).

[204]   E-Commerce Dir., Art. 15. Though see Case C-275/06, *Productores de Música de España (Promusicae)* v. *Telefónica de España SAU* (29 January 2008). Here the ECJ held that member states were not required to lay down an obligation to communicate personal data in order to ensure effective protection of copyright in the context of civil proceedings, following the refusal of an ISP to disclose names and addresses of its customers alleged to be using file-sharing software. Noted by Christopher Kuner, [2008] *EIPR* 199–202.

[205]   E-Commerce Dir., Recital 46.

renewed confidence to the challenges posed by electronic commerce. At the same time, the Directive secures the legitimate interests of users, consumers and society at large.[206]

This is a broad claim, and difficult to substantiate.[207] The Information Society Directive sought to provide a more harmonised framework for copyright and related rights in the information society – one which reflected the rapid and profound technological developments of recent years.[208] Its other important aim was to transpose into Community law the main international obligations arising from the 1996 WIPO treaties on copyright and related rights (the WIPO Copyright Treaty and the WIPO Performances and Phonograms Treaty).[209] Like the E-Commerce Directive, the Lisbon Summit regarded the Information Society Directive as a priority. Its subject matter is of great concern to a diverse range of interest groups. Copyright products affected include: films, DVDs, radio and television programmes; CDs and other recordings; published books, magazines, newspapers, sheet music and photographs; and computer software, ranging from data processing applications to interactive games. Many industries are involved in creating copyright products as their primary business, and still more create, distribute or depend on copyright materials in other ways. As the Directive was debated – for over three years – all these groups sought to protect their interests by intense lobbying.

The proposals were rooted in a Commission Green Paper, *Copyright in the Information Society*.[210] The Commission hoped to ensure a clear, stable and coherent regulatory framework for the development of the information society. It saw the need for significant infrastructure investment in order to provide information highways. However, the Commission also recognised that investment would not be forthcoming unless there was adequate EU-wide protection for new services and products. The Green Paper grappled with important issues, such as: whether the act of digitisation should require the right holder's authorisation; which acts of communication should require prior authorisation; whether the rental right was adequate in a digital environment; whether an exclusive broadcasting right was necessary; whether collecting societies would facilitate sufficiently the licensing of right; whether moral rights should be harmonised. Consultations with other EU institutions, member states,

---

[206]   Press Release (9 April 2001), 'Commission welcomes adoption of the Directive on copyright in the information society by the Council' IP/01/528.

[207]   See section 2.3.10 below: Future Reforms.

[208]   Directive 2001/29 on Copyright and related rights in the Information Society [2001] OJ L 1767/10 (implementation date December 2002).

[209]   See section 2.2.6 above: The WIPO Internet Treaties.

[210]   COM(95) 382 final.

industry, right holders, users and all other interested parties followed, and over 350 submissions were received. In a follow-up Communication, the Commission outlined its legislative plan. Its proposals focused on the reproduction and distribution rights, the right of communication to the public, and protection against the circumvention of anti-copying devices. Although the details of each element were fiercely contested, the broad lines of this plan remain in the Information Society Directive. Other important issues (notably, the broadcasting right, copyright enforcement, collective rights management, and moral rights) were identified as needing further action or consideration. Some of these have been picked up again in later legislative initiatives.

The Information Society Directive leaves the earlier Directives essentially untouched.[211] It harmonises three basic exclusive rights: the reproduction right, the right of communication to the public and the distribution right. It attempts some harmonisation of the exceptions to copyright. In addition, it introduces obligations concerning anti-copying measures and rights management information.[212]

(i) Exclusive rights

Member states must provide for 'the exclusive right to authorise or prohibit direct or indirect, temporary or permanent reproduction by any means and in any form, in whole or in part'.[213] The reproduction right is the fundamental exclusive right, expressed here in broad but explicit form. Once copyright material is in digital form, it may be copied very readily, leaving right holders potentially vulnerable. On the other hand, digital technology automatically creates many copies of a work even for simple display operations, and there was anxiety that if the reproduction right covered temporary copies, this would give the right holder excessive control. This concern is addressed by the single mandatory exception in the scheme.[214] The reproduction right is expressed to be for authors in respect of their works, performers in respect of fixations of their performances, phonogram producers in respect of their phonograms, film

---

[211]   Info. Soc. Dir., Art. 1. The exception is the Term Directive, to which some small technical amendments are made by Art. 11.

[212]   In a brief preliminary report, the Commission examined 'the application of Articles 5, 6 and 8 in the light of the development of the digital market', though the report was limited to assessing how these Articles were transposed by the member states and applied by the national courts: Report to the Council, the European Parliament and the Economic and Social Committee on the application of Directive 2001/29/EC on the harmonisation of certain aspects of copyright and related rights in the information society SEC(2007) 1556. Available at: http://register.consilium.europa.eu/pdf/en/07/st16/st16140.en07.pdf.

[213]   Info. Soc. Dir., Art. 2(1).

[214]   Info. Soc. Dir., Art. 5(1).

producers of the first fixations of films in respect of originals and copies of their films and for broadcasting organisations in respect of fixations of their broadcasts, whether transmitted by wire or air, including cable and satellite transmissions.[215]

The new right of communication to the public covers the transmission and distribution of copyright works in a non-physical form. Unlike public performance, the public is not present at the place where the communication originates. This new right includes broadcast and cable distribution, and also online, on-demand distribution. This is regarded as an important growth area, with further technological developments likely – hence the desire to establish a clear and coherent system of EU-wide protection as a matter of priority. Authors must be granted 'the exclusive right to authorise or prohibit any communication to the public of their works, by wire or wireless means, including the making available to the public of their works in such a way that members of the public may access them from a place and at a time individually chosen by them'.[216] For performances, phonograms and broadcasts, the right is limited to the 'making available to the public', so does not cover broadcasts except through on-demand services.[217] The ECJ has given its first ruling on the right of communication to the public. The case concerned a hotel which received TV signals via its main aerial, and distributed them to the rooms of individual guests. This was held to constitute communication to the public within the meaning of Article 3(1) of the Directive, even though hotel rooms are in some sense private.[218]

The distribution right relates to distribution of the original work, or tangible copies of it. Prior to the Directive there were significant differences between member states as to the form of the distribution right, exceptions to it, and the point of its exhaustion. Under the Directive, authors must be granted 'in respect of the original of their works or of copies thereof, the exclusive right to authorise or prohibit any form of distribution to the public by sale or otherwise'. The normal rule of Community-wide exhaustion is applied.[219]

---

[215]   Info. Soc. Dir., Art. 2(2).
[216]   Info. Soc. Dir., Art. 3(1).
[217]   Info. Soc. Dir., Art. 3(2).
[218]   Case C-306/05, *Sociedad General de Autores y Editores de España (SGAE)* v. *Rafael Hoteles* [2006] ECR I-11519.
[219]   Info. Soc. Dir., Art. 4. For consideration of the meaning of 'distribution to the public by sale or otherwise' see Case C-456/06, *Peek & Cloppenburg* v. *Cassina* (17 April 2008).

(ii) Exceptions

Although the desire was to harmonise exceptions as far as possible, what has been achieved is comparatively limited. There is one single mandatory exception from the reproduction right, to cover temporary copying such as caching and browsing.[220] Temporary acts of reproduction 'which are transient or incidental [and] an integral and essential part of a technological process and whose sole purpose is to enable either a transmission in a network between third parties by an intermediary, or a lawful use of a work' fall within the exception, provided that they 'have no independent economic significance'.[221] The uncertainties inherent in this definition are likely to make it difficult to apply.[222] Note that the E-Commerce Directive provides more specific protection for service providers, for certain acts of transmission, hosting and caching.[223]

The Information Society Directive lays down an exhaustive list of 20 optional exceptions.[224] Member states are free to enact as many or as few of these as they wish, though they may not stray outside the list. This will necessarily undermine the effort at harmonisation, particularly as many of the exceptions are expressed to be quite broad in scope, and are therefore susceptible to a variety of methods of implementation. The permitted exceptions to the reproduction right are: reprographic copying (but not of sheet music) subject to the condition that right holders receive 'fair compensation';[225] copying 'by a natural person for private use and for ends that are neither directly nor indirectly commercial', again on condition that right holders receive fair compensation;[226] copying by public libraries, educational establishments, museums and archives, on condition that it is not for 'direct or indirect economic or commercial advantage';[227] ephemeral recordings of works made by broadcasting organisations by means of their own facilities and for their own broadcasts;[228] the reproduction of broadcasts made by social institutions such as

---

[220] Info. Soc. Dir., Recital 33.
[221] Info. Soc. Dir., Art. 5(1). Because the Directive leaves earlier Directives unaffected, this exception does not cover computer programs or databases: Info. Soc. Dir., Art. 1(2).
[222] See Michael Hart, 'The Copyright in the Information Society Directive: An Overview' [2002] *EIPR* 58–64, 59: P. Bernt Hugenholtz, 'Caching and Copyright: The Right of Temporary Copying' [2000] *EIPR* 482–93.
[223] E-Commerce Dir., Arts. 12–14. see section 2.3.7 above: E-Commerce Directive.
[224] Info. Soc. Dir., Art. 5.2, 5.3.
[225] Info. Soc. Dir., Art. 5.2(a).
[226] Info. Soc. Dir., Art. 5.2(b).
[227] Info. Soc. Dir., Art. 5.2(c).
[228] Info. Soc. Dir., Art. 5.2(d).

hospitals or prisons, again, on condition that right holders receive fair compensation.[229] 'Fair compensation' is not defined, although Recital 35 gives guidance:

> When determining the form, detailed arrangements and possible level of such fair compensation, account should be taken of the particular circumstances of each case. When evaluating these circumstances, a valuable criterion would be the possible harm to the rightholders resulting from the act in question. In cases where rightholders have already received payment in some other form, for instance as part of a licence fee, no specific or separate payment may be due. The level of fair compensation should take full account of the degree of use of technological protection measures referred to in this Directive. In certain situations where the prejudice to the rightholder would be minimal, no obligation for payment may arise.[230]

Although these criteria may seem somewhat cumbersome to apply, it is argued that such an approach may offer improvements on the levy systems in place in many member states, because the latter are necessarily much less focused. However, levy systems, even as they stand, are likely to be considered 'fair compensation', at least by the Commission.[231]

There is an even longer list of permitted exceptions to the reproduction right and right of communication to the public.[232] Use for the sole purpose of illustration for teaching or scientific research is permitted, although it must be 'non-commercial'. The source, including the author's name, must be indicated, 'unless this turns out to be impossible'.[233] There is a carefully targeted exception covering uses for the benefit of people with a disability. The uses must be directly related to the disability and of a non-commercial nature.[234] There are exceptions for the reporting of current events,[235] for the use of quotations for criticism and review,[236] for use for the purposes of public security or administrative, parliamentary or judicial proceedings,[237] for use of

---

[229] Info. Soc. Dir., Art. 5.2(e).
[230] Info. Soc. Dir., Recital 35.
[231] See 2.3.10 (ii) Copyright Levies below. For the Commission's gloss on fair compensation see Press Release (9 April 2001), 'Commission Welcomes Adoption of the Directive on Copyright in the Information Society by the Council' IP/01/528. For reflections on whether levies could in practice be replaced, given current technology, see P. Akester and R. Akester, 'Digital Rights Management in the 21st Century' [2006] *EIPR* 159–68.
[232] Info. Soc. Dir., Art. 5.3.
[233] Info. Soc. Dir., Art. 5.3(a).
[234] Info. Soc. Dir., Art. 5.3(b).
[235] Info. Soc. Dir., Art. 5.3(c).
[236] Info. Soc. Dir., Art. 5.3(d).
[237] Info. Soc. Dir., Art. 5.3(e).

political speeches and extracts of public lectures for informative purposes,[238] for use during religious or official celebrations,[239] for works of architecture or sculpture located permanently in public places,[240] for incidental inclusion,[241] for advertising the public exhibition or sale of artistic works,[242] for caricature, parody or pastiche,[243] for use in connection with the demonstration or repair of equipment,[244] use of artistic works for the purposes of reconstructing a building,[245] use of material on dedicated terminals in libraries, museums and archives for the purpose of research or private study by individual members of the public.[246] Finally, there is a 'grandfather' clause, permitting use in 'other cases of minor importance where exceptions or limitations already exist under national law, provided that they only concern analogue uses and do not affect the free circulation of goods and services within the Community'.[247] Where a member state provides for one of these exceptions to the right of reproduction, they may provide similarly for an exception to the right of distribution.[248] All exceptions are subject to the Berne three-step test.[249]

(iii)   Protection of technological measures and rights management information

One of the most politically controversial questions raised by the Information Society Directive was the stance to be taken regarding anti-copying devices. Article 11 of the WIPO Copyright Treaty requires Contracting Parties to

> provide adequate legal protection and effective legal remedies against the circum-vention of effective technological measures that are used by authors in connection with the exercise of their rights under this Treaty or the Berne Convention and that restrict acts, in respect of their works, which are not authorised by the authors concerned or permitted by law.

The difficulty is that any thoroughgoing legal protection for such technological measures risks making lawful exceptions to copyright meaningless. For example, if a user wishes to rely on the exception permitting copying of an

---

238   Info. Soc. Dir., Art. 5.3(f).
239   Info. Soc. Dir., Art. 5.3(g).
240   Info. Soc. Dir., Art. 5.3(h).
241   Info. Soc. Dir., Art. 5.3(i).
242   Info. Soc. Dir., Art. 5.3(j).
243   Info. Soc. Dir., Art. 5.3(k).
244   Info. Soc. Dir., Art. 5.3(l).
245   Info. Soc. Dir., Art. 5.3(m).
246   Info. Soc. Dir., Art. 3(n).
247   Info. Soc. Dir., Art. 3(o).
248   Info. Soc. Dir., Art. 5.4.
249   Info. Soc. Dir., Art. 5.5.

illustration for teaching purposes, this will not be possible in practice if an anti-copying device prevents such copying – the more so if circumventing that device is prohibited.

The Directive attempts a compromise. Firstly, member states must provide adequate legal protection against the deliberate circumvention of 'any effective technological measures'.[250] Protection must also be provided against 'the manufacture, import, distribution, sale, rental, advertisement for sale or rental, or possession for commercial purposes of devices, products or components or the provision of services which: (a) are promoted, advertised or marketed for the purpose of circumvention of, or (b) have only a limited commercially significant purpose or use other than to circumvent, or (c) are primarily designed, produced, adapted or performed for the purpose of enabling or facilitating the circumvention of, any effective technological measures'.[251] This approach gives right holders considerable security. The counterbalancing provisions address users' interests. Member states must take appropriate measures to ensure that, in relation to certain exceptions permitted under the Directive, right holders do in fact make available to the beneficiary of the exception the means of benefiting from it.[252] Voluntary measures taken by right holders may suffice. Member states may also take such measures in respect of the beneficiaries of a private copying exception.[253]

---

[250] Info. Soc. Dir., Art. 6.1. 'Technological measures' are defined to mean 'any technology, device or component that, in the normal course of its operation, is designed to prevent or restrict acts, in respect of works or other subject matter' which are not authorised by the right holder. Technological measures are deemed 'effective' where the use of a protected work or other subject matter is controlled by the right holders through application of an access control or protection process, such as encryption, scrambling or other transformation of the work or other subject matter or a copy control mechanism, which achieves the protection objective: Info. Soc. Dir., Art. 6.3. Note that Art. 6 does not apply to computer software.

[251] Info. Soc. Dir., Art. 6.2.

[252] Info. Soc. Dir., Art. 6.4.1. The exceptions specified are those for reprographic copying, copying by libraries, educational establishments or museums, ephemeral recordings made by broadcasting organisations, copying of broadcasts by non-commercial social institutions, copying for illustration for teaching or scientific research, copying for people with a disability and copying for purposes of public security or for the proper performance or reporting of administrative, parliamentary or judicial proceedings.

[253] Info. Soc. Dir., Art. 6.4.2. Arts. 6.4.1 and 6.4.2 do not apply to interactive on-demand services – 'works or other subject-matter made available to the public on agreed contractual terms in such a way that members of the public may access them from a place and at a time individually chosen by them': Art. 6.4.4. For criticism of this provision's lack of clarity see Michael Hart, 'The Copyright in the Information Society Directive: An Overview' [2002] *EIPR* 58–64, 62.

The Directive is supportive of the use of rights management information; a much less controversial subject than technological measures. Member states must provide for adequate legal protection against any person knowingly and without authority (a) removing or altering any electronic rights management information, or (b) distributing, importing for distribution, broadcasting, communicating or making available to the public works or other protected subject matter from which electronic rights management information has been removed or altered, if such person knows, or has reasonable grounds to know, that by so doing he is inducing, enabling, facilitating or concealing an infringement of any copyright or related right, or of the *sui generis* database right.[254] 'Rights management information' is defined as any information provided by right holders which identifies the work or other protected subject matter, the author or any other right holder, or information about the terms and conditions of use of the work, and any numbers or codes that represent such information.[255]

2.3.9 The Resale Right Directive

The artist's resale royalty, also known as the *droit de suite*, gives an artist a right to a share in the proceeds of any subsequent sale of an original work. Such a right is of particular importance to the works of visual artists, whose work may change in value very considerably as their reputation grows. The justification for the *droit de suite* is the belief that artists should be entitled to participate in the increasing value of their works as their reputation increases. It is also argued that this compensates artists for their inability to exploit their work through repeated sales (as authors could do) or performances (as composers could do). It is also said to counteract the imbalance of power between young artists and galleries or collectors. However, others argue strongly that the resale right acts simply to lower the initial sale price, and that its effect is not to support emerging artists but to reward established ones.[256]

---

[254] Info. Soc. Dir., Art. 7(1).
[255] Info. Soc. Dir., Art. 7(2).
[256] See data in Jeffrey C. Wu, 'Art Resale Rights and the Art Resale Market: A Follow-up Study', 46 (1999) *Journal of the Copyright Society of the U.S.A.* 531–51. According to the (American) Art Dealers Association, only 50 living American artists have a resale market for their works; 99% of all contemporary art depreciates in value. For more see: John Henry Merryman, 'The Proposed Generalisation of the Droit de Suite in the European Communities' [1997] *IPQ* 16–36; Simon Hughes, 'Equal Treatment for Artists under Copyright Law and the EU's Droit de Suite' in Lionel Bently and Spyros M. Maniatis, *Perspectives on Intellectual Property* Vol. 4 – Intellectual Property and Ethics (London: Sweet and Maxwell, 1998); Clare McAndrew and Lorna Dallas-Conte, 'Implementing Droit de Suite (artists' resale right)

The earliest legislation on the subject was passed by France in 1920, and others followed swiftly. Before the passage of the Directive, the right had been adopted by most EU states, though with notable exceptions (such as the UK, Ireland and Liechtenstein).

(i) Protection under the Berne Convention

The resale right is recognised in the Berne Convention, but it can only be claimed in countries whose laws provide for this, and then only on the basis of reciprocity. Article 14*ter* provides that:

> The author, or after his death, the persons or institutions authorised by national legislation, shall, in respect of original manuscripts of writers and composers, enjoy the inalienable right to an interest in any sale of the work subsequent to the first disposal of the work by the author.

It is an inalienable right, although it is an economic right. It applies only to subsequent sales of the work, and not the original sale, which is presumed to be made by the artist. The way in which the 'interest' on subsequent sales is to be calculated is not prescribed. The contracting state is free to determine the procedure for collection and the amounts to be collected. Some national laws give the artist a share of the increase in value of the work, and others give a share of the total price. It is not clear from Article 14*ter* whether all subsequent sales should be included, or only those made at public auctions.

(ii) Protection under the Resale Right Directive

The Commission was eager to harmonise the market in modern and contemporary art by applying a resale right uniformly throughout the EU. The Recitals to the Directive noted the 'lack' of a resale right in several member states, and the disparities between national systems which did recognise the resale right. These factors contributed to the creation of distortions of competition, as well as (it was argued) displacement of sales within the Community.[257] There was strong opposition to the proposal by a number of member states, including the UK. The central concern was that, since the burden of payment falls on the seller, harmonisation would lead to major art sales shifting from the European auction houses to countries which do not

---

in England' Research Report 23, The Arts Council of England, London (2002); Nobuko Kawashima, 'The Droit de Suite Controversy Revisited: Context, Effects and the Price of Art' [2006] *IPQ* 223–55; Simon Stokes, *Artist's Resale Right: Law and Practice* (Powys: Institute of Art and Law, 2006).

[257]   Resale Right Dir., Recitals 8–9. For criticism of the Commission's position see David L. Booton, 'A Critical Analysis of the European Commission's Proposal for a Directive Harmonising the Droit de Suite' [1998] *IPQ* 165–91.

apply the right (such as the US and Switzerland). A Directive was finally adopted in 2001, with an implementation date of 1 January 2006.[258] Although the Commission spoke of its satisfaction at the adoption of the Directive, it also expressed disappointment at the unusually long period before implementation, and at the extensive transitional provisions.[259]

The right applies to 'original works of art', defined to mean 'works of graphic or plastic art such as pictures, collages, paintings, drawings, engravings, prints, lithographs, sculptures, tapestries, ceramics, glassware and photographs, provided they are made by the artist himself or are copies considered to be original works of art'.[260] The resale right is granted to 'the author of an original work of art'. It is an inalienable right to receive a royalty based on the sale price obtained for any resale of the work, subsequent to the first transfer of the work by the author.[261] It applies to all acts of resale involving 'art market professionals' (such as salesrooms, galleries and dealers), whether acting as sellers, buyers or intermediaries.[262] The effect of this is to exclude sales between private individuals, largely because such a right would be extremely difficult to enforce. Nor does the right extend to resale by persons acting in their private capacity to museums which are not for profit and which are open to the public.[263]

The royalty is payable by the seller.[264] It is calculated on the sales price, net of tax.[265] Member states are free to set the threshold at which the resale right

---

[258]   Directive 2001/84 on the resale right for the benefit of the author of an original work of art [2001] OJ L 272/32.

[259]   Press Release (19 July 2001) 'Commission Welcomes Adoption of the Directive on Resale Rights for the Benefit of the Authors of Original Works of Art' IP/01/1036.

[260]   Resale Right Dir., Art. 2(1). Certain 'limited edition' copies are brought within the scheme of the Directive, this slippery concept being defined (rather vaguely) in Art. 2(2). Original manuscripts of writers and composers are outside the terms of the Directive: Recital 19. In practice, it will apply largely to sculptures and paintings, since sketches, engravings, and photographs are unlikely to exceed the minimum price threshold for operation of the right.

[261]   Resale Right Dir., Art. 1(1).

[262]   Resale Right Dir., Art. 1(2).

[263]   Resale Right Dir., Recital 18. It is common in the art world for dealers and galleries to purchase unsold works of new artists, and then to promote them. So as not to blight these promotional sales, member states may choose to exempt any resale which takes place within three years of acquisition, although (to protect the artist) the resale price must not exceed €10,000: Art. 1(3). This is sometimes known as the 'bought as stock' exemption.

[264]   Resale Right Dir., Art. 1(4). Member states may provide that the relevant art market professional 'shall alone be liable or shall share liability with the seller for payment of the royalty'.

[265]   Resale Right Dir., Art. 5.

comes into operation, provided that this does not exceed €3,000.[266] Royalty rates are set in bands, which taper off as the sale price increases. For the portion of the sale price up to €50,000 the rate is 4%. Then the rates are: 3% for the portion up to €200,000; 1% for the portion up to €350,000; a mere 0.5% for the portion up to €500,000, and a tiny 0.25% for any portion of the sale price exceeding €500,000. In addition, the total royalty is capped at €12,500.[267] The rates are set extremely cautiously in an attempt 'to reduce the risk of sales relocating and of the circumvention of the Community rules on the resale right'.[268] However, there is provision for revision of the Directive, in particular the minimum threshold and royalty rates.[269]

The royalty is payable to the author of the work, and to those entitled to claim under the author on death.[270] Member states may provide for compulsory or optional collective management of the royalty.[271] Third-country nationals are entitled to receive royalties if their home state offers reciprocal protection.[272] Authors may require any relevant art market professional to provide information necessary to secure payment of royalties on the resale.[273] The term is tied to the full copyright term.[274] However, there are generous transitional provisions for those member states (namely, the UK, Ireland, Liechtenstein) which did not have a resale right on the date of the Directive's entry into force (13 October 2001). During a transitional period expiring no later than 1 January 2010, these member states may choose not to apply the right for the benefit of the author's heirs – confining the benefits to living artists.[275] A further two years' grace may be negotiated.[276] The effect of these provisions regarding term is to limit the application of the Directive to modern and contemporary art.

---

[266]   Resale Right Dir., Art. 3. One argument is that below the minimum threshold the application of a royalty will entail disproportionately high collection and administration costs, as compared with the profit for the artist. However, member states are free to establish national thresholds lower than the Community threshold, and some consider this useful in promoting the interests of new artists: Recital 22.

[267]   Resale Right Dir., Art. 4(1). Member states may choose to apply a rate of 5% for the band up to €50,000. If a member state has chosen to set a national threshold for collection of the royalty below the Community minimum, the member state is free to determine the rate applicable to the portion of the sale price below the Community minimum, although it may not be lower than 4%: Arts. 4(2), 4(3).

[268]   Resale Right Dir., Recital 22.
[269]   Resale Right Dir., Art. 11(1).
[270]   Resale Right Dir., Art. 6(1).
[271]   Resale Right Dir., Art. 6(2).
[272]   Resale Right Dir., Art. 7(1).
[273]   Resale Right Dir., Art. 9.
[274]   Resale Right Dir., Art. 8(1).
[275]   Resale Right Dir., Art. 8(2).
[276]   Resale Right Dir., Art. 8(3).

Controversy regarding the resale right remains. One year after the Directive's implementation in the UK,[277] the Design and Artists Copyright Society reported with some fanfare that it had collected more than £1 million in royalties since the law took effect. However, art dealers who are required to administer the payments claim that the extra financial burden on them vastly outweighs the benefits for artists. Four hundred and twelve artists received payments in that first year. The artist David Hockney, who had opposed the law for fear it would damage the competitiveness of the UK market, was (as he had predicted) one of those who received the most. The royalty payments for a single work ranged from £13.77 to £7,283.[278]

2.3.10 Future Reforms

As has been noted, a clear majority of these Directives are sectoral, or focus on specific rights. The Information Society Directive is the most important exception, and does attempt a significant degree of general harmonisation of copyright law. However, laudable though the Information Society Directive's harmonising aims may have been, in many important areas these have not been realised. Its requirements are framed in broad terms, leaving member states considerable discretion in their implementation. This has contributed neither to harmonisation nor to legal certainty.[279] In 2004 the Commission launched consultations on simplifying existing EU legislation on copyright and related rights.[280] The consultations were based on a Commission working paper which concluded that there was no need for root and branch revision of the existing Directives but that fine-tuning was necessary to ensure that definitions – for

---

[277] For detail see Joanna Cave, 'An Overview of the European Artist's Resale Right Directive and its Implementation in the UK via the Artist's Resale Right Regulations 2005' [2006] *JIPL&P* 242–6; Charles Lewis, 'Implementing the Artist's Resale Right Directive' [2007] *JIPL&P* 298–304.

[278] Bob Sherwood, 'Artists Welcome Benefits of Royalty Rights' *Financial Times* 3 February 2007. Hockney's was the first name on a letter to *The Times*, 21 January 2006 which claimed: 'The arrival of this levy will do little or nothing for the vast majority of British artists. It will undoubtedly envelop the market, on which we as artists depend, in red tape and it will discourage art dealers from buying particularly the work of emerging artists but also of most artists who have not achieved "celebrity" status.'

[279] For more detail and persuasive criticism see the IViR's *Study on the implementation and effect in member states' laws of Directive 2001/29/EC on the harmonisation of certain aspects of copyright and related rights in the information society* (February 2007), available at: http://ec.europa.eu/internal_market/copyright/docs/studies/infosoc-study_en.pdf.

[280] For the working paper, SEC(2004) 995, see: http://ec.europa.eu/internal_market/copyright/docs/review/sec-2004-995_en.pdf.

example of the reproduction right – were consistent. However, responses to the working paper indicated that the online environment was putting serious pressure on traditional business models.

(i) Management of online rights

Consumers have readily embraced the technical advances which allow easy electronic dissemination of copyright works (by downloading or streaming). There is a growing demand for interactive and on-demand services. To ensure that the market for on-line delivery is as efficient and flexible as possible, some changes may be needed. For example, the rules on webcasting and simulcasting are not entirely harmonised by the Information Society Directive. They do not fall within the 'making available' right (because they are not fully interactive), and they remain governed by national rules on neighbouring rights. This acts as a disincentive to enter certain sectors of the market. Similarly, the 'making available' right will be of only limited benefit if jurisdictional differences make it difficult for right holders to grant multi-territorial licences. Even an apparently straightforward decision to offer a single music download will involve many right holders, and thus separate licences from various collective rights managers; the authors' society, the record producers' society, a performing rights society, and so on. Separate licences may also have to be acquired for each form of exploitation. The management and clearance of intellectual property rights have traditionally been organised along national lines. For online operators, rights clearance in 25 member states becomes a great burden, and, again, a disincentive.[281] This reaches beyond the simple harmonisation of laws, and implies a shift towards management and licensing at EU level.

In addition, the new digital rights management technologies (DRMs) facilitate identification and tracking of the use of works. Traditionally, collective management of copyright and related rights has provided a reasonably successful solution for the offline environment, in which right holders are unable to control effectively the uses of their works. DRMs have the potential

---

[281]   EDiMA, the organisation representing online music providers, estimates the direct cost of negotiating one single licence at €9.5 (20 internal man hours, external legal advice and travel expenses). Even assuming that mechanical rights and public performance rights in most member states can be cleared with one society, the overall cost of the requisite licences per member state would be 25 x €9.5 = €237.5. On the basis that a profit of €0.10 can be achieved per download, the online music provider would have to sell 2.37 million downloads merely to recover the cost associated with obtaining the requisite communication to the public and mechanical reproduction licences. Quoted in Commission Communication to the Council, the European Parliament and the European Economic and Social Committee on the Management of Copyright and Related Rights in the Internal Market, COM(2004) 261 final (para. 4.12).

to allow right holders to control the licensing of online uses much more tightly and directly, and to take on the collection and distribution of royalties. This has put pressure on the existing collective rights management organisations to justify the cost of their operations, and to defend the efficiency of multiple national bodies against calls for EU-wide licensing through one rights manager.[282] Following complaints from broadcasters, in February 2006 the Commission used its antitrust powers to send a formal Statement of Objections (SO) to the International Confederation of Societies of Authors and Composers (CISAC) and its 18 national collecting society members within the EEA. It concerned parts of the CISAC model contract and its implementation by CISAC members within the EEA, although only newer methods of exploitation: internet, satellite transmission and cable retransmission of music.[283] The Commission considered that certain aspects of the agreements might infringe Article 81. CISAC and the collecting societies offered certain commitments designed to meet the Commission's objections, and the Commission has invited comments from interested parties.[284]

However, following criticism of the proposals, the Commission issued a decision finding that the disputed clauses infringed Article 81(1) and requiring all EEA-based collecting societies that are members of CISAC to cease applying the membership and territoriality clauses.[285]

---

[282]   See Commission Communication to the Council, the European Parliament and the European Economic and Social Committee on the Management of Copyright and Related Rights in the Internal Market, COM(2004) 261 final (para. 4.12). Also, Commission Staff Working Document, 'Initative on the Cross-border Collective Management of Copyright' (7 July 2005): http://ec.europa.eu/internal_market/copyright/docs/management/study-collectivemgmt_en.pdf. Commission Staff Working Document, 'Impact Assessment Reforming Cross-Border Collective Management of Copyright and Related Rights for Legitimate Online Music Services' (11 October 2005) SEC(2005) 1254: http://ec.europa.eu/internal_market/copyright/docs/management/sec_2005_1254_en.pdf. For more details of national approaches, and comment on the Commission's earlier thinking, see Pavel Tuma, 'Pitfalls and Challenges of the EC Directive on the Collective Management of Copyright and Related Rights' [2006] *EIPR* 220–29.

[283]   Press Release (7 February 2006), 'Competition: Commission Sends Statement of Objections to the International Confederation of Societies of Authors and Composers (CISAC) and its EEA Members' MEMO/06/63.

[284]   Press Release (14 June 2007), 'Antitrust: Commission Market Tests Commitments from CISAC and 18 EEA Collecting Societies Concerning Reciprocal Representation Contracts' IP/07/829. If the results of the market test were positive, the Commission would adopt a decision under Article 9 of Regulation 1/2003, rendering the commitments legally binding. However, small and medium collecting societies are anxious that they will be sidelined if large collecting societies and content providers can offer a single EU-wide direct licence.

[285]   Comp/38.698. CISAC has already removed the disputed clauses from its

In 2005 the European Commission also adopted a Recommendation on the management of online rights in musical works, intended to improve the EU-wide licensing of copyright for online services.[286] Stakeholders were divided as to the appropriate model – whether to encourage cooperation among collecting societies allowing each society in the EU to grant an EU-wide licence covering the other societies' repertoires, or to give right holders the choice to appoint a collective rights manager for the online use of their musical works across the entire EU ('EU-wide direct licensing'). The Commission concluded that right holders and users should be permitted a free choice. The recommendation therefore proposes the elimination of territorial restrictions and customer allocation provisions in existing licensing contracts while leaving right holders who do not wish to make use of those contracts the possibility of tendering their repertoire for EU-wide direct licensing. The 2005 Recommendation also includes provisions on governance, transparency, dispute settlement and accountability of collective rights managers, intended to allow stakeholders to make an informed decision as to the licensing model best suited to their needs.

It is of course important that any changes in practice do not undermine the value of copyright and neighbouring rights. The new policy aims to strike a balance between rewarding creators and market entry, rather than starting a 'race to the bottom' in terms of IP protection. EU-wide online licensing is being promoted by the Commission as a way of disseminating different cultures and their repertoires across the EU, and it is hoped that the creative community will perceive these new online licences as an opportunity and not as a threat. However, Commissioner Charlie McCreevy has made it clear that if the soft-law, soft-touch approach does not deliver 'results', a binding legislative measure will be considered.[287] It also seems clear that, in the first instance, the Commission will favour the light touch methodology – impact studies, evaluation reports and recommendations – as it attempts to foster new

---

model contract. No fines were imposed. See also Press Release (16 July 2008), 'Commission Prohibits Practices which Prevent European Collecting Societies Offering Choice to Music Authors and Users' IP/08/1165.

[286]   Commission Recommendation of 18 October 2005 (2005/737/EC) on collective cross-border management of copyright and related rights of legitimate online music services [2005] OJ L 276.

[287]   Charlie McCreevy (European Commissioner for Internal Market and Services), 'Music Copyright: Commission Recommendation on Management of Online Rights in Musical Works' (SPEECH/05/588 7 October 2005). See also Tilman Lueder (Head of the Copyright Unit DG Internal Market and Services), 'How can Copyright Policy Foster Market Entry and Innovation?' (Speech, Vienna, March 2006): http://ec.europa.eu/internal_market/copyright/docs/docs/vienna_speech_en.pdf.

business models for the digital environment.[288] The European Parliament, although its preliminary position was one of agreement with the Commission's policy goals, has expressed concern that the use of Recommendations circumvents the democratic process.[289] Some MEPs in the Legal Affairs Committee have argued that cross-border music licensing should be regulated, requiring collecting societies to provide consumers with a diverse range of music products, in order to protect local and niche repertoires. The anxiety is that large collecting societies would capture the international commercially successful repertoire from national collecting societies, making it harder for the smaller societies to compete, and impacting their ability to represent local artists who have no international audience.[290] The Commission undertook a further public consultation to assess the development of Europe's online music sector, in the light of its 2005 Recommendation.[291]

More recently, the Commission has stated that 'EU citizens should be able to enjoy easier and faster access to a rich variety of music, TV programmes, films or games via the Internet, mobile phones or other devices' and that it 'encourages the content industry, telecoms companies and Internet service providers to work closely together to make available more content online, while at the same time ensuring a robust protection of intellectual property rights'.[292] Following public consultation, it has issued a Communication, 'Creative Content Online in Europe's Single Market', and has launched further consultation in order to prepare – by mid-2008 – a further EU

---

[288]   The industry itself would argue for minimum interference, on the grounds that it is already taking active steps to respond to the changing conditions. 'Policymakers have the responsibility to support developments of the still nascent market with as little intervention as possible': Florian Koempel, 'If the Kids are United' [2007] *JIPL&P* 371–6.

[289]   'Stakeholder consultation is not sufficient in an area such as this which affects society as a whole. Better legislation and less legislation are one thing, trying to legislate by the backdoor without any consultation or input from the representatives of the directly-elected Parliament is quite another. If the Commission considers that action is needed in a particular area where it has no power to take normative action, it should propose legislation.' Working document on the Commission recommendation of 18 May 2005 on collective cross-border management of copyright and related rights for legitimate online music services (recom. 2005/737/EC) (Committee on Legal Affairs): http://www.europarl.europa.eu/meetdocs/2004_2009/documents/dt/609/609817/60981 7en.pdf.

[290]   European Parliament Press Release, 'Online Music: Call for Binding EU Legislation' (27 February 2007).

[291]   http://ec.europa.eu/internal_market/copyright/docs/management/monitoring_ en.pdf. The Commission received over 80 replies from interested parties.

[292]   Press Release (3 January 2008), 'Commission Sees Need for a Stronger More Consumer-Friendly Single Market for Online Music, Films and Games in Europe' IP/08/5.

Recommendation on Creative Content Online for adoption by the European Parliament and the Council.[293] The 2005 Recommendation does seem to have had an impact on licensing practices, and there is clear evidence of increased EU-wide licensing. The Commission therefore seems to be in no hurry to intervene legislatively.[294]

(ii) Copyright levies

The Commission has also engaged in a consultation process regarding copyright levies, imposed by many countries on recording hardware and/or blank recording media. Levies offer a form of indirect remuneration for right holders, justified on the basis that it is not practical to license individual acts of private copying. Copyright levies were first introduced in the analogue environment, and are somewhat crude instruments. They do not reflect the number of copies actually made, and cannot be remitted to right holders accurately. Copyright levies are now increasingly applied to digital equipment and media as a form of compensation for right holders whose works are subject to private copying (an approach permitted by the Information Society Directive, Article 5(2)). The Commission is concerned that due account is not being given to the impact of new technologies and equipment, particularly DRM technologies, which can provide alternative ways of compensating right holders. It is also concerned at the lack of transparency in the application, collection and distribution of the copyright levies.[295] A questionnaire was distributed, and the replies have been published.[296] There are very strong views on both sides, and the Commission initially decided to postpone action. Opponents of the current system, notably the Copyright Levies Reform Alliance, threatened to force the issue by pressing complaints to the Commission, and perhaps ultimately moving the debate to the ECJ. In February 2008 the Commission announced

---

[293]   Commission Communication on Creative Content Online in the Single Market, COM(2007) 836 final: http://ec.europa.eu/avpolicy/docs/other_actions/col_en.pdf. See also accompanying Staff Working Document, SEC(2007) 1710: http://register.consilium.europa.eu/pdf/en/08/st05/st05279-ad01.en08.pdf.

[294]   European Commission, *Monitoring of the 2005 Music Online Recommendation* (Brussels, 7 February 2008): http://ec.europa.eu/internal_market/copyright/docs/management/monitoring-report_en.pdf.

[295]   See, for example, Charlie McCreevy, Address to the EABC/BSA (European-American Business Council/Business Software Alliance) Conference on Digital Rights' Management (Brussels, 12 October 2005).

[296]   Stakeholder consultation on copyright levies in a changing world (June 2006): http://ec.europa.eu/internal_market/copyright/docs/levy_reform/stakeholder_consultation_en.pdf. Replies at: http://circa.europa.eu/Public/irc/markt/markt_consultations/library?l=/copyright_neighbouring/copyright_reform&vm=detailed&sb=Title.

that it would relaunch the consultation process, with a view to finding a prag-matic and workable solution.[297]

(iii) Term of protection for recorded music

One further area of copyright law which has generated considerable publicity in the general press is the term of protection for recorded music, currently 50 years. There have been calls to extend the term of this neighbouring right, and align it with the authorial copyright term (the author's life plus 70 years), on the grounds that performances are similarly creative.[298] It has also been argued that the term should be aligned with the newly extended US term for sound recordings (95 years), to prevent the European music industry being disad-vantaged as compared to its US counterpart. High-profile submissions from performing artists such as Sir Cliff Richard and U2 brought the issue to the attention of the mainstream media. However, the Commission was not persuaded of the need for change, noting that practically all developed coun-tries, with the exception of the USA, have adopted the 50-year term. The term is already harmonised in the Community, and had been incorporated by the ten new member states. Moreover, the Commission has observed, 'it seems that public opinion and political realities in the EU are such as not to support an extension in the term of protection'.[299] It was therefore very surprising that in February 2008 the Commission announced its intention to bring forward a proposal to extend the term of protection for sound recordings to 95 years.[300]

---

[297] Press Release (14 February 2008), 'Commission to Launch Fresh Look at Copyright Levies' IP/08/238. See also Commission Background Document, 'Fair Compensation for Acts of Private Copying'(Brussels,14 February 2008):http:// ec.europa.eu /internal_ market/copyright/docs/levy_reform/background_en.pdf.

[298] 'It seems that performers are regarded by some people as mere "interpreters" of the works which they record. But making recordings is not simply a mechanical process. It is a creative process in its own right. Surely the creativity of the artists whose performances breathe life into the authors' works is worthy of recognition for at least the same period?': submission by Sir Cliff Richard to the European Commission on working paper SEC(2004) 995 (19 July 2004).

[299] Commission staff working paper on the review of the EC legal framework in the field of copyright and related rights, SEC(2004) 995 (19 July 2004) (para. 2.2.3.2).

[300] Press Release (14 February 2008), 'Performing Artists – No Longer Be the "Poor Cousins" of the Music Business' IP/08/240. For an empirical study which contra-dicts the Commission's reasoning in support of its proposal, see the *Review of the Economic Evidence Relating to an Extension of the Term of Copyright in Sound Recordings*, produced by the Centre for Intellectual Property and Information Law, University of Cambridge: http://www.hm-treasury.gov.uk/media/B/4/gowers_ cipilreport.pdf. The Report argues that no additional incentive effect could possibly be achieved by offering copyright term extensions to existing works, while such exten-sions would cause considerable damage to consumer welfare. The Report also indicates that the increased incentive from prospective extension is unlikely to be significant.

These potential reforms reflect the Commission's understandable priorities – fostering competitiveness by opening up markets and promoting innovation, with the aim of increasing growth and prosperity within the EU. The focus of copyright policy is no longer on the harmonisation of rights, but instead on how rights may be exploited commercially across boundaries.[301] Innovative business models will be encouraged, and risk-taking rewarded. The idea will be to offer creators incentives to exploit these freshly minted business models, and to take advantage of new rights management technologies and approaches. In such an environment, whether the straightforward objective of harmonising national copyright laws within the EU is a worthwhile or plausible one is a different question. To some, it may seem to be simply too troublesome to address thorny issues such as the harmonisation of authorship and ownership of copyright, or of moral rights. If the discrepancies between national systems do not disrupt the internal market overmuch, perhaps there will be little drive (certainly within the Commission) for harmonisation of these fundamental aspects of copyright law. On the other hand, it might be argued that without some common ground on such matters, the potential development of the internal market will be invisibly thwarted. The Term Directive asserts that:

> The level of protection of copyright and related rights should be high, since those rights are fundamental to intellectual creation. Their protection ensures the maintenance and development of creativity in the interest of authors, cultural industries, consumers and society as a whole.[302]

If this is true, and not mere window-dressing, then serious consideration needs to be given to the future of copyright law, in its widest aspects. These debates will continue.[303]

See also Natali Helberger, Nicole Dufft, Stef van Gompel and Bernt Hugenholtz, 'Never Forever: Why Extending the Term of Protection for Sound Recordings is a Bad Idea' [2008] EIPR 174–81; 'Creativity Stifled? A Joint Academic Statement on the Proposed Copyright Term Extension for Sound Recordings' [2008] EIPR 341–7.

[301]   Tilman Lueder (Head of the Copyright Unit DG Internal Market and Services), 'How Can Copyright Policy Foster Market Entry and Innovation?' (Speech, Vienna, March 2006): http://ec.europa.eu/internal_market/copyright/docs/docs/vienna_speech_en.pdf.

[302]   Term Dir., Recital 11.

[303]   For further thoughts see Michel M. Walter, 'Updating and Consolidation of the Acquis: The Future of European Copyright', available at:http://ec.europa.eu/internal_market/copyright/docs/conference/2002-06-santiago-speech-walter_en.pdf.

3. Patents and related rights

3.1 INTRODUCTION

If this chapter were to confine itself to Community patent law *senso stricto*, it would be very brief indeed. The ECJ recently observed that 'as Community law now stands, there is none'.[1] In spite of the importance which the Community attaches to patents, efforts (over decades) to create a Community patent have so far proved fruitless. Undeterred, the European Commission has recently set out a new vision for improving the patent system in Europe. Launching the Commission Communication, Internal Market and Services Commissioner Charlie McCreevy said:

> Patents are a driving force for promoting innovation, growth and competitiveness, but the single market for patents is still incomplete. Our 2006 stakeholder consultation showed that the EU simply must deliver, in particular on the Community patent and sound litigation arrangements, because in today's increasingly competitive global economy Europe cannot afford to lose ground in an area as crucial as patent policy.[2]

It is still far from certain that these endeavours will be successful. They will be discussed in detail later in the chapter.

As things currently stand, the effect of Community law on patent law is minimal. The Biotechnology Directive does regulate one self-contained element of patent law: the patentability of biotechnological inventions. There are Regulations which govern the grant of supplementary protection certificates for medicinal products and for plant protection products. These offer a form of *sui generis* protection, which does not extend the life of the patent as such (although it has a similar effect).[3] There is a regime for the Community

---

[1]   Case C-431/05, *Merck Genéricos – Produtos Farmacêuticos Ld^a* v. *Merck and Co. Inc., Merck Sharp and Dohme Ld^a* [2007] 3 CMLR 49 (para. 40).

[2]   Press Release (3 April 2007), 'Commission Sets Out Vision for Improving Patent System in Europe' IP/07/463.

[3]   Regulation 1768/92 concerning the creation of a supplementary protection certificate for medicinal products [1992] OJ L 182/1. Regulation 1610/96 concerning the creation of a supplementary protection certificate for plant protection products [1996] OJ L 198/30. See below section 3.3.3.2 Supplementary protection certificates.

protection of plant varieties, which although often and inevitably discussed in the context of patent law, is certainly distinct from the patent system.[4]

It seems, perhaps, very surprising that there is such a paucity of Community patent law, given the extent of successful Community harmonisation regimes in other fields of intellectual property. In part, the lack is due to the success of other international initiatives, notably the Patent Cooperation Treaty, and the European Patent Convention. The TRIPS Agreement is also influential, and the Convention on Biological Diversity provides a backdrop for discussions in certain areas. These various regimes have evolved in response to different needs; their objectives and content reflect this. Nevertheless, the economic importance of patents is such that there is great pressure for the various elements of the global patent environment to be at least consistent with each other to the extent that they overlap or interact, even if the patent world cannot be entirely unified. This chapter will therefore consider the provisions of these other international treaties in considerable detail. Community patent law, when it eventually emerges, could not possibly afford to ignore these powerful and successful pre-existing regimes.

What is a patent? A brief outline

A patent may be granted for an invention in any field of technology, if it is new, involves an inventive step and is capable of industrial application. The maximum period of protection is 20 years, which is comparatively short as compared to other intellectual property rights. But the monopoly conferred is strong. A patent does more than protect against copying. It prevents even independent devisers of the same idea from using that idea. To balance the strength of this right, a patentee is required to disclose the invention in the patent specification, which is available to the public. In modern systems, patents are intended to encourage innovation, and to promote developments which build on that inventiveness. The aim is that the grant of a patent will act as an incentive to inventors, who will consider the rewards sufficient to make it worthwhile disclosing their invention. Information about the latest technical advances thus becomes available for public consultation, thereby increasing efficiency, and in turn prompting further inventions. Of course, this is a very simple, summary account of a much more complex mechanism. There is a wealth of material exploring the appropriateness and effectiveness of the incentives offered by patent systems.[5]

---

4   Regulation 2100/94 on Community plant variety rights (CPVR) [1994] OJ L 227/1. See section 3.4 below: Plant variety rights.

5   See (for example) Fritz Machlup, *An Economic Review of the Patent System* (Study No. 15 of the Sub-Committee on Patents, Trademarks and Copyrights of the Committee on the Judiciary, US Senate 85th Congress, 2nd Session) (Washington,

The patent system has a long history. In Europe, the grant of state privileges was commonly used as a method of reward and control. Patentees might be given a patent privilege in return for loyal service, or in order to secure this. Often the aim was to attract valuable foreign technology (such as printing) into the state, to promote economic activity there. Since these privileges were usually granted on the basis of prerogative powers, they were increasingly criticised as harmful and arbitrary monopolies, which offered no benefits to the general public. In reaction to such pressures, in 1624 England's Statute of Monopolies prohibited the grant of patents by the Crown, unless for 'a new manner of manufacture'. Such patents were granted to the 'true and first inventor', and were limited to a term of 14 years. Gradually, patent systems throughout Europe reformed to take account of wider public policy goals.

It is important to note that patent policy can be used in a number of ways. Its role in offering incentives to invent has already been mentioned, and is commonly accepted. Patent policy may also be used negatively, for instance to exclude certain inventions from patent protection. A variety of subject matter has been denied patent protection by this route. Patents are not granted for methods of medical treatment, or for inventions which offend public policy or morality. The boundaries between patentable and unpatentable subject matter may be highly controversial, and fiercely contested.[6] The quest for innovation is not without downsides. For example: the patenting of biological resources may have unwelcome consequences for individuals, society and the environment; patent protection for drugs may reduce access to those drugs for some groups within the community. These wider considerations are being increasingly recognised, but agreement is not easily achieved as to the appropriate balance to be struck by the patent system.[7]

At a more detailed level, the drafting of patents is a difficult and highly technical task. As has been seen, patents fulfil a number of functions, which impose sometimes conflicting pressures. For example, to satisfy the disclosure requirement, a patent must enable a person 'skilled in the art' to make the invention. Knowing that the patent will be seen by potential competitors, the

---

1958); Fritz Machlup and Edith Penrose, 'The Patent Controversy in the Nineteenth Century' 10 (1950) *Journal of Economic History* 1–29; C.T. Taylor and Z.A. Silberston, *The Economic Impact of the Patent System* (Cambridge: Cambridge University Press, 1973); Kenneth W. Dam, 'The Economic Underpinnings of Patent Law' 23 (1994) *Journal of Legal Studies* 247–71; David J. Teece, *Managing Intellectual Capital: Organizational, Strategic, and Policy Dimensions* (Oxford: Oxford University Press, 2000); William M. Landes and Richard A. Posner, *The Economic Structure of Intellectual Property Law* (Cambridge, MA: Belknap Press of Harvard University Press, 2003); Matthew Fisher, 'Classical Economics and Philosophy of the Patent System' [2005] *IPQ* 1–26.

[6] See below (4) Excluded subject matter – Article 52(2) – Article 53.
[7] See below Compulsory licensing of pharmaceuticals – the Doha Declaration.

patentee will be reluctant to disclose anything more than the absolute minimum required. There is no incentive to disclose 'know-how'. But if the disclosure is insufficient, the patent may be revoked. The patentee has to steer a careful course. The same is true of the drafting of claims. Although there is a temptation to draft claims expansively (with a view to enjoying wider protection against infringers), this must be set against the risk of over-claiming, and seeing the patent declared invalid (because it is anticipated in the prior art or obvious as a result of it).

A patent will contain an abstract, a description of the invention, one or more claims, and any drawings referred to in the description or claims. The abstract gives a brief summary of the technical features of the invention. One important purpose of the abstract is to allow the relevant patent office to search effectively, and to assess whether any given patent should be examined more closely. The abstract also makes third parties aware of the patent application. Its purpose is to give 'technical information' only, and it is not regarded as forming part of the 'state of the art'. This is to avoid a situation in which the abstract would anticipate the patent and render it invalid for lack of novelty. The description must disclose the invention in a way that allows a person skilled in the art to perform it, and it must support the claims. The claims mark out the boundaries of the monopoly protection. They are usually arranged hierarchically, moving from the general (the 'principal' or 'generic' claim) to the particular ('dependent' or 'subsidiary' claims). Formulation of the claims is a crucial part of patent drafting. The drawings will provide a representation of the invention.

All this implies a system of examination and registration, both considered necessary for a number of reasons. Since a patent protects from even an independent deviser, it seems only fair to potential infringers to create a register open to public search. The process of filing also assists in establishing the priority of the invention. Most patent systems, including the European Patent Convention (EPC), grant patents to the first person to file a successful application.[8] Further, the EPC requires that applications are examined to ensure that they comply with the required formalities, and the criteria for patentability. This means that an application must not relate to excluded subject matter, and it must satisfy detailed requirements as to novelty, non-obviousness and suffi-

---

[8]   An alternative is to grant to the first person to invent (as in the United States), although this may necessitate administratively complex historical examinations of fact. The highly competitive race-to-file inevitably results in applications being filed without complete understanding of the invention, and without full knowledge of the prior art. See T. Nicolai, 'First-to-File vs. First-to-Invent: A Comparative Study Based on German and United States Patent Law' (1972) 3 *IIC* 103–38; William Kingston, 'Is the United States Right about 'First-to-Invent?' [1992] *EIPR* 223–6.

ciency. Most (though not all) national patent offices likewise require full examination as part of their national procedure. However, falling levels of national applications may perhaps persuade more national offices to offer unexamined patents, as a cheaper alternative to the European patent.

Challenges of harmonisation – overview

Various routes lead to patent protection, and the applicant's circumstances will determine the advantages and disadvantages of each. A national patent is valid only in the state where it is granted. These may be obtained by application directly to the relevant national patent office, or to the European Patent Office (EPO). As is explained later, the EPO grants a bundle of national patents, the choice of countries being at the request of the applicant. If protection is required in only one or a few countries, it will usually be cheaper to apply to the national offices. But if a larger number of countries is required, it will be cheaper to make a European application to the EPO, designating all the countries where protection is desired. Translation costs may well be a factor in the decision, because EPC member states may require that the patent be translated as a condition of validity.[9] Other strategic considerations may also be relevant, such as differences between the national legal systems. For example, some national offices have no examination requirement, whereas the EPC imposes a full examination. The EPC also allows for an opposition proceeding, which may result in the revocation of the European patent in all the designated states. If a patent is not strong, applicants may prefer to take their chances in various national offices individually. It is also possible to apply to these offices indirectly, via an international filing under the Patent Cooperation Treaty. This procedural route may also offer a number of advantages.[10] The Community patent – if and when it is ever agreed – would add yet a further layer of complexity to these legal structures.

---

[9]   The issue is highly contentious. Translation costs are a major expense for those seeking patents in Europe. The cost of a European patent is several times that of a patent in the United States and Japan: see EPO figures on the cost of a sample European patent, including a study on the cost of patenting, http://www.european-patent-office.org/epo/new/cost_analysis_2005_en.pdf. However, the public policy goal of making patent specifications readily understood in the relevant country is clearly an important one. Nevertheless, the cost of full translation of the entire patent into all the official languages of Europe would be astronomical. The problem has repeatedly defeated attempts to introduce a Community patent (see below section 3.3.3.1 The Community patent: context and history).

[10]   See below section 3.2.2 The Patent Cooperation Treaty.

3.2   THE GLOBAL PATENT ENVIROMENT

3.2.1   The Paris Convention

The first international convention was the Paris Convention for the Protection of Industrial Property, signed in 1883. Its signatories include most countries of the world and all European countries, and it has achieved harmonisation of a number of significant points.[11] One of the most important of these is the principle of national treatment. Each contracting state must grant the same protection to nationals of the other contracting states as it grants to its own nationals. Nationals of non-contracting states are also entitled to national treatment under the Convention if they are domiciled or have a real and effective industrial or commercial establishment in a contracting state.[12] Also very important is the 'right of priority', which ensures that an application for a patent in one contracting state does not prejudice later applications in other member states. Once an application has been filed in one of the contracting states, the applicant may, within 12 months, apply for protection in any of the other contracting states. These later applications will then be regarded as if they had been filed on the same day as the first application and will have priority over applications which may have been filed by others during this time. This means that these subsequent applications will not be rendered invalid by events during the priority period (such as publication or exploitation of the invention).[13] This allows the applicant to take time to decide on the countries in which to seek protection, and obviates the burdensome task of presenting every application at the same time. Patents granted in different contracting states for the same invention are independent of each other: the granting of a patent in one contracting state does not oblige the other contracting states to grant a patent; nor can a patent be refused, annulled or terminated in any contracting state on the ground that this has occurred in any other contracting state.[14]

The Convention establishes the Paris Union, which has an Assembly and an Executive Committee. The Assembly deals with all matters concerning the maintenance and development of the Union and the implementation of the

---

[11]   The Paris Convention ('Paris'), concluded in 1883, was revised at Brussels in 1900, at Washington in 1911, at The Hague in 1925, at London in 1934, at Lisbon in 1958, at Stockholm in 1967, and was amended in 1979. The Convention is open to all states, and there are currently over 170 signatories. It is administered by WIPO. For its text see: http://www.wipo.int/treaties/en/ip/paris/trtdocs_wo020.html.

[12]   Paris, Arts. 2 and 3.

[13]   Paris, Art. 4.

[14]   Paris, Art. 4*bis*.

Convention.[15] The Paris Convention provides a framework for a number of international patent agreements, including the Patent Cooperation Treaty, and the European Patent Convention.

3.2.2 The Patent Cooperation Treaty

The Patent Cooperation Treaty (PCT) aims to centralise and simplify international patent applications, thereby reducing costs. It provides for a system of international application and preliminary examination, so is essentially procedural rather than substantive. Signed in 1970, the PCT came into force in 1978.[16] It currently has 139 members, including all the important industrial countries, although somewhat fewer than the Paris Convention.[17] Countries that have acceded to the PCT are deemed to belong to the International Patent Co-operation Union. Applicants using the PCT route enjoy the benefit of using a single procedure to make many national applications, but the decision as to whether a patent is granted remains the responsibility of the relevant national offices. Although the applicant files what is known as 'an international application', the PCT does not result in an 'international patent'. The scheme has seen continuous growth since inception, with a record 156,100 applications filed in 2007, representing a 4.7% growth over the previous year.[18]

An applicant files an 'international application' at a local national patent office ('the Receiving Office'). The European Patent Office is a Receiving Office for this purpose.[19] The international application is checked for compliance with formalities, then sent to the International Bureau of WIPO in Geneva which acts as administrative office for the PCT. Applications may also be filed with WIPO directly. They may be filed by anyone who is a national or resident of a contracting state. Copies of the application are sent to one of the major patent offices designated as an International Searching Authority (ISA). The European Patent Office is one of those designated (and is a popular choice with PCT applicants, because of the quality of its search and preliminary examination). The ISA searches the prior art and sends an International Search

---

15 'The countries to which this Convention applies constitute a Union for the protection of industrial property': Paris, Art. 1. See also Paris, Arts. 13 and 14.

16 The PCT was concluded in 1970, amended in 1979, and modified in 1984 and 2001. It is open to states party to the Paris Convention for the Protection of Industrial Property (1883). For its text see http://www.wipo.int/pct/en/texts/.

17 Signatories as of 15 April 2008: http://www.wipo.int/export/sites/www/ treaties/en/documents/pdf/pct.pdf.

18 WIPO Press Release (21 February 2008), 'Unprecedented Number of International Patent Filings in 2007' PR/2008/536.

19 These so-called Euro-PCT applications are dealt with under Part X of the EPC 2000 (Arts. 150–53).

Report (ISR) to the International Bureau at WIPO and to the applicant. The ISR lists the citations of published documents that might affect the patentability of the invention claimed in the international application. The ISA will also prepare a written opinion on patentability. If the subject matter of the application is considered unpatentable under national laws, the ISA will not conduct a search. Excluded subject matter includes scientific and mathematical theories, plant and animal varieties, methods for treatment of the human or animal body, and computer programs.[20] On receipt of the ISR, the applicant can amend the claims if necessary (though not beyond the disclosure in the international application as filed). If the international application is not withdrawn, it is published (as is the ISR, though not the written opinion), and sent to the patent offices of the Designated States ('the Designated Offices'), again, including the EPO. The applicant may also opt for what is known as an international preliminary examination (under Chapter II of the PCT).[21] At this point the national offices take over from the PCT.

International applications may be filed with the Receiving Office in any language which it permits. However, the request has also to be filed in one of the publication languages under the PCT, that is, in Arabic, Chinese, English, French, German, Japanese, Russian or Spanish. If the language in which the international application is filed (in other words, the language used for description and claims) is not accepted by the ISA that is to carry out the international search, the applicant is required to furnish a translation into a language which is both a language accepted by the ISA and a language of publication.[22]

An international application must include a request that the application be processed under the PCT, a description, one or more claims, one or more drawings (where required), and an abstract. The description must disclose the invention in a manner sufficiently clear and complete for the invention to be carried out by a person skilled in the art. It must specify the technical field to which the invention relates and indicate the background art useful for the understanding, searching and examination of the invention. The claim or claims must define the matter for which protection is sought, must be clear and concise, and fully supported by the description. Drawings must be provided where they are necessary for the understanding of the invention. The applica-

---

[20]   PCT, Art. 17(2)(a)(i) and PCT, Rule 39.

[21]   This results in an international preliminary report on patentability, which analyses aspects of the general patentability of the invention. It too will be sent to the Designated Offices. Not all contracting states are bound by Chapter II. Only an applicant who is a resident or a national of a contracting state bound by Chapter II may opt for an international preliminary examination.

[22]   PCT, Rule 12.

tion must designate all states where the applicant requires patent protection. Priority may be claimed for one or more earlier applications.[23]

The centralised procedure of the PCT offers a number of advantages to applicants over multiple national applications, not least a reduction in the fees payable. It may take as long as 18 months for an international PCT application to be forwarded to the designated national patent offices. An applicant can use this period to gauge the invention's prospects, and to reflect on the desirability of seeking protection in foreign countries. The ISR will assist the applicant in assessing whether or not the invention is likely to be patented. If the invention seems likely to be successful, it may be worth the expense of appointing local patent agents, preparing the necessary translations, and paying the national fees. The ISR will also be helpful to third parties. The existence of an international search and examination procedure may be particularly useful for countries where the national patent offices are less well equipped than the ISAs to do this work.[24]

3.2.3 TRIPS

The TRIPS Agreement was negotiated at the end of the Uruguay Round of the General Agreement on Tariffs and Trade (GATT) in 1994. Because of the level of harmonisation which had already been achieved, the TRIPS Agreement's impact on European patent law was not dramatic. Members must make patents available for any inventions, whether products or processes, in all fields of technology without discrimination, subject to the normal tests of novelty, inventiveness and industrial applicability. It is also required that patents be available and patent rights enjoyable without discrimination as to the place of invention and whether products are imported or locally produced.[25]

Three exceptions are permitted. Members may exclude inventions from patentability, and from commercial exploitation, if this is 'necessary to protect *ordre public* or morality, including to protect human, animal or plant life or health or to avoid serious prejudice to the environment, provided that such exclusion is not made merely because the exploitation is prohibited by their law'.[26] Members may also exclude from patentability 'diagnostic, therapeutic and surgical methods for the treatment of humans or animals'.[27] Finally, they

---

[23] PCT, Arts. 3–8.
[24] For a more detailed appraisal of the PCT's achievements see Jay Erstling and Isabelle Boutillon, 'The Patent Cooperation Treaty: At the Center of the International Patent System' (2006) 32 *William Mitchell Law Review* 1583–602.
[25] TRIPS, Art. 27.1.
[26] TRIPS, Art. 27.2.
[27] TRIPS, Art. 27.3(a).

may exclude from patent protection 'plants and animals other than micro-organisms, and essentially biological processes for the production of plants or animals other than non-biological and microbiological processes'.[28]

Patentees are guaranteed various rights. The owner of a product patent has exclusive rights 'to prevent third parties not having the owner's consent from the acts of: making, using, offering for sale, selling, or importing' that product. Where the subject matter of a patent is a process, the owner has the exclusive right 'to prevent third parties not having the owner's consent from the act of using the process, and from the acts of: using, offering for sale, selling, or importing' products 'obtained directly by that process'. Patent owners also have the right to assign or transfer patents, and to conclude licensing contracts.[29] Limited exceptions to these exclusive rights are permitted, provided that such exceptions do not unreasonably conflict with a normal exploitation of the patent and do not unreasonably prejudice the legitimate interests of the patent owner, taking account of the legitimate interests of third parties (the three-step test).[30]

Patent applications must disclose the invention adequately.[31] The term of protection must be a minimum of 20 years from the filing date.[32] In this context, the ECJ has now held that EU member states are free to choose whether or not to give direct effect to the provisions of the TRIPS Agreement.[33] The case concerned a Portuguese patent, whose owner claimed it had been infringed, to be met with the response that the term of the national patent had expired after 15 years. In reply it was argued that Article 33 of the TRIPS Agreement provides for a minimum term of 20 years. The Portuguese court referred the matter to the ECJ, asking whether it was free to apply Article 33. Noting the absence of Community law in the particular field, the ECJ held that it was not contrary to Community law for

---

[28]   TRIPS, Art. 27.3(b). However, members must provide for the protection of plant varieties either by patents or by an effective *sui generis* system or by any combination thereof: see below section 3.4: Plant Variety Rights.

[29]   TRIPS, Art. 28. Members may provide for the exhaustion of intellectual property rights, subject to the obligations regarding national treatment and most-favoured-nation status.

[30]   TRIPS, Art. 30.

[31]   'in a manner sufficiently clear and complete for the invention to be carried out by a person skilled in the art': TRIPS, Art. 29(1).

[32]   TRIPS, Art. 33.

[33]   Case C-431/05, *Merck Genéricos – Produtos Farmacêuticos Ld^a* v. *Merck and Co. Inc.*, *Merck Sharp & Dohme Ld^a* [2007] 3 CMLR 49 (paras. 48–9). For criticism of the ECJ's decision, see Otto P. Swens and Titus A.F. Engels, 'Community Law, Patent Law and TRIPs: A Complicated Cocktail to Mix' *Pharmaceutical Law Insight* (March 2008).

Article 33 to be directly applied by a national court, subject to the conditions provided for by national law.[34]

Compulsory licensing of pharmaceuticals – the Doha Declaration

One ground of tension between industrialised countries and developing nations is the extent to which compulsory licensing of patents should be permitted. TRIPS attempts to find a point of balance, by permitting compulsory licensing, but only subject to conditions aimed at protecting the legitimate interests of the right holder.[35] In 2001 the issue arose in a very public arena, when pharmaceutical companies brought a legal challenge against South African legislation which would have allowed the import of generic versions of patented HIV/AIDS drugs, and their manufacture under compulsory licence in South Africa. South Africa is a member of the WTO, and has signed the TRIPS Agreement. Nevertheless the extent of the AIDS epidemic, and the lack of affordable medicines, cause understandably serious concern. Although the legal dispute was settled, pressure to address the underlying problems remained, and the matter was discussed at the fourth WTO Ministerial Conference, held in Doha in November 2001. At issue was whether the existing compulsory licensing provisions were adequate to ensure that public health was supported, especially in promoting affordable access to existing medicines, while also promoting research and development into new ones. There was anxiety that governments would fear pressure from other governments and the pharmaceutical industry, and would therefore feel inhibited in using the flexibility already built into the TRIPS Agreement. There was also disagreement as to whether the TRIPS Agreement could be used to control parallel imports.

In the Doha Declaration, WTO members acknowledged the gravity of the public health problems afflicting many developing and least-developed countries.[36] It was stressed that the TRIPS Agreement should be part of the wider national and international action to address these problems, whilst recognising that intellectual property protection is important for the development of new medicines. Although reiterating their commitment to the TRIPS Agreement,

---

[34] It should be emphasised that if there had been (or are in the future) Community rules in the sphere in question, then Community law will apply. In such circumstances, the ECJ will, so far as possible, attempt to interpret Community law consistently with the TRIPS Agreement, although no direct effect may be given its provisions: Case C-337/95, *Parfums Christian Dior SA* v. *Evora BV* [1997] ECR I-6013; [1998] ETMR 26 (paras. 44, 47, 49).

[35] TRIPS, Art. 31.

[36] WTO, *Declaration on the TRIPS Agreement and Public Health* (20 November 2001) WT/MIN(01)/DEC/2.

WTO members affirmed that it could and should be interpreted and implemented in a manner supportive of WTO members' right to protect public health and, in particular, to promote access to medicines for all. Thus, each member has the right to grant compulsory licences and the freedom to determine the grounds upon which such licences are granted, and each member has the right to determine what constitutes a national emergency or other circumstances of extreme urgency. In particular, public health crises, including those relating to HIV/AIDS, tuberculosis, malaria and other epidemics, can represent a national emergency or other circumstances of extreme urgency. In addition, the TRIPS Agreement leaves members free to establish their own regimes for the exhaustion of intellectual property rights, subject only to the most-favoured-nation and national treatment provisions.

Another thorny problem could not be resolved immediately. The TRIPS Agreement provides that where use of the subject matter of a patent is imposed by compulsory licence, the use should be 'predominantly for the supply of the domestic market of the Member authorizing such use'.[37] This acts to restrict WTO members without adequate manufacturing capabilities, since (for example) manufacture of a patented drug under compulsory licence in State A for sale in State B is not permitted. The Doha Declaration could do no more than acknowledge this, though the TRIPS Council was instructed to find an expeditious solution. The TRIPS Council was also instructed to extend until 1 January 2016 the deadline by which least-developed countries were obliged to apply provisions on pharmaceutical patents.[38]

After considerable debate, on 30 August 2003, the TRIPS Council agreed a 'waiver' of some of the obligations concerning compulsory licensing of pharmaceuticals for less-developed countries which could not manufacture the pharmaceuticals themselves.[39] The system established by the decision 'should be used in good faith to protect public health' and not as 'an instrument to pursue

---

[37]   TRIPS, Art. 31(f).

[38]   Least-developed countries will not have to protect pharmaceutical patents and test data until 1 January 2016: *Decision on the Extension of the Transition Period under Article 66.1 of the TRIPS Agreement for Least-Developed Country Members for Certain Obligations with Respect to Pharmaceutical Products*, adopted by the TRIPS Council on 27 June 2002. Nor will least-developed countries have to give exclusive marketing rights to pharmaceuticals that are the subject of a patent application until 1 January 2016: *Decision on Least-Developed Country Members – Obligations Under Article 70.9 of the TRIPS Agreement with Respect to Pharmaceutical Products*, adopted by the General Council on 8 July 2002.

[39]   WTO, *Implementation of paragraph 6 of the Doha Declaration on the TRIPS Agreement and public health* (1 September 2003) WT/L/540 and Corr.1 (decision of the General Council of 30 August 2003).

industrial or commercial policy objectives'.[40] It covers patented pharmaceutical products, pharmaceutical products manufactured through a patented process, as well as the active ingredients necessary for their manufacture, and diagnostic kits needed for their use. It waives the requirements of TRIPS Article 31(f), allowing a member to produce pharmaceutical products under compulsory licence, and then export them to a member which lacks the manufacturing capacity to produce them itself. Only the amount necessary to meet the needs of the importing member may be manufactured under the licence, and these needs must be notified to the TRIPS Council. The products must be clearly identified by labelling, and relevant information must be posted on a web site. Adequate remuneration must be paid. Importing members must 'take reasonable measures within their means, proportionate to their administrative capacities and to the risk of trade diversion' to prevent re-exportation of such products – so-called 'anti-diversion measures'. These are extremely important (particularly to pharmaceutical manufacturers), given the high value and easy portability of many pharmaceutical products. The decision remains in force until an amendment to the TRIPS Agreement itself, replacing the decision, takes effect. The decision has been implemented at EU level by means of a Regulation.[41]

A Protocol amending the TRIPS Agreement was adopted in December 2005, with the intention of converting the waiver into a permanent amendment.[42] The amendment will take effect when two thirds of the WTO's members have ratified the change. Although the aim was to achieve this by 1 December 2007, currently fewer than one third of WTO members have ratified the agreement, and the deadline has been extended to 31 December 2009.[43]

---

[40] WTO, *General Council Chairperson's statement* (13 November 2003) WT/GC/M/82 (Excerpt from the minutes of the General council meeting 30 August 2003 (paragraph no. 29)). For further comment see Peter Rott, 'The Doha Declaration – Good News for Public Health?' [2003] *IPQ* 284–311.

[41] Regulation 816/2006 on compulsory licensing of patents relating to the manufacture of pharmaceutical products for export to countries with public health problems [2006] OJ L 157/1. See also http://ec.europa.eu/internal_market/indprop/docs/medicines/ implementation_en.pdf.

[42] WTO, Amendment of the TRIPS Agreement (8 December 2005) WT/L/641 (decision of the General Council of 6 December 2005). A new Article 31*bis* will be inserted into the TRIPS Agreement, and a new annex will be added. For assessment of the impact of the system see Frederick M. Abbott and Jerome H. Reichman, 'The Doha Round's Public Health Legacy: Strategies for the Production and Diffusion of Patented Medicines under the Amended TRIPS Provisions' (2007) 10 *JIEL* 921–87.

[43] Once two thirds of members have formally accepted the amendment, it will take effect in those members, replacing the 2003 waiver. The waiver will continue to apply in the remaining members, unless and until they ratify the amendment. See also Gemma O'Farrell, 'One Small Leap or One Giant Leap towards Access to Medicines for All?' [2008] *EIPR* 211–15.

Plant and animal inventions – review of Article 27.3(b)

Another contentious area is that covered by Article 27.3(b). The general rule is that patents should be granted for inventions in all fields of technology, for both products and processes. Article 27.3(b) allows a limited exclusion from patentability for 'plants and animals other than micro-organisms, and essentially biological processes for the production of plants or animals other than non-biological and microbiological processes'.[44] The Article contained a requirement that these provisions should be reviewed. The review began in 1999, but the issues are contentious, and progress has been slow. Topics raised in TRIPS Council discussions include: the application of the existing TRIPS provisions, and whether they need to be modified; the handling of moral and ethical issues, such as whether and, if so, to what extent invented life forms should be eligible for protection; the commercial use of traditional knowledge and genetic material by those outside the communities or countries where these originate; the interaction between the TRIPS Agreement and the UN Convention on Biological Diversity (CBD).

Some have argued that the exceptions to patentability are unnecessary and that patent protection should be extended to all patentable inventions of plants and animals. Others consider Article 27.3(b) to be a well-balanced provision, preserving members' rights and flexibility to decide whether or not to exclude plants and animals from patentability in the light of their specific national interests and needs. There are also suggestions that certain terms should be better defined, particularly with a view to clarifying the differences between plants, animals and micro-organisms. At the other end of the spectrum are arguments that Article 27.3(b) should prohibit the patenting of all life forms – plants, animals, micro-organisms and all other living organisms and their parts, including genes as well as natural processes that produce plants, animals and other living organisms. It has also been suggested that the Article should be amended to prohibit the patenting of inventions based on traditional knowledge, or those that violate provisions of the Convention on Biological Diversity (CBD). The Doha Declaration sought to provide an even broader mandate for these discussions, requiring the TRIPS Council to examine the relationship between the TRIPS Agreement and the CBD, and to review the protection of traditional knowledge and folklore, taking fully into account the development dimensions.[45]

---

44   TRIPS, Art. 27.3(b), which also requires members to provide for the protection of plant varieties either by patents or by an effective *sui generis* system or by any combination thereof.

45   WTO, Doha Declaration (20 November 2001) WT/MIN(01)/DEC/1, para. 19. For overviews of these areas see the following, prepared by the TRIPS Secretariat: 'Review of the Provisions of Article 27.3(b): Summary of Issues Raised and Points

One concern is that although the CBD recognises that members have certain rights over their biological resources, the TRIPS Agreement allows the patenting of biological resources, but contains no provisions preventing acts of 'biopiracy' – where patent rights are claimed in one country over genetic resources that come from another country.[46] One group of countries, led by India and Brazil (and supported by the African group and some developing countries), has therefore suggested that the TRIPS Agreement should contain provisions ensuring the prior informed consent of the owners of the biological resources used in any invention, and should allow national regimes for fair and equitable sharing of benefits from the patenting of national genetic resources to be enforced in other countries. This could be achieved by requiring an applicant for a patent relating to biological materials or to traditional knowledge to disclose the source and country of origin of the biological resource and of the traditional knowledge used in the invention; to give evidence of prior informed consent under relevant national regimes; and to provide evidence of fair and equitable benefit sharing under the national regime of the country of origin.[47] Switzerland has proposed an alternative route for ensuring similar disclosure – through an amendment to WIPO's Patent Cooperation Treaty.[48] Both of these proposals locate the process of disclosure within the patent

---

Made' IP/C/W/369/Rev.1 (9 March 2006); 'The Protection of Traditional Knowledge and Folklore' IP/C/W/370/Rev.1 (9 March 2006); 'The TRIPS Agreement and Convention on Biological Diversity' IP/C/W/368/Rev.1 (8 February 2006) and IP/C/W/368/Rev.1/Corr.1 (9 March 2006). Available at: http://www.wto.org/english/tratop_e/trips_e/art27_3b_e.htm.

[46]   It may be very difficult to attribute 'ownership' to a biological resource, particularly since value may be added at many points. For example, the now ubiquitous 'kiwi fruit' originated in China. Introduced to several different countries at the beginning of the twentieth century (using Chinese seed), only in New Zealand did this result in the domestication of the plant, followed by the successful, worldwide marketing of the hitherto unknown fruit. Kiwi fruit orchards have now been established in many countries throughout the world. See Douglas C. Calhoun and John Robertson, 'Treaty on Biological Diversity: Ownership Issues and Access to Genetic Materials in New Zealand' [1995] *EIPR* 219–24.

[47]   See the Communication from Brazil, India and others, 'The Relationship between the TRIPS Agreement and the Convention on Biological Diversity and the Protection of Traditional Knowledge' IP/C/W/356 (24 June 2002). Norway also supports a mandatory disclosure requirement within the TRIPS Agreement: Communication from Norway, 'The Relationship between the TRIPS Agreement and the Convention on Biological Diversity and the Protection of Traditional Knowledge: Amending the TRIPS Agreement to Introduce an Obligation to Disclose the Origin of Genetic Resources and Traditional Knowledge in Patent Applications' IP/C/W/473 (14 June 2006).

[48]   See the Communication from Switzerland, 'The Relationship between the TRIPS Agreement and the Convention on Biological Diversity and the Protection of Traditional Knowledge' IP/C/W/400/Rev.1 (18 June 2003).

system, with the potential to refuse patents if conditions are not met. The EU's current position, although it is willing to entertain a requirement that patent applicants should disclose information on the geographic origin of genetic resources or traditional knowledge used in an invention, is that such a disclosure requirement should not act, *de facto* or *de jure*, as an additional formal or substantial patentability criterion. Its view is that if such a requirement is not respected, any legal consequences should lie outside the ambit of patent law.[49] The United States is very reluctant to see disclosure requirements within the patent system, arguing that it would disrupt an already delicate balance without accomplishing the stated objectives of ensuring access and equitable benefit-sharing, preventing misappropriation and preventing erroneously issued patents.[50]

Although little progress was made with the TRIPS review at the Fifth WTO Ministerial Conference in Cancún (September 2003), the Sixth Conference, held in Hong Kong in December 2005, was more fruitful. The Ministerial Declaration reaffirmed the Declarations and Decisions adopted at Doha, and expressed renewed resolve to complete the Doha Work Programme fully by

---

[49]   See the Communication from the European Communities and their member states, 'Review of Article 27.3(b) of the TRIPS Agreement, and the Relationship between the TRIPS Agreement and the Convention on Biological Diversity (CBD) and the Protection of Traditional Knowledge and Folklore' IP/C/W/383 (17 October 2002). Recital 27 of the Biotechnology Directive states that if an invention uses biological material, the patent application should, 'where appropriate', include information on its geographical origin (if known), although this is 'without prejudice to the processing of patent applications or the validity of rights arising from granted patents'. Recital 55 notes that the Community is party to the CBD, and requires EU member states to 'give particular weight' to the geographical origin and equitable sharing of benefits provisions of the CBD when implementing the Directive. The Commission is supportive of the idea of a disclosure requirement as a self-standing obligation under EU law, though not retroactive and not as an additional formal or substantial patentability criterion. The Commission is also keen to discuss constructively the imposition of a disclosure requirement at international level, and would be open to introducing this as a formal condition for patentability and not only as a self-standing obligation. See Commission Communication, *The Implementation by the EC of the 'Bonn Guidelines' on Access to Genetic Resources and Benefit-Sharing under the Convention on Biological Diversity* COM(2003) 821, p.18. See also *Second Report of the European Community to the Convention on Biological Diversity: Thematic Report on Access and Benefit-Sharing* (October 2002). Both available at: http://biodiversity-chm.eea.europa.eu/convention/.

[50]   See the Communication from the United States, 'Article 27.3(b), Relationship between the TRIPS Agreement and the Convention on Biological Diversity and the Protection of Traditional Knowledge' IP/C/W/434 (26 November 2004). See also Rahul Goel, 'Protection and Conservation – TRIPs and CBD: A Way Forward' [2008] *JIPL&P* 334–8.

the end of 2006.[51] The issue of the relationship between the TRIPS Agreement and the Convention on Biological Diversity was specifically mentioned, and the Director General was asked 'to intensify his consultative process' on this and all outstanding implementation issues, reporting to the TRIPS Council so that it could take any appropriate action no later than 31 July 2006.[52] In an attempt to move matters towards a conclusion, a group of countries, led by India and Brazil, have proposed a text for a disclosure of origin requirement.[53] At the TRIPS Council meeting in June 2007, support for the proposal came from the African Group, Venezuela and others, though there is opposition from some developed countries including the US, Korea, Japan and New Zealand. These states consider that there is no conflict between the TRIPS Agreement and the CBD, and that these agreements could and should be implemented in a mutually supportive manner without any need for amendment to the TRIPS Agreement.[54] No final agreement has yet been reached, therefore.

3.2.4   The Convention on Biological Diversity (CBD)

As the preceding discussion of the review of TRIPS Article 27.3(b) makes clear, although the CBD does not have a direct impact on patent law, its goals are highly relevant to the way in which certain patents are viewed. Governments and individuals alike have noted the rapid development of technology, and the inevitable pressure to offer legal protection for its fruits.[55] However, the patenting of biological resources is no longer viewed as unquestionably beneficial. Other aspects of these technologies are being more keenly examined; including potential unexpected negative effects on individuals, society and the environment. Increasingly, therefore, the intrinsic value of biodiversity is being recognised, and priority given to conservation, maintenance and recovery of biological resources.

---

[51]   Ministerial Declaration, 'Doha Work Programme' WT/MIN(05)/DEC (22 December 2005).

[52]   Ministerial Declaration, 'Doha Work Programme' WT/MIN(05)/DEC (22 December 2005), para. 39.

[53]   Communication from Brazil, China, Colombia, Cuba, India, Pakistan, Peru, Thailand and Tanzania, 'Doha Work Programme – The Outstanding Implementation Issue on the Relationship between the TRIPS Agreement and the Convention on Biological Diversity' IP/C/W/474 (5 July 2006).

[54]   WTO, TRIPS Council, Minutes of meeting 26 July 2007 IP/C/M/54.

[55]   For a case study of the interaction between patents and the CBD see Charles Lawson, 'Patents and Biological Diversity Conservation, Destruction and Decline? Exploiting Genetic Resources in Queensland under the Biodiscovery Act 2004' [2006] *EIPR* 418–28.

The CBD was one important outcome of the Earth Summit, held in Rio de Janeiro in June 1992. Run under the auspices of the United Nations, it currently has 190 members.[56] The Convention has three main goals: the conservation of biological diversity (or biodiversity), the sustainable use of its components, and the fair and equitable sharing of the benefits from the use of genetic resources.[57] It takes a very wide view, acknowledging 'the intrinsic value of biological diversity and of the ecological, genetic, social, economic, scientific, educational, cultural, recreational and aesthetic values of biological diversity and its components', and affirming that its conservation is 'a common concern of mankind'.[58] It aims to promote international, regional and global cooperation among states and intergovernmental organizations and the non-governmental sector for the conservation of biological diversity and the sustainable use of its components, and to provide financial resources for this.[59] It also acknowledges that developing countries have special needs in this respect, particularly since their overriding priorities are economic and social development and poverty eradication. Nevertheless, the CBD foresees a broad range of environmental, economic and social benefits following from its implementation, viewing conservation and sustainable use of biological diversity as of critical importance for meeting the food, health and other needs of the growing world population.[60]

---

[56]   As of March 2008: http://www.cbd.int/convention/parties/list.shtml.

[57]   CBD, Art. 1. 'Biological diversity' is defined as 'the variability among living organisms from all sources including, inter alia, terrestrial, marine and other aquatic ecosystems and the ecological complexes of which they are part; this includes diversity within species, between species and of ecosystems'. 'Biological resources' includes 'genetic resources, organisms or parts thereof, populations, or any other biotic component of ecosystems with actual or potential use or value for humanity'. CBD, Art. 2. For the text of the Convention see: http://www.cbd.int/convention/convention. shtml. For the argument that, notwithstanding the importance of the environmental and scientific issues, the word 'biodiversity' lacks the precision needed for a workable legal standard, see Fred Bosselman, 'A Dozen Biodiversity Puzzles' (2004) 12 *NYU Environmental Law Journal* 364–506.

[58]   CBD, Preamble. For more on the wider context see Secretariat of the Convention on Biological Diversity, 'How the Convention on Biological Diversity Promotes Nature and Human Well-Being': http://www.cbd.int/doc/publications/cbd-sustain-en.pdf. See also William Lesser, *Sustainable Use of Genetic Resources under the Convention on Biological Diversity: Exploring Access and Benefit Sharing Issues* (Wallingford: CAB International, 1998); Philippe G. Le Prestre (ed.), *Governing Global Biodiversity: The Evolution and Implementation of the Convention on Biological Diversity* (Aldershot: Ashgate, 2002); Natalie P. Stoianoff (ed.), *Accessing Biological Resources: Complying with the Convention on Biological Diversity* (The Hague; London: Kluwer Law International, 2004).

[59]   CBD, Art. 20. Developed countries have greater financial obligations than developing countries.

[60]   CBD, Preamble.

The CBD affirms that states have 'the sovereign right to exploit their own resources pursuant to their own environmental policies', although this is balanced by 'the responsibility to ensure that activities within their jurisdiction or control do not cause damage to the environment of other States or of areas beyond the limits of national jurisdiction'.[61] Signatories are required to develop national strategies, plans or programmes for the conservation and sustainable use of biological diversity, and to integrate the conservation and sustainable use of biological diversity into relevant sectoral or cross-sectoral plans, programmes and policies.[62] One particular concern addressed is access to genetic resources. The CBD recognises that states have sovereign rights over their natural resources, and that the authority to determine access to genetic resources rests with the national governments and is subject to national legislation. However, each signatory is tasked with facilitating access to genetic resources for environmentally sound uses by other signatories, and should not impose restrictions that run counter to the objectives of the Convention.[63] Access to and transfer of technology are regarded as priorities, and should be provided to developing countries on fair and most favourable terms – although these terms should be consistent with the adequate and effective protection of intellectual property rights.[64] It is specifically noted that patents and other intellectual property rights may have an influence on the implementation of the Convention, and that signatories should cooperate to ensure that such rights do not run counter to CBD objectives.[65]

On 29 January 2000, the Conference of the Parties to the Convention on Biological Diversity adopted a supplementary agreement to the Convention known as the Cartagena Protocol on Biosafety.[66] The Protocol seeks to protect biological diversity from the potential risks posed by living modified organisms resulting from modern biotechnology, adopting the precautionary

---

[61] CBD, Art. 3.

[62] CBD, Art. 6. It is recognised that each signatory state will have particular conditions and capabilities. For advocacy of a regional model of cooperation see Kanchana Kariyawasam, 'Access to Biological Resources and Benefit-Sharing: Exploring a Regional Mechanism to Implement the Convention on Biological Diversity (CBD) in SAARC Countries' [2007] *EIPR* 325–35.

[63] CBD, Art. 15. These obligations are fleshed out in the 'Bonn Guidelines': Secretariat of the Convention on Biological Diversity, *Bonn Guidelines on Access to Genetic Resources and Fair and Equitable Sharing of the Benefits Arising out of their Utilization.* (Montreal: Secretariat of the Convention on Biological Diversity, 2002). Available at: http://www.cbd.int/doc/publications/cbd-bonn-gdls-en.pdf .

[64] CBD, Art. 16.

[65] CBD, Art. 16(5).

[66] The Protocol entered into force on 11 September 2003. As of April 2008 it has over 140 members. Full text at http://www.cbd.int/biosafety/protocol.shtml.

approach set out in Principle 15 of the Rio Declaration on Environment and Development.[67] It applies to the transboundary movement, transit, handling and use of all living modified organisms that may have adverse effects on the conservation and sustainable use of biological diversity, taking also into account risks to human health.[68] It establishes an 'advance informed agreement' (AIA) procedure for ensuring that countries are provided with the information necessary to make informed decisions before agreeing to the import of such organisms into their territory.[69] Living modified organisms must be handled, packaged and transported safely, taking into consideration relevant international rules and standards.[70] The Protocol also establishes a Biosafety Clearing-House to facilitate the exchange of information on living modified organisms and to assist countries in the implementation of the Protocol.[71]

3.2.5   The Patent Law Treaty

The Patent Law Treaty (PLT) aims to harmonise and streamline formal procedures in respect of national and regional patent applications and patents, and thus to make such procedures more user-friendly (and cheaper).[72] It was signed in 2000, came into force in April 2005 and is administered by WIPO.[73] With the significant exception of the filing date requirements, the PLT specifies the maximum requirements which national and regional offices may apply. Requirements for obtaining a filing date have been standardised: there must be an indication that the elements received by the Office are intended to be an application for a patent for an invention; there must be indications that would allow the Office to identify or to contact the applicant; and there must be a part which appears to be a description of the invention. If these are present, a filing date must be accorded.[74] The formal requirements for national and regional applications have been standardised by the incorporation into the PLT of the PCT requirements, with the aim of eliminating or reducing procedural gaps between national, regional and international patent systems.[75] Other changes regarding (for example) representation, submission of docu-

---

67   Cartagena Protocol, Art. 1.
68   Cartagena Protocol, Art. 4.
69   Cartagena Protocol, Art. 7.
70   Cartagena Protocol, Art. 18.
71   Cartagena Protocol, Art. 20.
72   Text available at: http://www.wipo.int/treaties/en/ip/plt/trtdocs_wo038.html.
73   As of 15 April 2008 it had been ratified by 18 countries, though it has 60 signatories. The implementation of changes to detailed procedural matters in national offices understandably takes some time.
74   PLT, Art. 5.
75   PLT, Art. 6.

ments and evidence, and language requirements were also agreed, again with the aim of simplifying requirements. There is additional protection against unintentional loss of substantive rights as a result of the failure to comply with formality requirements or time limits.

The PLT was negotiated in WIPO's Standing Committee on the Law of Patents (SCP). This was created in 1998 and serves as a forum to discuss issues, facilitate coordination and provide guidance concerning the progressive international development of patent law. All member states of WIPO and/or of the Paris Union are members of this committee. Other member states (including members of the UN who are not members of WIPO or the Paris Union, as well as a number of intergovernmental and non-governmental organisations) may be given status as observers. The SCP also began work on a treaty aimed at harmonising substantive patent law. This is a considerable task. Initially it was agreed that the focus should be on issues of direct relevance to the grant of patents, in particular, the definition of prior art, novelty, inventive step/non-obviousness, industrial applicability/utility, the drafting and interpretation of claims and the requirement of sufficient disclosure of the invention. Other important matters (such as first-to-file versus first-to-invent systems, 18-month publication of applications and a post-grant opposition system) were to be left for consideration at a later stage. In May 2001, the SCP considered a first draft of the Substantive Patent Law Treaty (SPLT), with Regulations and Practice Guidelines. In November 2001, the SCP discussed revised draft provisions and agreed on an approach to establishing a seamless interface between the SPLT, the PLT and the PCT. It also agreed, on the basis of a proposal by the US, to create a Working Group on Multiple Invention Disclosures and Complex Applications. This Working Group was given the mandate to address: unity of invention; the linking of claims; the number of claims; the requirement of 'clear and concise' claims and special procedures to treat complex applications (such as mega-applications or large sequence listings).

In 2002 and 2003 the SCP continued to discuss further revised drafts of the SPLT. Following proposals by a number of delegations, the contents of the draft SPLT were progressively broadened. While the SCP agreed in principle on a number of issues (such as the scope of the SPLT, the right to a patent, novelty, inventive step/non-obviousness or the requirement of sufficient disclosure), certain provisions (such as patentable subject matter, and the exceptions to patentability) caused grave difficulty. Members were unwilling to cede the flexibility in respect of their national policies which they currently enjoy under existing international treaties. Also, there were differing views regarding disclosure of the origin of genetic resources and associated traditional knowledge in patent applications. Developing countries are concerned to secure provisions on technology transfer and anti-competitive practices, and to ensure that their governments have the power to act in the public interest (in response to serious health crises, for instance) where necessary. The complexity and sensitivity of these points led to stasis.[76]

Observing that, 'twenty years is far too long to have dwelled on a subject so important to the global economy, to the stakeholders of the patent system and to patent offices worldwide', in 2004 the US, Japan and the European Patent Office submitted a joint proposal, in an attempt to break the deadlock.[77] This advocated confining the work of the SCP to an initial package of priority issues (prior art, grace period, novelty, non-obviousness/inventive step) with a view to concluding a limited SPLT as quickly as possible. Although this trilateral group would have preferred a more expansive treaty, the more limited proposal was offered in the hope that it would offer the best opportunity for rapid agreement and results. The proposal found a measure of support, but others continued to insist that all provisions of the existing draft SPLT should be considered as a whole. No consensus could be reached for progress within WIPO.

Following informal consultations in 2005, there was a recommendation that prior art, grace period, novelty and inventive step should be addressed in the SCP, whereas the issues of sufficiency of disclosure and genetic resources should be discussed in the Intergovernmental Committee on Intellectual Property and Genetic Resources, Traditional Knowledge and Folklore. The importance of a robust, effective and actionable WIPO Development Agenda was emphasised. However, while delegations recognised the importance of the work of the SCP and emphasised that the work on patent law harmonisation should progress taking into account the interests of all parties, they did not reach agreement as to the future work of the Committee. Although WIPO is still exploring 'areas of common interest', little concrete progress has been made.

Frustrated by this, the so-called 'Group B+' came together. This comprises all members of WIPO Group B, plus member states of the European Union, the European Commission, member states of the European Patent Organisation, and the European Patent Office. Group B+ has been discussing substantive patent law harmonisation issues, and issues with regard to intellectual property and development, with a view to seeking a common basis for

---

[76]   For reflection see Andrew R. Sommer, 'Trouble on the Commons: a Lockean Justification for Patent Law' 87 (2005) *Journal of the Patent and Trademark Office Society* 141–70.

[77]   WIPO, *Proposal by the United States of America, Japan and the European Patent Office for Establishing a New Work Plan for the Standing Committee on the Law of Patents (SCP)* WO/GA/31/10.

further discussion in WIPO.[78] A number of meetings have been held. Discussions have been based on a variant of the compromise package offered to the SCP by the trilateral offices in 2004.[79] There is considerable will to reach agreement.[80] However, the matter is not uncontroversial. The Group by definition excludes the developing countries, which resisted the original compromise plan. There are concerns that the economic and political power of the B+ Group might result in its interests overshadowing those of the developing countries, and even the wider public interest.[81] Nevertheless, it has to be admitted that progress in WIPO had proved impossible.

3.3   THE EUROPEAN PATENT ENVIRONMENT

3.3.1   The European Patent Convention

3.3.1.1   History
After World War II, attempts to rebuild European industry drew attention to the significant differences between national patent systems. An EEC patent was considered in the early 1960s, but shelved when Britain failed in its candidacy for EEC membership. Fearing that the PCT would become dominant, France promoted a rejuvenated Community plan. This had two elements: firstly, a European Patent Convention, which would provide for a centralised granting system; secondly, a convention to provide a unitary Community patent. The first limb was not intended to promote freedom of trade within the EC, but to offer a system of examination which was more complete and more rigorous than the PCT. It would also seek to take advantage of economies of scale, and minimise the duplication of work by national patent offices. Like the PCT, the outcome would be a bundle of national patents, with each signatory free to maintain its national system. However, it was recognised that certain basic rules – particularly those on patentability and validity – would have to be harmonised if the granting process was to function effectively. Matters of infringement, enforcement, revocation, renewal and litigation were to remain the exclusive province of national law.

---

[78]   The group formed in February 2005: http://www.uspto.gov/main/homepagenews/bak08feb2005.htm. See also Heinz Bardehle, 'Patent Harmonization: Quo Vadis?' 88 (2006) *Journal of the Patent and Trademark Office Society* 644–8.

[79]   See William New and Tove Iren S. Gerhardsen, 'Group B+ Draft Patent Harmonisation Treaty Emerges', available at http://ip-watch.org/weblog/wp-track-back.php?p=448.

[80]   http://www.patent.gov.uk/policy/policy-notices/policy-notices-groupb.htm.

[81]   For further detail and discussion see Louise Davies, 'Global Patent Harmonisation and Nodal Governance' [2007] *IPQ* 467–88.

The European Patent Convention (EPC) was signed in Munich in 1973. Applications were first received by the European Patent Office in Munich in 1978. Since then, over 830,000 patents have been granted, from over 2 million applications. The United States and Japan produce a high proportion of these applications, with Germany being the leading EU state in terms of applications.[82] The EPC is an intergovernmental treaty, and its membership extends beyond the European Community. There are currently 34 member states.[83]

European patents are granted only to inventions which are new, involve an inventive step, and are susceptible of industrial application.[84] A European patent provides protection for 20 years from the date of filing the application.[85]

3.3.1.2 EPC 2000 – major changes

Significant revisions to the EPC have recently been agreed in a new Convention, known as the EPC 2000, which came into force on 13 December 2007.[86]

A number of objectives drove this process. One aim was to modernise the legal basis of the European patent system, although still within the framework of existing substantive and procedural law. There was a desire to streamline and simplify where possible, to ensure that the system functioned efficiently and could adapt in the future to changing conditions. It was felt that Europe's standing as an economic force in the global economy, and hence its competitiveness, would be enhanced by strengthened patent protection. In addition, as an immediate priority, the EPC had to be brought into line with TRIPS and the impending WIPO Patent Law Treaty. One controversial area – the protection of biotechnological inventions – was not addressed in detail. Although the importance and sensitivity of the issues were recognised, it was thought that, given the European Union's leading political and legislative role in this area, it was inadvisable to open up parallel discussions. It was felt that future diplomatic conferences would offer the appropriate forum for further discussions of biotechnology inventions, the protection for computer programs and the possible implementation of the Community patent.

Changes to substantive law are comparatively few, as was the intention. The core provision on patentability, Article 52(1), remains substantially the

82   European Patent Office, *Annual Report 2006* (Statistics).
83   As of 24 March 2008: http://www.epo.org/about-us/epo/member-states.html.
84   EPC 2000, Art. 52. These requirements are discussed more fully below.
85   EPC 2000, Art. 63.
86   Text of EPC 2000 at: http://www.epo.org/patents/law/legal-texts/epc.html. For more on the EPC 2000, and relevant texts, see http://www.european-patent-office.org/epo/dipl_conf/documents.htm.

same.[87] Previously this provided that 'European patents shall be granted for any inventions which are susceptible of industrial application, which are new and which involve an inventive step.' As revised to take account of Article 27(1) of the TRIPS Agreement, it now reads, 'European patents shall be granted for any inventions, in all fields of technology, provided that they are new, involve an inventive step and are susceptible of industrial application.'[88] This amendment already reflects the EPO's current practice regarding patentability, which requires inventions to have 'technical character', or to provide 'technical solutions' to 'technical problems'. There had been a proposal to delete computer programs from the list of non-patentable inventions in Article 52(2)(c), but the conference decided it should remain for the time being. The issue is a controversial one, and there is a commitment to further consultation on the future of legal protection in this area. Some changes have been made to confirm current practice. For example, the scope of the patent monopoly granted by Article 69 EPC has frequently been contested, resulting in a Protocol on its Interpretation, the precise ambit of which was likewise contested. The revised Protocol now expressly includes the so-called 'doctrine of equivalents', which did not appear explicitly in either Article 69 or the original Protocol, thereby clarifying its status. One notable change is that patent proprietors now have the option, in a central procedure before the EPO, of limiting the protection afforded by their patents. The availability of a central limitation procedure will allow proprietors to avoid going through the various national patent offices. The intention is that, should a patent as granted turn out not to be valid, it can be limited using this rapid and cheap procedure. The hope is that it will encourage proprietors to amend incorrectly granted patents promptly.

There are a number of important procedural amendments. For example, it is now possible to file patent applications in any language, since a translation into one of the official languages of the EPO is not required until a later date. During the procedure itself, applicants enjoy improved protection against inadvertent legal consequences arising from the non-observance of time limits.[89] In a practical change intended to increase productivity and efficiency, search and examination procedures have been brought together. Previously, the two tasks had been split between different locations and different patent

---

[87]   Footnotes will refer primarily to the EPC 2000, the text of the EPC now in force. However, references will also be made to the EPC 1973, and references to both texts given where necessary for purposes of comparison or for clarity.

[88]   EPC 2000, Art. 52(1).

[89]   EPC 2000, Arts. 121 and 122. Statement by Dr Roland Grossenbacher, Chairman of the Administrative Council of the EPO, 29 November 2000 (Press Release).

examiners. Given that the EPO's vast collection of search documentation is available at all its duty stations through its databases, there is no longer any need to separate these stages in the process.

At the institutional level, the EPO has been brought more firmly within the political responsibility of the member states, and regular conferences of ministers responsible for patent matters in the contracting states will now be held.[90] Significant and controversial issues remain outstanding, notably the protection of computer programs and biotechnological inventions, and these will require further analysis with a view to possible reform. The Administrative Council has been authorised to adapt the EPC to international treaties and European Community legislation, albeit with far stricter limitations than were originally envisaged.[91] Many detailed provisions have been transferred from the Treaty itself into the Implementing Regulations; the latter can be amended more readily by the Administrative Council, allowing for greater adaptability. There is now a legal basis for special agreements between the contracting states concerning the translation of European patents and the introduction of a central court system for the enforcement of European patents, issues which are also of importance for the Community patent proposed by the European Commission.[92]

3.3.1.3   EPC 2000: overview and procedure

The EPC 2000 provides for a single, centralised process for the grant of European patents. Applicants wishing to protect their inventions in more than one European country can take advantage of a single application and search procedure. A successful application will result in a single grant of a bundle of national patents in each of the countries designated by the applicant. Each European patent has, in each of the states for which it is granted, the effect of a national patent.[93] Its term is 20 years from the application filing date.[94]

Applications are made to the European Patent Office, whose headquarters are in Munich. Applications may also be filed through the national patent

---

[90]   EPC 2000, Art. 4(a). Decisions at these conferences will not be legally binding, but they will offer a forum for political cooperation.

[91]   EPC 2000, Art. 33. Art. 33(1)(b) gives the Administrative Council a new power to amend the EPC 2000 'to bring [it] into line with an international treaty relating to patents or European Community legislation relating to patents'. This will allow the EPC 2000 to be amended without the need for a diplomatic conference (and subsequent national ratification) where agreement has been reached at WIPO, WTO or EU level.

[92]   EPC 2000, Art. 149(a).

[93]   EPC 2000, Art. 2, Art. 64.

[94]   EPC 2000, Art. 63.

office of a contracting state, for forwarding to the EPO.[95] Unlike the PCT or the Paris Convention, an application may be filed by any natural or legal person, regardless of their place of residence.[96] Joint applications are permissible.[97] The right to a European patent belongs to the inventor.[98] For the purposes of proceedings before the EPO, the applicant is deemed to be entitled to exercise the right to the European patent.[99] Questions regarding entitlement to the patent are largely left to the national courts, because of the range and variety of legal concepts involved in disputes. For example, there are significant differences between member states' rules governing inventions by employees. Although the EPC's approach has the advantage that it is comparatively straightforward, it largely sidesteps the problem of harmonisation of the underlying rules.[100] However, to minimise ownership disputes and to prevent forum shopping, a Protocol to the EPC was agreed (Protocol on Jurisdiction and the Recognition of Decisions in Respect of the Right to the Grant of a European Patent). The Protocol provides that disputes are heard by only one member state. The Protocol also provides (in the absence of express agreement between the claimant and the applicant) that questions regarding entitlement will be determined by the tribunals (and the law) of the country where the applicant is resident, or has their place of business. If the applicant is from a non-EPC state, entitlement is determined by the tribunal of the country of the claimant. If a national tribunal makes a final determination as to entitlement, the successful claimant may either prosecute the application in place

---

[95] EPC 2000, Art. 75. Applications may be filed with the EPO in Munich, The Hague or Berlin, but not at the sub-office in Vienna: EPC 2000, Rule 35. Applications may be filed electronically, and many documents may be filed by fax.

[96] EPC 2000, Art. 58.

[97] EPC 2000, Art. 59. Under the terms of this Article it is also possible for two or more applicants to file an application designating different member states. See EPC 2000, Rule 72.

[98] Or his successor in title. If the inventor is an employee, then the entitlement to a European patent is usually determined in accordance with the law of the state in which the employer is mainly employed: EPC 2000, Art. 60.

[99] EPC 2000, Art. 60(3).

[100] The European Commission has noted that the application of these different rules by businesses has an impact on research work and management, and that this might affect freedom to provide services in the single market and/or the conditions of competition. This led the Commission to at least consider harmonisation at Community level. See *Promoting Innovation through Patents: Green Paper on the Community Patent and the Patent System in Europe* (1997), 17. However, following consultation, the Commission concluded that the differences in national laws did not justify harmonisation at Community level: Commission Communication, *Promoting Innovation through Patents: The Follow-up to the Green Paper on the Community Patent and the Patent System in Europe* (1999), 14–15.

of the applicant, file a new application or request that the application be refused.[101]

EPC 2000 significantly changes and simplifies the language requirements for applications. Previously, they had to be filed in one of the official languages of the EPO (English, French and German).[102] Now, however, they may be filed in any language, though if an official language is not used, a translation into one of these is required within two months of filing.[103] All proceedings are conducted in the relevant official language. Under the EPC 2000 there is no longer a requirement to designate expressly the states where protection is sought. All contracting states party to the EPC at time of filing are now deemed designated, although designations of individual states may be withdrawn at any time up to grant.[104] At the moment, a fee is paid for each designated state.[105] An applicant can claim priority for a European patent application based on an earlier patent application filed in any state party to the Paris Convention within the previous 12 months. The later application must relate to the same invention and contain the same subject matter as the application from which priority is being drawn.[106] The application must contain a description of the invention, one or more claims, any drawings referred to in the description of the claims and an abstract. Filing fees and search fees are payable.[107] The claims must define the matter for which protection is sought. They must be clear and concise and be supported by the description.[108] Simplicity is not a requirement: Article 84 offers no basis for objecting that a claim is not simple but complex and hence takes too long to understand, as complexity is not tantamount to lack of clarity of a claim.[109]

---

[101]   EPC 2000, Art. 61, Rules 14–18.
[102]   EPC 1973, Art. 14, which also specified the limited exceptions to this general rule.
[103]   EPC 2000, Art. 14; Rule 6(1). There are special concessions for natural or legal persons who reside or have their principal place of business within a contracting state whose language is not an official language. They may file documents in an official language of that state, though a translation will be required in due course: EPC 2000, Art. 14(4); Rule 6(2).
[104]   EPC 2000, Art. 79.
[105]   Currently €80 per state designated (Switzerland and Liechtenstein are designated jointly on payment of a single fee). Designation fees for all states are deemed paid if seven designation fees are paid.
[106]   EPC 2000, Art. 87(1) and 87(4).
[107]   EPC 2000, Art. 78.
[108]   EPC 2000, Art. 84. See also *Mycogen/Modifying plant cells*, T694/92 [1998] *EPOR* 114.
[109]   *Bayer/Safeners*, T1020/98 [2004] *EPOR* 20, para. 3.5.2. But see also *Oxy/Gel-Forming Composition*, T246/9 [1995] *EPOR* 526.

Claims are often categorised according to the type of subject matter which they protect, although there is no rigid or definitive subdivision, and the categories may overlap. Product claims are claims to products or substances, and they confer protection over all uses of the product, regardless of how it was derived.[110] Process claims, however, protect activities – such as methods, processes, uses. These may be patentable even if the product itself is not (say, if it is already known). If the subject matter of the patent is a process, the protection conferred by the patent extends to the products directly obtained by the process.[111] So-called 'product-by-process' patents claim a product produced by a particular method. The EPO does not recognise these except where 'the product cannot be satisfactorily defined by reference to its composition, structure, or other testable parameter'.[112] This might well be the case with natural products, or with new chemicals whose molecular structure is particularly complex, and as yet unidentified.[113] In other words, such claims should normally be regarded as product claims, unless it is impossible to define the product in any other way.

If an invention involves the use of or concerns biological material which is not available to the public and which cannot be described in the application in such a manner as to enable the invention to be carried out by a person skilled in the art, extra steps are necessary to comply with the requirement of disclosure. These include the deposit of a sample of the biological material with a recognised depositary institution not later than the date of filing of the application.[114] If a patent application discloses nucleotide or amino acid sequences, the description must contain a sequence listing conforming to certain prescribed standards.[115]

---

[110]   See *Mobil/Friction reducing additive*, G2/88 [1990] *OJEPO* 93; *Telectronics/Pacer*, T82/93 [1996] *EPOR* 386. In *Moog/Change of Category*, T378/86 [1988] *OJEPO* 386 the EPO explained: 'The division of patents into various categories (process or product) is legally important because the extent of protection depends to a crucial extent on the category selected, specific types of use being allocated to each category which in some cases differ substantially from each other. The difference in effect on the right conferred by a patent is the reason why it is at all justifiable to classify patents in categories.'

[111]   EPC 2000, Art. 64(2).

[112]   The Technical Board of Appeal has been firm in its stance: *IFF/Claim Categories*, T150/82 [1984] *OJEPO* 309, 310–11. The UK was for a considerable time alone amongst EPC member states in accepting such claims, but the House of Lords has now aligned UK practice with that of the EPO: *Kirin-Amgen* v. *Hoechst Marion Roussel* [2004] UKHL 46; [2005] RPC 9 (paras. 86–101).

[113]   *International Flavors and Fragrances Inc.* [1984] *OJEPO* 309.

[114]   EPC 2000, Rule 31. See also Rules 32–4.

[115]   EPC 2000, Rule 30.

Once the application is filed, the Receiving Section examines whether it satisfies the formal requirements, including payment of fees, and accords a date of filing.[116] The filing date will also be the priority date, unless there is a claim to an earlier date based on an earlier registration. The EPC 2000 broadens the definition of priority to include claims based on filings at offices in WTO members (in line with TRIPS, Article 2), as well as those in Paris Convention countries.[117] The priority date is of great importance, because it is the date at which the novelty and inventiveness of the invention are assessed. Once a priority date is established, the applicant may exploit the invention without fear of invalidating the patent by anticipating it.

The Search Division then draws up the European search report on the basis of the claims, with due regard to the description and any drawings.[118] This is a limited search for relevant prior art. The European search report does not contain reasons, and does not express any view about the patentability of the invention, although for applications filed after 1 July 2005 it will be accompanied by an opinion as to whether the application appears to meet EPC requirements.[119] The purpose of the search report is to identify the documents available to the EPO at the time of drawing up the report, which are relevant for novelty and inventive step.[120] Other documents of importance for other reasons (such as conflicting applications) may be noted, but the examiner will not spend a significant amount of time in searching for these documents unless there is a special reason for doing so in a particular case.[121] The application will also be examined to ensure that it relates to one invention, or to a group of inventions which form a single inventive concept – the requirement of 'unity of invention'.[122] This requirement aids those attempting to search the European Patent Register for prior art. As soon as it has been drawn up, the search report is sent to the applicant, together with copies of any cited docu-

---

[116]   EPC 2000, Art. 80, Art. 90.

[117]   EPC 2000, Art. 87 (and Arts. 88–9). Other countries may be recognised, by means of the Art. 87(5) procedure. The priority lasts for the 12-month period following the first filing in a Paris Convention, WTO or other recognised country. In member states, a European patent application which has been accorded a filing date is equivalent to a national filing: EPC 2000, Art. 66.

[118]   EPC 2000, Art. 92. Rule 61.

[119]   EPC 2000, Rule 62. The European search report and the opinion comprise the Extended European search report. The applicant may respond to the opinion during the examination procedure.

[120]   *Guidelines for Examination in the European Patent Office* (December 2007) ('*Guidelines*'), B-II, 2.

[121]   *Guidelines*, B-IV, 2.3.

[122]   EPC 2000, Art. 82, Rules 44 and 64. *Guidelines*, B-VII. *Draenert/Single General Concept*, W06/90 [1991] *EPOR* 516.

ments.[123] The application must be published as soon as possible after the expiry of a period of 18 months from the date of filing or the date of priority (if this has been claimed).[124] The European search report is included if available, but, in practice, this is not often the case. Once published, the patent enjoys provisional protection which must reach a minimum standard.[125] At this point the specification becomes part of the prior art (creating a danger of self-collision, if subsequent inventions are based on the same invention).

The next stage is the substantive examination. The Examining Division will consider, with the assistance of the search report, whether the application and the invention to which it relates meet the requirements of the EPC, and the rules of its Implementing Regulations.[126] This is a full examination of the validity of the patent. The invention must not therefore consist of excluded subject matter, it must be novel, must involve an inventive step, and be capable of industrial application.[127] The application must disclose the invention sufficiently, and the claims must be clear, concise and fully supported by the description. The examiner will take into account any amendments proposed, or comments made, by the applicant in reply to the search opinion, and then identify any requirements of the EPC which are not satisfied. The examiner will then write to the applicant giving reasons for any objections raised and inviting the applicant to file observations or submit amendments.[128] If re-examination shows that despite the applicant's submissions objections still persist and cannot be resolved, the application is likely to be refused immediately. However, re-examination may well indicate that there are good prospects of bringing the proceedings to a positive conclusion, in the form of a decision to grant. In such cases, if there are still objections to be met, they may be resolved by further communications, which may be written or oral.[129] If the Examining Division is of the opinion that the application and the invention to which it relates meet the requirements of the EPC, it will grant a

---

123   EPC 2000, Rule 65.

124   EPC 2000, Art. 93.

125   EPC 2000, Art. 67.

126   EPC 2000, Art. 94. Examination must be requested within six months of the publication of the search report: EPC 2000, Rule 70(1). The procedure for substantive examination is set out in Rule 71.

127   EPC 2000, Art. 52(1).

128   *Guidelines*, C-VI, 2.3. An application may not be amended in such a way that it contains subject matter which extends beyond the content of the application as filed: EPC, Art.123(2). See *British Biotech/Heterocyclic compounds*, T684/96 [2000] *EPOR* 190. Although addition of subject matter is unacceptable, reformulation of the same subject matter is permissible: *Xerox/Amendments*, T133/85 [1989] *EPOR* 116. See also *Alza/Infusor*, T514/88 [1990] *EPOR* 157.

129   *Guidelines*, C-VI, 4.3.

European patent for the designated contracting states. The applicant must approve the text in which the Examining Division intends to grant the patent, must have paid the relevant fees and must file translations of the claims in the two other official languages of the EPO.[130]

The grant of a European patent results in a bundle of national patents for the states designated in the application. Patent protection lasts up to 20 years from the filing date. Renewal fees are payable, and increase over time, to encourage patentees to let useless patents lapse.[131] European patents may be assigned or licensed.[132]

3.3.1.4   Opposition proceedings

Third parties may apply to revoke a European patent within nine months of its grant. If successful, opposition proceedings result in the revocation of the European patent in all the designated states.[133] This central procedure has obvious advantages for an opponent, since it is easier and cheaper to mount one single attack than to bring revocation proceedings in each of the designated states. Opposition may only be filed on the grounds that: the subject matter of the European patent is not patentable within the terms of Articles 52 to 57 EPC; the European patent does not disclose the invention in a manner sufficiently clear and complete for it to be carried out by a person skilled in the art; the subject matter of the European patent extends beyond the content of the application as filed.[134] This excludes objections on the grounds of lack of unity of invention, that the claims are not clear or concise or supported by description, or that the person is not entitled to the patent. The Notice of Opposition must include a written reasoned statement of the extent to which the European patent is opposed and of the grounds on which the opposition is based as well as an indication of the facts, evidence and arguments presented in support of these grounds.[135] The patent owner is provided with this statement, and invited to file observations and any amendments considered necessary. Amendments are limited to those occasioned by a ground for opposition, and the claims may not be amended in such a way as to add matter or extend

---

[130]   EPC 2000, Art. 97. Any member state may require a translation into one of its official languages, if the patent is not drawn up in one of these: EPC 2000, Art. 65. See below section 3.3.2.1 The London Agreement.

[131]   EPC 2000, Art. 86, Rule 51. Renewal fees are payable for the third and subsequent years. For the third year the fee is €400, rising to €1,065 for the tenth and subsequent years.

[132]   EPC 2000, Arts. 71–3.

[133]   EPC 2000, Art. 99. For effect of revocation see EPC 2000, Art. 68.

[134]   EPC 2000, Art. 100.

[135]   EPC 2000, Rule 76.

the protection conferred.[136] The Opposition Division may revoke the patent, maintain it, or maintain it in an amended form.[137] The EPC 2000 has introduced a new procedure by which the proprietor of a European patent may apply to revoke its own patent, or to limit its scope through amendment of the claims.[138]

APPEALS

There are three Boards of Appeal, which are responsible for the examination of appeals from the decisions of the Receiving Section, Examining Divisions, Opposition Divisions and of the Legal Division.[139] The Technical Board of Appeal hears appeals from the Examining Division concerning refusal or grant of a patent application, and from decisions of the Opposition Divisions. The Legal Board of Appeal hears appeals which are purely on a matter of law. The Enlarged Board of Appeal is responsible for deciding points of law referred to it by Boards of Appeal, for opinions on points of law referred to it by the President of the European Patent Office, and for deciding petitions for review of the decisions of the Boards of Appeal.[140] Its purpose is to ensure uniform application of the law, or to decide important points of law which arise.[141]

3.3.1.5 Substantive harmonisation – limits and definitional challenges

The EPC harmonises the national laws of member states to a significant extent in the fields of patentability and validity, up to the point of grant. It is the EPC which determines whether a European application is patentable, and European patents must confer on the proprietor the same rights as would be conferred by a national patent. They can only be revoked on grounds specified in the treaty. These are: that the subject of the European patent is not patentable; the European patent does not disclose the invention in a manner sufficiently clear and complete for it to be carried out by a person skilled in the art; the subject matter of the European patent extends beyond the content of the application as filed; the protection of the European patent has been extended; the proprietor

---

[136] EPC 2000, Art. 101, Rule 80, Art. 123(3). See *Moog/Change of Category*, T378/86 [1989] *EPOR* 85.

[137] EPC 2000, Art. 101.

[138] EPC 2000, Arts. 105a–c. A request for limitation or revocation may not be filed while opposition proceedings are pending.

[139] EPC 2000, Art. 21, Art. 106.

[140] EPC 2000, Art. 22. This Article has been amended to extend the Enlarged Board of Appeal's responsibilities to include decisions regarding petitions for review under the new Art. 112a procedure. This introduces limited judicial review of Board of Appeal decisions where a fundamental procedural defect or criminal act is alleged to have occurred.

[141] EPC 2000, Art. 112; the EBA's decision numbers are prefixed G.

of the European patent is not entitled to the patent.[142] The European patent must have the same prior right effect as a national patent application and a national patent.[143]

However, issues of validity and infringement post-grant are matters for national law and national courts.[144] Nor is there any appeal from a national patent office or court to the Boards of Appeal of the EPO (or any other international court). Similarly, decisions from the Boards of Appeal denying patent protection cannot be appealed to a national court. Consequently, a European patent may be interpreted differently in different countries, leading inevitably to fragmentation on important issues. Efforts to minimise this effect are made. The EPO examiners, national judges and national examiners meet each year. In addition, there is a Protocol on the Interpretation of Article 69 of the EPC, which offers guidance as to how patents should be interpreted.

3.3.1.6 Article 69 – interpretation of claims

A vital matter for all patentees is the scope of protection. If a defendant's device or process is identical, it will obviously infringe. If the two are very different, then it will not. Much more problematic are situations where there are only slight differences between the two, or where one aspect of the invention has been changed, or where a different means is used to achieve the same end result. It is in these situations that the scope of the patent monopoly is crucially important.

Before the EPC was agreed, member states approached the question of interpretation of patent claims in somewhat different ways. For example, the British 'fence-post' view was felt to be strict and literal in keeping the patentee to his claim. In contrast, other systems (such as in Germany) allowed 'signpost' claiming, which focused on specifying the essential inventive concept of the patent. Both approaches had an impact on the way that claims were drafted, and the differences threatened to undermine the harmonising effect of the EPC. In an attempt to overcome this difficulty, a Protocol was drafted to offer guidance on the way that patent claims should be interpreted. Article 69 of the EPC states:

> The extent of the protection conferred by a European patent or a European patent application shall be determined by the terms of the claims. Nevertheless, the description and drawings shall be used to interpret the claims.[145]

---

142   EPC 2000, Art. 138.
143   EPC 2000, Art. 139.
144   EPC 2000, Art. 64(3), Art. 74.
145   EPC 2000, Art. 69(1) – unchanged from EPC 1973.

This text appears to embody a 'fence-post' approach. However, the Protocol on the Interpretation of Article 69 offers an important qualification:

> Article 69 should not be interpreted in the sense that the extent of the protection conferred by a European patent is to be understood as that defined by the strict, literal meaning of the wording used in the claims, the description and drawings being employed only for the purpose of resolving an ambiguity found in the claims. Neither should it be interpreted in the sense that the claims serve only as a guideline and that the actual protection conferred may extend to what, from a consideration of the description and drawings by a person skilled in the art, the patentee has contemplated. On the contrary, it is to be interpreted as defining a position between these extremes which combines a fair protection for the patentee with a reasonable degree of certainty for third parties.

This formulation offers a middle way between two somewhat parodic extremes. In the UK it has been used to support a purposive approach to interpretation of claims, reading them through the eyes of a person skilled in the art, as opposed to a purely literal reading.[146] However, some have criticised this approach as inconsistent with the Protocol and it was perceived by some to be 'anti-patentee'. In *Improver* v. *Remington*, other national courts came to different conclusions from the UK court on the same patent. Thus a divergence remained, despite the existence of the Protocol.[147]

Another controversial issue is the scope of the so-called 'doctrine of equivalents'. To demonstrate infringement the patentee need not show that *every* element of the patented invention has been taken, but the defendant must take all of the *material* or *essential* elements – the *essential integers*. All patent systems must consider what the outcome should be when the defendant has substituted a material element with something functionally equivalent. In such a situation, a very literal reading of the claims will bear harshly on the patentee, allowing the defendant to avoid infringement by means of a minor variation. Equally, a generous approach to construction may well lead to an extension of the patentee's monopoly beyond the claims.[148] In England, a

---

[146]   *Catnic* v. *Hill and Smith* [1982] RPC 183; *Improver* v. *Remington* [1990] FSR 181.

[147]   For more see P. Mole, 'Beauty and the Beast: The Festo Case and the New Protocol to Article 69 EPC' [2003] *EIPR* 40; H. Dunlop, 'Court of Appeal Gets to Grips with the Protocol' [2003] *EIPR* 342.

[148]   This extension is frankly admitted in the United States, although it is balanced by a doctrine of 'prosecution estoppel', by which equivalence cannot be claimed for integers restricting the monopoly which have been included by amendment during the prosecution of the application in the patent office. The patentee is estopped from denying that he intended to surrender that part of the estoppel. Unfortunately, the effect of this is that the true scope of patent protection cannot be determined without an expensive investigation of the patent office file. See the United States Supreme Court's deci-

doctrine of infringement by use of the 'pith and marrow' of the invention was developed. Its nature was somewhat unclear, in the sense that the courts did not state whether the doctrine was merely a principle of construction, or whether it explicitly extended protection outside the claims.[149] In addition, there was no specific reference to a doctrine of equivalents in either Article 69 of the EPC, or in the Protocol on its interpretation. However, the EPC 2000 adds a new Article 2 to the Article 69 Protocol. It states that:

> For the purpose of determining the extent of protection conferred by a European patent, due account shall be taken of any element which is equivalent to an element specified in the claims.

This suggests an approach which does not go so far as the American doctrine of equivalents (which effectively extends protection outside the claims), but it does allow equivalence to form part of the background of facts known to the person skilled in the art, and thus is an aspect of the purposive approach to interpretation required by the Protocol.[150] Despite the revised Protocol, the extent to which protection and enforcement of European patents varies in different countries will remain a matter of anxiety, though national courts do look increasingly to the decisions of the EPO as they decide the cases before them.[151]

3.3.1.7   European patent – substantive requirements

'European patents shall be granted for any inventions, in all fields of technology, provided that they are new, involve an inventive step and are susceptible of industrial application.'[152] Certain subject matter is excluded from patentability.[153] The invention must be disclosed clearly and completely.[154]

---

sion in *Festo Corporation* v. *Shoketsu Kinzoku Kogyo Kabushiki* 535 US 722 (2002). For more see N. Fox, 'Divided by a Common Language: A Comparison of Patent Claim Interpretation in the English and American Courts' [2004] *EIPR* 528.

[149]   *Clark* v. *Adie* (1877) 2 App Cas 315, 320; *C Van Der Lely NV* v. *Bamfords Ltd* [1963] RPC 61.

[150]   For discussion see *Kirin-Amgen Inc.* v. *Hoechst Marion Roussel and Transkaryotic Therapies Inc.* [2004] UKHL 46 (esp. paras. 36–52); D. Curley and H. Sheraton, 'The Lords Rule in Amgen v. TKT' [2005] *EIPR* 154.

[151]   See Matthew Fisher, 'New Protocol, Same Old Story?: Patent Claim Construction in 2007; Looking Back with a View to the Future' [2008] *IPQ* 134–62.

[152]   EPC 2000, Art. 52(1).

[153]   EPC 2000, Arts. 52(2), 53.

[154]   EPC 2000, Arts. 83, 100(b).

(1) NOVELTY – ARTICLE 54

To be patentable an invention must be 'new'.[155] An invention is new if it does not form part of the 'state of the art'.[156] The state of the art is held to comprise everything made available to the public by means of a written or oral description, by use, or in any other way, before the invention's priority date.[157] If the invention is disclosed or 'anticipated' by the state of the art, no patent will be granted (or, if granted in error, is liable to be revoked).[158] The question is essentially a factual one – as to whether the invention has already been made public or not. The hurdle is a stringent one, because the EPC adopts a principle of 'objective novelty', meaning that all information available at the priority date is used to test novelty, regardless of where and in what form it was released. The harshness (and sometimes arbitrariness) of the test has been defended on the grounds that it avoids subjectivity and thus offers certainty.

The state of the art includes information made available anywhere in the world, by any means. The requirement that it has been 'made available to the public' does not imply that the public has actually seen it, but simply that members of the public may gain knowledge of the matter and there is no bar of confidentiality restricting the use or dissemination of such knowledge. For example, an inventor gave an oral presentation at an invitation-only meeting. Only certain members of the public had been invited to participate, but they were not subject to a secrecy agreement. As a result, everything that was said at the meeting was 'made available to the public'.[159] In another case, a journal was placed on the library shelves of the Royal Society of Chemistry one day before the priority date. It was held to have been made available to the public, and it was not necessary that any members of the public would have been aware that the document was available upon request on that day. It is sufficient if the document was in fact available to the public on that day, whether or not any member of the public actually asked to see it.[160] It is

---

[155] EPC 2000, Art. 52(1).

[156] EPC 2000, Art. 54(1).

[157] This is the date of filing of the European patent application: EPC 2000, Art. 54(2). The state of the art also includes European patent applications filed before but published after the date of filing: EPC 2000, Art. 54(3). Previously, later published European patent applications having earlier priority or filing dates were only considered part of the state of the art to the extent that the same states were designated in the earlier and later applications. This restriction no longer applies to European patent applications filed after the EPC came into force. These will now be considered prior art for the assessment of novelty in all EPC states.

[158] EPC 2000, Art. 138(1)(a).

[159] *Hooper Trading/T-Cell Growth Factor*, T877/90 [1993] *EPOR* 6.

[160] *Research Corporation/Publication*, T381/87 [1989] *EPOR* 138 EPO. The Board of Appeal distinguished a case in which a thesis had been placed in the archives

common for inventors to anticipate their own patents, in part because there is no grace period in which they can practise their inventions.

There are two non-prejudicial disclosures. The first is if the disclosure is due to 'an evident abuse in relation to the applicant or his legal predecessor'.[161] This somewhat vague formulation covers breaches of an obligation to maintain secrecy, at least theoretically. But applicants have found it difficult to rely on this exception. It is a condition that the disclosure take place 'no earlier than six months preceding the filing of the European patent application'.[162] The Enlarged Board of Appeal has held that the intention was to create a provision with a narrowly restricted time frame, and that 'in any case, breach of an obligation to maintain secrecy by disclosure relates more to the domain of the inventor and subsequent applicant than to that of the public in general and competitors in particular'. The Board therefore took the view that, since only the applicant can take suitable action to prevent unauthorised disclosure, it is not inherently unreasonable or inappropriate to resolve the prevailing conflict of interests to the applicant's disadvantage in the interests of legal certainty rather than to the public's disadvantage in the interests of individual justice.[163] The second non-prejudicial disclosure is when the applicant or his legal predecessor has displayed the invention at a relevant 'international exhibition'.[164] Again, the disclosure must have taken place within the six months preceding the filing date.

When determining what information has been disclosed by the prior art, documents are interpreted as if they were being read at the date of their publication. What is significant is the actual contents of their disclosure in the sense of a finite concrete technical rule, so it is important to avoid interpreting them

---

of a library a few days before the relevant priority date. The archives were not open to the public, and the thesis had not been indexed before the priority date, so no member of the public could have asked for it to be produced from the archives before the priority date. In these circumstances, it was held as a finding of fact that the document had not been published before the priority date.

[161]   EPC 2000, Art. 51(1)(a).

[162]   EPC 2000, Art. 51(1).

[163]   *University Patents/Materials and methods for herpes simplex virus vaccination*, G3/98 [2001] *OJEPO* 62, 81. For the calculation of the six-month period referred to in EPC 2000, Article 55(1), the relevant date is the date of the actual filing of the European patent application; the date of priority is not to be taken account of in calculating this period. A more positive expression of the provision is to be found in the *Guidelines*, which state that 'subject matter has not been made available to the public by use or in any other way if there is an express or tacit agreement on secrecy which has not been broken . . . or if the circumstances of the case are such that such secrecy derives from a relationship of good faith or trust': *Guidelines*, D-V, 3.1.3.2.

[164]   This means an exhibition falling within the terms of the Convention on international exhibitions signed at Paris on 22 November 1928 and last revised on 30 November 1972: EPC 2000, Art. 55(1)(b).

retrospectively.[165] To decide on the novelty of a feature claimed, it is necessary to determine whether the feature may be derived directly and unmistakably from a prior art document by a person skilled in the art. The skilled person is regarded as being used to seeing all the detailed information contained in a document in its technical context, so the technical disclosure in a prior art document should be considered in its entirety.[166] The skilled person can correct obvious errors or inconsistencies in documents.[167] It is not normally possible to combine (mosaic) different items from prior art, unless the documents would inevitably be read together.[168] Where the prior art is a product, a similar approach is taken, but some specific rules have been developed to deal with particular practical issues. A single sale is sufficient to make the product available to the public for the purpose of prior art, as long as the purchaser is not bound by an obligation of confidentiality. There is no need to prove that anyone was actually aware of the product, or had particular reasons for analysing it. Such a requirement would introduce an element of subjectivity which would lead to uncertainty, and is rigorously avoided in other areas of prior art. Nor is any account taken of the costs of the analysis, or the time required to undertake it. For disclosure by the prior art it is sufficient that a person skilled in the art can determine the structure of the product using the normal investigation capabilities used in that field, without additional inventive effort.[169] Where it is possible for the skilled person to discover the composition or the internal structure of the product and to reproduce it without undue burden, then both the product and its composition or internal structure become state of the art. However, extrinsic characteristics, which are only revealed when the product is applied in particular ways or under certain conditions (in order to provide a particular effect or result or to discover potential results or capabilities), are not regarded as having been made available to the public.[170]

For lack of novelty to be found, all the technical features of the claimed invention in combination must have been communicated to the public, or laid open for inspection.[171] This raises questions as to how precise a disclosure must be for it to be made available to the public. As the Technical Board of

---

[165] *Tektronix/Schottky Barrier Diode*, T694/91 [1995] *EPOR* 256; *Rhone-Poulenc/Taxoids*, T77/97 [1998] *EPOR* 256.

[166] *Scanditronix/Radiation Beam Collimation*, T6/87 [1990] *EPOR* 352; *Draco/Xanthines*, T7/86 [1989] *EPOR* 65.

[167] *ICI/Latex Composition*, T77/87 [1989] *EPOR* 246.

[168] *Amoco Corporation/Alternative Claims*, T153/85 [1988] *EPOR* 116; *Bayer/Diastereomers*, T12/81 [1979–85] B *EPOR* 308. *Guidelines*, C-IV, 7.1.

[169] *Thomson/Electron Tube*, T953/90 [1998] *EPOR* 415.

[170] *Availability to the Public*, G1/92 [1993] *EPOR* 241; *Packard/Liquid Scintillation*, T952/92 [1997] *EPOR* 457.

[171] *Mobil/Friction reducing additive*, G2/88 [1990] *EPOR* 73.

Appeal has noted, 'the concept of novelty must not be given such a narrow interpretation that only what has already been described in the same terms is prejudicial to it. The purpose of Article 54(1) EPC is to prevent the state of the art being patented again.'[172] Even where a prior art document fails explicitly to disclose something falling within a claim, availability in the sense of Article 54 may still be established if the inevitable outcome of what is literally or explicitly disclosed falls within the ambit of that claim.[173]

An interesting problem arises if the application relates to a secret or inherent use for a known product. Should this prior use anticipate the patent? On the one hand it can be argued that a new patent should not be able to prevent a person from using a product as before. On the other hand, since the use was secret, it can be argued that it has not been made available to the public, and should not be sufficient to destroy novelty. It is this latter approach which is taken.[174] Note that the EPO does not consider that novelty can be conferred on a known substance by a novel process for producing that substance, so a product-by-process claim will only be novel if the product itself is novel.[175]

A similar question arises in relation to a discovery that an old thing used in an old way had previously unknown advantages – so-called 'novelty of purpose' applications. Although historically these have not been recognised as novel by patent law, this approach has been very considerably eroded, first in the field of medical patents and then more widely. A very significant proportion of medical and biotechnological research now focuses on the discovery of new uses for known substances, and a special exception to the general rule on these was included in the EPC. This provides that a product for use in a method of medical or veterinary treatment does not lack novelty, even where the product is itself known and part of the state of the art, 'provided that its use

---

[172]   *Bayer/Diastereomers,* T12/81 [1979–85] B *EPOR* 308, 312.
[173]   In deciding what is or is not the inevitable outcome of an express literal disclosure in a particular prior art document, a standard of proof much stricter than the balance of probability is applied, and the matter must instead be 'beyond all reasonable doubt': *Allied Signal/Polyolefin Fiber,* T793/93 [1996] *EPOR* 104, 109.
[174]   'The question to be decided is what has been "made available" to the public: the question is not what may have been "inherent" in what was made available (by a prior written description, or in what has previously been used (prior use), for example). Under the EPC, a hidden or secret use, because it has not been made available to the public, is not a ground of objection to validity of a European patent. In this respect, the provisions of the EPC may differ from the previous national laws of some Contracting States, and even from the current national laws of some non-Contracting States': *Mobil/Friction reducing additive,* G2/88 [1990] *EPOR* 73, 88.
[175]   *IFF/Claim Categories* T150/82 [1979–85] C *EPOR* 629.

for any such method is not comprised in the state of the art'.[176] In other words, it is the new *purpose* which is regarded as novel, even though the substance is not novel. The same substance or composition cannot subsequently be patented for the same therapeutic effect.[177]

This provision was thought to apply only to the discovery of the *first* medical use of known products. Nevertheless, the Enlarged Board of Appeal later held that the Article did not prevent the patenting of second (or further) medical uses, if this application was new and inventive. However, whereas the inventor of a first medical indication could obtain purpose-limited product protection for a known substance or composition, for second and subsequent medical uses applicants had to use the so-called Swiss form of claims.[178] Such claims have to be in the form, 'use of a substance or composition X for the manufacture of a medicament for therapeutic application Z', to avoid possible objections that the invention is for a method of therapy. Thus the novelty lies in the further new therapeutic use which has been discovered, not the substance itself or in the first medical use. The justification given for allowing patent protection for second and subsequent medical uses is that there is no particular reason for drawing the line after the first medical use. However, not everyone is wholly convinced that second and subsequent medical use patents should be permitted.[179] Nevertheless, the EPC 2000 has endorsed them by amending Article 54(5) to allow for claims 'for any specific use', without any requirement to use Swiss-style claims.[180]

Articles 54(4) and 54(5) thus provide for an exception from the general principle that product claims can only be obtained for absolutely novel products. However, this does not mean that product claims for the first and further medical uses need not fulfil all other requirements of patentability, particularly that of inventive step.[181] It should also be remembered in this context that the EPC 2000 has removed methods of medical treatment from Article 52 EPC (the old version of which provided that these lacked industrial applicability)

---

[176]   EPC 2000, Art. 54(4); formerly EPC 1973, Art. 54(5).

[177]   *Hoffman-la Roche/Pyrrolidine Derivatives*, T128/82 [1979–85] B *EPOR* 591.

[178]   *Eisai*, G5/83 [1985] *OJEPO* 64; [1979–1985] B *EPOR* 241. See also *Genentech Inc./Method of administration of IGF-I*, T1020/03 [2006] *EPOR* 9.

[179]   As Buxton LJ observed in the UK Court of Appeal, 'This may seem to be merely a roundabout way of seeking to patent a medical process, and one that only doubtfully gives proper weight to the first sentence of Article 52(4)'. Nevertheless, recognising the undesirability of departing from decisions of the EPO, the Court of Appeal followed *Eisai*. *Bristol Myers Squibb* v. *Baker Norton Pharmaceuticals* [2001] RPC 1 (para. 81).

[180]   *Guidelines*, C-IV, 4.8. But see also Eddy D. Ventose, 'No European Patents for Second Medical Uses of Devices or Instruments' [2008] *EIPR* 11–16.

[181]   *Hoffman-la Roche/Pyrrolidine Derivatives*, T128/82 [1979–85] B *EPOR* 591.

and put them in Article 53 EPC 2000 (which provides, more straightforwardly, that they are excluded from patentability).[182]

The issue also arises in relation to non-medical patents. Should the discovery of further uses for a known product be patentable in all fields?[183] The issue was considered by the Enlarged Board of Appeal in *Mobil/Friction reducing additive*. In *Mobil* the claim was to the use of a known substance as a friction-reducing additive in lubricants. The substance was already known to inhibit rust, and the application was therefore opposed on the grounds that the invention was not novel. The Enlarged Board distinguished the medical use cases, as being relevant only with reference to Articles 52(4) and 54(5) EPC 1973, and refused to apply their reasoning directly here. This case instead raised general questions as to the interpretation of Article 54(1) and 54(2) EPC. The Enlarged Board held that if the claim was to the use of a known substance in a new way for a new purpose, then this might be novel, because the new way of using the substance amounted to a technical result. In contrast, a claim to the use of a known substance in a known way to achieve a new purpose would not include any novel technical feature. The only 'novelty' in such a case would be the mental state of the person carrying out the invention, so this was not an objective matter relevant to the determination of novelty under the EPC. However, a claim to the new use of a known substance in a known way could (in appropriate cases) be interpreted as including as a technical feature the function of achieving the new purpose (because this is the technical result). The question was whether the functional technical feature of the invention had been made available to the public. If the claim included a 'new means of realisation' by which the new purpose could be achieved, then this was a novel technical feature. The claim could be interpreted to include 'the function of achieving the new purpose (because this is the technical result)', so the fact that the substance achieved the new purpose would be a 'functional technical feature' of the invention. Thus on these facts, the functional technical feature was that the substance reduced friction, and, because the technical feature had not been previously made available to the public, the claimed invention was novel. This was so in spite of the fact that such a technical effect might have

---

[182] Specifically, EPC 1973, Art. 52(4) has been deleted, and its contents regarding methods of treatment transferred to EPC 2000, Art. 53(c).

[183] See Gerald D. Paterson, 'The Patentability of Further Uses of a Known Product under the European Patent Convention' [1991] *EIPR* 16–20; Sir Robin Jacob, 'Novelty of Use Claims' (1996) 27 *IIC* 170. In addition, speaking judicially, Jacob J noted, 'I am of course aware of the policy reasons behind *Mobil* (and that in *Eisai*) namely encouragement of research. But it may well be that it is not for patent law to be distorted with recourse to devices and sophistry': *Bristol-Myers Squibb* v. *Baker Norton Pharmaceuticals* [1999] RPC 253, 280.

taken place inherently in the course of carrying out what had previously been made available to the public.[184]

The *Mobil* decision thus makes it clear that the discovery of a new purpose for a known product used in an old way is potentially patentable, regardless of the technical field involved. The novelty lies in the discovery of the new purpose. Under Article 54(2) EPC the relevant question is what has been made available to the public, and not what may have been inherent in what was made available. A hidden or secret use, because it has not been made available to the public, is not a ground of objection to the validity of a European patent. The issue is whether the purpose claimed is actually new. What is important is that there are 'two distinctly different effects, two distinctly different applications or uses for the same substance, which can clearly be distinguished from each other'.[185]

Another problematic area is determining the novelty of so-called 'selection patents'. These are patent applications which claim a subset or 'selection' from within a larger known class, by showing that they share a feature peculiar to that sub-class. This is particularly relevant to the chemical and pharmaceutical industries. It is argued that if the substances disclosed in the generic group anticipate all sub-groups, this will act as a deterrent to further research. As a result, some jurisdictions allow selection patents and regard them as a distinct category, but others have been reluctant to do so. The EPO treats selection patents as it does any other patents. A generic disclosure does not usually take away the novelty of any specific example falling within the terms of that disclosure, but a specific disclosure does take away the novelty of a generic claim embracing that disclosure.[186] The question is whether the generic disclosure unequivocally makes available to the person skilled in the art those things claimed in the sub-group. If it does, the generic disclosure will be characterised as an enabling disclosure and will anticipate.[187]

(2)   INVENTIVE STEP – ARTICLE 56

To be patentable an invention must involve an inventive step.[188] The aim is to

---

[184]   *Mobil/Friction reducing additive*, G2/88 [1990] *EPOR* 73, 87–9.

[185]   *Robertet/Deodorant Compositions*, T892/94 [1999] *EPOR* 516, 525. See also *Bayer/Plant growth regulating agent*, G6/88 [1990] *EPOR* 257; *Ortho Pharmaceutical/Prevention of skin atrophy*, T254/93 [1999] *EPOR* 1.

[186]   So, a disclosure of copper takes away the novelty of metal as a generic concept, but not the novelty of any metal other than copper, and one of rivets takes away the novelty of fastening means as a generic concept, but not the novelty of any fastening other than rivets: *Guidelines*, C-IV, 9.5.

[187]   *Sanofi/Enantiomer*, T658/91 [1996] *EPOR* 24; *Bayer/Diastereomers*, T12/81 [1979–85] B *EPOR* 308. *Guidelines*, C-IV, 9.8.

[188]   EPC 2000, Art. 52(1).

ensure that there is a quantitative advance on the state of the art. An invention will be considered as involving an inventive step if, having regard to the state of the art, it is not obvious to a person skilled in the art.[189] Since the question of non-obviousness is one of fact, and thus a matter of the tribunal's judgement, it may be difficult to predict the outcome of cases. The EPO has favoured the so-called 'problem and solution approach', in an attempt to offer greater certainty to the parties involved.[190] By this, the inventive step is considered as 'a step from the technical problem to its solution'.[191] This approach requires identification of the technical field of the invention (which will also be the field of expertise of the person skilled in the art to be considered for the purpose of assessing inventive step), the identification of the closest prior art in this field, the identification of the technical problem which can be regarded as solved in relation to this closest prior art, and then an assessment of whether or not the technical feature(s) which alone or together form the solution claimed, could be derived as a whole by the skilled person in that field in an obvious manner from the state of the art.[192] Useful though the problem and solution approach often is, the Technical Board of Appeal has stressed that it is only 'one among other possible approaches, each of which has its own advantages and drawbacks'.[193]

The 'person skilled in the art' is presumed to be an ordinary practitioner aware of what was common general knowledge in the art at the relevant date. Such a person is the expert in the relevant field, possessed of average knowledge and ability, but no inventive capability. Such a person is also cautious, so would neither go against an established prejudice nor try to enter into sacrosanct or unpredictable areas nor take incalculable risks.[194] This notional person is presumed to have had access to everything in the state of the art, and

---

[189]   EPC 2000, Art. 56.
[190]   *Bayer/Carbonless Copying Paper*, T1/80 [1979–85] B *EPOR* 250. *Guidelines*, C-IV, 11.7. For comment see G.S.A. Szabo, 'The Problem and Solution Approach to Inventive Step' [1986] *EIPR* 293–303; Alan W. White, 'The Problem and Solution Approach to Obviousness' [1996] *EIPR* 387; Paul G. Cole, 'Inventive Step: Meaning of the EPO Problem and Solution Approach, and Implications for the United Kingdom' [1998] *EIPR* 214–18, 262–72.
[191]   *ICI/Containers*, T26/81 [1979–85] B *EPOR* 362, 365.
[192]   *Comvik/Two identities*, T641/00 [2004] *EPOR* 10 (para. 5).
[193]   *Alcan/Aluminium alloys*, T465/92 [1995] *EPOR* 501, 514. The Board noted in particular that the problem and solution approach relies on the results of a search made with actual knowledge of the invention, thus it is inherently based on hindsight, so care is required in its application in some circumstances. Also, where an invention breaks new ground, there will be no close prior art, and in such cases it is normally better to avoid formulating artificial and unrealistic technical problems, and to start from the technical problem identified in the patent itself.
[194]   *Genentech/Expression In Yeast*, T455/9 [1996] *EPOR* 85, 98.

to the normal means and capacity for routine work and experimentation.[195] When assessing inventive step, the subjective achievement of the inventor does not matter, so the history of the invention is irrelevant. What is assessed is the objective achievement – whether a person skilled in the art would consider the invention to be non-obvious.[196]

The nature of the skilled person's qualifications will depend on the technical field into which the invention falls. If the problem prompts the person skilled in the art to seek its solution in another technical field, the specialist in that field is the person qualified to solve the problem, and the assessment of whether the solution involves an inventive step will be based on that specialist's knowledge and ability. In *Fives-Cail Babock*, the question was whether it was obvious to use glass fibre to replace components in a conveyor-belt cleaning apparatus. Although this problem would have first confronted the conveying equipment specialist, it would inevitably have prompted resort to the field of materials science. Therefore the assessment of whether the problem's solution involved an inventive step had to be made by reference to the knowledge and ability of a materials specialist, not a conveying equipment specialist.[197] Sometimes (particularly in advanced technologies, or highly specialised processes) it will be more appropriate to think in terms of a group of persons, such as a research or production team, rather than a single person.[198] If an invention claims both technical and non-technical features, it is the technical part of the invention which is the basis for assessing inventive step, so the skilled person has expertise only in the technical fields. So, for example, if the technical problem is concerned with a computer implementation of a business, actuarial or accountancy system, the skilled person will be someone skilled in data processing, and not merely a businessman, actuary or accountant.[199] The exclusion of such skills as 'non-technical' makes it even more difficult to obtain patents for business methods, or for computer-related inventions.

For the purposes of determining obviousness, the state of art is conceived just as broadly as it is for the purposes of determining novelty. However, there are two important exceptions which apply when considering inventive step. Firstly, the prior art does not include national prior rights or earlier European patent applications published after the filing date of the application

---

[195] *Guidelines*, C-IV, 11.3; *Allied Colloids/Polymer Powders*, T39/93 [1997] *EPOR* 347.

[196] *BASF/Metal Refining*, T24/81 [1979–85] B *EPOR* 354.

[197] *Fives-Cail Babcock/Cleaning Apparatus for Conveyor Belt*, T32/81 [1979–85] B *EPOR* 377.

[198] *Guidelines*, C-IV, 11.3.

[199] *Comvik/Two identities*, T641/00 [2004] *EPOR* 10 (para. 7).

in question.[200] Secondly, it is possible to combine (that is, 'mosaic') information from different sources. This exception has various limits. It must be natural and logical for the skilled person to combine the teachings of the various documents. Although unrelated or conflicting documents may not be combined in an attempt to deny inventive step, it is permissible to consider documents together mosaically in order to prove a prejudice or a general trend pointing away from the invention.[201] The state of the art comprises everything made available to the public before the date of filing, regardless of language, date or extent of circulation.[202] But obviousness is judged from the point of view of the person skilled in the art, so the question is whether it would have been obvious to the skilled person to arrive at something falling within the terms of the claim. 'Obvious' means something which follows plainly or logically from the prior art, and does not require skill or ability beyond that to be expected of the person skilled in the art. But the skilled person is only expected to know about the information available in the relevant field, or in closely neighbouring fields. Nevertheless, a skilled person is expected to be aware of and refer to the state of the art in the general field of technology in which the same problems or problems similar to those in the special field of the application extensively arise. For the purposes of inventive step (as opposed to novelty), documents are construed in the light of subsequent knowledge and regard is had to all the knowledge generally available to the person skilled in the art before the filing date.[203] The sources of this general knowledge will depend on the nature of the technical field in question, but encyclopaedias and standard textbooks have been accepted as representing the common general knowledge.[204]

As has been explained, in assessing inventive step, the EPO will normally apply the 'problem-and-solution approach'. This has three stages: firstly, the 'closest prior art' is determined; secondly, the 'objective technical problem' to be solved is identified; finally, the examiner will consider whether or not the claimed invention, starting from the closest prior art and the objective technical problem, would have been obvious to the skilled person.[205] The closest prior art is that combination of features, disclosed in one single reference, which constitutes the most promising starting point for an obvious develop-

---

[200]   EPC 2000, Art. 56.
[201]   *Philip Morris/Tobacco Lamina Filler*, T323/90 [1996] *EPOR* 422; *Mobay/Methylenebis*, T2/81 [1979-85] B *EPOR* 280. See also *Discovision/Optical Recording*, T239/85 [1997] *EPOR* 171.
[202]   *Mitsuboshi/Endless Power Transmission Belt*, T169/84 [1987] *EPOR* 120.
[203]   *Guidelines*, C-IV, 11.4. *Mobius/Pencil Sharpener*, T176/84 [1986] *EPOR* 117.
[204]   *Mars II/Glucomannan*, T112/92 [1994] *EPOR* 249, 252.
[205]   *Guidelines*, C-IV, 11.7.

ment leading to the invention. In practice, the closest prior art is generally that which corresponds to a similar use and requires the minimum of structural and functional modifications to arrive at the claimed invention. The closest prior art must be assessed from the skilled person's point of view on the day before the filing date.[206]

The 'objective technical problem' is determined by looking at the patent application, the closest prior art and the distinguishing feature(s) of the invention. EPC rules require that the description should 'disclose the invention as claimed in such terms that the technical problem, even if not expressly stated as such, and its solution can be understood', so the description is the starting point.[207] In the context of the problem-and-solution approach, the technical problem means the aim and task of modifying or adapting the closest prior art to provide the technical effects that the invention provides over the closest prior art. The objective technical problem derived in this way may differ from 'the problem' presented in the application (which may not take into account the relevant prior art, or may be too ambitiously stated, for example).[208] A reformulation of the problem is permissible if the problem could be deduced by the person skilled in the art from the application as filed when considered in the light of the closest prior art.[209] The redefinition of the technical problem should not contradict earlier statements in the application about the general purpose and character of the invention.[210] The objective technical problem should not contain pointers to the solution, because it would lead to the assessment of inventive activity being made with hindsight.

Finally, it can be considered whether the invention is obvious or not. The question is whether there is any teaching in the prior art as a whole that would (not simply *could*, but *would*) have prompted the skilled person, faced with the objective technical problem, to modify or adapt the closest prior art while taking account of that teaching, thereby arriving at something falling within the terms of the claims, and thus achieving what the invention achieves. The point is not whether the skilled person *could* have arrived at the invention by adapting or modifying the closest prior art, but whether the skilled person *would* have done so in the hope of solving the objective technical problem or

---

[206] *Guidelines*, C-IV, 11.7.1.

[207] EPC 2000, Rule 42(1)(c). The abstract too 'shall be drafted in a way allowing the clear understanding of the technical problem': EPC 2000, Rule 47(2). See also *Pegulan/Surface Finish*, T495/91 [1995] *EPOR* 516.

[208] *Allied Colloids/Polymer powders*, T39/93 [1997] *EPOR* 347. *Guidelines*, C-IV, 11.7.2.

[209] *Sperry/Reformulation of the Problem*, T13/84 [1986] *EPOR* 289, 294.

[210] *Phillips Petroleum/Passivation of catalyst*, T155/85 [1988] *EPOR* 164, 169.

in expectation of some improvement or advantage.[211] If the problem can be solved by taking a series of obvious individual steps each generating only their predictable individual effects, this will not amount to an inventive step.[212] A particular approach may be obvious even if the skilled person is not absolutely certain that it will succeed. One relevant question is whether the skilled person would have used the approach with a reasonable expectation of success (as opposed to mere hope).[213] This is a useful test in technical situations where predictable methods are relied on to solve a particular problem, but inappropriate where the invention depends on a random technique (such as mutagenesis), luck, or chance.[214] A skilled person will be conditioned by the prior art and be cautious about entering unpredictable areas, challenging established (technical) prejudices, or taking incalculable risks. These avenues will thus not be obvious to try.[215] EPO Guidelines express this point positively:

> As a general rule, there is an inventive step if the prior art leads the person skilled in the art away from the procedure proposed by the invention. This applies in particular when the skilled person would not even consider carrying out experiments to determine whether these were alternatives to the known way of overcoming a real or imagined technical obstacle.[216]

If unforeseen difficulties can be overcome in a fairly straightforward manner the route will be obvious, but if inventiveness is required the invention will be patentable.[217] The discovery of a yet unrecognised problem may, in certain circumstances, give rise to patentable subject matter in spite of the fact that the claimed solution is retrospectively trivial and in itself obvious (so-called 'problem inventions'). However, the perception of the problem must be beyond the abilities of the person skilled in the art. The overcoming of recognised drawbacks and achieving resultant improvements are the normal task of the skilled person.[218] Where the invention solves a technical problem which workers in the art have been attempting to solve for a long time, or otherwise fulfils a long-felt need, this may be regarded as an indication of inventive

---

[211]   *Rider/Simethicone tablet*, T/83 [1979–85] C *EPOR* 715; *Genentech/ Expression in Yeast*, T455/9 [1996] *EPOR* 85. *Guidelines*, C-IV, 11.7.3.

[212]   *VDO Adolf Schindling/Illuminating Device*, T324/94 [1997] *EPOR* 146, 153.

[213]   *Mycogen/Modifying plant cells*, T694/92 [1998] *EPOR* 114.

[214]   *DSM/Astaxanthin*, T737/96 [2000] *EPOR* 557, 563.

[215]   *Genentech/Expression in Yeast*, T455/9 [1996] *EPOR* 85, 98. See also *Mobay/Methylenebis*, T2/81 [1979-85] B *EPOR* 280, 286.

[216]   *Guidelines*, C-IV, Annex, 4.

[217]   *Unilever/Chymosin*, T386/94 [1997] *EPOR* 184.

[218]   *Rider/Simethicone tablet*, T/83 [1979–85] C *EPOR* 715; *Boeing/General Technical Knowledge*, T195/84 [1986] *EPOR* 190.

step.[219] Although commercial success alone is not regarded as indicative of inventive step, evidence of immediate commercial success when coupled with evidence of a long-felt want is of relevance provided the success derives from the technical features of the invention and not from other influences (for example, selling techniques or advertising).[220]

(3) INDUSTRIAL APPLICATION – ARTICLE 57

Only inventions which are capable of industrial application are patentable under the EPC.[221] This is defined as meaning that the invention can be made or used in any kind of industry, including agriculture. There is no need to prove actual use; potential use in industry is sufficient.[222] 'Industry' includes any physical activity of a 'technical character', that is, an activity which belongs to the useful or practical arts as distinct from the aesthetic arts; it does not necessarily imply the use of a machine or the manufacture of an article. The definition of industrial application serves various aims of patent policy. Under Article 52(4) of the EPC 1973, it was specifically stated that methods for treatment of the human or animal body by surgery or therapy and diagnostic methods practised on the human or animal body were *not* regarded as inventions which are susceptible of industrial application.[223] The aim was that no one should be hampered in the practice of medicine by patent law. However, imposing a fiction that such inventions are not industrially applicable was a somewhat roundabout route of achieving the desired policy objective, and under the EPC 2000 methods of treatment and diagnosis are excluded from patentability directly, by Article 53(c).[224] No change of practice is expected to result.

The requirement of industrial application raises an important hurdle for the patenting of biological research, particularly the patenting of genes. It is not sufficient merely to identify a gene. In addition, a use for it which amounts to industrial application is required. The Biotechnology Directive also addresses this subject: Recital 23 states that a mere DNA sequence without any indication of a function does not contain any technical information and is therefore not a patentable invention. The Biotechnology Directive has been incorporated

---

[219] *Frisco-Findus/Frozen Fish*, T90/89 [1991] *EPOR* 42. *Guidelines*, C-IV, 9.10.3.

[220] *ICI/Fusecord*, T270/84 [1987] *EPOR* 357.

[221] EPC 2000, Art. 52(1).

[222] EPC 2000, Art. 57.

[223] EPC 1973, Art. 52(4). For case law see below 3.3.1.7 (4) (iv) Methods for treatment of the human or animal body.

[224] Art. 53(c), EPC 2000. See below 3.3.1.7 (4) (iv) Methods for treatment of the human or animal body.

into the Implementing Regulations of the EPC, in order to avert possible conflict between the EPC and the Directive. The Directive may also be used as a supplementary means of interpretation.[225]

(4)   EXCLUDED SUBJECT MATTER – ARTICLE 52(2)–ARTICLE 53
The EPC does not define positively what is meant by 'invention', but instead contains a list of what will *not* be regarded as inventions.[226] In addition, there are a number of specific exceptions to patentability.[227]

Article 52(2) excludes:

(a)   discoveries, scientific theories and mathematical methods;
(b)   aesthetic creations;
(c)   schemes, rules and methods for performing mental acts, playing games or doing business, and programs for computers;
(d)   presentations of information.

These provisions apply only to the extent to which the patent relates to these subject matters or activities *as such*. The primary intention seems to be to exclude things which are abstract, intellectual or non-technical, but this is not explicit in the Article itself. Computer programs were excluded because they were thought best protected by copyright law, but this has proved to be a troublesome provision nevertheless.[228]

Article 52 has an important policy role, in that it determines which types of inventions are patentable. However, there is little agreement even as to the purpose of the Article, and as to whether the Article 52(2) exclusions are disparate in nature or share a common purpose in terms of policy objectives. This area of patent policy touches on a range of highly contentious issues. Both the EPO and the European Union have strong interests and strong views regarding patentability within Europe. Understandably, their positions differ in certain respects. In addition, there is competition from the United States, where the threshold of patent protection is lower (notably, with respect to non-technical business methods). This brings pressure, from some quarters at least, to lower the bar in Europe also. At one end of the spectrum, there are concerns about the number of trivial patents granted. At the other, there is also concern

[225]   EPC 1973, Rule 23b; EPC 2000, Rule 26. See also *ICOS Corporation/Seven transmembrane receptor* [2002] *OJEPO* 293, 304 (para. 9); *ZymoGenetics, Inc./Hematopoietic cytokine receptor* T898/05. For more see below section 3.3.3.3 The Biotechnology Directive: the legal protection of biotechnological inventions.
[226]   EPC 2000, Art. 52(2).
[227]   EPC 2000, Art. 53.
[228]   See below 3.3.1.7 (4) (ii) Computer-related inventions.

as to the breadth and nature of certain biotechnological patents. On this latter subject, the Biotechnology Directive takes some account of this unease, but also notes that 'significant progress in the treatment of diseases has already been made thanks to the existence of medicinal products derived from elements isolated from the human body' and therefore concludes that 'research aimed at obtaining and isolating such elements valuable to medicinal production should be encouraged by means of the patent system'. Since the Biotechnology Directive has been incorporated into the Implementing Regulations of the EPC, it governs the EPC's stance on these matters.[229]

Some of these tensions are expressed in the different approaches used to decide whether an invention is unpatentable because it falls within Article 52. Before 2000 the EPO used the so-called 'contribution approach', expressed in *Vicom*: 'Decisive is what technical contribution the invention as defined in the claim when considered as a whole makes to the known art'.[230] With this came the expectation that inventions should have a technical character, and that those that did provide a technical contribution to the known art would be patentable. This avoids the difficulty of having to determine precisely what the subject matter of the invention is, and then deciding whether that is excluded subject matter.[231] The revised wording of Article 52(1), which now refers to the granting of patents for inventions 'in all fields of technology', provides a clear basis for the EPO's insistence on 'technical character'. One problem with the contribution approach, however, is that it introduces ill-defined considerations of novelty into Article 52(2), even though these are not mentioned there. Novelty and inventive step are independent requirements which must be considered according to the terms of their relevant Articles.[232] Thus in *Pensions Benefits* the EPO Board of Appeal held the contribution approach was not appropriate for deciding whether something is an invention, observing:

> There is no basis in the EPC for distinguishing between 'new features' of an invention and features of that invention which are known from the prior art when examining whether the invention concerned may be considered to be an invention within the meaning of Article 52(1) EPC. Thus there is no basis in the EPC for applying this so-called contribution approach for this purpose.[233]

---

[229]   In addition, under EPC Rules, the Directive is used as a supplementary means of interpretation: EPC, Rules 23b and 23e. For more see below section 3.3.3.3 The Biotechnology Directive: the legal protection of biotechnological inventions.

[230]   *VICOM/Computer-Related Invention*, T208/84 [1987] *EPOR* 74 (para. 16).

[231]   EPO Guidelines appear to expect that the application will disclose an invention, and state that it must be of a technical character, although it may be in any field of technology: *Guidelines*, C-IV, 1.2(ii) and 2.1.

[232]   There is, for example, no indication of what would comprise 'prior art' for the purposes of Art. 52(2).

[233]   *Pensions Benefit Systems Partnership*, T931/95 [2001] *OJEPO* 441 (para. 6).

On the facts of *Pensions Benefits*, the Board held that a computer system programmed for use in a particular way had 'the character of a concrete apparatus in the sense of a physical entity, man-made for a utilitarian purpose' and was thus an invention within Article 52(1) EPC. This sets a comparatively low hurdle, and the main focus of the patentability enquiry thus moves from Article 52(1) to the question of inventive step.

The EPO's approach has been set out very clearly recently, in *Duns Licensing Associates*.[234] The four requirements – invention, novelty, inventive step and susceptibility of industrial application – are essentially separate and independent criteria of patentability, which may give rise to concurrent objections. Novelty, in particular, is not a requisite of an invention within the meaning of Article 52(1), but a separate requirement of patentability. When examining patentability of an invention, the claim must be construed to determine the technical features of the invention, that is, the features which contribute to the technical character of the invention.

Following this general overview, some specific issues which arise in relation to the Article 52(2) exceptions will be considered.

(i)   The boundary between discoveries and inventions   The EPO Guidelines give examples of the Article 52(2) exclusions in operation. With respect to discoveries, if someone finds out a new property of a known material or article, that is mere discovery and unpatentable because discovery as such has no technical effect and is therefore not an invention within the meaning of Article 52(1).[235] If, however, that property is put to practical use, then this constitutes an invention which may be patentable. For example, the discovery that a particular known material is able to withstand mechanical shock would not be patentable, but a railway sleeper made from that material could well be patentable. To find a previously unrecognised substance occurring in nature is also mere discovery and therefore unpatentable. However, if a substance found in nature can be shown to produce a technical effect, it may be patentable. An example of such a case is that of a substance occurring in nature which is found to have an antibiotic effect. In addition, if a micro-organism is discov-

---

[234]   *Duns Licensing Associates/Method of estimating product distribution*, T154/04 (15 November 2006) (para. 5). The case is noted by David Rogers, 'EPO Decision on Exclusion of Methods of Business Research from Patentability, Requirement of Technical Character of an Invention' [2007] *JIPL&P* 641.

[235]   For an instructive case claiming a new 'magnetic force', which was said to falsify established theories of physics, including the Heisenberg uncertainty principle and Einstein's theory of relativity, see *Einstein-Bohr end*, T1538/05 (28 August 2006). The case is noted by David Rogers, 'Requirement of Industrial Application, Exclusion of Scientific Theories from Patentability, Perpetual Motion Machines' [2007] *JIPL&P* 62–3.

ered to exist in nature and to produce an antibiotic, the micro-organism itself may also be patentable as one aspect of the invention. Similarly, a gene which is discovered to exist in nature may be patentable if a technical effect is revealed, for example its use in making a certain polypeptide or in gene therapy.[236] Notwithstanding this guidance, it may be very difficult to draw an intellectually defensible distinction between discovery and invention, particularly in certain areas. Both are likely to involve a considerable investment in terms of time, skill and labour.

There is some assistance to be found in case law, and in the EPO Rules. The *Relaxin* case involved a patent for a hormone which relaxes the uterus during childbirth, and which, it was hoped, would reduce the need for caesarean deliveries. Relaxin from pigs was first described in 1926, but it was not until 1975 that the Howard Florey Institute in Australia isolated and determined the chemical structure of a human form of the hormone. Only human relaxin could be used for the medical purpose envisaged. Although it occurs naturally in the human ovary, a synthetic form was needed for therapeutic use. Having isolated the nucleotide sequence that coded for relaxin, recombinant DNA techniques were used to clone the gene, making it possible to produce synthetic relaxin. A patent was issued, but opposed by members of the Green Party in the European Parliament, in part on the grounds that the subject matter of the patent was a discovery and hence not patentable. The Opposition Division agreed that finding a substance freely occurring in nature would be mere discovery and therefore unpatentable. However, if a substance found in nature has first to be isolated from its surroundings and a process for obtaining it is developed, that process is patentable. Moreover, if this substance can be properly characterised by its structure and it is new in the absolute sense of having no previously recognised existence, then the substance *per se* may be patentable. Human H2-relaxin had no previously recognised existence, the patent proprietor had developed a process for obtaining it and the DNA encoding it, had characterised these products by their chemical structure and had found a use for the protein. The products were therefore patentable, and not excluded by Article 52(2).[237]

Nevertheless, anxieties regarding the use of the human body as a source of patentable material have led to a number of specific provisions on the subject. The human body, at the various stages of its formation and development, and the simple discovery of one of its elements, including the sequence or partial sequence of a gene, cannot constitute patentable inventions. However, an element isolated from the human body or otherwise produced by means of a

---

[236]   *Guidelines*, C-IV, 2.3.1.
[237]   *Howard Florey/Relaxin*, T74/91 [1995] *EPOR* 541. Now confirmed by EPC 2000, Rule 27(a). See also Biotech. Dir., Art. 3(2).

technical process, including the sequence or partial sequence of a gene, may constitute a patentable invention, even if the structure of that element is identical to that of a natural element. One important requirement for a patent concerning a sequence or partial sequence of a gene, is that its industrial application must be disclosed in the patent application.[238] In the *Icos* decision, the claim related to a purified and isolated polynucleotide encoding the amino acid sequence of the V28 protein. Although some potential uses were disclosed in the application, they were found to be speculative. The Opposition Division interpreted Recital 23 of the Biotechnology Directive as requiring that the indication of a function for a DNA sequence had to be more than speculative, and to be substantial, specific and credible. This application thus lacked industrial applicability, and was not patentable.[239] The issue of gene patenting causes considerable anxiety, both in the general public and with researchers. Although the requirement of industrial application imposes a significant threshold for those seeking patents, there remains concern that the disclosure of one use is sufficient to protect the patentee against *any* use by others, whether or not these uses had ever been contemplated by the patentee. Some therefore advocate the 'purpose-bound protection' model, which restricts the patent to the specific use disclosed in the patent application.[240]

(ii) Computer-related inventions   Article 52(2)(c) expressly excludes computer programs from patentability, and ordinary computer programs will normally be unpatentable.[241] However, many computer-related inventions have been granted patents. As computer technology spreads, more and more patent applications have a software element. Although a computer program *per se* remains unpatentable, applications which contain a computer program are *prima facie* patentable, if the invention as a whole makes a technical contribution to the art. The leading case for a considerable period was *Vicom*, notable for its formulation of the 'contribution approach' discussed earlier. On the particular facts, the Technical Board of Appeal said that:

---

[238]   EPC 1973, Rule 23e; EPC 2000, Rule 29. See also Biotech. Dir., Art. 5(2).
[239]   *Icos Corporation/Seven transmembrane receptor* [2002] *OJEPO* 293, 307.
[240]   For further reading see Sven Bostyn, 'The Patentability of Genetic Information Carriers' [1999] *IPQ* 1–36; Joseph Straus, 'Patenting Human Genes in Europe – Past Developments and Prospects for the Future' 26 (1995) *IIC* 920.
[241]   'The Board takes the view that, while an ordinary computer program used in a general-purpose computer certainly transforms mathematical values into electric signals with the aid of natural forces, the electric signals concerned amount to no more than a reproduction of information and cannot in themselves be regarded as a technical effect. The computer program used in a general-purpose computer is thus considered to be a program as such and hence excluded from patentability by Article 52(2)(c) EPC.': *Koch and Sterzel/X-Ray Apparatus*, T26/86 [1988] *EPOR* 72.

a claim directed to a technical process which process is carried out under the control of a program (be this implemented in hardware or in software), cannot be regarded as relating to a computer program as such within the meaning of Article 52(3) EPC, as it is the application of the program for determining the sequence of steps in the process for which in effect protection is sought.[242]

Here the technical benefit was a substantial increase in processing speed when using the claimed method for processing digital images.

More recently, however, EPO decisions have distanced themselves from *Vicom*. In *IBM/Computer programs*, it was held that determining the technical contribution of an invention with respect to the prior art was more appropriate for the purpose of examining novelty and inventive step than for deciding whether the invention was excluded subject matter.[243] A computer program product was not excluded from patentability under Article 52(2) and (3) EPC if, when run on a computer, it produced a further technical effect going beyond the 'normal' physical interactions between program (software) and computer (hardware). In the *Pensions Benefit* case, a method of controlling a pension benefits program was claimed, and also an apparatus for controlling a pension benefits system (in practical terms, a computer programmed in a particular way). The Board of Appeal held that this had 'the character of a concrete apparatus in the sense of a physical entity, man-made for a utilitarian purpose' and was thus an invention within the meaning of Article 52(1), and did not fall within Article 52(2)(c). No further technical contribution was required.[244] In *Hitachi/Auction method*, the Board observed that

> What matters having regard to the concept of 'invention' within the meaning of Article 52(1) EPC is the presence of technical character which may be implied by the physical features of an entity or the nature of an activity, or may be conferred to a non-technical activity by the use of technical means.[245]

---

[242] *VICOM/Computer-Related Invention*, T208/84 [1987] *EPOR* 74 (para. 12). For consideration of the scope of the exclusion of computer programs *as such* see *IBM/Computer programs*, T935/97 [1999] *EPOR* 301; *IBM/Computer programs*, T1173/97 [2000] *EPOR* 219. In both cases the Technical Board of Appeal distinguished between computer programs *as such* (which lacked technical character and were unpatentable), and computer programs which had a technical character (and were therefore patentable). This technical effect must go beyond the normal physical interactions between the program and the computer: *Guidelines* C-IV, 2.3.6.

[243] *IBM/Computer programs*, T1173/97 [2000] *EPOR* 219 (para. 8). See also *IBM/Computer programs*, T935/97 [1999] *EPOR* 301.

[244] *Pensions Benefit Systems Partnership*, T931/95 [2001] *OJEPO* 441.

[245] *Hitachi/Auction method*, T258/03 [2004] *EPOR* 55 (para. 4.5). See also *Computer controlled event ticket auctioning system*, T0688/05 (19 September 2007).

Apparent inconsistencies between these (and other) EPO decisions have caused tremendous doubt and difficulty.[246] The UK Court of Appeal has observed in this context that 'the provisions about what are not to be "regarded as inventions" are not easy'. In *Aerotel/Macrossan*, describing the decisions of the EPO Boards of Appeal as 'mutually contradictory', Jacob LJ said, 'surely the time has come for matters to be clarified by an Enlarged Board of Appeal'. Under Article 112(1)(b) of the EPC, the President of the EPO has the power to refer a point of law to an Enlarged Board where two Boards of Appeal have given different decisions on that question. Jacob LJ considered that this was now 'clearly the position', considering that there were 'at least four differing points of view'. The court even formulated questions, in the hope of encouraging a reference.[247] However, the President of the EPO considered that there were 'insufficient differences between current Board of Appeal decisions dealing with Article 52 EPC exclusions on important points of law that would justify a referral at this stage'.

Following the decision in *Duns Licensing Associates*, the divisions deepened further. Here the appellant had specifically requested the referral of a number of questions to the Enlarged Board of Appeal, several of them deliberately worded in identical terms to those posed in *Aerotel/Macrossan*. The Technical Board of Appeal considered that a referral to the EBA was not warranted, since 'the Board has no doubts how to answer the questions on the basis of the Convention, following the established case law on patentability of inventions'.[248] The Board was also highly critical of the UK Court of Appeal's approach in *Aerotel/Macrossan*, complaining that it confused the legal concept of 'invention' applied by the Boards of Appeal in the context of Article 52, with 'the layman's ordinary understanding of invention as a novel, and often also inventive contribution to the known art'.[249] The Board considered that the

---

[246]   See also *Microsoft/Data transfer*, T424/03 (23 February 2006).

[247]   *Aerotel Ltd* v. *Telco Holdings Ltd* and *Macrossan's Application* [2006] EWCA Civ. 1371; [2007] RPC 7 (paras. 8 and 25). For comment see Ian Karet, 'UK Courts Invite the EPO to Clarify Treatment of Excluded Inventions under Article 52 EPC' [2007] *JIPL&P* 63–7; William Cook and Geoff Lees 'Test Clarified for UK Software and Business Method Patents: But What about the EPO?' [2007] *EIPR* 115.

[248]   *Duns Licensing Associates/Method of estimating product distribution*, T154/04 (15 November 2006) (para. 2).

[249]   The technical effect approach is applied as follows, according to Jacob LJ. 'Ask whether the invention as defined in the claim makes a technical contribution to the known art – if no, Art. 52(2) applies. A possible clarification (at least by way of exclusion) of this approach is to add the rider that novel or inventive purely excluded matter does not count as a "technical contribution".' This is the approach adopted in *Vicom. Aerotel Ltd* v. *Telco Holdings Ltd* and *Macrossan's Application* v. *Telco Holdings Ltd* [2006] EWCA Civ. 1371 (para. 26).

'technical effect approach with rider' endorsed by Jacob LJ was 'not consistent with a good-faith interpretation of the European Patent Convention in accordance with Article 31 of the Vienna Convention on the Law of Treaties of 1969'.[250] The way in which the UK Intellectual Property Office (UKIPO) applied the four-step *Aerotel/Macrossan* approach led to the rejection of all computer program claims, creating a clear discrepancy between their application of the EPC provisions, and that adopted by the EPO.[251] This created a most unsatisfactory situation, the more so because computer program product applications were assessed differently depending on whether they were submitted to the EPO or the UK IPO.[252]

The UKIPO's approach was challenged in *Astron Clinica*. It was held that in *Aerotel/Macrossan* the specific point had not arisen, and so the court had not been required to consider what claims were permissible in the case of a computer-related invention which made a contribution extending beyond excluded subject matter. It was held that in a case where claims to a method performed by running a suitably programmed computer or to a computer programmed to carry out the method are allowable, then, in principle, a claim to the program itself should also be allowable. However, the claim to the computer program must be drawn to reflect the features of the invention which would ensure the patentability of the method which the program is intended to carry out when it is run.[253] The court in *Astron Clinica* noted that it was 'highly undesirable' for provisions of the EPC to be construed differently in the EPO from the way they are construed in the national courts of a contracting state. Although bound by *Aerotel/Macrossan*, the court sought to interpret it to produce a result consistent with that obtained by applying the reasoning of the Boards of Appeal in the *IBM/Computer programs* cases. This decision

---

[250] *Duns Licensing Associates/Method of estimating product distribution*, T154/04 (15 November 2006) (para. 12). The Board's objections are, firstly, that the Court of Appeal's formulation makes reference to the prior art (undefined by the EPC for the purposes of Article 52), and, secondly, its adoption of the rider that novel and inventive purely excluded matter does not count as a 'technical contribution'. The Board considers that this latter has no basis in the Convention and contravenes conventional patentability criteria. It takes the view that a non-technical feature might interact with technical elements so as to produce a technical effect.

[251] The four-step test (the 'technical effect with rider' approach) is as follows: 1. properly construe the claim; 2. identify the actual contribution; 3. ask whether it falls solely within the excluded subject matter; and 4. check whether the actual or alleged contribution is actually technical in nature (para. 40).

[252] See also Paul England, 'A Clash of Appeals over Patentability' [2007] *JIPL&P* 712–13.

[253] *Astron Clinica Limited and Others* v. *The Comptroller General of Patents, Designs and Trade Marks* [2008] EWHC 85 (Pat).

brought the UKIPO's practice with respect to computer program product claims back more closely into line with that of the EPO.[254]

Cases involving computer-related inventions may involve business methods, also. All the features of the method claim in *Pensions Benefit* were found to be steps of processing and producing information of a purely administrative, actuarial and/or financial character. The invention did not go beyond a method of doing business as such and, therefore, was excluded from patentability.[255] However, there has been some encouragement for those seeking patent protection for business methods. In *Sohei*, a system was intended to perform a number of independent and different types of management. The Technical Board of Appeal found that personnel management, 'as an administration kind of management', was of abstract character and so fell within the exclusion. But the Board suggested that construction management, 'dealing with works to be done, and having been done, by workers on construction sites', could be seen as comparable with management of manufacturing processes. These being technical processes, it was arguable that they would not fall under the business methods exclusion.[256]

Given that the United States has shown itself to be comparatively friendly to business methods patents (as have Australia, Singapore and Japan), there is continuing pressure for Europe to behave likewise.[257] But there is little agreement on the appropriate way forward. The revision of the EPC in 2000 brought no revolution. There was a proposal to delete 'computer programs as such' from the Article 52(2)(c) exclusions to patentable subject matter, but it was not accepted, delegates preferring to maintain the status quo pending the outcome of the European Commission's initiatives. As regards the EPC, therefore, the existing legal situation remains unchanged by the EPC 2000.[258] In 2002 the European Commission published a draft *Directive on the Patentability of Computer-Implemented Inventions*, with the intention of harmonising national

---

[254]   For the view that the UK's practice remains more stringent than that of the EPO see [2008] *JIPL&P* 279–81.

[255]   *Pensions Benefit Systems Partnership*, T931/95 [2001] *OJEPO* 441. See also, more recently, *Method for responding to mail returned to sender as undeliverable*, T388/04 (22 March 2006).

[256]   *Sohei/General-purpose management system*, T769/92 [1996] *EPOR* 253.

[257]   *State Street Bank & Trust* v. *Signature Financial Group* 149 F.3d. 1368 (1998); *AT&T Corporation* v. *Excel Communications, Inc.* 172 F.3d. 1352 (1999).

[258]   In 2002, the European Economic and Social Committee described the doctrinal premise of the European Patent Office's interpretation of Article 52(2) of the European Patent Convention as 'the product of legal casuistry'. For an assessment of this claim see Justine Pila, 'Dispute over the Meaning of "Invention" in Article 52(2) EPC – the Patentability of Computer-Implemented Inventions in Europe' 36 (2005) *International Review of Industrial Property & Copyright Law* 173–91.

approaches. It attempted to find a middle ground in a much-contested field, seeking to foster innovation without stifling competition or preventing the development of interoperable software. It sought to maintain the distinction between computer programs *as such*, and those which made a technical contribution.[259] However, there were strong objections from those opposed to software patents, and a campaign of opposition was organised.[260] After a battle of wills between the European Commission and the European Parliament, in July 2005 the proposed 'common position' was rejected by the Parliament, bringing to an end the Commission's initiative. Although some see the Community patent as offering a possible route to a solution, this is still a long way off.[261]

(iii) Biological subject matter – Article 53(b) This is another extremely controversial area, in which fast-moving technology puts great pressure on the law in the field. There is no general prohibition against the patenting of biological material or biotechnological inventions. But the EPC does not allow patents to be granted in respect of 'plant or animal varieties or essentially biological processes for the production of plants or animals', although 'this provision does not apply to microbiological processes or the products thereof'.[262] The Biotechnology Directive has been incorporated into the Implementing Regulations of the EPC, and the Directive may also be used as a supplementary means of interpretation.[263]

---

[259] Press Release (20 February 2002), 'Patents: Commission Proposes Rules for Inventions Using Software' IP/02/277. Although the Directive would have had no direct legal effect on the EPO, the intention was to resolve any inconsistencies with the EPC once the Directive had been implemented (as with the Biotech. Directive).

[260] For example, the Foundation for a Free Information Infrastructure (FFII) was a dedicated opponent of the Commission's position: http://www.ffii.org/Home.

[261] For further discussion see Jack George Abid, 'Software Patents on Both Sides of the Atlantic' 23 (2005) *John Marshall Journal of Computer and Information Law* 815; Robert Bray, 'The European Union "Software Patents" Directive: What is it? Why is it? Where are we now?' (2005) *Duke Law and Technology Review* 11; Martin Campbell-Kelly, 'Not all Bad: An Historical Perspective on Software Patents' (2005) *Michigan Telecommunications and Technology Law Review* 191; Grant C. Yang, 'The Continuing Debate of Software Patents and the Open Source Movement' 13 (2005) *Texas Intellectual Property Law Journal* 171; David S. Evans and Anne Layne-Farrar, 'Software Patents and Open Source: The Battle over Intellectual Property Rights' 9 (2004) *Virginia Journal of Law and Technology* 10; David Booton, 'The Patentability of Computer-Implemented Inventions in Europe' [2007] *IPQ* 92–116; Philip Leith, *Software and Patents in Europe* (Cambridge: Cambridge University Press, 2007).

[262] EPC 2000, Art. 53(b).

[263] EPC 1973, Rule 23b; EPC 2000, Rule 26. For more see below section 3.3.3.3 The Biotechnology Directive: the legal protection of biotechnological inventions. For further reading see Denis Schertenleib, 'The Patentability and Protection of Living Organisms in the European Union' [2004] *EIPR* 203–13.

The definition of 'animal variety' was considered in the widely discussed *Onco-mouse* decision. The Onco-mouse is a type of laboratory mouse that has been genetically modified using modifications designed to carry a specific gene called an activated oncogene. The activated oncogene significantly increases the mouse's susceptibility to cancer, and thus makes the mouse suitable for cancer research. Patent applications on the Onco-mouse were filed throughout the world. At the EPO, the claims related to a 'transgenic non-human mammalian animal' (in particular a mouse). The Examining Division took the view that the legislative intention behind Article 53(b) was that animal varieties were not appropriate subject matter for patent protection, and concluded that animals in general were excluded from patentability.[264] On appeal, the Technical Board of Appeal held that the Examining Division was wrong in concluding that Article 53(b) excluded the patenting of animals as such. As an exception to the rule on patentability, it should be construed narrowly. The proper issue was whether or not the subject matter of the application was an 'animal variety' (as expressed in the other official languages of the EPC, 'race animale', and 'Tierart').[265] On reconsideration, the Examining Division acknowledged that the meaning of the term 'animal variety' was not entirely clear, particularly in view of the differing meanings of the English, French and German terms. However, it could be stated with certainty that non-human mammals constitute a taxonomic classification unit much higher than species ('Tierart'). An 'animal variety' or 'race animal' is a sub-unit of a species and therefore necessarily ranks lower in the taxonomy. Since the claim related to non-human mammals, it did not relate to an animal variety, and did not fall within the Article 53(b) exclusion.[266] The patent was therefore granted.

The position remains the same under the Biotechnology Directive (as incorporated in the EPC).[267] Animal varieties are not patentable, but inventions which concern animals are patentable 'if the technical feasibility of the invention is not confined to a particular plant or animal variety'.[268] So, when considering an amended version of the *Onco-mouse* patent, the Opposition division cited both the EPC and Recital 31 of the Biotechnology Directive. It confirmed that living matter and in particular plants and animals could be patented. The equal linguistic treatment of plant and animal varieties in the

---

[264]   *Harvard/Onco-mouse* [1989] *OJEPO* 451; [1990] *EPOR* 4.
[265]   *Harvard/Onco-mouse* [1990] *EPOR* 501.
[266]   *Harvard/Onco-mouse* [1991] *EPOR* 525.
[267]   Directive 98/44 on the legal protection of biotechnological inventions ('Biotech. Dir') [1998] OJ L 213/13, Art. 4.
[268]   Biotech. Dir., Art. 4; EPC 1973, Rules 23b and 23c; EPC 2000, Rules 26 and 27.

EPC was seen as a clear indication that the purpose of the exclusions must have been the same for both. So, following *Novartis* (an Enlarged Board of Appeal decision on plant varieties), the Opposition Division concluded that the exclusion is limited to varieties only and does not extend to animals in general. Since the claim here was to transgenic rodents, and not to varieties *per se*, Article 53(b) was no bar to patentability.[269]

Plant varieties were excluded from the EPC because of the existence of the International Convention for the Protection of New Varieties of Plants (UPOV). The drafters wished to ensure that plant breeders would not obtain dual protection, so the conventions were drafted to achieve this, providing that either plant variety protection or patent could be granted, but not both.[270] This policy decision to maintain mutually exclusive schemes of protection was qualified in the 1991 revision of UPOV, but the exclusion of plant varieties remains in the EPC. The Biotechnology Directive confirms that plant varieties are not patentable, and provides that the concept of 'plant variety' is to be defined by reference to the Community Plant Variety Regulation.[271] In *Ciba-Geigy's Application*, the Technical Board of Appeal held that the plant variety exclusion covered only 'claims to individually characterized plants which would have the detailed taxonomy and the reproductive capacity which is required in general for a plant variety right'. What defined a plant variety was the features which distinguished it from other varieties, and these features needed to be stable enough to be passed on through subsequent generations. This application concerned a plant which had been treated with a chemical compound to protect it from the toxic side-effects of herbicides. The Technical Board of Appeal found that these were not claims to a 'plant variety', because the chemical treatment did not survive more than one generation.[272]

In *Plant Genetic Systems*, the claims involved plants, plant cells and seeds which contained a foreign gene which made them resistant to certain herbicides. The Opposition Division had found that the claims were not restricted to a specifically defined group of plants, but related to a much broader group

---

[269]   *Harvard/Onco-mouse* [2003] *OJEPO* 473, 499–500.

[270]   UPOV 1961, Art. 2(1).

[271]   Biotech. Dir., Art. 4, Art. 2(3). Regulation 2100/94 on Community Plant Variety Rights [1994] OJ L 227/1, Art. 5. 'Plant variety' means any plant grouping within a single botanical taxon of the lowest known rank, which grouping, irrespective of whether the conditions for the grant of a plant variety right are fully met, can be: (a) defined by the expression of the characteristics that results from a given genotype or combination of genotypes, (b) distinguished from any other plant grouping by the expression of at least one of the said characteristics, and (c) considered as a unit with regard to its suitability for being propagated unchanged.

[272]   *Ciba-Geigy/Propagating Material* application, T49/83 [1979–85] C *EPOR* 758; [1984] *OJEPO* 112.

of plants, so did not fall within the exclusion. But the Technical Board of Appeal reversed this decision. Since 'plant variety' was defined as 'any plant grouping within a single botanical taxon of the lowest known rank', then plant cells as such (which could be cultured in much the same way as bacteria and yeasts) could not be considered to fall within the definition of plant variety. A plant variety was 'characterized by at least one single transmissible characteristic distinguishing it from other plant groupings and which is sufficiently homogenous and stable in its relevant characteristics'. Although this much was consistent with *Ciba-Geigy's Application*, the Technical Board of Appeal in *Plant Genetic Systems* read the exclusion very expansively. Although claims relating to plant cells were potentially patentable, claims which 'encompassed' or were 'based on' a plant variety were not. The Board found that the subject matter of the claim applied to genetically altered plants which remained stable with regard to their altered character. Since the material forming the starting point for these alterations was derived from known plant varieties, the genetically altered plants derived from these varieties were to be construed as 'essentially derived varieties', and therefore within the UPOV definition of a plant variety, so excluded from patentability by Article 53(b). The effect of this decision was to exclude most plants produced by genetic engineering, since plant varieties are a common starting point for such techniques. The *Plant Genetic Systems* decision generated understandable concern within the plant-breeding industry, and was subject to considerable criticism.[273]

The effect of *Plant Genetic Systems* was limited, however, and it has now been overruled. Following the decision, the Biotechnology Directive was passed. This requires that 'inventions which concern plants . . . shall be patentable if the technical feasibility of the invention is not confined to a particular plant . . . variety'.[274] Claims which encompass more than plant variety are thus patentable, although a claim to a single plant variety will not be (and must be protected, if at all, under the UPOV Convention). The decision by the Enlarged Board of Appeal in *Novartis* reinforces this conclusion. It noted that the purpose of Article 53(b) had always been to define the boundary between patent protection and plant variety protection. The extent of the exclusion for patents is the obverse of the availability of plant variety rights. Plant variety rights are only granted for specific plant varieties (and not for technical teach-

---

[273]   *Plant Genetic Systems/Glutamine synthenase inhibitors*, T356/93 [1995] *EPOR* 357. For comment see Andreas Schrell, 'Are Plants (Still) Patentable?' [1996] *EIPR* 242–4; Tim Roberts, 'Patenting Plants around the World' [1996] *EIPR* 531–6; Ulrich Schatz, 'Patentability of Genetic Engineering Inventions in European Patent Office Practices' (1998) 29 *IIC* 2–16.

[274]   Biotech. Dir., Art. 4(2); EPC 1972, Rule 23c(b); EPC 2000, Rule 27(b).

ings which might be implemented in an indefinite number of plant varieties). The Technical Board of Appeal had been wrong to conclude that a claim is necessarily 'in respect of' a plant variety if it may comprise a plant variety. So, 'in the absence of the identification of a specific plant variety in a product claim, the subject-matter of the claimed invention is not directed to a plant variety or varieties within the meaning of Article 53(b) EPC'.[275]

Also excluded from patentability by Article 53(b) are 'essentially biological processes for the production of plants or animals'.[276] The exclusion affects only processes (not product claims or product-by-process claims). The Biotechnology Directive states that 'a process for the production of plants or animals is essentially biological if it consists entirely of natural phenomena such as crossing or selection'.[277] In *Lubrizol*, the claim was to a process for rapidly developing hybrids and commercially producing hybrid seeds. The Technical Board of Appeal considered that the question as to whether a process was 'essentially biological' had to be judged 'on the basis of the essence of the invention taking into account the totality of human intervention and its impact on the result achieved'. Here the claimed processes represented 'an essential modification of known biological and classical breeders processes', and the efficiency and high yield associated with the product showed 'important technological character'. Thus the process was not 'essentially biological', and not within the Article 53(b) exclusion.[278] The boundaries of this exclusion are currently being considered by the Enlarged Board of Appeal, in the context of an application relating to the crossing and selecting of plants.[279]

---

[275] *Novartis/Transgenic plant*, G1/98 [2000] *EPOR* 303, 319.

[276] See also Biotech. Dir., Art. 4(1)(b).

[277] Biotech. Dir., Art. 2(2); EPC 1973, Rule 23b(5); EPC 2000, Rule 26(5). EPO Guidelines explain that 'a method of crossing, inter-breeding, or selectively breeding, say, horses involving merely selecting for breeding and bringing together those animals having certain characteristics would be essentially biological and therefore unpatentable. On the other hand, a process of treating a plant or animal to improve its properties or yield or to promote or suppress its growth e.g. a method of pruning a tree, would not be essentially biological since although a biological process is involved the essence of the invention is technical': *Guidelines*, C-IV, 4.6.2.

[278] *Lubrizol/Hybrid plant*, T320/87 [1990] *EPOR* 173, 178–9. See also the various possible approaches offered by the Technical Board of Appeal in *Novartis/Transgenic plant*, T1054/95 [1999] *EPOR* 123, 135.

[279] The issue has arisen in relation to a patent for a method of producing broccoli having elevated levels of glucosinolates – a class of compounds with anti-cancer potential. The EBA has been asked by the TBA whether a non-microbiological process for the production of plants which contains the steps of crossing and selecting plants escapes the exclusion of Article 53(b) EPC merely because it contains, as a further step

The Article 53(b) exclusion does not apply to 'microbiological processes or the products thereof'. This is now defined as 'a microbiological or other technical process, or a product obtained by means of such a process other than a plant or animal variety'.[280] The original definition did not include the words 'technical process', which caused some difficulty in determining the application of the Article 53(b) exclusion when a combination of microbiological and technical steps were involved. Microbiological processes do not fall within the category of inventions excluded from patentability by Article 53(b), so if the concept is understood broadly it will soften considerably the impact of that Article. The inclusion of 'technical processes' confirms that the concept is not to be understood narrowly, and so will cover techniques such as genetic manipulation. This allows the patenting of much modern research involving biological subject matter, including genetically modified plants and animals. However, it was made clear in *Novartis* that genetically modified plant varieties were not to be regarded as outside the Article 53(b) exclusion (and therefore patentable) simply because they were the products of microbiological processes. The Enlarged Board of Appeal emphasised that the mere fact that a plant variety had been obtained by means of genetic engineering did not give its producers a privileged position relative to producers of plant varieties resulting from traditional breeding only.[281]

(iv)   Methods for treatment of the human or animal body – Article 53(c)   As has been mentioned, under the EPC 1973, it was specifically stated that methods for treatment of the human or animal body by surgery or therapy and diagnostic methods practised on the human or animal body were *not* regarded as inventions which are susceptible of industrial application.[282] The intention was to ensure that patent law did not hamper the practice of medicine,

---

or as part of any of the steps of crossing and selection, an additional feature of a technical nature. If not, then what are the relevant criteria for distinguishing excluded non-microbiological plant production processes from non-excluded ones? The TBA has reviewed and set out the issues with great care: *Plant Bioscience Limited/Method for selective increase of the anticarcinogenic glucosinolates in Brassica species*, T83/05. See also Michael A. Kock, 'Essentially Biological Processes: The Interpretation of the Exception under Article 53(b) of the European Patent Convention' [2007] *JIPL&P* 286–97.

[280]   EPC 1973, Rule 23c(c); EPC 2000, Rule 27(c).

[281]   *Novartis/Transgenic plant*, G1/98 [2000] *EPOR* 303, 321. The Board referred to Recital 32 of the Biotech. Directive, which states that 'if an invention consists only in genetically modifying a particular plant variety, and if a new plant variety is bred, it will still be excluded from patentability even if the genetic modification is the result not of an essentially biological process but of a biotechnological process'.

[282]   EPC 1973, Art. 52(4) see above (3) Industrial application – Article 57. See *Wellcome/Pigs I*, T116/85 [1988] *EPOR* 1.

although this goal was achieved by an unnecessarily indirect mechanism. In the EPC 2000 the policy goals are rendered explicit, and methods of treatment and diagnosis are excluded from patentability directly, by Article 53(c).[283] The exclusion applies only to *methods* of medical and veterinary treatment. It does not apply to products, in particular substances or compositions, for use in any of these methods. Hence, patents may be obtained for surgical, therapeutic or diagnostic substances and compositions (such as drugs), and for instruments or apparatuses for use in such methods.[284]

(v)   Morality – Article 53(a)   Although there has always been a provision in the EPC which allows patents to be refused on grounds of morality, it was not much used initially. More recently it has come under intense pressure, however. The rapid pace of scientific development, particularly in the field of biotechnology, has brought new challenges. The pursuit of scientific research

---

[283]   EPC 2000, Art. 53(c). For wider discussion of the issues see Alexandra Sim, 'The Case against Patenting Methods of Medical Treatment' [2007] *EIPR* 43–51; Elizabeth Verkey, 'Patenting of Medical Methods – Need of the Hour' [2007] *JIPL&P* 104–13; Amanda Odell-West, 'A Proposal to Amend the Medical Exclusion within Patent Law to Provide for the Patentability of Certain Methods of Treatment' [2007] *EIPR* 492–9; Eddy D. Ventose, 'Patent Protection for Methods of Medical Treatment in the United Kingdom' [2008] *IPQ* 58–81.

[284]   Interpretation and application of the provision is far from straightforward, and the former case law remains relevant. Therapy may be curative or prophylactic. It is often contrasted with mere cosmetic methods, which do not fall within the exclusion: *Du Pont/Appetite suppressant*, T144/83 [1987] *EPOR* 6. However, a method of treating plaque which had both cosmetic benefits *and* benefits for oral health was held not patentable: *ICI/Cleaning plaque*, T290/86 [1991] *EPOR* 157. On the application of the exclusion to diagnostic methods, see problems caused by the conflict between *Bruker/Non-invasive measurement*, T385/86 [1988] *EPOR* 357, and *Cygnus/Device and method for sampling substances*, T694/99 [2002] *OJEPO* 4. The recent decision of the EBA, *Diagnostic Methods*, G01/04 [2006] *OJEPO* 334, has gone some way to clarifying the position. Applied in *Australian National University/Method and apparatus for early detection of glaucoma*, T1197/02, and *Beth Israel Hospital Association/Non-invasive method for diagnosing Alzheimer's disease in a patient*, T143/04. For discussion see Sven J.R. Bostyn, 'No Contact with the Human Body Please! Patentability of Diagnostic Method Inventions after G01/04 [2007] *EIPR* 238–44. See also David Rogers, 'Exclusion from Patentability of Diagnostic Methods Practised on the Human Body: Article 52(4) EPC' [2007] *JIPL&P* 60–61. The application of the test in relation to methods of surgery has recently been referred to the Enlarged Board of Appeal: *Mediphysics/MR methods for imaging vasculature*, T992/03. See Eddy D. Ventose, 'Exclusion of Methods of Treatment of the Human or Animal Body by Surgery from Patent Protection' [2007] *JILP&P* 574–6; Amanda Odell-West, 'Protecting Surgeons and their Art? Methods for Treatment of the Human Body by Surgery under Article 52(4) EPC' [2008] *EIPR* 102–8; Eddy D. Ventose, 'Making Sense of the Enlarged Board of Appeal in *Cygnus/Diagnostic Method*' [2008] *EIPR* 145–50.

demands very significant investment, and solid protection for the results of such research is sought, particularly in the form of patents. In addition, the outcomes of this research – outcomes perhaps inconceivable when the legislation was drafted – have at times raised ethical issues as to the appropriateness and wisdom of undertaking such research at all. Thus, important and controversial questions arise as to whether a patent office is an appropriate place in which to take decisions regarding the morality of inventions, and, if it is, as to the basis on which such determinations should be made.[285]

Article 53(a) EPC 2000 prohibits the grant of European patents in respect of 'inventions the commercial exploitation of which would be contrary to *"ordre public"* or morality'.[286] This wording aligns the provision with the Biotechnology Directive, and with TRIPS.[287] The Biotechnology Directive also offers more detailed instructions regarding the unpatentability of certain biotechnological inventions (such as human cloning), and these are incorporated in the EPC.[288]

The scope of the Article 53(a) exclusion was first considered in the *Onco-mouse* decision (discussed above in relation to the animal varieties exclusion). The Onco-mouse had been genetically modified to increase the mouse's susceptibility to cancer, making it suitable for cancer research. The Examining Division noted that the idea of the patenting of higher organisms had encountered severe criticism (both for ethical and economic reasons), but concluded that patent law was not the right tool for regulating the range of problems that might arise from such research, and therefore did not use the exclusion to refuse the application.[289] In contrast, the Technical Board of Appeal felt that it was precisely in a case of this kind that the implications of Article 53(a) should be considered. It acknowledged that 'the genetic manipulation of mammalian animals is undeniably problematical in various respects', particularly where the effect would 'necessarily cause suffering'. It recognised the danger that the release of genetically manipulated animals might bring about 'unforeseeable and irreversible adverse effects'. The Board concluded that 'the decision as to whether or not Article 53(a) EPC is a bar to patenting the present invention

---

[285]　　See Shawn H.E. Harmon, 'The Rules Re-engagement: The Use of Patent Proceedings to Influence the Regulation of Science' [2006] *IPQ* 378–403.

[286]　　EPC 2000, Art. 53(a). The former provision used a slightly different formulation, prohibiting the patenting of 'inventions the publication or exploitation of which would be contrary to *"ordre public"* or morality': EPC 1973, Art. 53(a). For the difficulties which arise in seeking to apply this exception consistently and transparently see Amanda Warren-Jones, 'Vital Parameters for Patent Morality – a Question of Form' [2008] *JIPL&P* 832–46.

[287]　　Biotech. Dir., Art. 6(1); TRIPS, Art. 27.2.

[288]　　Biotech. Dir., Art. 6(1). EPC 1973, Rule 23d; EPC 2000, Rule 28.

[289]　　*Harvard/Onco-Mouse* [1990] *EPOR* 4, 10.

would seem to depend mainly on a careful weighing up of the suffering of animals and possible risks to the environment on the one hand, and the invention's usefulness to mankind on the other'.[290] The case was remitted to the Examination Division for reconsideration. It considered that the invention's usefulness to mankind was undeniable, given the widespread suffering caused by cancer. Because these mice were of a special type, fewer mice would be required than would be the case with conventional testing using ordinary mice. Animal testing was 'at present considered indispensable', and the intention was to use the mice in strictly controlled laboratory conditions. On balance, the Examining Division concluded that the invention was patentable.[291]

In the *Plant Genetic Systems* case, a patent had been granted for plants which had genetically modified to make them resistant to herbicides. Greenpeace sought revocation of the patent, arguing that the grant of a patent for plant life forms fell within the Article 53(a) exclusion, because plant genetic resources were the heritage of mankind, and because the exploitation of the patent presented serious, irreversible environmental risks. The Technical Board of Appeal acknowledged that the granting of patents in respect of plants and animals was the subject of intense debate in interested circles, and was giving rise to some public concern. But it also emphasised that seeds and plants did not fall within the Article 53(a) exclusion merely because they represented 'living' matter. The Board insisted that each particular case be examined on its merits, and observed that the so-called 'balancing exercise' of benefits and disadvantages was not the only way of assessing patentability with regard to the exclusion. The Board also observed that plant biotechnology was no more contrary to morality than traditional selective breeding, and that plant genetic engineering techniques could be used for constructive or destructive purposes. It would undoubtedly be against *ordre public* or morality to propose a misuse of such techniques, but that was not the case here. Although patent offices stood at the crossroads between science and public policy, there were also regulatory authorities who were charged with ensuring that the exploitation of a given technology took place within the relevant regulatory framework. Any inadequacies in that framework did not vest the EPO with authority to carry out tasks which should properly be the duty of regulatory bodies. On the evidence before it, the Board did not consider that the risks were such as seriously to prejudice the environment, and therefore revocation under Article 53(a) was not justified.[292]

---

290   *Harvard/Onco-Mouse* T19/90 *EPOR* 501, 503.
291   *Harvard/Onco-Mouse* [1991] *EPOR* 525, 528.
292   *Plant Genetic Systems/Glutamine synthenase inhibitors*, T356/93 [1995] *EPOR* 357.

More recently, in *Michigan State University/ Euthanasia Compositions*, the Board had to consider whether an invention relating to euthanasia compositions used for producing humane death in lower animals was contrary to Article 53(a).[293] Opponents had argued that the object of the invention was the provision of a composition for killing or for termination of life of all kinds of living beings, including all animals and human beings. They further argued that the avowed use indicated in the patent included the killing or euthanasia of all kinds of animals, including human beings. The Board held that the exclusion will only apply if either publication and/or exploitation of the invention would contribute causally to the infringement of the fundamental principles of *ordre public* and morality. Exploitation is to be construed as the normal avowed use indicated in the patent. Patent protection will only be denied if this would infringe *ordre public* or morality. It is not sufficient that the invention can also be exploited in this way. The mere possibility of abuse of the invention is not sufficient to deny patent protection pursuant to Article 53(a), if the invention can also be exploited in a way which does not and would not infringe *ordre public* and morality. The Board found that the use of the euthanasia compositions disclosed in the patent for any other conceivable purpose than for producing humane death in lower animals, had not been indicated, contemplated or foreshadowed. The Board therefore rejected the opponent's arguments, holding that the intended exploitation and publication of the invention was not contrary to *ordre public* or morality within the meaning of Article 53(a).

The question of gene patenting was raised in the *Relaxin* case. A synthetic form of a human hormone had been developed, following the isolation of relaxin DNA from tissue taken from pregnant women. The Green Party objected that this was an offence against human dignity in that it made use of pregnancy for profit. It also argued that patenting human genes was intrinsically immoral because it was patenting life, and that it amounted to a form of modern slavery involving the dismemberment of women and their piecemeal sale. The Opposition Division considered that Article 53(a) should be raised only rarely, when it was 'probable that the public in general would regard the invention as so abhorrent that the grant of patent rights would be inconceivable'. It emphatically rejected the Green Party's arguments, noting that the women who donated tissue consented to do so within the framework of necessary gynaecological operations, and that human tissue (blood, bone, etc.) was widely used as a source for useful products. Such practices were perfectly

---

[293]   *Michigan State University/Euthanasia Compositions*, T866/01 (11 May 2005). See also David Rogers, 'Exclusion from Patentability under Article 53(a) EPC upon "Morality" Grounds' *JIPL&P* [2007] 61–2.

acceptable to the vast majority of the public, and there was no reason to perceive them as immoral.[294] On the question of slavery, the Opposition Division stressed that patents covering DNA encoding a human gene conferred no rights whatever on individual human beings. In its opinion, DNA was not to be characterised as 'life', but as a chemical substance which carried genetic information and could be used as an intermediate in the production of proteins which were medically useful. The Opposition Division did acknowledge that the patenting of human genes was 'a controversial issue on which many people have strong opinions'. But it also noted that these opinions were often based 'rather on personal beliefs than on reasoned arguments', and that there was much confusion concerning the practical effects of a patent directed to a human gene. And it agreed with the Green Party that the EPO was 'not the right institution to decide on fundamental ethical questions'. Nevertheless, since the opposed patent did not offend against widely accepted moral standards of behaviour, nor was there a clear consensus among members of the public that patenting human genes was immoral, the patent did not fall within the Article 53(a) exclusion.[295]

Some of these issues were addressed in the EU's Biotechnology Directive, which was still in draft and a matter of fierce debate when the *Relaxin* decision was given in December 1994. The original proposal had been adopted in 1988, but it proved enormously difficult to reach agreement. The Commission sought to create a legal framework to encourage biotechnological research and its commercial development within the EU, whilst building in safeguards to acknowledge ethical concerns. Environmental groups such as Greenpeace lobbied against the Directive, arguing that it promoted the patenting of body parts, and thus would treat human life as fodder for economic interests. There was also great concern as to how biotechnological inventions should be controlled, whether by the patent system, other regulatory systems or a

---

[294] See also *17q-Linked breast and ovarian cancer susceptibility gene*, T1213/05 (27 September 2007). The invention related to the human BRCA1 gene isolated from the genome, mutant forms of that gene and its use in the diagnosis of predisposition to breast and ovarian cancer. The appellant argued that the absence of proof that the donors of the cells which had been critical to arriving at the claimed invention had given a previous informed consent to the use of said cells suggested a violation of *ordre public* or morality. The Board rejected this argument. The EPC contained no provision establishing a requirement for applicants to submit evidence of a previous informed consent or benefit-sharing agreement. Although the Biotechnology Directive states (Recital 26) that '. . . the person from whose body the material is taken must have had an opportunity of expressing free and informed consent thereto, in accordance with national law', the legislator had not provided for a procedure of verifying the informed consent in the framework of the grant of biological patents under the EPC.

[295] *Howard Florey/Relaxin*, T74/91 [1995] *EPOR* 541, 549–52.

mixture of both. The proposed Directive was rejected by the European Parliament in 1995, provoking strong criticism from the biotechnology industries, who argued that the lack of adequate harmonised protection in the EU put them at a competitive disadvantage as compared to America and Japan. Parliament eventually accepted a second proposal in 1998. The Directive confirms that inventions will not be patentable where their commercial exploitation would be contrary to *ordre public* or morality (reflecting Article 53(a) EPC).[296] In addition, the Directive lists a number of specific types of inventions which will definitely be considered unpatentable on this basis, and these have been incorporated in the EPC. These are:

(a) processes for cloning human beings;
(b) processes for modifying the germ line genetic identity of human beings;
(c) uses of human embryos for industrial or commercial purposes;
(d) processes for modifying the genetic identity of animals which are likely to cause them suffering without any substantial medical benefit to man or animal, and also animals resulting from such processes.[297]

The precise definitions of these processes continue to be contested. Human cloning refers to the production of genetically identical humans. This cloning can be done either by 'embryo splitting' or by 'nuclear transfer'. It has possible uses in infertility treatment. Reproductive cloning would produce a child genetically identical to an individual, and could be used when an infertile couple are unable to conceive a biologically related child via any other method. However, when this technique has been used in mammals, developmental abnormalities have occurred, though the levels of risk are disputed. Therapeutic cloning produces embryonic stem cells that are genetically identical to the patient's own. These stem cells can then be differentiated into precursor replacement cells to treat a variety of conditions from which the patient might suffer (for example, to repair spinal cord injuries, to treat diabetes, Parkinson's disease, osteoporosis or heart attacks). However, this procedure uses cloning to create a human embryo, and this embryo is then destroyed to obtain the embryonic stem cells. Any therapeutic benefits must be weighed against the ethical cost of destroying the early cloned embryo. Those who allocate to the early embryo the status of an individual with fundamental human rights consider the destruction of that embryo equivalent to murder. The matter is highly controversial, and different legal systems have taken different views of it.

---

[296] Biotech. Dir., Art. 6(1). For more see below section 3.3.3.3 The Biotechnology Directive: the legal protection of biotechnological inventions.
[297] Biotech. Dir., Art. 6(2). EPC 1973, Rule 23d; EPC 2000, Rule 28.

The Biotechnology Directive defines human cloning as 'any process, including techniques of embryo splitting, designed to create a human being with the same nuclear genetic information as another living or deceased human being'.[298] Much may depend on whether 'human being' is defined to exclude human embryos and embryonic tissue. The so-called 'Edinburgh Patent', granted by the EPO in 1999, offers a controversial illustration.[299] Its grant led to fierce protests and triggered a major public debate on the patenting of stem-cell technology. The invention concerns a method of genetically modifying animal stem cells so as to give them a survival advantage over unwanted differentiated cells. The original work was carried out on mouse cells, but the methods apply more widely and the patent covered methods carried out on human embryonic stem cells and also human embryonic stem cells which have been genetically modified so that they can be used in the selection process. The EPO described as an 'oversight' its failure to insist on limiting the term 'animal', which as a result could be interpreted as extending to humans. Greenpeace filed an opposition claiming the patent could and would be read so as to embrace human cloning and the creation of transgenic animals. Some European countries, including Germany (home of the EPO), have laws prohibiting embryo research. The German, Dutch and Italian governments hence also filed oppositions to the patent. Immediately after oppositions were filed, the University of Edinburgh stated that it had never intended the scope of the patent to extend to the creation of transgenic humans. The patent was maintained in an amended form, no longer including human or animal embryonic stem cells, but still covering modified human and animal stem cells other than embryonic stem cells. The Opposition Division took the view that the granted patent fell under the prohibition of immorality in Article 53(a), and also was caught by the prohibition on the use of human embryos for industrial or commercial purposes in Rule 23d(c) (now Rule 28(c)). After considering various recitals and articles of the Biotechnology Directive, the Opposition Division came to the conclusion that this Rule is to be interpreted broadly, and covers not only the use of embryos, but also the stem cells resulting from the use of embryos.[300] An appeal has been filed. The matter remains extremely controversial, the more so because of the possible benefits of stem-cell

---

[298]   Biotech. Dir., Recital 41.

[299]   This is the name commonly given to European patent No. 0695351, owned by the University of Edinburgh. Its title is 'Isolation, selection and propagation of animal transgenic stem cells'.

[300]   See EPO Press Release, 'Edinburgh Patent Limited after European Patent Office Opposition Hearing' (24 July 2002). Heike Vogelsang-Wenke, 'Patenting of Stem Cells and Processes Involving Stem Cells According to the Rules of the European Patent Convention' (2004) 23 *Biotechnology Law Report* 155–67.

research. Some countries permit embryonic stem-cell research, although often under strict (but varying) regulatory frameworks. Some national patent offices have therefore taken a different view to that taken by the EPO. For example, the UK Patent Office has stated that it will distinguish between inventions that relate to totipotent stem cells on the one hand (that is, cells which are individually capable of producing an entire human body), for which patents are not being granted, and pluripotent or multipotent stem cells on the other (that is, cells which are not individually capable of producing an entire human body), for which patents are being granted.[301]

The exclusion of germ line therapy is also debated. Gene therapy is the deliberate modification of the genetic material in cells of a patient in order to bring about a therapeutic effect. This raises ethical concerns (from 'designer babies' to eugenics), and a distinction is often made between therapy intended to correct a disease, and therapy intended to 'improve the human species'. These concerns also have led to the prohibition of germ line gene therapy, where the reproductive cells are modified, and all descendants of the patient will be affected. Somatic cell gene therapy is not caught by the prohibition. This deals with non-germ line cells, so all effects end with the life of the patient. Some have argued that the total ban on germ line therapy is disproportionate, and that it has the potential to eradicate serious diseases such as cystic fibrosis and Huntingdon's disease.[302] To be set against this are significant ethical and social concerns, as well as the potential risks.

Also excluded from patenting are 'processes for modifying the genetic identity of animals which are likely to cause them suffering without any substantial medical benefit to man or animal, and also animals resulting from such processes'. The reference to 'modifying' means that the exclusion does not affect the cloning of animals. This rule was considered in the *Onco-mouse* case, involving transgenic mice modified to make them unusually susceptible to cancer. The Opposition Division observed that 'if it is agreed that there is suffering, in accordance with [Rule 23d(d) EPC (now EPC 2000, Rule 28(d))] this suffering must be balanced by a substantial medical benefit'. The relevant date for assessing the benefit was the date of the patent application (as for all other patentability requirements), although the Opposition Division was willing to look at evidence of actual suffering after this date. Here it was undisputed that the mice would suffer when they developed tumours, but this had to

---

[301]   UK Patent Office: *Practice note: Inventions involving human embryonic stem cells* (April 2003). See also Graeme Laurie, 'Patenting Stem Cells of Human Origin' [2004] *EIPR* 59–66.

[302]   See Robin Nott, ' "You did it!": the European Biotechnology Directive at last' [1998] *EIPR* 347–51; Margaret Llewellyn, 'The Legal Protection of Biotechnological Inventions' [1997] *EIPR* 115–27.

balanced against the inventor's bona fide belief (in the light of the then existing techniques for medical cancer testing) that a substantial medical benefit could be expected. The Rule was therefore no bar to patentability.[303]

The debates seem certain to continue, as boundaries continue to be tested. For example, the high-profile scientist Craig Venter faced a great deal of criticism when he founded Celera Genomics, to generate genomic information for use for commercial purposes. Some members of the genetics community responded by redoubling their efforts to complete the Human Genome Project, and release the results for free public access, in a successful attempt to defeat Venter's plans to commoditise such information. Venter's team was the first to sequence the genome of a single identifiable individual – himself. More recently, as president of the J. Craig Venter Institute, he has applied for patent protection (worldwide, including at the EPO) on a synthetic bacterium. Its proposed name is *Mycoplasma laboratorium*, nicknamed 'Synthia' by Dr Venter. This would be the first life form created by man. It is hoped by those involved that this and similar bacteria could be genetically engineered to be used in making fuels, for instance. Opponents have expressed concerns that such microbes could be used negatively as well as positively. Objections have come from bioethics campaigners, one of whom observed, 'For the first time, God has competition'.[304]

(5) SUFFICIENCY OF DISCLOSURE

The patent application must disclose the invention in a manner sufficiently clear and complete for it to be carried out by a person skilled in the art.[305] This is a question of fact, and the amount of technical detail required will depend on the particular invention. The skilled person should, after reading the description, be able readily to perform the invention over the whole area claimed without undue burden and without needing inventive skill. For example, in *Icos*, the specification was insufficient because the skilled person seeking to identify the relevant compound would have had to test millions of available candidate compounds, and such an undertaking constituted an undue

---

[303]   *Harvard/Onco-mouse* [2003] *OJEPO* 473, 503.

[304]   See 'Patent Pending', *Economist*, 14 June 2007. For Venter's views see 'Sleep When You're Dead', an interview for the *New Scientist*, 20 October 2007 (issue 2626). For his opponents' views see (for example) ETC Group, 'Patenting Pandora's Bug: Goodbye, Dolly . . . Hello, Synthia! J. Craig Venter Institute Seeks Monopoly Patents on the World's First-Ever Human-Made Life Form', available at http://www.etcgroup. org/en/materials/publications.html?pub_id=631.

[305]   EPC 2000, Art. 83. Failure to do so is a ground of revocation, also: EPC 2000, Art. 100(b). For discussion of this requirement in relation to a perennial favourite of inventors, see Christopher Wadlow, 'Patents for Perpetual Motion Machines' [2007] *JIPL&P* 136–44.

burden.[306] A reasonable amount of trial and error is permissible when it comes to the sufficiency of disclosure in an unexplored field or where there are many technical difficulties, but there must be available adequate instruction in the specification or on the basis of common general knowledge which would lead the skilled person necessarily and directly towards success through the evaluation of initial failures or through an acceptable statistical expectation rate in case of random experiments.[307] The skilled addressee is expected to be aware of (and to use) the common general knowledge of the art but not to be aware of the whole state of the art.[308] In assessing inventive step and sufficiency of disclosure, the same level of skill is required from the person skilled in the art. However, whereas for the purpose of evaluating inventive step the skilled person has knowledge of the prior art only, for the purpose of evaluating sufficiency of disclosure the skilled person has knowledge both of the prior art and of the invention as disclosed.[309]

3.3.2   Other Legislative Initiatives in European Patent Law – The London Agreement and the EPLA

The EPC harmonises the national laws of member states significantly, but only up to the point of grant. Issues of validity and infringement post-grant are matters for national law and national courts.[310] Two matters have caused particular concern. The first is the high cost of translating the full patent specification into the national languages of the states where it will take effect. The second is the absence of a common European litigation scheme to deal with infringement and validity of European patents. Currently there is no appeal from a national patent office or court to the Boards of Appeal of the EPO (or any other international court). Likewise, decisions of the Boards of Appeal cannot be appealed to a national court. Inevitably, this may lead to a European patent being interpreted differently in different jurisdictions. This has obvious negative consequences for patentees, who must take advice and litigate in several places, who will face different rules of procedure and evidence, and

---

[306]   *Icos Corporation/Seven transmembrane receptor* [2002] *OJEPO* 293, 300.

[307]   *Unilever/Stable Bleaches*, T226/85 [1989] *EPOR* 18, 22. Here the inherent instability of the composition was such that the skilled person could only reproduce the invention with some luck, if at all. See also *Weyershause/Cellulose*, T272/95 [2001] *OJEPO* 1.

[308]   *ICI/Pyridine Herbicides*, T206/83 [1986] *EPOR* 232, 237.

[309]   *Mycogen/Modifying Plant Cells*, T694/92 [1998] *EPOR* 114, 120. See *Exxon/Fuel Oils*, T409/91 [1994] *EPOR* 149. See also *Unilever/Hexagonal Liquid Crystal Gel*, T435/91 [1995] *EPOR* 314; *Schering/Dipeptides*, T548/91[1995] *EPOR* 327.

[310]   EPC 2000, Art. 64(3), Art. 74.

uncertain timing of outcomes. This leads to high costs, and, inevitably, to forum shopping. Nor does this fragmented and inefficient system offer an attractive alternative to patents in the US, Japan and elsewhere. The EPO examiners, national judges and national examiners meet each year, in an attempt to minimise these effects. In addition, the Protocol on the Interpretation of Article 69 offers guidance on interpretation. Nevertheless, the underlying problems are serious.

Two Intergovernmental Conferences (Paris 1999 and London 2000) sought to address these difficulties, resulting in the London Agreement, and the draft European Patent Litigation Agreement (EPLA).

3.3.2.1 The London Agreement
The London Agreement, signed in October 2000, aims to reduce the cost of translation of European patents granted under the EPC. Ten contracting states signed in the first instance.[311] For the agreement to enter into force, the ratification of at least eight contracting states was required, including the three where the most European patents took effect in 1999 (France, Germany and the United Kingdom). France's ratification in October 2007 was the final trigger, and the London Agreement entered into force on 1 May 2008.[312] It aims to gives easier access to European patents – especially for small and medium-sized firms – by reducing translation costs for granted European patents.

Parties to the London Agreement undertake to waive (entirely, or nearly so) the requirement for translations of European patents to be filed in their national language. Each country will select one of the three official languages of the EPO, and the patent will issue in that language. This means in practice that European patent proprietors will no longer have to file a translation of the specification where a patent is granted for an EPC contracting state which is also party to the London Agreement, and which has one of the three EPO languages as an official language. If a state does not have one of the three EPO languages as its official language, it will nominate one of them, and the patent proprietor will have to submit a full translation of the specification in the national language only if the patent is not available in the nominated EPO language. Such states may require claims to be translated into their national

---

[311]   Denmark, France, Germany, Liechtenstein, Luxembourg, Monaco, Netherlands, Sweden, Switzerland, United Kingdom.

[312]   Agreement dated 17 October 2000 on the application of Article 65 EPC ('London Agreement'). So far, Denmark, France, Germany, Liechtenstein, Luxembourg, Monaco, the Netherlands, Sweden, Switzerland and the United Kingdom have ratified the London Agreement. Croatia, Iceland, Latvia, and Slovenia have acceded to it. For current status see: http://www.epo.org/patents/law/legislative-initiatives/london-agreement/status.html.

language, and, and, also, may require a full translation of the patent in the event of any dispute relating to it. It is hoped that this breakthrough on the translation issue will significantly reduce the cost of European patents: savings of perhaps 30% have been predicted.[313] Although this is a significant step, the London Agreement does not solve the translation problem in its entirety.[314] Validation of a European patent in countries that have not ratified the agreement (such as Greece, Italy, Portugal, Spain and Turkey) may still entail translation of the whole patent.

3.3.2.2 The European Patent Litigation Agreement (EPLA)

The draft European Patent Litigation Agreement (EPLA) has the aim of creating the first centralised European Patent Court. If agreed, it would be an 'optional protocol to the European Patent Convention committing its signatory states to an integrated judicial system, including uniform rules of procedure and a common appeal court'.[315] A Working Party on Litigation was tasked with preparing a draft text, and with defining 'the terms under which a common entity can be established and financed to which national jurisdictions can refer, with a view to obtaining advice, that part of any litigation relating to validity and infringement'. Perceiving an urgent need to remedy the shortcomings in the present system, the EPO participated actively in the Working Party's efforts.

By the end of 2003 there were two central proposals:

- A proposal to set up a European Patent Court (comprising a Court of First Instance, with a Central Division and a number of Regional Divisions, as well as a Court of Appeal) with jurisdiction to deal with infringement and revocation actions concerning European patents.
- A proposal to entrust the European Patent Court of Appeal (acting as 'Facultative Advisory Council') with the task of delivering, upon request, non-binding opinions on any point of law concerning European or harmonised national patent law to national courts trying infringement and validity actions.

---

[313]   Communication from the Commission to the European Parliament and the Council – Enhancing the patent system in Europe, COM(2007) 165 final, App. II.

[314]   France, Germany, Liechtenstein, Luxembourg, Monaco, Switzerland and the United Kingdom will waive their current requirement for translations into national languages. If a European Patent is filed in English, claims translations into the local language will be required in Croatia, Denmark, Iceland, Latvia, the Netherlands Slovenia and Sweden. A full translation will still be necessary if a European patent is granted in French or German. Additionally, Croatia, Denmark, Iceland, the Netherlands and Sweden prescribe English as the language of the description of the patent.

[315]   http://patlaw-reform.european-patent-office.org/epla/. Its formal title is 'the Draft Agreement on the establishment of a European patent litigation system'.

The basic legal instruments needed to achieve this were also agreed by the Working Party: a Draft Agreement on the establishment of a European patent litigation system, and a Draft Statute of the European Patent Court. Since then, the relevant provisions of the Enforcement Directive 2004/48/EC have been incorporated into the draft.[316] Although the Working Party considered that the proposed jurisdictional arrangement offered an optimum solution for users of the European patent system, and that the drafts constituted a suitable basis for convening a diplomatic conference to adopt the new court system, it also acknowledged that account had to be taken of the work being done by the EU to introduce a Community patent with a judicial system of its own. Implementation of the EPLA was therefore put on hold for a time, so that potential conflicts could be addressed. So far there has been little progress on the Community patent. Furthermore, even if a Community patent is introduced, it will not obviate the need for a workable litigation system covering European patents. Several hundred thousand of these are already in force in the EPC contracting states, and European patents will continue to be granted if and when Community patents become available. Efforts were therefore made to relaunch the EPLA, based on the revised text of December 2005.

The Draft Agreement provides for a new international organisation – the European Patent Judiciary (EPJ) – to be set up by those EPC states willing to commit themselves to an integrated judicial system. The organs of the EPJ would be the European Patent Court (comprising the Court of First Instance, the Court of Appeal and a Registry) and the Administrative Committee. The Court of First Instance would comprise a Central Division set up at the seat of the EPJ and a number of Regional Divisions. Regional Divisions would be set up upon request by an EPC state or group of EPC states.[317] The Court of Appeal, which would decide on appeals from decisions of the Court of First Instance and on petitions for review, would be set up at the seat of the EPJ. The Court of Appeal would also act as Facultative Advisory Council. The Administrative Committee, composed of representatives of the participating states, would supervise the European Patent Court, without prejudice to the Court's judicial independence. It would appoint the judges and the Registrar, and would exercise important legislative and budgetary powers. Judges would have to have 'sufficient experience of patent law', but could be either legally

---

[316] Working Party on Litigation, *Draft Agreement on the establishment of a European patent litigation system* (December 2005). For more on the Enforcement Directive see below Chapter 7.

[317] Larger EPC states may request that up to three Regional Divisions be set up within it, if the number of cases concerning European patents heard in that state warrants it.

or technically qualified.[318] The financial provisions of the Agreement are based on the assumption that the EPJ would be self-financing, funded by court fees. Nevertheless, provision is made for states to make contributions if necessary, it being recognised that access to the Court at reasonable cost is a necessity.

The substantive patent law (definition of infringing acts, etc.) contained in the Agreement is closely related to the corresponding provisions in the 1989 Agreement relating to Community patents. Those provisions of the European Patent Convention which apply to every European patent are deemed to be provisions of the Agreement. The EPC would deal with European patents effective in one or more of the participating states. It would have jurisdiction in respect of actions for actual or threatened infringement or for a declaration of non-infringement, actions or counterclaims for revocation, and actions for damages or compensation derived from the provisional protection conferred by a published European patent application. After a seven-year transitional period, the Court would have exclusive jurisdiction to try actions for revocation and actions for infringement where the alleged infringer is domiciled in a participating state or where all parties are in agreement. It would also have non-exclusive jurisdiction to try actions for infringement where the alleged infringement occurred in a participating state even though the alleged infringer is not domiciled in a participating state. Rules of Procedure would regulate the allocation of cases to the Central or a Regional Division of the Court of First Instance, taking account of the Brussels and Lugano Conventions as well as the Brussels Regulation.[319]

The application of Community law would be guaranteed by the ECJ, which on request by the EPC would issue preliminary rulings binding on the EPC in so far as its decision takes effect in a member state of the EU. Participating states would designate the EPC as their national court for cases concerning the infringement and validity of European patents, so that decisions of the Court would be directly enforceable in all contracting states. National courts would retain jurisdiction to order provisional and protective measures provided for

---

[318]   'Any person who has a good command of at least one of the official languages of the European Patent Office may be appointed as a judge of the European Patent Court, provided that he has sufficient experience of patent law and (a) has been or is a judge in one of the Contracting States to the European Patent Convention, (b) has been or is a member of a board of appeal of the European Patent Office or a national patent office of one of the Contracting States to the European Patent Convention, or (c) has other equivalent experience enabling him to act as a judge of the European Patent Court.': EPLA Draft Statute, Art. 2.

[319]   Regulation 44/2001 on jurisdiction and the recognition and enforcement of judgments in civil and commercial matters [2001] OJ L 012/1. See Chapter 7 below: section 7.24 Jurisdiction – the Brussels Regulation.

by their national law and to order provisional seizure of goods as security for damages, costs or any other payment resulting from proceedings before the EPC.

The Draft Agreement lays down basic procedural provisions (covering case management, conduct of proceedings, rules of evidence, costs etc.), and sets out the EPC's powers to order provisional and protective measures, and to impose sanctions and fines. Appeals would only be based on the grounds that the facts alleged by the parties were not correctly established, or that, based on the established facts, the law was not correctly applied. New facts or evidence would only be taken into consideration by the Court of Appeal in exceptional cases. The petition for review would not be a further appeal, but a limited judicial review based only on the grounds that a criminal act may have had an impact on the decision, or that a fundamental procedural defect has occurred in proceedings before the Court of Appeal. The Court of Appeal would also function as Facultative Advisory Council, to which national jurisdictions can refer, with a view to obtaining advice. The Draft Statute lays down rules on the composition of the panels, on the language regime (which would be English, French and German, as at the EPO) and on representation.

In October 2005, the European Patent Lawyers Association (EPLAW) and the EPO jointly organised a Forum for European Judges involved in patent cases. This led to the so-called Venice Resolution.[320] Signed by all the judges present, this supported the implementation of proposals broadly along the lines of those of the Working Party on Litigation for a European Patent Litigation Agreement as soon as practical. In November 2006 the Second Venice Resolution was agreed, adopting a set of principles for the Rules of Procedure of the European Patent Court. The guidelines had been drafted in Venice by a small committee of judges under the chairmanship of Sir Robin Jacob and were approved unanimously by all judges attending the Venice Forum.[321] Given the variety of procedural rules prevailing in European states, the expression of unanimity within the judiciary is striking. It reveals a sense of urgency felt by practitioners and judges which has not as yet been matched by political will to achieve practical reform.

The European Parliament debated the EPLA agreement in October 2006, and voted to postpone membership of the EPLA, whilst continuing participation in discussions.[322] Although recognising the importance of an efficient, competitive and cost-effective patent system, and acknowledging the deficiencies in the

---

[320]   http://www.eplaw.org/Downloads/Venice%20Resolution.pdf.

[321]   http://www.eplaw.org/Downloads/Second%20Venice%20Resolution%20 dated%204%20November%202006.pdf.

[322]   European Parliament resolution on future patent policy in Europe, Future action in the field of patents P6_TA(2006)0416.

Community patent proposals, the Parliament expressed serious reservations concerning the EPLA text. It sought reassurance with respect to democratic control, judicial independence and litigation costs, and regarded the proposal for the Rules of Procedure of the EPLA Court as unsatisfactory. It urged the Commission to explore all possible ways of improving the patent and patent litigation systems in the EU, whether via the EPLA or via revised proposals for the Community patent. It also asked its Legal Service 'to provide an interim opinion on EU-related aspects of the possible conclusion of the EPLA by the Member States in the light of overlaps between the EPLA and the *acquis communautaire*'. The Legal Service concluded that the EPLA governed matters on which the Community's competence is exclusive (including jurisdiction and the recognition of enforcement of judgments), and that individual member states would not be entitled to agree to it. Some member states are concerned that a new jurisdiction running in parallel with a Community patent jurisdiction would be over-complicated, leading to duplication and inconsistency. The political reality is that both the Community and the member states would have to agree if the EPLA is to be adopted.

The problem remains a pressing one. As Lord Justice Jacob has remarked,

Unless and until sensible judicial arrangements are put in place, the litigation of European patents in various national courts and the EPO will remain a messy, expensive and prolix business. One would hope that the politicians would find a way to put various national interests on one side for the sake of European industry as a whole. But despite attempt after attempt that has not yet been possible.[323]

3.3.3   Community Initiatives in the Field of Patent Law

3.3.3.1   The Community patent: context and history

The Commission regards patents as a driving force for promoting innovation, growth and competitiveness within the Community. A recent Commission study on the value of patents calculated that the so-called 'patent premium' amounts to over 1% of GDP, and notes a correlation between high innovation

---

[323]   *Unilin Beheer* v. *Berry Floor* [2007] EWCA Civ. 364 (para. 17). See also Anthony Arnull and Robin Jacob, 'European Patent Litigation: Out of the Impasse?' [2007] *EIPR* 209–14. For a robust appraisal of the difficulties, and the comparative merits of an EPLA or EU solution see Robin Jacob, 'The Judge's Perspective' (paper given at the EPLAW conference in Munich, June 2007), available at http://ipkitten. blogspot.com/2007/06/epla-or-bust-robin-jacob-speaks-out.html. See also *Research In Motion UK Ltd* v. *Visto Corporation* [2008] EWCA Civ. 153 (para. 3): 'The case is yet another illustrating the unsatisfactory state of the current arrangements for deciding European wide patent disputes. Too often one finds parties litigating as much about where and when disputes should be heard and decided as about the real underlying dispute.'

performance and high levels of patenting.[324] Yet there is still no single market for patents, and the EU lags behind the US and Japan in terms of patent activity.[325] Designating a European patent in, say, a dozen countries is many times more expensive than a US or Japanese patent. At least in theory, a centralised Community patent system would offer attractive benefits, notably: lower costs, legal uniformity and certainty, efficiency, and the elimination of forum-shopping. However, EU member states have been reluctant to cede control for a number of reasons, including fear of the effects on their own national patent systems. Discussions have dragged on for over 30 years with little evidence of progress.

As originally conceived, the Community patent was intended to complement the centralised granting procedure offered by the EPC. The aim was to establish a single Community patent, valid throughout the entire common market, and enforceable there by a single proceeding. The Luxembourg Convention establishing the Community Patent Convention (CPC) was signed in 1975. It provided for a Community patent which was of a unitary nature, in the sense that it could only be granted, transferred, revoked or allowed to lapse in respect of the whole Community.[326] It was intended that applications be made to the EPO, the applicant being obliged to provide translation of claims into all the official languages – eight at that time. But it did not enter into force, not being ratified by the required number of member states. In 1989 there was an attempt to revive the proposals, in an agreement relating to Community patents, which was an amended version of the CPC. At this conference it was proposed that the entire application – not just the claims – be translated into the official languages. This would have had serious implications for costs, whilst offering little advantage over a European patent other than cheaper renewal fees.

---

[324] Gambardellea et al., Study on patents: 'What Are Patents Actually Worth? The Value of Patents for Today's Economy and Society', available at http://ec.europa.eu/internal_market/indprop/docs/patent/studies/ final_report_lot2_en.pdf.

[325] The number of EPO patents per million population for the EU is 137, just behind the 143 for the US, and significantly behind the 174 for Japan. The number of so-called 'triadic' patents (those filed in the EU, the US and Japan) demonstrates a similar pattern: 33 per million population for the EU, 48 for the US and 102 for Japan. For these figures and further analysis see Maastricht Economic Research Institute on Innovation and Technology (MERIT) and the Joint Research Centre (Institute for the Protection and Security of the Citizen) of the European Commission, 'European Innovation Scoreboard 2006: Comparative Analysis of Innovation Performance' (European Commission, 2006), p. 13. See also Eurostat, 'Patent Statistics' *Statistics in Focus: Science and Technology* 17/2008: http://epp.eurostat.ec.europa.eu/cache/ITY_OFFPUB/KS-SF-08-017/EN/KS-SF-08-017-EN.PDF.

[326] CPC, Art. 2(2).

It was also intended that the Community patent would offer applicants the attraction of Europe-wide litigation and enforcement, in the form of a Community patent court. The 1975 Convention gave national courts responsibility for the scope of protection, leaving the Community court to deal with validity. But this approach was discarded in 1989. The proposed new approach bore the hallmarks of compromises demanded by vested interests, particularly in its complexity. It would have allowed challenges to validity either by application to a Revocation Division at the EPO, or in a counterclaim for revocation before a national community patent court. Appeal from either would have lain to a Community Patent Appeal Court (COPAC). Appeal from the national courts on other issues would have been to the relevant national appeal court. COPAC would also have made the final decisions on appeals from the EPO Administration and Revocation Divisions. The intention was for COPAC to be an independent organisation and not attached to the EPO or the ECJ. It would have been not only an appeal court, but would also have given preliminary rulings on the interpretation of the CPC, on request from national courts. However, with respect to remedies, the national rules of the member state where the infringement occurred would have applied. Again the revised CPC failed to gain the necessary ratifications.

In 2000, the European Commission proposed the creation of a Community Patent Regulation, stressing the views of the Lisbon and Feira European Councils that a Community patent was essential as part of Europe's efforts to harness the results of research to new scientific and technological developments and ensuring a competitive, knowledge-based economy in Europe. It was noted that the cost of a European patent was three to five times higher than that of Japanese and United States patents. Twenty-five per cent of this cost (€49,900) was attributable to translation costs. The proposal was that the patent application would be made in one of the working languages of the EPO (English, French, German), with the claims subsequently being translated into the other two. English was described as 'the universal language for patents'. To deal with the inevitable problems of legal certainty, given the potentially different interpretations of the EPC in the national courts, the Commission proposed a new centralised Community tribunal to deal with the Community patent.[327] It was intended to place the new court within the framework of the European Court of Justice, necessitating amendments which were put in place in the Treaty of Nice.[328]

---

[327]   Press Release (3 April 2007), 'Commission Proposes the Creation of a Community Patent' IP/00/714.
[328]   Treaty of Nice, Arts. 225a and 229a.

The proposal for a Community patent remained extremely controversial, particularly with respect to translations and jurisdictional arrangements. Nevertheless, political agreement was reached in March 2003.[329] However, in spite of great efforts, in March 2004, the Competitiveness Council failed to agree on the text of the Regulation. Aspects of the translation requirements (in particular, the treatment of infringements which might arise as a result of mistranslations) proved an insuperable stumbling block. Internal Market Commissioner Frits Bolkestein expressed his frustration forcefully:

> It is a mystery to me how Ministers at the so-called 'Competitiveness Council' can keep a straight face when they adopt conclusions for the Spring European Council on making Europe more competitive and yet in the next breath backtrack on the political agreement already reached on the main principles of the Community Patent in March of last year. . . . I can only hope that one day the vested, protectionist interests that stand in the way of agreement on this vital measure will be sidelined by the over-riding importance and interests of European manufacturing industry and Europe's competitiveness. That day has not yet come.[330]

In spite of this setback, the Commission regarded the issues as too important to ignore. In 2006 it launched 'a public consultation on how future action in patent policy to create an EU-wide system of protection can best take account of stakeholders' needs'.[331] The Commission stressed the need for a single market for patents, and declared that the Community patent remained central to its policy. Over 2,500 replies were received. Respondents insisted on the need to develop a comprehensive innovation policy in Europe, to respond to challenges from the US, Japan and emerging economic powers such as China and India. Industry gave priority to the quality of patents, and expressed concern that reducing costs might undermine the effectiveness of search and examination procedures. The Community patent was generally supported as a way forward, although there remained pockets of resistance. Nevertheless, stakeholders were unequivocal in rejecting the 2003 Common Political Approach, objecting to its language regime and jurisdictional arrangements. There are two extremes advocated for a possible language regime, from single

---

[329] MEMO/03/47, *Results of the Competitiveness Council of Ministers,* Brussels, 3rd March 2003.

[330] MEMO/04/58, *Results of the Competitiveness Council of Ministers, Brussels, 11th March 2004 Internal Market, Enterprise and Consumer Protection issues.*

[331] Press Release (16 January 2006), 'Internal Market: Commission Asks Industry and Other Stakeholders for their Views on Future Patent Policy' IP/06/38. See also a study commissioned by the European Parliament, Scientific Technology Options Assessment (STOA), 'Policy Options for the Improvement of the European Patent System' IP/A/STOA/FWC/2005-28/SC16. Available at: http://www.europarl.europa. eu/stoa/publications/studies/stoa16_en.pdf.

language grant, to full translations into all EU languages immediately on grant, with shades in between. However, it is clear that to compete with the EPC regime, the result must be unitary, affordable and offer legal certainty. Many respondents stressed that judges would have to have sufficient legal and technical experience. Critics have argued that a single court will in itself be no guarantee of uniformity, particularly if its personnel and resources are drawn without sufficient care from the existing resources in member states.

The Commission's conclusion following the public consultation was that although there was a widespread preference for the Community patent as a way forward, stakeholders did not want this 'at any price'. They sought 'a truly unitary high quality patent'.[332] Internal Market Commissioner Charlie McCreevy found it impossible to deliver a promised Communication immediately following the 2006 public consultation. In December 2006, EU industry and economics ministers (of France, notably) would not agree to support the EPLA. The Commission considered that its proposals on the Community patent, scheduled for discussion later in the month, were not worth pursuing. There are many competing proposals, there has been little consensus and McCreevy has questioned whether member states have the will to find a solution at EU level, since this will inevitably require compromise of national interests.[333] However, in April 2007 the Commission did issue a Communication, with proposals for reforming the patent system, hoping to 'revitalise the debate'.[334] It tackles the discrete issues of the Community patent, and patent jurisdiction, but also wider questions of patent policy such as patent quality, knowledge transfer and enforcement. A separate and comprehensive Communication on Intellectual Property Rights is promised for 2008, 'to complement the Patent Communication and address outstanding non-legislative and horizontal issues in all fields of intellectual property'.

The Patent Communication once again highlights the fact that Europe's current patent system is considerably more expensive than the US and Japanese systems. It asserts that a Community patent would be far more attractive than the existing system, which offers a bundle of national patents. This may true for some patentees, but certainly not all: many are content to cherry-

---

[332] 'Future Patent Policy in Europe, Public Hearing – 12 July 2006: Preliminary Findings' available at http://ec.europa.eu/internal_market/indprop/docs/patent/hearing/preliminary_findings_en.pdf.

[333] SPEECH/06/786 Charlie McCreevy, 'EU Patent Strategy' (PanEuropean Intellectual Property Summit, 7 December 2006).

[334] Press Release (3 April 2007), 'Patents: Commission Sets out Vision for Improving Patent System in Europe' IP/07/463. Communication from the Commission to the European Parliament and the Council – Enhancing the patent system in Europe, COM(2007) 165.

pick a few countries in which they wish to trade. Currently more than 90% of patent litigation in the Community takes place in just four member states (Germany, France, UK and the Netherlands).[335] The Communication acknowledges that the existing system of patent litigation in the EU, which may well entail patent litigation in several countries on a single patent issue, leads to unnecessary costs and lack of legal certainty.[336] The Commission sees an urgent need for action to provide a simple, cost-effective and high-quality patent system in Europe. It acknowledges the criticisms of the 2003 approach, which would have entailed high translation costs and excessive centralisation of the jurisdictional arrangements. The Commission still believes 'that a truly competitive and attractive Community patent can be achieved provided there is political will to do so', and describes this as 'a key objective for Europe'.[337]

Member states' views on patent jurisdictional arrangements are currently polarised, with some supporting the draft European Patent Litigation Agreement (EPLA) in the context of the European Patent Convention, and others favouring the establishment of a specific Community jurisdiction for patent litigation on European and Community patents based on the jurisdictional arrangements already in the EC Treaty. A specific judicial panel for patent litigation would be created (on the basis of Article 225a EC). This would include first instance courts with specialised judges located in the member states, with appeal to the Court of First Instance (CFI). There would be uniform rules of procedure, and the Community judges would apply not only Community law but also relevant provisions of the European Patent Convention. However, a number of member states (and some stakeholders) fear that an EU-wide patent court established within the Community framework would not be workable in practice, doubting in particular whether it would be possible to appoint technically qualified judges without full legal qualifications.

The Commission is advocating a compromise, seeking to build consensus on the basis of an integrated approach which combines elements of both the

---

[335] Communication from the Commission to the European Parliament and the Council – Enhancing the patent system in Europe, COM(2007) 165, p. 7.

[336] The Commission estimates that 'the cost of an average case heard by a unified patent jurisdiction is estimated at 10%–45% less than the cost of parallel litigation at first instance, and 11%–43% at second instance': Communication from the Commission to the European Parliament and the Council – Enhancing the patent system in Europe, COM(2007) 165, p. 8. The presumption (as yet untested) is that the quality of the unified jurisdiction will be satisfactory to litigants, who will consider outcomes as well as costs.

[337] Press Release (3 April 2007), 'Patents: Commission Sets Out Vision for Improving Patent System in Europe' IP/07/463. Communication from the Commission to the European Parliament and the Council – Enhancing the patent system in Europe, COM(2007) 165, p. 4.

EPLA and a Community jurisdiction. It proposes that a Community patent should be created, but avoiding competing jurisdictions. It suggests this might be achieved by creating a unified and specialised patent judiciary, competent to handle litigation involving both European patents and Community patents: 'Such a judicial system could be strongly inspired by the EPLA model, in particular as regards the specificities of patent litigation, but could allow for harmonious integration in the Community jurisdiction'.[338] What is envisaged by the Commission is a limited number of first instance courts, and a fully centralised appeal court to ensure uniformity of interpretation. The first instance courts could be created using existing national structures, and would form an integral part of the single jurisdictional system. Allocation of cases would be handled by the registry of the judiciary on the basis of clearly defined and transparent rules (such as the Brussels Regulation). The courts would be competent to hear infringement and validity actions, and to award damages and other remedies. The appeal court and first instance courts would share common rules of procedure based on best practices in the member states; the work done on the draft EPLA is cited as potentially helpful here. Judges could be legally or technically qualified. The Commission emphasises that the new patent courts would be obliged to respect the European Court of Justice as the final arbiter in matters of EU law, including questions related to the *acquis communautaire* and to the validity of future Community patents. The Commission believes that if there is adequate political will, the current differences between the member states can be overcome and an appropriate architecture for a unified and integrated EU-wide patent jurisdiction could be established.[339]

Both the German and Portuguese presidencies have made considerable efforts to move matters forward. Following preliminary informal discussions with member states and stakeholders there are now several working documents, including a *Draft Agreement on the European Patent Judiciary*, outlining the main features of the proposed EU patent jurisdiction, as well as remedies and procedures.[340] This *Draft Agreement* outlines what is necessary to set up a European Union Patent Court (EUPC) for litigation relating to the

---

[338] Communication from the Commission to the European Parliament and the Council – Enhancing the patent system in Europe, COM(2007) 165, p. 11.
[339] Communication from the Commission to the European Parliament and the Council – Enhancing the patent system in Europe, COM(2007) 165, p. 11.
[340] 13675/07, *Towards an EU Patent Jurisdiction – Points for discussion* (10 October 2007); 14492/07, *Towards an EU Patent Jurisdiction – Points for discussion* (30 October 2007); 5245/08, *EU Patent Jurisdiction – Remedies, procedures and other measures* (11 January 2008); 5954/08, *EU Patent Jurisdiction – Main features of the Court system (first part); Remedies* (4 February 2008); *European Union Patent Jurisdiction – Preliminary Set of Provisions for the future legal instrument* (19 March 2008); 9124/08, *Draft Agreement on the European Patent Judiciary* (14 May 2008),

infringement and validity of patents. It would be an integrated and exclusive court for Community patents and European patents designating any of the contracting parties. It would be open to all contracting states of the European Patent Convention.[341] It would comprise a Court of First Instance with local and regional divisions as well as one central division, a Court of Appeal and a Registry.[342]

Panels of three judges are envisaged, with five in the Court of Appeal. In the local divisions, two would come from the member states concerned, and would serve as permanent members of the EU patent jurisdiction. The third judge in a local division would come from a Community pool of patent judges consisting of legally and technically qualified judges covering all fields of technology. The regional division would have two permanent judges chosen from a regional list, whose habitual residence was within the division, and one judge from the pool whose habitual residence was elsewhere. Panels of the central division would consist of two legally and technically qualified judges. Any panel of the Court of Appeal would consist of five judges, three legally qualified and two technically qualified. The panel would be multinational.[343] Legally qualified judges would be qualified for judicial functions at national level. Technically qualified judges would have university-level qualifications in a field of technology.[344] Judges would be required to be independent and impartial. Legally qualified judges would not be precluded from exercising judicial functions at national level, and technically qualified judges could exercise other functions provided there is no conflict of interest.[345] The Court would be financed from its own fees, and (where necessary) by contributions from the Community budget and contracting parties which are not member states.[346]

In terms of substantive law, the Court would base its decisions on the provisions of the *Draft Agreement*; the Community Patent Regulation (yet to be agreed); those provisions of the European Patent Convention which apply to every European patent; provisions of national law enacted to implement EPC Articles 65, 67(2) and (3), 70(3) and (4) (relating to translations); the Regulation implementing the Doha Declaration;[347] and the Regulation creating

---

revised as 11270/08, *Draft Agreement on the European Union Patent Court* (30 June 2008) ('*EPC Draft Agreement*'). Available at http://register.consilium.europa.eu/.

[341]   *EPJ Draft Agreement*, Preamble, Arts. 1–3.
[342]   *EPJ Draft Agreement*, Arts. 4–8.
[343]   *EPJ Draft Agreement*, Art. 7.
[344]   *EPJ Draft Agreement*, Art. 10.
[345]   *EPJ Draft Agreement*, Art. 12.
[346]   *EPJ Draft Agreement*, Art. 18.
[347]   Regulation 816/2006 on compulsory licensing of patents relating to the manufacture of pharmaceutical products for export to countries with public health problems [2006] OJ L 157/1.

supplementary protection certificates for plant protection products.[348] The application of national law would be determined by reference to the existing agreements between contracting parties, including the 'Rome II' Regulation (on non-contractual obligations, which includes specific provision for intellectual property),[349] and the EC Convention on the Law Applicable to Contractual Obligations ('Rome I'). The definition of infringing acts is taken from the Draft Agreement on the establishment of a European patent litigation system, which in turn is closely related to the corresponding provisions in the 1989 Agreement relating to Community patents.[350] Provision is also made for the establishment of a patent arbitration and mediation centre.[351]

Uniform rules of procedure would be established.[352] The intention is to take account of the Enforcement Directive, and the work carried out in preparing the draft EPLA. The rules would aim to ensure expeditious and high quality judgments, and cost-effective procedures. The controversial question of the language of proceedings would be resolved in a compromise. In cases before a local/regional division, the language of proceedings would be the official European Union language(s) of the relevant member state, or the official language(s) of other contracting parties hosting the division, or the official languages designated by contracting parties sharing a regional division. Contracting parties would be free to designate one of the official languages of the EPO as the language of proceedings of their local or regional division. Parties would be entitled to agree on the use of the language in which the patent was granted as language of proceedings, subject to the division's approval. On request, and having heard both parties, the division would be free to choose a different language on the grounds of convenience and fairness. In all cases before the central division, the language of proceedings would be the language in which the patent was granted.[353] The language of proceedings before the Court of Appeal would be the language of proceedings before the Court of First Instance. However, the parties would be entitled to agree on the use of the language in which the patent was granted. In exceptional cases, the Court would be able to decide on another European Union official language or the official language of a contracting party (not a member state) as the

---

348 Regulation 1768/92 concerning the creation of a supplementary protection certificate for medicinal products [1992] OJ L 182/1. Regulation 1610/96 concerning the creation of a supplementary protection certificate for plant protection products [1996] OJ L 198/30.

349 Regulation 864/2007 on the law applicable to non-contractual obligations (Rome II) [2007] OJ L 199/40.

350 *EPJ Draft Agreement*, Arts. 14(a)–(f).

351 *EPJ Draft Agreement*, Art. 17.

352 *EPJ Draft Agreement*, Part III – Procedural Provisions.

353 *EPJ Draft Agreement*, Art. 29.

language of proceedings, subject to agreement by the parties.[354] Any division, and the Court of Appeal, would be able to dispense with translation requirements where appropriate.[355] There would be a written, interim and oral procedure, though the oral procedure could be dispensed with by agreement.[356]

The Court would have the power to order the production of evidence, to appoint technical experts to assist the Court, to grant preliminary and permanent injunctions, to make freezing orders, to order seizure or delivery up of goods suspected to be infringing, to order appropriate measures with regard to infringing goods, and to award compensatory damages against deliberate or negligent infringers.[357] The Court would be able to declare patents invalid in whole or in part, on the grounds listed in the European Patent Convention.[358] Appeals from decisions of the Court of First Instance would lie to the Court of Appeal on points of law or fact.[359] Further review by the ECJ would be possible on points of law only.[360] Decisions of the Court would have EU-wide effect for Community patents, and for European patents would have effect in the territory of those contracting parties for which the patent had been validated.[361]

The EU Competitiveness Council has reviewed the Commission's report, responding positively, if somewhat guardedly. It welcomed the progress achieved so far and agreed on the need to work towards solutions for a Europe-wide patent litigation system and a Community patent. Ministers agreed on the need for an efficient litigation system which ensures legal certainty and which is capable of reducing costs for users, especially for small and medium-sized enterprises (SMEs). There is nothing controversial in such statements. More ominously, the Council also noted that 'certain issues will require further in-depth discussions within the Council preparatory bodies'. As commentators have observed, 'Whether the Commission Communication results in advancement in the coming years depends largely on the political will of Member

---

[354]   *EPJ Draft Agreement*, Art. 30.
[355]   *EPJ Draft Agreement*, Art. 31.
[356]   *EPJ Draft Agreement*, Art. 32.
[357]   *EPJ Draft Agreement*, Arts. 34–41.
[358]   EPC, Art. 138(1) . These grounds are: that the subject of the European patent is not patentable; the European patent does not disclose the invention in a manner sufficiently clear and complete for it to be carried out by a person skilled in the art; the subject matter of the European patent extends beyond the content of the application as filed; the protection of the European patent has been extended; the proprietor of the European patent is not entitled to the patent.
[359]   *EPJ Draft Agreement*, Art. 45.
[360]   *EPJ Draft Agreement*, Art. 48.
[361]   *EPJ Draft Agreement*, Art. 16.

States'. The challenge is a demanding one, and it remains to be seen whether real progress can be made, given the many constraints.[362]

3.3.3.2 Supplementary protection certificates

Supplementary protection certificates (SPCs) acknowledge the fact that the increased regulatory framework surrounding certain products may lead to the patent proprietor's being disadvantaged, particularly with respect to the duration of the patent. It may take many years to receive regulatory approval for the marketing of a patented pharmaceutical (for example), thus eating into the effective term of the patent monopoly significantly, and perhaps even rendering its exploitation uneconomic. In 1984 the United States introduced patent term restoration for pharmaceuticals, and Japan followed in 1987. France responded in 1991 with a Certificate of Complementary Protection, and Italy soon followed suit.[363] It became obvious that this was a threat to the uniformity of the internal market, disadvantaging European pharmaceutical industries, and discouraging investment in pharmaceutical research. The Commission therefore proposed a harmonising regulation, conferring supplementary protection for medicinal products (SPC (MP) Reg.), which came into force in 1993. There is a similar regulation for plant protection products (SPC (PPP) Reg.), in force since 1997.[364] The regulations do not extend the life of the patent as such (to avoid conflict with the maximum term of patent protection specified in Article 63 EPC). Instead they provide for the grant of a *sui generis* supplementary protection certificate (SPC), which has much the same effect.[365]

SPCs are granted by national patent offices (not the EPO), and have effect only in the state in which they are granted. They are granted for 'products' which constitute the 'active ingredient', or combination of active ingredients, of a 'medicinal product'; or, the 'active substance', or combination of active

---

[362]   Victoria Hanley and Alain Strowel, 'Last-Ditch Attempt to Improve the EU Patent System' [2007] *JIPL&P* 577–8. For further comment see the notes of a panel discussion held at the Venice III conference of EPLAW: 'Brevets sans frontières: Update on European Initiatives', with Dr Jochen Pagenberg of Bardehle Pagenberg, Munich, and Dr Margot Fröhlinger, Director General Internal Market and Services of the European Commission. Available at http://www.eplaw.org/News.asp.

[363]   See Peter L. Kolker, 'The Supplementary Protection Certificate: The European Solution to Patent Term Restoration' [1997] *IPQ* 249–53.

[364]   Regulation 1768/92 concerning the creation of a supplementary protection certificate for medicinal products [1992] OJ L 182/1. Regulation 1610/96 concerning the creation of a supplementary protection certificate for plant protection products [1996] OJ L 198/30.

[365]   For Spain's challenge to the entire SPC regime, which was dismissed by the ECJ, see Case 350/92, *Spain* v. *Council of the European Union* [1995] ECR I-1985.

substances, of a 'plant protection product'.[366] The product must have received its first marketing authorisation – the authorisation necessary for compliance with the relevant EC Directives, and not any free-standing national requirements – and applications must be made within six months of receipt of this.[367] In addition, the product must be protected by a UK patent or European patent (the 'basic patent').[368]

An SPC takes effect at the end of the lawful term of the basic patent. The term of a certificate is equal to the period which elapsed between the filing date of the patent and the date of the first authorisation in the EC reduced by a period of five years. The term of a certificate may not exceed five years. The formulation ensures that all national SPCs will expire at the same time. An SPC extends the protection conferred by the basic patent beyond the term of that patent, but only in respect of the product covered by the marketing authorisation.[369] This does not mean, however, that the SPC is confined to the specific product for which authorisation was first secured. The SPC will cover the product 'in any of the forms enjoying the protection of the basic patent'.[370] This is to prevent the purpose of the SPC being frustrated. If any competitor could simply wait for the basic patent's expiry and then apply for marketing authorisation for a different version of the same active ingredient, medicinal products which were therapeutically equivalent to that protected by the SPC would be able to compete with it. Instead, the holder of the basic patent is ensured a period of exclusivity on the market extending beyond that patent's period of validity.

3.3.3.3 The Biotechnology Directive: the legal protection of biotechnological inventions

Like the Community patent, the Biotechnology Directive has had a difficult history. The initial Commission proposal to harmonise the patenting of biotechnological inventions was submitted to the Council in 1988. The Commission noted that there were significant differences between the laws of member states concerning this subject, and also considered that the level of

---

[366] SPC (MP) Reg., Art. 1. SPC (PPP) Reg., Art. 1. But see also Case C-431/04, *Massachusetts Institute of Technology* [2006] ECR I-4089.

[367] SPC (MP) Reg., Art. 7. SPC (PPP) Reg., Art. 7. A marketing authorisation which is issued by the Swiss authorities and automatically recognised by Liechtenstein (a member state of the EEA) is regarded as a first marketing authorisation for the purposes of SPC Regulations, even though Switzerland itself is not part of the EEA. See Joined Cases C-207/03 and C-252/03, *Novartis et al.* v. *Comptroller-General* and *Ministère de l'Economie* v. *Millennium Pharmaceuticals.*

[368] SPC (MP) Reg., Art. 3(a). SPC (PPP) Reg., Art. 3(1)(a).

[369] SPC (MP) Reg., Art. 4. SPC (PPP) Reg., Art. 4.

[370] Case C-392/97, *Farmitalia Carlo Erba Srl* [1999] ECR I-5553.

protection offered was significantly less than that available in competing patent systems such as those in the US and Japan. The intention was therefore both to harmonise national laws, and to increase protection for biotechnological inventions. The Commission's proposals were fiercely debated both in Council and in Parliament. In 1994 the Council adopted a common position on the Directive, but only by qualified majority; Denmark, Spain and Luxembourg voted against it. In 1995 the European Parliament rejected a joint text agreed following the consultation procedure, and it appeared unlikely that any compromise could be agreed. Members of the European Parliament were seriously concerned by the ethical and moral implications of patenting living matter. Nevertheless, in 1998 a Directive was agreed, to be implemented by 30 July 2000. The Netherlands challenged the Directive on a number of grounds, seeking its annulment, but the ECJ rejected all of its arguments.[371]

In order to allay the fears of MEPs, the Directive's Recitals spell out in considerable detail the aims of the legislation, and the safeguards built into it (some of which were already inherent in existing patent law). They note the importance of biotechnology and genetic engineering in a broad range of industries, and the importance of offering effective and harmonised legal protection to inventions in these fields, particularly since research and development may well entail considerable risk and investment. Without harmonisation, the existing differences between the laws of the member states would inevitably increase, and would act as a disincentive to industrial development in these fields in the Community. Although it was unnecessary to replace existing national patent laws, differences in their application to the protection of biotechnological and microbiological inventions had created uncertainty, so harmonisation would clarify these areas.

The positive effects of biotechnology are also stressed: its utility in developing more effective and less polluting methods of cultivation; its importance to developing countries, to promote health and combat disease, and to combat hunger. The EC and the member states have an obligation under the TRIPS Agreement to provide patent protection for products and processes in all areas of technology. The Community's legal framework for the protection of biotechnological inventions is limited to laying down certain principles as they apply to the patentability of biological material as such. These principles determine (*inter alia*) the difference between inventions and discoveries with regard to the patentability of certain elements of human origin, and the scope of protection conferred by a patent on a biotechnological invention. It is emphasised that the grant of a patent does not authorise the patentee to imple-

---

[371]   Case C-377/98, *Kingdom of the Netherlands* v. *Parliament and Council* [2001] ECR I-7079.

ment that invention, but merely entitles the patentee to prohibit third parties from exploiting it for industrial and commercial purposes. Thus substantive patent law cannot serve to replace or render superfluous national, European or international laws which impose restrictions or prohibitions on research, or on its use, or on the commercialisation of its results. Such laws might (for example) seek to safeguard public health, safety, environmental protection, animal welfare, the preservation of genetic diversity and compliance with ethical standards.

Neither the EPC nor any national law precluded *a priori* the patenting of biological matter. However, mere discoveries are not patentable. The Directive spells out the implications of this: that the human body, at any stage in its formation or development, including germ cells, and the simple discovery of one of its elements or one of its products, including the sequence or partial sequence of a human gene, cannot be patented. Nevertheless, medicinal products derived from elements isolated from the human body and/or otherwise produced have been valuable in the treatment of diseases, and research into these should be encouraged by means of the patent system. Such patents do not extend to the human body and its elements in their natural environment. The patenting of gene sequences is acknowledged to be controversial. The Directive stresses that such patents are subject to the same criteria of patentability as all other areas of technology: novelty, inventive step and industrial application. The industrial application of a gene sequence or partial sequence must be disclosed in the patent application, and a mere DNA sequence without indication of a function does not contain any technical information and is therefore not a patentable invention. If inventions are based on or use biological material of human origin, the person from whose body the material is taken must have had an opportunity of expressing free and informed consent thereto, in accordance with national law. If an invention is based on or uses biological material of plant or animal origin, the patent application should, where appropriate, include information on the geographical origin of such material, if known. The EPC excludes the patenting of plant and animal varieties, but permits the patenting of inventions concerning plants or animals provided that the technical feasibility of the invention is not confined to a single plant or animal variety. The Directive aligns itself with this position. It is stated explicitly that the Directive does not prejudice the provisions of national patent law whereby processes for treatment of the human or animal body by surgery or therapy and diagnostic methods practised on the human or animal body are excluded from patentability.

It is noted that the TRIPS Agreement allows members to exclude inventions from patentability if their commercial exploitation would be contrary to *ordre public* or morality. The Directive reasserts this principle, and offers an illustrative but non-exhaustive list of such inventions to serve as a guide to national courts and patent offices. Since there is consensus within the Community that interventions in the human germ line and the cloning of human beings offend against *ordre public* and morality, these are excluded from patentability unequivocally. Uses of human embryos for industrial or commercial purposes are also excluded from patentability, although this does not affect inventions for therapeutic or diagnostic purposes which are applied to the human embryo and are useful to it. The Directive also reasserts the EU's commitment to fundamental rights, both as guaranteed by the ECHR, and as general principles of Community law resulting from the constitutional traditions common to the member states. Recognising the impact of the life sciences and information technology on cultural, societal, economic and political change, in 1991 the Commission set up the Group of Advisers on the Ethical Implications of Biotechnology (GAEIB). The aim was to create an ethical body at Community level, to help policymakers assess the impact of these technologies on society, and to prevent any harmful developments. This group was replaced in 1998 by the European Group on Ethics in Science and New Technologies (EGE).[372] The Biotechnology Directive expresses a commitment to consult the EGE where biotechnology needs to be evaluated at the level of basic ethical principles. As under the EPC, processes for modifying the genetic identity of animals which are likely to cause them suffering without any substantial medical benefit in terms of research, prevention, diagnosis or therapy to man or animal, and also animals resulting from such processes, are excluded from patentability.

The Recitals also acknowledge the right of an inventor to prohibit the use of patented self-reproducing material for a limited time, expressing this as a reward to the inventor for his creative efforts. However, there is a derogation from those rights where propagating material is sold by the patentee to a farmer for farming purposes. In such cases the farmer must be able to save seed for use on the farm. Similarly, a farmer must be able to use patented livestock for agricultural purposes. There is provision for compulsory cross-

---

[372]   The EGE is independent, multicultural and multidisciplinary. Its 12 members represent a variety of different viewpoints and disciplines. On the basis of the principles laid down in the European Treaties (which make reference to the fundamental rights defined by the ECHR), the EGE endeavours to draw up common rules to enable the internal market to operate in accordance with Europe's ethical values. Its three main objectives are: 'to help break down barriers between disciplines in fields which require a multi-disciplinary approach, not only scientific and legal, but also philosophical, sociological and economic; to provide European decision-makers with clear and up-to-date basic information, enabling them to be properly informed in carrying out their duties; and to promote dialogue that stimulates mutual tolerance so that all viewpoints can be expressed before the Community authorities decide on appropriate regulations', http://ec.europa.eu/european_group_ethics/archive/1998_2000/intro_en.htm.

licensing, on payment of a fee, where new plant varieties resulting from genetic engineering represent significant technical progress of considerable economic interest. The final Recital notes the Community's obligations under the Convention on Biological Diversity.

The Articles express these principles and aims in often familiar legal form. Article 1 requires member states to protect biotechnological inventions under national patent law. However, obligations under the Directive are without prejudice to the obligations of the member states pursuant to international agreements, in particular the TRIPS Agreement and the Convention on Biological Diversity. Inventions which are new, which involve an inventive step and which are susceptible of industrial application are to be patentable even if they concern a product consisting of or containing biological material or a process by means of which biological material is produced, processed or used.[373] This includes biological material which is isolated from its natural environment or produced by means of a technical process, even if this previously occurred in nature.[374] Plant and animal varieties are not patentable, nor are essentially biological processes for the production of plants or animals.[375] However, inventions which concern plants or animals are patentable 'if the technical feasibility of the invention is not confined to a particular plant or animal variety'.[376] The human body, at the various stages of its formation and development, and the simple discovery of one of its elements, including the sequence or partial sequence of a gene, cannot constitute patentable inventions.[377] However, an element isolated from the human body or otherwise produced by means of a technical process, including the sequence or partial sequence of a gene, may constitute a patentable invention, even if the structure of that element is identical to that of a natural element.[378] The industrial application of a sequence or a partial sequence of a gene must be disclosed in the patent application.[379] Inventions will be considered unpatentable where their

---

[373] Biotech. Dir., Art. 3(1). 'Biological material' means any material containing genetic information and capable of reproducing itself or being reproduced in a biological system: Art. 2(1)(a).

[374] Biotech. Dir., Art. 3(2).

[375] Biotech. Dir., Art. 4(1). A process for the production of plants or animals is essentially biological if it consists entirely of natural phenomena such as crossing or selection: Art. 2(2). Compare EPC 2000, Art. 53(b). Microbiological processes are patentable: Art. 4(3). See above section 3.3.1.7 (4) (iii) Biological subject matter. See also Sven J.R. Bostyn, 'The Patentability of Genetic Information Carriers' 1 (1999) *IPQ* 1–36.

[376] Biotech. Dir., Art. 4(2).

[377] Biotech. Dir., Art. 5(1).

[378] Biotech. Dir., Art. 5(2).

[379] Biotech. Dir., Art. 5(3). See also Denis Schertenleib, 'The Patentability and Protection of DNA Based Inventions in the EPO and the European Union' [2003] *EIPR*

commercial exploitation would be contrary to *ordre public* or morality (though not merely because their exploitation is prohibited by law or regulation).[380] On this basis, the following are specifically excluded from patentability:

(a) processes for cloning human beings;
(b) processes for modifying the germ line genetic identity of human beings;
(c) uses of human embryos for industrial or commercial purposes;
(d) processes for modifying the genetic identity of animals which are likely to cause them suffering without any substantial medical benefit to man or animal, and also animals resulting from such processes.[381]

The Commission's European Group on Ethics in Science and New Technologies (EGE) is tasked with evaluating all ethical aspects of biotechnology.[382]

The protection given by biological patents for products and processes is stated to extend to any biological material derived from that biological material (through propagation or multiplication in an identical or divergent form) which possesses the same characteristics.[383] Similarly, the protection conferred by a patent on a product containing or consisting of genetic information extends to all material (subject to the exception in Article 5(1) regarding patentability of the human body) in which the product is incorporated and in which the genetic information is contained and performs its function.[384] There are a number of derogations from this protection. It does not extend to biological material obtained from the propagation or multiplication of biological material marketed in a member state by the patentee or with his consent, where the multiplication or propagation necessarily results from the application for which the biological material was marketed, provided that the material obtained is not subsequently used for other propagation or multiplication.[385] This permits a farmer who has bought seed from the patentee (or his licensee) to sow the seed, and harvest and sell the crop, but not to

---

125–38; Geertrui Van Overwalle, 'Gene Patents: A Different Approach' [2001] *EIPR* 505–6; A.W. White, 'Gene and Compound Per Se Claims: An Appropriate Reward' [2000/2001] 6 *Bio-Science Law Review* 239–48; R.S. Crespi, 'Gene and Compound Claims: Another View' [2000/2001] 1 *Bio-Science Law Review*, 3–8.
[380] Biotech. Dir., Art. 6(1).
[381] Biotech. Dir., Art. 6(2). Compare EPC 2000, Art 53(a). See above section (v) Morality – Article 53(a).
[382] Biotech. Dir., Art. 7.
[383] Biotech. Dir., Art. 8.
[384] Biotech. Dir., Art. 9. See Sven J.R. Bostyn, 'The Patentability of Genetic Information Carriers' 1 (1999) *IPQ* 1–36, 28.
[385] Biotech. Dir., Art. 10.

reuse the crop as seed. This provision seems to do little more than state the obvious, to emphasise for political purposes that normal farming activities will not be affected by the Directive. In addition, however, the sale of plant propagating material to a farmer by the patentee or with his consent for agricultural use implies authorisation for the farmer to use the product of his harvest for propagation or multiplication by him on his own farm. This is the 'farm saved seed' derogation familiar from the Community Plant Variety Regulation, and the extent and conditions of the derogation under the Biotechnology Directive correspond to those laid down there (including equitable remuneration).[386] Similarly, the sale of breeding stock or other animal reproductive material to a farmer by the patentee or with his consent implies authorisation for the farmer to use the protected livestock for an agricultural purpose. This includes making the animal or other animal reproductive material available for the purposes of pursuing his agricultural activity but not sale within the framework or for the purpose of a commercial reproduction activity. Here (in the absence of a Directive on animal variety rights), the extent and the conditions of the derogation are to be determined by national laws, regulations and practices (if any).[387]

A breeder who cannot acquire or exploit a plant variety right without infringing a prior patent may apply for a compulsory licence to exploit it, subject to payment of an appropriate royalty. In such circumstances the patent holder will be entitled to a cross-licence on reasonable terms to use the protected variety.[388] Similarly, where the holder of a patent concerning a biotechnological invention cannot exploit it without infringing a prior plant variety right, he may apply for a compulsory licence, subject to payment of an appropriate royalty. Again, the holder of the plant variety right will be entitled to a cross-licence on reasonable terms to use the protected invention.[389] In both of the above situations, applicants for compulsory licences must demonstrate: that they have applied unsuccessfully to the holder of the patent or of the plant variety right to obtain a contractual licence; and, that the plant variety or the invention constitutes significant technical progress of considerable economic interest compared with the invention claimed in the patent or the protected plant variety.[390]

---

[386] Biotech. Dir., Art. 11(1). CPVR, Art. 14(1). See below section 3.4 Plant variety rights: section 3.4.3 The Community plant variety right.

[387] Biotech. Dir., Art. 11(2).

[388] Biotech. Dir., Art. 12(1). The concept of 'plant variety' is that defined in Article 5 of the Community Plant Variety Regulation 2100/94: Biotech. Dir., Art. 2(3).

[389] Biotech. Dir., Art. 12(2).

[390] Biotech. Dir., Art. 12(3).

Where an invention involves the use of or concerns biological material which is not available to the public and which cannot be described in a patent application in such a manner as to enable the invention to be reproduced by a person skilled in the art, the description will be considered inadequate for the purposes of patent law unless the biological material is deposited in accordance with various conditions. Firstly, the biological material must be deposited no later than the date on which the patent application was filed with a recognised depositary institution (such as those recognised under the Budapest Treaty).[391] In addition, the patent application must contain such relevant information as is available to the applicant on the characteristics of the biological material deposited, and must state the name of the depository institution and the accession number.[392] Access to the samples is permitted only under strict conditions.[393]

The Directive puts in place a rigorous system of reporting. Every five years the Commission is required to send the Parliament and Council a report on any problems encountered with regard to the relationship between the Directive and international agreements on the protection of human rights to which the member states have acceded. Within two years of the Directive entering into force it was also required to send a report assessing the implications for basic genetic engineering research of failure to publish, or late publication of, papers on subjects which could be patentable (meaning, whether research is being hampered as a result of delays in publication due to the filing of patent applications). Finally, an annual report is required on the development and implications of patent law in the field of biotechnology and genetic engineering.[394]

---

[391]   The Budapest Treaty of 28 April 1977 on the international recognition of the deposit of micro-organisms for the purposes of patent procedure ('Budapest Treaty'), Art. 7.

[392]   Biotech. Dir., Art. 13(1).

[393]   Biotech. Dir., Art. 13(2) and (3). Supply of a sample is permitted: (a) up to the first publication of the patent application, only to those persons who are authorised under national patent law; (b) between the first publication of the application and the granting of the patent, to anyone requesting it or, if the applicant so requests, only to an independent expert; (c) after the patent has been granted, and notwithstanding revocation or cancellation of the patent, to anyone requesting it. The sample may be supplied only if the person requesting it undertakes, for the term during which the patent is in force: (a) not to make it or any material derived from it available to third parties; and (b) not to use it or any material derived from it except for experimental purposes, unless the applicant for or proprietor of the patent, as applicable, expressly waives such an undertaking. If the deposited material ceases to become available, a new deposit may be made on the same terms: Biotech. Dir., Art. 14.

[394]   Biotech. Dir., Art. 16.

The first to be published was a report on the interaction between publication of research and the filing of patent applications.[395] It considered the potential conflict for researchers between the twin strategies of 'protection' from disclosure which would prevent a patent being granted, and 'publication' to the scientific community and/or investors. A survey was conducted among public and private researchers and institutions in industry and public research, as well as those involved in intellectual property rights issues (for example, patent agents) to investigate the issue of publication delay. The results showed that only a very small fraction of researchers and organisations actually experienced a considerable delay in publication of research results which were the subject of a patent application. This fraction was lowest for the most experienced users of the patent system (10%), and highest for less experienced users (40%). The report concluded that providing patent protection for results of genetic engineering research usually facilitated publication and prevented secrecy strategies. The public research sector strongly favoured the introduction of a grace period and large industry strongly opposed it, with both positions being present in small and medium-sized enterprises. The possibility of filing a provisional patent application was attractive to both industry and academia, although understandably was a low priority for patent agents. The report concluded that the patent system should be made as easy to use as possible for academics and small and medium-sized enterprises. It recommended that support, advice and training should be available. It also endorsed the proposed Community patent.

The first report on the development and implications of patent law in the field of biotechnology and genetic engineering was submitted in October 2002.[396] The report noted the 'long and constructive debate' which preceded the adoption of the Biotechnology Directive. The background was a sector in full expansion, with 'new techniques of great promise for cures and foodstuffs' becoming established very rapidly. Although European legislators considered it essential not to hamper the sector's development, it was considered that there was a need to establish a sound legal framework which allowed European businesses to develop and market the products and processes deriving from genetic engineering. The sector had to be watched very closely 'in

---

[395] *Report from the Commission to the European Parliament and Council – An assessment of the implications for basic genetic engineering research of failure to publish, or late publication of, papers on subjects which could be patentable as required under Article 16(b) of Directive 98/44/EC on the legal protection of biotechnological inventions* COM(2002) 2 final.

[396] *Report from the Commission to the European Parliament and the Council – Development and implications of patent law in the field of biotechnology and genetic engineering* COM(2002) 545 final.

order to monitor its development and prevent any malfunctions'. The report concluded that the Articles relating to the patentability of plants and animals and the patentability of elements isolated from the human body or otherwise produced do take account of society's concerns and of the financing needed for research. These provisions were found to comply strictly with the ethical rules recognised in the European Community, whilst protecting inventions developed in that field. The report also noted that, since biotechnology and genetic engineering are not fixed and static sciences, it is incumbent on the Commission to identify and assess problems which have recently appeared or which have become more pressing. It therefore recommended that the Commission should, in particular, consider the scope of patents relating to sequences or part-sequences of genes isolated from the human body, and the patentability of human stem cells and of cell lines obtained from them. In response, the Commission announced that these two topics would be studied and analysed by a group of independent experts (specialising in the fields of economics, law and natural sciences), and their conclusions used in the preparation of the future progress reports. The Commission stressed that the group would not duplicate work by the European Group on Ethics (which delivered an opinion on ethical aspects of patenting inventions involving human stem cells),[397] but would focus on the scientific, legal and economic aspects of these questions.

The second report did not appear until July 2005.[398] It did address both the patenting of gene sequences, and stem cells. The conclusion in both cases was that the Commission should continue to monitor these difficult areas. With respect to gene sequences, the central question is whether the patentee should be allowed to claim an invention which covers all possible future uses of that sequence (the classical model of a patent claim), or whether the patent should be restricted so that only the specific use disclosed in the patent application can be claimed ('purpose-bound protection'). Although it can be argued from a plain reading of the provisions of the Directive that there are no objective grounds for limiting the traditional protection granted by patent law to inventions relating to sequences or partial sequences of genes isolated from the human body, other issues were raised. In particular, in two member states ethical considerations had led to the grant of only purpose-bound protection for inventions concerning material isolated from the human body (France) and

---

[397]   Opinion no. 16 (7 May 2002), *Ethical aspects of patenting inventions involving human stem cells.* Available from http://ec.europa.eu/european_group_ethics/avis/index_en.htm. See also R. Stephen Crespi, 'The Human Embryo and Patent Law – A Major Challenge Ahead?' [2006] *EIPR* 569–75.

[398]   *Report from the Commission to the European Parliament and the Council – Development and implications of patent law in the field of biotechnology and genetic engineering* COM(2005) 312 final.

human/primate gene sequences (Germany). There was also the economic question of whether it would be more valuable to society to allow the first inventor a broad scope of protection, with the result that others building on the invention would have to seek a licence, or to provide that a patent on a gene sequence would be limited in scope to allow future uses of such sequences to be patented freely. Since economic data were scarce, the Commission launched a study analysing the extent of human DNA patenting in Europe and its potential consequences on research and innovation.[399] Given this background, the Commission was not willing to take a position on the validity of transposition of the Directive on the basis of either classical or limited scope of protection for gene sequences. The Commission will, nonetheless, continue to monitor the situation, watching in particular for any economic consequences of possible divergences between member states' legislation. With respect to the patenting of stem cells, the Commission concluded that totipotent stem cells should not be patentable, on grounds of human dignity. However, it was considered inappropriate to come to a definitive conclusion on the question of the patentability of embryonic pluripotent stem cells. In the light of the clear divergences which currently exist between member states as regards the acceptability of research relating to embryonic stem cells, the continuing and rapid developments in this field, and the fact that the Directive itself provides for member states to refuse patents on grounds of *ordre public* or morality under Article 6(1), the Commission considered it premature to give further definition or provide for further harmonisation in this area. The Commission will continue to monitor developments in this area.

3.3.3.4 Utility models

Given that it is difficult to secure patent protection, because the conditions are onerous, some countries offer a lesser form of protection for certain inventions. These may be called petty patents, utility models, or some similar name. Usually there is no substantive examination of validity before grant, and the term is shorter than that of a patent. Some member states do not offer this form of protection at all. Such national schemes as there are vary considerably, particularly as to subject matter covered, and as to requirements for novelty and inventive step. Usually the aim is to provide for a threshold of inventiveness lower than that of patentability. Although attractive in theory, and useful in limited areas (such as technical design), such schemes have drawbacks. For example, the fact that the right is unexamined may lead to unjustified protection, and the differing standards of novelty may introduce confusion into the patent field.

---

[399]   *The Patenting of Human DNA: Global trends in commercial and public sector activity*: available at http://www.sussex.ac.uk/spru/1-4-14-1.html.

Given these national divergences, it is not surprising that the Commission was interested in harmonising such rights. In 1995 the Commission presented a Green Paper on the protection of utility models, and in 1997 it proposed a Directive. It argued that a harmonised system would improve the free movement of goods and prevent distortions of competition, making life easier for SMEs in particular.[400] The proposal was to grant utility models for any inventions which were susceptible of industrial application, new, and involved an inventive step. The applicant would have to show that, compared with the state of the art, the invention exhibited either: (a) particular effectiveness in terms of, for example, ease of application or use; or (b) a practical or industrial advantage. It would have been granted without examination, and would have lasted for no more than ten years. Although the European Parliament approved the broad outlines for the proposal, it suggested a number of significant amendments. The exchange of views served only to highlight fundamental concerns and differences of opinion, and the proposal made no significant progress.[401]

3.4 PLANT VARIETY RIGHTS

3.4.1 History of Protection

Plant variety rights (PVRs) are intellectual property rights granted to the breeder of a new variety of plant. Such varieties may be valuable for a number of reasons: increased yields, improved resistance to pests and diseases, or simply because they add to the range available. Breeding a new variety is skilled work, which is time consuming and costly. But once disclosed to the public, a new variety may be easily reproduced.

One famous pioneering agricultural scientist was the American, Luther Burbank. Inspired by Charles Darwin's, *The Variation of Animals and Plants under Domestication*, the 21-year-old Burbank bought a 17-acre plot of land

---

[400] *Proposal for a European Parliament and Council Directive approximating the legal arrangements for the protection of inventions by utility model* (12 December 1995).

[401] See *Amended proposal for a European Parliament and Council Directive approximating the legal arrangements for the protection of inventions by utility model* (12 July 1999) COM(1999) 309 final; Commission staff working paper, *Consultations on the impact of the Community utility model in order to update the Green Paper on the Protection of Utility Models in the Single Market (COM(95)370 final)* (26 July 2001) SEC(2001) 1307; *Summary report of replies to the questionnaire on the impact of the Community utility model with a view to updating the Green Paper on protection by the utility model in the internal market* (SEC(2001)1307) (1 March 2002).

in California and began to experiment. Using crossbreeding of foreign and native strains, painstaking cultivation techniques, and grafting, he sought to produce new and better breeds. In over 50 years of plant breeding, Burbank introduced more than 800 new varieties of plants, including over 200 varieties of fruits, many vegetables, nuts and grains, and hundreds of ornamental flowers. Still-famous names include the 'Shasta' daisy, July Elberta peach, Santa Rosa plum and Flaming Gold nectarine. His greatest success was the Russet Burbank potato (1871), better known as the 'Idaho' potato, which was introduced into Ireland to help combat the effects of the devastating potato blight of 1840–60. Burbank sold the rights to this for $150. These achievements, and Burbank's vision expressed in his book *How Plants Are Trained to Work for Man* (1921), inspired the US Plant Patent Act of 1930, which amended patent law to permit the patenting of new varieties of plants. The American inventor Thomas Edison observed that 'nothing that Congress could do to help farming would be of greater value and permanence than to give to the plant breeder the same status as the mechanical and chemical inventors now have through the law'.[402] It was realised that without protection, plant breeders had no financial incentive to experiment in search of improved varieties. Burbank himself was awarded 16 plant patents posthumously.

The question of whether patent protection is the appropriate method of protecting plant breeders is a contested one.[403] Plant breeding was regarded by many as outside the natural remit of patent law, being agricultural and artistic rather than scientific.[404] Now, of course, advances in genetic knowledge have

---

[402]   S.Rep. No. 315, 71st Cong., 2d Sess. 3 (1930) (Senate Report). Quoted in *Imazio Nursery, Inc.* v. *Dania Greenhouses* 69 F.3d 1560, C.A.Fed. (Cal.), 1995. See also Cary Fowler, 'The Plant Patent Act of 1930: A Sociological History of its Creation' 82 (2000) *Journal of the Patent & Trademark Office Society* 621–44.

[403]   For the underlying debate see Andrew Christie, 'Patents for Plant Innovation' [1989] *EIPR* 394–408; Stephen Crespi, 'Patents and Plant Variety Rights: Is there an Interface Problem?' 23 (1992) *IIC* 168–84; Natalie M. Derzko, 'Plant Breeders' Rights in Canada and Abroad: What are these Rights and How Much Must Society Pay for Them?' 39 (1993–4) *McGill Law Journal* 144–78; Tim Roberts, 'Patenting Plants around the World' [1996] *EIPR* 531–6; Joshua V. Funder, 'Rethinking Patents for Plant Innovation' [1999] *EIPR* 551–77; Matthew Rimmer, 'Franklin Barley: Patent Law and Plant Breeders' Rights' (December 2003) 10(4) *Murdock University Electronic Journal of Law*: http://www.murdoch.edu.au/elaw/issues/v10n4/rimmer104.html; William Kingston, 'Repairing Incentives to Invest in Plant Breeding' [2007] *IPQ* 294–311. One particularly thoughtful study is Dan Leskien and Michael Flitner, 'Intellectual Property Rights and Plant Genetic Resources: Options for a *Sui Generis* System' (June 1997) *Issues in Genetic Resources* No. 6: available at http://www.bioversityinternational.org/Publications/Pdf/497.pdf.

[404]   Paolo Palladino, 'Science, Technology, and the Economy: Plant Breeding in Great Britain, 1920–1970' 49 (1996) *Economic History Review* 116–36.

altered this situation significantly. Nevertheless, a major hurdle to the patenting of plant varieties is that most breeds are obvious, and do not fulfil the criterion of inventiveness. There are also anxieties about the public interest. A case can therefore be made for a *sui generis* system.

3.4.2 The UPOV Convention

There is a history of formal international cooperation in the seed and plant-breeding industries. The first International Seed Congress, which led to the establishment of the International Seed Trade Federation (*FIS*; the French acronym for *Fédération Internationale du Commerce des Semences*), was held in London in 1924. Further *FIS* congresses followed, and helped to establish strong links within the seed industry, and an agreed system of Rules and Usages for the Trade in Seeds for Sowing Purposes. *ASSINSEL*, the International Association of Plant Breeders for the Protection of Plant Varieties (*Association Internationale des Sélectionneurs pour la Protection de Obentions Végétales*) was established in 1938. Its main objective was the adoption of an international convention for the protection of new varieties of plants.[405] An international diplomatic conference to consider the protection of plant varieties was held in France in 1957, which led to the formation of UPOV.[406] Its mission is 'to provide and promote an effective system of plant variety protection, with the aim of encouraging the development of new varieties of plants, for the benefit of society'. The UPOV Convention was signed in Paris in 1961.[407]

The purpose of the UPOV Convention is to ensure that the members of the Union acknowledge the achievements of breeders of new varieties of plants, by granting to them an intellectual property right, on the basis of a set of clearly defined principles. To be eligible for protection, varieties have to be distinct from existing, commonly known varieties, sufficiently uniform, stable and new in the sense that they must not have been commercialised prior to

---

[405] *FIS* and *ASSINSEL* merged in 2002 to become ISF, the International Seed Federation. For more see: http://www.worldseed.org/en-us/international_seed/ history. html.

[406] The International Union for the Protection of New Varieties of Plants, known as 'UPOV' (*Union internationale pour la protection des obtentions végétales*). It is an intergovernmental organization with headquarters in Geneva. See: http:// www.upov.int/export/sites/upov/en/about/pdf/pub437.pdf.

[407] The Convention entered into force in 1968. It was revised in Geneva in 1972, 1978 and 1991. The 1991 Act entered into force on 24 April 1998. There were 65 members of UPOV as of April 2008. For more detail on UPOV's early history see UPOV, *The First Twenty-Five Years of the International Convention for the Protection of New Varieties of Plants* (1986).

certain dates established by reference to the date of the application for protection.[408] Member states are required to 'grant and protect breeders' rights'.[409] The Convention is based on the principle of national treatment.[410] An application in any member state gives a 12-month right of priority in the others.[411] The 1991 Act of the UPOV Convention does not specify the form of the breeder's right, which may therefore be a *sui generis* breeder's right, or may be called a 'patent' (or anything else) as long as it fulfils the minimum requirements of the Convention. The 1991 Act no longer contains the so-called 'ban on double protection', leaving member states free to offer additional protection, such as patents.[412] The Convention sets out a minimum scope of protection and offers members the possibility of taking national or regional circumstances into account in their legislation. It also defines acts concerning propagating material in relation to which the holder's authorisation is required.[413] There are important exceptions to the breeder's right, which does not cover acts done privately and for non-commercial purposes, acts done for experimental purposes and acts done for the purpose of breeding other varieties.[414] But member states may not restrict the exercise of the breeder's right once granted unless it is in the public interest to do so.[415] The minimum period of protection is 25 years for trees and vines, and 20 years for all other species.[416]

Member states are thus required to adopt legislation consistent with their obligations under the Convention. The UK, for example, enacted the Plant Variety and Seeds Act 1964. The TRIPS Agreement requires its member states to provide for the protection of plant varieties 'either by patents or by an effective *sui generis* system or by any combination thereof'.[417] Because the UPOV Convention has become the most widely recognised system for plant variety protection, most countries discharge their TRIPS obligation by

---

[408]   UPOV, Arts. 5–9. For text see http://www.upov.int/en/publications/conventions/1991/act1991.htm. For commentary on the 1991 Act see Barry Greengrass, 'The 1991 Act of the UPOV Convention' [1991] *EIPR* 466–72. See also Margaret Llewelyn, 'The Legal Protection of Biotechnological Inventions: An Alternative Approach' [1997] *EIPR* 115–27.

[409]   UPOV, Art. 2.

[410]   UPOV, Art. 4.

[411]   UPOV, Art. 11.

[412]   For example, both the US and Australia currently offer both breeders' rights and patent protection for plants. Overlaps in protection are resolved in the relevant jurisdiction, and not by UPOV.

[413]   UPOV, Art. 14.

[414]   UPOV, Art. 15.

[415]   UPOV, Art. 17(1).

[416]   UPOV, Art. 19.

[417]   TRIPS, Art. 27(3)(b).

adopting legislation which is compliant with it.[418] Since 1994 there has been a system for the protection of plant variety rights within the European Community.

3.4.3   The Community Plant Variety Right

The Community Plant Variety Regulation (CPVR) creates a Community plant variety right.[419] This is a unitary right which has uniform effect throughout the Community.[420] Cumulative national protection is prohibited: any variety which is the subject matter of a Community plant variety right may not enjoy either national plant variety right protection, or patent protection.[421] However, member states remain free to offer parallel national protection systems as an alternative, and most do so.[422] The Community scheme, which is based on a process of registration, is administered by the Community Plant Variety Office (CPVO) in Angers, France. In 2006, the CVPO received 2,735 applications for Community plant variety protection.[423]

Procedure
The first step is to file an application for protection either directly through the CPVO or through one of the national offices for transmission to the CPVO. An application for a Community plant variety right may be filed by any natural or legal person, or any body ranking as a legal person under the law applicable

---

[418]   For the particular problems faced by developing countries, see S.K. Verma, 'TRIPs and Plant Variety Protection in Developing Countries' [1995] *EIPR* 281–9. For anxiety concerning inappropriate harmonisation, see Enrico Bonadio, 'Crop Breeding and Intellectual Property in the Global Village' [2007] *EIPR* 167–71. For wider criticism, see P.R. Mooney, *Seeds of the Earth: A Private or Public Resource?* (Ottawa: Inter Pares, 1979).

[419]   Regulation 2100/94 on Community plant variety rights (CPVR) [1994] OJ L 227/1. For detailed reference see Gert Würtenberger, Paul van der Kooij, Bart Kiewiet and Martin Ekvad, *European Community Plant Variety Protection* (Oxford: Oxford University Press, 2006); Margaret Llewelyn and Mike Adcock, *European Plant Intellectual Property* (Oxford: Hart Publishing, 2006).

[420]   CPVR, Art. 2.

[421]   CPVR, Art. 92(1).

[422]   For the argument that national legislation should itself be harmonised, see Paul van der Kooij, 'Towards an EC Directive on Plant Breeder's Rights' [2008] *JIPL&P* 97–101.

[423]   CPVO Annual Report 2006, 8.1. The number of applications has remained relatively stable for a number of years. Although applications have been received from over 50 countries, more than one third of all applications received have originated from the Netherlands, and the top ten countries account for over 90% of applications.

to that body. Joint applications are permissible.[424] Varieties of all botanical genera and species, including, *inter alia*, hybrids between genera or species, may form the object of Community plant variety rights.[425] A 'variety' is defined as a plant grouping within a single botanical taxon of the lowest known rank, which grouping can be: defined by the expression of the characteristics that results from a given genotype or combination of genotypes; distinguished from any other plant grouping by the expression of at least one of the said characteristics, and; considered as a unit with regard to its suitability for being propagated unchanged.[426] The application must identify the botanical taxon, which must be of the lowest rank. This is to prevent claims for higher groupings in the taxonomical classification system (such as species), which are not protectable.[427]

The application must identify the applicant(s), give the name of the breeder, and give an assurance that, to the best of the applicant's knowledge, no one else has been involved in the breeding, or discovery and development, of the variety. If the applicant is not the breeder, documentary evidence must be provided showing entitlement to the Community plant variety right. The applicant must also give a provisional designation for the variety, a technical description of the variety, the geographic origin of the variety, details of any previous commercialisation of the variety, and details of any other application made in respect of the variety. Colour photographs are required for varieties of all fruit and ornamental species. A name must be proposed for the variety.[428] A formal examination of application follows, to see if it complies with these rules, whether any claim for priority is justified, and whether the relevant fees have been paid.[429]

---

[424]   CPVR, Art. 12. The rules have recently been simplified, to make the CPVR equally accessible to all: Council Regulation 15/2008 amending Regulation 2100/94 as regards the entitlement to file an application for a Community plant variety right [2008] OJ L 8/2.

[425]   CPVR, Art. 5(1).

[426]   CPVR, Art. 5(2).

[427]   Every individual plant is treated as belonging to an indefinite number of taxa of consecutively subordinate rank, among which the rank of species is basic. The principal ranks of taxa in descending sequence are: kingdom, division or phylum, class, order, family, genus and species: International Code of Botanical Nomenclature (Vienna Code 2006).

[428]   CPVR, Art. 50. See also Regulation 1239/95 establishing implementing rules for the application of Council Regulation (EC) No. 2100/94 as regards proceedings before the Community Plant Variety Office [1995] OJ L 121/37.

[429]   CPVR, Art. 53. The application fee is currently €900. Examination fees must be paid for each growing period, and vary from €1,020 to €2,380, depending on the type of crop. Annual renewal fees are €200 per variety. See Regulation 1238/95 establishing implementing rules for the application of Council Regulation (EC) No. 2100/94 as regards the fees payable to the Community Plant Variety Office [1995] OJ L 121/31.

Next comes the substantive examination. The CPVO examines whether the subject of the application fulfils the criteria for protection: whether it is a 'variety' according to the definition in Article 5; whether it is 'new' as required by Article 10, and whether the applicant is entitled to apply for a Community plant variety right.[430] The Office also determines whether the proposed variety denomination is 'suitable', according to a wide range of criteria. Obstacles include relevant prior rights, difficulties with user recognition, confusion with other variety denominations or commonly used designations, and denominations which are likely to mislead.[431]

Once a variety is protected, the designated variety denomination must always be used when variety constituents are offered or disposed of for commercial purposes. This requirement applies even after the termination of the Community plant variety right.[432]

The next step is the technical examination. The aim of this is to verify that the variety is distinct from others, uniform in its characteristics and stable in the long run – the so-called 'DUS' requirements.[433] The applicant must submit samples of propagating material which the CPVO can use to test these requirements by planting and growing the variety.[434] The work is normally carried out by designated examination offices all over the world. The decision as to where the examination of an individual variety will take place depends on the applicant's location, the variety's geographical origin, and the practical experience and completeness of the reference collection of a possible examination office in relation to the species to be tested. The decision is a matter entirely for the CPVO. The duration of the examination varies from one year for most ornamental species to six years for certain fruit tree varieties. The proposed variety denomination is also examined at this point.[435] Once the CPVO considers that the examination results are satisfactory and that all the other requirements have been fulfilled, it grants a Community plant variety right for a period of 25 years, and up to 30 years for vines, potatoes and trees.[436]

---

[430]   CPVR, Art. 54.
[431]   CPVR, Art. 63.
[432]   CPVR, Art. 17.
[433]   CPVR, Art. 55.
[434]   The Office determines, through general rules or through requests in individual cases, when, where and in what quantities and qualities the material for the technical examination and reference samples are to be submitted. More information about the submission of plant material is available on the CPVO web site: http://www.cpvo.europa.eu.
[435]   For more detail see CPVO *Notes for Applicants*: http://www.cpvo.europa.eu/documents/infodd/Notes_for_applicants_EN_2007.pdf. A list of examination offices is available in the CPVO Annual Report.
[436]   CPVR, Art. 19; Regulation 2470/96 providing for an extension of the terms of a Community plant variety right in respect of potatoes [1996] OJ L 335/10.

Criteria for validity

As has been explained, the variety must be 'new', and must fulfil the so-called DUS criteria (distinct, uniform, stable).[437]

Novelty The criteria for novelty in a plant variety are far less taxing than those applied in patent law. A variety is 'new' if variety constituents or harvested material of the variety have not been sold or otherwise disposed of within the Community earlier than one year prior to the application date. Sale or disposal outside the Community also has the potential to destroy novelty, but the time period is more generous. In these cases, a variety is still new if there is no sale or disposal earlier than four years prior to the application date (six years in the case of trees or vines).[438] This is a substantial period during which the plant breeder can prepare for potential commercial exploitation, without having to apply for a plant variety right. Note that only sale and disposal are destructive of novelty. Thus, mere use – by growing a plant, for instance – would not affect novelty. Similarly, the disposal of variety constituents to an official body for statutory purposes, or to others on the basis of a contractual or other legal relationship solely for production, reproduction, multiplication, conditioning or storage, is not regarded as a 'disposal', provided that the breeder preserves the exclusive right of disposal, and no further disposal is made.[439] Note also that only sale or disposal 'by or with the consent of the breeder' will destroy novelty.[440] Thus, acts of third parties who have independently developed the variety will not affect novelty for these purposes. The first to apply will be given the right.

Distinct, uniform and stable A variety is 'distinct' if it is 'clearly distinguishable by reference to the expression of the characteristics that results from a particular genotype or combination of genotypes, from any other variety whose existence is a matter of common knowledge on the date of application'.[441] For example, distinctiveness may arise from differences in character-

---

[437] CPVR, Art. 6. the *UPOV General Introduction to the Examination of Distinctness, Uniformity and Stability and the Development of Harmonised Descriptions of New Varieties of Plants* (and references therein) offers more detailed explanations of how the DUS criteria may be applied. Available at: http://www.upov.int/en/publications/tg-rom/tg001/tg_1_3.pdf.

[438] CPVR, Art. 10(1).

[439] CPVR, Art. 10(2). See also CPVR, Art. 10(3).

[440] CPVR, Art. 10(1).

[441] CPVR, Art. 7 (1). The existence of another variety is deemed to be a matter of common knowledge if it is the object of a plant variety right in the Community or any state, or in any intergovernmental organisation with relevant competence. Other examples are also possible. CPVR, Art. 7(2).

istics such as shape or structure, resistance to disease or particular climatic conditions.

A variety is 'uniform' if, 'subject to the variation that may be expected from the particular features of its propagation, it is sufficiently uniform in the expression of those characteristics which are included in the examination for distinctness, as well as any others used for the variety description'.[442] The idea here is that nearly all the examples of the variety should bear the characteristics that make the plant distinctive, without deviant strains.

A variety is 'stable' if 'the expression of the characteristics which are included in the examination for distinctness as well as any others used for the variety description, remain unchanged after repeated propagation or, in the case of a particular cycle of propagation, at the end of each such cycle'.[443] Again, the idea is that even subsequent generations of the variety should retain the characteristics that make the plant distinctive.

A Community plant variety right may be declared null and void by the CVPO if it is established that at the time of grant these conditions were not met, or if the right has been granted to a person who is not entitled to it.[444] The right may be cancelled if the variety is no longer uniform or stable.[445]

The effects of Community plant variety rights

The holder of a Community plant variety right has rights in relation both to variety constituents, and harvested material of the protected variety. Variety constituents are entire plants or parts of plants capable of producing entire plants – in other words, propagating material such as seeds, bulbs, rhizomes, grafts and so on. Acts of production or reproduction (multiplication), conditioning for the purpose of propagation, offering for sale, selling or other marketing, exporting from the Community, importing to the Community and stocking for any of these purposes, all require the authorisation of the holder.[446] These rights apply in respect of harvested material only if this was obtained through the unauthorised use of variety constituents of the protected variety, and unless the holder has had reasonable opportunity to exercise his right in relation to these variety constituents.[447] The Community plant variety right extends to varieties which are essentially derived from the protected vari-

---

442   CPVR, Art. 8.
443   CPVR, Art. 9.
444   CPVR, Art. 20(1).
445   CPVR, Art. 21(1). Failure to pay renewal fees is also a ground for cancellation.
446   CPVR, Art. 13(2).
447   CPVR, Art. 13(3).

ety, varieties which are not distinct from the protected variety; and varieties whose production requires the repeated use of the protected variety.[448]

Community plant variety rights are circumscribed in various important ways. They do not extend to acts done privately and for non-commercial purposes; acts done for experimental purposes; or acts done for the purpose of breeding, or discovering and developing other varieties.[449] They may not be exercised in a way which violates any provisions adopted on the grounds of public morality, public policy or public security, the protection of health and life of humans, animals or plants, the protection of the environment, the protection of industrial or commercial property, or the safeguarding of competition, of trade or of agricultural production.[450] The Community plant variety right is exhausted when protected material is 'disposed of to others by the holder or with his consent, in any part of the Community'.[451]

There is also a special derogation intended to safeguard agricultural production. This is known as the 'farm saved seed' derogation. For certain specific varieties, even though they are protected by Community plant variety rights, farmers may use 'in the field, on their own holding' the product of the harvest which they have obtained by planting that variety.[452] The list includes fodder plants such as field pea, common vetch and Persian clover; cereals such as oats, barley, rice and rye; potatoes; and oil/fibre plants such as rape.[453] Implementing rules safeguard the legitimate interests of the breeder and of the farmer. Small farmers are not required to pay the holder of the right, whereas other farmers are required to pay an equitable remuneration.[454]

Compulsory exploitation rights may be granted by the CPVO in respect of Community plant variety rights, but only on grounds of public interest and after consulting the Administrative Council. The right holder's interests must be taken into account, and reasonable conditions (such as the payment of an appropriate royalty as equitable remuneration to the holder) may be imposed. Member states may not grant such rights.[455]

---

[448] CPVR, Art. 13(5).

[449] CPVR, Art. 15(1).

[450] CPVR, Art. 13(8).

[451] CPVR, Art. 16.

[452] CPVR, Art. 14(1).

[453] CPVR, Art. 14(2).

[454] CPVR, Art. 14(3). See also Regulation 1768/95 implementing rules on the agricultural exemption provided for in Article 14(3) of Council Regulation (EC) No. 2100/94 on Community plant variety rights [1995] OJ L 173/14. The levels of remuneration were considered by the ECJ in Joined Cases C-7/05 to C-9/05, *Saatgut-Treuhandverwaltungs GmbH* v. *Ulrich Deppe (et al.)* (8 June 2006).

[455] CPVR, Art. 29.

4. Designs

4.1 INTRODUCTION – THE CONCEPT OF DESIGN

'Design' is a term which refers to the appearance and composition of an article, and to any preliminary drawings or models used. It is a hugely important aspect of the way we choose to live our lives, though this can sometimes be unacknowledged and unappreciated. Design touches a vast range of fields, for example: product design, packaging design, web design, software design, graphic design, theatrical design, colour design, architectural design, automotive design, environmental design, fashion design, furniture design, garden design, industrial design, interior design, urban design. As a widely based concept, covering both playful and functional designs, it presents a challenge to intellectual property law. How should such things be protected, if at all? If a design can be thought of as a work of art, then copyright protection is perhaps appropriate. But design protection is also demanded for industrial products, especially the aspects of shape and pattern which make them distinctive. If an item is mass-produced, should the designer or manufacturer be able to prevent others from producing a similar design? Should it make a difference whether the design has been copied or arrived at independently? And what sort of protection is appropriate?

One problem is that it may be difficult to separate the functional and the aesthetic aspects of a design. If something is entirely functional, like a petrol engine, but not sufficiently inventive to justify a patent, there is little reason for granting monopoly rights over it. But as soon as decorative additions turn an engine into a car, customers will start to consider appearance and design, in addition to the performance of the engine. The design features may or may not be intended for aesthetic purposes. The shape of car bodies will be determined partly with aerodynamics in mind, and partly with an eye to what the consumer will want. Consumers have grown more and more aware of design over recent decades, and style may well be the dominant factor in the purchase of basically functional articles such as furniture and lighting. As a result, manufacturers spend huge amounts of time and effort in deciding on design features, and it is this that leads to demands for their protection.

A number of forms of intellectual property have been used to protect designs, as well as a variety of specific design regimes. The difficulty is the breadth of the field, which results in a complex pattern of protection, and potential overlaps. Patent protection may be available if a new invention necessarily incorporates a particular design, although this is rare. Trade mark registration may cover distinctive shapes. Passing off and breach of confidence are also possibilities, in the right circumstances. Copyright protection, never intended to protect design features of mass-produced items, has been an important method of protection, particularly where designs are reproduced from drawings. Since copyright arises automatically, and lasts for a long time, the interface with design protection has to be considered. Specific design protection has a considerable history. In Britain, the Calico Printers' Act was passed in 1787, giving two months' protection to new and original patterns. Registered design protection for certain types of designs followed in the nineteenth century, co-existing with unregistered protection for other types of designs.[1] Other countries pursued their own approaches. The same arguments recurred as to the appropriate types of protection for useful and aesthetic designs, and for ornamental and functional designs. Fundamental philosophical differences ensured that there was little agreement as to the appropriate boundaries (or overlap) with copyright, or with patent, even where *sui generis* design systems were adopted.[2] International consensus was therefore very limited. The Paris Convention did not require members to protect industrial designs until the Lisbon revision of 1958, and left the mechanism of protection open, so copyright and unfair competition law could be used. The present text still contains no requirement that registered design protection be offered, although national treatment and priority periods are addressed.[3] The 1908 Berlin revision of the Berne Convention was the first to mention 'applied art', but did not grant it full protection as literary property. Berne Union members are still free to determine both the scope of protection for applied art and industrial designs and models, and any necessary formalities.[4]

4.2 FIRST STEPS TOWARDS EC HARMONISATION

This lack of consensus caused obvious difficulties for the EC. The fact that national laws had not been harmonised was noted in the early cases involving

---

[1] See Brad Sherman and Lionel Bently, *The Making of Modern Intellectual Property Law* (Cambridge: Cambridge University Press, 1999), 63–94.

[2] For more detail see J.H. Reichman, 'Design Protection in Domestic and Foreign Copyright Law: From the Berne Revision of 1948 to the Copyright Act of 1976' [1983] *Duke Law Journal* 1143–264.

[3] Paris Convention, Art. 2 (national treatment), Art. 4C(1) (priority periods).

[4] Art. 2(7). By Art. 7(4) the minimum term of protection is 25 years.

designs, and necessarily had an impact on the free movement of goods.[5] In 1991, the Commission published a Green Paper, with associated draft legislation.[6] It proposed a Community Design system, to include both registered and unregistered protection (requiring a Regulation). Additionally, it proposed that national designs would be harmonised, to some extent (requiring a Directive).[7] The aim was to find a middle way between the so-called 'patent' and 'copyright' approaches seen in national laws. The 'patent' approach involves registration, perhaps pre-examination, and offers a degree of legal certainty. The 'copyright' approach does not require formalities or fees, and is argued to be more designer-friendly as a result. The Green Paper instead laid out a scheme specifically tailored to designs.[8] After extensive consultation with interested parties, from both industry and practice, redrafts of both the Directive and the Regulation were produced.[9] The legislative process did not run smoothly, and the European Parliament suggested many amendments, which were incorporated in a further Proposal in 1996.[10] Although there were many points of dispute, the single most controversial issue was the appropriate protection for spare parts for cars. It proved impossible to reach agreement, and the Directive side-stepped the issue by establishing a 'stand-still' clause for spare parts, coupled with a commitment to a consultation exercise.

The Directive was adopted in July 1998.[11] It aims to 'approximate' the design protection laws of the member states, particularly those which most directly affect the functioning of the internal market.[12] The Directive therefore

---

    5   Case 144/81, *Keurkoop BV* v. *Nancy Kean Gifts BV* [1982] ECR 2853; Case 238/87, *Volvo AB* v. *Erik Veng (UK) Ltd* [1988] ECR 6211; Case 53/87, *Consorzio Italiano della Componentistica di Ricambio per Autoveicoli (CICRA) and Maxicar* v. *Régie Nationale des Usines Renault* [1988] ECR 6039.
    6   Green Paper on the Legal Protection of Industrial Design (June 1991) III/F/5131/91-EN.
    7   For further details see Audrey A. Horton, 'Industrial Design Law: The Future for Europe' [1991] *EIPR* 442–8. See also W.R. Cornish, 'Designs Again' [1991] *EIPR* 3–4.
    8   Herman M.H. Speyart, 'The Grand Design: An Update on the E.C. Design Proposals Following the Adoption of a Common Position on the Directive' [1997] *EIPR* 603–12, 605.
    9   See Audrey A. Horton, 'European Design Law and the Spare Parts Dilemma: The Proposed Regulation and Directive' [1994] *EIPR* 51–7; F.K. Beier, 'Protection for Spare Parts in the Proposal for a European Designs Law' (1994) 25 *IIC* 840.
    10   [1996] OJ C 142/5 (published with an explanatory memorandum as COM(96) 66 final, 21 February 1996).
    11   Directive 98/71 on the legal protection of designs ('Designs Dir.') [1998] OJ L 289/28. For more see Uma Suthersanen, *Design Law in Europe* (London: Sweet & Maxwell, 2000).
    12   Designs Dir., Recitals 1, 2, 3, 5.

harmonises the conditions for obtaining registration, the extent and term of protection, and the conditions for refusal or invalidation.[13] Provisions on sanctions, remedies and enforcement are left to national law, leaving member states free to fix the procedural provisions concerning registration, renewal and invalidation of design rights, and provisions concerning the effects of such invalidity. Member states may provide for additional protection through other regimes, such as unregistered design rights, trade marks, patents and utility models, and unfair competition.[14] The principle of cumulation of protection is insisted upon, meaning that registered design protection cannot pre-empt copyright protection. However, member states are free to establish the extent of copyright protection and the conditions under which it is conferred.[15]

The Regulation followed in December 2001.[16] The Recitals note the negative effect on competition of the wide variety of national design systems, and acknowledge the Directive's contribution to harmonising these. However, even approximated national laws divide the internal market. The better solution for these purposes is to have a single unitary design right, applicable throughout the Community.[17] It is also thought that enhanced protection for industrial design will encourage innovation and development of new products and investment in their production.[18] Nevertheless, in the absence of complete harmonisation, the principle of cumulation of protection remains (as in the Directive), leaving member states free to establish the extent and conditions of copyright protection.[19] The Regulation therefore established a Community-wide scheme of design protection, including both the Registered Community Design, and the Unregistered Community Design.[20] In both cases, eligible designs must be new and must have an individual character. Under the Registered Community Design (RCD) system, holders of eligible designs can register them with the Office for Harmonisation in the Internal Market (OHIM). There is no substantive examination procedure, to minimise

---

13 Designs Dir., Recitals 9, 10, 17, 21.
14 Designs Dir., Recitals 5, 6, 7.
15 Designs Dir., Recital 8, Art. 17. This failure to harmonise copyright protection for designs has been rightly criticised. Lionel Bently, 'The Shape of Things to Come: European Design Law', in Paul Coughlan (ed.), *European Initiatives in Intellectual Property Law: Papers from the I.C.E.L. Conference, November 1992* (Dublin: Irish Centre for European Law, Trinity College, 1993), 63, 86–7.
16 Regulation 6/2002 on Community designs ('CDR') [2002] OJ L/1.
17 CDR, Recitals 3, 4, 5.
18 CDR, Recital 7.
19 CDR, Recital 32, Art. 96(2).
20 The substantive provisions of the Regulation are aligned with the respective provisions in the Directive: CDR, Recital 9.

procedural burdens.[21] The Regulation confers exclusive rights to use the design concerned and to prevent any third party from using it within the European Union, for a period of up to 25 years. A Registered Community Design is protected against both deliberate copying and the independent development of a similar design. The validity of such designs may be challenged either in proceedings at OHIM, or in infringement proceedings in national courts. The Unregistered Community Design (UCD) offers short-term protection, for three years from the date of disclosure of designs to the public within the EU. That disclosure may occur through designs going on sale or through prior marketing or publicity. The relevant designs will be protected for three years. A UCD is protected only against deliberate copying.[22] OHIM began registering designs on 1 April 2003, and the UCD has been available since 7 March 2002. Since 2003 OHIM has received over 65,000 applications to register over a quarter of a million new designs.

The EU has now acceded to the Geneva Act of the Hague Agreement concerning the international registration of industrial designs (effective 1 January 2008). This allows, with a single application at WIPO, protection of a design not only throughout the EU, but also in the countries which are members of the Geneva Act of the Hague Agreement.[23] Instead of making a number of national or regional registrations, each with separate fees, numbers and renewal dates, the design owner may make one application, in a single language, with a single fee, giving a single registration valid for several territories.

4.3   REGISTERED COMMUNITY DESIGN

There are a number of advantages to registration. It offers the certainty of a formal filing date, which will establish priority over later designs. The Registered Community Design (RCD) gives a right to prevent even designs which were independently created, and lasts for a significantly longer period than the Unregistered Community Design (UCD). The decision to register will often be a practical matter, and may well depend on industry norms. If design fashions change rapidly and a short market life is predicted (clothes, shoes,

---

[21]   CDR, Recitals 18, 24.

[22]   See also Victor M. Saez, 'The Unregistered Community Design' [2002] *EIPR* 585–90.

[23]   Various preparations were required, including updating OHIM's IT systems to handle Hague Agreement filings. The Implementing Rules are in Regulation 876/2007 [2007] OJ L 193/13, and amendments to the Fee Regulation are in Regulation 877/2007 [2007] OJ L 193/16.

cosmetics, for example), there may be no need to bother with registration. On the other hand, registration at OHIM is cheap and simple – and certainly is much less onerous than patent registration. One of the fundamental objectives of the CDR is that the registration of Community designs should present the minimum cost and difficulty to applicants, so as to make it readily available to any applicant including small and medium-sized enterprises and individual designers.[24]

Application

An application for a Registered Community Design may be filed either at OHIM, or through one of the national offices.[25] It must contain a request for registration, the name and address of the applicant (and their representative, if any), a representation of the design, and an indication of the products in relation to which the design is intended to be used.[26] In addition, the application *may* contain an explanatory description, a request for deferment of publication, an indication of the design's intended classification, and a citation of the designer.[27] The examiner issues a notification of receipt without delay. If the application is complete, the notification may indicate that the Community design is accepted for registration. If the application is deficient in some way, these will be identified in an 'examination report' which may be included in the notification.[28] If the application does not contain the necessary information, it will not be accorded a filing date.[29]

The Regulation gives the designer the right 'to be cited as such before the Office and in the register'. If the design is the result of teamwork, the team may be cited.[30] Somewhat perplexingly, however, the implementing rules indicate that citation is in practice optional. The application *may* include a citation of the designer (or design team), or an indication that the right to be cited has been waived. Where neither a designer is cited nor a waiver of the right to be cited is indicated, no objection will be raised by the examiner.[31]

The representation

The representation of the design 'shall consist in a graphic or photographic

---

[24]   CDR, Recital 24.
[25]   CDR, Art. 35.
[26]   CDR, Art. 36; Examination Guidelines, Art. 11.
[27]   CDR, Art. 36(3); Regulation 2245/2002 implementing Regulation 6/2002 on Community designs ('CDIR') OJ L 341/28, Art. 1(2).
[28]   Examination Guidelines, Art. 3.2.
[29]   CDIR, Art. 10; Examination Guidelines, Art. 4.1.
[30]   CDR, Art. 18.
[31]   CDR, Art. 36(3)(e); CDIR, Art. 1(2)(d); Examination Guidelines, Art. 11.3.

reproduction of the design, either in black and white or in colour'.[32] So, drawings, photographs (except slides), computer-made representations or any other graphical representation are accepted, provided they are suitable for reproduction.[33] The representation must meet various size and presentational requirements. It should cover only one design. It may contain no more than seven different 'views' of that design.[34] It is the applicant's responsibility to submit a representation which includes a sufficient number of views to specify all the features of the design for which protection is sought. The examiner will not check whether the design has other features not shown in the views as submitted. Decisions as to the method of representing the design will affect the scope of protection. If a design is shown in colour, the colours are regarded as claimed. A simple drawing is likely to offer the widest protection. If a photo shows details such as the surface structure or material of the design, this will narrow the scope of protection. If many views are shown, again, this may limit protection.[35]

Where registration is sought for a design that consists of a repeating surface pattern, the representation of the design 'shall show the complete pattern and a sufficient portion of the repeating surface'.[36] If the application is for a design consisting of a 'typographic typeface', the representation of the design must include in a string all the letters of the alphabet (in both upper and lower case), all the arabic numerals and five lines of text.[37] The application may contain a single description per design (not exceeding 100 words) explaining the representation of the design or specimen. The description must relate only to those features which appear in the reproductions of the design, and must not contain statements regarding the design's purported novelty, individual character or technical value.[38] The description may be used to disclaim features shown in the representation, if these are also shown on the graphical representation.

Multiple applications

The Community Design Regulation allows for so-called 'multiple applications', in which several designs are combined in a single application. The intention is to make the system as accessible as possible to users, including those who produce large numbers of possibly short-lived designs, many of

---

32   CDIR, Art. 4(1).
33   Examination Guidelines, Art. 4.4.
34   CDIR, Art. 4(2); Examination Guidelines, Art. 11.4.
35   Martin Schlotelburg, 'The Community Design: First Experience with Registrations' [2003] *EIPR* 383–7.
36   CDIR, Art. 4(3); Examination Guidelines, Art. 11.5.
37   CDIR, Art. 4(4); Examination Guidelines, Art. 11.6.
38   CDIR, Art. 1(2)(a); CDR, Art. 36(3a); Examination Guidelines, Art. 9.2.

which perhaps will not be commercialised. Although in such cases unregistered Community design offers a solution, the multiple applications facility offers readier access to registration.[39] This route is also cheaper, since only the first design is subject to the full fee. The designs must be intended to be applied to products within the same class of the Locarno Convention, unless the design is ornamentation.[40] The number of designs contained in a multiple application is not limited.[41] A representation of *each* design, and an indication of the product to which it is to be applied, are required. After filing, each design in a multiple application constitutes a right on its own and may be transferred or licensed (etc.) individually.[42]

Priority

Priority may be claimed on the basis of a previous (first) application of a design or utility model (but not on the basis of a patent application) filed in or for a state which is party to the Paris Convention or a member of the WTO. Priority can only be claimed where the application for a Community design is filed within six months from the date of filing of the first application(s). Priority may be claimed either simultaneously with the filing of the application, or within one month subsequent to the date of filing.[43]

Examination

The Office examines whether the application complies with the formal requirements for filing laid down in Article 36 (and Article 37, for multiple applications), and whether the requirements concerning the claim to priority are satisfied (if a priority is claimed).[44] There is no substantive examination as to compliance with the requirements for protection (subject matter, novelty, individual character, etc.). This is to minimise the procedural burden on applicants, and to reduce costs.[45] It is argued that examination is an expensive and difficult exercise, and that a design is best tested in *inter partes* proceedings, when both parties will have a genuine interest, suggesting that the design is of some significance and value. Nevertheless, the Office will refuse an application in two situations: firstly, where the subject matter of the application does

---

[39]   CDR, Art. 37 and Recital 25.
[40]   CDR, Art. 37(1); CDIR, Art. 2. 'Ornamentation is an additional and decorative element capable of being applied to the surface of a variety of products without significantly affecting their contours': Examination Guidelines, Art. 8.3.
[41]   Examination Guidelines, Art. 8.1.
[42]   CDR, Art. 37(4).
[43]   CDR, Arts. 41 and 42; CDIR, Art. 8; Examination Guidelines, Art. 10.
[44]   CDR, Art. 45. See also Examination Guidelines, Art. 14.
[45]   CDR, Recital 18.

not correspond to the definition of a design laid down in Article 3(a); secondly, where the design is contrary to public policy or accepted principles of morality. In these cases, the applicant will be given the opportunity of withdrawing or amending the application, or of submitting observations before the examiner takes a decision.[46] If all these requirements are satisfied, and the fees have been paid, the examiner will take the decision that a design can be registered and will enter the date of entry into the Register. The applicant will be informed accordingly.[47]

Publication

Unless an application contains a request for deferment of publication, publication in the Community Designs Bulletin takes place immediately after registration.[48] Deferment of publication may only be requested in the application, and results in a delay before publication of up to 30 months.[49] The Regulation provides for this facility, because 'the normal publication following registration of a Community design could in some cases destroy or jeopardize the success of a commercial operation involving the design'.[50] In such cases, the design is registered but neither the representation of the design, nor the indications of the products to which it will be applied, nor any file relating to the application is open to public inspection.[51] A mention of the deferment of publication is published in the Community Designs Bulletin, with information identifying the right holder, the date of filing and registration, and the file number of the application.[52] At the end of the deferment period (or earlier, at the request of the right holder), the register entries and file are opened to public inspection, and the design is published in the Community Designs Bulletin.[53] An additional fee is payable.[54]

Deferment of publication has consequences for the design's protection, however. Legal proceedings may only be brought if the information contained

---

[46]   Examination Guidelines, Art. 2.4, Art. 5.

[47]   Examination Guidelines, Art. 14.2.

[48]   CDR, Art. 49; CDIR, Art. 14; Examination Guidelines, Art. 16.

[49]   The period is 30 months from the date of filing the application or, if a priority is claimed, from the date of priority: CDR, Art. 50(1).

[50]   CDR, Recital 26.

[51]   CDR, Art. 50(2); Examination Guidelines, Art. 15.2. Third parties wishing to inspect the entire file may ask to do so if they have obtained the applicant's approval beforehand, or may do so without consent if they can establish a legitimate interest in doing so. A legitimate legal interest is established if the holder of the registered Community design has taken steps with a view to invoking the right against that third party: CDR, Art. 74(1)(2).

[52]   CDR, Art. 50(3); Examination Guidelines, Art. 15.2.

[53]   CDIR, Art. 16.

[54]   CDIR, Art. 15.

in the register and in the file relating to the application has been communicated to the person against whom the action is brought.[55]

4.4 THE COMMUNITY DEFINITION OF 'DESIGN'

As has been noted, unregistered and registered Community designs are subject to the same basic requirements for protection, although the regimes differ in other important respects. It is therefore important to understand the Community definition of 'design'.

Design

'Design' is defined as 'the appearance of the whole or a part of a product resulting from the features of, in particular, the lines, contours, colours, shape, texture and/or materials of the product itself and/or its ornamentation'.[56] This focus on appearance acts to exclude (for example) the idea behind the design, or the 'design concept'. Equally, there is no requirement that the design be either functional or aesthetic.[57] The list of characteristics is broad, and non-exhaustive, in an attempt to encompass the wide range of design activities undertaken. The references to 'texture' and 'materials' suggest that 'appearance' includes the tactile as well as the visual.

Product

A 'product' (referred to in the definition of 'design') is 'any industrial or handicraft item, including *inter alia* parts intended to be assembled into a complex product, packaging, get-up, graphic symbols and typographic typefaces, but excluding computer programs'.[58] Again, the definition is very broad. However, the borderlines may prove difficult to patrol. Is a painting a work of handicraft, or a work of art? Is a building an 'industrial or handicraft item'? Although computer programs are specifically excluded (being protectable by copyright), icons will be included (as 'graphic symbols'), and the position of user interfaces is uncertain.[59] The topographies of semiconductor chips fall within the definition, creating an overlap in protection with the Directive requiring *sui generis* protection for these.[60]

---

[55] CDR, Art. 50(6).
[56] Designs Dir., Art. 1(a); CDR, Art. 3(a).
[57] Designs Dir., Recital 14; CDR, Recital 10.
[58] Designs Dir., Art. 1(b); CDR, Art. 3(b).
[59] For discussion see Charles-Henry Massa and Alain Strowel, 'Community Design: Cinderella Revamped' [2003] *EIPR* 68–78. See also Annette Kur, 'Protection of Graphical User Interfaces under European Design Legislation' (2003) 34 *IIC* 50.
[60] Directive 87/54 on the legal protection of semiconductor chips OJ L 24/36.

Complex products

A 'complex product' is 'a product which is composed of multiple components which can be replaced permitting disassembly and reassembly of the product'.[61] Designs applied to a component part of a complex product must reach a higher threshold of protection.[62] These provisions were intended to address the controversial problem of spare parts for cars, and to limit their design protection. The definition is readily applied to cars, which are complex, and have a number of components, several of which are likely to need replacement during the life of the product. Whether the definition encompasses items such as flat-pack furniture is less clear, although it is unlikely that this was intended. It is also questionable whether consumable items, such as printer cartridges, fall to be regarded as 'components'.

Exclusions

This very broad definition of 'design' is subject to a number of important exceptions.

(a)　DESIGNS DICTATED BY THEIR TECHNICAL FUNCTION

A design right 'shall not subsist in features of appearance of a product which are solely dictated by its technical function'.[63] The aim is that technological innovation should not be hampered by granting design protection to features dictated solely by a technical function. It does not carry the implication that a design must have an aesthetic quality. Also, if features are dictated by technical function, this indicates that there has been no design input, and it is thus appropriate to exclude such features from design protection. Such features are not taken into consideration for the purpose of assessing whether other features of the design fulfil the requirements for protection (novelty, and individual character).[64] One outstanding question is when a feature is 'solely dictated' by its technical function. It seems likely that the exclusion was intended to apply only when there is no other way of performing that technical result (sometimes called the 'mandatory approach'). Thus, if it can be shown that alternative features perform the same technical result, then the feature is not 'solely dictated' by technical function, and all may be protected.

The regimes are not always consistent. For more, see Iris H-Yu Chiu and Will W. Shen, 'A *Sui Generis* Intellectual Property Right for Layout Designs on Printed Circuit Boards? An Analysis of Current Intellectual Property Laws and Proposal for Reform' [2006] *EIPR* 38–50.

61　Designs Dir., Art. 1(c); CDR, Art. 3(c).
62　Designs Dir., Art. 3(3) and Art. 14; CDR, Art. 4(2) and Art. 110.
63　Designs Dir., Art. 7(1); CDR, Art. 8(1).
64　Designs Dir., Recital 14; CDR, Recital 10.

This would mean that the exclusion will apply only rarely.[65] However, when interpreting a similar provision in trade mark law, the ECJ held that the provision 'is intended to preclude the registration of shapes whose essential characteristics perform a technical function, with the result that the exclusivity inherent in the trade mark right would limit the possibility of competitors supplying a product incorporating such a function or at least limit their freedom of choice in regard to the technical solution they wish to adopt in order to incorporate such a function in their product'. This means that if the essential functional characteristics of the shape of a product are attributable solely to the technical result, it may not be registered, even if that technical result can be achieved by other shapes. The interpretation of the provision in Community design law must ultimately be determined by the ECJ.

(b) DESIGNS OF INTERCONNECTIONS
Similarly, a design right 'shall not subsist in features of appearance of a product which must necessarily be reproduced in their exact form and dimensions in order to permit the product in which the design is incorporated or to which it is applied to be mechanically connected to or placed in, around or against another product so that either product may perform its function'.[66] The aim is that the interoperability of products of different makes should not be hindered by extending protection to the features which allow mechanical parts to fit together. Such protection might allow a manufacturer to restrict competition in secondary markets (for accessories, or consumables, for instance). As a result, such features are not taken into consideration for the purpose of assessing whether other features of the design fulfil the requirements for protection (novelty, and individual character).[67] The exception does not apply to 'modular systems': 'a design right shall . . . subsist in a design serving the purpose of allowing multiple assembly or connection of mutually interchangeable products within a modular system'.[68] The ostensible justification for this saving is that 'the mechanical fittings of modular products may nevertheless

---

[65] An alternative would be to apply the exclusion whenever the design has been created with purely functional considerations in mind (even if the function could be achieved another way), protecting the design only if any of its features were not prompted by the technical function required. This was the approach adopted by the UK House of Lords in *Amp* v. *Utilux Pty* [1972] *RPC* 103. But the mandatory approach was used in several other member states (for example, Benelux law, German law), and the Commission explicitly favoured this approach in the EC Green Paper (para. 5.4.6.2).

[66] Designs Dir., Art. 7(2); CDR, Art. 8(2). Considered and applied to invalidate a Community Design in *UES AG* v. *Nordson Corporation*, ICD 000002970, 20 November 2007.

[67] Designs Dir., Recital 14; CDR, Recital 10.

[68] Designs Dir., Art. 7(3); CDR, Art. 8(3).

constitute an important element of the innovative characteristics of modular products and present a major marketing asset, and therefore should be eligible for protection'.[69] It was added as a result of lobbying by the Danish government, in the hope of securing some continued protection for Lego bricks. Other construction sets would also be covered, as would more conventional products such as modular seating and shelving.

(c) DESIGNS CONTRARY TO PUBLIC POLICY OR MORALITY

A design right 'shall not subsist in a design which is contrary to public policy or to accepted principles of morality'.[70] This is both a ground of refusal of registration (both at national and Community levels), and a ground of invalidity.[71] However, the Community regime does not attempt to harmonise national concepts of public policy or accepted principles of morality.[72]

4.5 GROUNDS OF INVALIDITY

To be protected, Community designs must demonstrate novelty and individual character. The Commission had originally intended to impose a higher threshold for protection – that of 'distinguishing character' – in order to offer a higher degree of protection to fewer designs. However, it was concluded that this standard was impractical, and confusingly similar to the concept of 'distinctive character' in the Trade Marks Directive.

The issues of novelty and individual character are tested only when the right is challenged. There is no opportunity for examining an unregistered design right until this point, and there is no substantive examination on application for a registered design right. A registered Community design may be declared invalid either in invalidity proceedings before OHIM, or as a counterclaim for proceedings for infringement before a Community design court. Community design courts have sole jurisdiction to determine invalidity with respect to unregistered Community designs.[73]

---

[69] Designs Dir., Recital 15; CDR, Recital 11.
[70] Designs Dir., Art. 8; CDR, Art. 9.
[71] Designs Dir., Art. 8; CDR, Art. 47(1)(b), Art. 25(1)(b).
[72] Designs Dir., Recital 16; CDR, Recital 11.
[73] CDR, Art. 24. Community design courts are national courts and tribunals designated by member states to perform the functions assigned to them by the Regulations. They have exclusive jurisdiction to deal with actions for the infringement of a Community design, whether registered or unregistered; actions for a declaration of invalidity of an unregistered Community design; and counterclaims for a declaration of invalidity of a Community design (whether registered or unregistered), in the context of an infringement action. CDR, Arts. 80, 81. Art. 82 determines which member state's Community design courts have jurisdiction in the proceedings.

4.5.1 Novelty

A design is considered new if no identical design has been made available to the public on the relevant date. In the case of an unregistered Community design, this is the date on which the design has first been made available to the public. In the case of a registered Community design, this is the date of filing of the application for registration of the design (or the priority date, if claimed). Designs are considered identical if their features differ only in immaterial details.[74]

A design is deemed to have been made available to the public if it has been published (following registration or otherwise), exhibited, used in trade or otherwise disclosed. If these events could not reasonably have become known in the normal course of business to the circles specialised in the sector concerned, the design is not regarded as having been made available to the public.[75] This so-called 'safeguard clause' is intended to exclude obscure disclosures from the state of the art. Although the clause was included from the best of intentions, a good deal of uncertainty has been generated as a result. For example, it is not yet definitively clear which is the 'sector concerned'.[76] Also, the clause may leave a design which has been disclosed outside the Community (perhaps even by the design proprietor) vulnerable. In such circumstances, the novelty for the purposes of the RCD will have been destroyed, without giving rise to a UCD.[77] Features dictated solely by technical function, or which allow for mechanical connection to another product, are to be left aside when considering both novelty and individual character

---

[74] Designs Dir., Art. 4; CDR, Art. 5. For rules on priority see CDR, Arts. 41–4. See, for example, *Heidelberger Druckmaschinen AG* v. *Microsoft Corporation*, ICD 000000743, 6 February 2006; [2006] ECDR 29, where Microsoft's RCD for a particular typeface was held invalid because it was considered identical to another typeface for which prior sales could be shown. Compare *Prodir SA* v. *Dariusz Libera* [2008] ECDR 7, where the designs of two almost-identical ballpoint pens did differ in at least two features, which could not be deemed immaterial.

[75] Designs Dir., Art. 6; CDR, Art. 7.

[76] The most likely answer is that the 'sector concerned' is the sector of the prior art, but some commentators have suggested it should be a single sector comprising both the sector of the registered design and the sector of the prior art, and others (much less plausibly) have argued that it should be the sector covered by the product class specified in the registration. For discussion of the point in a Community design court, see *Green Lane Products Ltd* v. *PMS International Group Ltd* [2008] EWCA Civ. 358.

[77] See Mariecke Hunfeld, 'Chinese Pre-Publication Precludes European Community Unregistered Design Right' [2007] *JIPL&P* 441–2. See also Charles-Henry Massa and Alain Strowel, 'Community Design: Cinderella Revamped' [2003] *EIPR* 68–78, 73 and 74. See also Victor M. Saez, 'The Unregistered Community Design' [2002] *EIPR* 585–90, 588.

(because neither is covered by design right).[78] Early case law indicates that a design or trade mark application published in an EU member state will disclose,[79] as will publication in the official journal of the Japanese Patent Office ('one of the world's most important industrial property offices in terms of volume of applications and registrations of designs'),[80] publication of a United States design patent,[81] and of an international patent application.[82] So far as the applicant is concerned, this is arguably rather a demanding interpretation of 'disclosure' in the 'normal course of business', suggesting that applicants will be expected to conduct extensive international searches. This approach risks making the right less accessible to individuals and SMEs.

Designs which are disclosed in breach of confidence are not regarded as having been made available to the public, and are thus also excluded from the state of the art.[83] The legislation is silent as to how conditions of confidentiality may arise (presumably expecting this to be a matter for national law). There is a specific exclusion for disclosures made available to the public 'as a consequence of an abuse in relation to the designer or his successor in title', though the disclosure must have taken place within the 12 months preceding the date of priority (or filing date, if relevant).[84] This covers, for example, a disclosure by a disgruntled employee. The designer is given a special 12-month 'grace period' preceding the priority date (or filing date, if relevant) during which the designer's own disclosures are not taken into consideration for the purpose of determining novelty (and individual character).[85] The aim

---

[78]   *Honda Giken Kogyo KK* v. *Kwang Yang Motor Co. Ltd*, ICD 000000990, 17 August 2006.

[79]   *Mafin Spa* v. *Leng-d'Or S.A.*, ICD 000000222, 22 October 2004; [2005] ETMR 106; [2005] ECDR 29. See also *C. Josef Lamy GmbH* v. *Sanford LP*, ICD 000000362, 27 October 2005; *Burberry Ltd* v. *Creaciones Camal SL*, ICD 000001568, 8 February 2006.

[80]   *Sunstar Suisse SA* v. *Dentaid SL*, ICD 000000420, 20 June 2005.

[81]   *Honda Giken Kogyo KK* v. *Kwang Yang Motor Co. Ltd*, ICD 000000990, 17 August 2006. OHIM found that in the normal course of business, circles specialised in the relevant sector in the European Community would be expected to keep themselves updated in relation to the competitor's registered designs at least in the most relevant countries, including the United States, particularly since the US patent databases are accessible online.

[82]   *Rodi Commercial SA* v. *Vvelta International SpA*, ICD 000000594, 20 December 2005.

[83]   For example, *Grupo Promer Mon-Graphic SA* v. *PepsiCo Inc.*, ICD 000000180, 1 July 2005. Note, though, that it is not sufficient to allege that a party is acting in bad faith and copied a design shown to it previously. Then the question is not whether one design has been copied from the other, but whether they produce the same overall impression (para. 25).

[84]   Designs Dir., Art. 6(3); CDR, Art. 7(3).

[85]   Designs Dir., Art. 6(2); CDR, Art. 7(2) and Recital 20.

is to allow designers to test products embodying the design in the marketplace before deciding whether to seek registered protection. The grace period does not allow the designer to backdate any future application to the time of the initial disclosure, nor does it establish priority against an independent design.

4.5.2 Individual Character

A design is considered to have 'individual character' if 'the overall impression it produces on the informed user differs from the overall impression produced on such a user by any design which has been made available to the public'.[86] The relevant dates are the same as those when assessing novelty. In the case of an unregistered Community design, this is the date on which the design has first been made available to the public. In the case of a registered Community design, this is the date of filing of the application for registration of the design (or the priority date, if claimed). 'Individual character' imposes a more exacting standard on the design than the test of novelty.[87] It is also a broader and more difficult test to apply.

The 'informed user' is a new category of person, considered to be more informed than the average consumer (and so more alert to possible differences), but less informed than an expert or design specialist. Where a design had been registered for 'meat foodstuffs', the informed user had to be a user and consumer of meat foodstuffs, rather than a designer, a manufacturer or a specialist in the food industry.[88] Such a person will be more objective than the creator of the design. Expert witnesses and market surveys may be useful in assessing the informed user's knowledge and characteristics. The informed user is aware of the existing design corpus, the nature of the product to which the design is applied or in which it is incorporated, the industrial sector to which it belongs and the degree of freedom of the designer in developing the design.[89] The comparison of the design in issue may be with either a single design or several designs from the design corpus. Overall impression is the

---

[86]   Designs Dir., Art. 5; CDR, Art. 6.

[87]   See *Prodir SA* v. *Dariusz Libera* [2008] ECDR 7, which concerned two almost-identical ballpoint pens. The challenged design did not lack novelty, but would be regarded by the informed user as a variant on the earlier design, and so did not produce a different overall impression.

[88]   R 1214/2006-3, *Atria Yhtyma Oyj* v. *HK Ruokatalo Group Oyj* [2008] ECDR 6 (para. 24).

[89]   CDR, Recital 14. A designer might be constrained by functional requirements, costs or other manufacturing and marketing considerations, previous design solutions and so on: EC Green Paper, para. 5.5.8.2. See also the Board of Appeal's discussion in *Grupo Promer Mon-Graphic SA* v. *PepsiCo Inc.*, ICD 000000180, 1 July 2005 (paras. 16, 20).

key, rather than analysis of individual details, although these too may be significant in creating the overall impression.[90]

In *Daka Research* v. *Ampel* the validity of a design for an 'underwater motive device' was challenged.[91] The Invalidity Division of the Office considered that two designs for 'underwater motive devices' were identical except for differences in their handles, but these were not 'immaterial details',[92] and therefore the RCD could not be said to lack novelty. However, the differences between the handles were not sufficient to mean that the designs produced a different overall impression on the informed user. Therefore, the contested RCD lacked individual character and was declared invalid. The Board of Appeal acknowledged that there was necessarily some overlap between the two requirements of novelty and individual character, but also stressed their important differences. The test for novelty 'is essentially of an objective nature', the task being simply to decide whether two designs are identical, except in 'immaterial details'. It described the test for individual character as 'less straightforward' and 'likely to give rise to slightly more subjective appraisals'. The contested RCD concerned the underwater device as a whole, even though the appellant could have sought design protection for the handle alone. The comparison had therefore to be between the whole of the prior disclosed design and the whole of the contested RCD. The Board concluded that they produced the same overall impression on the informed user, so the Invalidity Division's decision was confirmed.

4.5.3 Complex Products – Special Requirements

The controversy and conflict regarding the appropriate protection for car parts has had consequences throughout the Community design regime. It has already been seen that design protection is defined to exclude 'interconnections'.[93] There are also special rules regarding novelty and individual character. It was thought that protection should not be extended to those component parts which are not visible during normal use of a product, nor to those

---

[90] 'To assess the overall impression, the designs must be compared both on their various features taken individually and on the weight of the various features according to their influence on the overall impression': *Mafin Spa* v. *Leng-d'Or S.A.*, ICD 000000222, 22 October 2004; [2005] ECDR 29 (para. 28). For concerns as to the likely consistency of national decisions see Toby Headdon, 'Community Design Right: An Emerging Consensus or a Different Overall Impression' [2007] *EIPR* 336–9.

[91] R 196/2006-3 *Daka Research Inc.* v. *Ampel 24 Vertriebs-GmbH & Co. KG* (22 November 2006). See also José J. Izquierdo Peris, 'OHIM Practice in the Field of Invalidity of Registered Designs' [2008] *EIPR* 56–65.

[92] CDR, Art. 5(2).

[93] Designs Dir., Art. 7(2); CDR, Art. 8(2).

features of such part which are not visible when the part is mounted, or which would not, in themselves, fulfil the requirements as to novelty and individual character. Therefore, such design features are not taken into consideration for the purpose of assessing whether other design features fulfil the requirements for protection.[94] So, a design applied to or incorporated in a product which constitutes a component part of a complex product shall only be considered to be new and to have individual character:

(a) if the component part, once it has been incorporated into the complex product, remains visible during normal use of the latter; and

(b) to the extent that those visible features of the component part fulfil in themselves the requirements as to novelty and individual character.[95]

Normal use means 'use by the end user, excluding maintenance, servicing or repair work'.[96] This exclusion was intended to exclude 'under-the-bonnet' spare parts from design protection.[97] In *Honda* v. *Kwang Yang Motor*, a design had been registered in respect of 'internal-combustion engines', and Honda applied for a declaration of invalidity. The Board of Appeal found that such engines were 'component parts' of a 'complex product'. The design had to be considered after the engine had been installed on the complex product. During normal use it was primarily the upper side which remained visible, and secondarily the front and lateral sides. It followed that the individual character of the challenged design had to be assessed on the basis of the overall impression produced primarily by its upper side, and from the perspective of an informed user of the complex product. The design in question was found to lack individual character.[98]

4.5.4 Relative Grounds of Invalidity

The Designs Directive provides for five further grounds for invalidity. Two – lack of entitlement and conflict with a prior design – are mandatory. The remainder are optional.

---

[94] CDR, Recital 12.

[95] Designs Dir., Art. 3(3); CDR, Art. 4(2). See *Honda Giken Kogyo KK* v. *Kwang Yang Motor Co. Ltd*, ICD 000000990, 17 August 2006.

[96] Designs Dir., Art. 3(4); CDR, Art. 4(3).

[97] Herman M.H. Speyart, 'The Grand Design: An Update on the E.C. Design Proposals Following the Adoption of a Common Position on the Directive' [1997] *EIPR* 603–12, 606, 609.

[98] R 1380/2006-3, *Honda Giken Kogyo Kabushiki Kaisha* v. *Kwang Yang Motor Co.* [2008] ECDR 5.

(a) Lack of entitlement

The Designs Directive states that a design must be refused registration, or, if the design has been registered, be declared invalid if the applicant for or the holder of the design right is not entitled to it under the law of the member state concerned.[99] This ground may be invoked solely by the person who is in fact entitled to it.[100] Similarly, under the Regulation, a Community design may be declared invalid if, by virtue of a court decision, it is known that the right holder is not entitled to the Community design.[101] Again, this ground may be invoked solely by the person who is in fact entitled to the Community design.

(b) Conflict with prior design

The Designs Directive states that a design must be refused registration, or, if the design has been registered, be declared invalid if 'the design is in conflict with a prior design which has been made available to the public after the date of filing of the application or, if priority is claimed, the date of priority, and which is protected from a date prior to the said date by a registered Community design or an application for a registered Community design or by a design right of the Member State concerned, or by an application for such a right'. As a mandatory ground of invalidity, this ground may be invoked solely by the applicant for, or the holder of, the conflicting right. However, member states may choose to provide for this ground to be invoked by the appropriate authority of the member state on its own initiative.[102] This provision creates a 'first to file' system to determine priority between registrations in situations where the earlier application had not been published by the priority date of the later registration (for example, where there was deferred publication of the earlier Community registration).

The Regulation treats the conflicts provision as a ground only of invalidity. Relevant prior designs are earlier Community applications and registrations, and earlier applications and registrations for 'a registered design right of a Member State'. As a mandatory ground of invalidity (before OHIM), this ground may be invoked solely by the applicant for, or the holder of, the conflicting right. However, member states may choose to provide for this ground to be invoked (before a Community design court) by the appropriate authority of the member state on its own initiative.[103]

---

[99]   Designs Dir., Art. 11(1)(c).
[100] Designs Dir., Art. 11(3).
[101] CDR Art. 25(1)(c), Art. 14, Art. 25(2).
[102] Designs Dir., Art. 11(1)(d), (4), (6).
[103] CDR Art. 25(1)(d), 25(3), 25(5). For an example invalidated under this provision, see the first ever decision by the Invalidity Division: *Eredu S. Coop* v. *Arrmet Srl*, ICD 000000024, 27 April 2004; [2004] ECDR 24.

(c) Conflict with a distinctive sign

Member states may refuse registration, or, if the design has been registered, treat the design right as invalid, 'if a distinctive sign is used in a subsequent design, and Community law or the law of the Member State concerned governing that sign confers on the right holder of the sign the right to prohibit such use'. This ground may be invoked solely by the applicant for or the holder of the conflicting right.[104] The same provision appears in the Regulation.[105] These provisions would commonly cover earlier trade mark rights, but might also cover other regimes protecting 'distinctive signs', such as passing off, and possibly Protected Designation of Origins (PDOs), Protected Geographical Indication (PGIs), and even some personality rights.[106]

A trade mark owner mounted a challenge under this provision in *Honeywell Analytics Limited* v. *Hee Jung Kim*.[107] The case concerned four RCDs, consisting of very similar stylised logos including the word 'midas'. These were declared invalid on the basis of an earlier international trade mark registration of the word MIDAS, in a particular graphic font. On appeal, it was argued that a registered design cannot be assumed to exist for the purposes of distinguishing goods and services. This point was dismissed by the Board of Appeal. Although the essential purpose of a design is not to distinguish the products or services of an undertaking from those of other undertakings, in a commercial context, when applied to products, their packaging and get-up, or when used in advertising, the contested RCD might be perceived as a sign by the relevant public. The Board therefore considered whether there was a risk that the relevant public might believe that the goods or services in question came from the same undertaking, within the meaning of Article 5(1)(b) of the Trade Mark Directive. The signs were visually similar, and phonetically and conceptually identical. Since the logo might be applied to an infinite range of products and services, including the products covered by the trade mark registration, it was conceivable that the public would perceive the logo as an indication of the commercial origin of the products in question and not as a pure embellishment. The contested RCD was therefore liable to jeopardise the guarantee of origin which constitutes the essential function of the trade mark, and the respondent was entitled to prevent it. The RCD thus fell within Article 25(1)(e) and was invalid. This decision gives trade mark holders a considerable

---

[104] Designs Dir., Art. 11(2)(a), 11(4).
[105] CDR Art. 25(1)(e), 25(3).
[106] See, for example, R 137/2007-3, *Piotrowski* v. *Compagnie Gervais Danone SA* [2008] ETMR 27.
[107] Case R 609/2006-3, *Honeywell Analytics Limited* v. *Hee Jung Kim* (BoA, 3 May 2007).

breadth of protection against designs, since although under the Trade Mark Directive a registered mark can only be used to prevent use on goods which are the same or confusingly similar, the effect is to prevent its use as a design on all goods, since the RCD was invalidated in its entirety.

(d)　Conflicts with earlier copyright protected works

Member states may refuse registration, or, if the design has been registered, treat the design right as invalid, 'if the design constitutes an unauthorised use of a work protected under the copyright law of the Member State concerned'. This ground may be invoked solely by the copyright holder.[108] The same provision appears in the Regulation.[109]

(e) Conflicts with protected badges

Finally, member states may refuse registration, or, if the design has been registered, treat the design right as invalid, 'if the design constitutes an improper use of any of the items listed in Article 6*ter* of the Paris Convention', or of 'badges, emblems and escutcheons . . . which are of particular public interest in the Member State concerned'.[110] Article 6*ter* requires countries of the Paris Union to refuse or invalidate the registration of trade marks which are or contain armorial bearings, flags and other state emblems, official signs and hallmarks of Countries of the Union, or of international intergovernmental organisations. This ground may be invoked solely by the person or entity concerned by the use, unless a member state has chosen to permit an 'appropriate authority' to invoke it of its own initiative.[111] The parallel provision in the Regulation treats such conflicts as a ground for invalidity.[112]

4.6　THE DESIGN PROPRIETOR'S RIGHTS

4.6.1　Initial Entitlement

The right to the Community design vests 'in the designer or his successor in title'.[113] The 'designer' is not further defined, though the Regulation recognises that a design may be developed jointly – in which case the right to the

---

108　Designs Dir., Art. 11(2)(b), 11(4).
109　CDR, Art. 25(1)(f), 25(3).
110　Designs Dir., Art. 11(2)c).
111　Designs Dir., Art. 11(5), 11(6).
112　CDR, Art. 25(1)(g), 25(4).
113　CDR, Art. 14(1).

Community design vests in them jointly.[114] The role of the 'designer' differs from that of an 'author', being seen as more constrained by a range of circumstances, particularly the needs of industry and the marketplace. Where a design is 'developed by an employee in the execution of his duties or following the instructions given by his employer', the right to the Community design vests in the employer, unless otherwise agreed or specified under national law.[115] The position of those commissioning designs is not addressed explicitly in the Regulation, though of course the design right may be transferred by assignment if the parties wish. The Regulation does give the designer the right 'to be cited as such before the Office and in the register', although this right may be waived.[116]

In any proceedings, there is a presumption in favour of the registered holder of the design, that the person in whose name a registered Community design is registered is the person entitled to it.[117] There is provision for challenge by 'the person entitled to it', who may 'claim to become recognised as the legitimate holder of the Community design'.[118] OHIM has no specific power to resolve such disputes, so they will be determined by national courts, with jurisdiction governed by the Brussels Convention.[119] There is a limitation period of three years from the date of publication of a registered Community design or the date of disclosure of an unregistered Community design, unless the person who is not entitled was acting in bad faith.[120] The fact that legal proceedings have been instituted will be entered in the register, and after a final decision, any change in ownership will also be entered.[121] Similarly, a Community design may be declared invalid if, by virtue of a court decision, it is known that the right holder is not entitled to the Community design.[122]

4.6.2 Assignment and Licences

Since the Community design right is a unitary right, it can only be transferred in its entirety, for the whole Community territory. Any transfers will be subject to national rules, though the Regulation does specify which national law will

---

[114] CDR, Art. 14(2).
[115] CDR, Art. 14(3).
[116] CDR, Art. 18, Art. 36(3)(e). If the design is the result of teamwork, the team may be cited.
[117] CDR, Art. 17.
[118] CDR, Art. 15(1). The person may claim to become recognised as joint holder, if appropriate.
[119] CDR, Art. 79.
[120] CDR, Art. 15(3).
[121] CDR, Art. 15(4).
[122] CDR, Art. 25(1)(c), Art. 14, Art. 25(2).

apply. It will normally be the law of the member state where the right holder has their seat or domicile.[123]

(a) Registration

If a registered Community design is transferred, one of the parties may request that the transfer be entered in the register and published. Until this is done, the successor in title may not invoke the rights arising from the registration of the Community design.[124] A registered Community design may be given as security, or levied in execution, and these rights may be entered in the register if one of the parties requests this.[125] A Community design may only be involved in insolvency proceedings in the territory where the debtor's main interests are situated.[126]

(b) Licences

A Community design may be licensed for the whole or part of the Community. Licences may be exclusive or non-exclusive. An exclusive licensee may bring proceedings for infringement of a Community design if the right holder does not do so within an appropriate period, having been given notice. A non-exclusive licensee requires the consent of the right holder to bring infringement proceedings. A licence of a registered Community design may be entered in the register.[127]

4.6.3 Duration

The Designs Directive harmonised the term of protection for national design rights at a maximum of 25 years, granted in five-year periods from the date of filing.[128] Recital 17 noted that it was 'fundamental for the smooth functioning of the internal market to unify the term of protection afforded by registered design rights'. Note, though, that the 25-year figure was a compromise, and should be contrasted with copyright term, which was harmonised upwards to the highest then applicable in any member state. Although the majority of member states protected registered designs for 25 years or less, France did so

---

[123]   CDR, Art. 27(1). If the right holder has no seat or domicile, it will be the law of the member state where the holder has an establishment. There are provisions for joint holders, also. If none of the specific provisions of Art. 27 applies, it will be the law of the member state in which the Office is situated.

[124]   CDR, Art. 28.

[125]   CDR, Arts. 29, 30.

[126]   CDR, Art. 31. The competent national authority may request publication of the involvement in insolvency proceedings in the register.

[127]   CDR, Art. 32. For effects on third parties see Art. 33.

[128]   Designs Dir., Art. 10.

for 50 years. Setting the term of protection for intellectual property rights is inevitably contentious. Like copyright, registered designs cover a huge range of subject matter, from trivial to timeless. One consideration in setting the period for registered designs may have been that if works of applied art are protected by copyright in member states, the Berne Convention requires a minimum 25-year term.[129] The term of protection of the registered Community design was set at the same maximum 25-year term, again granted in five-year periods.[130] The unregistered Community design is protected for a much shorter period; three years from the date on which the design was first made available to the public within the Community. A design is made available to the public within the Community if it has been published, exhibited, used in trade or otherwise disclosed in such a way that, in the normal course of business, these events could reasonably have become known to the circles specialised in the sector concerned, operating within the Community. Confidential disclosures are not deemed to be 'making available to the public'. However, a disclosure in breach of confidence (or as the result of theft) will not prevent the UCD from arising if the design has thereby been made available to the public.[131]

4.6.4 Rights Conferred by the Design Right

Registered Community designs and registered national designs enjoy full monopoly rights. The right holder has the exclusive right to use the design and to prevent any third party using it without consent. Use covers, in particular, 'the making, offering, putting on the market, importing, exporting or using of a product in which the design is incorporated or to which it is applied, or stocking such a product for those purposes'.[132] Note that the infringing use may relate to a different product than the product to which the original design has been applied.

Unregistered Community designs, and registered designs which have not been published, are treated differently, and enjoy only a limited monopoly. The right holder again has the exclusive right to use the design and to prevent any third party using it without consent, but only if that use results from copying the protected design.[133] This will be a matter for the design proprietor to prove on the balance of probabilities. It is not considered appropriate that use of a design should be stopped where search of a central register would not have

---

[129] Berne Convention, Art. 7(4).
[130] CDR, Art. 12.
[131] CDR, Art. 11.
[132] Designs Dir., Art. 12; CDR, Art. 19.
[133] CDR, Art. 19(2), (3). See also Recital 21.

revealed that the design was protected. Protection therefore does not extend to design products which are the result of a design arrived at independently by a second designer. Thus the defendant's use of a design is not deemed to result from copying the protected design if it 'results from an independent work of creation by a designer who may be reasonably thought not to be familiar with the design made available to the public by the holder'.[134]

Scope of protection

Under both the harmonised and Community regimes, the scope of the protection conferred by a design right is defined to include 'any design which does not produce on the informed user a different overall impression'.[135] The 'informed user' was discussed earlier, as the concept is used when determining whether a design has 'individual character'. In assessing the scope of protection, the degree of freedom of the designer in developing the design shall be taken into consideration (again, as when determining individual character).[136] Where designers have a high degree of freedom, two similar designs are more likely to produce the same overall impression on the informed user.[137]

For registered designs, the representations will be the starting point for comparison. It should be recalled that features of designs dictated by their technical function and designs of interconnections are excluded from design protection and will not be considered.[138] For unregistered designs there will be no documents associated with the registration process to assist in the enquiry. In both cases the notional 'informed user' must decide whether or not the designs produce 'a different overall impression'. In *Honda* v. *Kwang Yang Motor*, the designs of two internal-combustion engines were compared. It was the overall impression on the informed user that was to be considered, based on the physical product and not on the technical drawings. The Board of Appeal found that the two designs showed an identical arrangement of components, which were similarly designed. The Invalidity Division had noted a number of differences, and found the overall impression of the challenged design to be different from that of the earlier design. However, the Board crit-

---

[134]   CDR, Art. 19(2).

[135]   Designs Dir., Art. 9(1); CDR, Art. 10(1).

[136]   Designs Dir., Art. 9(2); CDR, Art. 10(2); and see above section 4.5.2 Individual character.

[137]   R 1380/2006-3 *Honda Giken Kogyo Kabushiki Kaisha* v. *Kwang Yang Motor Co.* [2008] ECDR 5 (para. 37). See also *Holey Soles Holdings Ltd* v. *Crocs Inc.* [2008] ECDR 8.

[138]   Designs Dir., Art. 7; CDR, Art. 8.

icised this 'excessively detailed analysis', considering that the contested decision had 'lost the broader perspective of "the overall impression" '.[139]

4.6.5 Exceptions and Defences

The Community design regime mandates a number of 'limitations of the rights conferred'.[140] There are also provisions addressing exhaustion of rights, and the tricky issue of spare parts (repair of complex products).

(a) Acts done privately and for non-commercial purposes
Designs law has as its focus the market for the product embodying the design. Although the right holder has the exclusive right to 'use' the design, the non-exhaustive list of examples of use makes it clear that it is commercial use which is envisaged, primarily.[141] There is therefore an exception for acts done privately and for non-commercial purposes.[142]

(b) Acts done for experimental purposes
In many patent law systems there is a defence for acts done for experimental purposes relating to the subject matter of the patent. The Community design regime provides a parallel exception, for 'acts done for experimental purposes', although, given the subject matter of most designs, it seems likely that it will not be used particularly frequently.[143]

(c) Acts of reproduction for the purposes of making citations or of teaching
There is an exception covering 'acts of reproduction for the purposes of making citations or of teaching, provided that such acts are compatible with fair trade practice and do not unduly prejudice the normal exploitation of the design, and that mention is made of the source'.[144] The broad coverage of the Community design regime might have rendered innocuous activities infringing, and this limitation seeks to avert this danger.

---

[139] R 1380/2006-3 *Honda Giken Kogyo Kabushiki Kaisha* v. *Kwang Yang Motor Co.* [2008] ECDR 5.

[140] Designs Dir., Art. 13(1); CDR, Art. 20(1).

[141] Designs Dir., Art. 12; CDR, Art. 19: use covers, in particular, 'the making, offering, putting on the market, importing, exporting or using of a product in which the design is incorporated or to which it is applied, or stocking such a product for those purposes'.

[142] Designs Dir., Art. 13(1)(a); CDR, Art. 20(1)(a).

[143] Designs Dir., Art. 13(1)(b); CDR, Art. 20(1)(b).

[144] Designs Dir., Art. 13(1)(c); CDR, Art. 20(1)(c).

(d) Ships and aircraft
Design right may not be exercised in respect of: the equipment on ships and aircraft registered in another country when these temporarily enter the territory of the member state concerned; the importation in the member state concerned of spare parts and accessories for the purpose of repairing such craft; the execution of repairs on such craft.[145]

(e) Exhaustion of rights
Both the Directive and the Regulation provide for Community-wide exhaustion of rights. Thus, the design right will be exhausted 'when the product has been put on the market in the Community by the holder of the design right or with his consent'.[146] This is in line with the Community's policy on the free movement of goods, which precludes the barriers which would follow from purely national exhaustion. The specific provision of a Community-wide regime will prevent a member state from adopting an international exhaustion regime.

(f) Complex products
As has been mentioned, the passage of Community design legislation was seriously hindered by controversy regarding the appropriate protection for spare parts for cars. The Council had wanted to leave member states a free hand in this area, whereas Parliament had been keen to see a harmonised regime of fair and reasonable remuneration for right holders for any use of the design of a component part used in the repair of a complex product. It proved impossible to reach agreement, and the Directive side-stepped the issue by establishing a 'stand-still' clause for spare parts, coupled with a commitment to a consultation exercise.[147] The Directive therefore requires member states to 'maintain in force their existing legal provisions relating to the use of the design of a component part used for the purpose of the repair of a complex product so as to restore its original appearance and shall introduce changes to those provisions only if the purpose is to liberalise the market for such parts' – the so-called 'freeze plus' solution.[148] The Directive also mandated a Commission review of the consequences of the Directive, three years after implementation, 'particularly for the industrial sectors which are most affected, particularly manufacturers of complex products and component parts, for consumers, for competition and for the functioning of the internal market'. The Commission was required to propose any changes needed 'to complete the internal market

---

145   Designs Dir., Art. 13(2); CDR, Art. 20(2).
146   Designs Dir., Art. 15; CDR, Art. 21.
147   Designs Dir., Recital 19.
148   Designs Dir., Art. 14.

in respect of component parts of complex products' and any other necessary changes.[149] The Regulation has a transitional provision excluding from Community design protection 'a design which constitutes a component part of a complex product used . . . for the purpose of the repair of that complex product so as to restore its original appearance' – 'must match' spare parts – until a Commission proposal has clarified Community policy on the subject.[150] From the Community point of view, there is a clear pressure for liberalisation of the aftermarket in spare parts.[151] Automotive manufacturers continue to resist this option fiercely, however.[152]

The Commission proposal was published in September 2004.[153] The Commission described the prevailing system as 'totally unsatisfactory from an internal market point of view'. Nine member states have liberalised their design regimes, whilst 16 member states still offer design protection to spare parts. The automotive sector is the most affected, and automotive spare parts cannot be freely produced and traded within the Community. This affects consumer choice, and limits the efficiency of independent parts producers. The Commission's analysis indicated that the markets for various spare parts were 'systematically distorted', with prices 'significantly higher' (6–10%) in member states with design protection than in member states without it. Four alternative regimes for design protection were considered: the status quo; full liberalisation (meaning no design protection for spare parts); short-term design protection for spare parts; a remuneration system which allowed independent producers to produce spare parts in exchange for a reasonable remuneration to be paid to the holder of the design right; and a combination whereby a short period of full design protection would be followed by a remuneration system for a subsequent period. The Commission concluded that excluding design protection in the aftermarket for spare parts would be the only effective way

---

[149] Designs Dir., Art. 18.

[150] CDR, Art. 110. See also CDR, Recital 13.

[151] Regulation 1400/2002 on the application of Article 81(3) of the Treaty to categories of vertical agreements and concerted practices in the motor vehicle industry (OJ L 203/30) addressed some practical issues regarding the distribution of spare parts, attempting to protect effective competition in the market for repair and maintenance services, *inter alia* by allowing users to choose between competing spare parts. However, it does not deal directly with the crucial question of the protection or not of spare parts by an industrial property right.

[152] In 2000, the Commission undertook a consultation exercise on design protection for component parts of complex products in the motor vehicle sector, in the hope of reaching a voluntary agreement. After discussions with interested parties, the conclusion was that the positions of the parties would remain completely opposed.

[153] Commission Proposal for a Directive of the European Parliament and of the Council amending Directive 98/71/EC on the legal protection of designs, SEC(2004) 1097.

of achieving an internal market. In addition, the Commission noted that the main purpose of design protection is to grant exclusive rights to the appearance of a product, but not a monopoly over the product as such. However, protecting designs in the aftermarket for spare parts for which there is no practical alternative did in practice lead to a product monopoly.

The Commission has therefore proposed an amendment to Article 14 of the Designs Directive, to exclude design protection for 'must match' spare parts: 'Protection as a design shall not exist for a design which constitutes a component part of a complex product used . . . for the purpose of the repair of that complex product so as to restore its original appearance'.[154] The definition of 'must match' parts mirrors that used in the Regulation. Member states will also be required to ensure that consumers are informed about the origin of spare parts, so that they can make an informed choice between competing spare parts. The Commission's proposal affects only the secondary market for spare parts (replacements and repairs), and not the primary market (which concerns their use in the initial manufacturing process). The Commission considers that offering design protection in the primary market should be sufficient to reward manufacturers' investment in design and to maintain a strong incentive to innovate.[155]

The proposal has not made rapid progress. Although two Parliamentary Committees have voted in its favour (Economic and Monetary Affairs, and Internal Market and Consumer Protection), the Legal Affairs Committee was slow to do so. Vehicle manufacturers argued that the Commission's proposal ignored issues of the safety, quality and structural integrity of spare parts, claiming that the use of non-original body repair parts in a liberalised aftermarket could be 'unsafe'. The European Parliament's Legal Affairs Committee therefore commissioned a study to help determine whether existing legislation and regulation in Europe adequately protects the safety of road users. The study concluded that the existing approaches were 'more than adequate to ensure the safety of vehicles', and that vehicle manufacturers were unjustified in invoking a general risk to safety from the use of non-original parts to protect their profit margins.[156] Various radical options were consid-

---

[154]   Proposal for a Directive of the European Parliament and of the Council amending Directive 98/71/EC on the legal protection of designs, COM(2004) 582, Art. 1.

[155]   See 'Industrial Property: Commission Proposes More Competition in Car Spare Parts Market' Press Release, IP/04/1101 (14 September 2004). For more detail, see the Commission staff working document extended impact assessment, SEC(2004) 1097.

[156]   Autopolis/Thatcham Study, *The Consequences for the Safety of Consumers and Third Parties of the Proposed Directive Amending Directive 98/71/EC on Legal Protection of Design Rights* (September 2006): http://www.ecar-eu.com/documents/European ParliamentfinalE_001.pdf. However, the study did recommend

ered, such as giving vehicle manufacturers a spare parts monopoly which lasted as long as the relevant car model was in production, and allowing member states to liberalise the spare parts market by permitting reproduction subject to equitable remuneration.[157] However, in November 2007, the Legal Affairs Committee endorsed yet another solution, amending the proposed Directive to allow member states a five-year transitional period before full liberalisation. This softening of the Commission's proposal aims to acknowledge and take account of the tension between the various interested parties.[158] The dossier remains pending in the Council of Ministers.

(g) Prior use

Under the Regulation, a third party who has in good faith begun to use a design, or is preparing to use it, may be entitled to continue using it.[159] A right of prior use is conferred if the third party can establish that, before the date of priority, 'he has in good faith commenced use within the Community, or has made serious and effective preparations to that end'. The design must not have been copied from the registered Community design. The right only allows exploitation of the design 'for the purposes for which its use had been effected, or for which serious and effective preparations had been made', before the priority date. It will not therefore cover wider and different activities undertaken later. The right is a personal right, in the sense that it does not cover the grant of a licence to another person to exploit the design. It cannot be transferred except as part of a business.

---

that the type approval procedure should be extended to cover certain safety-related spare parts in order to guarantee their safety, and this has been done: Art. 31, Directive 2007/46 [2007] OJ L/263.

[157] Alexander Radwan, 'Draft Report on the Proposal for a Directive of the European Parliament and of the Council' 2004/0203(COD): http://www.europarl.europa.eu/meetdocs/2004_2009/ documents/pr/640/640008/640008en.pdf.

[158] Committee on Legal Affairs, 'Report on the Proposal for a Directive of the European Parliament and of the Council amending Directive 98/71/EC on the Legal Proection of Designs' A6-0453/2007 (22 November 2007).

[159] CDR, Art. 22 (also Recital 23).

5. Trade marks and related rights

5.1 INTRODUCTION

Trade marks have a long history.[1] In prehistoric times farmers would brand cattle and implements as a mark of their ownership. Similarly, early merchants used personal marks on goods, to indicate ownership. Later these marks came to be used as true trade marks, to indicate origin. As trade expanded beyond purely local markets, the value of such marks to both traders and purchasers was increasingly appreciated, and legally enforced penalties began to be imposed for abuses. By the sixteenth century, some countries (Britain, France and Germany, for example) had adopted recognisable systems of trade mark law. As industrialisation took hold, traders continued to apply marks to their manufactured goods, and began to use their marks in advertising. Purchasers in turn began to rely on marks to indicate the producer of the goods, and thus to offer some security as to their quality. This process of development continued, and by the early twentieth century some marks began to embody an allure or emotional appeal to the consumer. Thus the mark itself acquired an advertising function, and began to function as a symbol rather than a signal. Whereas the earlier function of the mark was to indicate origin, often thereby providing some guarantee of quality, the mark now gave the product its identity.[2] Reinforced by advertising, the trade mark could evoke the product's broader attributes and make it desirable to the consumer. This poetic function went far beyond the prosaic aims of identifying a product's manufacturer or its likely quality.

Today, marks convey extraordinarily complex levels of meaning, and consumers are highly sophisticated in their reading of them. Purchase of trade marked products can bring status and particular identities to consumers. Hence

---

[1]   Frank Schechter, *The Historical Foundations of the Law Relating to Trade Marks* (New York: Columbia University Press, 1925); Gerald Ruston, 'On the Origin of Trade-Marks' (1955) 45 *TM Rep.* 127–44.

[2]   Thomas D. Drescher, 'The Transformation and Evolution of Trademarks: From Signals to Symbols to Myth' (1992) 82 *TM Rep.* 301–40, 309–21; Sidney A. Diamond, 'The Historical Development of Trademarks' (1975) 65 *TM Rep.* 265–90; Per Mollerup, *Marks of Excellence: The History and Taxonomy of Trademarks* (London: Phaidon, 1997).

the power of modern brands. The iPod, for example, is far more than a digital music player, manufactured by Apple and known for its appealing design and ease of use. Nearly 120 million iPods have been sold since the product's launch in 2002; over 10 million of these were sold in the final quarter of 2007 alone.[3] Its phenomenal popularity in the market cannot be attributed solely to its functionality, however. This is the age of the iPod. Literally thousands of different accessories are available for it, the range including both the predictable (cases, docking stations, car chargers, speakers) and the capricious (pushchairs, belts and massage chairs, all with slots for iPods). This astonishing 'iPod ecosystem' indicates that the iPod is far more than just a product to consumers. The iPod brand conveys a way of life, a style, a 'personality' with which purchasers are delighted to interact. Definitions and theories of brands and branding are hotly debated, but it is nevertheless clear that brands influence customer choice. Brands are now thoughtfully and deliberately created and shaped. Look and feel, positioning, advertising strategy, all combine to give a brand a personality with which – it is hoped – customers will identify.[4] Brands are no longer merely local, but may have even global recognition. The top brands are worth a great deal of money. A survey in 2007 ranked Coca-Cola, Microsoft and IBM as the top three most valuable brands in the world, each worth in the region of $60 billion. The phenomenon is not confined to a few super-brands. Every brand in the top hundred was valued at over $3 billion.[5]

These changes have implications for legal systems of trade mark protection. Originally, when marks did little more than indicate origin (or qualities associated with that source), the law sought to protect traders and consumers from fraud and confusion. But since the function of trade marks has changed to such an enormous extent, and since it entails such economic significance, it is unsurprising that wider protection has been demanded. In the 1920s, commentators such as Frank Schechter began to argue that trade mark law should protect the identity of marks to a far greater extent.[6] Such thinking is now reflected in many national legal systems. The trade mark proprietor may enjoy protection against 'dilution' – the use of the mark on goods which are not similar – even in situations when there is no customer confusion. Trade marks are increasingly treated as assets, with legal attention focused on the

---

[3]   Press Release: 'Apple Reports Fourth Quarter Results', 22 October 2007.

[4]   Rochelle Dreyfuss, 'Expressive Genericity: Trademarks as Language in the Pepsi Generation,' (1990) 65 *Notre Dame Law Review* 397.

[5]   *Business Week*/Interbrand Survey (July 2007), *The 100 Top Brands 2007*, http://www.businessweek.com/pdfs/2007/0732_globalbrands.pdf.

[6]   Frank Schechter, 'The Rational Basis of Trade Mark Protection' (1927) 40 *Harvard LR* 813–33.

origin and advertising functions, rather than on consumer interest.[7] Trade marks do have social costs associated with them, particularly for other traders who are restricted from using the protected sign.[8] Others have argued that although the informational aspects of a trade mark's advertising function are valuable (in that they help consumers make informed choices), the persuasive element of trade marks works to add costs and insulate traders from competition and has a socially negative effect.[9] The more powerful forms of trade mark protection may even have implications for freedom of speech, because they allow the trade mark owner to control the sign's meaning and also the contexts in which it is used.[10] Trade mark law can thus have important societal effects, and its proper role remains contested and often controversial.

The international scene

As has been seen, the need for legally protected trade marks was tied to the expansion of trade beyond local markets. Growth in international and global trading has only emphasised these needs. There are two main strands which run through international initiatives. One seeks to facilitate the registration of trade marks in an international context. The other seeks to harmonise the standards of protection offered to trade marks.

These international efforts have a number of important focal points. One is the World Intellectual Property Organisation (WIPO), which seeks to promote the progressive development and harmonisation of legislation, standards and procedures in all fields of intellectual property law. Its history dates back to the Paris Convention, which it administers.[11] In the field of trade mark law, WIPO administers (*inter alia*) the 1891 Madrid Agreement, and the 1989 Madrid Protocol. Both of these are intended to centralise and simplify filing for trade marks worldwide. They do not offer an 'international mark' as such, but they

---

[7]　　Jennifer Davis, 'To Protect or Serve? European Trade Mark Law and the Decline of the Public Interest' [2003] *EIPR* 180–87.

[8]　　William M. Landes and Richard A. Posner, 'The Economics of Trademark Law' (1988) 78 *TM Rep.* 267–306.

[9]　　Ralph S. Brown, 'Advertising and the Public Interest: Legal Protection of Trade Symbols' (1948) 57 *Yale LJ* 1165–206; Sarah C. Haan 'The "Persuasion Route" of the Law: Advertising and Legal Persuasion' (2000) 100 *Columbia LR* 1281–326.

[10]　　Rosemary J. Coombe, 'Tactics of Appropriation and the Late Politics of Recognition in Late Modern Democracies' (1993) 21 *Political Theory* 411–33; Naomi Klein, *No Logo: Taking Aim at the Brand Bullies* (London: Flamingo, 2000); Rosemary J. Coombe, *The Cultural Life of Intellectual Properties: Authorship, Appropriation, and the Law* (Durham, NC; London: Duke University Press, 1998).

[11]　　The Paris Convention of 1883 was the first international convention for the protection of industrial property (including trade marks). It has over 170 signatories, including most countries of the world and all European countries. For its text, see: http://www.wipo.int/treaties/en/ip/paris/trtdocs_wo020.html.

do facilitate the acquisition of national marks. Under the terms of these treaties, applicants may obtain protection in a number of different countries by means of one single application, instead of having to file separate applications in each country. The TRIPS Agreement, administered by the WTO, has also mandated significant harmonisation of substantive trade mark law. The other important source of initiatives is the European Community. Its concerns include the free movement of goods and services within the EU, and the promotion of effective competition. This has led to two significant developments. The first was a Directive harmonising substantive national trade mark law to a considerable extent. The second was the establishment of a Community trade mark (CTM). The CTM offers uniform protection in all countries of the European Union, via a single registration procedure with the Office for Harmonisation of the Internal Market (OHIM).

Notwithstanding these efforts, significant diversity remains at national level, both substantive and procedural. Some countries maintain a first-to-use policy for trade marks, rather than the first-to-file system. Outside the Community it is less common for European countries to extend the protection of registered marks to similar or dissimilar goods, instead restricting it to the goods specified in the registration, or to the goods and services supplied in the course of the proprietor's business. There are considerable differences in the search and examination procedures, and in the approach to opposition. Attitudes to the assignment of marks also vary, some countries being reluctant to permit this without assignment of the underlying business. But the success of the various international regimes has acted as a catalyst for change, and national regimes are slowly converging.

5.2   TREATIES ADMINISTERED BY WIPO

5.2.1   The Paris Convention

This does not regulate the conditions for the filing and registration of trade marks, which are determined by the relevant national laws, whilst respecting the principle of national treatment.[12] It is primarily concerned with the harmonisation of substantive trade mark law, rather than of procedural matters. As an international convention, it has no force of law unless enacted in domestic legislation. All European countries have acceded to the Paris Convention, but not all of its requirements are necessarily fully reflected in their domestic law, and the detailed interpretation of particular provisions may differ at national level.

---

[12]   Paris Convention, Art. 6(1).

The Paris Convention sets out a number of important rules on trade marks which all member states must follow. One key advantage for those seeking to register a trade mark is that an application filed in a contracting state gives a priority of six months in which to file corresponding applications in other contracting states.[13] Since the Convention does not regulate procedural conditions (which are a matter for national law), no application for the registration of a mark filed by a national of a contracting state may be refused, nor may a registration be invalidated, on the ground that filing, registration or renewal has not been effected in the country of origin.[14] Once the registration of a mark is obtained in a member state, it is independent of its possible registration in any other country, including the country of origin; consequently, the lapse or annulment of the registration of a mark in one member state will not affect the validity of registration in other member states.[15] Where a mark has been duly registered in the country of origin, it must, on request, be accepted for filing and protected in its original form in the other member states. Nevertheless, registration may be refused in certain well-defined cases, such as when the mark would infringe acquired rights of third parties, when it is devoid of distinctive character, when it is contrary to morality or public order, or when it is of such a nature as to be liable to deceive the public.[16] Under Article 6*bis*, well-known marks enjoy special protection. Service marks and collective marks must both be granted protection.[17] Member states are also required to offer effective protection against unfair competition.[18]

All of the EC member states are parties to the Paris Convention, although the EC itself is not. As a result, the recitals to the Trade Mark Directive make it clear that its provisions are entirely consistent with those of the Paris Convention. There are also some explicit references to Paris Convention provisions in the text of the Directive and the Community Trade Mark Regulation.[19] Notwithstanding, the Paris Convention *per se* is not directly applicable in Community law.

5.2.2   The Madrid Agreement

The Paris Convention gives member states the right to make other special

---

[13]   Paris Convention, Art. 4.
[14]   Paris Convention, Art. 6(2).
[15]   Paris Convention, Art. 6(3).
[16]   Paris Convention, Art. 6*quinquies*.
[17]   Paris Convention, Art. 6*sexies*, Art. 7*bis*.
[18]   Paris Convention, Art. 10*bis*.
[19]   TMD, Recital 12. TMD, Arts. 3(1)(h), 3(2)(c), 4(2)(d). CTMR, Arts. 7(1)(h) and (i), 8(2)(c).

agreements for the protection of industrial property, in so far as these do not contravene the provisions of the Paris Convention itself. In 1891, shortly after the Paris Convention was agreed, the Madrid Arrangement for the International Registration of Marks ('the Madrid Agreement') was signed and ratified by four countries.[20] The intention was to provide an international procedure for applicants who had registered a trade mark at national level, and wished to acquire an 'international registration', recognised by all Madrid Agreement countries. Thus it is essentially a procedural convention, in contrast to the harmonising Paris Convention. The first international registration was made in 1893, and belonged to Swiss chocolate producer Russ Suchard et Cie. The oldest subsisting international registration, also first registered in 1893, belongs to Swiss watchmaker Longines. Fifty-six countries have now ratified the Madrid Agreement, including most European countries.[21]

Nationals of any of the contracting countries may, in all the other Madrid Agreement countries, secure protection for a mark already registered in the country of origin, by filing an international application with the International Bureau, at WIPO's headquarters in Geneva.[22] Only nationals of a Madrid Agreement country, or persons domiciled there, or legal persons having a real and effective industrial or commercial establishment there, are eligible to apply in this way.[23] The applicant designates the member states where protection is required, and, if procedural requirements are satisfied, the International Bureau must register the application immediately.[24] From the date of registration, the protection of the mark in each designated member state is the same as if the mark had been filed there directly.[25] National offices have the right to refuse protection, but only on the grounds set out in the Paris Convention, and they must do so within one year.[26] Registration of a mark at the International

---

[20]   The Madrid Agreement has been revised several times; most recently by the 1957 Nice revision, and the Stockholm revisions of 1967 and 1979. All states party to the Madrid Agreement are subject either to the Nice or the Stockholm revisions. The differences are relatively minor, and most European countries are bound by the Stockholm revisions. One set of regulations governs the text of both revisions. For the text of the Madrid Agreement see: http://www.wipo.int/madrid/en/legal_texts/trtdocs_wo015.html.

[21]   As of 28 April 2008: http://www.wipo.int/export/sites/www/treaties/en/documents/pdf/madrid_marks.pdf.

[22]   Madrid Agreement, Art. 1(2). The international application must be presented to the International Bureau of WIPO via the applicant's national trade mark office.

[23]   Madrid Agreement, Art. 1(2) and (3).

[24]   Madrid Agreement, Art. 3(4).

[25]   Madrid Agreement, Art. 4(1).

[26]   Paris Convention, Art. 6*quinquies*. Madrid Agreement, Art. 5(1) and (2).

Bureau is initially for 20 years, with the possibility of further 20-year renewal periods. However, if within five years the 'home' registration is struck off for any reason, all the registrations in the designated member states fall with it.[27] This is known as the 'central attack' provision.

A number of countries (including several, such as the United States, Japan and Canada, with very large numbers of trade mark filings) had serious objections to the Madrid Agreement, which undermined efforts to make it a truly international regime. The international mark followed a 'home' registration almost automatically (unless the Paris Convention grounds applied). This gave an advantage to nationals of states who could obtain a home registration comparatively easily. For example, some states offered registration merely on deposit, rather than thorough examination. Some states, notably the United States, require use of a mark before registration, thus disadvantaging their nationals against those of states without such a requirement. Countries (such as the UK) which did conduct a thorough search considered the 12-month window for refusal of a mark to be too short. Others objected to the 'central attack' provision. The only official language of the Agreement was French, posing a barrier for English-speaking countries. There was also discontent at the fee distribution for international applications, which was significantly less than that received from most domestic applications. Because of these drawbacks, several countries (including the United Kingdom, Australia, the USA and Japan) refused to ratify the Madrid Agreement, making it unattractive to applicants. The majority of 'home' registrations came from EC member states. When the EC began to make plans for a unitary Community trade mark, WIPO realised that the Madrid Agreement would become even less relevant and appealing. It therefore proposed a new treaty, the Madrid Protocol, to run in parallel with the Madrid Agreement.

5.2.3   The Madrid Protocol

A diplomatic conference in June 1989 resulted in the adoption of The Protocol Relating to the Madrid Agreement Concerning the International Registration of Marks ('the Madrid Protocol').[28] It has been signed by many Madrid Agreement countries, but also by countries unable to sign the Agreement

---

[27]   Madrid Agreement, Art. 6(3). After this five-year period has expired, the international registration becomes independent of the national mark: Madrid Agreement, Art. 6(2).

[28]   The Madrid Protocol entered into force on 1 December 1995 and became operational on 1 April 1996. The Community trade mark system became operational on the same date. For text of the Madrid Protocol see: http://www.wipo.int/madrid/en/legal_texts/trtdocs_wo016.html.

(including the UK, Australia, the USA and Japan).[29] The EC is itself a signatory to the Convention.[30] The effect of this is twofold: Community Trade Mark (CTM) protection may be extended internationally, using a CTM application or a registered CTM as the basic mark for an international application; or, the EC may be designated in an international application.

Like the Agreement, the Protocol is administered by WIPO. Although there are similarities between the two, there are also key differences. Whereas under the Madrid Agreement a home registration is required, under the Protocol it is sufficient if a home application has been made.[31] The working language of the Protocol is French, but applications may be submitted in either French, English or Spanish (although the national office may restrict this choice to just one language). The national office must certify that the particulars appearing in the international application correspond to the particulars in the home application or registration.[32] The countries where protection is required must be designated. The national office then forwards the application to WIPO, which must register the mark immediately if it complies with the necessary formalities.[33] As with the Madrid Agreement, from the date of registration, the protection of the mark in each designated member state is the same as if the mark had been filed there directly.[34] Again, national offices have the right to refuse protection, but only on the grounds set out in the Paris Convention.[35] The time limit for refusal is normally 12 months (as under the Madrid Agreement), but if an extensive examination is undertaken, member states can declare that the period is 18 months.[36] The period of protection is only ten years, with the

---

[29]   Seventy-five members as of 28 April 2008: http://www.wipo.int/export/sites/www/treaties/en/documents/pdf/madrid_marks.pdf.

[30]   Any state that is a party to the Paris Convention may become party to the Protocol. In addition, any intergovernmental organisation may do so, provided that at least one of the member states of that organisation is a party to the Paris Convention, and the organization has a regional office for registering marks: Madrid Protocol, Art. 14(1). The intention was to allow the Community Trade Mark Office (OHIM) to be designated, and thus allow the Protocol to be used to obtain a CTM. The EC's accession entered into force on 1 October 2004. This was the first time that the EC as such had acceded to a WIPO treaty. See also Jörg Weberndörfer, 'The Integration of the Office for Harmonization in the Internal Market into the Madrid System: A First Field Report' [2008] *EIPR* 216–21.

[31]   Madrid Protocol, Art. 2.

[32]   Madrid Protocol, Art. 3(1).

[33]   Madrid Protocol, Art. 3(4), Art. 2.

[34]   Madrid Protocol, Art. 4.

[35]   Madrid Protocol, Art. 5(1).

[36]   Madrid Protocol, Art. 5(2)(b). National offices may also declare that applications may be refused even after the 18-month period, if opposition proceedings have

possibility for renewal of further ten-year periods.[37] The 'central attack' provision remains, and has been extended in certain circumstances. Normally the international registration becomes independent five years from the date of international registration. But if opposition, rejection, cancellation or revocation proceedings have begun before the expiry of this five-year period, the Protocol permits the central invalidation of an international registration even after this date.[38] To soften the effect of this, the Protocol permits the transformation of a centrally invalidated international application into a national or regional application.[39] Such transformed applications maintain the priority date of the failed international registration.

The Madrid Agreement and the Protocol work in parallel, but separately. International applications from Protocol countries can only designate states which have acceded to the Protocol, and similarly, international applications from states which have only ratified the Agreement can only designate Agreement countries. If an international application comes from a state which has ratified both, the Protocol applies to Protocol-only countries, and the Agreement to others.[40] Nine hundred thousand marks have now been registered under the Madrid system, and WIPO anticipates that the one millionth mark will be registered in 2009.[41]

5.2.4   The Trademark Law Treaty

In this context the Trademark Law Treaty (TLT 1994) merits a brief mention. Also administered by WIPO, it was signed on 28 October 1994, and entered into force on 1 August 1996. Originally there were ambitious hopes that the Treaty would address significant issues of substantive law, but the diversity of national legal regimes rendered this aim impossible. The result is a treaty

---

been started against the applicant. Notification of refusal based on the opposition must be made not later than seven months from the date on which the opposition period began: Madrid Protocol, Art. 5(2)(c).

[37]   Madrid Protocol, Arts. 6 and 7.
[38]   Madrid Protocol, Art. 6(3).
[39]   Madrid Protocol, Art. 9*quinquies*.
[40]   Madrid Protocol, Art. 9*sexies*.
[41]   'WIPO Registers 900,000th Mark under the International Trademark System', WIPO Press Release 466 (Geneva, 27 October 2006). By the end of September 2006, about 465,000 international trade mark registrations belonging to some 150,000 different trade mark holders were in force in the international register. WIPO estimates that those international registrations represented the equivalent of some 5.1 million national registrations. For an appraisal of the Madrid System, see Roya Ghafele, 'Trade Mark Owners' Perspectives on the Madrid System: Practical Experiences and Theoretical Underpinnings' [2007] *JIPL&P* 160–69.

which harmonises various administrative procedures, important in trade mark practice.[42]

5.2.5   The Singapore Treaty on the Law of Trademarks

The Singapore Treaty on the Law of Trademarks was adopted in March 2006. It is not yet in force. Its objective 'is to create a modern and dynamic international framework for the harmonization of administrative trademark registration procedures'. It builds on the 1994 Trademark Law Treaty, having a wider scope of application, for example.[43] In other respects, the Singapore Treaty closely follows the TLT 1994. The two treaties are separate, and may be ratified or adhered to independently.[44]

5.3   TRIPS

The TRIPS Agreement lays down detailed requirements for substantive trade mark law.[45] Protectable subject matter is defined extremely broadly, and service marks must be protected in the same way as marks on goods.[46] The owner of a registered trade mark must be granted certain exclusive rights, including the right to prevent use on identical/similar goods where such use would result in a likelihood of confusion. The TRIPS Agreement also contains provisions on well-known marks, which supplement the protection required by Article 6*bis* of the Paris Convention. The provisions of Article 6*bis* must be applied also to services. Furthermore, the protection of registered well-known marks must extend to dissimilar goods or services, provided that use of the mark would indicate a connection between those goods or services and the owner of the registered trade mark, and the interests of the owner are likely to be damaged by such use.[47] Limited exceptions to these rights may be provided

---

[42]   For full text see http://www.wipo.int/treaties/en/ip/tlt/trtdocs_wo027.html.

[43]   Unlike the TLT 1994, the Singapore Treaty applies generally to marks that can be registered under the law of a contracting party. This is the first time that non-traditional marks have been explicitly recognised in an international instrument dealing with trade mark law. The Treaty is applicable to all types of marks, including non-traditional visible marks, such as holograms, three-dimensional marks, colour, position and movement marks, and also non-visible marks, such as sound, olfactory or taste and feel marks.

[44]   For more detail see http://www.wipo.int/treaties/en/ip/singapore/.

[45]   TRIPS, Arts. 15–21.

[46]   TRIPS, Art. 15.

[47]   TRIPS, Arts. 16.2, 16.3.

for.[48] Potentially, trade mark registration must be renewable indefinitely.[49] Cancellation of a mark on the grounds of non-use is restricted.[50] Compulsory licensing of marks is prohibited.[51]

Although the EC is a party to the TRIPS Agreement, its provisions are not directly applicable in Community law.[52]

5.4   COMMUNITY TRADE MARK LEGISLATION

5.4.1   Overview

The EU regards the protection of IP rights as of great importance for innovation, employment, competition and thus economic growth in the single market – which has over 350 million consumers. The Commission takes the lead on any initiatives. In the field of trade mark law, these have involved both traditional harmonising efforts intended to eliminate barriers to trade, and a project to create a unitary Community trade mark. Strong trade mark protection is also seen as a prerequisite to combat counterfeiting and product piracy. In addition, the Commission has been increasingly concerned to ensure that the EU adapts to changes in the information society, and leads wherever possible. Like other intellectual property rights, trade mark law is seen as an important tool in supporting this strategy.

Trade Mark Directive   The first stage was to harmonise national laws, via the 1988 Trade Mark Directive (TMD).[53] Whilst recognising that national trade mark laws contained disparities which might impede the free movement of goods and services and might distort competition within the single market, the Directive did not attempt full-scale harmonisation of the laws of member states. Instead, it was considered sufficient to focus on those provisions which most directly affect the functioning of the internal market. Thus the Directive harmonises the conditions for obtaining and continuing to hold a registered

48   TRIPS, Art. 17.
49   TRIPS, Art. 18.
50   TRIPS, Art. 19.
51   TRIPS, Art. 21.
52   See, to that effect, Case C-149/96, *Portugal* v. *Council* [1999] ECR I-8395 (paras. 42–8); Joined Cases C300/98 and C392/98, *Dior and Others* [2000] ECR I-11307 (paras. 44 and 45); Case C-245/02, *Anheuser-Busch* [2004] ECR I-10989 (para. 54); Case C-238/06 P, *Develey Holding GmbH* v. *OHIM* (25 October 2007).
53   Directive 89/104 to approximate the laws of the Member States relating to trade marks [1989] OJ L 040/1 ('TMD'). For text see: http://eur-lex.europa.eu/ LexUriServ/LexUriServ.do?uri=CELEX:31989L0104:EN:HTML.

trade mark, but leaves member states free to determine procedural provisions concerning registration, revocation and invalidity of trade marks. The substantive provisions regulating conflicts between confusingly similar marks and signs are also harmonised, although again various procedural matters are left to the member states.[54]

Community Trade Mark The next stage was to introduce a Community trade mark (CTM), by means of a Regulation.[55] Here the aim was to enable undertakings to adapt their activities to the scale of the Community, whether in manufacturing and distributing goods or in providing services. The Community trade mark offers the advantage of uniform protection in all countries of the European Union on the strength of a single registration procedure. It is valid for a period of ten years and may be renewed indefinitely. Because of its unitary character, when a CTM is registered, transferred or allowed to lapse, the effect of such action is Community-wide. The CTM co-exists with national trade marks, which remain useful for many undertakings. The CTMR uses very similar provisions to the Trade Mark Directive to control the conditions under which a CTM may be obtained and held. Once obtained, CTMs are enforced in national courts which have been designated 'community trade mark courts'.[56]

In order to implement the necessary administrative measures, an Office for Harmonization in the Internal Market (OHIM) was established in Alicante. Decisions made by OHIM may be appealed to one of its Boards of Appeal, and these decisions may in turn be appealed to the CFI, and ultimately the ECJ.[57] The Office opened in 1996, and by the end of 2006 it had received well over half a million applications, resulting in over 350,000 registrations. The greatest number of applications has come from the United States, the United Kingdom, and Germany. Predictably, therefore, the most popular first languages of application are English (42%) and German (19%).[58] OHIM is a self-financing agency of the EU, and its budget comes entirely from the fees paid by the businesses that use its services. It prides itself on its efforts to improve efficiency, increase the quality of its service, and introduce the most

---

54   TMD, Recitals.

55   Regulation 40/94 on the Community Trade Mark [1994] OJ L 11/1 ('CTMR'). For text see: http://eur-lex.europa.eu/LexUriServ/LexUriServ.do?uri=CELEX: 31994R0040:EN:HTML.

56   CTMR, Art. 91. See section 5.4.4 below: Infringement. Although a CTM may be revoked or declared invalid either in proceedings in a Community trade mark court, or by application to the Cancellation Division of the OHIM: CTMR, Art. 129.

57   CTMR, Recitals.

58   *OHIM Statistics of Community Trade Marks 2006*.

advanced information technology tools and resources. The CTM has been so successful that in 2005 OHIM was able to cut fees significantly.[59]

5.4.2 Applying for a Community Trade Mark

Any natural or legal person may be the proprietor of a Community trade mark.[60] However, for all proceedings other than the filing of an application, natural or legal persons not domiciled or having their principal place of business (or a real and effective industrial or commercial establishment) in the Community must be professionally represented.[61] CTM applications can be filed either directly at the OHIM or at any national trade mark office.[62] E-filing, by online application, is also available. A CTM application may be filed in any of the 22 languages of the Community. A second language must also be specified, which must be one of the five languages of the Office (Spanish, German, English, French or Italian).[63] The filing date of a CTM application is the date on which it was actually received at the OHIM (or, if filing through a national office, the date of actual receipt at that office), provided that the application fulfils the necessary conditions. The application must include a request for the registration of the mark as a CTM; information identifying the applicant; a list of the goods or services in respect of which the registration is requested; and a graphic representation of the trade mark. Classification of goods and services is according to the Nice Classification.[64] Although the EC is not party to the Nice Agreement, OHIM has adopted the use of the Nice Classification and its use is mandatory for CTM applicants.[65]

---

[59]   The CTM application fee was lowered from €975 to €900; the registration fee from €1,100 to €850; the renewal fee from €2,500 to €1,500. A further discount of 150 is available to those who file their applications or renewal requests online. IP/05/1289 'Trade Mark Protection in the EU Gets Cheaper' (Press Release, 17 October 2005).

[60]   CTMR, Art. 5.

[61]   CTMR, Art. 88(2). Professional representatives must be either a legal practitioner qualified in a member state to act as a representative in trade mark matters, or a professional representative recognised by OHIM: CTMR, Art. 89.

[62]   CTMR, Art. 25(2). The national office must forward the application to OHIM within two weeks of receipt. It then receives a filing date as if it had been filed direct in Alicante.

[63]   CTMR, Art. 115. The second language may be used in opposition and cancellation proceedings.

[64]   The Nice Agreement Concerning the International Classification of Goods and Services for the Purposes of the Registration of Marks (1957), administered by WIPO. Currently the ninth edition is in force. The Nice Classification is divided into classes of goods (classes 1 to 34) and services (classes 35 to 45).

[65]   *Guidelines Concerning Proceedings before the Office for Harmonization in the Internal Market (Trade Marks and Designs): Part B, Examination* (Draft,

There is no requirement (as there is in some national systems) that the applicant declare their intent to use the mark. Payment of the basic application fee is required within one month. The applicant may claim the priority of one or more previous trade mark applications; a national (or Benelux) application filed in or for a state party to the Paris Convention, a member of the TRIPS Agreement, a state for which the Commission has confirmed reciprocity, or a Community trade mark application.[66] The proprietor of an earlier national trade mark who applies for an identical CTM for identical goods or services may claim the seniority of that earlier mark. This has the effect of allowing the proprietor to surrender the national mark without suffering any disadvantage, and may produce a significant saving on renewal fees.[67]

Once a date of filing has been accorded, the process of examination begins. The application may be refused by OHIM only on the basis of the 'absolute' grounds (which regulate the characteristics of registrable trade marks).[68] OHIM (unlike some national systems) does not refuse applications on relative grounds – those relating to prior rights. The onus lies on third parties to raise relative grounds for refusal in opposition (or cancellation) proceedings. However, OHIM does draw up a search report on existing Community trade marks, and some national offices perform national searches.[69] The system was intended to help small and medium-sized firms for whom the monitoring of conflicting rights may involve prohibitive costs. The aim was to allow the applicant to take appropriate action even before publication, whether by amending or withdrawing the application, or by seeking agreement with the owner of a conflicting mark. In practice, the variable quality of the searches led the majority of applicants to conduct their own searches, and from March 2008 the national searches will be at the applicant's option, on payment of a separate fee.[70]

December 2007), 3.1. Figurative elements are classified according to the Vienna Classification system: the Vienna Agreement Establishing an International Classification of the Figurative Elements of Marks (1973). *Ibid.*, 3.7. See also Richard Ashmead, 'International Classification Class Headings: Illustrative or Exemplary? The Scope of European Union Registrations' [2007] *JIPL&P* 76–88.

[66] CTMR, Art. 29.

[67] CTMR, Art. 34.

[68] CTMR, Art. 38. The absolute grounds for refusal are stated in CTMR, Art. 7(1).

[69] CTMR, Art. 39. The relative grounds for refusal are stated in CTMR, Art. 8. Not all national offices search their national registers. France, Germany and Italy (for example) do not participate.

[70] For the defects in the system see Communication from the Commission to the Council, *Report on the operation of the system of searches resulting from Article 39 of the Community Trade Mark Regulation* (27 December 2002) COM(2002) 754 final. For the amendment to the procedure, see Regulation 422/2004 amending Regulation (EC) No. 40/94 on the Community trade mark.

If the application survives the examination procedure, it is published in the *Community Trade Marks Bulletin*, no less than one month after the applicant has been sent the search report. At this point OHIM informs the proprietors of any earlier CTMs (though not of prior national marks) that the application has been published.[71] Third parties may now submit 'observations' to OHIM, founded on the absolute grounds of refusal (Article 7), explaining why the trade mark should not be registered.[72] A narrow group of third parties may bring opposition proceedings, on the basis of the relative grounds of refusal (Article 8). These parties are: the proprietors of earlier trade marks and their licensees, the proprietors of trade marks whose agent has applied for registration in his own name without the proprietor's consent, the proprietors of well-known marks (seeking to rely on the anti-dilution provisions).[73] Notice of opposition must be given within three months. Both parties are then invited to file observations. Oral hearings are rare. The Opposition Division concludes the opposition procedure either by totally or partially refusing the application, or by rejecting the opposition and registering the trade mark. If no opposition is raised within a period of three months following publication, the trade mark is registered.[74] The initial registration period is ten years from the filing date, with the possibility of renewal for further periods of ten years.[75] A CTM may be revoked or declared invalid, either in proceedings in a Community trade mark court, or by application to the Cancellation Division of the OHIM.[76]

5.4.3   Criteria for Registration

The Trade Mark Directive and the Community Trade Mark Regulation impose very similar requirements for the registrability of trade marks. The regimes were intended to mirror each other as far as possible, and, in terms of substantive law, the wording of their provisions is often identical. Wherever it is feasible, the provisions of the Regulation are interpreted in the same way as the corresponding provisions of the Directive.

---

[71]   CTMR, Arts. 39 and 40.

[72]   CTMR, Art. 41. If 'serious doubts' are raised, OHIM will re-examine the application: Communication No. 1/00 of the President of the Office of 25 February 2000 concerning observations under Article 41 of the Community Trade Mark Regulation. Those submitting observations are not parties to the proceedings before the Office.

[73]   CTMR, Art. 42.

[74]   CTMR, Art. 45. A registration fee must be paid. The information in the Register is distributed in the OHIM *Community Trade Marks Bulletin*, available online.

[75]   CTMR, Arts. 46 and 47.

[76]   CTMR, Art. 129. For the grounds of revocation see CTMR, Arts. 50–52.

To be validly registered, a sign must satisfy three requirements:

- it must fall within the definition of a registrable mark;
- it must not be excluded by one of the absolute grounds of refusal;
- it must not be excluded by one of the relative grounds of refusal.

Each of these will be considered in turn.

(a) What is a registrable mark?

A trade mark may consist of 'any sign capable of being represented graphically, particularly words, including personal names, designs, letters, numerals, the shape of goods or their packaging, provided that such signs are capable of distinguishing goods or services of one undertaking from those of other undertakings'.[77]

SIGN

OHIM has indicated that this 'is to be interpreted as a very broad, "open" and general term encompassing all conceivable types of marks (including, for example, sound marks and three-dimensional marks)'.[78] There are nevertheless limits to what will be considered a sign. In *Dyson*, the ECJ held that the transparent collecting chamber of a bagless vacuum cleaner (in all conceivable forms, of which two examples were given) was insufficiently specific to be considered a sign.[79] The registration of shapes had not previously been permitted in some countries (including the UK), on the grounds that a trade mark is something which distinguishes goods rather than the goods themselves.[80] The more liberal approach to the understanding of marks has been appealing to trade mark proprietors, but raises other difficulties. One is evidentiary. Trade mark lawyers are accustomed to weighing up the impact of word and figurative marks for purposes of registrability and infringement. In contrast, notions

---

[77] TMD, Art. 2; CTMR, Art. 4.

[78] R 122/1998-3 *Wm. Wrigley/Light Green* [1999] ETMR 214 (para. 17).

[79] Case C-321/03. *Dyson* v. *Registrar of Trade Marks* [2007] ETMR 34. For discussion see Edward Smith, 'Dyson and the Public Interest: An Analysis of the Dyson Trade Mark Case' [2007] *EIPR* 469–73.

[80] *Re Coca-Cola Co.* [1986] 2 All ER 274. In the UK, resistance to the notion of shape registrations was strong. The Coca-Cola bottle had previously been registered as a design, but there followed an attempt to register the shape of the bottle as a trade mark. The application was rejected at every level. In the House of Lords, Lord Templeman observed that to win its appeal 'the Coca-Cola Co. must succeed in the startling proposition that a bottle is a trade mark. If so, then any other container or any article of a distinctive shape is capable of being a trade mark. This raises the spectre of a total and perpetual monopoly in containers and articles'.

of how colour, smell, shape or even movement marks should be assessed (to determine their distinctiveness, for example) are much less well developed and defined.[81]

GRAPHIC REPRESENTATION

This requirement is imposed for a number of reasons, including that of legal certainty. It ensures that the sign that is protected is delineated clearly and precisely, to define the extent of the trade mark owner's rights, and to assist those (including other traders) searching the register. In *Sieckmann*, the ECJ held that graphic representation must enable the sign to be represented visually, particularly by means of images, lines or characters. The representation must be 'clear, precise, self-contained, easily accessible, intelligible, durable and objective'.[82] For most marks, this requirement is easily met: word marks will be written, and figurative marks will be represented by pictures. The definition of sign is broad enough to encompass much more than these, however, and there have been efforts to register shapes, colours, smells, tastes, sounds, and so on.[83] For some of these, the requirement of graphic representation may present a significant hurdle.

Smells and tastes   OHIM's initial attitude to the graphic representation of olfactory marks was originally a generous one, permitting the registration of 'the smell of fresh-cut grass' for tennis balls.[84] However, the ECJ's approach in *Sieckmann* was significantly more restrictive. Here the application included a chemical formula, but since this represented the substance as such – rather than its odour – the formula did not satisfy the requirement of representation. In addition, the scent was described as 'balsamically fruity with a slight hint of cinnamon', and an odour sample was deposited with the application. The description was held to be graphic, but insufficiently clear, precise and objective. The odour sample was not a graphic representation, nor was it sufficiently stable or durable. These efforts, either on their own or in combination, did not

---

[81]   For discussion, see Robert Burrell and Michael Handler, 'Making Sense of Trade Mark Law' (2003) *IPQ* 388–410.

[82]   Case C-273/00, *Ralf Sieckmann* v. *Deutsches Patent-und Markenamt* [2002] ECR I-11737 (paras. 46–55).

[83]   The vast majority of the applications received to date have been for word marks (350,291) or figurative marks (198,138). But there are significant numbers of applications in other categories: 3D (4,339); colour (511); other (431); sound (65); hologram (11); olfactory (7). The numbers registered were: word marks (224,993); figurative (131,022); 3D (1,975); other (185); colour (103); sound (38); hologram (3); olfactory (1). *OHIM Statistics of Community Trade Marks 2006*.

[84]   R 156/1998-2, *Vennootschap Onder Firma Senta/The Smell of Fresh Cut Grass* [1999] ETMR 429.

satisfy the requirement of graphic representation.[85] The OHIM Board of Appeal has indicated that it would apply the same approach to tastes (gustatory signs), and that a description in written words would be insufficient.[86] An application to register 'the smell of ripe strawberries' was likewise rejected. There was evidence that the smell of strawberries varies from one variety to another, so the description was neither unequivocal nor precise, and did not eliminate all elements of subjectivity in the process of identifying and perceiving the sign claimed. The Court of First Instance noted that there is currently no generally accepted international classification of smells which would make it possible to identify an olfactory sign objectively and precisely through the attribution of a name or a precise code specific to each smell.[87] In the *IPF* case, an attempt was made to register a sign purporting to be a graphic representation of a particular fragrance. This was a coloured rectangle, containing red, green and blue stripes. An additional descriptive phrase had been added to the sign, and it was stated that samples of the fragrance could be obtained from the applicant's lawyers. The colour shades of the sign were produced by employing a particular protocol, commonly used in the fragrance industry, whereby electric signals from a scented source are digitised and processed, so that they can be used for identification and comparison. The OHIM Board of Appeal noted that, unlike professionals in the perfume industry, the relevant public would be unaware of this form of representation of olfactory nuances, and users of the register would not be able to reconstitute the fragrance in question. The representation was not sufficiently intelligible or self-contained, and the additional phrase of description did not make up for these deficiencies.[88] There is much industry pressure to protect the smell of perfumes. The global fragrance market is worth over ten billion US dollars, and manufacturers are anxious to use all possible legal avenues to defend their products. Trade mark law covers word and figurative marks straightforwardly, and may protect the shape of bottles and packaging. But, with the advent of so-called 'smell-alikes', what had been sought was protection for the smell of the perfume itself. After *Sieckmann*, trade mark protection seems a remote possibility. *Parfumeurs* have had only very limited success in seeking copyright protection for perfume, and it seems unlikely that one isolated decision by the Dutch

---

[85] Case C-273/00, *Ralf Sieckmann* v. *Deutsches Patent-und Markenamt* [2002] ECR I-11737 (paras. 69–73).

[86] R 120/2001-2, *Eli Lilly and Company/The Taste of Artificial Strawberry Flavour* [2004] ETMR 4.

[87] T-305/04, *Eden* v. *OHIM* [2006] ETMR 14.

[88] R 186/2000-4, *Institut Pour la Protection des Fragrances (IPF)'s Application* [2005] ETMR 42.

Supreme Court will provoke Community-wide change in that direction.[89] The problem of smell-alikes, and whether they are adequately covered by existing unfair competition law, has been referred to the ECJ.[90]

Colours   Similar issues affect the registration of colour marks. In *Libertel*, the ECJ considered whether a single colour is capable of constituting a trade mark, and concluded that it could. Although a colour *per se* cannot be presumed to constitute a sign (normally being a simple property of things), depending on the context in which it is, a single colour is capable, in relation to a product or service, of constituting a sign. The ECJ made explicit reference to the *Sieckmann* requirements in relation to graphic representation of colour. Mere samples would be insufficiently durable to satisfy these, but a verbal description might do so, as might a description combined with a sample, particularly if accompanied by an internationally recognised identification code.[91] OHIM now recommends that where registration for a colour mark *per se* is applied for, the indication of the colour required should where possible include a designation from an internationally recognised identification code.[92] The requirement of distinctiveness is also a significant hurdle.

Sounds   Sound marks are not precluded from registration, although they must satisfy the requirement of graphic representation. In *Shield Mark*, the Hoge Raad (Supreme Court of the Netherlands) asked the ECJ a number of questions about how the requirement might be satisfied for sound marks.[93] The applicant had attempted to register two marks. One was the first nine notes of Beethoven's famous Bagatelle, 'Für Elise', which was represented in various ways: a musical stave with those notes; a description, 'Sound mark. The trade mark consists of the representation of the melody formed by the notes (graph-

---

[89]   The French Cour de Cassation has held that the fragrance of a perfume results from the mere implementation of know-how, so does not constitute the creation of a form of expression which is capable of enjoying copyright protection as a work of the mind: *Bsiri-Barbir* v. *Haarmann & Reimer* Civ. (1re ch.), 13 June 2006; [2006] ECDR 28. However, the Dutch Supreme Court considered that copyright could subsist in a perfume: *Kecofa* v. *Lancôme* [2006] ECDR 26. See Catherine Seville, 'Copyright in Perfumes: Smelling a Rat' (2007) 66 *Cambridge Law Journal* 49–52.

[90]   *L'Oreal* v. *Bellure* [2007] EWCA Civ. 968.

[91]   Case C-104/01, *Libertel Groep BV* v. *Benelux-Merkenbureau* [2003] ECR I-3793 (paras. 26–38).

[92]   Communication No. 06/03 of the President of the Office of 10 November 2003. The Communication acknowledges that such an indication may not always be possible, for example because the colour or shade of colour does not exist in the coding system. See also Regulation 2868/95 implementing Council Regulation (EC) No. 40/94 on the Community Trade Mark ('CTMIR'), Rule 3(5).

[93]   Case C-283/01, *Shield Mark BV* v. *Joost Kist* [2003] ECR I-14313.

ically) transcribed on the stave'; and the sequence of musical notes 'E, D#, E, D#, E, B, D, C, A' . The other was a cockcrow, again represented in different ways, including: 'Kukelekuuuuu', an onomatopoeic word suggesting (in Dutch) a cockcrow; and a description, 'Sound mark, the trade mark consists of an onomatopoeia imitating a cockcrow'. The ECJ again invoked the *Sieckmann* requirements. Verbal descriptions such as 'the first nine notes of *Für Elise*' or 'a cockcrow' lacked the necessary precision and clarity. Nor would onomatopoeic representations allow those searching the register to determine whether the protected sign is the onomatopoeia itself, as pronounced, or the actual sound or noise. The sequence of musical notes, without indications of pitch and duration, was also insufficient. However, appropriate musical notation (a stave divided into bars, clefs, musical notes including accidentals, rests) could determine the pitch and duration of the sounds, and might thus constitute a faithful representation of the sounds. Such a representation would satisfy the *Sieckmann* criteria. Although it would not be immediately intelligible to everyone, it would be easily intelligible, and would allow the competent authorities and the public (in particular traders) to know precisely what the sign was.

The Hoge Raad had asked whether sonograms, sound recordings or digital recordings would suffice, but since the applicant had not used any of these methods, the ECJ refused to rule on them. The position of sonograms was considered by the OHIM Board of Appeal in *MGM*, where the company sought to register a mark described as 'constituted by the sound produced by the roar of a lion' and 'represented' by a spectrogram. The Board was willing to contemplate the use of diagrams as graphic aids to represent sound marks graphically, comparing sonograms to representation using musical notation, since both reproduce pitch, volume and progression of the sound over time. The fact that training and practice would be required to read sonograms was not regarded as a convincing objection, since the same was true of musical notation. The particular sonogram submitted, however, was unacceptable because it lacked time and frequency scales and so could not be read.[94] Although this decision seemed to leave the door open for the use of sonograms as the basis for a sound mark application, this door now appears to have been shut. The Fourth Board of Appeal refused to register a mark consisting 'of the yell of the fictional character TARZAN, the yell consisting of five distinct phases, namely sustain, followed by ululation, followed by sustain, but at a higher frequency, followed by ululation, followed by sustain at the starting frequency'.[95] The application

---

94 R 781/1999-4, *Metro-Goldwyn-Mayer Lion Corporation's Application* [2004] ETMR 34 (paras. 23–8).
95 R 708/2006-4, *Edgar Rice Burroughs, Inc.* v *OHIM* (27 September 2007).

was accompanied by a spectrogram. A spectrogram did not meet the *Shield Mark* requirements, for a number of reasons. It was not 'self-contained', because it could not be read as such. The Board considered it unlikely 'that anybody, even a superior specialist of spectrograms, could, on the basis of the spectrogram alone and without technical means, reproduce the sound'. For the same reason, the representation was not clear or intelligible, nor easily accessible to a reader of the CTM Register. These deficiencies were not cured by the verbal clarifications offered. The Board considered that, in contrast, musical notation was not ambiguous.[96] However, the Board also noted that it was precisely because it is so difficult to offer a proper graphical reproduction of sounds – although they might function as a trade mark – that the CTM rules now allow the filing of sound files in an electronic CTM application.[97] Such sound files do fulfil the requirements of being easily accessible and self-contained, since the Office publishes the sound file in electronic format, allowing the reader of the CTM Bulletin to hear the sound readily.

Shapes   OHIM rules require that non-word marks shall be 'reproduced'.[98] A mere verbal description, not conveying the clear and precise appearance of the mark itself, will not suffice. Photographs or design drawings will be required. In *Antoni & Alison's Application/Vacuum Packaging*, the description 'The trade mark consists in the vacuum packing of an article of clothing in an envelope of plastics' was held to be inadequate for the purposes of graphic representation, and not remedied by furnishing a sample of the packaging.[99] In addition, there are specific provisions which prevent the registration of shapes which: result from the nature of the goods themselves; which are necessary to obtain a technical result; which give substantial value to the goods. These will be discussed with the other absolute grounds for refusal.[100]

---

[96]   OHIM accepted a second application for the Tarzan yell, supported by musical notation, because it complied with the required formalities and the 'yell' which it described was held to be distinctive. See Press Release (5 November 2007), 'Tarzan's Trade Mark Yell' CP/07/01.

[97]   CTMIR, Rule 3(6); Decision No. EX-05-3 of the President of the Office of 10 October 2005. A third application for the Tarzan yell, combining a sonogram with an MP3 sound file is currently going through the registration process. See Press Release (5 November 2007), 'Tarzan's Trade Mark Yell' CP/07/01.

[98]   CTMIR, Rule 3(2).

[99]   R 4/97-2, *Antoni & Alison's Application/Vacuum Packaging* [1998] ETMR 460. Similarly, although tactile marks may be represented graphically if the representation and/or description fulfil the relevant criteria, a sample will not be accepted as a substitute. See R 1174/2006-1, *DaimlerChrysler AG* (30 October 2007), where important elements which determined the tactile impression of the surface of the object (represented by a picture and a description) remained unknown.

[100]   See below 5.4.3 (b) (vi) The shape exclusions.

'CAPABLE OF DISTINGUISHING'

The sign must be 'capable of distinguishing the goods and services of one undertaking from the goods or services of another'.[101] A certain amount of confusion was generated by this requirement, in particular its relationship with the exclusion from registrability of signs 'devoid of distinctive character'.[102] If a sign passed the hurdle of being 'capable of distinguishing', then how could it be 'devoid of distinctive character'? Was it possible, for example, for a mark to be distinctive by its nature or in fact, but still to be regarded as not 'capable of distinguishing'? In *Philips* v. *Remington* the ECJ made it clear that this was not possible.[103] The Court observed that the essential function of a trade mark was to guarantee the identity of the origin of the marked product to consumers by enabling them, without any possibility of confusion, to distinguish the product or service from others which have another origin. Both of the requirements in issue acted to preclude the registration of signs which did not permit consumers to distinguish the goods or services in this way. It seems therefore that the provisions should be read not as separate grounds of refusal, but seen more globally, as interrelated provisions intended to assure the guarantee of origin.

THE PROTECTION OF RETAIL SERVICES AS SERVICE MARKS

A service mark identifies and distinguishes the services of one company from another, as a trade mark does for products. There has been significant resistance to allowing service marks to cover the provision of retail services, such as the provision of customer information, advice and assistance, air conditioning and background music, toilet and car parking facilities, credit facilities, delivery services, and child care. One objection is the lack of precision in the definition of such services, and the goods to which they relate. Another is that these services are merely ancillary to the sale of products, and paid for by customers indirectly, as part of their purchases of goods. Therefore, it is argued, a trader should simply register a trade mark for the relevant goods. The issue has been much debated, and practices in different jurisdictions differed widely, although the trend has been towards willingness to allow retail services to be registered as service marks. When the CTMR was first adopted, the Council and the Commission of the European Communities entered a joint statement in the minutes of that meeting: 'The Council and the Commission consider that the activity of retail trading in goods is not as such a service for which a Community trade mark may be registered under this Regulation'.

---

[101]　TMD, Art. 2; CTMR, Art. 4.
[102]　TMD, Art. 3(1)(b); CTMR, Art. 7(1)(b).
[103]　Case C-299/99, *Koninklijke Philips Electronics NV* v. *Remington Consumer Products* [2002] ECR I-5475 (paras. 39 and 40).

Subsequent OHIM guidelines reflected this policy, and applications which sought registration of retail services were refused. In *Giacomelli*, the examiner refused a figurative mark for 'Bringing together, for the benefit of others, of a variety of goods – excluding transport – to enable consumers to view and buy the products'. The examiner's view was that this was not a service because the activity was ancillary to the sale of products and, despite the words 'for the benefit of others', was in the interest of the applicant alone. However, the Second Board of Appeal of OHIM set aside that decision, taking a wide view of the concept of a service, and noting that 'it is a matter of common experience that the consumer prefers the service provided by one particular shop over that of another'.[104] The fact that a retailer was motivated to perform these activities by the desire to make or increase its profits, rather than to offer a service to the public, in no way altered the fact that a service was being provided. The Board of Appeal held that it was necessary for the applicant to describe the service with sufficient clarity, however, including a reference to the field in which the service was rendered. OHIM felt obliged to change its practice as a result of the *Giacomelli* decision, and retail services were accepted as eligible for registration as CTMs. A reference to the field of activity or the specific nature of the service was stated to be desirable, rather than a legal necessity. The Office expressed unease both at departing from the earlier joint statement, and at having to adopt such a position in the absence of unanimity from member states.[105]

The ECJ has now ruled on the matter (in the context of the Trade Mark Directive) following the German Patent and Trade Mark Office's refusal to register the word PRAKTIKER in relation to a service described as 'retail trade in building, home improvement and gardening goods for the do-it-yourself sector'. The German Office had taken the view that the concept of 'retail trade' did not denote independent services which possessed any autonomous economic significance and related only to the distribution of goods as such. The applicant appealed to the *Bundespatentgericht*, submitting that the economic trend towards a service society necessitated a reappraisal of retail trade as a service, and that such services provided in connection with retail trade enabled retailers to be distinguishable from their competitors, and so ought to be eligible for protection by service trade marks. The *Bundespatentgericht* sought a preliminary ruling on various questions. The ECJ acknowledged the importance of a uniform interpretation of the concept of 'services', and concluded that it did include services provided in connection with retail trade in goods. It observed that retail trade consists, *inter alia*, in

---

104   R 46/1998-2, *Giacomelli Sport SpA's Application* [2000] ETMR 277.
105   Communication No. 3/01 of the President of the Office of 12 March 2001 concerning the registration of Community trade marks for retail services.

selecting an assortment of goods offered for sale and in offering a variety of services aimed at inducing the consumer to conclude a transaction with the trader in question rather than with a competitor. There was no overriding reason to exclude such services from the concept of services within the TMD. The Court refused to adopt a restrictive definition of retail services, and so held that it is not necessary to specify in detail the service(s) in question. However, details must be provided with regard to the goods or types of goods to which those services relate, in order to facilitate searches and to define the scope of the mark clearly (for opposition and infringement purposes).[106]

(b) The absolute grounds for refusal

The absolute grounds for refusal to register a trade mark are set out in Article 3 of the TMD, and Article 7 of the CTMR. These cover inherent objections to a sign's distinctiveness, and various public interest objections, including bad faith. Signs which do not comply may not be registered, or, if registered, are liable to be declared invalid.

(i)   SIGNS WHICH DO NOT CONFORM TO THE REQUIREMENTS OF A TRADE MARK
Signs which do not fall within the definition of a trade mark just discussed (for instance because they are not capable of graphic representation, or are not 'capable of distinguishing') may not be registered.[107]

Trade marks which are not distinctive   There are three absolute grounds which address the distinctiveness of the mark. The most general requires that marks which are 'devoid of any distinctive character' shall not be registered. The following two grounds are more specific in their focus, acting to exclude descriptive marks and those which have become customary in the relevant trade. Although each ground of refusal is independent of the others and should be considered separately, in practice they will often be applied cumulatively, and a mark may be caught by more than one category. The case law of the ECJ on these provisions has caused a certain amount of confusion, seeming somewhat inconsistent in its approach, particularly as to the level of distinctiveness required. Another issue is how far these provisions (particularly that excluding descriptive marks) aim to protect the freedom of other traders to use descriptive signs and indications.

(ii)   'DEVOID OF ANY DISTINCTIVE CHARACTER'
Trade marks which are devoid of any distinctive character may not be

---

106   C-418/02, *Praktiker Bau- und Heimwerkermärkte* [2005] ECR I-5873.
107   TMD, Art. 2; CTMR, Art. 4. See above (a) What is a registrable mark?.

registered.[108] This is to exclude marks which are not 'capable of identifying the product as originating from a particular undertaking and thus distinguishing it from other undertakings'.[109] In order to assess whether or not a trade mark has any distinctive character, the overall impression given by it must be considered. It may be useful, in the course of that overall assessment, to examine each of the components of which the trade mark concerned is composed.[110] A trade mark's distinctiveness is assessed by reference to the goods or services listed in the application and to the perception of the relevant public. The relevant public consists of average consumers of the goods or services in question, who are reasonably well informed and reasonably observant and circumspect.[111] There is also an element of public interest, aimed at ensuring that other traders offering the same type of goods or services will not be unduly restricted.[112] The level of distinctiveness required is not challenging: the mark must be 'devoid' of distinctive character. There is no requirement that the sign should exhibit any particular level of linguistic or artistic creativity. But the trade mark must enable the relevant public to identify the origin of the goods or services protected by it, and to distinguish them from those of other undertakings.[113] If the mark is a compound mark, the whole of the mark must be assessed for distinctiveness. The mere fact that each element, considered separately, is devoid of distinctive character does not mean that their combination cannot present a distinctive character. Thus, an application for CARGO PARTNER for transport, packaging and storage of goods was rejected as devoid of distinctive character for these services: 'cargo' and 'partner' were generic words, and there was nothing in the sign as a whole to indicate that it had a meaning other than that of presenting a partner offering services of transport, packaging and storage of goods.[114] In contrast, SAT.2,

---

[108]   TMD, Art. 3(1)(b); CTMR, Art. 7(1)(b).

[109]   Joined Cases C-53/01 and C-55/0, *Linde AG, Winward Industries, Rado Uhren AG* [2003] ECR I-3161 (para. 47).

[110]   Case C-286/04 P, *Eurocermex* v. *OHIM* [2005] ECR I-5797 (paras. 22 and 23). The applicant cannot demand to determine the order in which the examination of the individual features takes place, nor the level of detail to which each feature is examined: Case C-238/06 P, *Develey Holding GmbH* v. *OHIM* [2008] ETMR 20.

[111]   Case C-363/99, *Koninklijke KPN Nederland NV* v. *Benelux-Merkenbureau* [2004] ECR I-1619 (para. 34).

[112]   Case C-329/02 P, *SAT.1 SatellitenFernsehen GmbH* v. *OHIM* [2004] ECR I-8317 (para. 26).

[113]   Case T-34/00, *Eurocool Logistik GmbH* v. *OHIM* [2002] ECR II-683. Case T-79/00, *Rewe Zentral AG* v. *OHIM* [2002] ECR II-705 (LITE); Case C-304/06 P, *Eurohypo AG* v *OHIM* (8 May 2008).

[114]   Case T-123/04, *Cargo Partner* v. *OHIM* [2005] ECR II-3979. See also Case C-37/03, *BioID AG* v. *OHIM* [2005] ECR I-7975.

for services connected with satellite broadcasting, was not devoid of distinctive character when considered as a whole.[115]

All signs are subject to the same tests for the purpose of assessing their distinctiveness.[116] It is nevertheless helpful to look at the way different types of signs are handled in practice.

Letters, numbers, geometric shapes A plain numeral alone, without any unusual or fanciful feature, will be regarded as devoid of distinctive character. It 'belongs in the public domain and forms part of the store of signs available to all traders'.[117] OHIM guidelines indicate that a trade mark consisting of one or two letters or digits, unless represented in an unusual fashion, would, except in special circumstances, be devoid of distinctive character.[118] Registration of an ordinary exclamation mark with no additional graphic element or feature has likewise been refused as devoid of distinctive character.[119] Simple designs such as circles or squares, whether on their own or in conjunction with descriptive elements, are generally considered to be devoid of distinctive character.[120] Numbers and letters may suggest to the average consumer that they are model or catalogue numbers, in which case the sign will not function as a trade mark, but as a means of distinguishing the applicant's various products from one another.[121]

---

[115] Case C-329/02 P, *SAT.1 SatellitenFernsehen GmbH* v. *OHIM* [2004] ECR I-8317 (para. 28). Compare Case T-88/06, *Dorel Juvenile Group, Inc.* v. *OHIM* (24 January 2008) (SAFETY 1ST).

[116] Joined Cases C-53/01 and C-55/0, *Linde AG, Winward Industries, Rado Uhren AG* [2003] ECR I-3161 (para. 42).

[117] R 63/1999-3, *Caterham Car Sales & Coachwork's Application/Numeral 7* (para. 2); [2000] ETMR 14, 17. Compare R 800/2004-2, *Level 3 Communications, Inc.*, where the Board of Appeal thought that the numeral '3' inside parentheses might be capable of functioning as a trade mark.

[118] But see R 294/2000-3, *Fuji Photo Film Co.* (DS registrable for cameras, because not descriptive). See also R 773/2002-1, *Sun Chemical Corporation* (SOS registrable for the applicant's very specialist range of services, namely, 'providing temporary use of on-line non-downloadable expert-system software for troubleshooting lithographic printing processes'). See also Case T-441/05, *IVG Immobilien AG* v. *OHIM* (13 June 2007), for sympathetic discussion of an application to register a figurative mark consisting of the letter I in a particular font and colour.

[119] R 1658/2006-1, *Seriosity, Inc.*

[120] See Case T-304/05, *Cain Cellars, Inc.* v. *OHIM* (12 September 2007): application to register a simple pentagon refused for lack of distinctive character, [2005] OJ C 257.

[121] R 63/1999-3, *Caterham Car Sales & Coachwork's Application/Numeral 7* (para. 22); [2000] ETMR 14, 19.

Colours[122] Though it may constitute a sign, normally a colour is a simple property of things. Consumers are not accustomed to making assumptions about the origin of goods on the basis of their colour or the colour of their packaging alone. Usually there is some additional graphic or textual element. As a result, a colour *per se* is not normally distinctive. In addition, the relevant public is rarely in a position directly to compare products in various shades of colour, so the number of colours which it is capable of distinguishing is limited. Thus the number of different colours that are in fact available as potential trade marks to distinguish goods or services is limited. A small number of trade mark registrations for certain services or goods could exhaust the entire range of the colours available. The ECJ has acknowledged that there is, in Community trade mark law, a public interest in not unduly restricting the availability of colours for other traders.[123] The Court noted that in the case of a colour *per se*, 'distinctiveness without any prior use is inconceivable save in exceptional circumstances, and particularly where the number of goods or services for which the mark is claimed is very restricted and the relevant market very specific'.[124] However, distinctive character may be acquired through use. In *Heidelberger Bauchemie*, the ECJ considered the registrability of combinations of colours. The application was for blue and yellow, the company's corporate colours, which it claimed were used 'in every conceivable form'. Following *Libertel*, the Court observed that colours 'possess little inherent capacity for communicating specific information', although they may be capable of acquiring distinctive character. In addition the application for registration must include 'a systematic arrangement associating the colours concerned in a predetermined and uniform way'.[125]

Shapes The criteria for assessing the distinctiveness of three-dimensional shape of product marks are no different from those to be applied to other trade marks.[126] Nevertheless, it may in practice be more difficult to establish

---

[122]   See also Charlotte Schulze, 'Registering Colour Trade Marks in the EU' [2003] *EIPR* 55–67.

[123]   Case C-104/01, *Libertel Groep BV* v. *Benelux-Merkenbureau* [2003] ECR I-3793 (paras. 54–5).

[124]   Case C-104/01, *Libertel Groep BV* v. *Benelux-Merkenbureau* [2003] ECR I-3793 (paras. 66–7). See also Case C-447/02 P, *KWS Saat AG* v *OHIM* [2004] ECR I-10107.

[125]   Case C-49/02, *Heidelberger Bauchemie GmbH.* [2004] ECR I-6129 (para. 42). See also Case T-316/00, *Viking-Umwelttechnik GmbH.* v. *OHIM* (green and grey) [2002] ECR II-3715, and R 1620/2006-2, *Mars UK Limited* (purple, for Whiskas cat food).

[126]   Case C-299/99, *Koninklijke Philips Electronics NV* v. *Remington Consumer Products* [2002] ECR I-5475 (para. 48). Joined Cases C-53/01 and C-55/0, *Linde AG, Winward Industries, Rado Uhren AG* [2003] ECR I-3161 (para. 49).

distinctiveness in relation to a shape mark than a word or figurative trade mark. The public is accustomed to perceiving word and figurative marks as identifying the trade origin of the goods, but may not regard shape as communicating anything at all. This will be particularly the case where the sign is indistinguishable from the product itself. In *Henkel* (Ovoid Dishwasher Tablet), an application was made to register a two-layer, bi-coloured dishwasher tablet. The relevant public was the average consumer, although, because these were everyday goods, the level of attention given to the shape and colours of such tablets was not expected to be high. The shape was a basic geometrical shape, and an obvious one for such use. The use of basic colours was commonplace for detergents. The ECJ observed that 'only a trade mark which departs significantly from the norm or customs of the sector and thereby fulfils its essential function of indicating origin' would not be devoid of distinctive character.[127] Variants of common shapes for a particular product are thus likely to be regarded as non-distinctive.[128] Although this explains why many shape marks are refused registration initially, such marks may still acquire distinctive character through use.[129] The ECJ has stressed that a shape

---

[127] Joined Cases C-456/01 P and C-457/01 P, *Henkel* v. *OHIM* [2004] ECR I-5089 (para. 39). See also Joined Cases C-468/01 P to C-472/01 P, *Procter & Gamble* v. *OHIM* [2004] ECR I-5141; Case C-286/04 P, *Eurocermex* v. *OHIM* [2005] ECR I-5797; Case C-144/06 P, *Henkel* v. *OHIM* (4 October 2007); T-358/04, *Georg Neumann* v. *OHIM* (12 September 2007). Similarly, Joined Cases T-241/05, T-262/05 to T-264/05, T-346/05, T-347/05, T-29/06 to T-31/06 *Procter & Gamble Co.* v. *OHIM* (23 May 2007).

[128] Case T-324/01, *Axion SA* v. *OHIM* [2003] ECR II-1897 (cigar and ingot shapes for chocolate not substantially different from a basic shape for these products commonly used in the trade); Case T-360/03, *Frischpack* v. *OHIM* [2004] ECR II-4097 (flat box for cheese 'only a slight and unremarkable variation on the typical shape'); Case T-15/05, *De Waele* v. *OHIM* [2006] ECR 1511 (no grounds for believing that manufacturers of gut for sausage-making sought to differentiate their goods by its shape, so manufacturers of charcuterie and consumers would not be capable of identifying the shape of gut and charcuterie as an indication of origin); Case T-140/06, *Philip Morris Products* v. *OHIM* (12 September 2007) (three-dimensional shape of a packet of cigarettes lacked distinctive character because it differed only slightly from 'standard' cigarette packets). But cf. Case T-128/01, *DaimlerChrysler Corp.* v. *OHIM* [2003] ECR II-701, where the CFI allowed registration of the shape of a vehicle grille, noting that grilles 'have become an essential part of the look of vehicles and a means of differentiating between existing models on the market made by the various manufacturers' (para. 42). See also Case T-305/02, *Nestlé Waters France* v. *OHIM* [2003] ECR II-5207 (water bottle design not commonplace when considered as a whole); Case T-460/05, *Bang & Olufsen A/S* v. *OHIM* (10 October 2007) (shape of loudspeaker, 'a vertical, pencil-shaped column, with a long, rectangular panel attached to one side', held to be 'truly specific', so 'cannot be considered to be altogether common' (paras. 39–40).

[129] Such marks would qualify for registration under the terms of the proviso: TMD, Art. 3(3); CTMR, Art. 7(3). See Case T-63/01, *Procter & Gamble Co.* v. *OHIM*

mark is essentially different from its two-dimensional graphic representation. So a picture of the product featured on the packaging, although it may sometimes facilitate awareness of the mark by the relevant public, will not necessarily amount to use of the mark.[130]

The public interest underlying this ground of refusal is that trade marks must be capable of fulfilling the essential function of a trade mark, which is to guarantee the identity of the origin of the marked product or service to the consumer or end-user, without any possibility of confusion. The question arose as to whether there was also a need to keep certain shapes freely available for others to use. In *Deutsche SiSi-Werke*, the ECJ made it clear that this was not the case. Such considerations were relevant only for the exclusion of descriptive marks.[131]

Names   In several member states the registration of common surnames has traditionally been viewed with caution, unless accompanied by evidence of acquired distinctiveness. The question has now been considered by the ECJ. An application was made to the UK Trade Marks Registry to register the surname *Nichols'* as a trade mark for vending machines, and food and drink dispensed through such machines. It was refused for food and drink products, on the grounds that the surname (and close equivalents) was common in the London telephone directory, and the mark was therefore not of itself capable of communicating the fact that such goods originated from a single undertaking. The public were unlikely to consider that there would be only one trader operating under that surname in such a wide market, so it was devoid of any distinctive character in respect of food and drink products. The UK Registry had taken the view that the registration of names, and particularly of common surnames, should be considered carefully to ensure that unfair advantage was not given to the first applicant for such a name. The more common the surname, the less willing the Registry had been to accept an application for registration without proof that that name had become distinctive in fact. However, the ECJ stated unambiguously that the criteria for assessing the

---

(Soap Bar Shape) [2002] ECR II-5255 (para. 40). See also Case C-136/02 P, *Mag Instrument* v. *OHIM*. There the ECJ noted that distinctive character would normally be acquired by familiarising the relevant public with the mark. The Court also recognised the possibility that evidence of the actual perception of the mark by consumers might contribute to the assessment of distinctiveness of a mark for the purposes of CTMR, Art. 7(1)(b). However, such evidence would have to show that consumers did not need to become accustomed to the mark through the use made of it, but that it immediately enabled them to distinguish the product's origin (para. 50).

[130]   Case C-24/05 P, *August Storck* v. *OHIM* [2006] ECR I-5677.
[131]   Case C-173/04, *Deutsche SiSi-Werke* v. *OHIM* [2006] ECR I-551 (paras. 60–63).

distinctiveness of trade marks which were personal names were the same as those applicable to the other categories of trade mark, and that stricter general criteria of assessment for names were not permitted. The ECJ acknowledged that it might be more difficult to establish the distinctive character of certain categories of trade marks (shapes, for example), but this did not justify the assumption that such marks were *a priori* devoid of distinctive character.[132]

Slogans   The ECJ has taken a similar approach to the registration of slogans, insisting that the criteria for assessing the distinctiveness of these are the same as for any other category of marks. Because the relevant public may not tend to perceive slogans as identifying trade origin, it may prove more difficult to establish distinctiveness in such cases, but this does not justify laying down specific criteria supplementing or derogating from the usual criterion of distinctiveness.[133] Thus, the term REAL PEOPLE, REAL SOLUTIONS was unregistrable for technical support services in the computer industry, because the relevant public would perceive only its obvious promotional meaning, and would not without prior knowledge regard it as a distinctive trade mark for those services.[134] Similarly, a figurative mark with the words BEST BUY superimposed on the shape of a coloured price tag would be immediately perceived as a mere promotional formula rather than an indication of the commercial origin of the services applied for.[135]

(iii)   DESCRIPTIVE MARKS

Descriptive trade marks may not be registered. These are trade marks which consist exclusively of signs or indications which may serve, in trade, to designate the kind, quality, quantity, intended purpose, value, geographical origin,

---

[132]   Case C-404/02, *Nichols Plc* v. *Registrar of Trade Marks* [2004] ECR I-8499 (paras. 25–30).

[133]   Case C-64/02 P, *OHIM* v. *Erpo Mobelwerk* [2004] ECR I-10031. Both the CFI and the ECJ rejected the Board of Appeal's approach in this case, which required that slogans display imaginativeness or conceptual tension.

[134]   Case T-130/01, *Sykes Enterprises Inc.* v. *OHIM* [2002] ECR II-5179. See also Case T-216/02. *Fieldturf Inc.* v. *OHIM* [2004] ECR II-1023 (LOOKS LIKE GRASS . . . FEELS LIKE GRASS . . . PLAYS LIKE GRASS for synthetic sports surfaces found to be incapable of being perceived immediately as an indication of origin, and merely a promotional slogan informing the consumer that the surface had properties similar to those of natural grass). Compare R184/2006-2, *Lavalife Inc.* (13 July 2006) (WHERE SINGLES CLICK registrable for online dating services).

[135]   Case T-122/01, *Best Buy Concepts Inc.* v. *OHIM* [2003] ECR II-2235. Likewise Case T-320/03, *Citicorp* v. *OHIM* [2005] ECR II-3411 (LIVE RICHLY for financial services). See also Case T-28/06, *RheinfelsQuellen H. Hövelmann GmbH* v. *OHIM* (6 November 2007), where the slogan 'Vom Ursprung her vollkommen' ('perfect because of its origin') for beers and waters was held to be descriptive.

the time of production of goods or of rendering of services, or other characteristics of goods or services.[136] This area of trade mark law has been the
subject of considerable controversy. The test for descriptiveness set out by the
ECJ in BABY DRY was criticised for setting a very low threshold for the
registration of descriptive marks, raising concerns that ordinary language
might be monopolised by a few traders.[137] The Court has qualified this position somewhat in more recent decisions such as POSTKANTOOR, and
BIOMILD.[138] It is now clear that this exclusion also has a public interest aim
– to ensure that descriptive signs may be freely used by all, unless they have
become distinctive through use.[139] The relevant question is whether, given the
meaning of the sign to the relevant public, there is a sufficiently direct and
specific relationship between the sign and the goods or services for which it is
to be registered.[140] A word mark which is descriptive of characteristics of
goods or services within the meaning of this provision is also, on that account,
necessarily devoid of any distinctive character.[141] Thus, the sign BASICS used
for artist's paints would be perceived by the target public as indicating that the
goods were the most useful and important of the artist's fundamental and
elementary materials. BASICS therefore describes, in a direct manner, one of
the characteristics of the goods in question, and could not be registered.[142]

A mark consisting of a neologism produced by a combination of elements
will not be regarded as descriptive merely because each of its components is
descriptive. The mark as a whole must be found to be descriptive. It is not
necessary for all possible meanings to fall within the exclusion. A word will
be refused registration if at least one of its possible meanings designates a

---

[136]   TMD, Art. 3(1)(c); CTMR, Art. 7(1)(c).

[137]   Ian Kilbey, '"BABY_DRY": A Victory for the Ephemera of Advertising'
[2002] *EIPR* 493–7; Andrew Griffiths, 'Modernising Trade Mark Law and
Promoting Economic Efficiency: An Evaluation of the Baby Dry Judgment' [2003]
IPQ 1–37.

[138]   Case C-363/99, *Koninklijke KPN Nederland NV* v. *Benelux-Merkenbureau*
(POSTKANTOOR) [2004] ETMR 57. Case C-265/00, *Campina Melkunie BV* v.
Benelux-Merkenbureau [2004] ECR I-1699 (BIOMILD). Both discussed below.

[139]   Case C-108/97, *Windsurfing Chiemsee Produktions- und Vertriebs GmbH* v.
Boots- und Segelzubehor Walter Huber [1999] ECR I-2779 (para. 25). Joined Cases C-
53/01 and C-55/0, *Linde AG, Winward Industries, Rado Uhren AG* [2003] ECR I-3161
(para. 73). Case C-104/01, *Libertel Groep BV* v. *Benelux-Merkenbureau* [2003] ECR I-
3793 (para. 52). The Court has refused to endorse the German doctrine of
Freihaltungsbedürfnis ('the need to keep it free').

[140]   Case T-28/06, *RheinfelsQuellen H. Hövelmann GmbH* v. *OHIM* (6 November
2007) (para. 31).

[141]   Case T-190/05, *Sherwin-Williams* v. *OHIM* (TWIST & POUR) (12 June 2007,
para. 39).

[142]   Case T-164/06, *ColArt/Americas, Inc.* v. *OHIM* (12 September 2007).

characteristic of the goods or services concerned.[143] The mere combination of descriptive elements will normally remain descriptive, even if the combination creates a neologism. To be registrable, there must be 'a perceptible difference between the neologism and the mere sum of its parts'. This might occur because for the relevant goods or services the combination of elements is sufficiently unusual that the word creates an impression which is 'sufficiently far removed from that produced by the mere combination of meanings lent by the elements of which it is composed, with the result that the word is more than the sum of its parts'.[144] Thus, the elements of BABY-DRY did allude to the function of babies' nappies, but their 'syntactically unusual juxtaposition' was not a familiar expression in the English language, either for designating nappies or for describing their essential characteristics. When considered as a whole, BABY-DRY was not descriptive, but a lexical invention which rendered the mark distinctive.[145] In contrast, DOUBLEMINT for chewing gum simply indicated a doubling of the mint flavour, so was unregistrable. Although this exclusion is commonly applied to word marks, there is nothing in principle to prevent its being applied to shape marks, or other marks.[146]

Geographical names fall to be considered under this provision. National trade mark laws have often been hostile to the registration of place names, to prevent a single trader from monopolising them. However, it is still possible to register geographic names in some circumstances. In *Windsurfing*, an application had been made to register CHIEMSEE, the name of the largest lake in Bavaria, for sports clothing. The ECJ noted that geographic names could indicate the quality and characteristics of goods, and might also influence consumer choice by associating the goods with a favourable message. The public interest underlying the provision was that such names should be freely

---

[143]   Case C-191/01, P *OHIM* v. *Wm Wrigley Jr Co.* [2003] ECR I-12447.

[144]   Case C-265/00, *Campina Melkunie BV* v. *Benelux-Merkenbureau* [2004] ECR I-1699 (para. 41). See also Case C-363/99, *Koninklijke KPN Nederland NV* v. *Benelux-Merkenbureau* (POSTKANTOOR) [2004] ETMR 57.

[145]   Case C-383/99 P, *Procter & Gamble Co.* v. *OHIM* [2001] ECR I-6251 (paras. 43–4).

[146]   Case C-191/01 P, *OHIM* v. *Wm Wrigley Jr Co.* [2003] ECR I-12447. See also Case T-183/03, *Applied Molecular Evolution Inc.* v. *OHIM* [2004] ECR II-3113 (APPLIED MOLECULAR EVOLUTION descriptive of the services claimed, given the highly specialised relevant public), but cf. Case C-273/05 P, *OHIM* v. *Celltech R&D Ltd* (19 April 2007) (CELLTECH, when considered as a whole, even understood as meaning 'cell technology', not shown to be descriptive of the relevant goods and services). Joined Cases T-178/03 and 179/03, *CeWe Color* v. *OHIM* [2005] ECR II-3105 (DigiFilmMaker and DigiFilm). Case T-289/02, *Telepharmacy Solutions Inc.* v. *OHIM* [2004] ECR II-2851. Case T-230/05, *Golf USA, Inc.* v. *OHIM* (6 March 2007); T-461/04, *Imagination Technologies Ltd* v. *OHIM* [2008] ETMR 10 (PURE DIGITAL descriptive of electronic goods).

available to all. The important question was whether the geographical name 'designates a place which is currently associated in the mind of the relevant class of persons with the category of goods concerned, or whether it is reasonable to assume that such an association may be established in the future'. The size and characteristic of the place, the relevant public's familiarity with it and the nature of the goods concerned would all be factors in determining this question. Registration would not be precluded if a particular geographical name was unknown to the relevant public (that is to say, unknown as a geographical location), or if the name was such that the relevant public would be unlikely to believe that the goods originated there (a mountain or lake, for example).[147] It is not necessary for the goods to be manufactured in the geographical location in order for them to be associated with it. A connection might be established by other ties, such as the fact that the goods were conceived and designed in the geographical location concerned. This approach was applied by the CFI to permit the registration of CLOPPENBERG. Although Cloppenberg was a small town, as far as the relevant public was concerned, the word did not present any link with the relevant services, nor was it reasonable to imagine that it might in the future designate the geographical origin of those services.[148]

Certain words may be distinctive in some member states, but descriptive in others. The question arose whether the Spanish trade mark MATRATZEN, registered for beds, could be cancelled on the grounds that it meant 'mattress' in German, and was descriptive. The CFI held that the registration, as a *national* trade mark, of a descriptive term borrowed from the language of another member state was permitted – unless the relevant public in the state of registration was capable of identifying the meaning of the term.[149]

(iv)　CUSTOMARY AND GENERIC MARKS

Trade marks which consist exclusively of signs or indications which have become customary in the current language or in the bona fide and established

---

[147]　Case C-108/97, *Windsurfing Chiemsee Produktions- und Vertriebs GmbH* v. *Boots- und Segelzubehor Walter Huber* [1999] ECR I-2779 (paras. 26–33).

[148]　Case T-379/03, *Peek & Cloppenburg KG* v. *OHIM* [2005] ECR II-4633. Compare Case T-295/01, *Nordmilch eG* v. *OHIM* [2003] ECR II-4365. Similarly, Case T-316/03, *Münchener Rückversicherungs-Gesellschaft AG* v. *OHIM* [2005] ECR II-1951 (MunichFinancialServices refused for financial services). Compare R 1461/2006-4, *Alvito Holdings Ltd's Application* [2008] ETMR 28: ('Not made in China' unregistrable as descriptive).

[149]　Case C-421/04, *Matratzen Concord AG* v. *Hukla Germany SA* [2006] ECR I-2303.

practices of the trade are not registrable.[150] In *Merz & Krell*, the German trade mark registry rejected an application to register BRAVO for writing implements, on the ground that this was a purely laudatory term and thus lacking in distinctive character. The ECJ agreed that a sign which did not possess distinctive character could not be registered, but emphasised that this question could not be considered in the abstract or separately from the goods or services applied for. The Court noted that the exclusion of customary marks overlapped with the exclusion of descriptive marks, but observed that customary signs would not necessarily be descriptive. Customary signs would by their nature be incapable of distinguishing, and it was of little consequence whether they were used as advertising slogans, indications of quality or incitements to purchase. It is for the national court to determine in each case whether the sign has become customary to designate the goods or services covered by the mark.[151] Similarly, in *Alcon*, the registration of BSS as a CTM for ophthalmic preparations was cancelled, because BSS was an abbreviation for 'balanced salt solution' or 'buffered saline solution', and had become customary in current usage among the relevant public (ophthalmologists and ophthalmic surgeons).[152]

(v) ACQUIRED DISTINCTIVENESS

There is an important exception to these rules. The above three absolute grounds of refusal (mark devoid of distinctive character, descriptive or customary) may be overcome if the mark has become distinctive in relation to the goods or services for which registration is requested in consequence of the use which has been made of it.[153] This recognises that, through use, an inherently unregistrable mark may become distinctive in fact, and thus registrable. For distinctive character to have been acquired through use, 'the mark must serve to identify the product in respect of which registration is applied for as originating from a particular undertaking, and thus to distinguish that product from goods of other undertakings'.[154] In other words, as always, the trade mark must enable the relevant public to identify the origin of the goods or services protected by it, and to distinguish them from those of other undertakings.

---

150 TMD, Art. 3(1)(d); CTMR, Art. 7(1)(d).

151 Case C-517/99, *Merz & Krell* v. *Deutsches Patent- und Markenamt* [2001] ECR I-6959.

152 Case C-192/03 P, *Alcon Inc.* v. *OHIM* [2004] ECR I-8993. See also Case T-322/03, *Telefon & Buch Verlagsgesellschaft* v. *OHIM* [2006] ECR II-835 (WEISSE SEITEN – 'white pages' – customary for private telephone directories).

153 TMD, Art. 3(3); CTMR, Art. 7(3).

154 Case C-108/97, *Windsurfing Chiemsee Produktions- und Vertriebs GmbH* v. *Boots- und Segelzubehor Walter Huber* [1999] ECR I-2779 (paras. 51–3).

Whether this is so will be determined by an overall assessment of the evidence. Important factors will include: the market share held by the mark; how intensive, geographically widespread and long-standing use of the mark has been; the amount invested by the undertaking in promoting the mark; the proportion of the relevant class of persons who, because of the mark, identify goods as originating from a particular undertaking; statements from chambers of commerce and industry or other trade and professional associations. If, on the basis of those factors, there is evidence that the relevant class of persons, or at least a significant proportion thereof, identifies goods as originating from a particular undertaking because of the trade mark, then it is registrable. Because the nature of the particular mark is relevant, predetermined percentages cannot be used as the basis of assessment. Opinion polls are not precluded as guidance in making this judgement.[155]

The assessment is a global one, and there is no *a priori* restriction on the way in which the mark must be used for acquired distinctiveness to be possible. The mark HAVE A BREAK was refused by the UK Registry, because it had always been used as part of the composite phrase, 'Have a break, Have a KIT KAT', and thus was used as an advertising slogan rather than to indicate origin. The ECJ held that there was no requirement that the mark be used independently.[156] However, although the definition of use is not constrained, not all use will lead to acquired distinctiveness – the relevant public must have come to understand that the sign indicates origin. In *Philips*, the applicant was at first the only seller of three-headed rotary shavers, and there was evidence that the public associated the shape with Philips. There was doubt as to whether this association had come about because of the pre-existing monopoly, or whether the shape was genuinely functioning as a trade mark. The ECJ acknowledged that extensive use of the shape might be sufficient to give the sign a distinctive character, but stressed that the national court would have to verify this on the basis of specific and reliable data.[157]

Showing acquired distinctiveness may be particularly challenging for a CTM applicant. In *Ford Motor*, the sign OPTIONS for insurance services was refused as devoid of distinctive character in English and French. Ford argued that there was no specific requirement that distinctiveness must be shown

---

[155]   Case C-108/97, *Windsurfing Chiemsee Produktions- und Vertriebs GmbH* v. *Boots- und Segelzubehor Walter Huber* [1999] ECR I-2779 (para. 46). See also Case C-299/99, *Koninklijke Philips Electronics NV* v. *Remington Consumer Products* [2002] ECR I-5475 (para. 65).

[156]   Case C-353/03, *Société des Produits Nestlé* v. *Mars UK* [2005] ECR I-6135 (para. 27).

[157]   Case C-299/99, *Koninklijke Philips Electronics NV* v. *Remington Consumer Products* [2002] ECR I-5475 (para. 65).

throughout the Community, and that it was sufficient that distinctiveness be acquired in a substantial part of the Community. The CFI rejected this argument. The CTM is of unitary character, which implies that it shall have equal effect throughout the Community. Consequently, in order to be accepted for registration, a sign must possess a distinctive character throughout the Community. Thus the requirement is to demonstrate acquired distinctive character in 'the substantial part of the Community where it was devoid of any such character'.[158]

In *Glaverbel*, the applicant submitted declarations as to its mark's distinctiveness from ten of the 15 member states (as at the date of filing of the application). Since those member states represented around 90% of the population of the Community, it argued that this was representative of the single market. OHIM argued that there was no reason to exclude the population of five member states of the Community from the consumer circles whose awareness and perception of the sign in question must be assessed, and the CFI agreed. The mark must have become distinctive through use in the Community as a whole, and must be refused registration if it is devoid of any distinctive character in part of the Community. Since that part of the Community may be comprised of a single member state, the evidence concerning distinctive character acquired through use for each member state should be examined separately.[159] This will represent an increasing hurdle as EU membership widens.

A similar approach was taken with an application to register EUROPOLIS as a Benelux trade mark for insurance and financial services, on the basis of acquired distinctiveness. The ECJ was asked whether the sign had to have acquired distinctiveness throughout the Benelux territory (that is, in Belgium, the Netherlands and Luxembourg), and whether it was necessary to take into account the language regions within that territory. The reply was that the trade mark had to have acquired distinctive character through use throughout the part of the territory of Benelux in which there existed a ground for refusal. If the ground for refusal existed only in one linguistic area, the mark had to have acquired distinctive character through use throughout that linguistic area.[160]

(vi)   THE SHAPE EXCLUSIONS
A product's design is crucial to its success in the market. Although design

---

[158]   Case T-91/99, *Ford Motor Co.* v. *OHIM* [2000] ECR II-1925 (paras. 23–7). See also Case T-16/02, *Audi AG* v. *OHIM* [2003] ECR II-5167 (paras. 50–54); Case T-164/06, *ColArt/Americas, Inc.* v. *OHIM* (12 September 2007).

[159]   Case T-141/06, *Glaverbel* v. *OHIM* (12 September 2007). See also Case C-24/05 P, *August Storck* v. *OHIM* [2006] ECR I-5677 (paras. 81–3).

[160]   Case C-108/05, *Bovemij Verzekeringen NV* v. *Benelux-Merkenbureau* [2007] ETMR 29.

rights and copyright may be available, these have limitations. Hence the increased demand for shape trade marks, which can provide indefinite protection for design elements. There is an obvious danger that such marks will hamper other traders who legitimately wish to use similar shapes. Shape marks, like other marks, must satisfy the general requirements for registrability, including distinctiveness. In addition, there are specific exclusions intended to prevent the registration of marks which will give their proprietors a monopoly on technical solutions or functional characteristics of a product, thus hampering competitors. The exclusions apply to signs which consist exclusively of: the shape which results from the nature of the goods themselves; the shape of goods which is necessary to obtain a technical result; the shape which gives substantial value to goods.[161] Unlike the previous absolute grounds for refusal, they may not be overcome by showing that they have acquired a distinctive character through use.[162] Not all goods possess an intrinsic shape (liquids, powder, granules, for example), and these must be packaged in order to be marketed. The packaging chosen inevitably imposes its shape on the goods. If a trade mark application involves goods of this sort, the ECJ has held that the packaging must be assimilated to the shape of the product for the purposes of examining that application.[163]

(i)   *The shape which results from the nature of the goods themselves*   As yet there is little EU case law on this subsection. The aim is to exclude basic shapes that should be available for use by all traders. A shape which results from the nature of the goods themselves will not be capable of distinguishing the trade origin of the goods, since other traders will necessarily be using that shape. OHIM draft guidelines state that the subsection 'is limited to those shapes which are identical to the goods, for example the shape of a football for a football'.[164] The definition of 'the goods themselves' will be important, because if drawn narrowly the shape exclusion is more likely to apply. Thus, in *Philips Electronics* v. *Remington* the first instance judge noted that if 'the goods' were 'rotary shavers having three equilateral heads and a face plate'

---

[161]   In interpreting the requirement that the sign must consist 'exclusively' of such shapes, the ECJ focused on the 'essential functional features' of the shape, to avoid the possibility that the addition of an arbitrary element would allow the applicant to escape the prohibition: Case C-299/99, *Koninklijke Philips Electronics NV* v. *Remington Consumer Products* [2002] ECR I-5475 (para. 4).

[162]   TMD, Art. 3(1)(e); CTMR, Art. 7(1)(e).

[163]   Case C-218/01, *Henkel* v. *Deutsches Patent- und Markenamt* [2004] ECR 1725.

[164]   *Guidelines Concerning Proceedings before the Office for Harmonization in the Internal Market (Trade Marks and Designs): Part B, Examination* (Draft, December 2007), 7.6.2.

then the shape resulted from the nature of the goods, but if 'the goods' were just rotary shavers, or more generally electric shavers or even more generally shavers electric or otherwise, then the shape did not result from the nature of the goods.[165] It is clear that the decision cannot be based unquestioningly on the applicant's categorisation of the goods. Similar difficulties arise when asking whether the shape results from the nature of the goods. In *Procter & Gamble (Soap Bar)*, an attempt was made to register a three-dimensional waisted bone shape for soaps. This did not fall foul of the exclusion, firstly, because the shape bent inwards along its length and had grooves which did not come about as a result of the nature of the product itself, and, secondly, because there were 'other shapes of soap bar in the trade without those features'.[166] The exclusion will be very narrow if it is only to be applied when there is no practical alternative for other traders.

(ii)   The shape of goods which is necessary to obtain a technical result   The leading authority on this exclusion is *Philips* v. *Remington*. In 1966 Philips developed a new type of three-headed rotary electric shaver. A graphic representation of the shape of the shaver-head, comprising three circular heads with rotating blades in the shape of an equilateral triangle, was registered as a trade mark in 1985. In 1995, Remington began selling a competing shaver, with three rotating heads forming an equilateral triangle, shaped similarly to the Philips shaver. Philips argued that there were many alternatives to the shape constituting the trade mark which would achieve the same technical result in terms of a close and effective shave, and so the mark did not fall within the exclusion. Remington argued that this was too narrow an interpretation. The ECJ held that the provision 'is intended to preclude the registration of shapes whose essential characteristics perform a technical function, with the result that the exclusivity inherent in the trade mark right would limit the possibility of competitors supplying a product incorporating such a function or at least limit their freedom of choice in regard to the technical solution they wish to adopt in order to incorporate such a function in their product'. If the essential functional characteristics of the shape of a product are attributable solely to the technical result, it may not be registered, even if that technical result can be achieved by other shapes.[167]

---

[165]   *Philips Electronics BV* v. *Remington Consumer Products* [1998] RPC 283 at 304.

[166]   Case T-122/99, *Procter & Gamble (Soap Bar)* v. *OHIM* [2000] ECR II-265 (para. 55).

[167]   Case C-299/99, *Koninklijke Philips Electronics NV* v. *Remington Consumer Products* [2002] ECR I-5475 (paras. 79–84). For discussion, see Uma Suthersanen, 'The European Court of Justice in *Philips* v *Remington*: Trade Marks and Market Freedom' [2003] *IPQ* 257–83.

This approach was applied in a case concerning the registration of the Lego brick for various goods, including construction toys. The Cancellation Division, following *Philips* v. *Remington*, found that each of the elements of the shape of the Lego brick, and the Lego brick as a whole, were necessary to obtain a technical result. The various features (studs, secondary projections, hollow skirt, overall brick shape, etc.) all performed particular technical functions ('clutch power', fixing versatility and arrangement, size for children, etc.). On appeal, the Grand Board of Appeal observed that although the fact that the mark had once been the subject of a patent was not in itself a bar to registration, a prior patent is 'practically irrefutable evidence that the features therein disclosed or claimed are functional'. Lego argued that the technical result exclusion did not necessarily inhibit the registration of a particular design which implements the technical solution, while at the same time being not essential to it. The Board rejected this argument, noting that if the exclusion did not preclude monopolies on visual embodiments or designs of a technical solution, it would be possible to circumvent the exclusion by registering not only the preferred embodiment of that solution (here, the Lego brick), but also every conceivable visual embodiment or design of that technical solution. The Lego brick's features were clearly adopted to perform utilitarian functions, and there was nothing arbitrary or ornamental present in it. Any 'eye appeal' merely stemmed from the aesthetics of a sound structural and functional form. Thus, in the words of *Philips* v. *Remington*, 'the essential functional characteristics of the shape' were 'attributable solely to the technical result'.[168]

In *Lamborghini*, this provision was applied to a movement mark, described as 'a typical and characteristic arrangement of the doors of a vehicle. For opening the doors are "turned upwardly", namely around a swivelling axis which is essentially arranged horizontally and transverse to the driving direction'. The application was refused as devoid of distinctive character, and under the technical solution exclusion. The applicant emphasised that the door movement was not a technical necessity, but a choice made by the designer, Ferruccio Lamborghini, and intended to represent an unmistakable sign of a Lamborghini. The Board of Appeal, applying *Philips* v. *Remington*, considered that the mark was a functional movement excluded from protection, and noted that the availability of alternative solutions achieving the same technical effect did not overcome the objection.[169]

(iii)   The shape which gives substantial value to the goods   This exclusion

---

168   R 856/2004-G, *Lego Juris* v. *Mega Brands* [2007] ETMR 11.
169   R 772/2001-1, *Automobili Lamborghini Holding* v. *OHIM* [2005] ETMR 43.

has seemed somewhat puzzling to many, and again there is little EU case law. Draft OHIM guidelines state that it 'is limited to shapes which exclusively realize an aesthetic function, such as the shape of an object of art for objects of art, and in particular has nothing to do with the commercial value of the goods'.[170] The question will usually arise in relation to well-designed products, however – furniture, and lighting, for example. Consumers buy Arne Jacobsen's renowned 'Egg' chairs because of their elegance as well as their functionalism. Philippe Starck's 'Ara' lamp, with its distinctive conical horn shape, is regarded as iconic in the field of modern design. It is argued that such products should be offered only design protection, rather than trade mark registration.[171] The article was mentioned in *Benetton Group* v. *G-Star International*, a case involving the design of jeans protected by shape marks.[172] However, on the facts, the ECJ did not need to discuss the article in any detail, simply confirming that if a sign falls within the Article 3(1)(e) exclusion, it cannot be saved by showing acquired distinctiveness under Article 3(3).

(vii)   THE REMAINING ABSOLUTE GROUNDS FOR REFUSAL

(i)   Public policy and morality   Trade marks which are contrary to public policy or to accepted principles of morality may not be registered.[173] OHIM draft guidelines define 'public policy' as 'the body of all legal rules that are necessary for a functioning of a democratic society and a state of law', and 'accepted principles of morality' as 'those that are absolutely necessary for the proper functioning of a society'. The provision is thus not concerned with bad taste or protection of the feelings of individuals, but trade marks which are 'directly against the basic norms of society'. The rationale is to preclude trade marks from registration where the grant of a monopoly would undermine the state of law.[174]

---

[170]   *Guidelines Concerning Proceedings before the Office for Harmonization in the Internal Market (Trade Marks and Designs): Part B, Examination* (Draft, December 2007), para. 7.6.2.

[171]   For attempts to grapple with the provision in national courts see *Philips Electronics* v. *Remington* [1998] RPC 283, and discussion on appeal [1999] RPC 809; *BMW Motorhaube (BMW engine hood)* (*Bundespatentgericht*, Germany) [2005] ETMR 77.

[172]   Case C-371/06, *Benetton Group SpA* v. *G-Star International BV* [2008] ETMR 104.

[173]   TMD, Art. 3(1)(f); CMTR, Art. 7(1)(f).

[174]   In Case T-140/02, *Sportwetten* v. *OHIM*, it was argued unsuccessfully that merely because a particular CTM could not be used in Germany (because German law prohibited the offering and advertising of betting services without a permit, which the proprietor did not have), the mark was therefore contrary to public policy. The CFI

The test is an objective one: the mark must have a clear offensive impact on people of normal sensitivity.[175]

Blasphemous, racist or discriminatory phrases are excluded, but trade marks that might be considered in poor taste are not. Thus DICK AND FANNY was registrable for clothing, the Board of Appeal finding it had 'a rather smutty flavour' but fell short of being contrary to public policy or accepted principles of morality.[176] In contrast, SCREW YOU was refused for clothing and other ordinary items marketed in outlets used by the general public. Use of the mark in relation to such goods 'would inevitably cause a significant section of that public to be upset and affronted'. However, SCREW YOU was allowed for artificial breasts and sex toys likely to be found only in sex shops or on web sites specialising in sex products, because people using such outlets were 'by definition, unlikely to be offended by a trade mark which contains crude, sexually charged language'.[177]

The general public in the Community will sometimes encounter words on imported goods and services which, if used conversationally in their own language, might be found shocking. Nevertheless, the Board of Appeal has suggested that they will be understood for what they are, 'namely as neutral foreign words carrying an unfortunate meaning in the native tongue'. An application to register a figurative mark containing the words REVA ELEC-TRIC CAR for electric vehicles – the word 'Reva' being an acronym for 'Revolutionary Electric Vehicle Alternative' – was refused by the examiner because it contained the Finnish word 'Reva', which is a vulgar word for female genitalia. The Board of Appeal allowed the applicant's appeal: 'No one in Finland is likely to believe that the applicant is intentionally trying to be abusive – and by the way, potentially ruining its business prospects in the process – by putting the word 'reva' on its cars . . . At worst the mark might carry an element of unintentional bad taste, but nothing more.'[178]

---

observed that this could not be considered as relating to the intrinsic qualities of the trade mark, and could not render the trade mark itself contrary to public policy: [2005] ECR 3247 (para. 29).

[175]   *Guidelines Concerning Proceedings before the Office for Harmonization in the Internal Market (Trade Marks and Designs): Part B, Examination* (Draft, December 2007), para. 7.8.1.

[176]   R 111/2002-4, *Dick Lexic Limited v. OHIM* (25 March 2003).

[177]   R 495/2005-G, *Screw You v. OHIM* [2007] ETMR 7. The applicant suggested that the acceptance of CTMs such as PISSTARGET, BILLY BASTARD, CRAP, BIG COCK (and device), BULLSHIT, BITCH, ORGASMUS and PORN STAR supported its argument that consumers would not consider its mark offensive. Marks refused under this provision include ROCK 'N FUCK, IBIZA FUCKIN ISLAND, KUNT and BOLLOX.

[178]   R 558/2006-2, *Reva Electric Car Co. (PVT) Ltd v. OHIM* (18 July 2006).

The provision also excludes all direct references to or incitements to commit criminal acts, and names of terrorist organizations (as they would be perceived as a direct support for them): both ETA and BIN LADEN have been refused.[179] OHIM has also rejected marks which name famous people without their consent; FIDEL CASTRO, BILLCLINTON, JOHANNES PAUL II. Though, after a change of practice, names of heads of state are no longer considered deceptive or contrary to public policy.[180]

(ii) Deceptive marks Trade marks which are of such a nature as to deceive the public, for instance as to the nature, quality or geographical origin of the goods or services, may not be registered.[181] Normally this is because they contain an allusion which is inaccurate when the goods or services registered are considered. The ECJ has stated that there must be either actual deceit or a sufficiently serious risk that the consumer will be deceived.[182] WINE OH! was refused for mineral waters because of the 'obvious' difference between water and wine in terms of the nature and quality of the goods.[183] ARCADIA for wines was initially refused as descriptive, because Arcadia was a Greek region known for its wine production. The applicant's offer to limit the specification of goods to exclude Greek wines or to include only Italian wines would have made the name deceptive, so it was not registered. Similarly, TITAN for portable buildings would have deceived the relevant public as to the nature of the goods. 'Titan' means 'titanium' in German, Swedish and Danish. Titanium is a metallic element which is resistant to corrosion and often used in strong lightweight alloys. Use of the word TITAN would therefore lead the German-speaking public to expect a building which used titanium, instead of the conventional non-metallic materials which were used in the applicant's product.[184] But I.T.@MANPOWER did not communicate a sufficiently specific message regarding the potential characteristics of the goods and services to be

---

[179] ETA: OHIM Refused Trade Marks (7 September 2004) see http://oami.europa.eu/search/legaldocs/la/EN_Refused_index.cfm. BIN LADEN (thus, and in Arabic characters): R 176/2004-2, *Falcon Sporting Goods* v. *OHIM* (29 September 2004).

[180] *Guidelines Concerning Proceedings before the Office for Harmonization in the Internal Market (Trade Marks and Designs): Part B, Examination* (Draft, December 2007), para. 7.8.2.

[181] TMD, Art. 3(1)(g); CMTR, Art. 7(1)(g).

[182] Case C-87/97, *Consorzio per la tutela del formaggio Gorgonzola* v. *Kaserei Champignon Hofmeister GmbH* [1999] ECR I-1301 (para. 41).

[183] R 1074/2005-4, *Wine OH!* v. *OHIM* (7 March 2006). The Board observed, 'Since Jesus Christ the Saviour turned water into wine at Kanaan, it is common ground that wine is superior in quality to water'.

[184] R 789/2001-3, *Portakabin Ltd* v. *OHIM* (23 January 2002).

deceptive.[185] Where a world-famous wedding-dress designer later assigned her mark ELIZABETH EMANUEL to another, along with the goodwill in that mark, and the business which made the goods, the ECJ found that the name Elizabeth Emanuel could not be regarded in itself as being of such a nature as to deceive the public as to the nature, quality or geographical origin of the product it designated.[186]

Marks which falsely imply that they convey official approval will be regarded as deceptive. INTERNATIONAL STAR REGISTRY was refused, because it was likely to mislead consumers into believing that the applicant was an authoritative body empowered to give names to stars. In fact, the names it allocated to stars were not recognised by the astronomical community.[187] References to official recognition such as 'by Royal Appointment' will be deceptive if the applicant cannot prove they are true, although the word 'Royal' is not regarded as promising any official status. In contrast, THE ECOMMERCE AUTHORITY for services related to electronic commerce was regarded as merely laudatory, rather than likely to deceive the public into believing that the applicant was an authorised regulatory body.[188]

OHIM draft guidelines state that the mark will not be refused if there is a possible non-deceptive use.[189] Nor does the provision apply where the mark is merely suggestive.[190]

Marks for wines and spirits which contain or consist of a geographical indication identifying wines will not be registered unless they do have that origin. Marks which contain or consist of a designation of origin or a geographical indication may not be registered as a CTM.[191]

(iii)   Special emblems and marks prohibited by law   Article 6*ter* of the Paris Convention forbids the registration of various state and other emblems, includ-

---

[185]   R 124/2004-4, *MP Temporärpersonal GmbH* v. *OHIM* (5 April 2005).

[186]   Case C-259/04, *Elizabeth Emanuel* v. *Continental Shelf 128 Ltd* [2006] ECR 3089. It was for the national court to determine whether the applicant had intended to make consumers believe that Elizabeth Emanuel was still involved in the design of the books, and whether such conduct might be fraudulent. But such practices would not affect registrability.

[187]   R 468/1999-1, *International Star Registry of Illinois* v. *OHIM* (4 April 2001). The applicant's web site and advertising reinforced the impression that the names given would be officially recognised.

[188]   R 803/2000-1, *Gomez Advisors, Inc.* v. OHIM (11 July 2001).

[189]   *Guidelines Concerning Proceedings before the Office for Harmonization in the Internal Market (Trade Marks and Designs): Part B, Examination* (Draft, December 2007), para. 7.8.2.

[190]   METAL JACKET for metal coatings and rust-proofing products only suggestive and not deceptive: R 314/2002-1, *Lord Corporation* v. *OHIM* (23 October 2002).

[191]   CTMR, Arts. 7(1)(j) and (k).

ing flags. A list of these is kept by WIPO. The TMD and CTMR therefore provide protection for these symbols.[192] The flag of the European Union is included in the list.[193] Protection extends beyond exact representation to cover trade marks containing the emblems or heraldic imitations of them.[194]

The CTMR also protects trade marks which include badges, emblems or escutcheons other than those covered by Article 6*ter* of the Paris Convention and which are of particular public interest, unless the consent of the appropriate authorities to their registration has been given. Member states are free to offer such protection, and to protect signs of high symbolic value (such as religious symbols).[195] In addition, member states may prohibit the registration of marks where use of the mark would be unlawful under national law or Community law.[196]

(iv) Bad faith Member states may provide that a trade mark shall not be registered if the application is made in bad faith by the applicant.[197] However, under the CTMR this is a ground of invalidity and not a ground of refusal.[198]

(c) Relative grounds for refusal

Marks which conflict with earlier marks or signs may not be registered. In part this is to protect the earlier trade mark owner, but it also safeguards the guarantee of origin – if both marks were protected, then neither would be able to indicate origin. The relative grounds for refusal mirror the provisions concerned with infringement. The effect is that the owner of an earlier mark may prevent the registration of a later mark where use of that mark would infringe the rights of the earlier mark owner. As a result of this symmetry, much of the case law on infringement is relevant to the relative grounds for refusal.

---

[192] TMD, Art. 3(1)(h); CTMR, Art. 7(1)(h). See Case T-215/06, *American Clothing Associates* v. *OHIM* (Representation of a maple leaf) (28 February 2008).

[193] See the decision of the Cancellation Division of 19 October 2007, *European Community* v. *Motorpress-Iberica* (CTM No. 4 081 014).

[194] See Case T-127/02, *Concept Anlagen und Gerate nach GMP fur Produktion und Labor GmbH* v. *OHIM (ECA)* [2004] ECR II-1113.

[195] CTMR, Art. 7(1)(h) and (i); TMD, Art. 3(2)(c). See R 315/2006-1, *Cruz Roja Española* v. *SF Unternehmensbeteiligungsgesellschaft mbH* (28 June 2007) (orange cross of a contested CTM distinct from the Red Cross emblem).

[196] TMD, Art. 3(2)(a) and (b). Under national law, this might prevent the registration of (for example) hallmarks, plant varieties or marks which would offend fair-trading law. Under Community law, this might cover 'protected designations of origin' (PDOs) and 'geographical indications' (GIs).

[197] TMD, Art. 3(2)(d); CTMR, Art. 51(1)(b).

[198] TMD, Art. 3(2)(d); CTMR, Art. 51(1)(b). See below section 5.4.4 Cancellation of a mark: invalidity.

The existence of earlier rights is a significant risk for applicants. There are over three million registered trade marks in the member states of the European Union (including international trade marks in those member states party to the Madrid Agreement). In addition, the identification of unregistered trade marks and signs is extremely difficult.

1. EARLIER TRADE MARKS

(i) Identical trade mark and identical goods A trade mark applied for shall not be registered if it is identical to an earlier trade mark and the goods or services for which registration is applied for are identical with the goods or services for which the earlier trade mark is protected.[199] In these cases of 'double identity' there is no need to prove anything further: it is assumed that confusion will result.

WHAT IS AN EARLIER TRADE MARK? Earlier marks are (taking account of priority dates where appropriate): earlier Community trade marks; registered national trade marks and international trade marks having effect (under the Madrid Agreement or the Madrid Protocol) in one of the EU member states; well-known trade marks within the meaning of Article 6a of the Paris Convention.[200]

ARE THE MARKS IDENTICAL? If the contested sign and goods are identical to the earlier mark, there will be no need to prove confusion. The notion of identity is therefore construed narrowly. There is identity between the sign and the trade mark 'where the former reproduces, without any modification or addition, all the elements constituting the latter'. However, the perception of identity between the sign and the trade mark must be assessed globally with respect to an average consumer who is deemed to be reasonably well informed, reasonably observant and circumspect. Direct comparison is rarely possible, and the consumer's level of attention is likely to vary according to the nature of the goods or services. As a result, 'insignificant differences between the sign and the trade mark may go unnoticed by an average consumer', and these will be ignored when assessing whether the sign and the mark are identical.[201] This qualification has been criticised, as potentially blurring the bright line between cases of identity, and cases of similarity.[202]

---

[199] TMD, Art. 4(1)(a); CTMR, Art. 8(1)(a).
[200] TMD, Art. 4(2); CTMR, Art. 8(2).
[201] Case C-291/00, *LTJ Diffusion SA* v. *Sadas Vertbaudet SA* [2003] ECR 2799 (paras. 50–54).
[202] Belinda Isaac and Rajiv Joshi, 'What Does Identical Mean?' [2005] *EIPR* 184–7.

ARE THE GOODS AND SERVICES IDENTICAL? This provision will not be infringed unless the goods and services for which registration is sought are identical with those for which the earlier mark is protected. Goods may be regarded as identical if either the goods designated by the earlier mark fall within a more general category designated by the trade mark application, or vice versa.[203] The question will be a practical one of how the goods are regarded for the purposes of trade.

(ii) Confusingly similar marks and goods A mark will not be registered if, because of its identity with or similarity to the earlier trade mark and the identity or similarity of the goods or services covered by the trade marks, there exists a likelihood of confusion on the part of the public in the territory in which the earlier trade mark is protected. The likelihood of confusion includes the likelihood of association with the earlier trade mark.[204]

GLOBAL ASSESSMENT The ECJ has stated that the likelihood of confusion must be appreciated globally, taking into account all factors relevant to the case. The concept of similarity is interpreted in relation to the likelihood of confusion, the appreciation of which depends on the recognition of the trade mark on the market and the degree of similarity between the mark and the sign and between the goods or services identified. This implies some interdependence between the relevant factors. Accordingly, a lesser degree of similarity between the goods or services may be offset by a greater degree of similarity between the marks, and vice versa. The more distinctive the earlier mark, the greater the risk of confusion.[205] To determine distinctiveness, an assessment is made of the mark's capacity to identify the goods or services for which it has been registered as coming from a particular undertaking, and thus to distinguish those goods and services from those of other undertakings.[206] Marks

---

[203] Case T-133/05, *Meric* v. *OHIM* (7 September 2006) (para. 29).

[204] TMD, Art. 4(1)(b); CTMR, Art. 8(1)(b).

[205] In *Sabel*, the Court noted that where a mark was well known to the public and/or the image was particularly imaginative, mere conceptual similarity might give rise to a likelihood of confusion. Case C-251/95, *Sabel BV* v. *Puma AG* [1997] ECR 6191 (paras. 24 and 25). Compare Case T-31/01, *Éditions Albert René* v. *OHIM* [2003] ECR II-4625, where the fame of the ASTERIX mark made confusion with STARIX unlikely.

[206] In making that assessment, account should be taken, in particular, of the inherent characteristics of the mark, including the fact that it does or does not contain an element descriptive of the goods or services for which it has been registered; the market share held by the mark; how intensive, geographically widespread and long-standing use of the mark has been; the amount invested by the undertaking in promoting the mark; the proportion of the relevant section of the public which, because of the mark,

with a highly distinctive character, either *per se* or because of the reputation they possess on the market, may therefore enjoy broader protection than marks with a less distinctive character. However, even if the earlier mark is highly distinctive, it is essential to show that the goods or services are similar. This is to avoid an overlap with the provisions dealing with dissimilar goods.[207]

ARE THE MARKS SIMILAR?   When assessing the similarity of marks, their visual, aural or conceptual similarity is considered. Two marks are similar when, from the point of view of the relevant public, they are at least partially identical as regards one or more of these aspects.[208] The assessment must be based on the overall impression given by the marks, bearing in mind their distinctive and dominant components. What is relevant is the perception of marks in the mind of the average consumer of the type of goods or services in question. Whilst the average consumer normally perceives a mark as a whole and does not proceed to analyse its various details, in general it is the dominant and distinctive features of a sign which are more easily remembered – this is the concept of 'imperfect recollection'.[209] Much will depend on the circumstances of the case, including the nature of the marks.

Aural similarity may be sufficient, particularly if it is the dominant element of the mark.[210] ELS was held to be similar to iLS where there was no significant visual difference between the signs, and the pronunciation of the two acronyms was either very similar or identical (depending on whether they were pronounced in English or German).[211] MYSTERY and MIXERY were also held to be similar, where the goods might be ordered orally.[212] But

---

identifies the goods or services as originating from a particular undertaking; and statements from chambers of commerce and industry or other trade and professional associations. It is not possible to state in general terms, for example by referring to given percentages relating to the degree of recognition attained by the mark within the relevant section of the public, when a mark has a strong distinctive character. Case C-108/97, *Windsurfing Chiemsee Produktions- und Vertriebs GmbH* v. *Boots- und Segelzubehor Walter Huber* [1999] ECR I-2779 (paras. 49–52).

[207]   Case C-39/97, *Canon Kabushiki Kaisha* v. *Metro-Goldwyn-Mayer Inc.* [1998] ECR I-5507 (paras. 16–19).

[208]   Case T-6/01, *Matratzen Concord* v. *OHIM* [2002] ECR II-4335 (para. 30). Case T-34/04, *Plus Warenhandelsgesellschaft mbH* v. *OHIM* [2005] ECR II-2401 (para. 43).

[209]   Case C-251/95, *Sabel BV* v. *Puma AG* [1997] ECR 6191 (para. 23). Case T-117/03, *New Look* v. *OHIM* [2004] ECR II-3471 (para. 39).

[210]   Case C-342/97, *Lloyd Schuhfabrik Meyer* v. *Klijsen Handel BV* [1999] ECR I-3819 (LLOYD and LOINT'S for identical goods). Case T-133/05, *Meric* v. *OHIM* (7 September 2006) (PAM-PIM'S BABY-PROP confusingly similar to PAM-PAM for near-identical goods).

[211]   Case T-388/00, *Institut für Lernsysteme GmbH* v. *OHIM* [2002] ECR II-4301.

[212]   Case T-99/01, *Mystery Drinks GmbH* v. *OHIM* [2003] ECR II-43.

HOOLIGAN for clothing was not confusingly similar to OLLY GAN. Although the marks were phonetically similar, they were visually and conceptually different – the average French or Portuguese consumer would view OLLY GAN as a name, and clothing was usually examined visually at time of purchase.[213]

If a word mark is short, differences may be as important as similarities. So, the CFI found BASS to be dissimilar to PASH,[214] and likewise BUD was dissimilar to BIT.[215] But more importance is normally attributed to the first syllable of a mark, so BUDMEN was similar to BUD.[216] Similarly, applications for NLSPORT, NLJEANS, NLACTIVE, NLCOLLECTION were successfully opposed by the holder of NL mark (also for clothing) on the grounds that consumers might identify these marks as sub-brands of the NL mark.[217] But there was no likelihood of confusion between GALÁXIA and GALA: although the first four letters of each were identical, the two words were clearly different in length so visually dissimilar, and also aurally and conceptually dissimilar.[218] ECHINAID and ECHINACIN shared the same descriptive prefix 'echina', which referred to the plant 'Echinacea'. Here the average consumer was likely to pay more attention to the endings of the marks rather than the descriptive and insufficiently distinctive prefix, so there was no likelihood of confusion.[219] Endings are usually less significant. SISSI ROSSI and MISS ROSSI shared a common Italian surname, but it was placed at the end of the marks. The dominant elements of the marks were the words 'Sissi' and 'Miss', which had only an average or slight degree of similarity.[220] Although SELIZIONE ORO shared a word with two earlier marks, ORO, and ORO SAIWA, the ORO mark *per se* had little distinctiveness, merely hinting

---

[213]   Case T-57/03, *Société Provençale d'Achat et de Gestion (SPAG) SA* v. *OHIM* [2005] ECR 287. The CFI observed (para. 58), 'It is difficult to establish with certainty how the average consumer will pronounce a word from a foreign language in his own language'.

[214]   Case T-292/01, *Phillips Van Heusen Corp.* v. *OHIM* [2003] ECR II-4335. Conceptual differences were important here, also.

[215]   Case T-350/04, *Bitburger Brauerei Th Simon GmbH* v. *OHIM* (19 October 2006).

[216]   Case T-129/01, *Jose Alejandro SL* v. *OHIM* [2003] ECR II-2251.

[217]   Case T-117/03, *New Look Ltd* v. *OHIM* [2004] ECR II-3471. See also *Panrico SA* v. *Kevin Thomas Rogers* OHIM (Cancellation Div.) [2005] ETMR 73.

[218]   Case T-66/03, *Koffiebranderij en Theehandel 'Drie Mollen Sinds 1818' BV* v. *OHIM* [2004] ECR II-1765.

[219]   Case T-202/04, *Madaus AG* v. *OHIM* [2006] ECR II-1115.

[220]   Case C-214/05, *Sergio Rossi SpA* v. *OHIM* (18 July 2006). See also Case T-224/01, *Durferrit GmbH* v. *OHIM* [2003] ECR 1589 (NUTRIDE and TUFFTRIDE dissimilar); Case T-31/01, *Éditions Albert René* v. *OHIM* [2003] ECR II-4625 (ASTERIX and STARIX dissimilar).

at the positive characteristics of the goods. There were important visual and phonetic differences in the way consumers perceived the conflicting marks, and the mere presence of the word 'oro' was not capable of giving rise to similarity between them.[221]

The figurative mark FERRÓ (the word Ferró on a simple banner) was found by the Board of Appeal to be similar to FERRERO: the dominant verbal element was phonetically and visually similar. The CFI upheld the decision, noting that word and figurative marks both have graphic form capable of creating a visual impression, and so may be visually similar.[222] Although each mark must be considered as a whole, a compound trade mark (word and figurative) cannot be regarded as similar to another mark which shares one of its components unless that component forms the dominant element within the overall impression created by the compound mark.[223] Here the verbal element 'Ferró' was dominant, prevailing over the figurative banner which was of purely secondary importance and had no distinctive character. The signs could therefore be compared using the verbal elements alone. They shared the same letters in the same order, and the differing number of syllables did not detract from this visual similarity.[224] In contrast, the visual and phonetic similarities

---

[221]   Case T-344/03, *Saiwa SpA* v. *OHIM* [2006] ECR II-1097. Appeal to the ECJ dismissed by Order of 9 March 2007: C-245/06-P. See also Case C-234/06-P, *Il Ponte Finanziaria SpA* v. *OHIM* [2008] ETMR 13.

[222]   Case T-35/04, *Athinaiki Oikogeniaki Artopoiia AVEE* v. *OHIM, Ferrero Deutschland GmbH* [2006] ECR II-785, following Case T-110/01, *Vedial SA* v. *OHIM* [2002] ECR II-5275 (para. 51). Appeal to the ECJ dismissed by Order of 11 September 2007: C-225/06 P.

[223]   That is the case where that component is likely to dominate, by itself, the image of that mark which the relevant public keeps in mind, with the result that the other components of that mark are negligible within the overall impression created by it. Case T-6/01, *Matratzen Concord GmbH* v. *OHIM* [2002] ECR II-4335 (para. 33); Case T-31/03, *Grupo Sada* v. *OHIM* (11 May 2005) (para. 49); Case T-214/04, *Royal County of Berkshire Polo Club Ltd* v. *OHIM* [2006] ECR II-239 (para. 39); Joined Cases T-333/04 and T-334/04, *House of Donuts International* v. *OHIM & Panrico, SA* [2007] ETMR 53.

[224]   Case T-35/04, *Athinaiki Oikogeniaki Artopoiia AVEE* v. *OHIM* (15 March 2006) [2006] ECR II-785. See also Joined Cases T-183/02 and T-184/02, *El Corte Ingles, SA* v. *OHIM* [2004] ECR II-965 (MUNDICOLOR/MUNDICOR). The ECJ has stressed that a global assessment of the similarity between two marks 'means more than taking just one component of a composite trade mark and comparing it with another mark'. The comparison must be made by examining each of the marks as a whole. Although the overall impression conveyed to the relevant public by a composite trade mark may be dominated by one or more of its components, it is only if all the other components of the mark are negligible that the assessment of the similarity can be carried out solely on the basis of the dominant element: Case C-334/05 P, *OHIM* v. *Shaker di L. Laudato & C. Sas* (12 June 2007). See also Case C-193/06, P, *Société des Produits Nestlé SA* v. *OHIM, Quick Restaurants SA* (20 September 2007).

between PICARO and PICASSO were counteracted by the strong conceptual difference, since PICASSO would be well known to the relevant public as the name of a famous painter.[225]

Where a two-word mark contains a word identical (visually and aurally) to an earlier single-word mark which constitutes an earlier word mark, the marks will normally be regarded as similar where they have no conceptual meaning for the relevant public. Thus, KIAP MOU (meaning 'crispy pork' in Laotian and Thai) was similar to MOU for an Anglophone public, who would think all the words were invented words.[226] In *Medion* v. *Thomson Multimedia Sales*, Medion was objecting to the use of its trade mark LIFE in a composite sign THOMSON LIFE. Under the German doctrine of *Prägetheorie* (theory of the impression conveyed), a likelihood of confusion would be found where the shared element characterised the later composite mark to such an extent that the remaining components were secondary to the overall impression of the later mark, but not where the shared element merely contributed to that over-all impression of the later mark even if it had an 'independent distinctive role' in the later mark. However, the ECJ did not endorse this approach, and again stressed the importance of considering each of the marks as a whole. Although it might well be the case that a component of an earlier composite sign might dominate, even if it did not, it was still possible that the overall impression produced by a composite sign including a company name might lead the public to believe that the goods or services came from two companies which were linked economically. Dominance could not, therefore, be a condition precedent for a finding of confusion in such a case.[227]

ARE THE GOODS OR SERVICES SIMILAR? In assessing the similarity of the goods or services concerned, all the relevant factors relating to those goods or services themselves should be taken into account; their nature, their end-users and their method of use and whether they are in competition with each other or are complementary.[228] What is relevant is the *usual* circumstances in which

---

[225]   Case C-361/04 P, *Ruiz-Picasso* v. *OHIM* [2006] ECR 643. See also Case T-149/06, *Castellani SpA* v. *OHIM* [2008] ETMR 22; Case T-112/06, *Inter-Ikea Systems* v. *OHIM* (16 January 2008).

[226]   Case T-286/02, *Oriental Kitchen Sarl* v. *OHIM* [2003] ECR II-4953.

[227]   Case C-120/04, *Medion AG* v. *Thomson Multimedia Sales Germany & Austria GmbH* [2005] ECR 8551. See also Case T-434/05, *Gateway, Inc.* v. *OHIM* (27 November 2007). There appears to be some tension with the approach to compound (word and figurative) marks, discussed above: Case T-6/01, *Matratzen Concord GmbH* v. *OHIM* [2002] ECR II-4335 (para. 33).

[228]   Case C-39/97, *Canon Kabushiki Kaisha* v. *Metro-Goldwyn-Mayer Inc.* [1998] ECR I-5507 (para. 17). Case C-291/00, *LTJ Diffusion SA* v. *Sadas Vertbaudet SA* [2003] ECR 2799 (para. 33).

such goods are marketed, and not the circumstances in which a particular proprietor markets goods, since the latter are dependent on subjective factors and may change over time.[229] The fact that goods or services are registered in different classes is not conclusive. The Board of Appeal found 'buckles for footwear and garments' to be somewhat similar to 'clothing articles, including boots, shoes and slippers', because the products were 'logically connected' in the sense that they were normally meant to be used together.[230] But in *Sergio Rossi*, leather goods and bags were found to be dissimilar to footwear, 'shoes being used to dress feet and bags to carry objects'. It followed that the goods were not interchangeable and, therefore, not in competition.[231] Goods or services are complementary if there is a close connection between them, in the sense that one is indispensable or important for the use of the other in such a way that customers may think that the responsibility for the production of those goods or for the provision of those services lies with the same undertaking.[232] This acts as a useful limit. In *Alecansan*, the proprietor of COMP USA for transport services opposed the registration of a figurative COMP USA mark as a CTM for computer-related goods and services. The opposition was rejected on the basis that, despite the near identity of the marks, there was no similarity whatsoever in the goods and services. On appeal, Alecansan argued that since the applicant sold computer goods on the internet, it would use transport services in order to get those goods to ultimate purchasers, and so their services were complementary. This imaginative argument was dismissed by the CFI.[233]

In *Venticinque*, the similarity of goods and retail services had to be assessed. Venticinque's mark THE O STORE was held for various leather goods, clothing, headgear and footwear. Oakley obtained a CTM for O STORE, covering a wide range of retail and wholesale services. The Cancellation Division noted that in such a case a finding of similarity is more likely where the retail services concern the same goods as the earlier mark, since the signs are more likely to be encountered in the same outlets. Although retail services were intangible and goods tangible, they could share the same distribution channels. Thus Oakley's retail services were similar to Venticinque's goods to the extent that they concurred in their distribution channels.[234]

---

229 Case C-171/06P, *TIME* v. *OHIM* (15 March 2007) [2007] ETMR 38.

230 R 267/1999-1 *Zanella* v. *Zanella Confezione SpA* [2000] ETMR 69.

231 Case T-169/03, *Sergio Rossi SpA* v. *OHIM* [2005] ECR II-685 (para. 57).

232 See also to that effect Case T-85/02, *Díaz* v. *OHIM* [2003] ECR II-4835 (para. 36).

233 Case T-202/03, *Alecansan SL* v. *OHIM* [2006] ETMR 93. A further appeal to the ECJ was dismissed by Order of 9 March 2007: C-196/06-P, *Alecansan SL* v. *OHIM*.

234 *Venticinque Ltd* v. *Oakley Inc.* (OHIM Cancellation Division, 18 June 2004) [2005] ETMR 115.

LIKELIHOOD OF CONFUSION   Likelihood of confusion presupposes both that the
mark applied for and the earlier mark are identical or similar, and that the
goods or services covered in the application for registration are identical or
similar to those in respect of which the earlier mark is registered. These conditions are cumulative.[235] The requirement is that 'there exists a likelihood of
confusion on the part of the public', and so the perception of marks in the mind
of the average consumer of the type of goods or services in question plays a
decisive role in the global appreciation of the likelihood of confusion.[236] The
average consumer normally perceives a mark as a whole and does not proceed
to analyse its various details. The average consumer of the category of products concerned is deemed to be reasonably well informed and reasonably
observant and circumspect, although their level of attention is likely to vary
according to the category of goods or services in question.[237] So, in the
PICASSO case, it was noted that the degree of attention of the relevant public
would be particularly high as regards goods such as motor vehicles, which are
expensive, and highly technological in character.[238] If a sign is already in use,
the relevant time for assessing the perception of the public concerned is the
time when the infringing sign began to be used. This prevents the sign's owner
from claiming that the earlier mark had become less distinctive after this point,
perhaps in part because of that user's activities.[239]

The ECJ has held repeatedly that the essential function of the trade mark is
to guarantee the identity of the origin of the marked product to the consumer
or end-user by enabling him, without any possibility of confusion, to distinguish the product or service from others which have another origin. Therefore,
'likelihood of confusion' is the risk that the public might believe that the goods
or services in question come from the same undertaking, or from economically
linked undertakings.[240] Likelihood of confusion is defined such that it
'includes the likelihood of association with the earlier trade mark'. This
proved extremely controversial. The issue was whether mere association could
ground an earlier proprietor's opposition, even when there was no likelihood
of confusion as to origin. The question was considered in *Sabel*, which

---

[235]   Case C-39/97, *Canon Kabushiki Kaisha* v. *Metro-Goldwyn-Mayer Inc.* [1998]
ECR I-5507 (para. 22). Case C-106/03 P, *Vedial SA* v. *OHIM* [2004] ECR I-9573 (para.
51).
[236]   Case C-251/95, *Sabel BV* v. *Puma AG* [1997] ECR 6191 (para. 23).
[237]   Case C-342/97, *Lloyd Schuhfabrik Meyer* v. *Klijsen Handel BV* [1999] ECR
I-3819 (para. 26).
[238]   Case C-361/04 P, *Ruiz-Picasso* v. *OHIM* [2006] ECR 643 (para. 23).
[239]   Case C-145/05 *Levi Strauss & Co.* v. *Casucci SpA* [2006] ECR I-3703 (para.
18).
[240]   Case C-39/97, *Canon Kabushiki Kaisha* v. *Metro-Goldwyn-Mayer Inc.* [1998]
ECR I-5507 (para. 29).

involved two pictorial marks of bounding felines. The referring court's provisional view was that there was no likelihood of confusion, but it sought guidance as to the importance of the semantic content of the marks in determining the likelihood of confusion. Would the mere association which the public might make between the two marks, through the idea of a bounding feline, justify the earlier proprietor's opposition? The ECJ held that 'the concept of likelihood of association is not an alternative to that of likelihood of confusion, but serves to define its scope'. The terms of the provision itself exclude its application where there is no likelihood of confusion on the part of the public.[241] This position is not inconsistent with *Canon*, which states that marks with a highly distinctive character enjoy broader protection. The ECJ has confirmed that the reputation of a mark does not give grounds for presuming the existence of likelihood of confusion simply because of the existence of likelihood of association in the strict sense.[242]

The appreciation of likelihood of confusion 'depends on numerous elements and, in particular, on the recognition of the trade mark on the market, of the association which can be made with the used or registered sign, of the degree of similarity between the trade mark and the sign and between the goods or services identified'.[243] The likelihood of confusion must therefore be appreciated globally, taking into account all factors relevant to the circumstances of the case.[244] However, a finding that there is a likelihood of confusion must be based on the perception by the public of the goods covered by the mark of the proprietor, and the goods covered by the allegedly infringing sign. It is not relevant that there is a need for the sign to be available for other traders. The ECJ has observed that signs which must, generally, remain available for all economic operators are likely to be used abusively with a view to creating confusion in the mind of the consumer. The application of Article 5(1) (the infringement provision) would be undermined if a third party could rely on a requirement of availability to use a sign which is nevertheless similar to the trade mark.[245]

The issue arose in relation to the Adidas three-stripe mark, which Adidas alleged was being infringed by various two-stripe marks. The national court found that Adidas' three-stripe motif was not very distinctive *per se*, but that because of Adidas' investment in advertising its marks it had acquired consid-

241   Case C-251/95, *Sabel BV* v. *Puma AG* [1997] ECR 6191 (para. 18).
242   Case C-425/98, *Marca Mode CV* v. *Adidas AG* [2000] ECR I-4861.
243   TMD, Recital 10.
244   Case C-251/95, *Sabel BV* v. *Puma AG* [1997] ECR 6191; Case C-425/98, *Marca Mode CV* v. *Adidas AG* [2000] ECR I-4861; Case C-120/04, *Medion AG* v. *Thomson Multimedia Sales Germany & Austria GmbH* [2005] ECR 8551.
245   Case C-102/07, *Adidas AG* v. *Marca Mode CV* (10 April 2008) (para. 31).

erable distinctive character and become well known. It therefore found that the three-stripe logo enjoyed wide protection. However, the national court considered that stripes and simple stripe logos are, generally, signs which must remain available. It therefore considered that the Adidas marks could not afford any protection against the use of two-stripe motifs. However, the ECJ ruled this out as an irrelevant consideration. Although stripe motifs are available and may used in a vast number of ways by all traders, this does not authorise Adidas' competitors to infringe its three-stripe logo by using stripe motifs which are so similar to the registered mark that there is a likelihood of confusion in the mind of the public.[246] The Court also stressed that the public's perception that a sign is a decoration cannot constitute a restriction on the protection conferred by Article 5(1)(b) if that sign is so similar to the registered trade mark that the relevant public is likely to perceive that the goods come from the same undertaking.[247] The assessment is a matter of fact for the national court.

(iii)   Marks with a reputation   The owner of any registered mark can resist use of identical or similar marks on identical or similar goods and services. However, both the TMD and the CTMR offer broader protection for marks 'with a reputation' – recognising implicitly that trade marks do more than simply indicate origin. A mark may not be registered as a CTM where:

- it is identical with, or similar to, an earlier mark; and
- it is to be registered for goods or services which are not similar to those for which the earlier mark is registered; and
- the earlier mark has a reputation in the Community, or, in the case of an earlier national trade mark, in the member state concerned; and
- the use of the later trade mark without due cause would take unfair advantage of, or be detrimental to, the distinctive character or the repute of the earlier trade mark.[248]

Under the TMD, member states have the option of providing that national trade marks will be subject to the same conditions.[249]

In *Davidoff* v. *Gofkid*, the ECJ was asked whether this broader protection applied *only* where the competing goods and services were 'not similar' (as the wording of the provisions would appear to suggest), or whether it could apply when the competing goods and services were identical or similar to those

---

[246]   Case C-102/07, *Adidas AG* v. *Marca Mode CV* (10 April 2008) (para. 32).
[247]   Case C-102/07, *Adidas AG* v. *Marca Mode CV* (10 April 2008) (para. 34).
[248]   CTMR, Art. 8(5).
[249]   TMD, Art. 4(3).

covered by the mark. Rejecting AG Jacobs's text-based approach, the ECJ's interpretation sought to acknowledge the overall objectives of the Community's trade mark regime. The Court considered that the provisions could not be interpreted to give 'well-known marks' less protection where a sign was used for identical or similar goods or services than where a sign was used for non-similar goods or services. Under the other relative grounds, protection for identical goods is absolute, but protection for similar goods requires a likelihood of confusion. Thus the protection for marks with a reputation could be relied on whether the goods were identical, similar or dissimilar.[250] This approach was affirmed in *Adidas-Salomon AG* v. *Fitnessworld*. If member states opt to confer protection on marks with a reputation, they must do so for all types of goods. The ECJ also confirmed that likelihood of confusion was not a requirement for this provision. It is enough that the marks are sufficiently similar that the relevant section of the public establishes a link between them.[251]

The earlier mark must have a 'reputation'. If the public has sufficient knowledge of the earlier mark, then, when confronted by the later trade mark, it may make an association between the two trade marks, even when used for non-similar products or services. This may lead to damage to the earlier trade mark. The relevant public is that concerned by the trade mark, and will depend on the underlying goods or services. The earlier mark must be known by a significant part of that public. The assessment must be based on all the relevant facts of the case, in particular the market share held by the trade mark, the intensity, geographical extent and duration of its use, and the size of the investment made by the undertaking in promoting it. Mere quantitative criteria (such as a percentage of the public knowing the mark) are insufficient. The reputation need not cover the entire territory, but it must exist in a substantial part of it.[252]

---

[250]   Case C-292/00, *Davidoff & Cie SA* v. *Gofkid Ltd* (C292/00) [2003] ECR I-389 (paras. 24–30). For comment (both positive and negative), see Andrew Griffiths, 'The Impact of the Global Appreciation Approach on the Boundaries of Trade Mark Protection' [2001] *IPQ* 326–60; Helen Norman, '*Davidoff* v. *Gofkid*: Dealing with the Logical Lapse or Creating European Disharmony?' [2003] *IPQ* 342–54; Christopher Morcom, 'Extending Protection for Marks having a Reputation: What is the Effect of the Decision of the European Court of Justice in *Davidoff* v. *Gofkid*?' [2003] *EIPR* 279–82 (response from Jane Cornwell [2003] *EIPR* 537–8).

[251]   Case C-408/01, *Adidas-Salomon AG* v. *Fitnessworld Trading Ltd* [2003] ECR I-12537 (para. 31). See also Anna Carboni, 'Two Stripes and You're Out!: Added Protection for Trade Marks with a Reputation' [2004] *EIPR* 229–33.

[252]   Case C-375/97, *General Motors Corporation* v. *Yplon SA* [1999] ECR I-5421; Case C-328/06, *Alfredo Nieto Nuño* v. *Leonci Monlleó Franquet* [2008] ETMR 12.

Use of the later mark must take unfair advantage of the earlier mark, or be detrimental to its distinctive character or repute. The existence of a link between the marks is an essential condition – the relevant public must make a connection between them. The existence of such a link must be appreciated globally, taking into account all factors relevant to the circumstances of the case. There is no requirement that certain signs be left available for use by other traders. Such a requirement would be extraneous both to the assessment of the degree of similarity between the mark with a reputation and the sign used by the third party, and to the link which may be made by the relevant public between that mark and the sign. It cannot therefore constitute a relevant factor for determining whether the use of the sign takes unfair advantage of, or is detrimental to, the distinctive character or the repute of the trade mark.[253] The stronger the earlier mark's distinctive character and reputation, the easier it will be to accept that detriment has been caused to it. However, the earlier mark holder must do more than establish that the relevant public links the two marks – this is mere non-origin association, and insufficient to establish unfair advantage or detriment. Although the proprietor of the earlier mark is not required to demonstrate actual and present harm to the mark, there must be *prima facie* evidence of a future risk, which is not hypothetical, of unfair advantage or detriment.[254] There is no need to prove intention to take unfair advantage, or to damage distinctive character or reputation.

The concept of taking unfair advantage of the distinctive character or the repute of the earlier mark is intended to encompass instances where there is clear exploitation and free-riding on the coat-tails of a famous mark or an attempt to trade upon its reputation.[255] Thus the Board of Appeal held that use of COSMOPOLITAN COSMETICS would take advantage of COSMOPOLITAN for women's magazines. Much of the magazine consisted of advertisements for cosmetics, and readers might associate the cosmetics marketed under the COSMOPOLITAN COSMETICS brand with the magazine. Since the magazine was better known than the applicant's goods in the relevant territory, the reputation of the first mark could be used as a vehicle for facilitating the sale of the latter goods. This would result in an unfair advantage for the applicant, because it would be based on the opponent's fame, rather than on the applicant's own marketing efforts.[256] In a similar case, an attempt to register a

---

[253] Case C-102/07, *Adidas AG* v. *Marca Mode CV* (10 April 2008) (para. 43).

[254] Case T-67/04, *Monopole SpA* v. *OHIM* [2005] ECR 1825 (paras. 40–41).

[255] Case T-67/04, *Monopole SpA* v. *OHIM* [2005] ECR 1825 (para. 51).

[256] R 552/2000-4, *Mülhens GmbH & Co. KG* v. *The Hearst Corporation* (26 July 2001). See also R 472/2001-1, *Hachel International Foundation* v. *Excelsior Publications* (8 February 2002); R 530/2004-2, *Marie Claire Album (SA)* v. *Marie Claire SA* (6 March 2006).

figurative mark D'NICKERS for footwear, was opposed by the proprietor of the NIKE 'swoosh' mark. The Board of Appeal noted the close connection between the relevant goods, the similarity of the signs and the high reputation of the earlier trade mark, concluding that the applicant sought to exploit the distinctive character and reputation of the earlier mark: 'the advantage for the opponent is a substantial saving on investment in promotion and publicity for its own mark, since it benefits from that which has made the earlier mark highly famous and it is unfair because it is done in a parasitic way'.[257] Likewise, registration of ABBSOLUTE for sunglasses was successfully opposed by the proprietor of ABSOLUT, a leading brand of vodka. ABSOLUT had an image as 'a young, stylish and fashionable brand', and had invested 'enormous amounts of time, effort and money' in sponsorship of the fashion industry. In adopting the ABBSOLUTE mark, the applicant 'manifestly looks to take unfair advantage of the reputation of the mark ABSOLUT and the stylish, fashionable and dynamic image associated with it'.[258]

Detriment to the distinctive character of a mark is known as 'dilution' or 'blurring'. This is based on the belief that use of the earlier mark on other goods may erode its distinctiveness (although some argue that unless there is either actual confusion or tarnishment of the mark, there is no real damage). If taken to extremes, this argument would prevent the registration of all marks identical or similar to a mark with a reputation – this is not the approach taken under EU law. The question is one of degree. There is detriment where the earlier mark is no longer capable of arousing immediate association with the goods for which it is registered and used.[259] The argument that the distinctive character of the 'Smarties-tube' shape was diluted from the moment that a rival tube was launched on the marketplace was rejected by the Board of Appeal, which noted that the concept of dilution must be something more than a likelihood of confusion. Although the specific 'Smarties-tube' did have enhanced distinctive character, it did not follow that competitors could be prevented from using any cylindrical container shapes in relation to the relevant goods.[260]

---

[257]   R 301/2005-2, *Nike International, Ltd* v. *Fina Calzados, SL* (19 May 2006). See also R 470/2001-2, *J Floris Limited* v. *Istrad Limited* (27 May 2004); R 308/2003-1, *Mango Sport System SRL* v. *Diknah, SL* (12 March 2004).

[258]   R 1204/2004-1, *V&S Vin & Sprit AB* v. *Hoya Corporation* (12 July 2005). See also Case T-47/06, *Antartica Srl* v. *OHIM, The Nasdaq Stock Market Inc.* ETMR [2007] 77, where the proprietor of NASDAQ for financial services successfully opposed the use of a very similar sign for sports equipment.

[259]   Case T-67/04 *Monopole SpA* v. *OHIM* [2005] ECR 1825 (paras. 40 and 43).

[260]   R 0506/2003-2, *Société des Produits Nestlé, SA* v. *Mars Inc.* (30 August 2004).

Detriment to the reputation of a mark is known as 'tarnishment'. This detriment is made out where the goods for which the mark applied for is used appeal to the public's senses in such a way that the earlier mark's power of attraction is diminished.[261] In the *Hollywood* case, the Board of Appeal stated that a trade mark is tarnished when the consumer's ability to associate it with the goods or services for which it is registered is reduced by the fact that:

(a) it is linked with goods of poor quality or which evoke undesirable or questionable mental associations which conflict with the associations or image generated by legitimate use of the trade mark by its proprietor;
(b) it is linked with goods which are incompatible with the quality and prestige associated with the trade mark, even though it is not a matter of inappropriate use of the trade mark in itself;
(c) its word or figurative element is amended or altered in a negative way.

The *Hollywood* case itself is an example of the first of these. An attempt to register HOLLYWOOD for tobacco products was successfully resisted by the proprietor of the same mark for chewing gum. The Board noted the 'image of health, dynamism and youth' enjoyed by the earlier mark, which contrasted strikingly with the negative connotation conveyed by tobacco, observing that 'no worse association can be imagined for a confectionery manufacturer than one with products capable of causing death'.[262] But where the proprietor of SPA for mineral waters was objecting to the use of SPA-FINDERS for travel services, the CFI noted there was no 'antagonism' between the goods and services covered by the marks which might be detrimental to the repute of SPA mineral waters.[263]

If a trade mark proprietor shows that its earlier mark has a reputation, and the use of the later mark will take unfair advantage of, or be detrimental to, that earlier mark, then the burden is on the other party to show 'due cause' for their use.[264] The Board of Appeal has indicated that this hurdle is very high:

it must generally be imposed as a condition for due cause that the trade mark applicant should be obliged to use the sign in question, such that, notwithstanding the detriment caused to the proprietor of the earlier trade mark, the applicant cannot reasonably be required to abstain from using the trade mark, or that the applicant has a specific right to use this sign, over which the right of the earlier trade mark's proprietor does not take precedence. In particular, the condition of due cause is not

---

[261] Case T-67/04, *Monopole SpA* v. *OHIM* [2005] ECR 1825 (para. 46).
[262] R 283/1999-3, *Hollywood SAS* v. *Souza Cruz SA* (25 April 2001).
[263] Case T-67/04, *Monopole SpA* v. *OHIM* [2005] ECR 1825 (para. 48).
[264] R 145/2003-2, *Deutsche Telekom AG* v. *Comité International Olympique* (1 March 2004).

fulfilled merely by the fact that (a) the sign is particularly suitable for identifying the products for which it is used, (b) the applicant has already used this sign for these products or similar products within and/or outside the relevant territory of the Community, or (c) the applicant invokes a right ensuing from a filing over which the filing by the proprietor of the opposing trade mark takes precedence.[265]

2. EARLIER RIGHTS (NON-TRADE MARK)

The CTMR provides that, in addition to the earlier trade marks rights just discussed, specific non-registered earlier rights protected at member state level, that is, non-registered trade marks and other signs used in the course of trade (sometimes referred to as 'business identifiers') of more than mere local significance, can be invoked in opposition proceedings. Such rights must confer on their proprietors the right to prohibit the use of a subsequent trade mark.[266] The common characteristics of these rights are: that they are based on use rather than on registration; that they are trade or business-related and thus outside of the sphere of mere individual or personal rights; that they serve as distinguishing signs in the course of trade, unlike patents or copyrights or design rights, which protect technical or artistic achievements or the 'appearance' as such; and that they are exclusive rights conferring on their proprietors an ownership or at least an ownership-like position.[267] The onus is on the opponent to state the specific national laws relied on as entitling it to prohibit use of a subsequent trade mark (to protect *inter alia* the applicant's right of defence).[268]

Member states may also provide that non-registered earlier rights may be invoked to prevent the registration of national trade marks (and also to render them liable to be declared invalid). Both non-registered trade marks and other earlier rights (in particular: a right to a name; a right of personal portrayal; a

---

[265]   R 283/1999-3, *Hollywood SAS* v. *Souza Cruz SA* (25 April 2001) (para. 101). See also R 552/2000-4, *Mülhens GmbH & Co. KG* v. *The Hearst Corporation* (26 July 2001) (where the applicant argued it had been inspired to choose its mark by the name of an affiliate company).

[266]   CTMR, Art. 8(4). As a result of CTMR, Art. 52(1)(c), these Art. 8(4) rights can also be invoked in invalidity proceedings directed against a registered CTM, as a relative ground for invalidation. Additionally, Art. 52(2) covers certain other earlier rights, including a right to a name, a right of personal portrayal, copyright and industrial property rights (such as a design right). These may be not be invoked in opposition proceedings, but only after registration of the CTM concerned, by filing a request for a declaration of invalidity (see below).

[267]   *Guidelines Concerning Proceedings before the Office for Harmonization in the Internal Market (Trade Marks and Designs) Part C: Opposition*, Part 4.

[268]   R 964/2005-2, *Corporacion Habanos, SA* v. *Paolo Brunelli* (29 November 2006); R 0191/2004-4, *Tomy Company Limited* v. *Tomy Inc.* (8 September 2006).

copyright; an industrial property right) are covered.[269] In the UK, as a result of this provision, an opponent can prevent registration where the use of the applicant's mark would be restrained under the law of passing off.[270]

5.4.4 Cancellation of a Mark

A mark may be revoked, or declared invalid, in cancellation proceedings. For CTMs, such proceedings are never initiated by OHIM, but only by an applicant for cancellation. In the event of revocation and to the extent it is revoked, a CTM will be deemed not to have the effects specified in the CTMR as from the date of application for revocation. An earlier date on which one of the grounds for revocation occurred may be fixed by the Cancellation Division if this is requested by one of the parties. In the event of a declaration of invalidity a CTM, to the extent it is declared invalid, will be deemed not to have had effect from the outset.[271]

Invalidity

A CTM may be declared invalid if it was registered in breach of one of the absolute or relative grounds for invalidity. The absolute grounds are: that it was registered in breach of the provisions of Article 7 (absolute grounds of refusal not overcome by acquired distinctive character); or that it was registered in bad faith. Where the ground for invalidity exists in respect of only some of the goods or services for which the CTM is registered, it is declared invalid as regards those goods or services only.[272] The relative grounds are that the mark was registered in breach of the provisions of Article 8 (relative grounds of refusal). A CTM may also be declared invalid where its use may be prohibited pursuant under a national law protecting earlier rights. If the proprietor of an earlier right consents expressly to the registration of the CTM, it will not be declared invalid.[273] If the proprietor of an earlier mark has acquiesced in the use of a later mark for five years, the right to bring opposition or invalidity proceedings is lost, unless the mark was applied for in bad faith.[274] Similarly, under the TMD, a national mark may be declared invalid if it was registered in breach of one of the absolute or relative grounds for invalidity.[275]

---

[269] TMD, Art. 4(4)(b) and (c).
[270] Trade Marks Act 1994, s. 5(4).
[271] CTMR, Art. 54.
[272] CTMR, Art. 51.
[273] CTMR, Art. 52.
[274] CTMR, Art. 53.
[275] TMD, Arts. 3 and 4.

The issue of bad faith applications is a serious one for trade mark owners, particularly if filings are made with a view to preventing market access, demanding compensation for vacating the mark or profiting from the reputation enjoyed by another's trade mark. Enlargement presents a particular challenge. The EU is seeking to minimise possible conflicts between CTM and national marks by introducing more advanced and rapid information systems.[276] Neither the CTMR nor the Implementing Regulation provides any guidance as to what actually constitutes bad faith. OHIM has published some guidance, which states that bad faith can be considered (*inter alia*) to mean 'dishonesty which would fall short of the standards of acceptable commercial behaviour'.[277] The relevant time for assessing this is the filing date, although subsequent events may shed light on the question.

In its case law, the Cancellation Division has held that bad faith is the opposite of good faith, generally implying or involving, but not limited to, actual or constructive fraud, or a design to mislead or deceive another, or any other sinister motive. Conceptually, bad faith can be understood as a 'dishonest intention'. A finding of bad faith 'should not be established lightly': there should be no doubt, based on the facts at hand, that there has indeed been bad faith on the part of the applicant/proprietor of the CTM.[278] There is bad faith when the CTM applicant intends through registration to lay claim to a trade mark of a third party with which it had contractual or pre-contractual relations. In *East Side Mario's*, the CTM owner was found to have acted in bad faith when applying for the challenged CTM, because he did so with full knowledge of the other party's trade mark rights (held for many years in the US and Canada), and with the intention of either blocking the development of those marks in Europe or forcing the grant of a franchise to himself.[279] Unlike some jurisdictions, a genuine intention to use a CTM is not required, although if it is not used within five years from registration it may be revoked.[280]

Revocation

The grounds for revocation are:

---

[276]   See http://oami.europa.eu/en/enlargement/mechanisms.htm.

[277]   *Guidelines Concerning Proceedings before the Office for Harmonization in the Internal Market (Trade Marks and Designs): Part D, Section 2: Cancellation Proceedings, Substantive Provisions* (Final version: November 2007), para. 4.3.2.

[278]   Decision of the Cancellation Division of 10 October 2004 (CTM ER No. 2386126).

[279]   R 582/2003-4, *Slater* v. *Prime Restaurant Holdings, Inc.* (13 December 2004). See also decision of the Cancellation Division of 25 August 2003 (CTM POGGIO AL CASONE No. 1302306).

[280]   See decision of the Cancellation Division of 14 December 2004 (CTM NAKED No. 1628395).

1. non-use;
2. that the mark has become the common name in trade for the goods and services for which it is registered;
3. that the mark has become deceptive.[281]

1. NON-USE

If marks are not used, their owners forfeit legal protection. Such marks convey nothing to consumers, and their presence on the register inhibits other traders from using identical or similar marks. The requirement that marks be used also deters the hoarding of marks. If a mark has not been put to genuine use within a continuous period of five years between registration and the filing of the request for cancellation, then it will be revoked unless there are proper reasons for non-use.[282] If there is use relating only to some of the goods and services for which it is registered, the revocation will be limited to those which are not being used.[283] The burden of providing evidence of genuine use, or demonstrating that there are proper reasons for non-use, rests on the proprietor.

Although neither the CTMR nor the CTMIR defines 'genuine use', the ECJ offered guidance in *Ansul BV* v. *Ajax Brandbeveiliging BV*.[284] It must be actual use of the mark, not use that is merely token, serving solely to preserve the rights conferred by the mark. It entails use of the mark relating to goods or services already marketed or about to be marketed and for which preparations to secure customers are under way, particularly in the form of advertising campaigns. The mark must be linked directly with the goods protected. Only this sort of use will be consistent with the trade mark's function as a guarantee of origin. Use as a company name or shop name will not suffice.[285] Where T-shirts with the MALIBU logo were given away at promotional events, this was regarded as use to advertise the drink for which the mark was registered, rather than use of the mark in connection with clothing, and the opposition to the applicant's very similar mark for clothing was therefore refused.[286] All

---

[281] CTMR, Art. 50; TMD, Art. 12.
[282] CTMR, Art. 50(1)(a); TMD, Art. 12(1). Use that commences or resumes within the three-month period before the filing of the application for revocation will be disregarded if the preparations for use occur only after the proprietor of a CTM becomes aware that an application for revocation may be filed. The onus for proving that the proprietor was so aware rests on the applicant for revocation.
[283] Case T-126/03, *Reckitt Benckiser (Espana) SL* v. *OHIM* (ALADDIN/ALADIN) [2005] ECR II-2861; Case T-256/04, *Mundipharma AG* v. *OHIM* (RESPICUR/RESPICORT) (13 February 2007).
[284] Case C-40/01, *Ansul BV* v. *Ajax Brandbeveiliging BV* [2003] ECR I-2439.
[285] Decision No. 1042/2001, *Magrinya* v. *Sportsmania Ltd* (MANIA/Sportsmania (fig.)) (Opposition Division).
[286] Decision No. 374/2001, *Twelve Islands Shipping Company Ltd* v. *Henrique & Oliveira, Lda* (Malibu (fig.)/ coconut tree (fig.)) (Opposition Division).

relevant facts and circumstances must be considered, such as the nature of the goods or services, the characteristics of the market, and the scale and frequency of use of the mark. There is no *de minimis* rule, in the sense of an abstract, quantitative threshold.[287] Genuine use may be found when the mark has been used in only one part of the Community, such as a single member state or part thereof. This rule ensures that large enterprises are not favoured over small ones.[288]

Proper reasons for non-use refer to circumstances unconnected with the trade mark owner which prohibit use of the mark, rather than to commercial difficulties.[289] Lack of resources, financial problems, insolvency, lack of staff or marketing problems are not proper reasons, because they are regarded as a natural part of running a business. The difficulties must have arisen independently of the owner's will or power, for example because of war, embargoes, *force majeure*, or other crises.[290] Borrowing the language of TRIPS, the ECJ has held that 'obstacles having a direct relationship with a trade mark which make its use impossible or unreasonable and which are independent of the will of the proprietor of that mark constitute "proper reasons for non-use" of the mark'.[291] This is a matter for the national court or tribunal to determine, in the light of this guidance.

---

[287] Case C-40/01, *Ansul BV* v. *Ajax Brandbeveiliging BV* [2003] ECR 2439. See also Case C-259/02, *La Mer Technology Inc.* v. *Laboratoires Goëmar SA* [2004] ECR I-1159, applied in Case T-418/03, *La Mer Technology* v. *OHIM – Laboratoires Goëmar* (27 September 2007) [2008] ETMR 9. See also Case T-131/06, *Sonia Rykiel v. OHIM* (30 April 2008).

[288] *Guidelines Concerning Proceedings before the Office for Harmonization in the Internal Market (Trade Marks and Designs): Part D, Section 2: Cancellation Proceedings, Substantive Provisions* (Final version: November 2007), para. 3.1.3.

[289] Case T-156/01, *Laboratorios RTB SL* v. *OHIM* [2003] ECR II-2789 (para. 41). The CTMR does not define 'proper reasons'.

[290] Decision No. 120/2001, *Ercros, SA* v. *Bordercross Marketing & Consulting GmbH* (Opposition Division).

[291] Case C-246/05, *Häupl* v. *Lidl Stiftung & Co. KG* [2007] ETMR 61 (para. 55). TRIPS, Art. 19(1) states that 'Circumstances arising independently of the will of the owner of the trade mark which constitute an obstacle to the use of the trade mark, such as import restrictions on or other government requirements for goods or services protected by the trade mark, shall be recognised as valid reasons for non-use'. This would also cover a state monopoly which impedes any kind of use, or a state prohibition of the sale of goods for reasons of health or national defence (such as regulatory procedures). See Decision No. 3767/2002, *Tomen Corporation v. REWE-Zentral AG* (CENTURION/CENTURIO) (Opposition Division); Decision No. 1507/2001, *Almirall-Prodesfarma, SA* v. *Alza Corporation* (DIADUR/VIADUR) (Opposition Division).

2. GENERIC MARKS

A mark may be revoked if it has become a generic term. That is, 'if in consequence of acts or inactivity of the proprietor, the trade mark' has become the common name in trade for a product or service for which the mark was registered.[292] It is argued that in such cases the mark has lost its ability to indicate origin. The burden of proof is on the person seeking to have the mark revoked.

The mark must have become the common name for the good or service not just amongst some people, but amongst the large majority of the relevant public, including those involved in the trade in the good or service in question. It is not sufficient for the mark to be used as a synonym or shorthand for a particular good or service while the relevant public also recognises the term as a mark designating the goods or services of a particular enterprise. OHIM guidelines offer the example of a person saying that they will 'google' something: but this habit in itself does not render the GOOGLE CTM a generic term, because it continues to designate goods and services from a particular enterprise.[293] The ECJ has stated that although a trade mark's origin function is of primary importance to the consumer or end-user, it is also of significance to intermediaries who deal with the product commercially. As a result, the relevant public for determining whether a mark has become generic will be principally consumers and end-users, but, depending on the features of the product market concerned, the influence of intermediaries on decisions to purchase, and thus their perception of the trade mark, must also be taken into consideration.[294]

The mark may only be revoked if it becomes generic 'in consequence of acts or inactivity' of the trade mark proprietor. This might happen, for instance, because the proprietor used the mark as a descriptive term in their own advertising or labelling. But where the proprietor has done that which could reasonably be expected in a particular case (for example, placing warnings on labels, using appropriate advertising, using Article 10 CTMR to control reproduction of the mark in dictionaries), the mark cannot be cancelled.

---

[292] CTMR, Art. 50(1)(b); TMD, Art. 12(2)(a).

[293] *Guidelines Concerning Proceedings before the Office for Harmonization in the Internal Market (Trade Marks and Designs): Part D, Section 2: Cancellation Proceedings, Substantive Provisions* (Final version: November 2007), para. 3.2.2. Compare the decision of the Cancellation Division of 30 January 2007, *Osotspa Co., Ltd* v. *Red Bull GmbH* (CTM STIMULATION partially revoked, including for energy drinks).

[294] Case C-371/02, *Björnekulla Fruktindustrier AB* v. *Procordia Food AB* [2004] ECR I-5791. See also Case C-412/05 P, *Alcon Inc.* v. *OHIM, Biofarma SA* [2007] ETMR 68.

3. MISLEADING MARKS

A mark may be revoked if 'in consequence of use made of the mark by the proprietor or with his consent the mark is liable to mislead the public particularly concerning the nature, quality or geographical origin of the goods or services for which it is registered'.[295] Again, there is a requirement of fault, in that the mark must have become misleading either as a result of the use made of it by the proprietor of the trade mark or the use made of it with his consent (by licensees, for example).

There are obvious parallels with the absolute ground for refusal covering descriptive marks, but this provision allows for the possibility that a mark may become misleading after it has been registered. For example, if a distinctive figurative mark contains the words 'Goat's cheese' and is registered for goat's cheese, if it is used for both goat's and sheep's cheese it is liable to be revoked. Similarly if a distinctive figurative mark contains the words 'pure new wool' and is registered for clothing, if it is used for clothing manufactured from artificial fibres it will be liable to revocation.[296] It seems that the mere act of licensing or assignment will not be regarded as misleading as to trade origin. Where a world-famous wedding-dress designer later assigned her mark ELIZABETH EMANUEL to another, along with the goodwill in that mark, and the business which made the goods, the ECJ found that this alone did not render the mark liable to revocation. Although a consumer might be influenced to purchase a trade marked garment by the belief that the designer was involved in its design, the garment's characteristics and qualities would remain guaranteed by the undertaking which owned the trade mark. Thus the name Elizabeth Emanuel could not be regarded in itself as being of such a nature as to deceive the public as to the nature, quality or geographical origin of the product it designated.[297]

5.4.5   Infringement

CTMs are registered for a period of ten years from the date of filing of the application, and registration may be renewed for further periods of ten years.[298] The rights conferred by a CTM may be enforced against third parties

---

[295]   CTMR, Art. 50(1)(c); TMD, Art. 12(2)(b).

[296]   *Guidelines Concerning Proceedings before the Office for Harmonization in the Internal Market (Trade Marks and Designs): Part D, Section 2: Cancellation Proceedings, Substantive Provisions* (Final version: November 2007), para. 3.3.2.

[297]   Case C-259/04, *Elizabeth Emanuel v. Continental Shelf 128 Ltd* [2006] ECR 3089.

[298]   CTMR, Arts. 46 and 47.

from the date of publication of registration of the trade mark.[299] CTMs are enforced in national courts which have been designated 'community trade mark courts', and not by OHIM.[300] They apply the provisions of the CTMR, or, on matters not covered by the CTMR, their own national law.[301] A Community trade mark court may grant provisional and protective measures which are applicable in the territory of any member state.[302] Proceedings are normally brought in the member state where the defendant is domiciled.[303]

Article 9 of the CTMR provides that:

1. A Community trade mark shall confer on the proprietor exclusive rights therein. The proprietor shall be entitled to prevent all third parties not having his consent from using in the course of trade:
   (a) any sign which is identical with the Community trade mark in relation to goods or services which are identical with those for which the Community trade mark is registered;
   (b) any sign where, because of its identity with or similarity to the Community trade mark and the identity or similarity of the goods or services covered by the Community trade mark and the sign, there exists a likelihood of confusion on the part of the public; the likelihood of confusion includes the likelihood of association between the sign and the trade mark;
   (c) any sign which is identical with or similar to the Community trade mark in relation to goods or services which are not similar to those for which the Community trade mark is registered, where the latter has a reputation in the Community and where use of that sign without due cause takes unfair advantage of, or is detrimental to, the distinctive character or the repute of the Community trade mark.

---

[299] Reasonable compensation may, however, be claimed in respect of acts following publication of the application and registration: CTMR, Art. 9(3).

[300] CTMR, Art. 91.

[301] CTMR, Art. 97.

[302] CTMR, Art. 99(2).

[303] CTMR, Art. 90 enacts a modified form of the Brussels Convention, in an attempt to reduce forum-shopping. The basic rule is that the claimant must bring the action in the jurisdiction where the defendant is domiciled. The CTMR extends this to defendants with an establishment in the jurisdiction. If the defendant is not domiciled in the Community, the action should be brought where the claimant is domiciled. If neither is domiciled nor established in the Community, the action should be brought where OHIM is situated (in Alicante). Although the claimant may opt to bring an action in the member state where the infringement took place, that court can only grant relief within that territory, making this route much less attractive. If the action is brought on the basis of the defendant's domicile, the court may grant relief throughout the EU. CTMR, Arts. 93 and 94.

For national marks, the TMD adopts a parallel approach (although protection for national marks with a reputation against dissimilar goods is optional).[304] It will be seen that the rights conferred mirror the relative grounds for refusal. The concepts used to determine whether a mark has been infringed are just the same as those used to determine whether a mark falls within one of the relative grounds for refusal. These concepts have already been discussed.[305]

The question of what amounts to 'use in the course of trade' is an important and controversial one. There is a non-exhaustive list of situations where a sign is used, and the use may be prohibited:

(a) affixing the sign to the goods or to the packaging thereof;
(b) offering the goods, putting them on the market or stocking them for these purposes under that sign, or offering or supplying services thereunder;
(c) importing or exporting the goods under that sign;
(d) using the sign on business papers and in advertising.[306]

In *Arsenal* v. *Reed*, the ECJ found that a sign had been used 'in the course of trade', because the use had taken place 'in the context of commercial activity with a view to economic advantage and not as a private matter'.[307] Not all uses are prohibited, though a use which is liable to jeopardise the guarantee of origin may be prevented, because this guarantee constitutes the essential function of the mark. In contrast, if the use of a sign cannot affect the trade mark proprietor's interests, having regard to the mark's functions, it may not be prohibited. Thus certain uses for purely descriptive purposes are excluded, because they do not affect any of the interests which these provisions aim to protect, and do not therefore fall within the concept of use.[308] In *Hölterhoff* v. *Freiesleben*, the proprietor of the trade marks SPIRIT SUN and CONTEXT CUT for 'precious stones for further processing as jewellery' alleged infringement when Hölterhoff sold two stones, using these names in oral negotiations to describe the 'spirit sun' cut. Neither party had understood the term as indicating origin. The ECJ held that the exclusive right could not be relied on 'where a third party, in the course of commercial negotiations, reveals the origin of goods which he has produced himself and uses the sign in question solely to denote the particular characteristics of the goods he is offering for

---

[304] TMD, Arts. 4 and 5.
[305] See above 5.4.3 (c) Relative grounds for refusal.
[306] CMTR, Art. 9(2); TMD, Art. 5(3).
[307] Case C-206/01, *Arsenal Football Club Plc* v. *Reed* [2002] ECR 10273 (para. 40).
[308] Case C-206/01, *Arsenal Football Club Plc* v. *Reed* [2002] ECR 10273 (para. 54).

sale so that there can be no question of the trade mark used being perceived as a sign indicative of the undertaking of origin'.[309]

In the *Arsenal* case, Arsenal FC, which owned the trade mark ARSENAL for clothing and footwear, was objecting to sales of scarves bearing the mark from stalls outside Arsenal's football ground. Reed's stall displayed a large sign indicating clearly that the scarves were not official Arsenal merchandise, and the evidence indicated that the marks were perceived by the public as 'badges of support, loyalty or affiliation' to Arsenal FC, rather than as a guarantee of origin. The ECJ focused on the guarantee of origin, and regarded the factual situation as 'fundamentally different' from that in *Hölterhoff*, because the use of the sign was 'obviously not intended for purely descriptive purposes'. The use of the ARSENAL sign was 'such as to create the impression that there is a material link in the course of trade between the goods concerned and the trade mark proprietor'. The disclaimer on Reed's stall, even if effective for initial purchasers, would not reach consumers who came across the goods after they had been taken away. Such use was liable to jeopardise the guarantee of origin which constitutes the essential function of the mark, and could be prevented by the trade mark proprietor. Once this conclusion has been reached, it was immaterial that in the context of that use the sign was perceived as a badge of support for or loyalty or affiliation to the proprietor of the mark.[310]

Somewhat different considerations come into play when the mark is used by a third party to refer to the trade mark owner's own goods. In *Deenik*, the ECJ held that use of the BMW trade mark (registered for cars) by a garage owner to indicate that he was a specialist in second-hand sales and repair of BMW cars (goods and services) fell within Article 5(1)(a) of the Directive (identical goods, identical marks).[311] Since these were genuine BMW goods, under the rules of exhaustion in Article 7 BMW could not prohibit the use of its mark by a reseller of its goods unless it could show a legitimate reason for opposition (for instance, that a commercial connection with BMW was implied).[312] This 'informative' use of marks is considered necessary to guarantee the right of resale under Article 7.[313] The advertisements relating to

---

[309] Case C-2/00, *Hölterhoff* v. *Freiesleben* [2002] ECR 4187 (paras. 16–17).

[310] Case C-206/01, *Arsenal Football Club Plc* v. *Reed* [2002] ECR 10273 (paras. 55–62).

[311] Case C-63/97, *Bayerische Motorenwerke AG* v. *Deenik* [1999] ECR 905.

[312] See, for example, *Aktiebolaget Volvo* v. *Heritage (Leicester) Ltd* [2000] FSR 253; *Volvo Ltd* v. *DS Larm Ltd* [2000] ETMR 299 (Swedish Supreme Court).

[313] Case C-63/97, *Bayerische Motorenwerke AG* v. *Deenik* [1999] ECR 905 (para. 54). Note, in this context, AG Mengozzi's Opinion in Case C-533/06, *O2 Holdings Limited & O2 (UK) Limited* v. *Hutchison 3G UK Limited* (31 January 2008), where he described the ECJ's case law in this area as not at all consistent, and observed

repair services fell within Article 6, which permits a third party to use a mark in the course of trade where this is 'necessary to indicate the intended purpose of a product or service, in particular as accessories or spare parts' provided that the mark is used 'in accordance with honest practices in industrial or commercial matters'.

However, more recently the ECJ has sought to confine *Deenik* to a very limited set of situations. In *Adam Opel* v. *Autec*, Autec was using the Opel logo (registered by Opel for motor vehicles and toys) on remote-controlled scale model replica cars. Opel argued that this infringed its mark for motor vehicles, being use of an identical mark on identical goods, since Autec was using the Opel mark to identify Opel cars as the subject matter of the Autec scale model. The ECJ rejected this reasoning. It conceded that *Deenik* had been concerned with an identical trade mark for services which were not identical, but that the use had nevertheless been held to fall within Article 5(1)(a). However, this was a special case, because the BMW-marked cars constituted the subject matter of the third party's repair services, resulting in a 'specific and indissociable link between the products bearing the trade mark and the services provided by the third party'. Other than in this specific case (use of a trade mark by a third-party provider of services having as subject matter the products bearing that trade mark), Article 5(1)(a) covers only the use of a sign identical to the trade mark in respect of goods marketed or services supplied by the third party which are identical to those in respect of which the trade mark is registered.[314] Here, since Autec did not sell motor vehicles, there was no use of the Opel logo by Autec as a trade mark registered for motor vehicles, and the situation did not fall within Article 5(1)(a).

Autec's use of the Opel logo for toys did fall squarely within Article 5(1)(a). However, Autec also used its own 'Cartronic' and AUTEC trade marks, and argued that it was obvious to the public that the scale model did not come from Opel. As in *Arsenal*, the ECJ emphasised that the exclusive right was conferred in order that the trade mark could fulfil its functions and, therefore, that its exercise must be reserved to cases in which a third party's use of the sign affects or is liable to affect the functions of the trade mark – in particular the essential function of guaranteeing to consumers the origin of the goods. Autec's use of the Opel mark could not be prohibited unless it did this. This was a matter of fact for the national court, but the referring court had indi-

---

that the examination of the conditions in which Articles 5(1)(a) and (b) apply was a task 'bristling with difficulties' (paras. 20 and 28). See also, Paul Reeskamp, 'Is Comparative Advertising a Trade Mark Issue?' [2008] *EIPR* 130–37.

[314]   Case C-48/05, *Adam Opel AG* v. *Autec AG* [2007] ETMR 35 (paras. 27 and 28). For wider discussion see Ilanah Simon, 'Nominative Use and Honest Practices in Industrial and Commercial Matters – A Very European History' [2007] *IPQ* 117–47.

cated that the relevant public did not perceive Autec's use of the Opel sign as an indication that the scale models came from Opel.[315] Following the ECJ's ruling, the Nuremburg District Court dismissed the car manufacturer's trade mark infringement complaint.

5.4.6 Defences

Use of own name and address
It is a defence to a claim of infringement that a person is using 'his own name or address', although this is subject to the proviso that he uses them 'in accordance with honest practices in industrial or commercial matters'.[316] The provision applies also to business and company names.[317]

Descriptive uses
A registered mark is not infringed by the use of indications concerning the kind, quality, quantity, intended purpose, value, geographical origin, the time of production of the goods or of rendering of the service, or other characteristics of

---

[315] Case C-48/05, *Adam Opel AG* v. *Autec AG* [2007] ETMR 35. For further discussion see Noam Shentov, '"Trade Mark Use" in Europe' [2007] *JIPL&P* 557–63; Po Jen Yap, 'Making Sense of Trade Mark Use' [2007] *EIPR* 420–27; Tobias Cohen Jehoram and Maarten Santman, '*Opel/Autec*: Does the ECJ Realize What it Has Done?' [2008] *JIPL&P* 507–10. The issue was considered by the ECJ in relation to the adoption of a company or trade name identical to an existing trade mark, in connection with the marketing of identical goods: Case C-17/06, *Céline Sarl* v. *Céline SA* ETMR [2007] 1320. It held that this would constitute use which the proprietor of that mark is entitled to prevent in accordance with Art. 5(1)(a) 'where the use is in relation to goods in such a way as to affect or to be liable to affect the functions of the mark'. In such a case, Art. 6(1)(a) would prevent the operation of Art. 5(1)(a) only if the third party's use of the name was in accordance with honest practices in industrial or commercial matters. The judgment provides little guidance as to how this interpretation should be applied by the national court in relation to particular facts. The Court also observed that the purpose of a company, trade or shop name is not, of itself, to distinguish goods or services. The purpose of a company name is to identify a company, whereas the purpose of a trade name or a shop name is to designate a business which is being carried on. As a result, where the use of a company name, trade name or shop name is limited to identifying a company or designating a business which is being carried on, such use cannot be considered as being 'in relation to goods or services' within the meaning of Art. 5(1). Citing *Arsenal* and *Adam Opel*, the Court noted that conversely, there is use 'in relation to goods' within the meaning of Art. 5(1) 'where a third party affixes the sign constituting his company name, trade name or shop name to the goods which he markets' (paras. 21–2). The case is noted by Tom Scourfield, [2008] *EIPR* 71–4.
[316] CTMR, Art. 12(a); TMD, Art. 6(1)(a).
[317] Case C-17/06, *Céline Sarl* v. *Céline SA* (11 September 2007).

the goods or services.[318] Again this is subject to the proviso that they are used in accordance with honest practices in industrial or commercial matters. In *Gerolsteiner Brunnen* v. *Putsch*, the claimant bottled mineral water and produced soft drinks with a mineral water base under the mark GERRI, registered in Germany. The defendant marketed soft drinks in Germany, with labels including the words KERRY SPRING, because the goods were manufactured in Ireland by a company called Kerry Spring Water and contained water from Kerry Spring. In infringement proceedings, the Bundesgerichtshof found that there was a likelihood of aural confusion between the two marks, but sought a ruling as to whether the defences to trade mark infringement under Article 6(1)(b) of the TMD could apply in such circumstances. The ECJ noted that the words KERRY SPRING were being used as an indication of geographical origin. This could only be prevented if that use was not in accordance with honest practices in industrial or commercial matters, and this was a matter of fact for the national court to determine. The mere fact that there was a likelihood of aural confusion between the earlier registered mark and the indication of geographical origin from another member state did not mean that the defendant's use of the indication in the course of trade was not in accordance with honest practices. The ECJ observed that because of the diversity of languages within the European Union, there is a high likelihood of phonetic overlap between marks in some countries and indicators of geographical origin in others.[319]

Use to indicate the intended purpose of a product or service

A registered mark is not infringed by the use of the mark 'where it is necessary to indicate the intended purpose of a product or service, in particular as accessories or spare parts'. As before, this is subject to the proviso of use in accordance with honest practices in industrial or commercial matters.[320] This defence recognises that traders may have a legitimate need to refer to a trade mark, even though they have no legal or economic link to the trade mark proprietor. This would be the case, for example, if the trader sells spare parts for a specific product, or repairs particular brands of goods. This defence was considered in *BMW* v. *Deenik*. BMW-authorised dealers are allowed to use BMW trade marks only if they reach very high standards of technical competence. BMW was therefore objecting to use of their marks by Deenik's garage business, which specialised in the sale of second-hand BMWs and the repair and servicing of BMWs, although he was not an authorised distributor. The

---

[318]   CTMR, Art. 12(b); TMD, Art. 6(1)(b).
[319]   Case C-100/02, *Gerolsteiner Brunnen GmbH & Co.* v. *Putsch GmbH* [2004] ECR I-691 (paras. 24–6).
[320]   CTMR, Art. 12(c); TMD, Art. 6(1)(c).

ECJ noted that if an independent trader carries out the maintenance and repair of BMW cars or is in fact a specialist in that field, that fact cannot in practice be communicated to his customers without using the BMW mark. The condition requiring use of the mark in accordance with honest practices in industrial or commercial matters was to be regarded as the expression of a duty to act fairly in relation to the legitimate interests of the trade mark owner. Use of the mark in a way that might create the impression that there is a commercial connection between the other undertaking and the trade mark proprietor, for example by suggesting that the two businesses are affiliated in some way, would not satisfy the proviso.[321]

Similarly, in *Gillette v. LA–Laboratories* Gillette was objecting to the use of its marks on the packaging of the defendant's razor blades. LA–Laboratories' packaging stated, 'all Parason Flexor and Gillette Sensor handles are compatible with this blade'. Gillette argued that this gave the consumer the impression that the third party was licensed to use its trade marks. The ECJ explained that third-party use of a trade mark is permitted where it constitutes the only means of providing consumers with 'comprehensible and complete information on the intended purpose of the product'. Such use is 'necessary' in cases where information about the third party's product cannot in practice be communicated to the public without reference being made to the trade mark, although the precise circumstances in each case are a matter of fact to be determined by national courts. The ECJ also clarified that Article 6(1)(c) could be applied when appropriate to permit third-party use of a mark on a primary product, not just on spare parts and accessories. Reiterating its position in *Deenik*, the ECJ stressed that third-party users must not give the impression that there is a commercial connection between themselves and the trade mark owner, nor discredit or denigrate the mark. In determining these factual matters, the national court should take into account the overall presentation of the product, and in particular whether the third party has made an effort to ensure that consumers can distinguish its products from those of the trade mark owner.[322]

Application of national laws to prevent use of Community Trade Marks
The proprietor of an earlier national mark may use its national rights in a national forum to prevent use of a subsequent CTM.[323] However, this will not be the case if that proprietor has acquiesced, for a period of five successive

---

[321]   Case C-63/97, *Bayerische Motorenwerke AG v. Deenik* [1999] ECR I-905 (paras. 58–64).
[322]   Case C-228/03, *Gillette Co. v. LA-Laboratories Ltd Oy* [2005] ECR I-2337.
[323]   CTMR, Art. 106.

years, in the use of the subsequent CTM in the member state where the earlier national mark is protected.[324]

Exhaustion

Trade mark rights are by their nature territorial, national and exclusive. Because they can be used to prevent the importation of marked goods into the territory where the right is granted, they act as barriers to trade. The holder of parallel national rights can use a right granted in state A to exclude goods from state B, and vice versa. This may allow them to partition the market, and maintain price differentials between the various member states. If goods are not protected by intellectual property rights, parallel importers will seek to buy in the cheapest market, and resell elsewhere, undercutting the original seller. The original seller may then choose to lower prices to a level where the parallel importer no longer makes a profit. In theory, this is good for the consumer, who benefits from cheaper prices. Intellectual property rights make it easier for sellers to resist parallel importation, and thus have a tendency to hamper the free movement of goods. Yet trade mark owners may well have good reasons for opposing parallel importation, and these must be acknowledged. Furthermore, intellectual property rights are guaranteed protection under EU law. Nevertheless, since the free movement of goods is one of the fundamental freedoms of the EU, solutions have had to be found, and compromises made. The subject is of such importance to all intellectual property rights that it merits separate and full discussion.[325] However, since the issues very frequently arise in relation to trade marks, an outline of the law will be given here also.

The principle of exhaustion expresses a balanced compromise between the rights of the trade mark holder, and the need for the free movement of goods. It provides that a trade mark will not be infringed by use of the mark in relation to goods which have been put on the market in the Community under that trade mark by the proprietor or with his consent. This means that trade mark rights may not be relied upon to prevent further circulation within the Community of goods which the trade mark proprietor has already sold. Parallel importers are thus free to exploit price differentials within the Community if they wish to do so. The trade mark proprietor must take the consequences of the choice to make the initial sale at a particular price. However, as has been mentioned, the trade mark proprietor may have justifiable grounds for objecting to further dealings in the marked goods. As a result, the principle of exhaustion does not apply 'where there exist legitimate

---

[324]   CTMR, Art. 53(2). The CTM proprietor may not oppose use of the earlier right, even if there has been acquiescence by the national proprietor.

[325]   See below Chapter 6 Intellectual Property and Free Movement of Goods.

reasons for the proprietor to oppose further commercialisation of the goods, especially where the condition of the goods is changed or impaired after they have been put on the market'.[326]

5.4.7 Other EU Harmonisation Initiatives Relevant to Trade Marks

A number of EU measures have been enacted as part of a wide framework of consumer protection objectives. Several of these affect the use of trade marks.

(a) Misleading Advertising

In 1984 a Directive on Misleading Advertising was adopted.[327] The national laws on misleading advertising differed widely, affecting the establishment and functioning of the common market, particularly conditions of competition, and the free movement of goods. The economic welfare of consumers was also affected. The first step was to harmonise provisions on misleading advertising. In 1997 a further Directive was passed, to bring comparative advertising within this structure.[328] Comparative advertising can assist consumer choice by demonstrating objectively the merits of comparable products, and thus stimulate competition between suppliers of goods and services to the consumer's advantage. A harmonised regime is essential, to ensure that firms are not exposed to forms of advertising developed by competitors to which they cannot respond in a like manner. The Directive therefore requires member states to permit comparative advertising, but under carefully harmonised conditions. These are that:

(a)   it is not misleading according to Articles 2(2), 3 and 7(1);[329]

---

[326]   CTMR, Art. 13; TMD, Art. 7.

[327]   Directive 84/450 relating to the approximation of the laws, regulations and administrative provisions of the Member States concerning misleading advertising [1984] OJ L 250. Directive 84/45 was repealed by a new codifying Directive 2006/114 with effect from 12 December 2007.

[328]   Directive 97/55 amending Directive 84/450/EEC concerning misleading advertising so as to include comparative advertising [1997] OJ L 290. For more detail see Ansgar Ohly and Michael Spence, *The Law of Comparative Advertising: Directive 97/55/EC in the United Kingdom and Germany* (Oxford: Hart, 2000).

[329]   By Art. 2(2) 'misleading advertising' means 'any advertising which in any way, including its presentation, deceives or is likely to deceive the persons to whom it is addressed or whom it reaches and which, by reason of its deceptive nature, is likely to affect their economic behaviour or which, for those reasons, injures or is likely to injure a competitor'. Art. 3 states that in determining whether advertising is misleading, account shall be taken of all its features, and in particular any information it contains on various listed matters. Art. 7 permits members states to provide more extensive protection, in certain cases.

(b)   it compares goods or services meeting the same needs or intended for the same purpose;

(c)   it objectively compares one or more material, relevant, verifiable and representative features of those goods and services, which may include price;

(d)   it does not create confusion in the marketplace between the advertiser and a competitor or between the advertiser's trade marks, trade names, other distinguishing marks, goods or services and those of a competitor;

(e)   it does not discredit or denigrate the trade marks, trade names, other distinguishing marks, goods, services, activities or circumstances of a competitor;

(f)   for products with designation of origin, it relates in each case to products with the same designation;

(g)   it does not take unfair advantage of the reputation of a trade mark, trade name or other distinguishing marks of a competitor or of the designation of origin of competing products;[330]

(h)   it does not present goods or services as imitations or replicas of goods or services bearing a protected trade mark or trade name.

Since comparative advertising is intended solely to distinguish between marks, and to highlight differences in their products and services objectively, it does not breach the trade mark proprietor's exclusive rights. Nevertheless, comparative advertising is often unwelcome to trade mark proprietors. In *Pippig*, the discount optician Hartlauer circulated widely an advertising leaflet which compared its prices very favourably with prices for spectacles and lenses supplied by traditional opticians. Some of the price comparisons did not highlight the fact that different brands were concerned. Traditional opticians tended to stock well-known high-value brands, and Hartlauer offered less known low-end brands. The ECJ held that the advertiser is in principle free to state or not to state the brand name of rival products in comparative advertising, but noted that the omission of a better known brand name might be misleading if the brand was a very important element of the buyer's choice, and there was a major difference in how well known the brand names were. The ECJ also observed that comparing rival offers, particularly as regards price, is the very nature of comparative advertising. Therefore, comparing

---

[330]   See Case C-59/05, *Siemens AG* v. *VIPA* [2006] ECR 2147; Case C-112/99, *Toshiba Europe GmbH* v. *Katun Germany GmbH* [2001] ECR 7945; Case C-381/05, *De Landtsheer Emmanuel SA* v. *Comité Interprofessionnel du Vin de Champagne & Veuve Clicquot Ponsardin SA* (19 April 2007) [2007] 2 CMLR 1146.

prices cannot in itself entail the discrediting or denigration of a competitor who charges higher prices.[331]

The ECJ has taken a pragmatic approach to the details of price comparison. In *Lidl Belgium* v. *Colruyt*, a supermarket chain had sent out a mailshot which stated: 'Last year, 2003, you were able once again to make significant savings with Colruyt. On the basis of our average price index for the past year we have calculated that a family spending EUR 100 each week in Colruyt stores saved between EUR 366 and EUR 1129 by shopping at Colruyt's rather than at any other supermarket.' Similar comparisons were made on the back of till receipts. Following objections by a rival supermarket, the ECJ interpreted the Directive as 'not precluding comparative advertising from relating collectively to selections of basic consumables sold by two competing chains of stores in so far as those selections each consist of individual products which, when viewed in pairs, individually satisfy the requirement of comparability laid down by that provision'. However, consumers had to be able to verify the claims readily if they wished to. This ruling allows price comparisons to be made on a generalised basis, rather than requiring a list of every single price in respect of every single item of every single retailer.[332]

The ECJ has recently held that trade mark law remains relevant to certain cases of comparative advertising. In the *O2* case, Advocate General Mengozzi took the view that the Comparative Advertising Directive provided an exhaustive regime. By this analysis, use of a competitor's mark in a comparative advertisement either did not comply with the Comparative Advertising Directive's conditions and was prohibited by that Directive, or it complied with that Directive's conditions and could not be prohibited under Articles 5(1)(a) or (b) of the Trade Mark Directive. However, the ECJ held that use of an identical or similar mark *will* fall within Articles 5(1) and 5(2). If a third party using the mark satisfies all the conditions of the Comparative Advertising Directive, then this affords a complete defence, and the trade mark proprietor cannot prevent such use. In contrast, if the use of the mark gives rise to a likelihood of confusion under Article 5(1)(b), then the conditions of the Comparative Advertising Directive cannot be met, and the use may be prevented.[333]

---

[331] Case C-44/01, *Pippig Augenoptik GmbH & Co. KG* v. *Hartlauer Handelsgesellschaft mbH* [2003] ECR 3095 (paras. 56 and 80).

[332] Case C-356/04, *Lidl Belgium GmbH & Co KG* v. *Etablissementen Franz Colruyt NV* (16 September 2006) [2007] 1 CMLR 9 (para. 39).

[333] C-533/06, *O2 Holdings Limited & O2 (UK) Limited* v. *Hutchison 3G UK Limited* (12 June 2008). The ECJ was not asked to consider Article 5(2) of the TMD, and did not do so. However, it did make it clear that if the third party's conduct complied fully with the conditions of the Comparative Advertising Directive then it

(b)   Unfair Commercial Practices Directive

The law in this area will change shortly, when the Unfair Commercial Practices Directive comes into force.[334] The Directive establishes a single, common and general ban on unfair commercial practices which distort consumers' economic behaviour. It lays down rules for determining whether a commercial practice is unfair and provides a short list of misleading practices which are prohibited throughout the European Union. The two criteria used to determine whether a practice is unfair are: if the practice is contrary to the requirements of professional diligence, and if it materially distorts the economic behaviour of consumers. The Directive makes a distinction between two types of unfair practices: those which are misleading and those which are aggressive.

The rules on misleading advertising in the Unfair Commercial Practices Directive will replace the business-to-consumer rules in the Misleading Advertising Directive. The Misleading Advertising Directive will remain applicable but its scope will be limited. It will cover business-to-business misleading advertising and comparative advertising which may harm a competitor but where there is no direct consumer detriment (for example, denigration). The new Directive provides that a commercial practice shall be regarded as misleading 'if, in its factual context, taking account of all its features and circumstances, it causes or is likely to cause the average consumer to take a transactional decision that he would not have taken otherwise', and it involves 'any marketing of a product, including comparative advertising, which creates confusion with any products, trade marks, trade names or other distinguishing marks of a competitor'.[335] Recital 14 states, however, that: 'it is not the intention of this Directive to reduce consumer choice by prohibiting the promotion of products which look similar to other products unless this similarity confuses consumers as to the commercial origin of the product and is therefore misleading'. This has obvious relevance for brand owners who object to 'lookalike' products.[336]

---

would not infringe Art. 5(2). There are likely to be more questions referred to the ECJ on this point – particularly since questions of detriment, dilution and unfair advantage are very likely to be raised in a case concerning comparative advertising.

[334]   Directive 2005/29 concerning unfair business-to-consumer commercial practices in the internal market ('Unfair Commercial Practices Directive') [2005] OJ L 149. The Directive is due to be implemented in member states by 12 June 2007, and applicable by 12 December 2007.

[335]   UCPD, Art. 6(2)(a).

[336]   For further discussion, see Gill Grassie, 'The EU Directive on Unfair Commercial Practices – A UK Perspective' [2006] *JIPL&P* 107–12.

(c)   Domain names

The EU has recently established the top-level domain, '.eu', and this may have some interest and relevance for trade mark owners. A certain amount of background is necessary to understand why this is so.

An immense amount of business is done over the internet. Domain names may be acquired very easily, on a first come, first served basis. In contrast to trade marks, there is no requirement that domain names be limited to a particular class of goods or services. These features generate intense competition for particularly desirable names. Trade mark owners are often the target of 'cyber-squatters', who register domain names identical or similar to trade marks or company names in the hope of selling them at a profit to those with trading interests in them. Trade mark owners object to this practice, arguing that cyber-squatters have no legitimate interest in using the name, and are free-riding on the reputation built up by the trade mark owner's investment. It is difficult to forestall such behaviour, because it would be virtually impossible for a business to acquire all the myriad variants of a mark or name which might be registered as a domain name. There have been a number of legal responses to this practice. One is the use of national laws directed against passing off or unfair competition.[337] The other has been the creation of 'cyber-jurisdictions', based on contractual relationships, in which cyber-squatters may be ordered to transfer the domain names they hold to those considered to be better entitled to them.

ICANN (Internet Corporation for Assigned Numbers and Names) is the registration body for the major generic top-level domains (TLDs), such as .com, .org, .int. ICANN also administers the Uniform Domain Name Dispute Resolution Policy (UDRP). The UDRP is based on recommendations made by WIPO in the Report on the First WIPO Internet Domain Name Process, which examined the problems caused by the conflict between trade marks and domain names. Anyone registering a domain name must agree to abide by UDRP terms. A trade mark owner who considers that a domain name registration infringes on its trade mark may initiate a proceeding under the UDRP. There are a number of adjudication services, of which the most commonly used is WIPO's.[338] Complainants must specify the domain name in question, the respondent or holder of the domain name, the registrar with whom the domain name was registered and the grounds for the complaint. The complainant must show: that the domain name is identical or similar to a trade

---

[337]   See, for example, *British Telecommunications* v. *One in a Million* (UK CA) [1999] FSR 1.

[338]   For recent figures, see WIPO Press Release (12 March 2007), 'Cybersquatting Remains on the Rise with Further Risk to Trademarks from New Registration Practices', PR/2007/479.

mark in which the complainant has rights; that the respondent should be considered as having no rights or legitimate interests in respect of the domain name; and that the domain name should be considered as having been registered and used in bad faith. The respondent is offered the opportunity to defend itself against the allegations. The arbitration body appoints a panellist who decides whether or not the domain(s) should be cancelled or transferred. Damages are not available, nor is injunctive relief; these are only available through legal action in national courts.[339]

Assignment of top-level domains (TLDs) was originally based roughly on the activities carried out by an organisation – the generic domains such as, .com (commercial organisations), .net (networks), .org (other organisations) and more recently, .biz (business), .info (information).[340] National agencies have now been given the power to grant 'country code' domains (ccTLDs) with a geographical suffix; such as, .uk, .de, .fr. The Commission initiated a process which resulted in the creation of the TLD .eu, thereby signalling the importance to the EU of electronic commerce and the information society. The aim is not to replace the existing national country code TLDs in the EU, but to complement them, by offering users the additional option of pan-European internet identity for their web sites and e-mail addresses. Registration is open to all EU residents and organisations with a registered seat in the EU. The .eu TLD is run by a private, non-profit organisation known as EURid. Well over 2.5 million '.eu' domain names have been registered, and .eu is currently the eighth most popular TLD worldwide.[341]

5.4.8   Community Trade Marks as Objects of Property

Community trade marks are objects of property.[342] However, national laws regarding a great many transactions relevant for the exploitation of trade marks (for example, transfers, assignments, security interests, testamentary

---

[339]   The ICANN system is itself under pressure, and is regarded as obsolete by some. See Oleksandr Pastukhov, 'Internationalised Domain Names: The Window of Opportunity for Cybersquatters' [2006] *IPQ* 421–30; Christopher T. Varas, 'Sealing the Cracks: A Proposal to Combat Advertising-Based Cybersquatting' [2008] *JIPL&P* 246–61. For more detail on the domain name system, and on individual jurisdictions, see Torsten Bettinger, *Domain Name Law and Practice: An International Handbook* (Oxford and New York: Oxford University Press, 2005).

[340]   See Simon Chapman and Jenny Holmen, 'New gTLDs – Protection or Threat for IP Owners?' [2006] *EIPR* 315–20.

[341]   Press Release (4 April 2008), 'Over 300,000 .eu Web Domains Created in 2007' IP/08/530. See also http://www.eurid.eu/.

[342]   CTMR, Art. 16.

disposition, bankruptcy and insolvency) are not harmonised.[343] The CTMR therefore provides that transactions regarding CTMs will normally be governed by the law of the most appropriate member state (usually, the member state where the trade mark proprietor is domiciled). Co-ownership of CTMs is permitted.[344] A CTM may be transferred, independently of any transfer of the undertaking which owns or has used it, in respect of some or all of the goods or services for which it is registered, but geographically it must be 'dealt with in its entirety, and for the whole area of the Community'.[345] An assignment of a CTM must be made in writing and must be signed by all the parties to the contract.[346] OHIM will not register transfers which are likely to mislead the public as to the nature, quality or geographical origin of the goods or services in respect of which it is registered.[347] A CTM may be licensed for some or all of the goods or services for which it is registered and for the whole or part of the Community. A licence may be exclusive or non-exclusive. The proprietor of a CTM may invoke the rights conferred by that trade mark against a licensee. Normally a licensee may bring proceedings for infringement of a CTM only with the proprietor's consent, although an exclusive licensee may do so if the proprietor does not do so within an appropriate period.[348] Transactions affecting CTMs should be registered as soon as possible to be fully effective. Transfers, grants of security and licences of CTMs shall only have effects *vis-à-vis* third parties in all the member states after entry in the Register, unless that third party knew of the act at the date on which the rights were acquired.[349] Until a transfer has been entered in the Register, the transferee may not invoke the rights arising from the registration of the CTM.[350]

---

[343]   A CTM may be mortgaged: CTMR, Art. 19. It may pass on the death of the proprietor either by will or according to the rules applicable on intestacy. Normally, the only insolvency proceedings in which a Community trade mark may be involved are those opened in the member state in the territory of which the debtor has his centre of main interests: CTMR, Art. 21. The effects *vis-à-vis* third parties of bankruptcy are governed by the law of the member state in which such proceedings are first brought: CTMR, Art. 23(4).

[344]   CTMR, Art. 16(3).
[345]   CTMR, Art. 17(1) & 16(1).
[346]   CTMR, Art. 17(3).
[347]   CTMR, Art. 17(4).
[348]   CTMR, Art. 22.
[349]   CTMR, Art. 23(1).
[350]   CTMR, Art. 17(6).

5.5 GEOGRAPHICAL INDICATIONS OF ORIGIN

5.5.1 Introduction

A geographical indication is a sign used on goods that have a specific geographical origin and possess qualities or a reputation that are due to that place of origin. Often, a geographical indication consists of the name of the place of origin of the goods. They are commonly used in relation to agricultural products. These typically have qualities that derive from their place of production and are influenced by specific local factors, such as climate and soil. These rights may have a considerable history. For example, Roquefort, the favourite cheese of Charlemagne, is made exclusively from the milk of the red Lacaune ewes that graze in the Aveyron region. The village Roquefort-sur-Soulzon sits above natural caves where a blue mould, *Penicillium roqueforti*, permeates the cheeses as these age for a minimum of four months. In 1411, King Charles VI of France gave rights to the ageing of Roquefort to Roquefort-sur-Soulzon alone. Other well-known regional products include Tuscan olive oil, Parma ham, Feta cheese, and so on. However, the use of geographical indications is not limited to agricultural products. They may also underline specific qualities of a product which are attributable to other factors found in their place of origin, such as specific manufacturing skills and traditions. Examples of this include Murano glass, Toledo steel and Swiss watches. But in all cases a geographical indication points to a specific place or region of production that determines the characteristic qualities of the product that originates therein, showing that there is a clear link between the products and their original place of production.

Geographical indications are thus understood by consumers to denote the origin and the quality of products. They may have very significant reputations. Without adequate protection, there is a risk that consumers will be misled, and legitimate producers harmed in consequence. A wide range of legal methods have been used to protect them, including trade marks, passing off/unfair competition law and certification marks. There are also a number of specifically tailored regimes, such as the French 'appellation d'origine contrôlée' (AOC), which is a government certification granted to certain French geographical indications for wines, cheeses, butters and other agricultural products. Geographical designations are usually regarded as a form of intellectual property, being unique, but intangible.

5.5.2 International Treaties

At the international level, a number of treaties administered by the WIPO provide for the protection of geographical indications. The Paris Convention specifically includes 'indications of source or appellations of origin' within its remit.[351] It provides that 'direct or indirect use of a false indication of the source of the goods or the identity of the producer, manufacturer, or merchant' may result in seizure of the goods on importation.[352] The Madrid Agreement for the Repression of False or Deceptive Indications of Source on Goods (1891) is directed at all goods bearing a false or deceptive indication of source, which must be seized or prohibited from import. It is a matter for member states whether an appellation has become generic (although regional appellations for wine may not be declared generic). The Madrid Agreement has to a considerable extent been superseded.[353] It currently has 35 signatories.

The Lisbon Agreement for the Protection of Appellations of Origin and their International Registration (1958) aims to provide for the protection of appellations of origin. These are defined as the 'geographical name of a country, region, or locality, which serves to designate a product originating therein, the quality and characteristics of which are due exclusively or essentially to the geographic environment, including natural and human factors'.[354] If such names are protected at national level, they may be registered at WIPO, on the application of the competent authorities of the interested member state. The appellation is published, and other member states are notified. A member state may declare, within one year, that it cannot ensure the protection of a registered appellation. If it does not do so, the appellation must be protected, so long as it is protected in the country of origin. A registered appellation may not be declared to have become generic in a member state as long as it continues to be protected in the country of origin. The Lisbon Agreement protects 'against any usurpation or imitation, even if the true origin of the product is indicated or if the appellation is used in translated form or accompanied by terms such as "kind," "type," "make," "imitation," or the like'.[355] This is in contrast to the Madrid Agreement, which sought to prevent consumers from being misled. The Lisbon Agreement offers wider protection, and would thus prevent the sale of 'Roquefort-style cheese', for example. The Lisbon Agreement currently has only 26 members, however.[356]

---

[351] Paris Convention, Art. 1(2).
[352] Paris Convention, Arts. 10(2), 9.
[353] The Madrid Agreement was of greater importance when the Paris Convention did not protect indications of source unless there was fraudulent intent. However, at the Lisbon revision of the Paris Convention in 1858, Article 10 was revised to protect indications of source even where fraud was not shown.
[354] Lisbon Agreement, Art. 2.
[355] Lisbon Agreement, Art. 3.
[356] Valuable protection may nevertheless arise from the fact that appellations of origin registered under the Lisbon Agreement are regarded as prior rights which allow

5.5.3 TRIPS

The TRIPS Agreement, negotiated under the umbrella of the WTO, is perhaps the most significant international treaty for geographic indications, in part because its membership is so wide. TRIPS requires member states to offer protection against (a) the use of any means in the designation or presentation of a good that indicates or suggests that the good in question originates in a geographical area other than the true place of origin in a manner which misleads the public as to the geographical origin of the good; (b) any use which constitutes an act of unfair competition within the meaning of Article 10*bis* of the Paris Convention.[357] TRIPS offers additional protection for geographical indications for wines and spirits, preventing use of a geographical indication for these even where the true origin of the goods is indicated, or the geographical indication is used in translation, or is accompanied by expressions such as 'kind', 'type', 'style', 'imitation' or the like.[358] TRIPS also provides for negotiations towards the establishment of a multilateral system of notification and registration of geographical indications for wines.[359]

At the 2001 WTO Ministerial Conference in Doha, pressure was exerted by an EU-led group of countries, aimed at actually delivering a multilateral system, and extending the extra protection enjoyed by wines and spirits to all agricultural products. A commitment to do so was expressed in the Doha Declaration.[360] The Doha Declaration's deadline for completing the negotiations was the Ministerial Conference in Cancún in 2003. Since this was not achieved, the negotiations are now taking place within the overall timetable for the round. A number of proposals have been put forward. The EU submitted a Communication in June 2005, calling for an amendment to TRIPS.[361] It proposes that when a geographical indication is registered, this would establish a 'rebuttable presumption' that the term is to be protected in other WTO member states, unless a reservation (on permitted grounds only, such as that the term has become generic) is lodged within a specified period. An alternative proposal has been put forward by a group of countries (including

---

their holders to oppose conflicting Community trade mark applications under certain circumstances: CTMR, Art. 8(4). For an attempt to do so, see Joined Cases T-53/04 to T-56/04, T-58/04 and T-59/04, *Budějovický Budvar, národní podnik* v. *OHIM* (12 June 2007). This case is only one of many in the bitter fight between the holders of the (American) trade mark 'Budweiser' and the (Czech) GI Cesky Budejovicky Budvar.

[357]   TRIPS, Art. 22(1).
[358]   TRIPS, Art. 23.
[359]   TRIPS, Art. 23(4).
[360]   WTO WT/MIN(01)/DEC/1 (20 November 2001), paras. 12, 18. WTO documents are available from http://docsonline.wto.org.
[361]   WTO TN/IP/W/11.

Australia, Canada, Japan, New Zealand, Chinese Taipei and the United States) strongly opposed to the EU plan.[362] Instead of amending the TRIPS Agreement, it suggests that the TRIPS Council should set up a voluntary system where notified geographical indications would be registered in a database. Those governments choosing to participate in the system would have to consult the database when taking decisions on protection in their own countries. Non-participating members would be 'encouraged' but 'not obliged' to consult the database. Hong Kong and China have proposed a compromise, under which a registered geographical indication would enjoy a more limited 'presumption' than under the EU proposal, and only in those countries choosing to participate in the system.[363] The EU proposal also advocates extending the 'higher level of protection' (currently given by Article 23 only to wines and spirits) to other products. Again the issue is contentious, and not all agree even that discussions are covered by the Doha mandate.[364]

There are strong feelings on both sides of the debate, and member states are deeply divided. Those in favour of the EU proposal see the higher level of protection as a way to improve the marketing of their products by differentiating them more effectively from their competitors, and they object to other countries 'usurping' their terms. The EU has produced a list of 41 EU regional quality products (including Champagne, Cognac, Parma ham, Parmigiano Reggiano) whose names it wants to 'recuperate'. These names are included in the EU's register of GIs, and were selected because in many third countries they are claimed to be generic terms, and/or are registered as trade marks by local producers. The choice was deliberately slanted to cover third countries where these kinds of 'abuses' were more frequent, and to reflect the most important markets for these products. EU Farm Commissioner Franz Fischler defended the EU against accusations of protectionism, arguing that it was a matter of fairness. He said, 'It is simply not acceptable that the EU cannot sell its genuine Italian Parma Ham in Canada because the trade mark "Parma Ham" is reserved for a ham produced in Canada'. EU Trade Commissioner Pascal Lamy summed up the EU's position as follows:

> Geographical Indications offer the best protection to quality products which are marketed by relying on their origin and reputation and other special characteristics linked to such an origin. They reward investment in quality by our producers.

---

362   WTO TN/IP/W/10.
363   WTO TN/IP/W/8. All three proposals are compared in a Secretariat paper, WTO TN/IP/W/12 (14 September 2005).
364   For comment, see Bernard O'Connor, 'The EC Need Not Be Isolated on GIs' [2007] *EIPR* 303–4.

Abuses in third countries undermine the reputation of EU products and create confusion for consumers. We want this to cease for the most usurped products in the world.[365]

Those opposing the proposal argue that the existing level of protection is adequate. They consider that enhanced protection would be burdensome, and would disrupt existing legitimate marketing practices. Former colonies, in particular, resent the accusation of usurpation. From their perspective, migrants have simply taken the methods of making the products and the names with them to their new homes and have been using them in good faith. Many countries therefore feel they have little to gain and much to lose by the implementation of the EU proposal. Although discussions are continuing, the problems have so far proved intractable, and no agreement is in prospect.[366]

5.5.4   The EU Regime

In 1992 the EU adopted a Regulation 2081/92 to protect the geographical indications and designations of origin for agricultural products and foodstuffs.[367] It came into force in July 1993. The United States and Australia considered that the Regulation did not meet the EU's WTO obligations, contravening the principle of national treatment, by discriminating against foreign geographical indications and failing to protect US trade marks.[368] The Regulation did cover third countries, but only under various conditions.[369] On 19 April 2005, the World Trade Organization's Dispute Settlement Body ruled in favour of the

---

[365]   Press Release (28 August 2003), 'WTO Talks: EU Steps Up Bid for Better Protection of Regional Quality Products' IP/03/1178. This includes an Annexe of the 41 products. See also http://ec.europa.eu/trade/issues/sectoral/intell_property/argu_en.htm.

[366]   For a factual account of the arguments presented, see WTO TN/IP/W/12/Add.1 (4 May 2007). See also WTO WT/GC/W/546 and TN/C/W/25 (18 May 2005). See also Nina Resinek, 'Geographical Indications and Trade Marks: Coexistence or "First in Time, First in Right" Principle?' [2007] *EIPR* 446; Marsha A. Echols, *Geographical Indications for Food Products* (London: Kluwer Law International, 2008). For wider discussion, see Rhonda Chesmond, 'Protection or Privatisation of Culture? The Cultural Dimension of the International Intellectual Property Debate on Geographical Indications of Origin' [2007] *EIPR* 379.

[367]   Regulation 2081/92 on the protection of geographical indications and designations of origin for agricultural products and foodstuffs [1992] OJ L 208/1 'GI Regulation (2081/92)'.

[368]   Complaints by the United States (WT/DS174) and Australia (WT/DS290). Full documentation is available on the WTO web site (www.wto.org), under dispute settlement. For deeper analysis, see Marsha A. Echols, *Geographical Indications for Food Products* (London: Kluwer Law International, 2008).

[369]   GI Regulation (2081/92), Art. 12.

United States and Australia, that certain provisions of the Regulation did contravene the European Union's obligations under GATT and the TRIPS Agreement. The Panel recommended that the European Union should amend the Regulation to bring it into line with the European Union's obligations. In response to the WTO Panel Ruling, Regulation 510/2006 was adopted, replacing Regulation 2081/92.[370] It entered into force on 31 March 2006. Applications for registration of PDOs and PGIs by producers in third countries, and objections to applications by individuals in third countries, can now be made directly to the Commission.

Regulation 510/2006 establishes the rules for protecting designations of origin and geographical indications for agricultural products and foodstuffs intended for human consumption.[371] If there is a link between the characteristics of a product and its geographical origin, it may qualify for the protection of either a designation of origin (PDO)[372] or a geographical indication (PGI). There are corresponding EU symbols which may be used on the labels of these products, to inform consumers and those in the trade. The scheme also aims to benefit rural economies, encouraging investment in quality local production.[373] However, the system is not without its critics. One commentator has complained that Community policies in this area 'give little weight to innovation and product choice, and instead emphasise the virtues of settled local interests and traditional products', dividing rather than integrating the Community's marketplace for foods, and hindering rather than promoting nutritional improvements.[374] Others have noted that the idyllic picture of the rural farm may, in an increasingly industrialised agricultural industry, be just a vision, and that efforts to support rural economies might be focused more effectively on promoting alternatives to this form of employment.[375]

---

[370] Regulation 510/2006 on the protection of geographical indications and designations of origin for agricultural products and foodstuffs [1996] OJ L 93/12 'GI Regulation (510/2006)'.

[371] GI Regulation (510/2006), Art. 1(1). The Regulation covers agricultural products intended for human consumption listed in Annex I to the Treaty, foodstuffs listed in Annex I to the GI Regulation, and agricultural products listed in Annex II to the GI Regulation. The GI Regulation does not apply to wine-sector products, except wine vinegars, or to spirits (which are separately regulated).

[372] The translation of *Appellation d'Origine Contrôlée* (AOC).

[373] GI Regulation (510/2006), Recital 2.

[374] Charles Lister, 'The Naming of Foods: The European Community's Rules for Non-Brand Food Products' (1993) 18 *ELRev* 179–201.

[375] Marina Kolia, 'Monopolising Names of Foodstuffs: The New Legislation' [1992] *EIPR* 333–4; Marina Kolia, 'Monopolising Names: EEC Proposals on the Protection of Trade Descriptions of Foodstuffs' [1992] *EIPR* 233–8.

The two designations, PDO and PGI, are different in nature. A designation of origin is defined as the name of a region, a specific place or, in exceptional cases, a country,[376] used to describe an agricultural product or a foodstuff. To be protected, the product must originate in that region, specific place or country. It must be shown that the quality or characteristics of the product are essentially or exclusively due to a particular geographical environment with its inherent natural and human factors. Natural factors might include the soil or subsoil, and the geography of the area (its relief and slope, climate and micro-climates, vegetation and landscape). Human factors might include the choice of area in which to plant (perhaps areas protected from the wind), adaptation of the geographical area to suit the production method, special constructions for production (for example, mills, terraces, irrigation ditches) as well as the development of local know-how or special production skills. The production, processing and preparation of the product must all take place in the defined geographical area.[377] Well-known examples include Mozzarella di Bufala Campana (Italy), Kalamata olives (Greece), Prosciutto di Parma (Italy).[378] A geographical indication is defined as the name of a region, a specific place or, in exceptional cases, a country, used to describe an agricultural product or a foodstuff. To be protected the product must originate in that region, specific place or country. The product must possess a specific quality, reputation or other characteristics attributable to that geographical origin. It is also necessary to show that at least one of the stages of production, processing or preparation of the product takes place in the defined geographical area.[379] The link with the area is therefore less strong than for PDOs. UK GIs include Scotch Beef, Rutland Bitter and Whitstable Oysters. Questions concerning the nature of this link have been referred to the ECJ, in a case involving Melton Mowbray pork pies.[380]

---

[376]   This provision was introduced to take account of very small countries, such as Luxembourg. See Case C-325/00, *Commission v. Germany* (AG Jacobs' Opinion, 14 March 2002) [2002] ECR I-9977.

[377]   GI Regulation (510/2006), Art. 2(1)(a). Notwithstanding the requirements of Art. 2(1)(a), geographical designations which were recognised as designations of origin in the country of origin before 1 May 2004 will be treated as designations of origin for the purposes of the Regulation, even if the raw materials for the products concerned come from a geographical area larger than, or different from, the processing area, provided that: the production area of the raw materials is defined; special conditions for the production of the raw materials exist; and there are inspection arrangements in place. GI Regulation (510/2006), Art. 2(1)(3).

[378]   UK PDOs include Cornish clotted cream, West Country farmhouse Cheddar cheese, Shetland lamb, Jersey Royal potatoes. For the complete list of PDOs and GIs see: http://ec.europa.eu/agriculture/qual/en/1bbaa_en.htm.

[379]   GI Regulation (510/2006), Art. 2(1)(b).

[380]   *R. on the Application of Northern Foods Plc v. Secretary of State for the*

Note that there is an exception to the general rule that only geographic names are registrable. 'Traditional' names, whether geographical or non-geographical, may be considered as designations of origin or geographical indications if they fulfil the above conditions.[381] Feta cheese, has – somewhat controversially – been registered as a result of this rule.[382]

Exclusions

Article 3 of the Regulation prevents the registration of generic names, names which conflict with the names of plant varieties, animal breeds, homonyms and trademarks.

(i) GENERIC NAMES

A 'name that has become generic' is defined as 'the name of an agricultural product or a foodstuff which, although it relates to the place or the region where this product or foodstuff was originally produced or marketed, has become the common name of an agricultural product or a foodstuff in the Community'. This excludes (for example) cheeses such as Brie, Camembert, Cheddar, Edam, Emmentaler and Gouda, and Dijon mustard.[383] When determining whether or not a name has become generic, account must be taken of all factors, including the situation in the member states and in areas where the product is consumed. If there are relevant national or Community laws, these too must be taken into account.

In the *Feta Cheese* case, 'feta' had been registered as a PDO in Greece, on the basis that it was a 'traditional' non-geographical name. In prolonged litigation, a number of governments objected that 'feta' had become a generic term. In its final determination, the ECJ concluded that 'several relevant and important factors' indicated that the term had not become generic. The ECJ acknowledged that feta had been lawfully produced (in significant quantities) in other countries, but noted that the production of feta had remained concentrated in Greece. More than 85% of Community consumption of feta, per capita and per year, took place in Greece. The majority of consumers in Greece consider that the name 'feta' carries a geographical and not a generic connotation, although

---

Environment, Food and Rural Affairs & The MMPPA, Minute of Order (14 March 2006). For discussion see Dev Gangjee, 'Melton Mowbray and the GI Pie in the Sky: Exploring Cartographies of Protection' [2006] *IPQ* 291–309.

381 GI Regulation (510/2006), Art. 2(2).

382 Case C-465/02, *Germany* v. *Commission* [2005] ECR 9115.

383 GI Regulation (510/2006), Art. 3(1). See Joined Cases C-289/96, C-293/96 and C-299/96, *Kingdom of Denmark* v. *Community* [1999] ECR I-1541. Although names which are generic *per se* may not be registered, a geographical name which incorporates a generic name may qualify for registration. For example, West Country farmhouse Cheddar Cheese is a PDO, though Cheddar is a generic form of cheese.

in Denmark the majority of consumers believe that the name is generic. The ECJ also noted that, in member states other than Greece, feta is commonly marketed with labels referring to Greek cultural traditions and civilisation. From this the Court inferred that these consumers perceived feta as a cheese associated with the Hellenic Republic, even if it had in fact been produced in another member state. The finding that the name 'feta' is not generic in nature bears heavily on existing producers outside Greece. Descriptive uses, such as 'Danish feta', 'Yorkshire feta', or 'feta-style ewe's milk cheese' will no longer be permitted (following a transition period).[384] The decision is also controversial, because much of the non-Greek feta had been imported into Greece, to address shortfalls in supply. The debate continues as to whether this decision creates an unwarranted monopoly for Greek feta producers, or simply acknowledges an ancient Greek cultural tradition.[385]

(ii) PLANT OR ANIMAL NAMES

A name may not be registered if it conflicts with the name of a plant variety or an animal breed and as a result is likely to mislead the consumer as to the 'true origin' of the product.[386]

(iii) HOMONYMOUS NAMES

Names which are wholly or partially homonymous (which are spelt or pronounced in the same way) with a name already registered under the Regulation may be registered, but only with due regard for local and traditional usage and the actual risk of confusion. In particular, a homonymous name which misleads the consumer into believing that products come from another territory shall not be registered even if the name is accurate as far as the actual territory, region or place of origin of the agricultural products or foodstuffs in question is concerned. In addition, a registered homonymous name may only be used if there is a sufficient distinction in practice between it and the homonym registered subsequently. Regard must be had to the need to treat the producers concerned in an equitable manner and not to mislead the consumer.[387]

(iv) TRADE MARKS

A designation of origin or geographical indication will not be registered

---

[384] Case C-465/02, *Germany* v. *Commission* [2005] ECR 9115.
[385] For comment, see Jeremy Reed, 'Feta: A Cheese or a Fudge?' [2006] *EIPR* 535–8; Dev Gangjee, 'Say Cheese! A Sharper Image of Generic Use through the Lens of Feta' [2007] *EIPR* 172–9.
[386] GI Regulation (510/2006), Art. 3(2).
[387] GI Regulation (510/2006), Art. 3(3).

where, in the light of a trade mark's reputation, renown and the length of time it has been used, registration is liable to mislead the consumer as to the true identity of the product.[388]

Registering a product name

In outline, the steps are as follows. A group of producers defines the product according to precise specifications. The application, including the specifications, is then sent to the relevant national authority where it will be scrutinised, and then, if appropriate, transmitted to the Commission. Here the application is scrutinised again, and, if it meets the requirements, will be published in the Official Journal. If there are no objections from those interested, the name is published in the Official Journal, now as a protected product name.

(i) THOSE ELIGIBLE TO APPLY FOR REGISTRATION

PDOs and PGIs must be registered. Applications for registration may only be made by a group of producers or processors or, in exceptional cases, natural or legal persons. A 'group' is defined as 'any association, irrespective of its legal form or composition, of producers or processors working with the same agricultural product or foodstuff'.[389] A group may lodge a registration application only for the agricultural products or foodstuffs which it produces or obtains.[390] If a name designates a trans-border geographical area, several groups may lodge a joint application.[391] If the application concerns a cross-border area, it may be made in conjunction with several groups.[392]

(ii) PRODUCT SPECIFICATION

The application for registration must include a 'product specification'. Without this the product will not be eligible for protection as a PDO or PGI.[393] The specification contains the detailed definition of the protected product drawn up by the producers concerned. This definition determines the conditions under which the protected name may be used, and, as a corollary, the

---

[388]   GI Regulation (510/2006), Art. 3(4).

[389]   GI Regulation (510/2006), Art. 5(1). Other interested parties may participate in the group. A natural or legal person may be treated as a group in accordance with the detailed rules referred to in Art. 16(c).

[390]   GI Regulation (510/2006), Art. 5(2).

[391]   GI Regulation (510/2006), Art. 5(1). Other interested parties may participate in the group. A natural or legal person may be treated as a group in accordance with the detailed rules referred to in Art. 16(c).

[392]   GI Regulation (510/2006), Art. 5(1). They must follow the detailed rules referred to in Art. 16(d).

[393]   GI Regulation (510/2006), Art. 4(1).

scope of protection against third parties' use of the name.[394] Article 4(2) gives a non-exhaustive list of the information required in a product specification, which must include:

(a) the name of the agricultural product or foodstuff comprising the designation of origin or the geographical indication;
(b) a description of the agricultural product or foodstuff, including the raw materials, if appropriate, and principal physical, chemical, microbiological or organoleptic[395] characteristics of the product or the foodstuff;
(c) the definition of the geographical area;
(d) evidence that the agricultural product or the foodstuff originates in the defined geographical area;
(e) a description of the method of obtaining the agricultural product or foodstuff and, if appropriate, the authentic and unvarying local methods as well as information concerning packaging, if the applicant group determines and gives reasons why the packaging must take place in the defined geographical area to safeguard quality or to ensure the origin of the product or to ensure control;
(f) details bearing out the link between the quality or characteristics of the agricultural product or foodstuff and the geographical environment (for a PDO), or the link between a specific quality, the reputation or other characteristic of the agricultural product or foodstuff and its geographical origin (for a PGI);
(g) the name and address of the relevant competent inspection authority;[396]
(h) any specific labelling requirements;
(i) any additional requirements laid down by Community or national law.

The product specification may be amended to take into account technical or scientific developments, or to redefine the relevant geographical area. A temporary change in the specification may be requested following the imposition of obligatory sanitary or phytosanitary measures by public authorities. Applications for amendments may be made using procedures similar to those for registering a designation.[397]

---

[394] Case C-108/01, *Consorzio del Prosciutto di Parma* v. *Asda Stores* [2003] ECR I-5121 (paras. 46–7).
[395] Something organoleptic has an effect on one of the organs of sense, such as taste or smell. It is an adjective commonly used to indicate the taste and aroma properties of a food or chemical.
[396] See GI Regulation (510/2006), Art. 10.
[397] GI Regulation (510/2006), Art. 9.

(iii) THE APPLICATION PROCEDURE

Where the application relates to a geographical area in a member state, the application is addressed to that member state, which scrutinises the application to check that it is 'justified' and meets the conditions of the Regulation. Member states must initiate a national objection procedure ensuring adequate publication of the application, and providing for a reasonable period within which any interested parties established or resident on its territory may lodge an objection to the application.[398] If, having considered any objections, the member state considers that the requirements of the Regulation are met, it approves the application and forwards it to the Commission for a final decision. If the member state's decision is favourable, this must be made public, and any person with a legitimate interest must have means of appealing the decision.[399] If an application for registration concerns a geographical area in a third country, it is sent to the Commission, either directly or through the authorities of that third country. The requirements for such an application are the same, although there must, additionally, be proof that the name in question is protected in its country of origin.[400]

The Commission then checks that the application is 'justified' and that it meets all the necessary conditions. This check must be carried out within 12 months. Each month, the Commission publishes the list of the names for which registration applications have been submitted. If the conditions are met, it publishes a summary (including a reference to the published product specification) in the Official Journal. If the conditions are not met, the Commission will reject the application.[401]

Objections may be lodged within six months of the date of publication in the Official Journal, by any member state, third country, or natural or legal person with a legitimate interest.[402] Proof must be given that either the product specification fails to meet the required conditions for protection under Article 2, or that the name conflicts with a trade mark, the name of a plant variety or an animal breed, a homonymous PDO or PGI, that it is in lawful use, is renowned and is economically significant for similar agricultural products or foodstuffs or that it has become a generic name.[403] If the Commission receives no admissible objection, it will register the name. Where the

---

[398] GI Regulation (510/2006), Art. 5(4), 5(5).
[399] GI Regulation (510/2006), Art. 5(5). The member state must ensure that the version of the specification on which its favourable decision is based is published, and assure electronic access to the specification.
[400] GI Regulation (510/2006), Art. 5(9).
[401] GI Regulation (510/2006), Art. 6.
[402] GI Regulation (510/2006), Art. 7(1), (2).
[403] GI Regulation (510/2006), Art. 7(3).

Commission judges that an objection is admissible, it will invite the interested parties to engage in appropriate consultations. If these parties reach an agreement within six months, they notify the Commission of all the factors that enabled that agreement to be reached, including the opinions of the applicant and the objector. If no agreement is reached, the Commission takes a decision, bearing in mind traditional fair practice and the actual likelihood of confusion.[404] The Commission maintains a Register of protected designations of origin and protected geographical indications.

Use of registered names

Although application for registration is made by a particular group, a registered name may be used by *any* operator marketing products which conform to the relevant specification. If the products originate within the EU, the terms 'protected designation of origin' and 'protected geographical indication', or the associated EU symbols, must appear on the product's label. These may appear on the labels of registered products originating in third countries.[405]

Scope of protection

Registered names are protected against commercial use of a registered name in respect of products not covered by the registration if they are 'comparable' to the products registered under that name or if this use exploits the reputation of the protected name.[406] They are also protected against any misuse, imitation or evocation, even if the true origin of the product is indicated or if the protected name is translated or accompanied by an expression such as 'style', 'type', 'method', 'as produced in', 'imitation' or something similar.[407] The notion of 'evocation' was considered in the *Gorgonzola* case.[408] A consortium of Gorgonzola producers was objecting to the sale of another soft blue cheese, called 'Cambozola'. Gorgonzola was registered as a PDO. The ECJ held that 'evocation' covers situations where the term used to designate a product incorporates part of a protected designation, so that 'when the consumer is confronted with the name of the product, the image triggered in his mind is

---

404   GI Regulation (510/2006), Art. 7(5).
405   GI Regulation (510/2006), Art. 8.
406   GI Regulation (510/2006), Art. 13(1)(a).
407   GI Regulation (510/2006), Art. 13(1)(b). Where a registered name contains within it the name of an agricultural product or foodstuff which is considered generic, the use of that generic name on the appropriate agricultural product or foodstuff does not fall within either Art. 13(1)(a) or Art. 13(1)(b). See Case T-291/03, *Consorzio per la tutela del formaggio Grana Padano, supported by the Italian Republic v. OHIM, Biraghi SpA* [2008] ETMR 3.
408   Case C-87/97, *Consorzio per la Tutela del Formaggio Gorgonzola v. Kaserei Champignon Hofmeister* [1999] ECR I-1301.

that of the product whose designation is protected'. It was possible 'for a protected designation to be evoked where there is no likelihood of confusion between the products concerned and even where no Community protection extends to the parts of that designation which are echoed in the term or terms at issue'. The Court noted that Cambozola was a soft blue cheese not dissimilar in appearance to Gorgonzola, and that there was obvious phonetic and visual similarity between the two terms. It was therefore reasonable to conclude that the protected name had been 'evoked'.[409]

Protection is also provided against 'any other false or misleading indication as to the provenance, origin, nature or essential qualities of the product, on the inner or outer packaging, advertising material or documents relating to the product concerned, and the packing of the product in a container liable to convey a false impression as to its origin'.[410] Finally, the Regulation prohibits 'any other practice liable to mislead the consumer as to the true origin of the product'.[411] Member states are required to set up inspection structures to ensure the effectiveness of the Regulation. However, responsibility for ensuring compliance with any particular PDO specification lies with the authorities or private bodies in the member state of origin, not with the inspection authorities in a member state where an alleged infringement takes place.[412]

Note that secondary uses – such as grating, slicing and packaging of a product – may be protected by the registration. This matter has been somewhat controversial. In the *Parma Ham* case, decided under the GI Regulation as originally worded, the supermarket chain Asda sold pre-sliced ham described as 'Parma ham'. The ham had been purchased boned but not sliced from an Italian producer who was entitled to use the PDO 'Prosciutto di Parma', and sliced for Asda by an intermediary. The packet stated (accurately) that the ham had been produced in Italy, and packed in the UK for Asda. The specification on the basis of which the PDO 'Prosciutto di Parma' was registered expressly mentions a requirement to slice and package the product in the region of production for ham marketed in slices. It was common ground that this condition did not apply to retail sale and restaurant sale, but objection was made to slicing and packaging operations carried out upstream of retail or restaurant sales. The ECJ considered that the condition was intended to safeguard the quality and authenticity of the product, and consequently the reputation of the PDO. Parma ham is consumed mainly in slices, so the slicing and packaging of the ham are important operations. If they are carried out in conditions that

---

[409] Case C-87/97, *Consorzio per la Tutela del Formaggio Gorgonzola v. Kaserei Champignon Hofmeister* [1999] ECR I-1301 (paras. 25–7).

[410] GI Regulation (510/2006), Art. 13(1)(c).

[411] GI Regulation (510/2006), Art. 13(1)(d).

[412] Case C-132/05, *Commission v. Germany* (26 February 2008) (para. 78).

result in a product which does not possess the organoleptic qualities (flavour, colour and texture) expected by consumers, this may harm the reputation of the PDO. The specification of the PDO establishes detailed and strict rules regulating the three stages which lead to the marketing of pre-packaged sliced ham. Technical operations and strict checks control the authenticity, quality, hygiene and labelling of the ham. The ECJ accepted that checks performed outside the region of production would provide fewer guarantees of the quality and authenticity of the product than checks carried out in the region of production in accordance with the procedure laid down in the specification. The condition of slicing and packaging in the region of production was therefore justified, and not contrary to the Treaty provisions on the free movement of goods.[413] The ECJ took a very similar approach in the *Ravil* decision, which concerned grated 'Grana Padano' cheese.[414] The matter is addressed specifically in the amended GI Regulation. The product specification may include 'information concerning packaging', allowing the applicant to give reasons why packaging of a product must take place in the defined geographical area, 'to safeguard quality or ensure the origin or ensure control'.[415]

Once protected, names may not become generic.[416] However, a mark may be cancelled in certain circumstances. If the Commission takes the view that compliance with the conditions of the specification 'is no longer ensured', it will initiate the procedure for the cancellation of the registration.[417] Alternatively, any natural or legal person having a legitimate interest may request cancellation of the registration, giving reasons for the request.[418] Notifications of cancellations are published in the Official Journal.

---

[413] Case C-108/01, *Consorzio del Prosciutto di Parma* v. *Asda Stores* [2003] ECR I-5121 (paras. 65–81).

[414] Case C-469/00, *Ravil* v. *Bellon Import* [2003] ECR I-5053 (paras. 52–62).

[415] GI Regulation (510/2006), Art. 4(2)(e).

[416] GI Regulation (510/2006), Art. 13(2). Though see Case C-132/05, *Commission v. Germany* (26 February 2008) (para. 36).

[417] GI Regulation (510/2006), Art. 12(1), Art. 15(2).

[418] GI Regulation (510/2006), Art. 12(2). In the case of the PGI 'Newcastle Brown Ale', the applicant who had originally sought registration later requested cancellation. Production at the site in Newcastle-upon-Tyne was no longer commercially viable, and the manufacturers, Scottish & Newcastle Plc, had decided to close the Newcastle brewery and move to another site in the north-east of England, meaning that the specification's delimitation of geographical area was no longer accurate. In this unusual case, only one single producer was entitled to use the protected name, because the PGI specification included ingredients (the strain of yeast, the particular blend of water and salt) which were trade secrets held by Scottish & Newcastle. Scottish & Newcastle made it clear that there would be no circumstances in which it would be willing to make public details of the ingredients or to consent to any other producer's

Conflicting rights

The Regulation permits limited transitional protection under national rules (a maximum of five years) for undertakings who have used a name for which registration is sought, but who will not meet the terms of the specification.[419] At Community level, the Commission may in certain circumstances allow a registered name and an identical unregistered name to co-exist. For this to occur, a number of conditions must be met. The identical unregistered name must have been in legal use consistently and equitably for at least 25 years before the entry into force of the GI Regulation (24 July 1993). The purpose of its use must not at any time have been to profit from the reputation of the registered name. It must be shown that the public has not been nor could be misled as to the true origin of the product. Finally, the problem resulting from the identical names must have been raised before registration of the name. If all these conditions are met, the registered name and the identical unregistered name concerned may co-exist for a period not exceeding 15 years, after which the unregistered name may no longer be used. Use of the unregistered geographical name concerned will be authorised only where the country of origin is clearly and visibly indicated on the label.[420]

Once a PDO or PGI has been registered, the name cannot be registered as a trade mark if it relates to the same class of product, and (if registered as a trade mark) would fall within the scope of protection offered to the PDO or PGI under the Regulation. Trade marks registered in breach of this provision will be invalidated.[421]

5.5.5 Traditional Specialities Guaranteed

The EU has adopted a further scheme, which is not directed at geographical origin, but aims to bring added value to products made from traditional ingredients, or by a method of traditional production. A 'Traditional Speciality Guaranteed' (TSG) therefore focuses on traditional character, either in the

---

use of them. Since the conditions laid down in the GI Regulation concerning the usage of the PGI 'Newcastle Brown Ale' could not be met, cancellation was sought: [1996] OJ C 280/13.

[419] GI Regulation (510/2006), Art. 13(3). The undertakings must be established in the member state or third country in which the geographical area is located, must have legally marketed the products in question, using the names concerned continuously for at least five years, and have noted this during the national or Community objection procedure.

[420] GI Regulation (510/2006), Art. 13(4).

[421] GI Regulation (510/2006), Art. 14(1). In certain limited circumstances, a trade mark which pre-dates the PDO or PGI may co-exist with a geographical indication or a designation of origin: GI Regulation (510/2006), Art. 14(2).

composition of the product, or in its means of production. The scheme was established in 1993 by a Regulation on 'certificates of specific character for agricultural products and foodstuffs', and the term 'traditional speciality guaranteed' was introduced by a further implementing Regulation.[422] With the aim of clarifying and simplifying the scheme, a new Regulation has been adopted (the 'TSG Regulation'), which abandons the term 'certificate of specific character' in favour of 'traditional speciality guaranteed'.[423] As with geographical indicators, the intention is to diversify agricultural production and benefit the rural economy, particularly in less-favoured or remote areas, both by improving the income of farmers and by retaining the rural population in these areas. It is thought that the scheme enhances the market value of traditional products, by making them distinctive, whilst protecting consumers against improper practices.[424] The scheme has so far proved less popular than that concerned with geographical designations, however. Products which are protected include Mozzarella (cheese), Jamón Serrano (ham), 'Traditional Farmfresh Turkey' (the only UK product currently protected).[425]

The register of products

The Commission keeps a register of TSGs recognised at Community level. There are two lists of TSGs, those where the use of the name is reserved to those producers who comply with the product specification, and those where this is not the case.[426] A product may only be registered if it is either produced using traditional raw materials, or it is characterised by a traditional composition or method of production and/or processing that reflects a traditional production and/or processing method.[427] 'Traditional' means proven usage on the Community market for a period showing transmission between genera-

---

[422]   Regulation 2082/92 on certificates of specific character for agricultural products and foodstuffs [1992] OJ L 208/9 (in force 24 July 1993). Regulation 1848/93 laying down detailed rules for the application of Regulation 2082/92 [1993] OJ L 168/35.
[423]   Regulation 509/2006 on agricultural products and foodstuffs as traditional specialities guaranteed [1996] OJ L093/1. The Regulation lays down the rules under which a traditional speciality guaranteed may be recognised for the agricultural products intended for human consumption listed in Annex I to the Treaty, and the foodstuffs listed in Annex I to the Regulation.
[424]   TSG Regulation, Recitals 2–3.
[425]   http://ec.europa.eu/agriculture/qual/en/1bbb1_en.htm.
[426]   TSG Regulation, Art. 3. If the name is not reserved, registered names may be used in labelling, even if they do not correspond to the product specification. However, in such cases, neither 'traditional speciality guaranteed', 'TSG', or the TSG symbol may be used: TSG Regulation, Art. 13.
[427]   TSG Regulation, Art. 4(1).

tions (at least 25 years).[428] In order to be registered, a name must be either specific in itself, or express the 'specific character' of the agricultural product or foodstuff.[429] 'Specific character' means the characteristic or set of characteristics (such as taste, or the specific raw materials) which distinguishes an agricultural product or a foodstuff clearly from other similar products or foodstuffs of the same category. Specific character does not consist in a particular presentation of the product (for example, uniquely luxurious or attractive packaging), a composition or mode of production simply meeting the requirements of mandatory rules or voluntary standards (unless these have been established in order to define the specificity of a product), or the product's provenance or geographic origin.[430]

A specific name must be clearly distinguished from other names, and will often be untranslatable; for example, Gueuze (beer), pumpernickel, haggis. It must be traditional and comply with national provisions or be established by custom. A name expressing specific character may not be registered if it refers only to claims of a general nature used for a set of agricultural products or foodstuffs, or to those provided for by particular Community legislation. Names which are likely to mislead consumers cannot be registered.[431] The Regulation applies without prejudice to Community rules or those of member states governing intellectual property, in particular those concerning geographical indications and trade marks. The name of a plant variety or breed of animal may form part of the name of a TSG, provided that it is not misleading as regards the nature of the product.[432]

A product specification must be submitted, which must include:

- the name of the product;
- a description of the product (including its main physical, chemical, microbiological or organoleptic characteristics);
- a description of the production method that the producers must follow (including where appropriate the nature and characteristics of the raw materials or ingredients used);
- the key elements that define the product's specific character;
- the key elements that prove the product's traditional character;
- the minimum requirements and procedures to check the specific character.[433]

---

[428] TSG Regulation, Art. 2(1)(b).
[429] TSG Regulation, Art. 4(2).
[430] TSG Regulation, Art. 2(1)(a), (2).
[431] TSG Regulation, Art. 4(3).
[432] TSG Regulation, Art. 5.
[433] TSG Regulation, Art. 6.

The product specification may later be amended, at the request of a member state or a group.[434]

In contrast to the scheme for PDOs and PGIs, an application for registration may be made only by a group of producers or processors. A joint application may be submitted by several groups originating from different member states or third countries. A group may lodge an application only for the products it produces or obtains.[435] The application must include: the group's name and address; the product specification; details of the authorities or bodies verifying compliance with the provisions of the product specification and their specific tasks; documents that demonstrate the specific nature and traditional character of the product.[436] Applications are submitted to the competent authority in the member state where the group is established. The examination must allow for publication of the application, and provide a reasonable period for interested parties to lodge objections. If the requirements are met, the completed application is forwarded to the Commission.[437] Applications from groups in third countries are sent to the Commission either directly, or through the competent authorities in the relevant third country.[438] Documents sent to the Commission must be in one of the official languages of the Community, or be accompanied by a certified translation in one of those languages.[439]

The application is then examined by the Commission, to ensure it is justified and meets all the necessary conditions. If so, the main elements of the application are then published in the Official Journal. If not, the application will be rejected.[440] Objections may be lodged within six months from the date of publication in the Official Journal.[441] A duly substantiated statement must show that either the conditions for registration have not been met, or that the name is already in lawful use, is renowned and is economically significant for similar agricultural products or foodstuffs.[442] If there are no admissible objections, the Commission will register the name, and publish it in the Official Journal. If there are objections, the Commission invites the interested parties to engage in consultations in an attempt to reach agreement within six months. If they do so, they notify the Commission of all the factors that enabled that

---

[434]   TSG Regulation, Art. 11. A legitimate economic interest must be demonstrated, and justification for the amendments must be given.
[435]   TSG Regulation, Art. 7(1), (2).
[436]   TSG Regulation, Art. 7(3).
[437]   TSG Regulation, Art. 7(4), (5), (6).
[438]   TSG Regulation, Art. 7(7).
[439]   TSG Regulation, Art. 7(8).
[440]   TSG Regulation, Art. 8.
[441]   TSG Regulation, Art. 9(1), (2). Objections are permitted from any member state or third country, or from any natural or legal person having a legitimate interest.
[442]   TSG Regulation, Art. 9(3).

agreement to be reached. If no agreement is reached, the Commission takes a decision, bearing in mind traditional fair practice and the actual likelihood of confusion.[443] A TSG registration may subsequently be cancelled if the Commission considers that compliance with the conditions of the specification is no longer ensured.[444]

Scope of protection

Only producers who comply with the product specification may use the TSG on labelling or in advertising. If reference is made to a TSG on labelling, the registered name must be used, and it must be accompanied either by the Community symbol or the words 'traditional speciality guaranteed'.[445] Registered names may be used in labelling, even if they do not correspond to the product specification. However, in such cases, neither 'traditional speciality guaranteed', 'TSG' nor the TSG symbol may be used. As has been seen, at the applicant group's request, a TSG may be registered with reservation of the name, unless the same name is already in lawful use, is renowned and is economically significant for similar agricultural products or foodstuffs. In such cases, the registered name may not be used on labelling unless the product meets the registered specification, even when unaccompanied by reference to the 'TSG' scheme.[446] Member states must take measures to prevent misuse of the term 'traditional speciality guaranteed', 'TSG' and the associated Community symbol. Registered names must be protected against imitation, and practices liable to mislead the public.[447]

---

[443]   TSG Regulation, Art. 9(4), (5). The Commission's decision is published in the Official Journal.
[444]   TSG Regulation, Art. 10.
[445]   TSG Regulation, Art. 12.
[446]   TSG Regulation, Art. 13.
[447]   TSG Regulation, Art. 17.

6. Intellectual property and free movement of goods

Intellectual property poses a particular challenge for the European Community. The protection of intellectual property is seen as an essential element in the success of the single market: 'In our growing knowledge-based economies the protection of intellectual property is important not only for promoting innovation and creativity, but also for developing employment and improving competitiveness'.[1] On the other hand, to create a genuine single market in Europe, restrictions on freedom of movement and anti-competitive practices must be eliminated or reduced as much as possible, whilst maintaining an environment favourable to innovation and investment. The difficulty is finding the correct balance between competing demands.

6.1 INTRODUCTION

6.1.1 Overview of the Problem – Three Typical Cases

The outline facts of three illustrative trade mark cases reveal some of the recurring problems which the Community faces in reconciling competing priorities. The legal aspects of all three cases will be discussed in more detail in what follows.

6.1.1.1 Pharmaceuticals: *Hoffmann-La Roche* v. *Centrafarm*

Valium, a tranquilliser belonging to the benzodiazepine family, was launched by Hoffmann-La Roche in 1963. It proved a huge therapeutic and commercial success. The first of the so-called 'blockbuster' drugs, it was the top-selling prescription drug during the 1970s, and achieved near-iconic status in popular culture. At its peak in 1978, nearly 2.3 billion pills were sold. Its fame as a cure for anxiety is still widespread, and the phrase 'Take a Valium!' is in general

---

[1]   EUROPA (portal site of the European Union): http://ec.europa.eu/internal_market/top_layer/index_52_en.htm.

310

use as an exhortation to calm down.[2] The events which led to the legal action took place during the heady times of the 1970s, when Valium was still under patent. Valium was marketed in Germany by Hoffmann-La Roche for individual buyers in packages of 20 or 50 tablets, and for hospitals in batches of five packages containing 100 or 250 tablets. Its British subsidiary, which manufactured the same product, marketed it in packages of 100 or 500 tablets at considerably lower prices than those in Germany. A Dutch company, Centrafarm, a manufacturer and wholesaler of largely unbranded pharmaceuticals, had made something of a specialism of parallel imports. Centrafarm imported into the Netherlands quantities of Valium which it had purchased in Britain in the original packages. The drug was then put up into new packages of 1,000 tablets, to which Centrafarm affixed Hoffmann-La Roche's trade mark, together with a notice giving its own name and address as vendor. Centrafarm began marketing these packages in Germany, and gave notice of its intention to repack the tablets into smaller packages intended for sale to individuals.

This is the classic behaviour of a parallel importer. Parallel importers exploit price differentials, buying in the cheapest market, and reselling in the dearest, hoping to make a profit as they do so. To prevent this, the original seller must eliminate these differentials, usually by cutting prices. The prevailing economic theory, at least within the Community, is that the activities of parallel importers should be welcomed, because they aid the efficiency of the market, and enhance consumer welfare.[3] Intellectual property rights complicate this picture. They are, by their nature, territorial, national and exclusive. They can be used to prevent the importation of protected goods into the territory where the right is granted, so act as barriers to trade. The holder of parallel national rights can use a right granted in state A to exclude goods from state B, and vice versa. If such rights are left unconstrained, this might well allow the right holder to partition the single market, and maintain price differentials between the various member states. Intellectual property rights thus allow sellers to resist parallel importation. National legal systems are necessarily territorial in their scope, and the strength of national intellectual property rights against parallel imports was of course welcome to national right holders. But how should the Community respond to such a situation?

Various points of view need to be taken into account. The right holder, Hoffmann-La Roche, was concerned about unwelcome competition in the

---

2   Ian Sample, Obituary of Leo Sternbach, *Guardian*, 3 October 2005. For more, see Alex Baenninger, *Good Chemistry: The Life and Legacy of Valium Inventor Leo Sternbach* (New York: McGraw-Hill, 2004).

3   For more detail on the policy arguments, for and against, see Christopher Stothers, *Parallel Trade in Europe* (Oxford: Hart Publishing, 2007), 17–24.

distribution of its own product, because this had implications for pricing. It was also concerned about the integrity and image of its trade mark. Repackaging posed a risk to the original condition of the product; both the Valium itself, and the way in which it was presented to the consumer. Consumer confidence in a branded pharmaceutical is extremely important to its manufacturer. Finally, Hoffmann-La Roche was concerned that Centrafarm's activities might make it harder to identify counterfeit drugs (a serious problem in the 1970s, which has become only more so).[4] The consumer, whether wholesale or individual, wants a guarantee that Valium is safe and effective. For branded pharmaceuticals, the trade mark forms an important part of this guarantee. Repackaging poses an obvious threat to this guarantee, since the product no longer moves directly from the manufacturer to the consumer, instead being subject to the active intervention of an intermediary. If the product is damaged during the repackaging process, the consumer must have someone to look to for redress. The consumer will also have some interest in the price, although for pharmaceuticals the provision of state medical care will affect this sensitivity. The parallel importer is motivated by profit, and will prefer an environment with as few legal and regulatory restrictions as possible. The Community seeks a genuine single market in pharmaceuticals, meaning a competitive market with no barriers to trade. Consumer protection is also a high priority. In addition, the Community must maintain a reputation as a good place for companies to do business, which entails offering adequate protection to trade marks.

The ECJ held that the essential function of a trade mark was to guarantee the identity of the trade marked product to the consumer, by enabling him to be sure of the product's origin, and to be certain that the product had not been subject to interference by a third person without the authorisation of the trade mark proprietor. So Hoffmann-La Roche seemed to be justified, at first sight, in preventing the marketing of repackaged Valium. However, the Treaty's exception for industrial property does not cover a disguised restriction on trade, and the Court thought that such a restriction might arise if the variation in packaging formed part of a marketing strategy to compartmentalise the

---

4   Although the existence of a link between parallel trade and counterfeiting is far from well established. See, for example, REMIT Consultants, *Impediments to Parallel Trade in Pharmaceuticals within the European Community*, report to DGIV of the European Commission (May 1991); Trade and Industry Committee, *Trade Marks, Fakes and Consumers*, Eighth Report of Session 1998–9 (HC 380, London: The Stationery Office, 1999), para. 109. Individual instances may be cited, however. In the UK, the MHRA recalled parallel distributed stock of Eli Lilli's Zyprexa (May 2007), and AstraZeneca's Casodex Tablets (June 2007), following the discovery of counterfeit tablets in the legitimate supply chain. See also Christopher Stothers, 'Counterfeit Pharmaceuticals Enter the Parallel Supply Chain' [2008] *JIPL&P* 797–8.

market. The ECJ therefore stipulated three conditions which a parallel importer must satisfy before the trade mark proprietor can be prevented from exercising the right:

(1) repackaging must have been carried out in a way which did not affect the original condition of the product;
(2) the proprietor of the mark must be given prior notice of the marketing of the repackaged product;
(3) the new packaging must indicate the person by whom the operation has been performed.[5]

These conditions make some attempt to address the concerns about repackaging which the ECJ considered to be legitimate. They make it clear that market partitioning will not be tolerated without good reason.

Should the same approach apply to all cases of repackaging where intellectual property rights are involved?

6.1.1.2 Premium alcoholic drinks: *Loendersloot* v. *George Ballantine & Son*

The heritage of Ballantine's Scotch whisky can be traced back to 1827, when farmer's son George Ballantine set up a small store in Edinburgh. In 1895 Queen Victoria awarded George Ballantine & Son its first Royal Warrant. In 1938 the company received its Grant of Heraldic Arms, recognising George Ballantine & Son as an 'incorporation noble on the Noblesse of Scotland'. The heraldic arms that decorate the Grant ('The Ballantine's Crest') have appeared on every bottle of Ballantine's Scotch whisky to this date. Ballantine's is now a major global brand; one of the five best-selling blended whiskies worldwide, and the best-selling Scotch whisky in Europe. It is said that every second, two bottles are sold.[6] Loendersloot is a transport and warehousing firm established in the Netherlands. Its customers include traders who engage in parallel trade. Ballantine brought proceedings seeking an order restraining Loendersloot from various acts affecting their whisky bottles, in particular: removing the labels bearing the Ballantine trade marks and reapplying them by reaffixing the original labels or replacing them with copies; removing the identification numbers on or underneath the original labels and on the packaging of the bottles; removing the English word 'pure' and the name of the importer approved by Ballantine from the original labels, and then exporting the altered

---

[5] Case 102/77, *Hoffmann-La Roche & Co. AG* v. *Centrafarm Vertriebsgesellschaft Pharmazeutischer Erzeugnisse mbH* [1978] ECR 1139.
[6] http://www.whisky.com/brands/ballantines.html.

products to traders in France, Spain, England, the United States and Japan. Loendersloot argued that such actions did not infringe trade mark rights, and were necessary to allow parallel trade in the products in question on certain markets.[7]

As in *Hoffmann-La Roche*, the right holder was concerned about unwelcome competition in the distribution of its own product, and the integrity and image of its trade mark. Since the whisky was not rebottled, its original condition was unaffected, although its presentation was. Counterfeit Scotch presents a serious problem to legitimate traders, and lot numbering is one method of discouraging and detecting this. The consumer here will be concerned to ensure that the product is genuinely the brand stated on the label, and the price will be a significant factor in their purchase. The parallel importer will again be motivated by profit, and will prefer as few restrictions as possible. The Community's interests in a genuine single market and high levels of consumer protection remain. As before, the Community will wish to encourage business, which will require a careful consideration of the needs of the trade mark and those of the parallel importer – both of whom make a valuable economic contribution to the Community.

An important question is whether precisely the same rules should apply to whisky as apply to pharmaceuticals. For simplicity and consistency, the answer would be, yes. But, on the other hand, it might seem appropriate to make the conditions for parallel trade in whisky less stringent than those for pharmaceuticals. The first *Hoffmann-La Roche* condition would be satisfied here, because there was no alteration in the original condition of the product, although, Ballantine would argue, there had been considerable interference with its outward appearance. The need for prior notice, and for the name and address of the relabeller, remains, although perhaps this would be less imperative than in the case of pharmaceuticals. The conditions can certainly be applied in such a case, but they achieve slightly different purposes, and perhaps leave other purposes unaddressed. One obvious difficulty with tailoring the conditions to each product is the complexity of such an approach. If the ECJ were to be asked to rule on the conditions for every category of goods, it would stultify parallel trade. Advocate General Jacobs addressed this point explicitly in *Loendersloot*:

> The Court's case-law on repackaging hitherto has been developed in relation to pharmaceutical products, whereas the present case is concerned with the relabelling of alcoholic drinks, notably whisky. I see no basis for making any distinction, so far as the essential principle is concerned, between different categories of product. The

---

[7]   Case C-349/95, *Frits Loendersloot, trading as F. Loendersloot Internationale Expeditie* v. *George Ballantine & Son Ltd* [1997] ECR I-6227.

underlying rationale remains the same: the right of the trade-mark owner to determine the mode of presentation of his goods must in certain circumstances give way to the requirements of the free movement of goods, subject always to certain conditions which are necessary to preserve the essential function of the trade mark. But the way in which the principle applies may vary according to the circumstances. Different considerations may apply to different products . . . In any event, this Court would in my view be going beyond its functions under Article 177 of the Treaty if it were to rule on all aspects of repackaging and relabelling which might be undertaken by parallel importers in relation to different types of product. Once the Court has spelt out the essential principle or principles, it must be left to the national courts to apply those principles in the cases before them.[8]

The ECJ took a middle path, reiterating the conditions it had laid down, but indicating that both the circumstances and the nature of the product concerned should affect the precise way in which the national court applied those conditions to the case in front of it.

A parallel importer's activities have implications for the brand owner which go beyond the mere resale of imported goods. The feature of parallel imports is that they are cheaper than the authorised distribution channels, and parallel importers – understandably – wish to draw this fact to the attention of consumers. The parallel importer's advertisements may be particularly irritating to certain brand owners, whose products are aimed at the very top of their market sector.

6.1.1.3 Luxury consumer goods: *Dior* v. *Evora*

Parfums Christian Dior owns some of the leading fragrance brands in the world. Its products command premium prices, and in 2005 Dior's revenues from perfumes comfortably exceeded €1 billion.[9] Evora operates a chain of shops under the name of its subsidiary, Kruidvat. Kruidvat is currently the market leader in the health and beauty retail sector in the Netherlands. Under the banner 'Always surprising, always cheaper', it aims to supply a wide selection of products, combining high quality with competitive pricing. Originally a grocery company founded in 1928, Kruidvat was among the first to open supermarkets in the Netherlands. The first Kruidvat health and beauty store opened in 1975. Dior products are distributed in the Netherlands by a selective distribution system, which means that Dior products are sold only to selected retailers who are under an obligation to sell Dior products only to ultimate consumers and never to resell to other retailers unless they are also selected to sell Dior products. Although they have not been appointed as

---

[8] Case C-349/95, *Frits Loendersloot* v. *George Ballantine & Son Ltd* [1997] ECR I-6227 (AG Jacobs, paras. 30–33).

[9] *Christian Dior Group Annual Report 2005.*

distributors by Dior Netherlands, the Kruidvat shops sell Dior products obtained by means of parallel imports. The legal action arose from a Christmas promotion run by Kruidvat in 1993. It advertised for sale the Dior products Eau Sauvage, Poison, Fahrenheit, Dune and Svelte, depicting their packaging and bottles in advertising leaflets. Dior took the view that this advertising did not correspond to the luxurious and prestigious image of the Dior marks, and brought proceedings for infringement of its trade marks. Dior also claimed that the advertising infringed its copyright.[10]

Again as in *Hoffmann-La Roche*, the right holder was concerned about unwelcome competition in the distribution of its own product, the integrity and image of the product and its trade marks, and the identification of counterfeit goods. However, for Dior, the elite brand image was of exceptional importance. Without the aura of luxury and exclusivity, the products would not command premium prices. The consumer whom Dior intends to reach will purchase on the basis that the product is so luxurious that other consumers will not be able to access it. Lavish advertising and opulent distribution outlets are key to maintaining this image. If Dior products are freely to be had at a discount price in supermarkets, then there is little incentive for consumers to purchase from a selective distributor and pay top prices. For a while, the brand will be bought by a different set of customers, but ultimately (Dior would argue) the brand will be pulled down-market, and will lose its deluxe connotations. Thus, there are two categories of consumer at issue here. The brand holder's intended consumer is comparatively insensitive to price, so long as the product is perceived to be exceptionally desirable. The parallel importer's customers want the brand's cachet without the cost. Luxury perfumes are particularly appealing to parallel importers: the products are well known and attractive to consumers, they are easy to transport, and the retail mark-up is considerable. As in all cases, the parallel importer is put off by restrictions. Limitations on the ability to advertise the goods makes the operation less tempting. Yet again, the Community has to balance the fundamentals of free movement against the economic contribution of the top global brand owners. The referring Dutch court therefore asked in particular if there were special considerations where the advertising function of a trade mark is endangered by the manner in which the reseller uses it, damaging the luxurious and prestigious image; or where the goods' allure, prestigious image and aura of luxury – a consequence of the trade mark owner's presentation and advertising – is changed or impaired. The ECJ observed:

> where a reseller makes use of a trade mark in order to bring the public's attention to further commercialization of trade-marked goods, a balance must be struck

---

[10]   Case C-337/95, *Parfums Christian Dior SA* v. *Evora BV* [1997] ECR I-6013.

between the legitimate interest of the trade mark owner in being protected against resellers using his trade mark for advertising in a manner which could damage the reputation of the trade mark and the reseller's legitimate interest in being able to resell the goods in question by using advertising methods which are customary in his sector of trade.[11]

The ECJ concluded that, in general, a parallel importer who was free to resell goods should also be free to advertise them. However, if the parallel importer's use of the trade marks seriously damaged the reputation of the mark, the trade mark proprietor could resist such use.

In all three of the cases just discussed, finding the appropriate balance lies at the heart of the problem. The ECJ's solutions will be discussed in detail in what follows. The aim so far has been simply to expose the issues. It should also be stressed that in each of these cases the manufacturer was seeking to prevent the resale of *their own goods*, not counterfeit goods. It is uncontentious that the trade mark owner should be able to prevent the sale of counterfeit goods. But if the resale of the trade mark owner's own goods is being inhibited, different considerations obtain. Free movement of goods is a fundamental aim of the Community. Intellectual property laws by their nature act to prevent or inhibit the free movement of goods – but are a vital means of protection for certain types of property.

6.1.2   Intellectual Property Rights – Different Rights Have Different Purposes

Intellectual property rights allow their owners to prohibit third parties from performing various acts. The range of intangible property rights includes patents, trade marks, copyright, design rights, designations and indications of origins. These rights have different aims, and their nature and content varies accordingly. It is important to acknowledge these differences, and to distinguish between the various rights. Their definitions are complex and subtle. The purposes of the different rights are hotly debated, particularly in their details and at their margins, so it is impossible to give a definitive account. The indications which follow are brief, but necessarily very simplified.

Patents   Patents protect invention, with the aim of rewarding the inventor, and thus encouraging investment in research, innovation and new technology. The grant of a patent is dependent on public disclosure of the new invention, allowing future inventors to build from the newest point, and thus benefiting

---

[11]   Case C-337/95, *Parfums Christian Dior SA* v. *Evora BV* [1997] ECR I-6013 (para. 44).

society in general. The patent monopoly is strong, protecting the patentee from even an independent deviser of the same invention. But the patent term is relatively short, as compared to other intellectual property rights – generally 20 years.

Trade marks   Personal brands and marks have been used for centuries to indicate ownership. They then came to be used as true trade marks, to indicate origin. This helped to prevent fraud and confusion. Consumers have come to understand that marks indicate the producer of the goods, and thus offer some guarantee of likely quality. Trade mark protection aims to stimulate fair competition and to protect consumers, by enabling them to make informed choices between various goods and services. Modern trade marks may also evoke a product's broader attributes and make it desirable to the consumer. Modern consumers are highly adept at reading this advertising function, understanding trade marks to convey sophisticated messages. Trade mark protection may last indefinitely, provided the mark continues to be used and to be distinctive.

Copyright   Copyright in its classic form protects aesthetic creations – literary, dramatic, musical and artistic works of various sorts – against copying. Computer programs fall within the modern definition. Copyright protects the form of expression rather than the idea underlying the work. Protection is offered against copying, but not against someone who creates the same work independently. Copyright gives creators incentives and recognition, providing both economic and non-economic rights. It seeks to protect creators by preventing unauthorised copying and distribution of copyright works. With a secure legal right, creators can sell the rights to their works, for marketing to a wider audience. Within the EU, the right lasts for the author's life plus 70 years. Rights have also been granted to performers (such as actors and musicians) in their performances, to producers of sound recordings in their recordings, and to broadcasters in their radio and television programmes. These rights are somewhat similar to copyright, but are often called neighbouring rights, to distinguish them.

Design rights   Design rights protect the original, ornamental and non-functional features of an industrial product. If the technical features of an industrial product are similar across manufacturers, consumers will choose on the basis of price and aesthetic appeal. Thus design rights aim to protect the distinctive visual elements of a product which will distinguish it in the market. Offering this legal protection acts as an incentive to invest in design activities. Designs can generally be protected only if they are new or original. Registered design rights enjoy a comparatively short period of protection (a maximum of 25 years under the EU Directive).

GEOGRAPHICAL INDICATIONS, DESIGNATIONS OF ORIGIN, TRADITIONAL SPECIALITIES

Certain terms for food, agricultural products, spirits, wines and other forms of alcohol are protected as a form of intellectual property, under a variety of regimes. A Protected Designation of Origin (PDO) is used to describe products which are produced, processed and prepared in a given geographical area, where the quality or characteristics of the product are essentially or exclusively due to that particular geographical environment. A Protected Geographical Indication (PGI) indicates a somewhat similar link with the area (though reputation alone will suffice), but it need only be in one of the stages of production, processing or preparation. The link with the area is therefore stronger for PDOs. Wines, spirits and aromatized drinks have their own specific regimes, which control the use of geographic indications for these products. A Traditional Speciality Guaranteed (TSG) is not geographically based, instead focusing on traditional character of a product, either in its composition, or in its means of production.[12]

6.2 INTELLECTUAL PROPERTY IN THE COMMUNITY – THE FREE MOVEMENT OF GOODS

6.2.1 The Treaty: The Basic Legal Framework

Provision was made both for the free movement of goods, and for the protection of intellectual property, in the founding treaties of the EU.

THE BASIC RULE: ARTICLE 28 EU (FORMERLY ARTICLE 30 EEC)

Article 28 provides that:

> Quantitative restrictions on imports and all measures having equivalent effect shall . . . be prohibited between Member States.

Advocate General Jacobs expressed the 'guiding principle' underlying this article as the principle 'that all undertakings which engage in a legitimate economic activity in a Member State should have unfettered access to the whole of the Community market, unless there is a valid reason for denying them full access to a part of that market'.[13] This is one of the four fundamental freedoms guaranteed by the Treaty.[14] Article 29 provides that quantitative restrictions on exports shall likewise be prohibited.

---

[12] See above section 5.5 Geographical indications of origin.

[13] Case C-412/93, *Société d'importation Edouard Leclerc-Siplec* v. *TF1 Publicité SA & M6 Publicité SA* [1995] ECR I-179 (AG Jacobs, 24 November 1994).

[14] Art. 3 EU.

EXCEPTIONS: ARTICLE 30 EU (FORMERLY ARTICLE 36 EEC)

Discriminatory trade rules may only be justified on the grounds specified in Article 30, which include specifically the protection of intellectual property:

> The provisions of Articles 28 and 29 shall not preclude prohibitions or restrictions on imports, exports or goods in transit justified on grounds of public morality, public policy or public security; the protection of health and life of humans, animals or plants; the protection of national treasures possessing artistic, historic or archaeological value; or the protection of industrial and commercial property. Such prohibitions or restrictions shall not, however, constitute a means of arbitrary discrimination or a disguised restriction on trade between Member States.

The Article provides a closed list of exceptions, which has been strictly construed. The second sentence of the Article is extremely important. It imposes a proportionality requirement. A member state seeking to justify a discriminatory measure must show that it represents the least restrictive way possible of attaining this aim.

NATIONAL AUTONOMY REGARDING PROPERTY RIGHTS: ARTICLE 295 EU (FORMERLY ARTICLE 222 EEC)

Article 295 provides:

> This Treaty shall in no way prejudice the rules in Member States governing the system of property ownership.

Member states have argued that, in the absence of Community harmonisation measures, this Article guarantees them exclusive competence over intellectual property. The ECJ has certainly made it clear that, in the absence of harmonising measures, it is for the national legislature to determine the conditions and rules regarding the protection of intellectual property. However, the Court has also stressed that, when read with Articles 28 and 30, Article 295 'cannot be interpreted as reserving to the national legislature, in relation to industrial and commercial property, the power to adopt measures which would adversely affect the principle of free movement of goods within the common market as provided for and regulated by the Treaty'.[15]

6.2.2 Early Case Law: The Distinction between Existence and Exercise of Rights

National intellectual property rights, if left completely unchecked, would

---

[15] Case C-30/90, *Commission* v. *United Kingdom* [1992] ECR I-829 (para. 18).

almost inevitably partition the single market. The problem was set out clearly in an early case, *Parke Davis* v. *Probel*:

> The national rules relating to the protection of industrial property have not yet been unified within the Community. In the absence of such unification, the national character of the protection of industrial property and the variations between the different legislative systems on this subject are capable of creating obstacles both to the free movement of the patented products and to competition within the common market.[16]

Because of their territorial nature, intellectual property rights can act as barriers to trade in the Community, particularly when defended aggressively, as is often the case. Parallel importers are hampered. An obvious solution, as indicated by the ECJ in *Parke Davis* in 1968, is to harmonise intellectual property regimes throughout the Community. Although there has been considerable harmonisation since that time, even now it is far from complete. When *Parke Davis* was decided, there were no intellectual property harmonisation measures in place.

The ECJ therefore developed a judicial solution to this problem, by distinguishing between the *existence* of a right (whose protection is assured by Article 295), and the *exercise* of a right:

> whilst the Treaty does not affect the existence of rights recognized by the legislation of a Member State in matters of industrial and commercial property, yet the exercise of those rights may nevertheless, depending on the circumstances, be restricted by the prohibitions in the Treaty. Inasmuch as it provides an exception to one of the fundamental principles of the common market, Article 36 [now Article 30] in fact admits exceptions to the free movement of goods only to the extent to which such exceptions are justified for the purpose of safeguarding rights which constitute the specific subject matter of that property.[17]

This approach reflects the fact that an intellectual property right is not merely a single right, but represents a bundle of rights, whose particular content may vary somewhat under national regimes. The ECJ interpreted the Article 30 exception as covering only the 'specific subject matter' of the right – sometimes described as the essential core of the right. The *existence* of an intellectual property right – its specific subject matter – is guaranteed, thus meeting the requirements of Article 295. However, the Article 30 exception will not apply where the Court considers that the particular rights claimed are not part of the specific subject matter of that type of right. So the *exercise* of

---

16 Case 24/67, *Parke Davis & Co.* v. *Probel* [1968] ECR 55.
17 Case C-119/75, *Terrapin (Overseas) Ltd* v. *Terranova Industrie CA Kapferer & Co.* [1975] ECR 1039.

a national intellectual property right can only be guaranteed in so far as it conforms with the Court's definition of specific subject matter. If the particular national intellectual property right is defined more broadly than this, or is exercised in a way which seeks to go beyond the specific subject matter, its use may be restricted. Thus, the intellectual property derogation in Article 30 has been confined to rights which the Court considers constitute the specific subject matter, or essential core, of the property in question. Exercise of such a right is tolerated, even if it impedes trade or competition, because otherwise it would no longer be possible to say that the property was receiving protection. But rights which the Court considers incidental to the property are not allowed to interfere with the project of unifying the market.

Both the distinction between existence and exercise of rights, and the Court's definition of specific subject matter, have been criticised as lacking in basis, artificial and inconsistent.[18] Nevertheless, the utility of the concept in the Court's jurisprudence has been considerable, in a situation where solving the problem by political means would have been considerably harder. The approach is, in theory, of only transitional importance. Harmonisation of national intellectual property regimes would solve these problems. However, the reality is that the process of harmonisation is slow and difficult, although considerable progress has been made, particularly in relation to some rights.

6.2.3 Specific Subject Matter: Definitions

The specific subject matter of the various intellectual property rights differs, because the rights have different purposes. There is a certain artificiality to these definitions, because they are directed towards the restriction of conduct which the ECJ considers incompatible with Community policy in this area, rather than towards defining the rights in a way that an intellectual property lawyer would recognise. Nevertheless, the concept is important, and often referred to in the Court's judgments.

Patents   In *Centrafarm* v. *Sterling* the ECJ held that:

> In relation to patents, the specific subject matter of the industrial property is the guarantee that the patentee, to reward the creative effort of the inventor, has the

---

[18]   Guiliano Marenco and Karen Banks, 'Intellectual Property and the Community Rules on Free Movement: Discrimination Unearthed' (1990) 15 *European Law Review* 224–56. See also Peter Oliver, *Free Movement of Goods in the European Community* 4th ed. (London: Sweet & Maxwell, 2003), 323; David Keeling, *Intellectual Property Rights in EU Law* Vol. I – Free Movement and Competition Law (Oxford: Oxford University Press, 2004), chapter 6; Valentine Korah, *Intellectual Property Rights and the EC Competition Rules* (Oxford: Hart Publishing, 2006), 3–4.

exclusive right to use an invention with a view to manufacturing industrial products and putting them into circulation for the first time, either directly or by the grant of licences to third parties, as well as the right to oppose infringements.[19]

This definition expresses clearly the idea that a patent is not a single right, but a bundle of rights, the most central of which are listed here. Note that the specific subject matter does not include a right to control sales of the product after the initial sale.

Trademarks In *Centrafarm* v. *Winthrop*, decided shortly after *Centrafarm* v. *Sterling*, the ECJ held that:

> In relation to trade marks, the specific subject matter of the industrial property is the guarantee that the owner of the trade mark has the exclusive right to use that trade mark, for the purpose of putting products protected by the trade mark into circulation for the first time, and is therefore intended to protect him against competitors wishing to take advantage of the status and reputation of the trade mark by selling products illegally bearing that trade mark.[20]

It also covers use likely to impair the guarantee of origin.[21] Although there are similarities to the definition of patent specific subject matter, important differences reflect the different nature and purpose of trade marks. Again, no right to control products after the initial sale is mentioned.

Copyright The definition of the specific subject matter of copyright is much more controversial than that of patents and trade marks. In an early case, *Deutsche Grammophon*, the ECJ wisely side-stepped the task of offering a positive definition. Reiterating that derogations from the principle of free movement were only permissible to the extent to which they are justified for the purpose of safeguarding rights constituting the specific subject matter of a right, the Court simply observed that if copyright (or a related right) were to be used to prevent parallel imports and promote partitioning of the market, this would not fall within the derogation for intellectual property, because it would amount to a disguised restriction on trade between member states.[22]

In *Warner Brothers* v. *Christiansen*, the ECJ affirmed that 'the two essential rights of the author, namely the exclusive right of performance and the exclusive

---

19 Case 15/74, *Centrafarm BV* v. *Sterling Drug Inc.* [1974] ECR 1147 (para. 9).

20 Case 16/74, *Centrafarm BV* v. *Winthrop BV* [1974] ECR 1183 (para. 8).

21 Case 102/77, *Hoffmann-La Roche & Co. AG* v. *Centrafarm Vertriebsgesellschaft Pharmazeutischer Erzeugnisse mbH* [1978] ECR 1139 (para. 7).

22 Case 78/70, *Deutsche Grammophon Gesellschaft GmbH* v. *Metro SB Grossmarkte GmbH & Co. KG* [1971] ECR 487 (paras. 11 and 12).

right of reproduction, are not called in question by the rules of the Treaty'.[23] In *GEMA*, the French government argued that copyright should not be subject to the same rules on its exercise as patents and trade marks, because it comprised not just economic rights, but also the extended protection given by moral rights. The ECJ acknowledged that copyright comprised moral rights, but held that this was no reason to make a distinction between copyright and other industrial and commercial property rights with regard to economic rights, which were the subject of the case. It therefore confirmed that copyright, like other intellectual property rights, could not be used to entrench the isolation of national markets by restricting parallel imports. Again, neither of these cases offered any positive definition of the specific subject matter of copyright.[24]

However, in the *Magill* cases, a competition case concerned with the use of copyright in television programme listings, the CFI observed that copyright's 'essential function' is 'to protect the moral rights in the work and ensure a reward for the creative effort, while respecting the aims of, in particular, Article 86'.[25] This definition is contentious for many reasons, and was not endorsed by the ECJ in the appeals which followed. The emphasis given to moral rights would not be universally accepted in all member states, by any means. Nor does the reference to ensuring 'a reward' appear to respect the reproduction right which is central to copyright (as the ECJ acknowledged in *Warner Brothers* v. *Christiansen*). It suggests that, instead of a right to prevent copying, a right to compensation for exploitation is all that can be expected. On appeal, the ECJ again confined itself to finding that the broadcasting companies had abused their dominant position, without entering into discussion regarding the nature of the specific subject matter of copyright.[26]

In the *Phil Collins* case, the ECJ took a more conventional line, explaining that the specific subject matter of copyright:

> is to ensure the protection of the moral and economic rights of their holders. The protection of moral rights enables authors and performers, in particular, to object to any distortion, mutilation or other modification of a work which would be prejudicial to their honour or reputation. Copyright and related rights are also economic in

---

[23] Case 158/86, *Warner Brothers Inc.* v. *Christiansen* [1988] ECR 2605 (para. 13).

[24] Joined Cases 55/80 and 57/80, *Musik-Vertrieb Membran GmbH* v. *GEMA* [1981] ECR 147 (paras. 11–12 and 18).

[25] Case T-69/89, *Radio Telefis Eireann* v. *Commission* [1991] ECR 485 (para. 71); Case T-76/89, *Independent Television Publications Ltd* v. *Commission* [1991] ECR II-575 (para. 56).

[26] Joined Cases C-241/91 P and C-242/91 P, *Radio Telefis Eireann (RTE) and Independent Television Publications Ltd (ITP)* v. *Commission* [1995] ECR 743.

nature, in that they confer the right to exploit commercially the marketing of the protected work, particularly in the form of licences granted in return for payment of royalties.[27]

The description of moral rights draws on the language of the Berne Convention, and the reference to economic rights echoes the definitions given for the specific subject matter of patents and trade marks in *Centrafarm* v. *Sterling*, and *Centrafarm* v. *Winthrop*.

More recently, in *IMS Health*, the President of the CFI skilfully folded the remarks made in the *Magill* cases into an affirmation of the importance of the reproduction right, noting that:

> The fundamental rationale of copyright is that it affords the creator of inventive and original works the exclusive right to exploit such works (*Warner Brothers*), thereby ensuring that there is a 'reward for the creative effort' (*Magill* cases). Copyright is of fundamental importance both for the individual owner of the right and for society generally. To reduce it to a purely economic right to receive royalties dilutes the essence of the right and is, in principle, likely to cause potentially serious and irreparable harm to the rightholder.[28]

This is an important acknowledgement of the centrality of the reproduction right. Both the *Magill* cases and *IMS* will be discussed further in the context of competition law.

Design rights   The ECJ made it clear in *Keurkoop* v. *Nancy Kean Gifts* that design rights fell within the scope of Article 30's protection for industrial and commercial property, although it did not define the specific subject matter of such rights.[29] In *CICRA* v. *Renault*, the ECJ noted that 'the authority of a proprietor of a protective right in respect of an ornamental model to oppose the manufacture by third parties, for the purposes of sale on the internal market or export, of products incorporating the design or to prevent the import of such products manufactured without its consent in other Member States constitutes the substance of his exclusive right'.[30] This was expressed more helpfully in *Volvo* v. *Veng*:

---

[27]   Joined Cases C-92/92 and C-326/92, *Phil Collins* v. *Imtrat* [1993] ECR I-5145 (para. 20).

[28]   Case T-184/01 R, Order of the President of the Court of First Instance of 26 October 2001, *IMS Health Inc.* v. *Commission* [2001] ECR II 3193 (para. 125).

[29]   Case 144/81, *Keurkoop* v. *Nancy Kean Gifts* [1982] ECR 2853.

[30]   Case 53/87, *Consorzio Italiano della Componentistica di Ricambio per Autoveicoli (CICRA)* and *Maxicar* v. *Régie nationale des usines Renault* [1988] ECR 6039.

the right of the proprietor of a protected design to prevent third parties from manufacturing and selling or importing, without its consent, products incorporating the design constitutes the very subject-matter of his exclusive right. It follows that an obligation imposed upon the proprietor of a protected design to grant to third parties, even in return for a reasonable royalty, a licence for the supply of products incorporating the design would lead to the proprietor thereof being deprived of the substance of his exclusive right.[31]

Designations and indications of origin   Although these forms of protection do not in themselves restrict parallel trade in genuine goods, they may work to impede parallel exports from a region, for instance, if the relevant PDO or PGI requires goods to be processed within the region. The ECJ originally took a somewhat restrictive approach when assessing whether such terms were within the Article 30 exception for the protection of industrial and commercial property.[32] But in more recent cases, such as the *Parma Ham* and *Ravil* decisions, the ECJ has been more sympathetic to claims that processing (such as slicing, grating and packaging) has an effect on the characteristics of the product, and should be done within the relevant region:

> Designations of origin fall within the scope of industrial and commercial property rights. The applicable rules protect those entitled to use them against improper use of those designations by third parties seeking to profit from the reputation which they have acquired. They are intended to guarantee that the product bearing them comes from a specified geographical area and displays certain particular characteristics . . . The reputation of designations of origin depends on their image in the minds of consumers. That image in turn depends essentially on particular characteristics and more generally on the quality of the product.

The Court found that the specification of the PDO 'Prosciutto di Parma' required the slicing and packaging of Parma ham to be carried out in the region of production, in order to safeguard the quality and authenticity of the product, and to control the way in which the product appeared on the market. Such a condition 'must be regarded as compatible with Community law despite its restrictive effects on trade if it is shown that it is necessary and proportionate and capable of upholding the reputation of the PDO'.[33]

But if member states attempt simply to reserve the use of particular names to domestic producers, where there is no link between the quality or charac-

---

[31]   Case 238/87, *Volvo v. Erik Veng (UK) Ltd* [1988] ECR 6211 (para. 8).

[32]   Case 12/74, *Commission* v. *Germany* [1975] ECR 181; Case C-47/90, *Etablissements Delhaize Frères* v. *Promalvin* [1992] ECR I-3669.

[33]   Case C-108/01, *Consorzio del Prosciutto di Parma* v. *Asda Stores* [2003] ECR I-5121 (paras. 64–6). See also Case C-388/95, *Belgium* v. *Spain* [2000] ECR I-3123; Case C-469/00, *Ravil* v. *Bellon Import* [2003] ECR I-5053 (paras. 52–62).

teristics of a product and its provenance, the measure will be regarded as discriminatory, and will not fall within the exception. Thus, in *Pistre*, French legislation effectively confined the use of the word 'montagne' (mountain) to products manufactured on national territory and prepared from domestic raw materials. The ECJ held that the description 'mountain', could not be regarded as a designation of origin or geographical indication, because it was so general in character, and did not serve to inform consumers as to the product's provenance, in terms of a particular place, region or country. Such a description was 'too remote' from the substantive subject matter of the scheme covering geographical indications, because the link between the product's mountain origins and its perceived qualities was too general and abstract.[34]

It is clear from all of these examples that the specific subject matter of a right does not encompass the right to erect barriers to free trade by preventing parallel imports of a right holder's own goods, if they have been marketed by the right holder or with the right holder's consent. To do so would allow partitioning of the market where no such restriction is necessary to guarantee the specific subject matter of the right. If a right,

> is relied upon to prevent the marketing in a Member State of products distributed by the holder of the right or with his consent on the territory of another Member State on the sole ground that such distribution did not take place on the national territory, such a prohibition, which would legitimize the isolation of national markets, would be repugnant to the essential purpose of the Treaty, which is to unite national markets into a single market.[35]

This is the principle of exhaustion of rights.

6.2.4 What Is 'Consent' for the Purposes of Exhaustion of Rights?

The concept of consent is central. In situations where a right holder has obviously consented to marketing, and is simply seeking to resist parallel imports, the situation is straightforward: free movement of goods prevails. But other scenarios may present difficulties.

TRADE MARKS AND THE RETREAT FROM COMMON ORIGIN
In 1990, the Court of Justice delivered its judgment in *HAG II*, a case involving

---

[34] Case C-321/94, *Criminal proceedings against Jacques Pistre* [1997] ECR I-2343 (paras. 35–7). See also Case 12/74, *Commission v. Germany* [1975] ECR 181 (para. 7).
[35] Case 78/70, *Deutsche Grammophon Gesellschaft GmbH v. Metro SB Grossmarkte GmbH & Co. KG* [1971] ECR 487 (para. 12).

the protection of trade marks and the free movement of goods.[36] The Court abandoned the so-called 'doctrine of common origin' and effectively reversed its previous heavily criticised decision in *HAG I*, which related to the same legal issue between the same parties. The judgment in *HAG II* puts consent of the owner of the right as the most important consideration in determining whether a right has been exhausted. The judgment marked a welcome acknowledgement of the importance of trade marks in the Community, and an acknowledgement of the need to protect them. It also created a precedent for the reversal of case law in the Court of Justice.

The facts were unusual. The German company HAG ('HAG Germany') produced decaffeinated coffee, made by a process which its founder invented. It held several trade marks in the Federal Republic of Germany – the oldest registered in 1907 – all including the word 'HAG'. In 1908 it registered two trade marks in Belgium including the word 'HAG'. In 1927, it established a wholly owned subsidiary company in Belgium ('HAG Belgium'), to which it transferred its Belgian trade marks. In 1944 HAG Belgium was seized as enemy property, and the company was sold. In 1972, HAG Germany began selling its products in Luxembourg, which ultimately led to the ruling in *HAG I*. The Court could not apply the concept of exhaustion as understood in such cases as *Deutsche Grammophon*, because there was no question of legal or economic link, and therefore no question of consent. However, the Court ruled that the use of trade mark rights to block the imports from Germany was nevertheless not justified, because the trade marks had a common origin. The Court observed that the exercise of trade mark rights tended to contribute to market partitioning, and thus affect the free movement of goods – the more so because trade mark rights have the potential to last indefinitely. Accordingly, it reasoned, a trade mark proprietor could not be allowed to rely on a trade mark right to prevent the marketing of goods produced legally under an identical trade mark in another member state, if the trade marks had a 'common origin'. Such a prohibition would legitimise the isolation of national markets, potentially indefinitely. Although recognising the possibility of consumer confusion as to origin, the Court considered that consumers could be informed by other means less harmful to the free movement of goods.[37] It was confirmed in *Terrapin* v. *Terranova* that the fact that the subdivision of a trade mark was involuntary made no difference: the trade mark could not be relied on to resist imports if the original right had been subdivided. The Court took the view that the guarantee of origin had already been undermined by the

[36]   Case C-10/89, *Cnl-Sucal NV SA* v. *HAG GF AG* [1990] ECR I-3711.
[37]   Case 192/73, *Van Zuylen Frères* v. *HAG AG* [1974] ECR 731.

subdivision of the right, regardless of its cause, so there was no legitimate interest in insulating the national markets.[38]

In 1985, HAG Belgium decided to launch a counter-attack on HAG Germany, by selling its products in the German market. HAG Germany sued for trade mark infringement in the German courts, which put various questions to the ECJ by way of preliminary reference, in substance asking if *HAG I* could legitimately be distinguished. But rather than attempting to distinguish its earlier decisions, the Court accepted Advocate General Jacob's opinion that the doctrine of common origin needed reconsideration. He was critical of 'signs of an unduly negative attitude to the value of trade marks' in the earlier case law, noting invidious comparisons with patents, and stressing that 'trade marks are no less important, and no less deserving of protection, than any other form of intellectual property'.[39] Trade marks reward the manufacturer who consistently produces high-quality goods and they thus stimulate economic progress. They do this because they act as a guarantee, to the consumer, that all goods bearing a particular mark have been produced by, or under the control of, the same manufacturer and are therefore likely to be of similar quality. Although the guarantee of quality is not absolute, the manufacturer will suffer the consequences in the marketplace if it declines. Consumers act on these guarantees every day. Advocate General Jacobs emphasised that a trade mark can only fulfil this role if it is exclusive. Once the mark is shared with a competitor, control over the goodwill associated with the mark is lost, and the reputation of the original proprietor will be harmed if the competitor sells inferior goods. Consumers will be confused and misled as to the origin of the products.

The Court in *HAG II* described trade mark rights as 'an essential element in the system of undistorted competition which the Treaty seeks to establish and maintain'. The guarantee of origin was a crucial part of this, and took

---

[38]   Case 119/75, *Terrapin (Overseas) Ltd* v. *Terranova Industrie CA Kapferer & Co.* [1975] ECR 1039.

[39]   Case C-10/89, *Cnl-Sucal NV SA* v. *HAG GF AG* [1990] ECR I-3711 (Opinion of AG Jacobs, para. 17). In Case 40/70, *Sirena* v. *Eda* [1971] ECR 69, Advocate General Dutheillet de Lamothe remarked that 'Both from the economic and from the human point of view the interests protected by patent legislation merit greater respect than those protected by trade marks . . . From the human point of view, the debt which society owes to the "inventor" of the name "Prep Good Morning" [a brand of shaving cream] is certainly not of the same nature, to say the least, as that which humanity owes to the discoverer of penicillin.' A similar tone can be detected in the Court's judgment: 'a trade mark right is distinguishable in this context from other rights of industrial and commercial property, inasmuch as the interests protected by the latter are usually more important, and merit a higher degree of protection, than the interests protected by an ordinary trade mark' (para. 7).

priority. HAG Germany had not consented to HAG Belgium's activities, and HAG Belgium was not legally or economically dependent on HAG Germany. Hence, the essential function of the trade mark would be undermined if HAG Germany could not use its German trade mark rights to block imports of HAG Belgium's products. Consumers would not be able to identify the source of the product with any degree of certainty and the trade mark owner could be held responsible for the quality of products over which it had no control. Thus, provided the trade mark rights fulfilled an independent role in the two member states, both owners could rely on their rights to block imports marked by the other without their consent.[40] The *HAG II* decision was welcome, both for its more positive attitude to trade marks, and because it restored the question of consent to a central position in the process of determining whether a right has been exhausted.

The question then arose, in *Ideal Standard*, as to whether the assignment of a trade mark amounted to consent to the assignee's activities. The 'Ideal Standard' trade mark was originally held by the American Standard group, via its French and German subsidiaries, and used for sanitary ware and heating equipment. The French subsidiary was in financial trouble, and sold the trade mark – for heating equipment only – to another French company, Compagnie Internationale du Chauffage (CICh), which had no legal or economic links with American Standard. CICh's German subsidiary, IHT, then began marketing goods with the Ideal Standard trade mark in Germany. Ideal Standard's German subsidiary brought infringement proceedings in Germany, and the German court found in its favour, holding that there was a risk of confusion between the use of the mark on the two groups of products (sanitary ware and heating equipment). IHT appealed, and the German court referred various questions to the Court of Justice, asking, essentially, whether the splitting of a trade mark by voluntary assignment constituted the consent required for the application of the doctrine of exhaustion of rights.

Advocate General Gulmann argued that it should do so. Separate territorial assignments for the various member states would lead to territorial protection, which might last indefinitely, and would necessarily imply an obstruction to free movement of goods and partitioning of the internal market contrary to the aims of the Treaty. Although a decision on this basis would in practice limit the trade mark proprietor's ability to conclude separate assignments, this ability was not an essential part of the rights associated with a mark. A trade mark proprietor should be expected to take the consequences of a decision to conclude separate assignments. A full assignment would be more in keeping with the objectives of the single market, and with the aim of promoting a

---

40   Case C-10/89, *Cnl-Sucal NV SA* v. *HAG GF AG* [1990] ECR I-3711.

Community trade mark. Nor was there any consumer interest which justified a right to protect the distinguishing function of a trade mark by means of import prohibitions (rather than, say, labelling or other indications).[41] This conclusion would have caused considerable concern to trade mark owners, who frequently assign their marks for single national territories, and may well not be equipped to tackle the entire Community market.

However, the Court of Justice did not follow Advocate General Gulmann's recommendation, noting that the principle of independent assignment of trade marks was respected in both the Paris Convention and the Madrid Agreement. The principle of exhaustion of rights acted to prevent the application of national laws, allowing trade mark rights to be used to prevent the free movement of a product which bore a trade mark under the control of the same entity. A contract of assignment in itself (in the absence of any economic link) did not give the assignor any means of controlling the quality of products which are marked and marketed by the assignee. Therefore, although some sort of consent was implicit in any assignment, this was not the sort of consent which would trigger the doctrine of exhaustion. For that, the owner of the right in the importing state had to be able (directly or indirectly) to determine the products to which the trade mark could be affixed, and to control their quality. No such control existed following the assignment of a trade mark to a third party which had no economic link to the former owner.

The Court acknowledged explicitly that the result of *HAG II* had been to 'insulate' markets in cases where there are two economically separate owners within the Community. However, the Court rejected the invitation to distinguish ownership divided by sequestration (*HAG II*) from voluntary division of ownership (*IHT*). Such a distinction was contrary to the reasoning in *HAG II*, where it had been stressed that the free movement of both types of marked goods would undermine the essential function of the trade mark, thus leaving consumers unable to identify the origin of goods purchased, and rendering the proprietor of one trade mark potentially liable to criticism for the quality of goods for which he was not responsible. The Court also noted that the Community trade mark was merely superimposed on national rights, and that undertakings were not obliged to take out Community trade marks.[42] In addition, the holder of a national mark was entitled to oppose the grant of a CTM for identical or similar goods, and so the assignment of national trade marks for one or more states of the Community only could not be precluded. Such a sanction could not be introduced through case law, because it would impose

---

[41]   Case C-9/93, *IHT Internationale Heiztechnik GmbH* v. *Ideal Standard GmbH* (Opinion of Advocate General Gulmann, 9 February 1994).

[42]   CTMR, Recital 5.

on member states a positive obligation to render such assignments void. If such a thing were to be done, it would be a matter for the Community legislature.

The Court therefore held that it was not contrary to the Treaty to prevent the use of confusingly similar trade marks where one had been acquired by assignment from the undertaking opposing the importation, if there was now no economic link between them. However, where an economic link exists (products put into circulation by the same undertaking, by a licensee, by a parent company, by a subsidiary of the same group or an exclusive distributor), then exhaustion will apply.[43] This approach may not be evaded by otherwise independent undertakings agreeing between themselves a pattern of assignments convenient for their various marketing purposes: market-sharing agreements will be considered anti-competitive, and will fall foul of Article 81.

PATENT RIGHTS AND THE NATURE OF CONSENT

The same general approach to consent is taken with patents. As explained earlier, *Centrafarm* v. *Sterling* laid down a rule that a patentee could not use parallel patents to prevent the sale of goods marketed in another member state by the patentee or with his consent. The patentee therefore has to take the consequences of a decision to market patented goods in an unprotected market.[44] However, where sales by a third party take place as the result of a compulsory licence, the patentee is not deemed to have consented to this.[45]

COPYRIGHT AND NEIGHBOURING RIGHTS: EXHAUSTION BEYOND THE DISTRIBUTION RIGHT?

With respect to the distribution right, copyright and neighbouring rights are again treated in the same way as patents and trade marks. In *Deutsche Grammophon* v. *Metro*, the holder of rights in various sound recordings was objecting to parallel imports into Germany of records sold with its consent in France; the price in Germany was protected by a retail price maintenance scheme. The Court stressed that such behaviour would legitimise the isolation of national markets, was repugnant to the essential purpose of the Treaty and

---

[43]   Case C-9/93, *IHT Internationale Heiztechnik GmbH* v. *Ideal Standard GmbH* [1994] I-ECR 2789 (paras. 34 and 41). See also Andrea Filippo Gagliardi, 'Trade Mark Assignments under E.C. Law' [1998] *EIPR* 371–8.

[44]   Case 187/80, *Merck & Co. Inc.* v. *Stephar BV* [1981] ECR 2063. Confirmed in Joined Cases C-267/95 and 268/95, *Merck & Co. Inc.* v. *Primecrown Ltd* [1996] ECR I-6285.

[45]   Case 19/84, *Pharmon BV* v. *Hoechst AG* [1985] ECR 2281.

could not be permitted.[46] In *GEMA*, a German copyright management society sought to rely on German rights not to exclude imports altogether, but to claim additional royalties. The recordings had been marketed in other member states with the right holder's consent, and the appropriate royalty for the territory had been paid, although these royalty rates were not as high as the rate prevailing in Germany. On import into Germany, GEMA argued it should be entitled to claim the difference between the lower and higher royalty rates, as would have been permissible under German national law. The Court emphasised that the right holder was free to choose where the goods were put into circulation, a decision based on a number of factors. Differing royalty rates did not justify the legal protection of a national right to additional payment: such a practice was incompatible with the rules concerning free movement of goods.[47] This argument can only be carried so far, however. In *EMI* v. *Patricia*, EMI, as holder of rights in sound recordings by Cliff Richard, was objecting to the import into Germany of records originally sold in Denmark. The records had been lawfully marketed in Denmark because the copyright period had already expired. The Court distinguished *GEMA*, because the marketing in Denmark was due 'not to an act or the consent of the copyright owner or his licensee, but to the expiry of the protection period provided for by the legislation of that Member State'.[48] The problem therefore stemmed from a lack of harmonisation of Community law, and this was 'inseparably linked to the very existence of the exclusive rights'. Restrictions due to disparities between national laws

---

[46] Case 78/70, *Deutsche Grammophon Gesellschaft GmbH* v. *Metro SB Grossmarkte GmbH & Co. KG* [1971] ECR 487.

[47] Case C-55/80, *Musik-Vertrieb Membran GmbH* v. *GEMA* [1981] ECR 147. Note, in this context, Case C?244/06, *Dynamic Medien Vertriebs GmbH* v. *Avides Media AG* [2008] 2 CMLR 651. Avides Media had sold Japanese 'anime' cartoons on DVD, by mail order via its internet site. The DVDs had been imported by them into Germany from the United Kingdom, where the relevant authorities had classified them as 'suitable only for 15 years and over'. The DVDs were labelled to indicate this. Dynamic Medien, a competitor of Avides Media, sought to prevent their sale on the grounds that German law on the protection of young persons prohibits the sale by mail order of DVDs which have not been examined in Germany, and which do not bear an age-limit label corresponding to a classification decision from a competent authority. The German courts agreed, but sought guidance from the ECJ as to whether such a law was precluded by the provisions on the free movement of goods. The ECJ held that Art. 28 does not preclude such national rules, unless the procedure for examination, classification and labelling of DVDs is not readily accessible or cannot be completed within a reasonable period, or if decisions are not open to challenge before the courts. Although this case does not involve consideration of an intellectual property right *per se*, it does affect the sale of goods whose intellectual property rights would normally have been exhausted by first sale within the Community.

[48] Case C-341/87, *EMI Electrola GmbH* v. *Patricia Im- und Export Verwaltungsgesellschaft mbH* [1989] ECR 79 (para. 10).

could therefore be justified, if they did not amount to a means of arbitrary discrimination or a disguised restriction on trade.

However, the exhaustion principle does not extend to rental and lending rights, or to rights in performances, or the right of communication to the public.

RENTAL AND LENDING RIGHTS

In *Warner Brothers* v. *Christiansen*, the manager of a video hire shop in Copenhagen went to London, where he bought a copy of the film *Never Say Never Again*, intending to hire it out in Denmark. Danish law prohibited the hiring out of videos without the consent of the author or producers of the recording. UK law did not. Christiansen argued that the right holder had consented to marketing in the UK, and, on the basis of *GEMA*, had to take the consequences of that decision. Advocate General Mancini agreed with Christiansen. The Court took a different view. It noted that a market had quite recently emerged for the hire of recordings, as distinct from their sale, and offered great potential as a source of revenue for makers of films. If royalties were mandatory only on sales, this did not guarantee film makers a remuneration which reflected the number of occasions on which the videos were hired out, so did not secure them a satisfactory share of the rental market. A number of national laws had recognised this by providing specific protection of the rental right. Such a right would be rendered worthless if it could be exhausted merely by sale in a member state without such a right, and such a repercussion could not be allowed.[49] Although at this time there was no provision for rental rights under Community law, this was in contemplation. The Court was doubtless influenced by the importance which the Commission attributed to rental rights, and its desire to see them regulated by a Community regime.

Not long afterwards, Directive 92/100 (now repealed and replaced by Directive 2006/115) harmonised the provisions relating to rental and lending rights, providing for exclusive rights to authorise or prohibit the rental and lending of copyright works. These rights (in copyright works, recorded performances, sound recordings and films) 'shall not be exhausted by any sale or other act of distribution of originals and copies of copyright works and other subject matter'.[50] The same approach had been taken to the rental of computer programs: the Computer Programs Directive provides explicitly for exhaustion of the distribution right in a copy of a computer program by first sale, but not the rental right.[51] This is unaffected by the Rental Directive.[52] Thus, the

---

[49] Case 158/86, *Warner Brothers Inc.* v. *Christiansen* [1988] ECR 2605.
[50] Rental Dir., Art. 1(2).
[51] Directive 91/250 OJ [1991] L 122/42 ('Software Dir.'), Art. 4(c).
[52] Rental Dir., Art. 4.

rental right remains one of the prerogatives of the right holder, notwithstanding sale of a physical copy of the work. The argument is that the rental right would be rendered meaningless if it were to be exhausted immediately a copy of the work was offered for rental. True though this is, the effect of this policy is to permit copyright holders to impose different prices and conditions for rental in different member states, at least as far as the free movement provisions are concerned.[53] However, such pricing strategies may still offend against competition law, if the factual circumstances are appropriate.

RIGHTS IN PERFORMANCES

Rights in performances (including the rights given to producers of sound recordings, and to broadcasters) are approached in a similar way to rental and lending rights. In *Coditel I*, a French film production company, Les Films La Boetie, had given exclusive distribution rights in the film *Le Boucher* to Ciné Vog, to cover Belgian territory.[54] Ciné Vog began showing the film in Belgian cinemas. The following year, Les Films La Boetie gave permission for the film to be shown on German television. This channel could be picked up in Belgium, and Coditel (a group of Belgian cable television companies) began to distribute it to subscribers. Ciné Vog argued that Coditel was infringing its copyright, to be met with the argument that this in turn infringed Coditel's freedom to provide services under Article 49. The ECJ noted that films – unlike books and records – are made available to the public 'by performances which may be infinitely repeated'. The film copyright holder therefore has a legitimate interest in calculating its licence fee on the basis of the actual or probable number of performances, and in holding back television broadcasts until after a period of cinema showings. The right to require fees for any showing of a film is therefore 'part of the essential function of copyright' for this type of copyright work. Article 49 does not permit the use of national intellectual property rights as a means of arbitrary discrimination or a disguised restriction on trade, as, for example, if copyright assignments were to be used in an attempt to isolate national markets. However, noting that television is organised largely on the basis of legal broadcasting monopolies given over national territories, the ECJ acknowledged that granting assignments on anything other than a geographical basis would often be impracticable. Thus Ciné Vog was entitled to enforce its rights, and would not breach Article 49 by doing so.

---

[53]   See Case C-200/96, *Metronome Musik* v. *Music Point Hokamp* [1998] ECR I-1953; Case C-61/97, *Foreningen af danske Videogramdistributører* v. *Laserdisken* [1998] ECR I-5171.

[54]   Case 62/79, *Coditel* v. *Cine Vog Films* [1980] ECR 881.

In *Basset* v. *SACEM*, the owner of a French discotheque was objecting to the levels of royalties being demanded by the French copyright collecting society, SACEM. The purchase of a record involved the payment of a reproduction royalty, and a performance royalty. Under French law it was permissible to grant a reproduction right relating only to private use, and to charge a supplementary mechanical reproduction fee for subsequent public use. In other countries, only a single royalty was payable, which was not severable into private and public uses. The question was whether the charging of a supplementary royalty in France was contrary to the provisions on the free movement of goods. At first sight, therefore, the case resembled *GEMA*, where differing royalty rates did not justify the legal protection of a national right to additional payment, and the right holder had to accept the consequences of a decision to market in another member state. In *Basset*, however, the ECJ characterised the supplementary reproduction fee as 'part of the payment for an author's rights over the public performance of a recorded musical work', rather than (as in *GEMA*) payment for the distribution right. Such a fee was thus part of the normal exploitation of copyright, and did not in itself amount to a means of arbitrary discrimination or a disguised restriction on trade for the purposes of Articles 28 and 30.[55]

These two strands – the free movement of services and the free movement of goods – were brought together by the ECJ in *Ministère Public* v. *Tournier*.[56] Again, the owner of a discotheque was objecting to the rates of royalties being charged by SACEM. The majority of the complaints involved issues of competition law, but the question of exhaustion was also raised by the referring court. Following *GEMA*, the ECJ confirmed that a national copyright management society could not 'charge a levy on products from another Member State where they have been put into circulation by the copyright owner or with his consent and thus to impose a charge on the importation of sound recordings which are already in free circulation in the common market as a result of the fact that they cross an internal frontier'. In such a situation, the distribution right would be exhausted. However, as in *Coditel I*, the ECJ again distinguished the exploitation of the performance right, where the copyright owner has 'a legitimate interest' in calculating the fees due under a licence (for example) on the basis of the actual or probable number of performances. Sound recordings fell into both categories, being products covered by the provisions on the free movement of goods, but also capable of being used for public performance of the underlying copyright work. In such circumstances, the ECJ held,

---

55   See Case 402/85, *Bassett* v. *SACEM* [1987] ECR 1747.
56   Case 395/87, *Ministère Public* v. *Jean-Louis Tournier* [1989] ECR 2521.

the requirements relating to the free movement of goods and the freedom to provide services and those deriving from the observance of copyright must be reconciled in such a way that the copyright owners, or the societies empowered to act as their agents, may invoke their exclusive rights in order to require the payment of royalties for music played in public by means of a sound-recording, even though the marketing of that recording cannot give rise to the charging of any royalty in the country where the music is played in public.[57]

In other words, the performance right could still be relied on once the distribution right had been exhausted. The abusiveness or otherwise of the royalty rates is a matter for competition law, and will not be a factor in determining whether a national rule is compatible with Articles 28 or 49.

RIGHT OF COMMUNICATION TO THE PUBLIC
Similarly, the right of communication to the public, guaranteed by Article 3 of the Information Society Directive, will not be exhausted by the sale of an article embodying the work. Thus, although the distribution right relating to a copyright work on a CD or DVD (for example) will be exhausted by consent to marketing with the Community, the right holder retains the right of communication to the public.

6.3   REPACKAGING: BALANCING THE PRINCIPLE OF FREE MOVEMENT AGAINST THE TRADE MARK OWNER'S RIGHTS

6.3.1   Pharmaceuticals

The parallel trade in pharmaceuticals is attractive and potentially highly profitable. Pharmaceuticals are high value and easy to transport, and there are wide price fluctuations within the Community, caused in part by government price controls in individual member states. The Association of the British Pharmaceutical Industry (ABPI) has estimated that in 2005 parallel trade cost the UK pharmaceutical industry nearly £1.4 billion, and that in the same year more than one in 17 prescriptions in the UK were filled by a parallel-imported product, accounting for more than 14% of sales. The ABPI claims that parallel trade benefits only parallel importers themselves, and does not deliver lower prices to purchasers (such as the National Health Service) or patients. It also argues that parallel trade can affect the safety and quality of medicines,

---

[57]   Case 395/87, *Ministère Public* v. *Jean-Louis Tournier* [1989] ECR 2521 (para. 13).

and bring about an increased risk of counterfeiting and piracy. It regards repackaging as presenting a particular danger to the integrity of the product, and suggests that patients may be confused by instructions in a foreign language.[58] Such suggestions do not go unchallenged, by any means, however.

As has been discussed, in *Hoffmann-La Roche*, the Court of Justice held that the essential function of a trade mark was to guarantee the identity of the trade marked product to the consumer, by enabling him to be sure of the product's origin, and to be confident that the product had not been subject to interference by a third person without the authorisation of the trade mark proprietor. However, the Treaty's exception for industrial property would not cover a disguised restriction on trade, for example, if a variation in packaging was used simply as a strategy to compartmentalise the market. For repackaging to be permitted regardless of any objections by the trade mark proprietor, the parallel importer had to meet three conditions: the repackaging must not affect the original condition of the product; the trade mark proprietor must be given prior notice of the marketing of the repackaged product; the new packaging must give the name and address of the repackager.[59] In *Pfizer* v. *Eurim-Pharm*, the parallel importer took Pfizer's blister strips of capsules, and sealed each one into a box without altering the strip or its contents. The original trade mark was visible on each strip through a transparent window in the box, which also named Eurim-Pharm as packager. A leaflet was inserted in the box, giving details required for the target market. Pfizer was given advance warning of Eurim-Pharm's intention to market the repackaged drug. This met all of the *Hoffmann-La Roche* conditions, and could not be resisted.[60]

The question arose as to whether a parallel importer could replace one trade mark with another, thereby rebranding the product. Taking a very similar approach to that used in *Hoffmann-La Roche*, in *Centrafarm* v. *American Home Products* the Court of Justice found that, in some circumstances, rebranding could be justified. AHP sold a tranquilliser in various member states under different trade marks; SERENID in the UK, and SERESTA in the Benelux countries. Its chemical composition and medical effects were identical, but the flavourings were slightly different. Centrafarm imported UK SERENID into the Netherlands, removed the SERENID mark, and remarked it SERESTA. The Court again emphasised that the essential function of a trade mark is to guarantee the product's origin to the consumer. This guarantee

---

[58]   Association of the British Pharmaceutical Industry (ABPI) Media Briefing 2006:   http://www.abpi.org.uk/press/media_briefings_06_ntfrs_0c5204e4/green_parallel_trade06.pdf.

[59]   Case 102/77, *Hoffmann-La Roche & Co. AG* v. *Centrafarm Vertriebsgesellschaft Pharmazeutischer Erzeugnisse mbH* [1978] ECR 1139.

[60]   Case C-1/81, *Pfizer Inc.* v. *Eurim-Pharm GmbH* [1981] ECR 2913.

would be compromised if anyone other than the trade mark proprietor was permitted to mark the product. However, notwithstanding, the exercise of the trade mark right might constitute a disguised restriction on trade between member states, and thus fall within the proviso. A manufacturer may have valid reasons for using different marks in member states, but, if the practice is part of a market-splitting strategy, the trade mark proprietor cannot rely on the mark to resist rebranding. It is for the national court to decide if the right is being legitimately exercised.[61]

The Trade Mark Directive: the approach to the problem does not change

The Court's initial approach to repackaging was based entirely on interpretation of the EC Treaty, and relevant case law. Since these early cases were decided, the Trade Mark Directive has come into force, requiring significant harmonisation of national trade mark laws. Article 5 of the Directive confers exclusive rights in a registered trade mark on the proprietor. Article 7 of the Directive establishes the principle of exhaustion of rights in a legislative form:[62]

> 1. The trade mark shall not entitle the proprietor to prohibit its use in relation to goods which have been put on the market in the Community under that trade mark by the proprietor or with his consent.
> 2. Paragraph 1 shall not apply where there exist legitimate reasons for the proprietor to oppose further commercialisation of the goods, especially where the condition of the goods is changed or impaired after they have been put on the market.

Its application was considered in *Bristol-Myers Squibb*, where a number of repackaging cases were considered together.[63] The question immediately arose as to whether the extensive Article 36 case law retained its relevance. The Court stressed that, since the Directive was a harmonisation measure, national laws in the field had to be assessed in the light of its provisions. However, like any secondary legislation, the Directive had to be interpreted in

---

[61]   Case 3/78, *Centrafarm BV* v. *American Home Products Corp.* [1978] ECR 1823.
[62]   The Community Trade Mark Regulation contains an identical provision: CTMR, Art. 13.
[63]   Joined Cases C-427/93, C-429/93 and C-436/93, *Bristol-Myers Squibb* v. *Paranova A/S*; *C.H. Boehringer Sohn, Boehringer Ingelheim KG and Boehringer Ingelheim A/S* v. *Paranova A/S*; *Bayer Aktiengesellschaft and Bayer Danmark A/S* v. *Paranova A/S* [1996] ECR I-3457. See also Joined Cases C-71/94, C-72/94 and C-73/94, *Eurim-Pharm Arzneimittel GmbH* v. *Beiersdorf AG and Others*; Case C-232/94, *MPA Pharma GmbH* v. *Rhone-Poulenc Pharma GmbH* (judgments given the same day).

the light of the Treaty rules on the free movement of goods and in particular Article 36. The case law thus remains important.

All the cases considered involved trade marked pharmaceutical products marketed by the trade mark owner within the Community. These products were purchased by parallel importers, and repackaged in a form suitable for the importer's target market. In each case, the trade mark was re-affixed by the importer, although the precise nature of the repackaging varied. In most cases the get-up of the product was mimicked to some extent (particularly the distinctive colours of the original packaging), and often the original instructions were replaced with an appropriate translation. In one case, a spray not manufactured by the trade mark owner was inserted into the packaging. The Court spelled out the meaning of Article 7(1), interpreting it in line with the earlier case law, and rejecting the suggestion that the parallel importer only had the right to resell products as originally marketed by the trade mark owner. Article 7(1) was held to preclude the owner of a trade mark from relying on that mark to prevent an importer from marketing a product which was put on the market in another member state by the trade mark owner or with his consent, unless Article 7(2) applies.

Article 7(2) provides that a trade mark owner may oppose further commercialisation of products where there is a legitimate reason for doing so. Changes which affect the condition of the product will provide a legitimate reason for such opposition, but other reasons may qualify. Again the Court took its own case law 'as a basis' for determining the meaning of the Article. It repeated its previous statements concerning the specific subject matter of a trade mark, and the trade mark's essential function as a guarantee of origin. The manufacturers' argument that the prevailing distortions in the pharmaceutical market provided a legitimate reason for opposing parallel imports was firmly dismissed. Whilst acknowledging that in the pharmaceutical market price differences between member states may well result from factors over which trade mark owners have no control (such as divergent rules on the fixing of maximum prices, the profit margins of pharmaceutical wholesalers and pharmacies, or the maximum amount of medical expenses which may be reimbursed under sickness insurance schemes), such distortions were a matter for the Community authorities to remedy.[64]

In the remainder of the judgment, the Court set out in some detail its views on particular forms of repackaging. Again previous case law formed the starting point. The three conditions from *Hoffmann-La Roche* were explicitly reit-

---

[64]   For studies of the effects of parallel trade in pharmaceuticals, see Christopher Stothers, *Parallel Trade in Europe* (Oxford: Hart Publishing, 2007), 17 n. 45. See also Margaret K. Kyle, 'Strategic Responses to Parallel Trade' (London Business School; NBER Working Paper).

erated and approved. The requirement that the owner's use of the trade mark will contribute to the artificial partitioning of the markets between member states (previously derived from the proviso to the Treaty exception for intellectual property) was now expressed as a preliminary condition. Thus, Article 7(2) gave the trade mark owner a right to oppose further marketing of a pharmaceutical product which had been repackaged and re-marked, unless five conditions were met ('the BMS conditions').

(i)   ARTIFICIAL PARTITIONING OF THE MARKETS BETWEEN MEMBER STATES

The use of different package sizes is a common practice which contributes to the partitioning of markets, particularly where national rules authorise packages of only certain sizes. The trade mark owner cannot object to repackaging in new external packaging where this is necessary to allow marketing in the member state of importation. However, the parallel importer's freedom is to do only what is necessary: if the importer can achieve marketable packaging by other means, such as additional labels or extra user instructions, the trade mark owner may resist the use of new external packaging. There is no need for the importer to prove that the trade mark owner deliberately sought to partition markets.

(ii)   EFFECT ON THE ORIGINAL CONDITION OF THE PRODUCT

This concerns the condition of the product inside the packaging, rather than the external presentation of the product. The trade mark owner may oppose any repackaging involving a risk of the product inside the package being exposed to tampering or to influences affecting its original condition. For pharmaceuticals, repackaging must be carried out in circumstances not capable of affecting the original condition of the product. If the repackaging affects only an external layer, leaving the inner packaging intact (as in *Pfizer*), or where the repackaging is carried out under the supervision of a public authority, there is no risk to the original condition. Similarly, the removal of blister packs, flasks, phials or ampoules from their original external packaging, and replacement in new external packaging, did not affect the original condition of the product in the packaging. Nor is the original condition affected by the addition of self-stick labels, information leaflets or even extra articles. The pharmaceutical companies argued that new larger packages might contain products from different batches, or that products might have exceeded their use-by dates. The Court did not regard this 'hypothetical risk of isolated error' as sufficient to give the trade mark owner a right to oppose repackaging. The Court was even prepared to contemplate the cutting of blister packs, and the reprinting of batch numbers, if done in a manner which excluded any real risk to the original condition of the tablets inside. It was, however, acknowledged that the original condition of the product might be indirectly affected if the new packaging omitted important information, or gave inaccurate information about the product. Likewise, an extra article which did not comply with the method of use and dosing envisaged by the manufacturer could have an indirect effect on the original condition of the product. In each case, this was a matter for the national court to decide on the facts.

(iii)   REQUIREMENT TO INDICATE WHO IS RESPONSIBLE FOR THE REPACKAGING

The parallel importer must indicate who has repackaged the product, and this information must be printed in such a way as to be understood by a person with normal eyesight, exercising a normal degree of attentiveness. This prevents consumers being misled into thinking that the repackaging has been done by the trade mark owner, which would threaten the guarantee of origin. It is not necessary to require an express statement that repackaging was undertaken without the authorisation of the trade mark owner, since this might imply that the repackaged product was not entirely legitimate. If the importer has added an extra article to the package, its origin must be made clear, to dissociate it from the trade mark owner. It may also be necessary to indicate the manufacturer's name, to ensure that the consumer does not believe that the importer is the owner of the trade mark.

(iv)   PRESENTATION NOT SUCH AS TO DAMAGE THE TRADE MARK'S REPUTATION

The Court acknowledged that, even if the identity of the repackager was made clear, the reputation of the trade mark might suffer if the repackaged product was presented inappropriately. In such a case, the trade mark owner has a legitimate interest, related to the specific subject matter of the trade mark right, in being able to oppose the marketing of the product. In the case of pharmaceutical products, the Court recognised that the public is particularly demanding as to the quality and integrity of the product, and that defective, poor quality or untidy packaging could damage the trade mark's reputation. The demands on a parallel importer will be less onerous if the products are administered to patients by professionals, 'for whom the presentation of the product is of little importance'. It would be for the national court to decide whether, say, the cutting of blister packs had been carried out in such a manner as to threaten the trade mark's reputation. It has become increasingly common for pharmaceutical products to be packaged in 'memory packs', which label each pill with a day of the week to aid the consumer. Advocate General Jacobs suggested in his opinion that the owner should be entitled to object if such packs were severed, and the national court thought that this would cause unacceptable confusion for the consumer, or endanger health, or that this would be detrimental to the reputation of the trade mark.

(v) PRIOR NOTICE

The importer must give notice to the trade mark owner before the repackaged product is put on sale. In *Bristol-Myers Squibb*, the Court stated that the importer should supply a specimen on demand, in order that the trade mark owner could object to any error or deficiency. These requirements were spelled out in greater detail in *Boehringer Ingelheim* v. *Swingward*. There the defendant parallel importers had argued that it would be disproportionate to allow the trade mark owner to oppose imports merely for lack of notice, unless there was a risk to the specific subject matter of the right. The ECJ nevertheless insisted on prior notice by the parallel importer, and the provision of a sample on request. This safeguarded legitimate interests of the proprietor, enabling checks on the condition of the product, the presentation of the packaging, and affording protection against counterfeiting. The trade mark proprietor must have a reasonable time to react to the intended repackaging, and this is a matter for the national court. However, the ECJ did indicate that a period of 15 working days was likely to constitute such a reasonable time, if a sample of the repackaged pharmaceutical was supplied.[65]

Bristol-Myers Squibb thus expresses a continued and firm refusal to allow the principle of free movement of goods to give way, in spite of admitted distortions in the pharmaceutical market. It also offers guidance as to what forms of repackaging are acceptable. Nevertheless, the wider issue of lack of harmony in the EU pharmaceutical market remains extremely problematic, and the application of the rules is continually being tested and explored. The decision was followed straightforwardly in a case involving similar facts, *Phytheron* v. *Bourdon*.[66] The Court then confirmed in *Pharmacia & Upjohn* v. *Paranova* that the *Bristol-Myers Squibb* approach applied to rebranding as to repackaging. Upjohn marketed an antibiotic, clindamycin, in a variety of forms. It used the trade mark 'Dalacin' in Denmark, Germany and Spain, 'Dalacine' in France, and 'Dalacin C' in the other member states. The use of different marks was explained in part by difficulties in securing registration of 'Dalacin C' in some countries, and also by an agreement whereby American

---

[65] Case C-143/00, *Boehringer Ingelheim KG* v. *Swingward Ltd* [2002] ECR I-3759 (paras. 61–7). Where a trade mark proprietor had been given 77 days' notice, the Helsinki District Court found that the company would be considered to have approved the packaging, and had lost its right to invoke its trade mark rights against that packaging: *NV Organon* v. *Paranova Oy* (Helsinki District Court, Finland) [2008] ETMR 7. See also *Aspirin II* (German Federal Supreme Court decision 1 ZR 147/04, 12 July 2007), where it was held that a trade mark owner had lost the right to object to further commercialisation, having failed to object to repackaging in a timely manner, following notification by the parallel importer.

[66] Case C-352/95, *Phytheron International SA* v. *Jean Bourdon SA* [1997] ECR I-1729.

Home Products had agreed not to object to Upjohn's use of the mark 'Dalacin' in Uruguay if Upjohn would use 'Dalacine' and 'Dalacin C' where possible in the Community. Paranova purchased Upjohn's 'Dalacine' capsules in France, for repackaging and marketing in Denmark as 'Dalacin'. It also purchased Upjohn's 'Dalacin C' injection phials in Greece, for repackaging and marketing in Denmark as 'Dalacin'. The Court found that there was 'no objective difference between reaffixing a trade mark after repackaging and replacing the original trade mark by another which is capable of justifying the condition of artificial partitioning being applied differently in each of those cases'.[67] This is a robustly practical view, which recognises that the practice of using different trade marks contributes to market partitioning in much the same way as using different packaging, and that in each case the parallel importer is using another's trade mark.[68] If the circumstances prevailing at the time of marketing make it 'objectively necessary' to replace the original trade mark by that of the importing member state in order to place the product on the market in that state, the parallel importer may do so.

When is repackaging 'necessary'?
In explaining the condition of necessity in *Pharmacia & Upjohn* v. *Paranova*, the Court said that the question is whether 'effective access' to the market would be hindered if the trade mark were not replaced. However, replacement is not 'necessary' if it is explicable solely by the parallel importer's attempt to secure a commercial advantage. These are matters for the national court.[69] The ECJ was asked for further clarification in *Boehringer Ingelheim* v. *Swingward (Boehringer I)*. The Court reaffirmed its previous approach. Access to the market might be impeded, for example, if products in their original packaging could not be marketed because of national rules or practices relating to packaging, or where sickness insurance rules made reimbursement of medical expenses dependent on a certain packaging or where well-established medical prescription practices are based on standard sizes recommended by profes-

---

        [67]   Case C-379/97, *Pharmacia & Upjohn SA* v. *Paranova A/S* [1999] ECR I-6927 (para. 37).
        [68]   The Court did not give weight to the trade mark proprietor's argument that the situations should be distinguished because the parallel importer is affixing a mark never used by the proprietor. Also, it was argued, there is no exhaustion within the strict meaning of Article 7(1), because the goods were not put on the market in the Community 'under *that* trade mark' by the proprietor or with his consent (emphasis added). For criticism see Marleen Van Kerckhove and David Rosenberg, '*Upjohn* v. *Paranova*: Utterly Exhausted by a Trip Too Far' [1999] *EIPR* 223-227.
        [69]   Case C-379/97, *Pharmacia & Upjohn SA* v. *Paranova A/S* [1999] ECR I-6927 (paras. 42–5).

sional groups and sickness insurance institutions.[70] The trade mark proprietor may oppose replacement packaging where the parallel importer could re-use the original packaging by relabelling it, because in such a case repackaging would be explicable solely as an attempt to secure a commercial advantage. However, if there is strong resistance to relabelled pharmaceutical products from a significant proportion of consumers, this will be a hindrance to effective market access. In such circumstances, repackaging would be permitted, because it would not be explicable solely as an attempt to secure a commercial advantage.[71]

The ECJ's approach to the necessity of repackaging is relatively broad, in that it includes obstacles of fact, as well as legal obstacles. Assessment of any issues of fact are matters for the national court, and, because of the importance of this sector, many cases do reach national courts. For example, in *Boehringer Ingelheim Danmark* v. *Orifarm* the parallel importer relabelled supplies of a laxative marketed in Portugal as GUTALAX, for sale in Denmark as LAXOBERAL. Although it was a non-prescription drug, it was most often sold on the recommendation of a health professional, and in Denmark the name LAXOBERAL was most frequently used. The Danish court held that this did not amount to a prescription practice which made it necessary to sell the products under the same name. Nothing prevented sales under the name GUTALAX, and the fact that the parallel importer might obtain higher sales by using the name LAXOBERAL did not justify the repackaging.[72] The rules were applied by the German courts in *Boehringer Ingelheim* v. *Eurim-Pharm* to prevent the repackaging of BERODUAL for distribution in Germany. Eurim-Pharm's reasons for repackaging did not relate to access to the German market (which could have been achieved simply by rebundling), but to its desire to improve product presentation by including the company's own logo

---

[70] Case C-143/00, *Boehringer Ingelheim KG* v. *Swingward Ltd* [2002] ECR I-3759 (para. 47). It is sufficient for there to be an impediment in respect of one type of packaging used by the trade mark proprietor in the member state of importation.

[71] Case C-143/00, *Boehringer Ingelheim KG* v. *Swingward Ltd.* [2002] ECR I-3759 (paras. 48–52). See, for example, Case C-443/99, *Merck, Sharp & Dohme* v. *Paranova Pharmazeutika* [2002] ECR I-3703, where the referring national court stated that Austrian consumers are not accustomed to being offered pharmaceutical products which have clearly been put on the market in another state, where a different language is used, and might well regard such products with the same suspicion as those with untidy or poor-quality packaging.

[72] *Boehringer Ingelheim Danmark A/S, C.H. Boehringer Sohn and Boehringer Ingelheim KG* v. *Orifarm A/S* (Court of Odense, Denmark) [2002] ETMR 20. See also Case T-10375-99, *Aventis Pharma* v. *Paranova Läkemedel* (Stockholm Tingsrätt) [2001] ETMR 60.

and using specially designed colours and shapes for the new box.[73] Likewise, Boehringer successfully resisted the repackaging of its CATAPRESAN in 'Euro packages' where other parallel importers imported the same product in bundled packages without repackaging.[74] Parallel importers have sought to rely on the ECJ's comments in *Boehringer I* that significant consumer resistance to relabelled products might amount to a hindrance to market access. In *Paranova* v. *Boehringer*, the parallel importer had commissioned a survey which purported to demonstrate that pharmacists and patients generally preferred to use pharmaceutical products which had been repackaged and rebranded rather than those which had been relabelled without there being any rebranding. The Danish Supreme Court found that the survey did not prove that Paranova, if it tried to market its product in a relabelled and non-rebranded format, would have experienced such a barrier to efficient access to the market that the repackaging and rebranding was necessary.[75]

National courts have on occasions struggled to apply the ECJ's principles to the facts, however. The ruling in *Boehringer I* in part concerned a case referred by the English High Court, *Glaxo* v. *Dowelhurst*. That court had found as a fact that there was substantial resistance to the use of over-stickered imported packaging, and that it was objectively necessary for importers to repackage the goods in order to obtain effective access to the United Kingdom market. The court also reached the preliminary view that a trade mark proprietor could object to repackaging only if it inflicted real and substantial damage on the specific subject matter of the mark, but sought clarification from the ECJ. The ruling in *Boehringer I* made it clear that repackaging had to be 'necessary', and offered the guidance just discussed. When the case returned to the High Court for the ECJ's ruling to be implemented, that ruling was interpreted as meaning that repackaging was deemed to be prejudicial to the specific subject matter, even if there was no effect on the quality of the goods and there was no real adverse impact on the mark's function as an indication of origin. Mr Justice Laddie termed this 'an irrebuttable legal fiction unconnected with the facts', and as a result concluded that the trade mark proprietor could object to any repackaging of its product 'no matter what its nature and

---

[73]   *Boehringer Ingelheim Pharma KG* v. *Eurim-Pharm Arzneimittel GmbH* (Bundesgerichtshof) [2003] ETMR 39.

[74]   *Boehringer Ingelheim Pharma KG* v. *MTK Pharma Vertriebs GmbH, Kohlpharma GmbH* (Hanseatisches Oberlandesgericht) [2003] ETMR 82. See also *Boehringer Ingelheim Pharma GmbH & Co. KG* v. *Munro Wholesale Medical Supplies Ltd* (Court of Session, Scotland) [2004] ETMR 66.

[75]   *Paranova A/S* v. *C.H. Boehringer Sohn GmbH, Boehringer Ingelheim KG and Boehringer Ingelheim A/S* [2004] ETMR 24 (Hoge Raad).

no matter how inoffensive it may be'.[76] However, he understood this to be subject to the rule that the trade mark proprietor cannot object to repackaging where this is necessary to allow effective market access by the parallel importer. This was an issue of fact to be determined by the national court, although here the finding had already been made. But there was the further consideration that the ECJ had held that the repackaging must not be such as to harm the reputation of the mark. Reading this in conjunction with the earlier 'irrebutable presumption' that repackaging was prejudicial to the specific subject matter of the mark, Mr Justice Laddie concluded 'that all repackaging must be treated as harmful and only to be tolerated to the extent that it can be shown to inflict the minimum collateral damage on the claimant's mark'. Such a conclusion had serious implications for parallel importers seeking to de-brand (remove the original mark from all or part of the packaging) or co-brand (add their own brand to the packaging). In contrast, Mr Justice Laddie understood the ECJ to say that if products were over-stickered or relabelled (as opposed to being repackaged), there was no presumption of damage to the specific subject matter.[77]

On appeal, the Court of Appeal noted that there was a substantial disparity of views across the EU. A number of national courts of member states at the highest level appeared to believe that the test of 'necessity' applied not only to repackaging as such but also to the details of the manner of repackaging. This had led to a number of decisions where parallel imports had been successfully resisted because the repackaging featured the brand or get-up of the distributor, and this was not held to be 'necessary'. In contrast, the EFTA Court had indicated that adding a decorative feature (such as stripes in a particular 'house' colour) to product packaging did not seem likely to damage the trade mark's reputation, and stated that the mere fact that a parallel importer gained additional advantage from a particular type of graphic design was, in itself, immaterial. The Commission of the European Communities took a similar view, arguing that the necessity test applied to the act of repackaging, and not to the presentation of the repackaged product.[78] The Court of Appeal therefore referred more questions to the ECJ, making *Boehringer* the only case ever to be referred twice.

Boehringer II: the BMS conditions clarified

In her Opinion in *Boehringer II* , Advocate General Sharpston observed:

---

[76] *Glaxo Group Ltd* v. *Dowelhurst Ltd* [2003] EWHC (Ch.) 110 (para. 15).

[77] *Glaxo Group Ltd* v. *Dowelhurst Ltd* [2003] EWHC (Ch.) 110 (esp. para. 20).

[78] *Boehringer Ingelheim KG & Others* v. *Swingward Limited* [2004] EWCA Civ. 129 (paras. 86–95).

It seems to me that after 30 years of case-law on the repackaging of pharmaceutical products it should be possible to distil sufficient principles to enable national courts to apply the law to the constantly replayed litigation between manufacturers and parallel importers. I will attempt to articulate such principles in this Opinion. I would then hope that national courts will play their part robustly in applying the principles to the facts before them without further requests to fine-tune the principles . . . It should not however in my view be for the Court of Justice to adjudicate on such detail for evermore.[79]

The ECJ patiently addressed the questions, nevertheless. It held that the five BMS conditions applied to relabelling as to repackaging, because this too was prejudicial to the specific subject matter of the mark, creating 'real risks' for the guarantee of origin.[80] The condition that packaging be necessary is directed only at the fact of repackaging the product – whether by re-boxing or over-stickering – for the purposes of allowing it to be marketed in the importing state. It is not directed at the manner or style in which the product has been repackaged.[81] It was a BMS requirement that the presentation of the repackaged product not be such as to damage the reputation of the trade mark or its proprietor. Defective, poor quality or untidy packaging were examples which were liable to cause damage, but (following *Dior*) other inappropriate presentation could do so 'by detracting from the image of reliability and quality attaching to such a product and the confidence it is capable of inspiring in the public concerned'.[82] The ECJ also considered the national court's list of questionable presentations. It held that de-branding, co-branding, obscuring the proprietor's trade mark, failing to state on the additional label that the trade mark belongs to the proprietor, and printing the name of the parallel importer in capital letters are all, in principle, liable to damage the trade mark's reputation. However, the Court emphasised that the question is one of fact for the national court to decide in the light of the circumstances of each case.[83] Although the ECJ's reluctance to stray into the national court's area of compe-

---

[79] Case C-348/04, *Boehringer Ingelheim KG* v. *Swingward Ltd* [2007] ETMR 71 (AG Sharpston's Opinion, 6 April 2006).

[80] Case C-348/04, *Boehringer Ingelheim KG* v. *Swingward Ltd* [2007] ETMR 71 (para. 30).

[81] Case C-348/04, *Boehringer Ingelheim KG* v. *Swingward Ltd* [2007] ETMR 71 (para. 38).

[82] Case C-348/04, *Boehringer Ingelheim KG* v. *Swingward Ltd* [2007] ETMR 71 (para. 43).

[83] Case C-348/04, *Boehringer Ingelheim KG* v. *Swingward Ltd* [2007] ETMR 71 (paras. 45–6). Applying this reasoning in a co-branding case, the Maritime and Commercial Court of Copenhagen found that the co-branding in question was harmful to the trade marks, as it was likely to indicate a special relationship between the trade marks and the parallel importer: *C.H. Boehringer Sohn* v. *Paranova* [2008] ETMR 6.

tence is entirely correct and explicable, its refusal to offer more specific guidance on these matters of detail leaves them open to dispute in the national courts.[84]

It is for the parallel importers to prove that the BMS conditions have been fulfilled. However, as regards the two requirements concerning the original condition of the product, and the presentation of the product, it is sufficient that the parallel importer furnishes evidence that leads to the reasonable presumption that these have been fulfilled. It will then be for the proprietor of the trade mark to show that the product's condition has been altered, or that the repackaging is liable to damage his reputation and that of the trade mark.[85]

Finally, the ECJ considered whether, in the absence of prior notice, a trade mark proprietor was entitled to claim the same financial remedies as if the goods had been counterfeit. It noted that, in the absence of specific Community sanctions, it was for member states to choose the most appropriate measures to ensure the effectiveness of the Directive, though the measures had to be proportionate, effective and a sufficient deterrent. Where parallel imports had been marketed in breach of the requirement of prior notice, the situation was no different from a case where counterfeit goods had been marketed – in neither case should the products have been marketed. Thus, a national measure which entitles a trade mark proprietor to claim financial remedies for lack of notice on the same basis as if the goods had been counterfeit is not in itself contrary to the principle of proportionality. However, it is for the national court to determine the amount of the financial remedies

---

[84] Further difficulties arose when these cases returned to the Court of Appeal: *Boehringer Ingelheim KG* v. *Swingward Ltd* [2008] EWCA Civ. 83. Applying the ruling in *Boehringer II*, the Court held that the defendants had complied with the BMS conditions, and found that their activities by way of re-boxing and relabelling had not caused and would not cause damage to the reputation of the claimants' trade marks. However, a further reference to the ECJ about repackaging remains pending, from the Austrian Supreme Court in Case C-276/05, *Wellcome* v. *Paranova*. The Austrian court has asked whether the presentation of new packaging is to be measured against a principle of minimum intervention, or (only) against whether it is such as to damage the reputation of the trade mark and its proprietor. The Court of Appeal considered that this question had already been answered in *Boehringer II*, and that any 'principle of minimum intervention' would in effect be a new and additional condition. The court was also concerned that such a test 'could be nearly unworkable'. However, given that the ECJ had agreed to take the case, instead of referring the Austrian court to its ruling in *Boehringer II*, the Court of Appeal felt it could not rule out the possibility that, notwithstanding the absence of any damage in fact, there was some further rule about minimum intervention. It therefore acceded to the claimants' request to defer making a final decision.

[85] Case C-348/04, *Boehringer Ingelheim KG* v. *Swingward Ltd* [2007] ETMR 71 (paras. 52–3).

according to the circumstances of each case, in the light of, in particular, the extent of damage to the trade mark proprietor caused by the parallel importer's infringement and in accordance with the principle of proportionality.[86]

6.3.2 Repackaging Principles – Application to Other Products?

In *Loendersloot*, the ECJ confirmed that the case law on the repackaging of pharmaceutical products also applied to other products – in this case, bottles of Scotch whisky. Three BMS conditions applied unchanged. The owner of trade mark rights may rely on those rights to prevent a third party from removing and then re-affixing or replacing labels bearing the trade mark, unless:

(1) it is established that the use of the trade mark rights by the owner to oppose the marketing of the relabelled products under that trade mark would contribute to the artificial partitioning of the markets between member states;

(2) it is shown that the repackaging cannot affect the original condition of the product; and

(3) the presentation of the relabelled product is not such as to be liable to damage the reputation of the trade mark and its owner.

However, the ECJ observed that the task of the national courts differed for pharmaceutical products and cases such as *Loendersloot*. In relation to pharmaceutical products, the national courts must consider whether circumstances in the markets of their own states make repackaging objectively necessary. In *Loendersloot*, however, the national court was required to assess 'whether the relabelling is necessary to protect the sources of supply of the parallel trade and to enable the products to be marketed on the various markets of the Member States for which they are intended'.[87] Loendersloot had argued that

---

[86]   Case C-348/04, *Boehringer Ingelheim KG* v. *Swingward Ltd* [2007] ETMR 71 (paras. 57–63). For further comment see Gill Grassie, 'Parallel Imports and Trade Marks' [2006] *EIPR* 474–9 and 513–16; Kathleen Harris, 'Parallel Imports: The Never-Ending Saga on Repackaging and Use of Trade Marks May Finally Be Ending . . . and Not Before Time' *JIPL&P* [2006] 564–7; Lucy Harrold, 'National Courts Will Have Final Word on Pharmaceutical Repackaged Parallel Imports' [2007] *EIPR* 395–8.

[87]   Case C-349/95, *Frits Loendersloot* v. *George Ballantine & Son Ltd* [1997] ECR I-6227 (para. 38). See also Joined Cases C-260/06 and C-261/06, *Criminal proceedings concerning Escalier* and *Criminal proceedings concerning Bonnarel* (8 November 2007). The cases concerned imports of pesticides for personal use, which had marketing authorisation in Spain (from where they were purchased) but not in France. In the course of its judgment, the ECJ observed that a requirement to attach a brand name or trade name to such a parallel imported product would be inappropriate and unnecessary in the particular circumstances (paras. 44–6).

removal of identification numbers was necessary to prevent artificial partitioning, because their suppliers feared sanctions from the product's producers.
Yet identification numbers might be used for legitimate purposes, such as
consignment identification for product recall, or anti-counterfeiting measures.
Where identification numbers are used for both legitimate and illegitimate
purposes, the Court held that parallel importers had to seek the protection of
Community competition law. Even if relabelling is justified in particular
circumstances, it must cause as little prejudice as possible to the specific
subject matter of the trade mark right. In relation to the other BMS conditions
(prior notice, stating the name and address of the repackager, supply of
samples), the Court acknowledged that they had been formulated in the light
of the particular nature of pharmaceutical products. Here the trade mark
owner's interests would be given sufficient weight if the parallel importer gave
prior notice that the relabelled products were to be put on sale.

Note in this context the ECJ's approach in *Pall*.[88] Although this case
involved a trade marked product, the Court did not focus on exhaustion of
trade mark rights, because this was not the primary issue. Dahlhausen
marketed, in Germany, blood filters which it had imported from Italy. The
Italian producer had marked the filters and their packaging with the trade mark
'Miropore', and the symbol ® to indicate that 'Miropore' was a registered
trade mark. Pall, a competitor, objected that this amounted to misleading
advertising, and was contrary to German unfair competition law, because the
mark was not registered in Germany. The Court found that the German rule
was an indistinctly applicable measure, which required Dahlhausen to repackage its products, and considered whether it could be justified by the mandatory
requirement of consumer protection. The Court held that it could not. Even
assuming that some consumers might be misled, this risk could not justify so
considerable an obstacle to the free movement of goods, since the consumer's
primary interest is in the qualities of a product rather than in the place of registration of the trade mark. Similarly, with regard to the mandatory requirement
of unfair commercial practice, the principal aim of registration is to obtain
legal protection for the trade mark in the relevant territory, and use of the
symbol ® is ancillary to this. The German rule therefore breached Article 28.

6.4   USE OF ANOTHER'S TRADE MARK IN ADVERTISING

The ECJ has stressed repeatedly that a trade mark's essential function is as a

---

[88]   Case C-238/89, *Pall Corp.* v. *P.J. Dahlhausen & Co.* [1990] ECR I-4827.

guarantee of origin: 'a guarantee that all products which bear it have been manufactured under the control of a single undertaking to which responsibility for their quality may be attributed'. Crucial though the origin function is, trade marks also perform an *advertising* function, and trade mark owners spend enormous sums on promoting and positioning their brands on the strength of this. One important question in *Dior* was how far the ECJ would protect this advertising function. As discussed above, a discount supermarket had obtained supplies of Dior perfumes on the parallel market, and was advertising them by means of leaflets. Dior considered that this form of advertising did not correspond to the luxurious and prestigious image of the Dior marks, and brought infringement proceedings. The referring court asked whether the rules on exhaustion were different in cases where the trade mark's advertising function is endangered by the way in which the reseller uses the mark. In particular, the national court asked about cases where a reseller's advertisements change or impair the 'mental' condition of the goods; here, the allure, prestigious image and aura of luxury which they have as a result of Dior's advertising strategy.

The preliminary position was straightforwardly dealt with. If the exclusive right under Article 5 is exhausted once the marked goods have been put on the market by the trade mark proprietor or with his consent, the same applies as regards the right to use the trade mark for the purpose of bringing to the public's attention the further commercialisation of those goods. If this were not the case, the principle of exhaustion laid down in Article 7 would be undermined. So, once trade mark rights are exhausted, a reseller, besides being free to resell those goods, is also free to make use of the trade mark in order to bring to the public's attention the further commercialisation of those goods. Article 7(2) does provide that a trade mark owner may oppose further commercialisation of products where there is a legitimate reason for doing so, 'especially where the condition of the goods is changed or impaired after they have been put on the market' – hence Dior's complaint regarding the 'mental' condition of their products. However, the ECJ considered that a balance had to be struck between the trade mark owner's legitimate interest in being protected against resellers using the mark for advertising in a manner which could damage the reputation of the trade mark, and the reseller's legitimate interest in being able to resell the goods by using advertising methods customary in that sector of trade. In a case such as *Dior*, the reseller must not act unfairly in relation to the legitimate interests of the trade mark owner, and must endeavour to prevent his advertising from affecting the value of the trade mark by detracting from the allure and prestigious image of the goods in question and from their aura of luxury. However, the fact that a reseller uses advertising methods which, though customary in his own trade sector, are different from those used by the trade mark owner does not constitute a legitimate reason for opposing that advertising, unless it is established that it seriously damages the reputation of the trade mark.[89] In this context, the ECJ also held that if a product is protected by both trade mark and copyright, the copyright may not be used to broaden the ambit of trade mark protection beyond its usual limits.[90]

In his opinion in *Dior*, Advocate General Jacobs observed that 'trade mark owners should not, as a general rule, be entitled to object to respectable advertising by respectable traders, even if it can be shown that there is some damage to the product's luxurious image by virtue of the fact that such advertising is inferior to that of selected distributors'. A reseller could not be expected to comply with the same conditions as selected distributors. However, there might be exceptional circumstances in which advertising 'positively degraded the product's image, as opposed to simply falling short of the standards of advertising imposed on selected distributors'.[91] This is essentially a question of fact for the national court. A similar case, again involving Dior products, reached the Madrid Court of Appeal. It illustrates the problem well. The defendant ran a chain of self-service wholesale stores, located in industrial estates, without a specialised perfume section, and without specialised staff. Their supplies of Dior products were advertised in catalogues alongside non-luxury products such as dog food, sugar, fresh pork bellies, peanuts and cooked ham. The Madrid court held that this created a serious and direct prejudice to the image of Dior's products. It ordered that any future advertising of such products had to be done through a separate booklet specifically dedicated to luxurious perfume products, or in a general booklet with a section absolutely differentiated from that for general products.[92]

---

[89] Case C-337/95, *Parfums Christian Dior SA* v. *Evora BV* [1997] I-ECR 6013. For criticism of this position, see the remarks of Laddie J in *Zino Davidoff SA* v. *A&G Imports Ltd. (No. 1)* [2000] Ch. 127 (para. 52): 'The words used by the Court of Justice in the *Parfums Christian Dior* case . . . if taken at face value, do appear to entitle a trade mark proprietor to use his trade marks to prevent further commercialisation by a reseller who engages in a form of business which "detracts from the image which the trade mark owner has succeeded in creating around his trade mark." In the case of luxury goods sale at low price, in large volume and through down-market outlets can be said to be the most effective way of detracting from the image of such goods. If so, the proprietor will be entitled to use his trade marks to enforce a market discipline which, as far as I can see, is contrary to the commercial objectives of the E.U. Treaty and has little to do with the proper subject matter of trade mark rights.'

[90] Case C-337/95, *Parfums Christian Dior SA* v. *Evora BV* [1997] ECR I-6013 (para. 58). Though in certain circumstances it may be possible to recover for breach of moral rights in addition to damages for trade mark infringement: *Lancôme Parfums, Beauté & Cie* v. *Kruidvat Retail BV* [2005] ETMR 26 (Court of Appeal, Amsterdam).

[91] Case C-337/95, *Parfums Christian Dior SA* v. *Evora BV* [1997] ECR I-6013 (AG General Jacobs' Opinion, 29 April 1997).

[92] *Christian Dior* v. *Makro Autoservicio Mayorista* [2003] ETMR 81. See also *Clarins Paris* v. *Supermercados Sabeco* [2005] ETMR 110.

It should be noted that this approach is not confined to use of a mark on parallel imports. In *Deenik*, the defendant's garage business specialised in the sale of second-hand BMW cars, and in the repair and maintenance of BMW cars.[93] Although authorised BMW dealers are entitled to use the BMW mark, they must meet high standards of technical quality. Deenik's business was not part of the BMW dealer network, and BMW was objecting to his use of their mark in his advertising, which contained phrases such as 'repairs and maintenance of BMWs', and 'BMW specialist'. The advertisements for second-hand BMWs were judged according to the principles on exhaustion laid down by Article 7, as interpreted in *Dior*. These were genuine BMW cars, marketed in the Community by BMW, and BMW could not prohibit the use of its mark by Deenik for the purpose of informing the public that he was a specialist in the sale of second-hand BMW cars, unless it could show a legitimate reason for opposition under Article 7(2). If the advertising gave the impression that there was a commercial connection between Deenik and BMW, in particular that Deenik was an authorised BMW dealer, this would constitute a legitimate reason for opposition.[94] However, the mere fact that a reseller derives an advantage from using the mark in advertisements which are in other respects honest and fair, perhaps because use of the mark lends an aura of quality to the reseller's business, does not constitute a legitimate reason for opposition. A reseller who genuinely has specialised in the sale of second-hand BMW cars cannot communicate such information to customers without using the BMW mark. This 'informative' use of the BMW mark is necessary to guarantee the right of resale under Article 7, and does not take unfair advantage of the mark's distinctive character or repute.

The advertisements relating to repair and maintenance of BMW cars did not fall within Article 7, because they did not affect further commercialisation of the goods. Instead they fell within Article 6, which permits a third party to use a mark in the course of trade where this is 'necessary to indicate the intended purpose of a product or service, in particular as accessories or spare parts', provided that the mark is used 'in accordance with honest practices in industrial or commercial matters'. The ECJ held that the same reasoning applied to the use of the mark, whether the use fell under Article 6 or Article 7. The proprietor could not object to a third party's use of the mark to inform the public that he carries out the repair and maintenance of such goods, unless there was a legitimate reason for opposition, such as that the advertising

---

[93]   Case C-63/97, *Bayerische Motorenwerke AG* v. *Deenik* [1999] I-ECR 905.

[94]   See, for example, *Aktiebolaget Volvo* v. *Heritage (Leicester) Ltd.* [2000] FSR 253; *Volvo Ltd* v. *DS Larm Ltd* [2000] ETMR 299 (Swedish Supreme Court). See also *Gulf International Lubricants Ltd* v. *Gulf Estonia AS* (Supreme Court, Estonia (Civil Chamber)): [2008] ETMR 26.

implied a commercial connection with the trade mark proprietor. This offers an appropriate balance between the interests of the trade mark proprietor, and the fundamental interest of free movement.[95]

Again, the question arises as to what precisely is *necessary*. In *Gillette*, the defendant made razor blades which fitted the claimant's razors, and put a sticker on its packaging stating that 'Gillette Sensor handles are compatible with this blade'. When challenged by the trade mark owner, the defendant relied on Article 6. Following a reference from the Finnish Supreme Court, the ECJ held that third-party use of a trade mark is permitted where it constitutes the only means of providing consumers with 'comprehensible and complete information as to the intended purpose of the product'. Third party use of a trade mark is 'necessary' in cases where information about the third party's product cannot in practice be communicated to the public without reference being made to the trade mark.[96] This is a matter of fact for the national court to determine, taking account of the nature of the public for which the product is intended.

The condition of 'honest use' is the expression of a duty to act fairly in relation to the legitimate interests of the trade mark owner and is similar to that imposed on a parallel importer using another's trade mark to advertise the resale of marked products.[97] The reseller must not suggest a commercial connection with the trade mark proprietor, nor affect the value of the trade mark by taking unfair advantage of its distinctive character or repute, or discredit or denigrate the mark. This is a matter of fact for the national court, which should take account of the overall presentation of the product, particularly the circumstances in which the mark is displayed, any distinction made between the mark and the third party's mark, and efforts made to ensure that consumers distinguish the third party's products from those of the trade mark owner. Following this ruling, the Finnish Supreme Court dismissed Gillette's action. The reference to Gillette's marks was the only way to inform

---

[95]   See also Case C-44/01, *Pippig Augenoptik* v. *Hartlauer* [2003] ECR I-3095. Here, a manufacturer was objecting to advertising by a competitor whose supplies had been obtained through parallel importing rather than official distribution channels. The ECJ was asked whether this could have an impact on the lawfulness of comparative advertising, for the purposes of the Comparative Advertising Directive. The Court held that it could not, stressing the important role played by parallel imports in completing the internal market, and noting 'that advertising is a very important means of creating genuine outlets for all goods and services throughout the Community' (paras. 63–4).

[96]   Case C-228/03, *Gillette Co.* v. *LA-Laboratories Ltd Oy* [2005] ECR I-2337 (paras. 34 and 35).

[97]   Case C-337/95, *Parfums Christian Dior SA* v. *Evora BV* [1997] ECR I-6013 (para. 45); Case C-63/97, *Bayerische Motorenwerke AG* v. *Deenik* [1999] ECR 905 (para. 61).

consumers about the intended purpose of LA-Laboratories' razor blades. LA-Laboratories' packaging highlighted its own brand name with prominent lettering, and the sticker simply clarified that those blades could be used with Gillette's razors also. Such use gave no impression that there would be a commercial link between these two undertakings.

6.5   GOODS IN TRANSIT ARE NOT 'ON THE MARKET'

Exhaustion cannot begin until goods are placed on the market. Important questions arise regarding the status of trade marked goods in transit through the EU.

In *Class International*, a consignment of genuine AQUAFRESH toothpaste was shipped from South Africa to the Netherlands, and placed in a customs warehouse. The trade mark owner, having been informed that the goods might be counterfeit, had the goods detained by the Dutch customs authorities under the Community legislation prohibiting the entry of counterfeit and pirated goods for customs warehousing and external transit procedures.[98] Since the goods were in fact genuine, Class International applied for their release. The question then arose as to whether the trade mark proprietor could prevent the introduction of original marked goods into the Community, as an infringement of the mark, if those goods were subject either to the external transit procedure or the customs warehousing procedure. The ECJ held that the mere physical introduction of such goods into the territory of the Community did not amount to 'importing' within the meaning of Article 5(3)(c) of the Trade Mark Directive and Article 9(2)(c) of the Trade Mark Regulation, and does not entail using the mark 'in the course of trade' within the meaning of Article 5(1) of the Directive and Article 9(1) of the Regulation. If such goods are offered for sale to a third country, the trade mark proprietor's right to control the initial marketing in the Community is not adversely affected, and there is no infringement. On the other hand, if the offering for sale (or sale) necessarily

---

[98]   Customs warehousing is a procedure enabling importers to store imported goods, even though they do not at that time know how the goods will eventually be disposed of. If they are re-exported, no import duties will be payable. If they are released for free circulation, import duties are payable at that point. The external transit procedure affects goods moving from one location to another within the Community customs territory, either to be subsequently exported (if Community goods), or re-exported (if non-Community goods) from the internal market. Goods placed under this procedure are subject to the legal fiction that they have never entered the Community territory, so are not subject to import duties or any other measures of commercial policy: Case C-383/98, *Polo/Lauren Co. LP* v. *PT Dwidua Langgeng Pratama International Freight Forwarders* [2000] ECR I-2519.

entails putting the marked goods on the market in the Community, the trade mark proprietor's exclusive rights will be adversely affected, and it may be opposed. This is the case even if the contract of sale imposes restrictions on resale of the goods. The fact that the buyer engages in parallel trade, or that the buyer is likely to put them on the market in the Community, is not sufficient. The burden of proof is on the trade mark proprietor to show that non-Community goods have been released for free circulation, or are being offered for sale in circumstances which necessarily entail putting the specific goods on the market in the Community.[99]

Similar issues arose in *Montex Holdings* v. *Diesel*. Montex makes jeans by exporting the different pieces from Ireland (where Diesel has no trade mark protection) to Poland, where they are sewn together. Montex then reimports the completed jeans into Ireland. In 2000 (before Poland joined the European Union), the German customs office held back a consignment of jeans marked DIESEL intended for delivery to Montex. They were to have been transported by lorry from the Polish factory through German territory, and were to have been in uninterrupted transit from the Polish customs office to the Dublin customs office, protected against any removal in the course of transit by a customs seal fixed to the lorry by the Polish authorities. Diesel argued that the transit through German territory amounted to an infringement of its trade mark rights because of the danger of the goods being placed on the market in the country of transit. The ECJ reiterated its stance in *Class International* – that the trade mark proprietor can oppose the offering for sale of original goods bearing the trade mark which are subject to the external transit procedure if this necessarily entails their being put on the market in the Community. Here, the mere risk that the goods could fail to reach their destination, and that they could theoretically be marketed fraudulently in Germany, was insufficient to justify prohibition by the trade mark proprietor.

Diesel had also argued (as had the German government and the Commission) that a trade mark proprietor should be able to oppose any form of transit if the goods had been manufactured in a third country in infringement of the rights which a trade mark confers on its proprietor in that state. Previous ECJ rulings on related subjects had given different signals. In *Commission* v. *France* and *Rioglass*, the ECJ considered national measures which allowed customs authorities to detain goods suspected of infringing intellectual property rights, although they were merely in transit through that member state. The Court had given primacy to free movement under Article

---

[99]   Case C-405/03, *Class International BV* v. *Colgate-Palmolive Co.* [2005] ECR 8735. For reservations regarding this approach, see Olivier Vrins and Marius Schneider, 'Trade Mark Use in Transit: EU-phony or Cacophony?' [2005] *JIPL&P* 43–50. Applied in *Eli Lilly & Co.* v. *8 pm Chemists Ltd* [2008] EWCA Civ. 24.

28, and refused to apply the Article 30 exception because the specific subject matter of a right was not affected by mere physical transportation, as opposed to marketing, of protected goods.[100] In *Polo/Lauren* and *Rolex*, the Court considered the Customs Regulation, which lays down measures for preventing the release of counterfeit and pirated goods.[101] These cases held that counterfeit or pirate goods intercepted at borders while in transit through Community territory could be detained by customs authorities in the member state of transit, the implication apparently being that mere transit may constitute the use of a sign for the purposes of trade mark law.[102] In *Montex*, however, the ECJ held that it was irrelevant whether the goods had been manufactured lawfully or unlawfully. What mattered was whether, during the external transit procedure, they had been subject to the act of a third party which necessarily entailed their being put on the market. This was not inconsistent with the *Rolex* decision respecting the Customs Regulation, because its purposes expressly include the need to prohibit the release of counterfeit goods into free circulation in the Community, and the Regulation therefore specifies the steps which customs authorities may take in relation to suspected goods. The Regulation did not, however, introduce a new criterion for ascertaining the existence of an infringement of trade mark law or determining whether there is a use of the mark liable to be prohibited because it infringes that law. It is thus clear from the *Montex* decision that trade mark infringement is defined no more broadly under the Customs Regulation than it is under the Trade Mark Directive. The judgment is 'transit-friendly', although trade mark owners are spared the prospect of shipping their goods via routes selected to avoid countries where local rights might lead to local trade mark disputes.

---

[100]   Case C-23/99, *Commission* v. *France* [2000] ECR I-7653. Case C-115/02, *Rioglass and Transremar* [2003] ECR I-12705.

[101]   Council Regulation 3295/94 laying down measures to prohibit the release for free circulation, export, re-export or entry for a suspensive procedure of counterfeit and pirated goods [1994] OJ L 341/8 amended in 1999. This was replaced by Council Regulation 1383/2003 concerning customs action against goods suspected of infringing certain intellectual property rights and the measures to be taken against goods found to have infringed such rights, which came into force on 1 July 2004 [2003] OJ L 196/7.

[102]   Case C-383/98, *Polo/Lauren Co. LP* v. *PT Dwidua Langgeng Pratama International Freight Forwarders* [2000] ECR I-2519. Case C-60/02, *Montres Rolex and Others* [2004] ECR I-651.

6.6 EXHAUSTION: NATIONAL, COMMUNITY-WIDE OR INTERNATIONAL?

One controversial issue is whether the current principle of Community-wide exhaustion is appropriate. The original regime of national exhaustion has been superseded. A holder of national intellectual property rights may not prohibit further commercialisation of goods which have been put on the market *in the Community* by the right holder or with his consent. This regime was devised to ensure the free movement of goods within the EU, and to prevent national barriers to trade. It therefore permits a right holder to prevent importation into the Community of goods marketed for the first time *outside* the Community, unless consent has been given. It is argued that trade mark holders (in particular) take advantage of this to block parallel imports of branded goods into the Community, allowing them to maintain higher prices within the EU than prevail in the rest of the world. Right holders can thus partition the Community-wide market from the rest of the world market, and prevent parallel importers from operating to level out differences in the market. This is precisely the state of affairs that the Community has been anxious to prevent *within* its boundaries. A regime of international exhaustion – where sales anywhere in the world would exhaust the right – would (it is argued) prevent such behaviour, and forestall accusations of protectionism and hypocrisy at differential treatment. The Commission has therefore come under some pressure to propose changes to the exhaustion regime. Others contend that the effects of such a regime on pricing would be small or negligible, but would have other undesirable consequences: on product quality and availability, for example.

Early responses to the issue of international exhaustion
The nature and extent of the exhaustion regime has not always been clear. In an early case, *Polydor v. Harlequin*, the ECJ considered a free trade agreement (FTA) which was almost identically worded to the EEC Treaty. Some case law regarding the exhaustion of rights had been developed in the context of the Treaty provisions, but the Court refused to transpose this to the FTA, reasoning that their purposes were quite different. The FTA merely made provision for the unconditional abolition of certain restrictions on trade between the Community and Portugal, whereas the EEC Treaty sought to unite national markets into a single market reproducing as closely as possible the conditions of a domestic market. It followed that, in the context of an FTA, restrictions on trade in goods might be justified on the ground of the protection of industrial and commercial property in situations in which their justification would not be possible within the Community.[103]

---

[103]   Case 270/80, *Polydor Ltd v. Harlequin Record Shops Ltd* [1982] ECR 329.

The issue first arose in the EEA context in *Mag Instrument*, where the holder of the Norwegian trade mark for Maglite flashlights was objecting to parallel imports from the United States for sale in Norway. Article 2 of Protocol 28 to the EEA requires contracting parties to provide for 'such exhaustion of intellectual property rights as laid down in Community law', including ECJ rulings given before the date of the Agreement. The ECJ had not at that time dealt with the question of whether Article 7(1) of the Trade Mark Directive prohibited individual member states from allowing for international exhaustion, although cases on the subject were pending. The EFTA Court noted that 'the principle of international exhaustion is in the interest of free trade and competition and thus in the interest of consumers'. It was also compatible with the guarantee of origin, since the imports were of genuine goods marketed by the trade mark proprietor. The EFTA Court concluded that although national exhaustion was precluded, international exhaustion was not. The Commission (and several governments) had argued that permitting individual states to provide for international exhaustion would lead to internal disparities in the Community, so the same principle had to apply to all member states, and for the EEA. The EFTA Court rejected this argument in so far as it concerned the EFTA states, since, unlike the EC Treaty, the EEA Agreement does not establish a customs union but a free trade area. It therefore concluded that it was for the EFTA states to decide whether to introduce or maintain the principle of international exhaustion of rights.[104]

The approach in *Silhouette*, and its aftermath

Shortly afterwards, the ECJ ruled on the question in *Silhouette International v. Hartlauer*. Silhouette is an Austrian company which manufactures expensive high-fashion spectacles. Hartlauer sold spectacles in many outlets, and was known primarily for its low prices. Silhouette considered that Hartlauer's retail practices would be harmful to the Silhouette image, and did not supply to them. The case concerned a consignment of 21,000 out of date Silhouette frames, sold, as Silhouette thought, for resale only in Bulgaria or states of the former Soviet Union. Hartlauer later acquired them and offered them for sale in Austria. Silhouette sought an order prohibiting their marketing, arguing that they had not been sold in the EEA by Silhouette or with its consent. Hartlauer

---

[104]   E-2/97 *Mag Instrument Inc.* v. *California Trading Co.* [1997] EFTA CR 127. Article 65(2) of the Agreement on the European Economic Area of 2 May 1992 (OJ 1994 L 1, p. 3) provides that specific provisions and arrangements in the EEA concerning intellectual, industrial and commercial property are contained in Annex XVII to that Agreement. Point 4 of Annex XVII refers to the Trade Mark Directive, and adapts Article 7(1) by replacing the term 'in the Community' with the words 'in a Contracting Party'.

denied being bound by any restriction on resale or importation, and argued that Silhouette's rights had been exhausted. Silhouette further argued that the question of exhaustion was irrelevant since the frames had been first put on the market outside the EEA. The Austrian court referred a number of questions to the ECJ. These were, essentially, whether Community law required member states to provide only for Community-wide exhaustion, or whether member states might (or must) provide for international exhaustion.

The Trade Mark Directive does not explicitly preclude member states from adopting a principle of international exhaustion. Did it leave it open to an individual member state to choose to adopt it? Advocate General Jacobs argued that it did not. If some member states adopt a principle of international exhaustion while others do not, there will be barriers to trade within the internal market which it was precisely the object of the Directive to remove. Although acknowledging the policy considerations, AG Jacobs dismissed them:

> There is of course a powerful argument based on the concern for free trade at the international level. To some commentators the exclusion of international exhaustion will appear protectionist and therefore harmful. Commercial policy considerations may however be more complex than they allow for . . . In any event it is no part of the Court's function to seek to evaluate such policy considerations.[105]

Price competition and other benefits to consumers which might follow from international exhaustion had to be set against the threat to the integrity of the internal market. He therefore concluded that Article 7(1) of the Directive precludes member states from adopting the principle of international exhaustion. The ECJ agreed. The Trade Mark Directive embodies a complete harmonisation of the rules relating to the rights conferred by a trade mark, and cannot be interpreted as leaving the member states free to provide for a principle of international exhaustion. Unless international exhaustion was precluded, the functioning of the internal market could not be safeguarded.[106]

The Court reiterated the *Silhouette* approach to international exhaustion in *Sebago*, a decision which also repeated that consent within the meaning of Article 7(1) must relate to each individual item of the product in respect of

---

[105]   Case C-355/96, *Silhouette International Schmied GmbH & Co. KG* v. *Hartlauer Handelsgesellschaft mbH* [1998] ECR 4799 (Opinion of AG Jacobs, para. 51).

[106]   Case C-355/96, *Silhouette International Schmied GmbH & Co. KG* v. *Hartlauer Handelsgesellschaft mbH* [1998] ECR 4799. Predictably, the case provoked differing views amongst commentators as to the appropriate policy. For two notably thoughtful responses, see William R. Cornish, 'Trade Marks: Portcullis for the EEA?' [1998] *EIPR* 172–7; David Edward, 'Trade Marks, Descriptions of Origin and the Internal Market: The Stephen Stewart Memorial Lecture 2000' [2001] *IPQ* 135–45.

which exhaustion is pleaded; that is, the actual goods involved in the parallel import, as opposed to goods of that type, merely.[107] The ECJ has likewise confirmed that the same approach prevails for copyright works (the distribution right), under the Information Society Directive.[108]

Nevertheless, hostility to the principles underlying the *Silhouette* decision remained, and the issue continued to be tested. In a UK case, *Zino Davidoff* v. *A & G Imports*, Laddie J attempted to circumvent the position regarding international exhaustion by using the notion of implied consent.[109] Davidoff was objecting to sales within the EEA of its products originally sold (at much cheaper wholesale prices) for the Asian market. Laddie J acknowledged that Community law (*Silhouette* and *Sebago*) allowed the trade mark proprietor to retain the ability to prevent the importation of goods marked with his registered trade mark into the Community, but stressed that the proprietor also had the right to consent to such importation. Here, therefore, he regarded the case as turning on the question of fact as to whether Davidoff had consented to importation. Nothing in either *Silhouette* or *Sebago* had made clear the ways in which a proprietor could effectively object to this. Laddie J considered that there was no presumption that the trade mark proprietor should be taken to object to unfettered distribution of his goods sold on the open market outside the EEA unless express consent had been given. Davidoff had been free to place the goods on the market with effective restraint on their further sale, but had not done so. Purchasers in the chain of distribution were therefore free to market Davidoff's goods wherever they liked, including within the EEA, and Davidoff was to be treated as having consented to this. Laddie J stated that, to avoid this conclusion, full and explicit contractual restrictions would have had to be imposed on the purchasers at the time of the purchase. He criticised the policy prevailing in the Community:

> Thus the effect of the Silhouette case is to enable a trade mark proprietor to exclude the goods from the E.E.A., whatever mark they carry. The only option is for the importer to sell the goods with no trade mark at all. In many cases, and particularly where high margin fashion goods are concerned, this will make the goods virtually unsaleable. In my view this illustrates how the *Silhouette* case has bestowed on a trade mark owner a parasitic right to interfere with the distribution of goods which bears little or no relationship to the proper function of the trade mark right. It is

---

[107]   Case C-173/98, *Sebago Inc. and Ancienne Maison Dubois & Fils SA* v. *G-B Unic SA* [1999] ECR I-4103.

[108]   Art. 4(2) Directive 2001/29 on Copyright and related rights in the Information Society [2001] OJ L 1767/10. See Case C-479/04, *Laserdisken ApS* v. *Kulturministeriet* [2006] ECR 8089.

[109]   *Zino Davidoff SA* v. *A & G Imports Ltd (No. 1)* [2000] Ch. 127.

difficult to believe that a properly informed legislature intended such a result, even if it is the proper construction of Article 7(1) of the Directive.[110]

Also controversially, Laddie J was dismissive of Davidoff's complaints that the removal of its product codes had impaired the 'mental condition' of its goods (although he did not consider *Loendersloot*), and refused to grant Davidoff's request for summary judgment. He ordered a reference to the ECJ on the issues of implied consent and the scope of Article 7(2).[111]

The ECJ focused again on the nature of the trade mark owner's consent. Because Articles 5 to 7 of the Trade Mark Directive embody a complete harmonisation of the rules relating to the rights conferred by a trade mark, the concept of consent was no longer a matter for the national laws of the member states, and it was for the Court to supply a uniform interpretation of it. Article 5 gives the trade mark proprietor exclusive rights, including the right to prevent third parties from importing marked goods without consent. Article 7(1) contains an exception to that rule, by providing that where goods have been put on the market within the EEA by the proprietor or with his consent, the proprietor's rights are exhausted. Consent is therefore the decisive factor in the extinction of the exclusive right, and must be expressed in a way which demonstrates unequivocally that the proprietor has renounced his rights. An express statement of consent will normally be sufficient, but consent can, in some cases, be inferred. However, consent must be expressed positively and the factors taken into consideration in finding implied consent must unequivocally demonstrate that the trade mark proprietor has renounced any intention to enforce his exclusive rights. It is for the trader alleging consent to prove it and not for the trade mark proprietor to demonstrate its absence. Implied consent cannot be inferred from the mere silence of the trade mark proprietor,

---

[110] *Zino Davidoff SA* v. *A & G Imports Ltd. (No. 1)* [2000] Ch. 127, at 143. Extrajudicially, Mr Justice Laddie has been quoted as saying, 'I think that my Davidoff decision has been somewhat misunderstood. I know that there are some people who think that it was an attack on the jurisprudence of the European Court of Justice and in particular the decision in *Silhouette*, which said that the Trade Mark Directive allowed trade mark owners to prohibit parallel import from outside the European Union. I am afraid this is not what my judgment was saying. I have little doubt that the decision of the European Court of Justice on the construction of the Trade Mark Directive was right. My objection, as one believing in the importance of a free market, was to the European legislature because it had passed legislation which seemed to allow trade mark owners to split up the international market that way. In other words, I was hostile to international exhaustion, but I do not believe the European Court of Justice was wrong in construing the Trade Mark Directive in the way it did.' [2003] *EIPR* 528–36 at 534.

[111] A number of national courts, including the Scottish Court of Session, adopted a different approach to implied consent. See Robert Swift, '*Davidoff*: Scottish Court Declines to Follow English Ruling on Parallel Imports' [2000] *EIPR* 376–8.

or from the fact that the goods do not carry any warning that they may not be
marketed within the EEA, or from the fact that they were sold without contractual restrictions, or from the fact that the law governing the contract includes
a right of resale in the absence of such reservations. A rule of national law
which proceeded upon the mere silence of the trade mark proprietor would not
recognise implied consent but rather deemed consent. This would not meet the
need for consent positively expressed required by Community law.[112]

In *Peak Holding* v. *Axolin-Elinor*, the trade mark proprietor had offered
clothing from old collections in its Danish sister store, but some remained
unsold even after cut-price sales.[113] These goods were sold to a French
company, Peak Holding said, on condition that they were not to be resold in
European countries other than Russia and Slovenia, with the exception of 5%
of the total quantity, which could be sold in France. The goods were acquired
by a Swedish company, which contested the existence of such a restriction,
and submitted that, in any event, it had no knowledge of it when it purchased
the consignment. The ECJ had to consider whether by importing goods with a
view to sale in the EEA, or by offering them for sale in the EEA, the trade
mark proprietor's rights had been exhausted, even if the goods were not actually sold. It held that they had not. Such acts do not amount to putting the
goods on the market within the meaning of Article 7(1), because they do not
transfer to third parties the right to dispose of the goods bearing the trade
mark, and therefore do not allow the proprietor to realise the economic value
of the trade mark. Peak Holding had also argued that a sale subject to a stipulation that trade mark rights would be retained did not exhaust those rights,
and that if the stipulation were not complied with the goods would not have
not been put on the market with the trade mark proprietor's consent, so that
exhaustion should not supervene. The Court did not agree. Exhaustion is a
legal matter, and a right is exhausted following a sale by the proprietor.
Exhaustion is not subject (additionally) to the proprietor's consent to further
marketing. So the right is exhausted even if the goods are resold in breach of
a prohibition, and the trade mark proprietor must rely on contractual remedies.[114]

Parallel importers have sought to rely on the trade mark proprietor's

---

[112]   Joined Cases C-414/99 to C-416/99, *Zino Davidoff* v. *A & G Imports* [2001]
ECR I-8691. For comment see Dina Kallay, '*Levi Strauss* v *Tesco*: At a Difficult
Juncture of Competition, IP and Free Trade Policies' [2002] *European Competition
Law Rev.* 193–9.

[113]   Case C-16/03, *Peak Holding* v. *Axolin-Elinor* [2004] ECR I-11313.

[114]   This is problematic for those wishing to sell their goods outside the
Community, who will put themselves at risk unless they go to the trouble of transfer-
ring the goods to a party outside the Community. The judgment has been criticised for

implied consent in a number of other situations, although these have not yet been considered by the ECJ. In *Mastercigars*, the parallel importer had argued that since the trade mark proprietor allowed individual sales in Cuba of $25,000 worth of cigars, a level absurdly high for individual consumption, it must therefore be aware that purchasers would sell on the cigars. At first instance, the English High Court held that the $25,000 limit on individual sales did point to consent to the subsequent commercial disposal of the cigars in the hands of the purchaser, or at least the turning of a blind eye, but that did not amount to proof that the trade mark proprietor had unequivocally renounced its rights within the meaning of the *Davidoff* decision. But the Court of Appeal held that 'unequivocal' did not refer to the standard of proof. 'Unequivocal' signified that an act which could be seen either as consistent with consent, or consistent with its absence, would not suffice. What mattered was what was really happening, the actual knowledge and actual, practical control or the right of control by the trade mark owner. Here the trade mark proprietor had unequivocally consented to the sale of the cigar consignments in Europe, by permitting Cuban retailers to sell commercial quantities of cigars to foreigners, and providing them with documentation so that they could go through Customs and take them home to sell. That behaviour led to the conclusion that consent to the use of the trade marks on the purchaser's home market had been given, and this applied as much to purchases by Europeans for sale within Europe as it did elsewhere.[115] In *Honda* v. *Neesam*, the parallel importer had obtained supplies of Honda motorbikes, which he claimed had been bought from authorised Honda dealers outside the EEA. He submitted that the consent of a Honda subsidiary or dealer to importation amounted to the consent of Honda, the trade mark proprietor. Honda dealers were expressly prohibited from selling their bikes outside their respective territories. The English High Court held that a dealer which had exceeded its authority or broken its contract by consenting to import into the EEA could not saddle Honda with the consequences of that breach. Neesam also argued that Honda not only connived at parallel imports, but actively facilitated it. It was held that even assuming that there had been knowledge by Honda that the bikes were being exported, such knowledge did not amount to consent by Honda. A failure to police restrictions could not amount to the unequivocal renunciation of

---

its interpretation of 'consent' in such a context: 'It is indeed tantamount to saying that even if a trade mark proprietor does (explicitly) refuse to "consent" to the sale of goods bearing the trade mark in the EEA his trade mark rights will still be exhausted just because the contract of sale is concluded with an operator "established in the EEA" '. See Nicolas Clarembeaux and Thierry Van Innis, 'EU: Trade Marks – Exhaustion without Consent' [2005] *EIPR* N65–6.

[115] *Mastercigars Direct Ltd* v. *Hunters & Frankau Ltd* [2007] EWCA Civ. 176.

rights to import.[116] It has also been held that the presence of the CE mark does not indicate consent to marketing within the EEA. CE marking indicates that a product has been formally approved for sale in the EU under the relevant regulatory and approval regimes and applies to countries of the EEA. It does not indicate the consent of the trade mark proprietor to the placing of the products on the market in the EU.[117]

A parallel importer cannot avoid liability simply by setting up a web site outside the EEA, if it is directed at EEA customers. In *Sony* v. *Pacific Game Technology*, Pacific was incorporated and had its registered office in Hong Kong. It supplied Sony PlayStation games consoles marked 'FOR SALE AND USE IN JAPAN ONLY' to customers in the UK. The Court noted that: the web site was in English, with English as its default language; prices were quoted in pounds sterling, with promotions in sterling also; PlayStation manuals were available on the web site in various European languages including English; the web site featured testimonials from UK purchasers; Pacific ran a free shipping promotion until the day before the PlayStationPortable Console was launched in Europe; a spurious EC Certificate of Conformity was included with the product shipped to Europe. It was held that the offer for sale had taken place not in Hong Kong but in the EEA, and the fact that the offer to sell was made via the intermediary of a web site did not mean that the offer had not been made within the EEA. The judge observed: 'it would make no sense if intellectual property rights in the EEA could be avoided merely by setting up a website outside the EEA crafted to sell within it. Were the acts of which complaint is made to have been committed physically within the EEA they would unarguably have been infringing acts. I cannot see how the electronic intermediary of a website which focussed at least in part on the EEA would make them any less so.'[118]

Note that the decision in *Davidoff* does not prevent the application of competition law to parallel imports from outside the EEA. In *Javico* v. *Yves St Laurent Parfums*, the parties had entered into distribution agreements which

---

[116]   *Honda Motor Company Limited* v. *Neesam* [2006] EWHC 1051 (Ch.). Summary judgment was granted against three defendants. For the trial of the action against the fourth defendant, see *Honda Motor Co. Ltd* v. *Neesam and Others* [2008] EWHC 338 (Ch.).

[117]   *Roche Products Ltd.* v. *Kent Pharmaceuticals Ltd* [2006] EWCA Civ. 1775.

[118]   *KK Sony Computer Entertainment* v. *Pacific Game Technology* [2006] EWHC (Ch.) 2509. Sony pressed for full judgment rather than summary judgment, hoping to make enforcement of its rights in Hong Kong easier. One week after the judgment, Pacific announced it would be shutting down. The decision was followed in *Independiente Ltd* v. *Music Trading On-Line (HK) Ltd* [2007] EWHC 533 (Ch.), a case involving CD WOW!, the popular online budget CD and DVD retailer based in Hong Kong.

committed Javico to sell YSL products only in Russia and the Ukraine, or in Slovenia. YSL discovered the relevant products in the UK and elsewhere in the EEA, so terminated the contracts.[119] The referring French court asked whether the contractual prohibition was contrary to Article 85(1) (now Article 81(1)). The ECJ focused on whether the prohibition restricted competition within the common market, and whether it might affect trade between member states to a significant extent. This would be assessed with reference to the position and the importance of the parties on the market for the products concerned. Here, the territorial stipulations were construed not as intending to exclude parallel imports and marketing of the contractual product within the Community, but as designed to enable the producer to penetrate a particular market outside the Community. So the agreement's object was not to restrict competition within the common market, nor was it capable of affecting, as such, trade between member states. It might, though, have an effect on competition within the common market, within the meaning of Article 85(1). This was a matter for the national court to determine, by looking at the agreement in its economic and legal context (in the usual way). Such an effect might be found if the relevant product market within the EU is oligopolistic, or if there is a significant difference in the price of the product inside and outside the EU. But intra-Community trade cannot be appreciably affected if the products intended for markets outside the Community account for only a very small percentage of the total market for those products in the EU. In such cases, Community competition rules do not apply. In addition, given *Davidoff*'s insistence that consent to marketing within the EU must be positively expressed before exhaustion occurs, there is in practice less need for the trade mark proprietor to have recourse to restrictions on distribution in these cases. There is also a risk of infringing Article 82 by enforcing an intellectual property right in circumstances which involve 'abusive conduct', for instance if prices within the EU are considered excessive when compared to those outside the EU.[120]

The burden of proof

If goods have been placed on the market for the first time outside the EEA, then a parallel importer must show the trade mark owner's consent to subsequent sale in the EEA. But if there is a dispute between them as to the facts, further issues arise. As a matter of policy, it is not straightforward to decide who should bear the burden of proof when determining whether trade mark rights have been exhausted. Normally, one would expect the person relying on

---

[119] Case C-306/96, *Javico International* v. *Yves Saint Laurent Parfums SA* [1998] ECR I-1983.

[120] See Case T-198/98, *Micro Leader Business* v. *Commission* [1999] ECR II-3989 (para. 56).

a defence to prove the conditions for its application, which would suggest that the parallel importer be required to show consent. But if parallel importers have the full burden of proving exhaustion, they will have to reveal their sources. The trade mark proprietor could then use this information to patch up leaky distribution systems, perhaps even bringing court actions for this purpose alone, though knowing full well that the goods had been offered for sale within the EEA. Under those circumstances, there is a significant risk that the trade mark proprietor will use the trade mark to partition national markets. Also, although parallel importers are likely to be able to show how the goods came into their hands, they will not be able to compel their supplier to reveal the rest of the distribution chain.

The *Van Doren* case offers a characteristic set of facts. Van Doren is the exclusive distributor for Stüssy clothing within Germany. Stüssy clothing is sold all over the world, without any indication as to where it may be marketed. The defendant sold legitimate Stüssy clothing in Germany, which it had not obtained from Van Doren. Van Doren sued for trade mark infringement in German courts, alleging that the clothes sold by the defendant had come from the United States, and were imported into the EEA without the trade mark owner's consent. The defendant alleged that the trade mark owner's rights had been exhausted, claiming that they had purchased the goods within the EC, and that the goods had been sold with the trade mark proprietor's consent. Appreciating the difficulties inherent in the situation, the Bundesgerichtshof asked the ECJ whether a possible solution would be to impose the burden of proof on the parallel importer only if the manufacturer had first used reasonable means to distinguish goods which had been marketed in the EEA by him or with his consent, from goods which had been marketed outside the EEA. The Court held that a rule of evidence which required the parallel importer to prove the conditions for exhaustion was consistent with Articles 5 and 7 of the Directive, and with *Davidoff*. However, the need to ensure the free movement of goods, enshrined in Articles 28 EC and 30 EC, might mean that the rule had to be qualified. Accordingly, if a parallel importer establishes that there is a real risk of partitioning of national markets if he bears the burden of proof, particularly where the trade mark proprietor markets his products in the EEA using an exclusive distribution system, it is for the proprietor of the trade mark to establish that the products were initially placed on the market outside the EEA by him or with his consent. If such evidence is adduced, it is for the third party to prove the consent of the trade mark proprietor to subsequent marketing of the products in the EEA.[121]

---

[121]   Case C-244/00, *Van Doren + Q GmbH* v. *Lifestyle Sports + Sportswear*

International exhaustion and other intellectual property rights

Subsequent Community legislation in other fields of intellectual property specifically prohibits international exhaustion. The Computer Programs Directive has followed this course, as has the Rental Right Directive, the Regulation on Plant Variety Rights, the Database Directive, the Designs Directive and Community Design Regulation, and the Information Society Directive.[122] It would seem very unlikely that any future harmonisation initiatives (such as the Community patent) would adopt a different course.

Continuing policy challenges

In the aftermath of *Silhouette*, the question of exhaustion of trade mark rights again became an important political issue. Member states and stakeholders were divided in their views. Those critical of the prevailing Community exhaustion regime argued that it acted as a barrier to parallel trade, reducing competition, and allowing the maintenance of artificially high prices within the EU. On this view, trade marks are there to protect the consumer, and not to give the trade mark holder an element of monopoly within the product market. Thus, trade mark law should be directed primarily at ensuring that marks function as a guarantee of origin, and should not be used as an instrument of market control and segmentation. Others argued that Community exhaustion was necessary for the promotion of investment in innovation and in high-quality goods, because it offers a higher economic reward to firms that invest in the quality or style of their products. This incentive helps to maintain the range of products and the quality of goods and associated service that EU consumers expect. Manufacturers and authorised dealers may invest considerable sums in goodwill of various sorts, and parallel importers 'free-ride' on this.[123] If products

---

Handelsgesellschaft mbH [2003] ECR I-3051. See Christian Rosner, 'Trade Mark Exhaustion' [2002] *EIPR* 604–7; Peter Dyrberg, 'For EEA Exhaustion to Apply, Who Has to Prove the Marketing of the Trade Marked Goods in the EEA – the Trade Mark Owner or the Defendant' [2004] *EIPR* 81–4.

[122] Dir. 91/250 on the legal protection of computer programs [1991] OJ L 122/42, Art. 4(c). Dir. 2006/115 on rental right and lending right and on certain rights related to copyright in the field of intellectual property (codified version) [2006] OJ L 376/28 (covering recordings of performances, audio recordings, films and recordings of broadcasts), Art. 9. Reg. 2100/94 on Community plant variety rights [1994] OJ L 227/1, Art. 16. Dir. 96/9 on the legal protection of databases [1996] OJ L 077/20, Arts. 5(c) and 7(2)(b). Directive 98/71 on the legal protection of designs [1998] OJ L 289/28, Art. 15. Reg. 6/2002 on Community designs [2002] OJ L 3/1, Art. 21. Dir. 2001/29 on the harmonisation of certain aspects of copyright and related rights in the information society [2001] OJ L 167/10, Art. 4(2).

[123] NERA report, 'The Economic Consequences of the Choice of Regime of Exhaustion in the Area of Trademarks': 2.4.3. http://ec.europa.eu/internal_market/indprop/docs/tm/report_en.pdf.

differ between member states (most obviously, difference in packaging and labelling due to language or regulatory differences, but also, perhaps, because of different national preferences), consumer confusion is possible, potentially undermining the guarantee of origin. Relevant after-sales services and guarantees may be unavailable for parallel imports. A link between parallel imports and counterfeiting is often alleged.[124] It was also argued that a change to international exhaustion would reduce the value of intellectual property and put European companies at a disadvantage *vis-à-vis* countries applying other regimes.

The Commission responded by ordering a report from external consultants (the 'NERA report') on the impact of any change, and held hearings for representatives of interested parties and member states. The NERA report indicated that although the short-term effects of a change to international exhaustion appeared small in macroeconomic terms, the longer-term dynamic consequences were likely to be both more important and more difficult to predict. It indicated that the issue of exhaustion is very complex and may have an impact not only on prices, but also on product quality, product availability, after-sales services (guarantees), employment, distribution agreements, market segmentation and so on. The study showed that the impact of a change in the existing Community exhaustion regime would have different consequences in different sectors, perhaps even on different products within a single sector. The study calculated that the lowering effect on prices would range from 'negligible' (soft drinks) to 'small' (around 1% for footwear, musical recordings, motor cars) or 'moderate' (around 2% for consumer electronics).[125] The dynamic effects of any change were hard to predict, perhaps offsetting any benefits, or perhaps causing more fundamental changes in business models as trade mark holders reacted to the new regime.

Following discussions with interested parties, the Commission produced a working document, setting out some of the options if a change to the exhaustion regime were to be implemented. Many of these raised difficulties. The introduction of a full international exhaustion scheme for trade marks would have required a change to both the Directive (for national marks) and the Regulation (for the Community mark).[126]

---

[124] Though it is not always substantiated. Christopher Stothers, *Parallel Trade in Europe* (Oxford: Hart Publishing, 2007), 22–3.

[125] NERA report, 'The Economic Consequences of the Choice of Regime of Exhaustion in the Area of Trademarks', table 6.10.

[126] Note that the Commission's original proposal for the Trade Mark Directive provided for international exhaustion, but it was later persuaded that Community-wide exhaustion was appropriate for both the Directive and the Regulation. Its anxiety was that third countries would not reciprocate, thus allowing parallel imports of goods

Politically, approval for neither change could be guaranteed, raising the unwelcome prospect of divergent regimes for different types of mark. The possibility of introducing international exhaustion for trade marks only was considered, but this too had drawbacks. Many products would be covered by a number of IP rights, allowing manufacturers to rely on non-trade mark rights to prevent parallel imports. It would also be possible to apply different exhaustion regimes to different sectors, either by introducing international exhaustion only for specific products, or, by introducing a principle of international exhaustion subject to exclusions for specific products. Identifying these sectors and products would, in practice, be extremely contentious. Another consideration was whether to introduce international exhaustion unilaterally, on the basis of bilateral agreements with third countries, or on the basis of a multilateral agreement (in the context of the WTO, for example). Unilateral international exhaustion would have been the easiest to implement, but offered the highest risk of disadvantage to EU trade. Negotiation of bilateral or multilateral agreements inevitably entails legal and political complexity.[127]

In May 2000, the Commission announced that for the moment it had decided not to propose any change to the current Community-wide exhaustion regime. It noted that new technologies and e-commerce were likely to give consumers access to a greater choice of products at lower prices, regardless of a change of exhaustion regime. The future enlargement of the EU would, it was thought, also have a considerable impact on the Union's internal market by lowering consumer prices. In any event, the NERA report had shown that a change to international exhaustion would not lead to a significant fall in consumer prices. It was thought likely that a number of member states would resist any change, possibly leading to two different schemes, creating confusion in the marketplace. The EU exhaustion policy had been developed to foster the integration of the single market, and was supported by other legislation and policy initiatives to ensure a certain uniformity throughout the EU. The same conditions did not prevail at the international level, and therefore an international exhaustion policy might put EU companies at a competitive disadvantage. The Commission's decision was said to be strongly supported by only four member states, eight regretting the decision and emphasising the need for change, the rest reserving their position.[128] Nevertheless, stubborn

---

marketed in the Community to be blocked. For more, see Christopher Stothers, 'Parallel Trade and Free Trade Agreements' [2006] *JIPL&P* 578–92.

[127]   'Exhaustion of Trade Mark Rights': working document from the Commission Services: http://ec.europa.eu/internal_market/indprop/docs/tm/exhaust_en.pdf.

[128]   Communiqué from Commissioner Bolkestein on the issue of exhaustion of trade mark rights, 7 June 2000: http://ec.europa.eu/internal_market/indprop/docs/tm/comexhaust_en.pdf.

criticism of the Commission's position remained, on the grounds that it protected European manufacturers from parallel trade, rather than opening up markets and generating competition which would benefit consumers.[129]

In a further working paper in 2003, the Commission considered possible abuses of trade mark rights within the EU in the context of Community exhaustion. It studied competition cases involving alleged abuses of trade marks, and sent questionnaires to over 60 interested parties, chiefly organisations representing rights holders, consumers and parallel traders asking for their experiences of abuses. There were three broad categories of possible abuses: problems relating to selective distribution systems; problems of abusive refusal to license trade marks; and problems of trade mark infringement. The Commission concluded that existing competition law and trade mark law provide an effective means of preventing restrictions on the free movement of goods within the Community, whilst protecting the legitimate rights of the trade mark holder.[130] Although such a response was understandable, given the complexity of the issues and the political practicalities, criticism persists. Similar considerations pertain at international levels. The issue of exhaustion of IP rights under the GATT is somewhat unclear, although it seems unlikely that a doctrine of exhaustion between WTO members is required. Article 6 of TRIPS explicitly disclaims any effect on the issue of exhaustion, although the Doha Declaration reaffirmed that members were free to establish exhaustion regimes of their choice.[131] Although the international climate is on the whole favourable to free trade, some private barriers remain stubbornly in place. The policy challenges are considerable, given the strength and diversity of the various interest groups.

---

[129]   See 'Draft Report on the Problem of the Exhaustion of Trademark Rights' by the Committee on Legal Affairs and the Internal Market (Rapporteur: Hans-Peter Mayer). It advocated 'a properly thought out transition from Community-wide exhaustion to international exhaustion' and called on the Commission to submit legislative proposals to this effect: Parliament doc. PE 298.407(19). The draft report itself was heavily criticised, and the final report was substantially changed, to ask for a much more limited response from the Commission.

[130]   Commission staff working paper, *Possible Abuses of Trade Mark Rights within the EU in the Context of Community Exhaustion* SEC(2003) 575: http://ec.europa.eu/internal_market/indprop/docs/tm/sec-2003-575_en.pdf.

[131]   TRIPS, Art. 6: 'For the purposes of dispute settlement under this Agreement . . . nothing in this Agreement shall be used to address the issue of the exhaustion of intellectual property rights'. For further detail and discussion, see Christopher Stothers, 'Parallel Trade and Free Trade Agreements' [2006] *JIPL&P* 578–92.

6.7 COMPETITION LAW AND INTELLECTUAL PROPERTY

As has been discussed, national intellectual property rights are territorial and exclusive.[132] This makes them very likely to partition markets, and tension with competition law is predictable. The ECJ has stressed repeatedly that intellectual property rights are not *per se* anti-competitive. However, the way in which they are exercised may be restricted, if they are used to frustrate the Community's rules on competition. The Commission enforces Community competition law, as do national competition authorities (where appropriate). National courts may apply Community competition law in the course of litigation.

There are two central provisions in the Treaty which are used to control anti-competitive behaviour considered incompatible with the common market.

Article 81(1) (formerly Article 85(1)) prohibits:

> all agreements between undertakings, decisions by associations of undertakings and concerted practices which may affect trade between Member States and which have as their object or effect the prevention, restriction or distortion of competition within the common market

unless they fall within the provision for exemption under Article 81(3).

Article 82 (formerly Article 86) states that:

> Any abuse by one or more undertakings of a dominant position within the common market or in a substantial part of it shall be prohibited as incompatible with the common market in so far as it may affect trade between Member States.

There is no provision for exemption under Article 82.

The potential clash between intellectual property rights and competition rules was observed early on. In *Consten and Grundig*, the German manufacturer appointed Consten its exclusive distributor in France. Consten agreed to take minimum quantities of Grundig's electronic products, and to provide publicity and post-sales service, including repairs. Consten also agreed not to sell products made by Grundig's competitors, and to refrain from selling Grundig products outside France. Grundig in turn agreed that it would not supply its products to other French distributors and imposed a prohibition on export on all its other distributors. This contractual attempt to secure absolute territorial protection was reinforced by an agreement allowing Consten to

---

132   See above section 6.2.2. Early case law: the distinction between existence and exercise of rights.

register the Grundig trade mark, GINT, so that Consten could object to unauthorised sales within France. A parallel importer nonetheless obtained supplies, which it sold to retailers in France at prices undercutting Consten's. Consten's legal action in the French courts led the Commission, and ultimately the ECJ, to examine the exclusive distribution contract. The Court upheld the Commission's finding that the agreement breached Article 81. The Court also noted that Consten's right to register the GINT trade mark was made possible only by virtue of an agreement with Grundig. The purpose of the registration was to deter parallel imports, and thus to restrict competition. This agreement too was therefore held to be unlawful, because it pursued the same object as the exclusive distribution agreement. This finding did not affect the grant of the national trade mark right, but merely limited its exercise to the extent necessary to give effect to the Article 81 prohibition.[133]

For competition law purposes, as it does in the context of the free movement of goods, the Court distinguishes between the *existence* of an intellectual property right (protected by Article 222) and its *exercise*:

> In the sphere of provisions relating to the free movement of products, prohibitions and restrictions on imports justified on the grounds of protection of industrial and commercial property are allowed by Article 36, subject to the express condition that they 'shall not, however, constitute a means of arbitrary discrimination or a disguised restriction on trade between Member States'. Article 36, although it appears in the chapter of the Treaty dealing with quantitative restrictions on trade between Member States, is based on a principle equally applicable to the question of competition, in the sense that even if the rights recognized by the legislation of a Member State on the subject of industrial and commercial property are not affected, so far as their existence is concerned, by Articles 85 and 86 of the Treaty, their exercise may still fall under the prohibitions imposed by those provisions.[134]

Thus, to trigger an infringement of the competition articles there must be an extra element – something more than the mere possession of an intellectual property right. For Article 81, this will be an agreement, decision or concerted practice. For Article 82, it will be the abuse of a dominant position.[135]

6.7.1 Article 81

Although an intellectual property right does not in itself amount to a restrictive practice, its exercise may do so. This commonly occurs in relation to assignments and licences of intellectual property rights.

---

[133]   Joined Cases 56/64 and 58/64, *Établissements Consten and Grundig-Verkaufs* v. *Commission* [1966] ECR 299.
[134]   Case 40/70, *Sirena* v. *Eda* [1971] ECR 69 (para. 5).
[135]   Case C-24/67, *Parke Davis & Co.* v. *Probel* [1968] ECR 55.

Assignments

Article 81 will apply, for instance, when an intellectual property right holder attempts to assign its rights in order to secure a network of exclusive territorial protection. If there is an agreement which prevents parallel imports between assignees, the agreement will infringe. In *Sirena* v. *Eda*, an American company had assigned its rights in the Italian trade mark 'Prep Good Morning', for shaving cream, to the Italian company Sirena. It later allowed a German company to use 'Prep Good Morning' (this time the German mark, again for shaving cream) in Germany. When the German company began selling in Italy at prices which undercut Sirena, as the Italian assignee, it sought to prevent this. The ECJ had to consider whether, 'when a trade-mark right is exercised by virtue of assignments to users in one or more Member States', such use led to a situation falling within Article 85 (now Article 81). It concluded that if a combination of assignments to different users of national trade marks protecting the same product had the result of re-enacting impenetrable frontiers between member states, this practice might well affect trade between states, and distort competition in the common market. Article 85 was therefore applicable in such circumstances.[136] This analysis seeks to avoid the objection that once an assignment has been completed, the formal agreement underlying it will have been discharged. The Court therefore focuses on the continuing consequences of such agreements.

A similar situation arose in *EMI* v. *CBS*. The COLUMBIA trade mark belonged originally to an American company, which in 1917 transferred the mark to its English subsidiary in respect of the states which, at the time of the case, comprised the Community. It retained the mark for the United States and other third countries. The English subsidiary changed hands several times, and the UK mark reached the hands of EMI. In the United States, it was owned by CBS. EMI was objecting to CBS's sales in the Community, which it undertook through its subsidiaries. The Court acknowledged that the assignment agreements were no longer in force, but held that for Article 85 to apply it would be sufficient that they continued to produce its effects. This would only be the case, however, if a concerted practice could be inferred from the behaviour of those involved. Here, the effects flowed 'from the mere exercise of the national trade-mark rights', so EMI could resist CBS imports under the COLUMBIA mark.[137] This approach was confirmed by the ECJ in *IHT*. If independent undertakings make trade mark assignments following a market-sharing agreement, the prohibition of anti-competitive agreements under Article 85 of the Treaty applies and assignments which give effect to such an

---

[136] Case 40/70, *Sirena* v. *Eda* [1971] ECR 69 (para. 10).
[137] Case 51/75, *EMI Records Ltd* v. *CBS United Kingdom Ltd* [1976] ECR 811.

agreement will be void in consequence. However, in each case, it would be necessary to analyse the factual context, the commitments underlying the assignment, the intention of the parties and the consideration for the assignment.[138]

Licensing agreements

A licence is a mechanism by which the owner of an intellectual property right grants permission for a third party to exploit that right, usually in return for payment. Licences can be extremely productive for the right holder, who may not have the resources to exploit the right to the full without assistance. Greater efficiency may result if the licensor's technology is combined with the assets and technologies of the licensee. The ECJ has acknowledged the importance of licences by including the right to grant licences within the specific subject matter of intellectual property rights.[139]

Licences are commonly granted to allow third parties to manufacture or distribute protected products. The terms of licences vary enormously. Most licence agreements do not restrict competition, but some will attempt to protect the licensee from competition from other licensees. In certain cases, this may be justifiable, in order to make the licences attractive to licensees. But if the result is to insulate the parties entirely from the effects of competition, Article 81 will be triggered.

Nungesser is illustrative.[140] The case involved contracts between Eisele, a German supplier of seeds, and INRA, a French institute for agricultural research. These gave Eisele exclusive rights in Germany to certain hybrid maize seeds which had been developed by INRA after a long period of experimentation and research. INRA had also agreed that it would not itself market the seed in Germany, and would prevent third parties from doing so. Eisele could use his exclusive rights to prevent all imports of the seeds into Germany, and all exports to other member states. It was argued that no supplier would take the risk of launching seeds in a new market without protection from direct competition from the holder of the breeders' rights and other licensees. The Court distinguished between two types of licence. Under an open exclusive licence, the right holder merely undertakes not to grant other licences in respect of the same territory and to refrain from competition with the licensee on that territory. In contrast, an exclusive licence with absolute territorial

---

138   Case C-9/93, *IHT Internationale Heiztechnik GmbH* v. *Ideal Standard GmbH* [1994] ECR 2789 (para. 59). It would seem more practical for an offending assignment to remain valid, but unenforceable against parallel imports.

139   Case C-15/74, *Centrafarm BV* v. *Sterling Drug Inc.* [1974] ECR 1147 (para. 9).

140   Case 258/78, *LC Nungesser KG* v. *Commission* [1982] ECR 2015.

protection seeks to eliminate all competition from third parties (such as parallel importers, or licensees from other territories). The Court accepted that without a certain amount of protection from competition, potential licensees might be deterred from taking on the new seeds. This would be damaging to the dissemination of a new technology and would prejudice competition in the Community between the new product and similar existing products. Given this, the grant of an open exclusive licence, if it did not affect the position of third parties such as parallel importers and licensees for other territories, was not in itself incompatible with Article 81(1). However, absolute territorial protection which allowed a licensee to control or prevent parallel imports was contrary to the Treaty because it resulted in the artificial maintenance of separate national markets.

The Court will consider whether the particular terms in a licensing agreement fall within the specific subject matter of the right. If they do not, then they will infringe Article 81(1). In *Windsurfing*, an American company held a German patent for a rig used on a sailboard. It had concluded licences with a number of firms in the Community, but the Commission had objected to a number of conditions in these licences. Licensees were required to use the rigs only on approved boards, Windsurfing arguing that this was necessary to ensure quality and safety. The Court observed that such controls 'do not come within the specific subject matter of the patent unless they relate to a product covered by the patent', since their sole justification is that they ensure that technical instructions described in the patent are put into effect by the licensee. Here, the German patent did not cover the board. In any event, such controls 'must be effected according to quality and safety criteria agreed upon in advance and on the basis of objectively verifiable criteria', to prevent the licensor imposing its own selection of models on licensees. The Court considered that Windsurfing's real interest 'lay in ensuring that there was sufficient product differentiation between its licensees' sailboards to cover the widest possible spectrum of market demand'. Another clause required licensees to sell the rigs only as part of a complete sailboard. The Court observed that since the patent was for the rig only, 'it cannot be accepted that the obligation arbitrarily placed on the licensee only to sell the patented product in conjunction with a product outside the scope of the patent is indispensable to the exploitation of the patent'. This was therefore a form of tying, and contrary to Article 81(1). Similarly, a clause requiring licensees to mark sailboards 'licensed by windsurfing international' encouraged uncertainty as to whether or not the board too was covered by the patent and thereby diminished the buyer's confidence in the licensees in order to give Windsurfing a competitive advantage. This sort of clause would only fall within the specific subject matter of the patent if the notice were placed only on components protected by the patent.

Windsurfing insisted that licensees acknowledge its trade marks (WIND-SURFING, WINDSURFER) as valid, arguing that this was necessary in order to prevent them from becoming generic. The ECJ held that this 'could not be safeguarded by means of a clause which clearly did not come within the specific subject matter of the patent and was imposed on the licensees in the agreements relating to the exploitation of the patent even though the subject matter of the clause was quite different'. The licensees were also required not to challenge the validity of the licensed patents. The ECJ again took the view that 'such a clause clearly does not fall within the specific subject matter of the patent' because it was in the public interest to eliminate any obstacles to economic activity which resulted from patents being granted in error.[141] All of these conditions fell outside the specific subject matter of the relevant patent right, and would only be lawful if brought within an exemption.

Copyright licensing – individual and collective

The same considerations apply to copyright licences, particularly if there is distribution of a physical copyright product. However, where copyright services are involved (online communication of copyright works, for example), the absence of a distributor may mean that there is only one undertaking, and hence Article 81 will not apply. Article 81 may sometimes be relevant, though, as in *Coditel II*.[142] Ciné Vog, a Belgian film distribution company, had acquired exclusive rights to distribute the film *Le Boucher* in Belgium. It faced competition in Belgium when a German television broadcast of the film was picked up by the Belgian cable television provider Coditel, and distributed to Coditel's subscribers. The ECJ stated that copyright in a film and the right of exhibiting the film, were not, as such, subject to the prohibitions contained in Article 81. But the exercise of those rights could fall within Article 81 if the effect of the economic or legal circumstances was to restrict film distribution to an appreciable degree or to distort competition in the film market. It was for national courts to determine whether or not the exercise of the exclusive right to exhibit a film created barriers which were artificial and unjustifiable in terms of the needs of the cinematographic industry, and whether or not the right's exercise within a given geographic area is such as to prevent, restrict or distort competition within the common market.[143] More recently, the Commission has sent a Statement of Objections to major record companies and Apple in relation to agreements (between each record company and Apple) that restrict music sales. Consumers can only buy music downloads

---

[141]   Case 193/83, *Windsurfing International Inc.* v. *Commission* [1986] ECR 611.
[142]   Case 262/81, *Coditel* v. *Ciné Vog Films (Coditel II)* [1982] ECR 3381.
[143]   Case 262/81, *Coditel* v. *Ciné Vog Films (Coditel II)* [1982] ECR 3381 (paras. 17–19).

from the iTunes' online store in their country of residence (verified by credit card details). Thus their choice of where to buy music is restricted, as is the range of music available, and the price they must pay. The UK consumers' association, Which?, had complained that users in the UK were being charged substantially more than users in France and Germany. The Commission alleges that these agreements violate Article 81.[144] Apple has said that it had always wanted to offer a fully pan-European service, but 'were advised by the music labels and publishers that there were certain legal limits to the rights they could grant us'.

Given the particular difficulties that individuals face in monitoring use of their works, collecting societies have developed to facilitate the licensing and enforcement of copyrights and related rights. Although this approach is generally considered an appropriate and economically beneficial way of overcoming these difficulties, it gives significant market power to the collecting societies, which raises issues of competition law. These factors are magnified by the fact that collecting societies have traditionally been organised on national lines, and have been accustomed to operating a network of reciprocal arrangements with their counterparts in other countries. Collecting societies have been accused of charging excessive royalty rates, amounting to an abuse of their dominant position.[145]

There have also been incidents where foreign collecting societies have refused to license their repertoires directly in other member states. National collecting societies frequently conclude reciprocal representation contracts with other societies, giving both parties the right to grant licences for the other's repertoire in their own territory, under the terms of the local agreement. This has the result that all works protected in a particular member state are subject to the same conditions, and allows each national collecting society to focus on its own local arrangements for granting licences and monitoring usage, relying on other societies for the administration of its interests outside that local territory. In *Lucazeau* v. *SACEM*, the ECJ acknowledged that such agreements are not restrictive of competition *per se*. However, the reciprocal representation contracts in question had previously contained exclusive representation clauses, which had been removed at the request of the Commission. Furthermore, the Commission observed that the removal of these clauses had

---

[144] Press Release (3 April 2007), 'Competition: European Commission Confirms Sending a Statement of Objections against Alleged Territorial Restrictions in On-line Music Sales to Major Record Companies and Apple' MEMO/07/126. The Statement of Objections does not allege that Apple is in a dominant market position.

[145] For example, Case 402/85, *Bassett* v. *SACEM* [1987] ECR 1747; Case 395/87, *Ministère Public* v. *Tournier* [1989] ECR 2521; Joined Cases 110/88, 241/88 and 242/88, *Lucazeau* v. *SACEM* [1989] ECR 2811.

not resulted in any change in behaviour by the collecting societies, who were still refusing to license their repertoires to anyone except the relevant local collecting society. This raised questions as to whether the collecting societies had in fact retained their exclusive rights by means of a concerted practice. The collecting societies argued that it would be far too burdensome for them to set up a system of direct collection of royalties in each local territory, and that it was economically and administratively sensible to entrust these activities to the local society. The ECJ noted that mere parallel behaviour may amount to strong evidence of a concerted practice if it leads to conditions of competition which do not correspond to the normal conditions of competition. but that concerted action could not be presumed where the parallel behaviour could be accounted for by other reasons. The task of determining whether concerted action had taken place was a matter of fact for the relevant national court.[146]

Current anxieties have focused on the ability to obtain an EU-wide licence for electronic use of works. In November 2000, the International Federation of the Phonographic Industry (IFPI) applied to the Commission for negative clearance or, alternatively, an individual exemption under Article 81(3), in respect of a model reciprocal agreement between record producers' rights administration societies for the licensing of simulcasting.[147] This was defined by the parties as 'the simultaneous transmission by radio and TV stations via the Internet of sound recordings included in their broadcasts of radio and/or TV signals'. The aim was to facilitate the grant of international licences to radio and TV broadcasters who wished to engage in simulcasting. Given the novelty of both the technology and the type of licence, the agreement was proposed for a trial period ending in 2004. The original proposal would have allowed national societies to grant international simulcasting licences only to parties broadcasting from that national territory. But a revised agreement allowed any simulcaster located in the EEA to seek a multi-territorial licence from any of the national collection societies established in the EEA. A further amendment provided for transparency in the charging system, whereby the collecting societies would specify which part of the tariff was an administration fee, and which part was the royalty payment. The intention was to allow each society to function as a one-stop-shop, granting a multi-territorial simul-

---

146   Joined Cases 110/88, 241/88 and 242/88, *Lucazeau* v. *SACEM* [1989] ECR 2811. See also Case 395/87, *Ministère Public* v. *Tournier* [1989] ECR 2521. Direct complaints about the practice made to the Commission were rejected, although the CFI annulled the decision in part for failure to give reasons: Case T-5/93 *Tremblay* v. *Commission* [1995] ECR II-185.

147   Case No. COMP/C2/38.014, Decision 2003/300, *IFPI 'Simulcasting'* [2003] OJ L 107/58.

cast licence, including the repertoire of other collecting societies, on the same conditions for all users in the same country. IFPI argued that, as a result, administration costs would be lower, and that these efficiencies would benefit both the holder of the rights, and the user.

The Commission was clear that the administration of copyright and neighbouring rights by collecting societies could, under certain circumstances, infringe Article 81(1). Here, the effect of the unamended agreement would have been to reduce price competition between the national societies significantly. The changes to the proposed agreement were made in response to the Commission's previously expressed concerns. It is notable that the collecting societies did not have in place administrative and accounting structures which allowed them to separate the copyright royalty from the administration fee, even though operating expenses were known to account for the most marked differences between collecting societies. But the Commission was prepared to accept the parties' commitment to implement such a separation, and considered that this allowed for sufficient price competition to offset other concerns, given the acknowledged benefits of the agreement. An individual exemption was therefore granted, to expire at the end of the agreement.

The Commission is demonstrably hostile to copyright licensing agreements which restrict price competition, or impose territorial restrictions on users which force them to seek licences from the member state where the works will be used.[148] It is keen to see cross-border collective management of copyright, particularly for new forms of technology, wherever possible.[149] The Commission has therefore adopted a recommendation on the management of online rights in musical works, intended to improve the EU-wide licensing of

---

[148] Press Release (2 February 2006), 'Competition: Commission Sends Statement of Objections to the International Confederation of Societies of Authors and Composers (CISAC) and its EEA Members' MEMO/06/63; Press Release (4 October 2006), 'Competition: Commission Renders Commitments by Music Publishers and Collecting Societies Legally Binding' IP/06/1311; Press Release (14 June 2007), 'Antitrust: Commission Market Tests Commitments from CISAC and 18 EEA Collecting Societies Concerning Reciprocal Representation Contracts' IP/07/829.

[149] See Commission Communication to the Council, the European Parliament and the European Economic and Social Committee on the Management of Copyright and Related Rights in the Internal Market, COM(2004) 261 final (para. 4.12). Also, Commission Staff Working Document, 'Initiative on the Cross-Border Collective Management of Copyright' (7 July 2005): http://ec.europa.eu/internal_market/copyright/docs/management/study-collectivemgmt_en.pdf. Commission Staff Working Document, 'Impact Assessment Reforming Cross-Border Collective Management of Copyright and Related Rights for Legitimate Online Music Services' (11 October 2005) SEC(2005) 1254: http://ec.europa.eu/internal_market/copyright/docs/management/sec_2005_1254_en.pdf.

copyright for online services.[150] It proposes the elimination of territorial restrictions and customer allocation provisions in existing licensing contracts, while leaving right holders who do not wish to make use of those contracts the possibility to tender their repertoire for EU-wide direct licensing. The recommendation also includes provisions on governance, transparency, dispute settlement and accountability of collective rights managers, intended to allow stakeholders to make an informed decision as to the licensing model best suited to their needs. The benefits in efficiency gains from collective management are universally recognised, as are the risks of excessive licence fees resulting from the abuse of monopoly power or from management inefficiency. The debate is as to the appropriate point of balance, and the Commission's determination to promote EU-wide licensing is far from uncontroversial. Some commentators have noted the difficulty of pursuing a regulatory approach in practice, given the territorial nature of copyright and the sheer complexity of licensing activities at international level, given the need to promote local cultures and diversity in a linguistically and culturally fragmented market, given the lack of uniformity in the national collective management systems, given the wide variety of rights involved and their differing contexts, and given the difficulty of defining management efficiency in such an environment. Others argue that even more intervention is needed.[151]

Unilateral action and Article 81(1)
Restrictions on parallel trade conflict with the Community's fundamental aim of market integration. Understandably therefore, ECJ case law shows a consistent hostility towards attempts to curb parallel trade, and many of these examples have fallen within Article 81(1). In *Bayer*, the Court considered whether arrangements intended to limit parallel trade within the EU, which had been devised and implemented unilaterally by Bayer, could be regarded as anticompetitive agreements within Article 81.[152] Bayer, one of the leading European pharmaceutical companies, manufactured and marketed the drug ADALAT through national subsidiaries throughout the EU. In most member states, the price is directly or indirectly fixed by the national health authorities.

---

[150]   Commission Recommendation of 18 October 2005 (2005/737/EC) on collective cross-border management of copyright and related rights for legitimate online music services OJ L 276, 21/10/2005. See Chapter 2, section 2.3.10 (i) Management of online rights.

[151]   KEA European Affairs, *The Collective Management of Rights in Europe: The Quest for Efficiency* (Brussels: KEA European Affairs, July 2006), esp. pp. 50–51. See also Conan Chitham, 'In the Slow Lane?' (2006) 158 *Copyright World* 13–15.

[152]   Joined Cases C-2/01 P and C-3/01 P, *Bundesverband der Arzneimittel-Importeure eV* v. *Bayer AG* [2004] ECR 23.

Between 1989 and 1993, the prices fixed by the Spanish and French health services were, on average, 40% lower than prices in the UK. Exports by wholesalers from these countries caused Bayer's UK subsidiary to suffer a very substantial loss of turnover, and thus a serious loss of revenue for Bayer (100 million DM). Bayer then refused to meet all the increasingly large orders placed with Bayer's French and Spanish subsidiaries by the French and Spanish wholesalers.

Following complaints by some of the wholesalers concerned, the Commission investigated, and concluded that Bayer France and Bayer Spain had infringed Article 85(1). It considered that their conduct amounted to an export ban, imposed as part of their commercial relations with the wholesalers. The Commission held that the conduct of the wholesalers showed that they had not only understood that an export ban applied to the goods supplied, but also that they had aligned their conduct on that ban, thereby demonstrating acceptance of it. The CFI annulled the Commission's decision, considering Bayer's response to be a genuinely unilateral measure, and so not within Article 85(1). The fact that the wholesalers had changed their policy on orders to obtain supplies by other routes could be construed only as a negation of their alleged acquiescence to an agreement. The ECJ agreed, observing that 'to hold that an agreement prohibited by Article 85(1) of the Treaty may be established simply on the basis of the expression of a unilateral policy aimed at preventing parallel imports would have the effect of confusing the scope of that provision with that of Article 86 of the Treaty'. Although an agreement to achieve an anti-competitive goal could in some circumstances be concluded by tacit acceptance, here the policy had been imposed on the wholesalers without their cooperation, and in the face of their opposition.[153]

Dual pricing

Pharmaceutical manufacturers continue to seek means of restricting the parallel trade which flourishes in the sector because of the significant price differentials between member states. They argue that the price differences are due to national interventions and purchasing policies, and therefore beyond their control. Further, they argue that the activities of parallel importers undermine national price regulation, reduce the resources available for research and development, and bring no benefit to either national health services or the ultimate consumer. They regard parallel importers as traders engaged in arbitrage, and consider themselves justified in seeking to prevent their activities. *GlaxoSmithKline Services Unlimited* concerned one of these attempts. The

---

[153]   Joined Cases C-2/01 P and C-3/01 P, *Bundesverband der Arzneimittel-Importeure eV* v. *Bayer AG* [2004] ECR 23 (para. 101).

leading pharmaceutical company GlaxoSmithKline (GSK) sought to impose a dual pricing system on Spanish wholesalers, covering a long list of its pharmaceuticals, several of which were prime candidates for parallel trade. Its General Sales Conditions provided for two different prices: one price for products financed by Spanish public funds and sold in Spain to pharmacies and hospitals, and a higher price for all other products (in effect, those sold outside Spain). In the first case, the price was guaranteed not to exceed the price set as the reimbursement price by the Spanish health authorities. In the second case, GSK stated that the price would be fixed 'according to real, objective and non-discriminatory economic criteria and completely irrespective of the destination of the product determined by the purchasing warehouse'. The vast majority of GSK's Spanish wholesalers accepted these conditions. GSK sought either negative clearance or an exemption from the Commission (under a system no longer in force). There were a number of complaints from wholesalers, both at national level and to the Commission. The Commission adopted a decision in which it found that the dual pricing system infringed Article 81, its object being to distort competition, and that it did not qualify for exemption. Although the Commission imposed no fine, it ordered an immediate end to the infringement.[154] GSK appealed to the CFI.[155]

The CFI was clear that there was an agreement between GSK and the Spanish wholesalers. Although some of the Spanish wholesalers had expressed doubts as to the legality of the General Sales Conditions, they had not distanced themselves from the agreement to the point where there was no longer a joint intention to collude. There was no dispute that GSK's intention was to limit parallel trade, so in principle the agreement had to be considered to have as its object the restriction of competition, but only if it could be presumed to deprive final consumers of the advantages of that competition. This was not the case here. The wholesalers were economic agents operating at an intermediate stage of the value chain and were free to keep most if not all of any price advantage which resulted from parallel trade. Prices of pharmaceuticals reimbursed by national health insurance schemes are not determined as a result of a competitive process throughout the Community, but are directly fixed following an administrative procedure in most member states, and indirectly controlled by the other member states. Pricing criteria differ

---

[154]   Decision 2001/791/EC of 8 May 2001, relating to a proceeding pursuant to Article 81 of the EC Treaty (Cases: IV/36.957/F3, *Glaxo Wellcome* (notification), IV/36.997/F3 *Aseprofar and Fedifar* (complaint), IV/37.121/F3, *Spain Pharma* (complaint), IV/37.138/F3, *BAI* (complaint), IV/37.380/F3, *EAEPC* (complaint)) [2001] OJ L 302/1.

[155]   Case T-168/01, *GlaxoSmithKline Services Unlimited* v. *Commission* [2006] ECR II-2969.

between member states, depending on their public health policies. Differences between the national provisions cause significant price differentials between member states, and thus cause parallel trade in pharmaceuticals. The Commission had not examined these 'specific and essential characteristics of the sector', which was 'to a significant extent shielded from the free play of supply and demand'. The CFI called this a 'largely unprecedented situation' and went on to consider the effects of the agreement. It hampered the ability of Spanish wholesalers to engage in parallel trade, which would put some downward pressure on prices. It was acknowledged that in practice the competition would be marginal, because Spanish wholesalers would undercut wholesalers in other member states only as much as was necessary to attract custom, and would pocket the difference between this price and the Spanish reimbursement price.

Since the dual pricing system could have the effect of restricting competition within the meaning of Article 81(1), the CFI went on to consider whether the Commission was right to conclude that it was not eligible for exemption under Article 81(3). GSK had argued that dual pricing would make it possible to secure advantages both upstream of the relevant market, by encouraging innovation, and on the market itself, by optimising the distribution of medicines. It was for the Commission to examine whether the factual arguments and the evidence submitted showed convincingly that the agreement would bring 'appreciable objective advantages', and, if so, to evaluate whether these advantages would offset the disadvantages entailed for competition. GSK's central argument was that parallel trade undermined its ability to fund research and development activities, and that its dual pricing system would allow it to increase such activities. The CFI noted that GSK's factual arguments and supporting evidence appeared to be 'relevant, reliable and credible', and were corroborated on a number of significant aspects by documents originating with the Commission. It found that the Commission had failed to carry out a proper examination of the arguments and evidence, and did not adequately substantiate its conclusion that an exemption was not justified. This part of the decision was therefore annulled, and the case remitted to the Commission for further consideration.

The CFI's finding that limitation of parallel trade does not amount to a *per se* violation of competition law is significant, and, if it stands, will force a change in the Commission's practice. The CFI also seemed to give considerable weight to the evidence and arguments pressed by GSK as to the exceptional conditions prevailing in the pharmaceutical sector. An interesting comparison can be made with the Advocate General's similarly sympathetic assessment in *Syfait*. That case involved a GSK stock allocation system intended to prevent parallel trade, which wholesalers had argued amounted to abuse of GSK's dominant position, although GSK had again sought to justify their conduct by reference to the particular conditions in the sector.[156] Although a change in attitude would be welcome to pharmaceutical manufacturers, it has not yet been endorsed by the ECJ. Both GSK and the Commission have lodged appeals against the CFI's decision in *GlaxoSmithKline Services Unlimited*. The Advocate General's opinion in a further reference from the Greek courts, again concerning GSK's response to parallel trade, is somewhat less favourable to the pharmaceutical manufacturers. It indicates that an undertaking in a dominant position which refuses to meet in full the orders of wholesalers of pharmaceutical products, with a view to reducing the harm caused by parallel trade, thereby engages in abusive conduct. Although an undertaking may be able to provide objective justification for its conduct by showing that the regulation of the market compels it to behave in that manner in order to protect its legitimate business interests, the Advocate General found no such justification in these cases.[157] Even if the CFI's approach is adopted by the ECJ, the legality of deliberate action to limit parallel trade will still have to be proved in the circumstances of each particular case.[158]

Block exemptions – the Technology Transfer Regulation

The licensing of intellectual property rights offers obvious advantages to those involved, but also offers opportunities for anti-competitive behaviour, as has been seen. Another increasingly important and controversial method of licensing is the patent pool, whereby two or more companies agree to cross-license patents relating to a particular technology. Patent pools allow their members to reduce risk and negotiation costs. The result of the combination may be to make the total pool very significantly more valuable than the individual patents would have been if free-standing. Although this is attractive to members, non-members may complain that the pool is used as a mechanism to exclude them from the market. Some industries, such as the telecommunications technology industry, use open pooling arrangements which, in effect, set standards for the industry.[159] Under open pooling, anyone may join on the

---

[156]   Case C-53/03, *Synetairismos Farmakopoion Aitolias & Akarnanias (SYFAIT)* v. *Glaxosmithkline Plc* [2005] ECR 4609 (AG Jacobs' Opinion, 28 October 2004). The ECJ found it had no jurisdiction to answer questions from the Greek Competition Commission which was hearing the case, because it was not a court or tribunal within the terms of the Treaty. See below: Should the pharmaceutical sector be treated as a special case for the purposes of Article 82?

[157]   Advocate General's Opinion in Joined Cases C-468/06 to C-478/06, *Sot. Lélos Kai Sia EE (and Others)* v. *GlaxoSmithKline* (1 April 2008).

[158]   See also Christopher Stothers, 'Who Needs Intellectual Property? Competition Law and Restrictions on Parallel Trade within the EEA' [2005] *EIPR* 458–66.

[159]   On this subject, note the Commission's pursuit of the US company Rambus,

same terms. Although some patent pools have positive effects for the relevant market, there is understandable suspicion lest they be used as a disguised means of excluding or disadvantaging other competitors.

Patent and know-how licences are granted with the aim of enhancing the licensor's position in the market for the relevant product. They do not, by themselves, limit competition between rival products. They may well, however, limit competition between the licensor and licensees. Given that one of the Community's fundamental priorities is to break down barriers to free trade, it is understandable that exclusive selling rights were viewed with grave suspicion, particularly if they inhibited parallel imports. However, there is increasing recognition that certain vertical limitations may promote healthy competition between brands. This general shift in attitude is reflected in the legislation controlling patent and know-how licensing, which attempts to strike a balance between the advantages and drawbacks of these arrangements.

The Commission first offered guidance in the form of a non-binding notice, 'Announcement on Patent Licensing Agreements, December 24, 1962'. This indicated certain clauses which it would not regard as falling within Article 85(1), and others which would require individual exemption, or which would be unacceptable. Uncertainty later ensued, as the Commission appeared to adopt a tougher line in the 1970s. In an attempt to define the balance point between protection and competition more clearly, the Commission adopted two block exemption regulations – one on patent licensing and one on know-how licensing.[160] They adopted a somewhat softer approach, in response to pressure from governments and industry interests. These were then combined in a single regulation, the Technology Transfer Regulation – an 'old style'

---

designer of high bandwidth chip connection technologies for computers, and a wide range of consumer electronic and communication products. Rambus participated in a standard-setting process for the ubiquitous DRAM chip, without disclosing the existence of its patents or patents-pending relating to the relevant technologies. As a result, any manufacturer wishing to produce DRAM chips to this important industry standard must acquire a licence (or contest the patents) – a so-called 'patent ambush'. The Commission's preliminary view is that Rambus has abused its dominant position, because the royalties it charges are unreasonable: Press Release (23 August 2007), 'Commission Confirms Sending a Statement of Objections to Rambus' MEMO/07/330. See also Piotr Staniszewski, 'The Interplay between IP Rights and Competition Law in the Context of Standardization' [2007] *JIPL&P* 666–81; Pat Treacy and Sophie Lawrance, 'FRANDly Fire: Are Industry Standards Doing More Harm than Good?' [2008] *JIPL&P* 22–9.

[160]   Regulation 2349/1984 on the application of Article 85(3) of the Treaty to certain categories of patent licensing agreements; Regulation 556/1989 on the application of Article 85(3) of the Treaty to certain categories of know-how licensing agreements.

block exemption, which has now itself been replaced.[161] Covering patent licensing agreements, pure know-how licensing agreements and combined patent and know-how licensing agreements, its approach was more permissive than that of the previous regulations. Agreements which fell within the scope of the block exemption were therefore not anti-competitive under Article 81. The Regulation set out a 'white list' of exempt terms, a 'black list' of prohibited terms and a 'grey list' of terms which, if an agreement contained any of them, had to be notified to the European Commission. If the Commission did not object to the agreement's terms within four months, then the agreement was deemed to be cleared. The Commission also had the power to withdraw the benefit of the block exemption where individual cases merited this. A somewhat crude instrument, it took little account of economic criteria, or the competitive relationship between the parties to the agreement. In addition, the lists of 'black', 'grey' and 'white' clauses were detailed and complicated. Parties preferred to follow them closely rather than risk falling foul of the Regulation, which led to a lack of flexibility in drafting agreements – the so-called 'strait-jacket' effect.

Following extensive consultation, the Commission adopted a revised Regulation and Guidelines on the application of Article 81(3) to categories of technology transfer agreements.[162] These came into force on 1 May 2004, replacing the existing technology transfer block exemption regulation. It covers patent licensing, know-how licensing, software licensing and mixed agreements. For these purposes, the term 'patents' covers not only patents and patent applications, but also utility models, designs, topographies of semiconductor products, supplementary protection certificates and plant breeder's certificates.[163] The new Regulation is much more flexible in its approach, moving away from a narrowly text-based assessment, to one which more closely reflects the economic realities of the situation. This is consistent with the new approach in Community competition policy more generally, which focuses on market impact rather than imposing a legal strait-jacket.[164] Block

---

[161]   Regulation 240/1996 of on the application of Article 85(3) of the Treaty to certain categories of technology transfer agreements.

[162]   Commission Regulation 772/2004 on the application of Article 81(3) of the Treaty to categories of technology transfer agreements [2004] OJ L 123/11 (Tech. Transfer Reg.). Guidelines on the application of Article 81 of the EC Treaty to technology transfer agreements (Tech. Transfer Guidelines) [2004] OJ C101/2.

[163]   Tech. Transfer Reg. 772/2004, Art. 1(1)(b) and (1)(h).

[164]   See the Commission Regulation 2790/1999 on the application of Article 81(3) to categories of vertical agreements and concerted practices [1999] OJ L 336. Similarly, Commission Regulation 2658/2000 on the application of Article 81(3) of the Treaty to categories of specialisation agreements; Commission Regulation 2659/2000 on the application of Article 81(3) of the Treaty to categories of research and development agreements [1999] OJ L 304.

exemption of categories of technology transfer agreements is based on the presumption that such agreements – to the extent that they are caught by Article 81(1) – fulfil the four conditions laid down in Article 81(3). It is thus presumed that the agreements give rise to economic efficiencies, that the restrictions contained in the agreements are indispensable to the attainment of these efficiencies, that consumers within the affected markets receive a fair share of the efficiency gains and that the agreements do not afford the undertakings concerned the possibility of eliminating competition in respect of a substantial part of the products in question.[165]

The aim is to offer a 'safe harbour' to agreements which will not have anticompetitive effects, when judged according to various market share thresholds. What is considered is the relevant technology market or product market. If the parties are competitors, the revised block exemption will only apply if the combined market share of the parties is not more than 20%. The 'safe harbour' is larger for agreements between non-competitors. Here the revised block exemption will apply if the market share of *each* of the parties is not more than 30%.[166] Provided that the thresholds are satisfied initially, they may be exceeded for up to two years. The Regulation applies to agreements primarily for the manufacture or provision of 'contract products' (products manufactured or services provided with the licensed technology). However, it also applies to software copyright licensing agreements (an addition to the existing provision for patent or know-how licensing), as well as to mixed agreements for the licensing of technology involving all or any of these. 'Patents' is defined widely, to include (*inter alia*) designs, utility models and semiconductor topographies. As before, the new Regulation does not apply to research and development agreements or to technology pools (although these latter are made subject to the Guidelines).

If the parties pass the market share assessment, then any contractual restrictions are analysed. The new approach is simpler: any provision not expressly excluded from the exemption is covered by its 'safe harbour'. There are two classes of restriction that would or might (unless severable) cause the agreement to be non-exempt. Firstly, there are 'hardcore' restrictions, which will render the whole agreement illegal and unenforceable.[167] These will vary depending on whether the agreement is between competitors or non-competitors, but cover pricing, output, sales and territorial restrictions, as well as reciprocal cross-licensing agreements between competitors. Such clauses are not regarded as creating objective economic benefits, or benefits for consumers.

---

165 Tech. Transfer Guidelines, 35.
166 Tech. Transfer Reg. 772/2004, Art. 3.
167 Tech. Transfer Reg. 772/2004, Art. 4.

Secondly, there are 'excluded restrictions'. These are not block exempted and require individual assessment of their anti-competitive and pro-competitive effects. The inclusion of any of these restrictions does not prevent the application of the block exemption to the rest of the agreement. It is only the individual restriction in question that is not block exempted, implying that individual assessment is required. So, if the restriction is severable from the rest of the agreement, the rest of the agreement could remain exempt. These 'excluded restrictions' include obligations on the licensee to grant exclusive licences-back (or assignments-back) of severable improvements or new applications, non-challenge clauses, obligations limiting the ability of the licensee to exploit its own technology and restrictions on either party's research and development activities.[168]

There is a set of Guidelines which accompany the Regulation. These elaborate on issues that relate to the application of the Regulation, as well as on the application of Article 81 to individual technology transfer agreements falling outside the scope of the block exemption. Outside the safe harbour created by the market share thresholds individual assessment is required. The fact that market shares exceed the thresholds does not give rise to any presumption either that the agreement is caught by Article 81(1) or that the agreement does not fulfil the conditions of Article 81(3). In the absence of hardcore restrictions, market analysis is required. Guidance is also provided on the application of Article 81 to technology pooling agreements. The Regulation only covers the licensing of other types of intellectual property such as trade marks and copyright, other than software copyright, to the extent that they are directly related to the exploitation of the licensed technology and do not constitute the primary object of the agreement. This ensures that agreements covering other types of intellectual property rights are only block exempted to the extent that these rights enable the licensee to better exploit the licensed technology.[169] However, the Commission has said that it considers copyright licensing of copyright for the purpose of reproduction and distribution of the protected work (that is, the production of copies for resale) to be similar to technology licensing, and to raise comparable issues. As a general rule, therefore, the Commission will apply the principles set out in the Regulation when assessing such licences under Article 81. In contrast, the licensing of rights in performances and other rights related to copyright is considered to raise different issues and the Regulation will not be applied by analogy. Nor will the Regulation's principles be extended to trade mark licensing, which is generally regarded as more akin to distribution agreements than

---

168   Tech. Transfer Reg. 772/2004, Art. 5.
169   Tech. Transfer Guidelines, 50.

technology licensing, and thus likely to fall within the Regulation on Vertical Agreements.

A number of concerns regarding the Regulation were flagged by practitioners at the time of its adoption, for example: the difficulty and expense of analysing market share data, both prior to and during the life of the agreements; the difficulty of assessing whether parties to an agreement are competitors (or potential competitors); the reliability of the safe harbour, and the status of the Guidelines, particularly for those seeking to rely on the Regulation before national competition authorities and national courts. Several of these predicted difficulties have materialised. In particular, the required effects-based economic analysis can be expensive and difficult to carry out, resulting in reduced legal certainty. There is little further information available from the Commission, because the public feedback which resulted from notifications to the Commission for negative clearance or individual exemption under Article 81(3) is no longer available. It appears that the Commission has received very little comment on the Regulation since it was adopted, and it is not currently investigating any technology transfer agreements other than some patent pools. Although the Commission's modernisation agenda requires parties to live with these costs and uncertainties, there remain concerns that there may be a chilling effect on research and development and licensing efforts in the Community.[170]

6.7.2 Article 82

Article 82 provides that 'any abuse by one or more undertakings of a dominant position within the common market or in a substantial part of it shall be prohibited as incompatible with the common market in so far as it may affect trade between Member States'. Merely holding an intellectual property right is therefore insufficient to trigger Article 82. The ECJ has used the same distinction between existence and exercise of the right in the context of both Article 81 and Article 82. As the Court explained early on in *Parke Davis*,

> For this prohibition to apply it is thus necessary that three elements shall be present together: the existence of a dominant position, the abuse of this position and the possibility that trade between Member States may be affected thereby. Although a patent confers on its holder a special protection at national level, it does not follow that the exercise of the rights thus conferred implies the presence together of all three elements in question. It could only do so if the use of the patent were to degenerate into an abuse of the abovementioned protection.[171]

---

[170] See Benedict Bird and Adrian Toutoungi, 'The New EC Technology Transfer Regulation One Year On' [2006] *EIPR* 292–6.

[171] Case C-24/67, *Parke Davis & Co. v. Probel* [1968] ECR 55 (p. 72).

Complaints may be triggered by a refusal to license an intellectual property right, but this in itself is insufficient to amount to a breach of Article 82. In *Volvo* v. *Veng*, Volvo was objecting to sales of imitations of its car body panels, which were protected by registered design rights. Because Volvo refused to license the design rights, consumers were forced to purchase Volvo parts, which, Veng alleged, were excessively priced. The national court asked whether a refusal to license the design right, even for a reasonable royalty, was *prima facie* an abuse of a dominant position. The Court held that the right to prevent third parties from manufacturing, selling or importing products incorporating the design without consent constituted the very subject matter of the design right. An obligation to grant licences to third parties, even in return for a reasonable royalty, would lead to the right holder being deprived of the substance of the exclusive right, and so a refusal to grant such a licence cannot in itself constitute an abuse of a dominant position. However, the Court also held that the *exercise* of a design right could fall within Article 82 if the undertaking held a dominant position, and engaged in abusive conduct:

> such as the arbitrary refusal to supply spare parts to independent repairers, the fixing of prices for spare parts at an unfair level or a decision no longer to produce spare parts for a particular model even though many cars of that model are still in circulation, provided that such conduct is liable to affect trade between Member States.[172]

'Abuse' may take a variety of forms. Where Tetra Pak had a near-monopoly position (90–95% market share, buttressed in other ways) in the market for aseptic milk packaging, its behaviour came under close scrutiny by the Commission. A new sterilisation technique was patented by a third party, and licensed exclusively to Liquipak, which worked with Elopak (a competitor of Tetra Pak's), to produce a machine to exploit it. Tetra Pak then acquired Liquipak, and hence the exclusive licence. The Commission found that, in the particular circumstances of the case, by acquiring an exclusive patent licence to the alternative process, Tetra Pak had impeded the entry of new competitors into the aseptic packaging market, and was thus in breach of Article 82.[173]

---

[172]   Case 238/87, *Volvo AB* v. *Erik Veng (UK) Ltd* [1988] ECR 6211 (paras. 8 and 9). See also Case 53/87, *Consorzio Italiano della Componentistica di Ricambio per Autoveicoli (CICRA) and Maxicar* v. *Régie Nationale des Usines Renault* [1988] ECR 6039. See more recently the so-called 'patent ambush' attempted by the US company Rambus, designer of DRAM chip technologies: Press Release (23 August 2007), 'Commission Confirms Sending a Statement of Objections to Rambus' MEMO/07/330.

[173]   Case COMP IV/31.043, *Tetra Pak I (BTG licence)*; [1990] 4 CMLR 47. The decision was upheld by the CFI in Case T-51/89, *Tetra Pak Rausing SA* v. *Commission* [1990] ECR II-309.

More controversial was the Commission's finding of abuse in the *Magill TV Guide* case. This concerned an Irish firm, Magill, which wished to publish and sell a weekly magazine containing TV listings for all channels which could be received in the area. TV listings are protected by both English and Irish copyright law (as compilations). The BBC, ITP and RTE TV stations each published their own weekly listing magazines, featuring only their own programmes. They also granted free licences to publish their listing information to anybody who was prepared to agree to the licence terms – the most important of which was that only one day's information was to be published at a time, except at weekends or on public holidays. As a result, to get a complete weekly schedule it was necessary to buy all three of the TV stations' guides. When Magill began publishing a complete weekly guide, the TV stations obtained an injunction to prevent further copyright infringement. Magill made a complaint to the Commission, alleging abuse of a dominant position. The Commission found that the broadcasters each held a factual monopoly in their individual programme listings, strengthened into a legal monopoly by copyright. Since there was no competition from third parties on these markets, this amounted to a dominant position. The Commission took the view that the broadcasters were using that position to prevent the introduction onto the market of a comprehensive weekly TV guide, which amounted to an abuse. Furthermore, copyright was being used 'as an instrument of an abuse, in a manner which falls outside the scope of the specific subject matter of that intellectual property right'.[174] The Commission decision required the broadcasters to supply third parties with advance weekly listings, and to permit their reproduction on payment of a reasonable royalty.

On appeal to the CFI, the broadcasters sought to rely on *Volvo* v. *Veng*, arguing that refusal to grant a licence could not in itself constitute an abuse of a dominant position, and that the Commission's requirement that they should license the listings deprived them of the very substance of their copyrights. The CFI conceded that failure to license was not in itself an abuse, but considered that the copyright was being exercised to pursue an aim manifestly contrary to the objectives of Article 86. Such conduct was not necessary to protect copyright's 'essential function', which was 'to protect the moral rights in the work, and ensure a reward for the creative effort, while respecting the aims of, in particular Article 86'.[175] This might be seen as implying that a right to a royalty ('reward') should be considered adequate, which would undercut the reproduction right fundamentally. Also, puzzlingly, the CFI appears to be

---

[174]   Case COMP IV/31.851, *Magill TV Guide/ITP, BBC and RTE* [1989] 4 CMLR 757.
[175]   Case C-241/91 P, *Radio Telefis Eireann* v. *Commission* [1991] ECR 485 (para. 71).

treating the free movement of goods exception (under which specific subject matter was devised) as in some sense applicable in the context of the competition provisions. For this and a number of other reasons, this is a highly contentious definition of the specific subject matter of copyright, and it was not adopted by the ECJ in the appeal which followed. The ECJ's analysis concentrated entirely on competition law. Following *Volvo* v. *Veng*, it confirmed that the right of reproduction forms part of copyright, so that refusal to grant a licence cannot in itself constitute abuse of a dominant position. However, the exercise of an exclusive right by the proprietor might, 'in exceptional circumstances', involve abusive conduct. Here the broadcasters had sought to monopolise a downstream market without justification, and this did amount to an abuse.[176]

The ruling in *Magill*, if taken to mean that a refusal to license to prevent emergence of a new product is an abuse, is potentially of extremely wide ambit. Other cases have stressed its exceptional nature.[177] The issue arose again in relation to intellectual property in the *IMS* case. IMS is a market research company which provides data report services to interested pharmaceutical companies. This case involved regional wholesaler data reports on sales of pharmaceutical products by pharmacies throughout Germany, provided to interested pharmaceutical companies through IMS's German subsidiary. The reports were based on the so-called '1860 brick structure', which divided the country into artificial geographic areas. The 1860 brick structure had been developed over decades, by a working group which included both IMS employees and representatives of the pharmaceutical industry. Considerable resources had been invested in it. In 2000, IMS sued Pharma Intranet Information (PI), a competitor, in the German courts for breach of copyright. PI had been founded by former IMS senior employees,

---

[176]   Joined Cases C-241/91 P and C-242/91 P, *Radio Telefis Eireann (RTE) and Independent Television Publications Ltd (ITP)* v. *Commission* [1995] ECR 743.

[177]   This raises a wider aspect of competition law, the 'essential facilities doctrine', found in US antitrust law, whereby the owner of an essential facility may be forced to share it with a competitor if the competitor cannot practically or reasonably duplicate the essential facility, and without access to it competition in a market is impossible or seriously impeded. The ECJ has been cautious in its attitude to this approach. See Case C-7/97, *Oscar Bronner GmbH & Co. KG* v. *Mediaprint Zeitungs- und Zeitschriftenverlag GmbH & Co. KG, Mediaprint Zeitungsvertriebsgesellschaft mbH & Co. KG* [1998] ECR I-7791; Case T-504/3, *Tiercé Ladbroke SA* v. *Commission* [1997] ECR II-923; Cases T-374, 375, and 388/94, *European Night Services Ltd* v. *Commission* [1998] ECR II-3141. For further discussion, see Frank Wooldridge, 'The Essential Facilities Doctrine and *Magill II*: The Decision of the ECJ in *Oscar Bronner*' [1999] 2 *IPQ* 256–64. For a US perspective, see Gregory V.S. McCurdy, 'Intellectual Property and Competition: Does the Essential Facilities Doctrine Shed Any New Light? [2003] *EIPR* 472–80.

and was found to be selling its services based on copies of the 1860 brick structure. The Frankfurt Regional Court granted an interim injunction preventing PI from using the brick structure, on the basis that the brick structure was covered by copyright, and also referred a number of questions to the ECJ. PI was acquired by National Data Corporation (NDC), which requested but was refused a licence to use the brick structure, so complained to the Commission that this was an infringement of Article 82.

The Commission issued an interim decision requiring IMS to license the 1860 brick structure forthwith, on the grounds that: there was a reasonably strong *prima facie* case establishing an infringement; there was a likelihood of serious and irreparable harm to the applicants unless the measures were ordered; and there was an urgent need for protective measures. It regarded the brick structure as a *de facto* industry standard. IMS appealed against the decision, and asked for interim suspension of it. The President of the CFI held that there was a serious dispute as to whether the Commission had correctly interpreted the notion of exceptional circumstances referred to in *Magill*. IMS also argued that the intellectual property in the painstakingly developed 1860 brick structure was a core feature of its competitiveness, and that its service would be devalued into a generic offering indistinct from the competing services if it were forced to share it. The President of the CFI noted that 'the fundamental rationale of copyright is that it affords the creator of inventive and original works the exclusive right to exploit such works', and that 'to reduce it to a purely economic right to receive royalties dilutes the essence of the right and is, in principle, likely to cause potentially serious and irreparable harm to the rightholder'. This was a significant interference with the specific subject matter of the right. An interim stay of the decision was granted, pending the decision of the CFI on the main issues.[178] A few months later, the Frankfurt Higher Regional Court gave a judgment upholding the injunction against PI on the grounds of German unfair competition law. It held that IMS could prevent use of a copied structure, but it could not prevent third parties from developing independently a brick structure based on districts and postcodes, nor could it expect third parties to adopt variations simply to distance themselves from the IMS product, particularly if the technical needs of the task required some overlap. Although the Court acknowledged that there was copyright in the brick structure, IMS did not have standing to enforce the copyright on these facts, because under German law copyright was owned by the members of the working group, and not IMS. The Commission at this point withdrew its

---

[178] Case T-184/01 R, *IMS Health Inc.* v. *Commission* [2001] ECR II-2349 and 3193 (orders of 10 August and 26 October 2001). A further appeal by NDC to the President of the ECJ was unsuccessful: Case C-481/01 P(R), *NDC Health* [2002] ECR I-3401 (order of 11 April 2002).

interim measures decision, on the grounds that there was no longer proven urgency requiring the prevention of irreparable damage to NDC and to the public interest in competition.[179]

The ECJ's ruling on the German court's questions offered a tighter and more structured definition of the 'exceptional circumstances' referred to in *Magill*. It reiterated that the exclusive right of reproduction forms part of the rights of the owner of an intellectual property right, so that refusal to grant a licence, even by an undertaking holding a dominant position, cannot in itself constitute abuse of a dominant position. Nevertheless, exercise of an exclusive right by the owner may, in exceptional circumstances, involve abusive conduct (*Volvo* v. *Veng*; *Magill*). For the refusal by an undertaking which owns a copyright to give access to a product or service indispensable for carrying on a particular business to be treated as abusive, it is sufficient that three cumulative conditions be satisfied, namely, that that refusal is preventing the emergence of a new product for which there is a potential consumer demand, that it is unjustified and is such as to exclude any competition on a secondary market.[180] It is not entirely clear when a right holder's refusal may be justified, and analogies with other compulsory licensing cases involving access to physical infrastructure are not particularly helpful. In practice, the matter will fall to be determined by national courts and competition authorities.[181]

The Commission's well-known action against Microsoft, although its central focus is the alleged abuse of a dominant position, also has relevance for intellectual property. Sun Microsystems had complained that Microsoft was abusing its dominant position in the market for client PC operating systems by refusing to supply interoperability information for Windows work group servers. The Commission agreed that there had been an infringement of Article 82, and required Microsoft to make the relevant interoperability infor-

---

[179]   Case COMP D3/38.044, *NDC Health* v. *IMS Health* (OJ 2003 268/69); [2003] 15 CMLR.

[180]   Case C-418/01, *IMS Health GmbH & Co. KG* v. *NDC Health GmbH & Co. KG* [2004] ECR I-5039 (paras. 34–8).

[181]   For further discussion see Alessandra Narciso, 'IMS Health or the Question Whether Intellectual Property Still Deserves a Specific Approach in a Free Market Economy' [2003] *IPQ* 445–68; David Aitman and Alison Jones, 'Competition Law and Copyright: Has the Copyright Owner Lost the Ability to Control his Copyright' [2004] *EIPR* 137–47; Christopher Stothers, 'IMS Health and its Implications for Compulsory Licensing in Europe' [2004] *EIPR* 467–72; Burton Ong, 'Anti Competitive Refusals to Grant Copyright Licences: Reflections on the IMS Saga' [2004] *EIPR* 505–14; Estelle Derclaye, 'The IMS Health Decision and the Reconciliation of Copyright and Competition Law' [2004] *ELRev* 687–97; Thomas Eilmansberger, 'The Essential Facilities Doctrine under Art. 82: What Is the State of Affairs after *IMS Health* and *Microsoft*?' (2005) 16 *KCLJ* 329–46.

mation available. The decision also required Microsoft to offer an 'unbundled' version of WINDOWS, without Windows Media Player.[182] The Commission insisted that the unbundled product should carry both the Microsoft and Windows trade marks, and also objected to Microsoft's proposal that it should be called 'Windows Reduced Media Edition'. It has instead been named 'Windows XP N', the 'N' indicating that Windows Media Player is not included. It has been argued on Microsoft's behalf that the Commission has in effect required it to use its world-famous trade mark for products which Microsoft would not have chosen to produce, of lower functionality and quality than the premium products its customers had learned to expect.[183] The Commission returned to the notion of specific subject matter to justify its decision, repeating its highly contentious view from *Magill* that 'the central function of intellectual property rights is to protect the moral rights in a right-holder's work and ensure a reward for the creative effort'. It continued:

> But it is also an essential objective of intellectual property law that creativity should be stimulated for the general public good. A refusal by an undertaking to grant a licence may, under exceptional circumstances, be contrary to the general public good by constituting an abuse of a dominant position with harmful effects on innovation and on consumers.[184]

The Commission here adopts a notion of the intellectual property 'bargain', as a rationale underpinning the grant of intellectual property rights. This approach works well for patent law. Patent law grants the patentee strong monopoly protection for a limited time, as a *quid pro quo* of disclosure to the public. The aim is to promote innovation, and the economic benefits which flow from it. However, a literal transfer of the patent model to copyright presents serious difficulties.[185] In addition, the Commission's reasoning seems

---

[182]   Case COMP C-3/37.792, *Microsoft*, C(2004)900 final; [2005] CMLR 19. For comment, see Daniel Byrne, 'Compulsory Licensing of IP Rights: Has EC Competition Law Reached a Clear and Rational Analysis Following the IMS Judgment and the Microsoft Decision?' [2007] *JIPL&P* 324–30; Steven Anderman, 'Does the *Microsoft* Case Offer a New Paradigm for the "Exceptional Circumstances" Test and Compulsory Copyright Licenses under EC Competition Law?' (2004) 1 *Competition Law Review* 7–23; James Killick, 'IMS and Microsoft Judged in the Cold Light of IMS' (2004) 1 *Competition Law Review* 23–47.

[183]   Christian Rohnke, 'Whose Trade Mark Rights? What the Microsoft Case Means for Trade Mark Owners' [2006] *JIPL&P* 861–6.

[184]   Case COMP C-3/37.792, *Microsoft* (para. 711). This extremely controversial 'definition' has here been widened to encompass *all* intellectual property, and not merely copyright.

[185]   See Catherine Seville, 'Copyright's Bargain – Defining our Terms' (2003) *Intellectual Property Quarterly* 312–41.

somewhat circular, and even arbitrary: exclusive intellectual property rights stimulate creativity for the public good, yet where the public good requires it they must be non-exclusive. For this reason, the Commission's decision in *Microsoft* has been attacked for espousing a 'convenient facilities' doctrine, in contrast to the ECJ's cautious approach to the 'essential facilities' doctrine in *Oscar Bronner*, and the carefully delimited 'exceptional circumstances' described by the ECJ in *IMS*.[186] Nevertheless, the Commission's decision was very largely upheld by the Court of First Instance.[187]

The interface between competition law and intellectual property law seems likely to continue to raise issues, given the pervasiveness of both. See, for example, the *Grüne Punkt* case. Germany introduced a law aimed at reducing packaging waste. Manufacturers could comply in various ways, including by contracting with suitable undertakings who would collect and recover their packaging. DSD ran the Grüne Punkt (Green Dot) scheme, which was the only one operating throughout Germany, although there were other regional schemes. Participating manufacturers were permitted to use the Grüne Punkt logo on all recoverable packaging, and a fee was charged for all packaging marked with the logo, whether or not the packaging was recovered by DSD, or by some other compliant route. The Commission found this to be an abuse of DSD's dominant position, because the fee was not calculated on the basis of actual use of the scheme. The effect was to discourage use of other schemes by other providers. The Commission required that no licence fee should be charged where manufacturers could show that the Grüne Punkt scheme had not been used, and that their obligations had been fulfilled by another scheme (such as a regional scheme, or a self-managed scheme). The CFI upheld the Commission's decision. The central focus of the case was the compatibility of DSD's scheme with Article 82. But DSD also argued that the Commission's required solution undermined both the specific subject matter and the distinctiveness of its mark. DSD objected that the Grüne Punkt logo would be affixed to packaging which would not in fact be recovered by DSD, enabling competitors to benefit unfairly, by what amounted to a compulsory licence. DSD also argued that the purpose of the logo was to distinguish packaging covered by the DSD scheme from that covered by any other scheme, and considered that use of the Grüne Punkt mark on packaging, which might not be recovered by the DSD scheme, would undermine the mark's distinctiveness. The CFI held that the function of the Grüne Punkt mark was to make consumers aware of

---

[186]   See Derek Ridyard, 'Compulsory Access under EC Competition Law – A New Doctrine of "Convenient Facilities" and the Case for Price Regulation' [2004] *ECLR* 669–73.

[187]   Case T-201/04, *Microsoft Corp.* v. *Commission* [2007] 5 CMLR 11. For comment, see Ian Eagles and Louise Longdin [2008] *EIPR* 205–8.

the *possibility* of having the packaging recovered by the DSD scheme, not to indicate an *exclusive* choice of DSD. Manufacturers were free to opt for a mixed system, so the logos of other schemes might be affixed on the same packaging. The exclusivity which DSD claimed would prevent use of mixed systems, and would legitimise the possibility that DSD would be paid for a service which it could be proved it did not actually provide. This could not be permitted. The specific subject matter of the Grüne Punkt mark was not adversely affected, and all DSD's arguments founded on trade mark law were therefore rejected. The decision did not give third parties the right to use the Grüne Punkt mark, so this could not amount to a compulsory licence.[188]

Both the *Microsoft* and *Grüne Punkt* cases highlight the difficulties posed when competition law remedies impinge, albeit indirectly, on the use of a trade mark.

Should the pharmaceutical sector be treated as a special case for the purposes of Article 82?

As has been discussed, attempts to limit parallel trade are normally viewed with great disfavour by the Community. When the trade mark holders in *Bristol-Myers Squibb* attempted to defend their resistance to parallel imports by arguing that distortions in the pharmaceutical market provided a legitimate reason for their opposition, the ECJ was unequivocal in its response. Even though price differences may result from factors over which trade mark owners have no control, distortions caused by divergent pricing rules in one member state must be remedied by measures at Community level, and not by action at national level incompatible with the free movement of goods.[189] Nevertheless, there has been a suggestion that these distortions may be used to defend a dominant pharmaceutical company's refusal to supply customers, even if the object is to limit parallel trade. In *Syfait*, GlaxoSmithKline (GSK) pharmaceutical products were sold to wholesalers in Greece, who exported them in large quantities to other member states where prices were much higher. GSK stopped supplying these wholesalers, saying that it would supply hospitals and pharmacies directly. After complaints to the Greek Competition Commission (GCC), GSK notified the GCC, and sought clearance that its behaviour was not anti-competitive. The GCC referred two questions to the ECJ, asking whether and in what circumstances a dominant pharmaceutical

---

[188] Case T-151/01, *Der Grüne Punkt-Duales System Deutschland GmbH* v. *Commission* [2007] 5 CMLR 4.

[189] Joined Cases C-427/93, C-429/93 and C-436/93, *Bristol-Myers Squibb* v. *Paranova A/S*; *C.H. Boehringer Sohn, Boehringer Ingelheim KG and Boehringer Ingelheim A/S* v. *Paranova A/S*; *Bayer Aktiengesellschaft and Bayer Danmark A/S* v. *Paranova A/S* [1996] ECR I-3457 (para. 46).

company may refuse to fulfil the orders it receives from wholesalers in order to limit parallel trade.

In his Opinion, Advocate General Jacobs reviewed not only the standard competition cases involving failure to supply an existing customer, but also *Volvo* v. *Veng*, *Magill* and *IMS*. He noted that although a dominant undertaking will sometimes be obliged to supply its products or services, that obligation is not unqualified. An intention to limit parallel trade will ordinarily render abusive a dominant undertaking's refusal to supply. But even if conduct is *prima facie* an abuse, Community law allows for the possibility that objective justification for such conduct may be shown. The Advocate General noted that the characteristics of the European pharmaceutical sector 'set it apart from all other industries engaged in the production of readily traded goods'. He thought it relevant to take a number of factors into account. Firstly, the pharmaceutical sector is subject to pervasive and diverse regulation at both national and Community levels. As a result, the price of pharmaceutical products in some member states is typically much higher than in others, and these price differentials create the opportunities for parallel trade. The distribution of pharmaceuticals is subject to a high degree of regulation, so that normal conditions of competition do not prevail. The Advocate General considered that in these circumstances, when pharmaceutical undertakings attempt to block parallel trade, they are not thereby seeking to entrench price differentials of their own making, but rather to avoid the consequences which would follow if the very low prices imposed upon them in some member states were generalised across the Community. He also took the view that dominant undertakings' legal and moral obligations to maintain supply in each member state cast doubt on the reasonableness and proportionality of requiring them to supply wholesalers in low-price member states intending to export the quantities supplied.[190] Secondly, it was important to consider the economics of the innovative pharmaceutical industry, where the price of pharmaceuticals must reflect the high fixed costs of research and development, as well as low marginal cost of production. In these economic conditions, parallel trade might have potentially negative consequences for competition, the common market and incentives to innovate. Finally, it had to be acknowledged that profit from parallel trade went to those in the distribution chain, rather than to consumers and purchasers. The main purchasers (often public bodies) could

---

[190]   Community legislation now requires pharmaceutical producers and their distributors to 'ensure appropriate and continued supplies of that medicinal product to pharmacies and persons authorised to supply medicinal products so that the needs of patients in the Member State in question are covered': Dir. 2001/83 on the Community code relating to medicinal products for human use [2001] OJ L 311/67, as amended by Dir. 2004/27 [2004] OJ L 136/34.

negotiate prices directly, but parallel trade tended to undermine those agreed pricing levels, without benefiting consumers. Enlargement is likely to emphasise these effects. The Advocate General therefore concluded that, in such circumstances, a dominant pharmaceutical undertaking refusing to meet orders in full might be able to justify that refusal.[191]

Although AG Jacobs was careful to stress that his conclusions were highly dependent on the very particular nature of the pharmaceutical industry, his Opinion displayed an unusual readiness to acknowledge the impact of these distortions on pharmaceutical manufacturers. Inevitably, there was a great deal of curiosity as to whether the ECJ would adopt the same approach.[192] However, the ECJ found that it had no jurisdiction to answer the questions referred to it by the GCC, because it was not a 'Court or Tribunal' within the meaning of Article 234 EC.[193] Given the change in attitude proposed by the Advocate General's Opinion, it is unfortunate that no ruling was given, because both legal and commercial uncertainty remain. It is likely that there will be guidance from the ECJ eventually, though, since a number of references from Greek courts on very similar questions are pending.[194]

---

[191]   Case C-53/03, *Synetairismos Farmakopoion Aitolias & Akarnanias (SYFAIT)* v. *Glaxosmithkline Plc* [2005] ECR 4609 (AG Jacobs' Opinion, 28 October 2004). For comment on the case, see Gavin Robert and Stephanie Ridley, 'Parallel Trade in the Pharmaceutical Sector: Scourge or Benefit?' [2006] *ECLR* 91–5; Anthony Dawes, 'Neither Head nor Tail: The Confused Application of EC Competition Law to the Pharmaceutical Sector' [2006] *ECLR* 269–78. For consideration of the problem, see Dermot Glynn, 'Article 82 and Price Discrimination in Patented Pharmaceuticals: The Economics' [2005] *ECLR* 135–43.

[192]   The ECJ has previously been wary of taking notice of 'ethical obligations' to supply pharmaceutical products, considering that these are 'difficult to apprehend and distinguish from commercial considerations': Joined Cases C-267/95 and 268/95, *Merck* v. *Primecrown* [1996] ECR I-6285 (para. 53).

[193]   Case C-53/03, *Synetairismos Farmakopoion Aitolias & Akarnanias (SYFAIT)* v. *Glaxosmithkline Plc* [2005] ECR 4609 (Judgment, 31 May 2005). The GCC has followed the Advocate General's guidance, as have a number of other national authorities, holding that a refusal to supply is not necessarily abusive. Nevertheless, pharmaceutical companies will want reassurance from the ECJ.

[194]   Cases C-468–478/06, *Sot. Lélos kai Sia* v. *GlaxoSmithKline*. The Advocate General's Opinion (1 April 2008) is that an undertaking in a dominant position which refuses to meet in full the orders of wholesalers of pharmaceutical products, with a view to reducing the harm caused by parallel trade, thereby engages in abusive conduct. However, it may be possible for the undertaking to provide an objective justification for its conduct by showing that the regulation of the market compels it to behave in that manner in order to protect its legitimate business interests (although in this particular case it is not possible for GlaxoSmithKline to rely on the pricing system for medicinal products, the duty to supply or the impact on innovation incentives). The wholesalers had argued that the Commission should take back responsibility for the

It will doubtless be difficult to persuade the Commission that the pharmaceutical industry deserves its sympathy. In the first Article 82 case involving pharmaceuticals, the Commission described a novel form of abuse, and fined the pharmaceutical giant AstraZeneca €60 million.[195] Patented in Europe in 1979, Losec was a pioneer in its field (of so-called 'proton pump inhibitors'), and for a time was the world's best-selling prescription medicine. The Commission held that between 1993 and 2000, AstraZeneca had blocked or delayed market access for generic versions of Losec, and blocked parallel imports. At that time, generic products could only be marketed (and parallel importers could only obtain import licences) if there was an existing reference market authorisation for the original corresponding product – here, Losec capsules. The Commission found that AstraZeneca had misused rules and procedures applied by the National Medicines Agencies, and selectively deregistered market authorisations for Losec capsules, replacing the capsule with Losec tablets. Although generic companies might have been able to obtain licences on the basis of published information, this was more difficult than relying on 'essential similarity' to an existing market authorisation. Although AstraZeneca continued to sell the capsules in low price member states, once the capsules had been deregistered in a particular member state (usually a high price member state), parallel importers could not obtain licences to import capsules. The practical result was that Losec was not subject to competition from generic substitutes even though it was out of patent, and that competition from parallel imports (previously very strong) was stopped. This practice, of extending monopoly rights beyond the original period of patent protection by introducing a new form of the patented product, is known as 'evergreening'.[196] AstraZeneca has lodged an appeal, arguing in part that the law was unclear,[197] and also claiming that its purpose in replacing Losec

---

cases from the Greek Competition Authority, because national procedures would take too long, and also because the complaints raised new and fundamental questions of EC competition law. The Commission refused to do so (Decision D/201953 EAEPC/Glaxo Greece (Imigran, Lamictal, Severent) (10 April 2006)), although this refusal is being appealed to the CFI: Case T-153/06, *European Association of Euro-Pharmaceutical Companies* v. *Commission* [2006] OJ C 178/68.

[195]   Case COMP A.37.507/F3 (*AstraZeneca*) [2006] 5 CMLR 6. For criticism of the decision, see Maria Isabel Manley and Anna Wray, 'New Pitfall for the Pharmaceutical Industry' [2006] *JIPL&P* 266–71.

[196]   Evergreening is a mechanism commonly associated with the manufacturers of 'blockbuster' drugs, and is intended to maximise monopoly profits for as long as possible. Some time after the active ingredient has been patented, 'new use' patent claims are filed for the process of manufacture, delivery mechanism or dosage regime. If this technique is successful, the period of patent protection is effectively extended, delaying the entry of generic substitutes into the market.

[197]   The relevant rules concerning marketing authorisations have since changed,

capsules with tablets was a commercial one, based on sound business reasons, and was not intended to block generic companies and parallel importers.

Pharmaceutical manufacturers will of course adapt their behaviour to prevailing market conditions. Where price distortions exist, they will seek both to defend themselves where necessary, and to exploit the situation where possible. Health care spending represents a major part of the budget of all member states, and health care policy is a matter of great national importance. Given the political difficulties in negotiating a harmonised approach to pharmaceutical pricing, it seems likely that variations on the old arguments between manufacturers and parallel importers will continue for the foreseeable future. The Commission has recently launched a sector inquiry into competition in the pharmaceuticals sector, and has been conducting inspections at the premises of a number of pharmaceutical companies. The Commission has described the inquiry as 'a response to indications that competition in pharmaceutical markets in Europe may not be working well', noting that 'fewer new pharmaceuticals are being brought to market, and the entry of generic pharmaceuticals sometimes seems to be delayed'.[198] The inquiry will examine whether agreements between pharmaceutical companies, such as settlements in patent disputes, infringe Article 81. It will also investigate whether pharmaceutical companies have created artificial barriers to entry, whether through the misuse of patent rights, vexatious litigation or other means, and whether such practices infringe Article 82. The Commission has stated that 'vigorous competition in this sector is crucial for the public, as it ensures both access by patients to state-of-the-art medicines, and value for money for health spending by individuals, private health schemes and government health services in Europe'. The interaction between competition law and intellectual property in the pharmaceutical sector remains a highly sensitive issue, since the economic stakes are so high.

---

so that such behaviour is no longer possible. See also Sophie Lawrance and Pat Treacy, 'The Commission's AstraZeneca Decision: Delaying Generic Entry is an Abuse of a Dominant Position' [2007] *JIPL&P* 7–8.

[198]   Press Release (16 January 2008), 'Commission Launches Sector Inquiry into Pharmaceuticals with Unannounced Inspections' IP/08/49.

7. Enforcement of intellectual property rights

For intellectual property rights to be effective, they need to be enforced. Remedies must be quickly and cheaply available. The environment is no longer simply a national one. The economic value of protected products is enormous. Piracy and counterfeiting is a major trade, with many operations highly organised and professional. With global trading, any deficiencies in enforcement methods are highlighted and exploited. In some countries, piracy has been rampant, and even condoned at government level. The scale of unauthorised use of intellectual property is therefore very considerable, and appropriate methods are needed to combat this.

7.1 TRIPS

Before the TRIPS Agreement, international intellectual property rules were to be found largely in WIPO Treaties, such as the Paris and Berne Conventions. Although these had (and have) considerable merits as harmonising instruments, they were well understood to have significant shortcomings with regard to the enforcement of rights. Detailed rules providing for the enforcement of rights in national courts simply did not exist. Nor was there any mechanism for establishing that states were in breach of their obligations, or for resolving disputes at state level. This was the background to the Uruguay Round of GATT. Although the inclusion of intellectual property in the negotiating mandate was a significant step forward, very considerable challenges still remained to be overcome. The text was signed at Marrakech in 1994 and entered into force on 1 January 1996. It is probably the most significant achievement in international intellectual property law of the twentieth century.

TRIPS sets normative standards for a wide range of intellectual property rights, including: copyright and related rights, trade marks, geographical indications, industrial designs, patents, plant varieties, layout designs of integrated circuits and trade secrets. In addition, an important set of provisions deals with domestic procedures and remedies for the enforcement of intellectual property rights.

The Agreement lays down certain general principles which apply to all intellectual property enforcement procedures. Member states must ensure that their enforcement procedures permit effective action against any act of infringement of intellectual property rights covered by the TRIPS Agreement, including expeditious remedies to prevent infringements and remedies which constitute a deterrent to further infringements. The procedures must be applied in a way which avoids the creation of barriers to legitimate trade, and provides for safeguards against their abuse. Enforcement procedures must be fair and equitable, must not be unnecessarily complicated or costly, or entail unreasonable time-limits or unwarranted delays. Decisions should preferably be in writing and reasoned, and based only on evidence in respect of which the parties could be heard. Judicial review of final administrative decisions must be available, and also of at least the legal aspects of initial judicial decisions on the merits of a case. However, there is no obligation to provide an opportunity for review of acquittals in criminal cases.[1]

Civil judicial proceedings must be available for the enforcement of any right covered by TRIPS. Defendants must be given adequate and timely written notice. Parties must be allowed representation by independent legal counsel, and procedures must not impose overly burdensome requirements concerning mandatory personal appearances.[2] All parties must be entitled to substantiate their claims and present all relevant evidence.[3] Injunctions must also be available. TRIPS defines this as a judicial power 'to order a party to desist from an infringement, *inter alia* to prevent the entry into the channels of commerce in their jurisdiction of imported goods that involve the infringement of an intellectual property right, immediately after customs clearance of such goods'. The requirement is grounded on infringing conduct: there is no obligation to make an injunction available if the defendant did not know or have reasonable grounds to know that dealing in the subject matter would infringe an intellectual property right.[4] Hence, provisional remedies are also provided for. Judicial authorities must be able 'to order prompt and effective provisional measures to prevent an infringement of any intellectual property right from occurring', and in particular 'to prevent the entry into the channels of commerce in their jurisdiction of goods, including imported goods immediately after customs clearance'.[5] Provisional measures must also be available to

---

[1]   TRIPS, Art. 41.
[2]   In some jurisdictions, only the chief executive may represent a legal person. This is considered unreasonable for routine judicial proceedings.
[3]   TRIPS, Art. 42. Judicial authorities must have power to order discovery in appropriate cases, subject to conditions which ensure the protection of confidential information where necessary: TRIPS, Art. 43(1).
[4]   TRIPS, Art. 44(1).
[5]   TRIPS, Art. 50(1)(a).

'preserve relevant evidence in regard to the alleged infringement'.[6] *Ex parte* actions must be available in serious cases (for example, where delay is likely to cause irreparable harm to the right holder, or where there is a demonstrable risk of evidence being destroyed), these being in practice the only realistic mechanism against the worst infringers.[7] To protect the defendant, a list of safeguards is provided for, comparable to those required for search orders (formerly known as Anton Piller orders) in the UK.[8]

Compensatory damages must be available against infringers who engage in infringing activity 'knowingly, or with reasonable grounds to know' that they are doing so.[9] An account of profits may be available even against an innocent infringer.[10] Delivery up and destruction of infringing goods (and materials used in creating them) may also be available. Simple removal of a trade mark from counterfeit goods will not be sufficient to allow their release into the channels of commerce, save in exceptional cases.[11] Infringers may be required to provide information about third parties involved in the production and distributions of the infringing goods, unless this would be out of proportion to the seriousness of the infringement.[12]

Border measures must be available. Members states must 'adopt procedures to enable a right holder, who has valid grounds for suspecting that the importation of counterfeit trademark or pirated copyright goods may take place, to lodge an application in writing with competent authorities, administrative or judicial, for the suspension by the customs authorities of the release into free circulation of such goods'.[13] Since this type of procedure was unfamiliar in many WTO member states, a detailed scheme (designed to protect the rights of all parties) is set out.[14] Member states are also obliged to apply criminal procedures and penalties, at the minimum in cases of wilful trade mark counterfeiting and copyright piracy on a commercial scale. Remedies must include imprisonment and/or fines sufficient to provide an appropriate deterrent.[15]

---

6   TRIPS, Art. 50(1)(b).
7   TRIPS, Art. 50(2).
8   TRIPS, Art. 50(3)–(7).
9   TRIPS, Art. 45(1). Costs are also recoverable.
10 TRIPS, Art. 45(2). This might cover, for example, acts of unfair competition or passing off.
11 TRIPS, Art. 46.
12 TRIPS, Art. 47.
13 TRIPS, Art. 51.
14 TRIPS, Arts. 52–60.
15 TRIPS, Art. 61.

7.2 EUROPEAN COMMUNITY MEASURES

The Community treats counterfeiting and piracy very seriously, considering them a real threat to the proper functioning of the single market. They have the potential to affect trade and investment adversely, and to distort competition. Their repercussions may be felt not only in the economic sphere, but also in the realms of consumer protection, public health and safety.

The Commission launched a wide-ranging consultation exercise in October 1998 through its Green Paper, *Combating Counterfeiting and Piracy in the Single Market*.[16] This uncovered a widespread dissatisfaction with the bureaucratic complexities, delays and haphazard responses associated with the enforcement mechanisms in member states. The prospect of action at Community level was therefore welcomed. What respondents sought was the availability of substantial penalties in all cases, rather than a few exemplary actions. It was thought that only punitive penalties, regularly applied, would deter those engaged in aggressive piracy and counterfeiting. Although it was difficult to gather reliable data, it was estimated that 5–7% of world trade was counterfeit, costing those concerned €200–300 billion per annum, with global job losses of 200,000 jobs. A number of sectoral studies were considered: industries most severely affected were software, textiles, clothing, toys, music, perfumes, publishing, pharmaceuticals, phonographic/CD recordings, videos, car parts and sports goods. Although the figures were somewhat speculative, it seemed reasonable to conclude that the scale of counterfeiting was huge, and also that it was on the increase. Links with organised crime were suspected. The point was made that counterfeiting was so profitable and the penalties so low that it made an attractive alternative to drugs crime.[17] As a result of these responses to the Green Paper, the Commission presented an 'ambitious' action plan, including a proposed Directive for the enforcement of intellectual property rights.[18] Other initiatives put in place immediately included: training for law enforcement officials; public information and awareness activities; efforts to define a methodology for collecting, analysing and comparing data on counterfeiting and piracy. The Commission also committed itself to exploring administrative cooperation between national authorities and the Commission, and to examining the need for harmonised minimum thresholds for criminal

---

[16] COM(98) 0569 final.

[17] *Report on Responses to the European Commission Green Paper on Counterfeiting and Piracy* (1999). Available at http://ec.europa.eu/internal_market/ indprop/docs/piracy/piracy_en.pdf.

[18] *Communication from the Commission to the Council, the European Parliament and the Economic and Social Committee – Follow-up to the Green Paper on combating counterfeiting and piracy in the single market* COM(2000) 0789 final.

sanctions. Alongside this came a proposal for a Regulation to facilitate seizures by customs of counterfeit goods from outside the EU.[19]

7.2.1   The Enforcement Directive

There was some resistance to the Commission's proposals, particularly those involving the imposition of criminal sanctions. There was also scepticism as to the need for a separate set of remedies for intellectual property protection, and concern at the Draft Directive's broad scope, and hence its potential impact on national procedural systems.[20] The text of the Directive as passed was significantly modified to meet these concerns, and the provision on criminal sanctions was dropped.[21] Nevertheless, the Commission remains convinced that criminal measures are required in order to counter the most serious infringements.[22] The Enforcement Directive concerns the measures, procedures and remedies necessary to ensure the enforcement of intellectual property rights, including industrial property rights.[23] It applies to any

---

[19]   This became Regulation 1383/2003 concerning customs action against goods suspected of infringing certain intellectual property rights and the measures to be taken against goods found to have infringed such rights [2003] OJ L 196/7. See also Regulation 1172/2007 amending Regulation 1891/2004 laying down provisions for the implementation of Regulation 1383/2003 [2007] OJ L 261/12. There has been a version of this Regulation in place since 1986, though it has been refined several times.

[20]   See William R. Cornish, Josef Drexl, Reto Hilty and Annette Kur, 'Procedures and Remedies for Enforcing IPRs: The European Commission's Proposed Directive' [2003] *EIPR* 447–9; Charles-Henry Massa and Alain Strowel, 'The Scope of the Proposed IP Enforcement Directive: Torn between the Desire to Harmonise Remedies and the Need to Combat Piracy' [2004] *EIPR* 244–53; Annette Kur, 'The Enforcement Directive – Rough Start, Happy Ending?' (2004) 35 *IIC* 821–30. Note also the reservations of the European Economic and Social Committee concerning the draft text: *Proposal for a Directive of the European Parliament and of the Council on measures and procedures to ensure the enforcement of intellectual property rights* COM(2003) 46 final.

[21]   Directive 2004/48 on the enforcement of intellectual property rights ('Enforcement Dir.') [2004] OJ L 195/16.

[22]   See below section 7.2.2 The Draft Criminal Enforcement Directive.

[23]   Enforcement Dir., Art. 1. The Commission considers that at least the following intellectual property rights are covered by the scope of the Directive: copyright, rights related to copyright, *sui generis* right of a database maker, rights of the creator of the topographies of a semiconductor product, trademark rights, design rights, patent rights (including rights derived from supplementary protection certificates), geographical indications, utility model rights, plant variety rights, trade names (in so far as these are protected as exclusive property rights in the national law concerned): [2005] OJ L 94/37. For the Directive's implementation in the UK, see Gwilym Harbottle, 'The Implementation in England and Wales of the European Enforcement Directive' [2006] *JIPL&P* 719–27.

infringement of intellectual property rights as provided for by Community law and/or by the national law of the member state concerned (though without prejudice to legislation more favourable to right holders).[24] It acknowledges the common standards imposed by TRIPS, and does not affect member states' international obligations.[25] The Directive seeks to remove some of the remaining disparities between national systems which affect the enforcement of intellectual property rights, particularly in relation to provisional measures. Member states remain free to apply additional sanctions, including criminal sanctions, if they wish to do so.[26] Member states are required to encourage the development of codes of conduct at Community level (say, by trade or professional associations), where these aim to contribute towards the enforcement of intellectual property rights.[27]

The Directive requires member states to provide for the measures, procedures and remedies necessary to ensure the enforcement of intellectual property rights. Measures, procedures and remedies must be fair and equitable, must not be unnecessarily complicated or costly, or entail unreasonable time-limits or unwarranted delays.[28] They must also be effective, proportionate and dissuasive, and applied so as to avoid the creation of barriers to legitimate trade and to provide for safeguards against their abuse.[29] Enforcement may be sought by right holders, licensees, collective rights management bodies and professional defence bodies.[30] In relation to literary or artistic works, and neighbouring rights, there is a rebuttable presumption of authorship or ownership if a name appears on the work.[31]

Where there is reasonable evidence of infringement, judicial authorities must be able to order disclosure (subject to the protection of confidential information). If the alleged infringement is committed 'on a commercial scale', disclosure of the defendant's banking, financial or commercial documents must be available (again, subject to the protection of confidential information).[32] The Directive retains its commitment to prohibitory and corrective measures in serious cases, aimed at preventing further infringements of intellectual property rights. However, their use must take account of the interests

---

[24] Enforcement Dir., Art. 2(1). Existing provisions relating to the enforcement of rights in the Software Directive and the Information Society Directive are also stated to be unaffected: Art. 2(2).
[25] Enforcement Dir., Art. 2(3)(b).
[26] Enforcement Dir., Art. 16.
[27] Enforcement Dir., Art. 17.
[28] Enforcement Dir., Art. 3(1).
[29] Enforcement Dir., Art. 3(2).
[30] Enforcement Dir., Art. 4.
[31] Enforcement Dir., Art. 5.
[32] Enforcement Dir., Art. 6.

of third parties, and would be disproportionate where infringement is committed unintentionally and without negligence.[33] So, although measures for preserving evidence must be available, *ex parte* if necessary, safeguards to protect the defendant (such as a right to appeal against the measures, or the lodging of adequate security) are also required.[34] If an infringement is 'on a commercial scale', disclosure of information on the origin and distribution networks of goods or services must be available.[35] Interlocutory injunctions, seizure and delivery up must be available.[36] If the infringement is on a commercial scale, and recovery of damages is uncertain, there must be the possibility of precautionary seizure of the alleged infringer's movable and immovable property, including the blocking of bank accounts and other assets.[37] These must be available *ex parte* if necessary, in particular where any delay would cause irreparable harm to the right holder.[38]

Once an infringement has been established, 'appropriate measures' must be available to deal with infringing goods, and materials used in their manufacture. Such measures must include recall and removal from the channels of commerce, or destruction. These must be carried out at the expense of the infringer, unless there are particular reasons not to do so. Remedies must be proportional, given the seriousness of the infringement, and rights of third parties must be taken into account.[39] Injunctions must also be available, against both the infringer and intermediaries whose services are used to infringe an intellectual property right.[40] Where the infringer has acted unintentionally and without negligence, pecuniary compensation may be ordered in lieu of these measures, if execution of the measures would cause disproportionate harm to the infringer.[41]

Where an infringer acts knowingly, or with reasonable grounds to know, the right holder is entitled to 'damages appropriate to the actual prejudice suffered by him/her as a result of the infringement'.[42] The quantum must be set taking into account all appropriate aspects, such as the negative economic consequences, including lost profits, which the injured party has suffered, any unfair profits made by the infringer and, in appropriate cases, elements other than economic factors, such as the moral prejudice caused to the right holder by the

---

[33] Enforcement Dir., Recitals 24 and 25.
[34] Enforcement Dir., Art. 7.
[35] Enforcement Dir., Art. 8.
[36] Enforcement Dir., Art. 9(1).
[37] Enforcement Dir., Art. 9(2).
[38] Enforcement Dir., Art. 9(4).
[39] Enforcement Dir., Art. 10.
[40] Enforcement Dir., Art. 11.
[41] Enforcement Dir., Art. 12.
[42] Enforcement Dir., Art. 13(1).

infringement. A reasonable royalty may be appropriate in some cases.[43] With respect to innocent infringers, member states may provide for an order of account of profits, or damages (which may be pre-established).[44] Costs should be borne by the unsuccessful party, unless this is inequitable.[45] Appropriate measures for the dissemination of the decision must be available.[46]

The Enforcement Directive was considered in *Promusicae*.[47] Promusicae (a Spanish music and audiovisual association) sought information from a telecoms and internet provider, Telefónica, regarding the names and addresses linked to computers which were using peer-to-peer file-sharing software. It wished to use this personal data in civil actions against the file-sharers. Telefónica refused, claiming that it could only turn over such information as part of a criminal prosecution or in matters of public security and national defence. The ECJ was asked whether Community law (in particular, the Information Society Directive, E-Commerce Directive, or Enforcement Directive) required member states to communicate such data. Having considered the matter in the light of the Directives on protection of personal data,[48] and the ECHR, the Court concluded that member states were not required to lay down an obligation to communicate personal data in order to ensure effective protection of copyright in the context of civil proceedings. However, Community law did require that, when transposing those Directives, the member states take care to rely on an interpretation of them which allows a fair balance to be struck between the various fundamental rights protected by the Community legal order. In addition, when implementing the measures transposing those Directives, the authorities and courts of the member states must not only interpret their national law in a manner consistent with those Directives but also make sure that they do not rely on an interpretation of them which would be in conflict with those fundamental rights or with the other general principles of Community law, such as the principle of proportionality.

---

43   Enforcement Dir., Art. 13(1).
44   Enforcement Dir., Art. 13(2).
45   Enforcement Dir., Art. 14.
46   Enforcement Dir., Art. 15.
47   Case C-275/06, *Productores de Música de España (Promusicae)* v. *Telefónica de España SAU* (29 January 2008).
48   Directive 95/46 on the protection of individuals with regard to the processing of personal data and on the free movement of such data [1995] OJ L 281/31; Directive 2002/58 concerning the processing of personal data and the protection of privacy in the electronic communications sector [2002] OJ L 201/37.

7.2.2   The Draft Criminal Enforcement Directive

The Commission continues to believe strongly that in appropriate cases, in addition to the civil and administrative measures, procedures and remedies provided for in the Enforcement Directive, criminal penalties should constitute a means of enforcing intellectual property rights. It notes 'major disparities' in national laws, which do not allow the holders of intellectual property rights to benefit from an equivalent level of protection throughout the Community. In particular, as regards criminal penalties, it notes 'considerable differences, particularly as regards the level of punishment laid down by national legislation'. In July 2005, it therefore resubmitted its scheme of criminal penalties, in the form of a proposal for a Directive on criminal measures aimed at ensuring the enforcement of intellectual property rights ('Draft Criminal Enforcement Directive'), and a proposal for a Council Framework Decision to strengthen the criminal law framework to combat intellectual property offences.[49]

As in the Enforcement Directive, the Commission sought to ensure that the Draft Criminal Enforcement Directive would apply to any infringement of intellectual property rights as provided for by Community law and/or by the national law of the member states.[50] It would have obliged member states to regard all intentional infringements of intellectual property rights on a commercial scale as a criminal offence.[51] It would also have covered attempting, aiding or abetting and inciting such offences. The 'commercial scale' criterion is borrowed from TRIPS, Article 61. For such offences, member states would be obliged to provide for custodial sentences when committed by natural persons, and fines and confiscation when committed by natural and/or legal persons. In appropriate cases, destruction of infringing goods, total or partial closure of the establishment used primarily to commit the offence, a permanent or temporary ban on engaging in commercial activities, placing under judicial supervision, judicial winding-up, a ban on access to public assistance or subsidies, and publication of judicial decisions would also have to be available.[52]

The Council has already adopted a Framework Decision on Confiscation of Crime-Related Proceeds, Instrumentalities and Property,[53] and in January

---

[49]   COM(2005) 276 final; SEC(2005) 848.
[50]   Draft Criminal Enforcement Dir., Art. 1.
[51]   Draft Criminal Enforcement Dir., Art. 3.
[52]   Draft Criminal Enforcement Dir., Art. 4.
[53]   2005/212/JHA of 24 February 2005. Member states have not been enthusiastic: see Press Release (18 December 2007), 'Member States Dragging their Heels When it Comes to Applying Community Legislation Aimed at More Widespread Confiscation of the Proceeds of Crime' IP/07/1948.

2005 the Commission adopted a Proposed Framework Decision on combating organised crime.[54] The July 2005 Draft Framework Decision sought to harmonise the level of sentencing for criminal offences under the Draft Criminal Enforcement Directive, including the rules concerning prison sentences, fines and confiscation. It proposed that offences falling within Article 3 of the Draft Directive (intentional infringements of intellectual property rights on a commercial scale) should be punishable by 'a maximum sentence of at least four years' imprisonment when committed under the aegis of a criminal organisation within the meaning of Framework Decision . . . on the fight against organised crime, or where they carry a health or safety risk'. In addition, such offences were to be punishable by 'effective, proportionate and dissuasive penalties', including criminal and non-criminal fines 'to a maximum of at least €100,000 for cases other than the most serious cases', to a maximum of at least €300,000 when committed under the aegis of a criminal organisation, with the possibility of more serious sentences (for example, in the case of risk of death or infirmity).[55] Extended powers of confiscation were required, at least where the offences are committed under the aegis of a criminal organisation, or where they carry a health or safety risk.[56] Member states would have been required to ensure that the holders of intellectual property rights were allowed to assist the investigations carried out by joint investigation teams into offences.[57] Coordination of criminal proceedings would also have been required, with the aim, if possible, of centralising proceedings in a single member state.[58]

The extent of these proposals was extremely controversial. Whilst they were being considered, the ECJ issued a judgment in which it held that although as a general rule, neither criminal law nor the rules of criminal procedure fell within the Community's competence, this did not, however, 'prevent the Community legislature, when the application of effective, proportionate and dissuasive criminal penalties by the competent national authorities is an essential measure for combating serious environmental offences, from taking measures which relate to the criminal law of the Member States which it considers necessary in order to ensure that the rules which it lays down on environmental protection are fully effective'.[59] The Court reiterated that the

---

[54]   MEMO/05/25.

[55]   Proposal for a Council Framework Decision to strengthen the criminal-law framework to combat intellectual property offences 2005/0128(CNS) ('Proposed Framework Decision'), Art. 2.

[56]   Proposed Framework Decision, Art. 3.

[57]   Proposed Framework Decision, Art. 4.

[58]   Proposed Framework Decision, Art. 5.

[59]   Case C-176/03, *Commission v. Council* [2005] ECR I-7879 (para. 48).

choice of the legal basis for a Community measure must rest on objective factors which are amenable to judicial review, including in particular the aim and the content of the measure. Since the principal aim and content of the framework decision at issue in the case in question was environmental protection, it should have been based on Article 175 of the ECT (first pillar) and not on Title VI TEU (third pillar). The Commission has taken a broad view of this ruling, and understands it to mean that there are no restrictions on adopting provisions relating to criminal matters under the first pillar in any potentially relevant area of Community competence. This interpretation is controversial in itself. The Commission's understanding is that the provisions of criminal law required for the effective implementation of Community law come under the first pillar, while horizontal criminal law provisions (police and judicial cooperation, measures on the harmonisation of criminal law in connection with the area of freedom, security and justice) belong to the third pillar.[60]

The Commission therefore decided to amend the 2005 proposal for a Directive and to withdraw the proposal for a framework decision. In April 2006, the Commission produced a new proposal for a Directive on criminal measures aimed at ensuring the enforcement of intellectual property rights, incorporating, updating and amalgamating the provisions of the two previous initiatives.[61] In particular, the proposals relating to the level of penalties and the broad powers of confiscation previously contained in the proposal for a framework decision were now incorporated in the new proposal for a Directive. Although somewhat fuller in its detail, the structure of the Directive is broadly similar to the earlier version of the Directive. Article 1 sets out the subject matter and scope of the Directive; Article 2 defines the concept of a legal person for the purposes of the Directive; Article 3 obliges member states to treat specified types of behaviour as criminal offences; Articles 4 and 5 specify the nature and the level of criminal penalties; Article 6 deals with powers of confiscation; Article 7 provides for joint investigation teams to combat counterfeiting; Article 8 obliges member states to ensure that investigations and prosecution of the offences defined in the Directive do not need to be instigated by the persons whose rights are infringed; Articles 9 and 10 deal with transposition and entry into force. The only provisions not incorporated in the new proposal were those relating to jurisdiction and the coordination of proceedings.[62]

---

[60]   *Communication from the Commission to the European Parliament and the Council on the implications of the Court's judgment of 13 September 2005 (Case C-176/03 Commission v. Council)* COM(2005) 0583 final.

[61]   Amended proposal for a directive of the European Parliament and of the Council on criminal measures aimed at ensuring the enforcement of intellectual property rights, COM(2006) 168 final.

[62]   The Commission plans to take a horizontal approach to this subject under its

The European Parliament's Legal Affairs Committee expressed concerns about some of the substantive provisions which were widely held.[63] The proposed Directive covers all intellectual property rights, including patents. It is thought by many that applying criminal penalties at Community level to infringements of patent rights would be inappropriate, as well as inconsistent with the approach taken by other recent Community legislation. Since many member states already impose criminal penalties, there seems no need for urgent action, and Community measures would lead to duplication in many cases. Furthermore, since Community legislation in the field of patents is extremely limited, it was thought inappropriate to intervene in this very partial way in an area of great complexity.

Although the European Parliament approved the Draft Directive in April 2007, it approved a text with significant amendments.[64] Patents (including plant variety rights and supplementary protection certificates) were excluded from the scope of the Directive. The definition of 'infringements on a commercial scale' was carefully defined as 'any infringement of an intellectual property right committed to obtain a commercial advantage', specifically excluding 'acts carried out by private users for personal and not-for-profit purposes'. Although it was agreed that all intentional infringements of an intellectual property right on a commercial scale, and aiding or abetting and inciting the actual infringement, should be treated as criminal offences, an amendment made it clear that parallel imports of original goods with the consent of the right holder would not be subject to criminal sanctions. In addition, member states would be required to ensure that the fair use of a protected

---

Green Paper on conflicts of jurisdiction and the principle of *ne bis in idem* in criminal proceedings, adopted 23 December 2005, COM(2005) 696 final.

[63]   Committee on Legal Affairs, *Report on the amended proposal for a directive of the European Parliament and of the Council on criminal measures aimed at ensuring the enforcement of intellectual property rights* (27 March 2007) A6-0073/2007.

[64]   *Enforcement of intellectual property rights (criminal measures)* (25 April 2007) P6_TA(2007)0145. See also the European Parliament's resistance to the strategy being adopted in France, the so-called 'Olivennes Agreement'. This 'Agreement for the Development and Protection of Cultural Works and Programmes on New Networks' calls for a 'three strikes, and you're out' policy, directed against French internet users who repeatedly download illegal content. Those who persistently ignore warnings could face suspension or termination of their accounts by ISPs. In France, the Agreement is a result of negotiations between the French government, ISPs and content owners, with the support of online retailers. A European Parliament resolution on the Cultural Industries in Europe calls on the Commission and the member states 'to avoid adopting measures conflicting with civil liberties and human rights and with the principles of proportionality, effectiveness and dissuasiveness, such as the interruption of Internet access'. The resolution also states that 'criminalising consumers who are not seeking to make a profit is not the right solution to combat digital piracy': P6_TA(2008)0123 (10 April 2008).

work, 'including such use by reproduction in copies or audio or by any other means, for purposes such as criticism, comment, news reporting, teaching (including multiple copies for classroom use), scholarship or research', does not constitute a criminal offence. A number of additional safeguards were added, to prevent misuse of criminal sanctions, and to ensure that the rights of defendants would be duly protected and guaranteed. The Directive remains very controversial, however, and serious criticism of it can be expected when it goes before the Council for consideration.

7.2.3   Counterfeiting: Future Measures

The Commission continues to express serious concern about counterfeiting. Modern, sophisticated and readily available techniques allow pirates to manufacture counterfeit products of remarkable quality, hardly distinguishable from genuine goods. Although it is extremely difficult to obtain accurate figures, counterfeit goods are estimated to account for perhaps 3–9% of world trade. Thus counterfeiting appears to offer a serious alternative to other forms of organised crime, though the risk of incurring criminal charges is comparatively low. The Commission also notes effects on European businesses and the internal market. Counterfeits affect trade between member states, and the conditions for competition, generating negative repercussions for competitiveness and growth and creating significant distortions in the market. The labour market is also affected. VAT and customs duties are evaded. Counterfeiting and piracy may also threaten the health and safety of consumers. However, the public perception appears to be that counterfeiting is not a serious problem.[65] A Commission Communication in 2005 emphasised the need for urgent action, calling for 'a more far-reaching and comprehensive approach', looking beyond seizures towards investigations to cut off production, distribution and sale of counterfeit items. Cooperation with business and customs authorities in third countries was also emphasised.[66] More recently, the Commission has sought a mandate from member states to negotiate a new Anti-Counterfeiting Trade Agreement (ACTA) with major trading partners, including the US, Japan, Korea, Mexico and New Zealand.[67] Its proposals were supported by figures showing that in 2006, 130 million 'fake objects' were intercepted at the EU's external borders – an increase of 40% since 2005.

---

[65]   Press Release (12 July 2005), 'Counterfeiting: State of Play' MEMO/05/250.

[66]   *Communication from the Commission to the Council, the European Parliament and the European Economic and Social Committee on a Customs response to latest trends in Counterfeiting and piracy* (11 October 2005) COM(2005) 479 final.

[67]   Press Release (23 October 2007), 'European Commission Seeks Mandate to Negotiate Major New International Anti-Counterfeiting Pact' IP/07/1573.

An OECD study released in 2007 estimated that the annual value of international physical trade in counterfeited consumer goods was $200 billion, an amount equivalent to 2% of world trade and higher than the GDP of 150 countries.[68]

7.2.4 Jurisdiction – the Brussels Regulation

Within the EU, the international jurisdiction of national courts is determined by the so-called 'Brussels Regulation'.[69] The aim of these common rules is to facilitate the recognition and enforcement of judgments, and thus to increase efficiency and reduce forum-shopping. The Regulation covers all the main civil and commercial matters, apart from certain well-defined exceptions. The basic rule is that the action should be brought in the member state where the defendant is domiciled.[70]

There are a number of exceptions. If the matter involves tortious harm, then the action may be brought in the place where the harmful event occurred.[71] If the proceedings are concerned with the registration or validity of patents, trade marks, designs or other similar rights required to be deposited or registered, the courts of the member state of registration or deposit have exclusive jurisdiction.[72] If there are a number of co-defendants, the action may be brought in the country where any one of them is domiciled.[73] Special provision is made for pending actions (*lis pendens*). Where proceedings involving the same cause of action between the same parties are brought in the courts of different member states, the court first seised of the matter has priority.[74] This is so even if the action is brought in the first court with the deliberate intention of taking advantage of its slow procedures, thereby 'torpedoing' the action.[75] Where related actions are pending in the courts of different member states, any court other than the court first seised may stay its proceedings or decline jurisdiction: the aim is to hear and determine the actions together to avoid the risk of

---

[68]   'Fact Sheet: Anti-Counterfeiting Trade Agreement' (23 October 2007).

[69]   Regulation 44/2001 on jurisdiction and the recognition and enforcement of judgments in civil and commercial matters [2001] OJ L 12/1.

[70]   Brussels Regulation, Art. 2.

[71]   Brussels Regulation, Art. 5(3).

[72]   Brussels Regulation, Art. 22(4). See also Case C-4/03, *Gesellschaft für Antriebstechnik mbH (GAT)* v. *Lamellen und Kupplungsbau Beteiligungs KG (LUK)* [2006] ECR I-6509.

[73]   Brussels Regulation, Art. 6(1). But see Case C-539/04, *Roche Nederland BV* v. *Primus* [2006] ECR I-6535.

[74]   Brussels Regulation, Art. 27.

[75]   Case C-116/02, *Erich Gasser* v. *MISAT* [2003] ECR I-14693.

irreconcilable judgments resulting from separate proceedings.[76] Provisional and protective measures are subject to different rules, on the grounds that the local court is best placed to assess the circumstances of the case.[77]

Once a judgment has been given in a member state, it must be recognised in other member states without further proceedings.[78] This basic rule is subject to a number of exceptions; for example, if the judgment is manifestly contrary to public policy, or if it is irreconcilable with a judgment given in a dispute between the same parties in the member state in which recognition is sought.[79]

---

[76] Brussels Regulation, Art. 28.
[77] Brussels Regulation, Art. 31.
[78] Brussels Regulation, Art. 33.
[79] Brussels Regulation, Art. 34.

Index